THE RIGHTS OF
AMERICANS

What They Are—What They Should Be

ESSAYS COMMEMORATING THE 50TH ANNIVERSARY
OF THE AMERICAN CIVIL LIBERTIES UNION

THE RIGHTS OF AMERICANS

What They Are–
What They Should Be

EDITED BY NORMAN DORSEN

PANTHEON BOOKS, A Division of Random House, New York

Library of Congress Catalog Card Number: 72–128005

ISBN: 0-394-46790-6

Manufactured in the United States of America
by The Book Press, Brattleboro, Vermont

2 4 6 8 9 7 5 3

First Edition

ABOUT THE EDITOR

Norman Dorsen is a professor at New York University School of Law (where he directs the Arthur Garfield Hays Civil Liberties Program) as well as General Counsel of the American Civil Liberties Union. An honor graduate of Harvard Law School, he served as an assistant to Joseph Welch during the Army-McCarthy Hearings and as law clerk to Justice John Marshall Harlan of the Supreme Court. Professor Dorsen is the author of *Frontiers of Civil Liberties* (Pantheon, 1968), and co-author of the two-volume work *Political and Civil Rights in the United States* (Little, Brown, 1967). A frequent advocate before the United States Supreme Court, he is currently Director of the Project on Courtroom Conduct of the Association of the Bar of the City of New York.

ACKNOWLEDGMENTS

I am grateful to Nicholas B. Waranoff, a law student, for valuable assistance with citations and other editorial matters; to Mary Lou Edwards, for ready secretarial support; to two old friends, Irwin Feinberg, M.D., and Daniel A. Rezneck, Esq., for helpful comments on a draft of the Introduction; and to my wife, Harriette, for (among other things) perceiving an original and logical organization for the chapters of this book.

Above all, I wish to express appreciation to the contributors to this volume, who on short notice prepared an outstanding series of essays. They not only have assured the quality of this book and provided welcome support to the American Civil Liberties Union, but they have, I think, contributed to the health and vigor of civil liberties in the United States during a particularly uneasy period.

N.D.

CONTENTS

Section III
The Right of Personal Autonomy

Section IV
Rights Against Government Process

Section V
The Rights of Particular Groups

INTRODUCTION

THE FIFTIETH ANNIVERSARY OF THE AMERICAN
Civil Liberties Union provides an appropriate occasion to assess
the current state of individual freedom in our country. The
moment is, unfortunately, doubly appropriate in that it coincides
with an apparent watershed in the trends regarding individual
rights. The sweeping progress of the past fifteen years, spear-
headed by the Supreme Court under Earl Warren, has come to
a jarring halt. Our confident forward march seems suddenly on
the verge of disorderly retreat.

The ideas underlying the gains of recent years seem to have
penetrated neither the hearts of men nor the seats of power. Hate,
rancor, suspicion, and violence pervade the American nation.
Even more ominously, the mood of government is—one cannot
avoid the term—repressive. We have witnessed official threats to
the mass media; prosecutions under statutes infringing the right
of free speech; accelerating invasions of privacy through wiretapping, electronic eavesdropping, and the new menaces of computer
data banks and indiscriminate government dossiers; bills to authorize preventive detention; retrenchment in respect of the rights
of black people; and failure to satisfy the minimum economic
needs of poor people. The atmosphere has been further embit-
tered by outright violence: the beating of young people in Chicago streets, the shooting of students at Jackson State and Kent
State, and the police raids on Black Panthers in several cities.

A salient feature of all these instances, including much of the
violence, is that they reflect open or covert government policy; in
no sense are they casual, sporadic, or accidental interferences
with the proper functioning of the system. Perhaps this is why

Henry Steele Commager observed in the summer of 1970, "If repression is not yet as blatant or as flamboyant as it was during the McCarthy years, it is in many respects more pervasive and more formidable."

In the search for a convincing explanation of this change in climate, surface reasons such as the end of the Warren Court or the election of Richard Nixon do not suffice. The malaise goes deeper, to the people themselves, particularly the comfortable middle class and the newly secure skilled worker. Conscious of the decline of old values, besieged by pornography and protest, fearful for their physical safety, horrified and angered by heretical doctrine, mystified and repelled by the new aggressiveness of the blacks, many Americans have had enough of social change and judicial activism. They want to be left alone to enjoy the fruits of position and labor. No more noise; no more trouble!

This state of mind is, in part, a regrettable example of what some logicians call the fallacy of the constant pie—the assumption that an increase in liberty means an inevitable decrease in security, and vice versa. But this is not a true relationship; we can either enhance or reduce *both* liberty and security. At the present time, guided by the contrary assumption, government at every level attempts to solve serious community and national problems by restricting the rights of accused criminals, unpopular dissenters, and racial and other minorities.

Simultaneously, events occur that reinforce the general mood. The man in the street is bombarded almost daily by the harsh rhetoric of the new Pied Pipers of revolution, those who blithely, even playfully, urge a call to arms. There may in fact be little chance of apocalyptic confrontation, but the visible—and increasing—violence against police and others feeds deep-seated fears and often provokes severe countermeasures. And so the difficulties mount.

There is a tendency in certain quarters to view threats to liberty as exclusively the problem of outsiders—racial minorities, political and cultural dissenters, and suspected criminals. This is a superficial judgment. True, these are the vulnerable groups that most often suffer weak enforcement of the Bill of Rights. But solid members of the silent majority also value the right to protest and even they may find themselves, from time to time, involved in criminal cases where they wholeheartedly embrace the protections fashioned by the Supreme Court. Moreover, there is a universal interest in certain rights—the privacy of one's home, and relief against Comstockian sex laws and Draconian drug laws. Finally, widely disparate groups—for instance, women, students, and servicemen—are now rebelling against ancient discriminations and seeking the full protection of the law. In short, the security of individual rights is, or should be, of universal concern. As John Donne recognized long ago, no man's freedom may be diminished without reducing the freedom of all.

The everyday affronts to our sense of justice are amply documented in the pages of this book. The agenda of tasks to be completed and wrongs to be righted is endless. To select almost at random, we could be busy for decades remedying the deficiencies in education and housing, the virtually invisible rights of mental patients, the gross inequalities of access to the mass media, and the failure of government to cope adequately with a polluted environment and polluted consumer goods. But instead of making progress along these lines, we may be occupied for some years in merely holding our own.

Many of the chapters range beyond the traditional role of civil liberties. This should be apparent from some topics already mentioned, and there are still others that do not fall into textbook categories. Despite the novel nomenclature and the new subject matter, virtually all that is written here derives from a few fundamental principles. These are the government's obligation to be fair in the use of state power; its duty to assure each individual an opportunity to secure the necessities of life and to participate effectively in the formulation of policy and opinion; and its obligation to leave the individual alone in matters of private concern and to safeguard him against the arbitrary wielding of the great private powers of employers, unions, landlords, and others. It is no simple matter to define individual rights in life's diverse spheres, but that is one of the major tasks of this volume.

Section I, on the "essentials of life," includes discussions not only of education, employment, housing, and welfare, but also the rights to legal services and a habitable environment, the rights of consumers, and the right to special treatment. A decade ago these would scarcely have been considered problems of civil liberties, but there are now solid grounds for including these subjects. The *Gideon* case established a right to counsel for defendants in serious criminal cases; courts and legislatures have so developed the principle that the main battlefield has now shifted to civil cases. For example, indigent juveniles already have the right to a lawyer in delinquency hearings. Persons involuntarily committed to mental institutions deserve the same right, and a natural further development would be to extend the right of representation to poor people for whom other important interests are in jeopardy. The right to a habitable environment and the rights of consumers also rest upon a practical awareness of the vital importance of assuring clean air and water, healthful food, and other necessaries to the residents of a planet speedily gaining in both population and pollution. The chapter on special treatment deals comprehensively with the difficult problem of adjusting the rights of individual blacks (who are members of a race long denied equality) and individual whites (who may not be personally responsible for the historic deprivations).

Section II is concerned with the citizen's influence on government and public opinion. It contains chapters on the well-established rights to vote, protest, associate, and publish as well as on the newer concept of the "right to participate," which has been pressed vigorously as more and more people feel powerless to influence the overburdened bureaucracies in the schools, police, and health services. The sense of being an insignificant object in an impersonal system poisons the lives of many and has stimulated broad if still embryonic efforts to involve the average person in decisions affecting his life. Also in Section II is a discussion of another right struggling to be born: equality of access to the mass media. At a time when rhetoric has spotlighted the central role of radio and television in public affairs, civil libertarians seek ways to enable relatively impecunious spokesmen for the public interest, such as conservationists and consumer groups, to be heard over the media and to participate in the decisions regarding allocation of scarce radio and television licenses.

Section III, on personal autonomy, deals with an assortment of individual rights. Although none except those relating to religion are mentioned in the Constitution, the Supreme Court has now established rights of privacy and travel, and has held that a drug-user cannot be punished merely because he is an addict. Prevailing mores and morality will be tested further (as is discussed in this section) as efforts proceed to broaden the sphere of personal autonomy by protecting homosexuals, users of marijuana, women seeking abortions, and others.

Section IV deals with defenses against government process, and includes chapters on the rights of suspects and defendants in criminal trials, matters of great preoccupation on the part of the Supreme Court in the Warren years. The emphasis is now shifting to the recently recognized rights of juveniles, mental patients, young men subject to the draft, and—a most neglected group—prisoners, each the subject of a separate article.

Finally, Section V concerns special groups, some of whom—teachers, union members, aliens—have long contested their legal rights before courts and legislatures. The others—women, students, servicemen—are still at the take-off stage, and the articles on these subjects accordingly probe much uncharted territory.

Several chapters deal with economic matters—for example, the rights of consumers, and the rights to housing and equal employment. The article on welfare rights contains the most far-reaching suggestions for a general redistribution of economic resources, and therefore it will be most open to the charge of wandering from the traditionally narrow road of civil liberties to the broad avenues of social justice and economic policy. One need not embrace Marxism to recognize this as a false dichotomy. The effective exercise of liberty requires, in Professor Paul Freund's phrase, "a degree of command over material resources." Ramsey Clark puts the point more broadly, following Anatole France's immortal observation that the law in its majestic equality forbids the rich as well as the poor to sleep under bridges, to beg in the streets, and to steal bread. The former Attorney General states, "Where there is social and economic disparity there cannot be justice."

We do not, therefore, apologize for including among individual rights the enjoyment of minimal economic security. It may be asked, however, why there is no chapter on "The Right to Private Property"; after all, the Constitution prohibits the government from depriving persons of property "without due process of law" and from taking property for public use "without just compensation." The omission is not due to any lack of appreciation of the important relationship between financial security and civil liberty. Indeed, several chapters consider the extent to which property is protected under the Bill of Rights. For instance, the one on the right of association explores the protections accorded those seeking to carry on a trade or profession in the face of challenges to their "loyalty" or "security," and the one on the right of privacy discusses many aspects of the protection accorded private homes and possessions.

Nevertheless, it is true that the book lacks systematic analysis of the ways in which the rights of property-owners, of employers, or of manufacturers are protected by the Constitution. One reason is that in recent decades the emphasis has shifted sharply, that previously unfettered rights of property are now limited by other individual rights. For example, employees have secured the right to organize and to equal treatment against employers, consumers have gained leverage against purveyors of food and other necessaries, and the public generally has acquired certain rights to a habitable environment against manufacturers and builders and other potential despoilers of the landscape. Of equal importance has been the recent recognition, largely due to the writings of Professor Charles Reich, that individuals can be held in virtual bondage because of economic dependence on government largesse, and that a major civil liberties effort now must be to develop procedural and substantive protections to mitigate impairments to freedom flowing from this unequal relationship.

The discerning reader will observe that the present contributors grace their subjects with rather different styles. Some express their argument in scholarly and detached prose. Others are more intense, even more passionate, as they press hard to justify maximum protection for the individual. The two styles reflect the different experiences of civil libertarians. Lawyers in the field, used to the often fierce battle in the courtroom, government hearing, police station, or storefront legal office, are bound to be just a bit hotter, a bit more polemical, a bit more audacious, and perhaps a trifle less "balanced" than those who lack extensive front-line experience. Both these approaches are valid, both may be detected within the American Civil Liberties Union, and both are essential to the continuing dialogue that animates and refines the nature of civil liberty.

Many chapters in this book are concerned more with rights derived from legislation rather than with litigation. The reason for this is that the capacity of the judicial process to create wholly new rights and obligations is limited. From time to time judges have broken new ground, notably in establishing the rights of travel, privacy, and association. But these are dramatic and exceptional instances; the usual judicial practice leads to incremental rather than basic change. The fascinating and so far frustrating attempt to establish a general right to welfare—or, as it is sometimes called, a "right to life"—exemplifies the difficulties involved. Efforts to establish a constitutional right to an abortion, discussed in the chapter on control over the use of one's body, face similar obstacles. It is realistic rather than pessimistic to recognize that legislation is sometimes the only way to secure certain personal rights and that shifting majorities in the Supreme Court may result in periods during which legislation is the only possible source of change.

It is reasonably clear, moreover, that neither the Supreme Court nor the Congress alone is capable of guaranteeing the implementation of judicial or legislatively established rights. The article on the rights of suspects makes this point very well regarding the Supreme Court, but the point is also pertinent to other topics and, with some variation, to the practical impact of congressional action on individual rights. Although it is our principal lawmaker, Congress does not directly supervise the police, the military, or other agencies of government that actually impinge on the citizen on a daily basis.

There is, in other words, a large and persistent gap between the law as authoritatively uttered and the law as it finds its way to the public. Justice Frankfurter once plaintively inquired, "Does anybody know . . . where we can go to find light on what the practical consequences of these decisions have been?" A recent collection of materials by Professor Theodore Becker has shown that Supreme Court decisions frequently occasion noncompliance and misunderstanding on the part of government and the citizenry, and that they may exert differing effects on Congress and the President, the lower courts, local and state governments, and public opinion. We are still a long way from understanding the factors which determine effective implementation, but it is clear that legal pronouncements are but one step in the establishment of living freedoms.

If this introduction sketches the present position darkly, it is useful to remember that not long ago the situation was much worse and that civil liberties have expanded in theory—and often in practice—at a relatively steady and surprisingly rapid rate. Recall that when the ACLU was founded in 1920 Attorney General A. Mitchell Palmer was roaming the land in a hunt for "Reds," and when he found them, or thought he had, there was little or nothing by way of constitutional respect for free speech or due process to restrain the most outrageous practices of his lieutenants. Bear in mind, too, that it was not until 1923 that the Supreme Court invalidated a state criminal conviction for being inconsistent with the requirements of due process of law, and not until 1927 that the Court struck down a state law on the ground that it inhibited free speech. In addition, the situation of the blacks has, until recently, differed little from the virtual bondage to which they were returned following Reconstruction.

The Court's pace was unhurried during the 1930's and early 1940's, but even during this period it settled firmly its authority over state infringements of speech and religion and state treatment of suspected criminals that fell below general standards of due process. From 1946 to 1953, the years under Chief Justice Fred Vinson, there was little expansion of rights, and the latter part of this period—the heyday of Senator Joseph McCarthy—was marked by a general passivity on the part of the Court, as it failed to shield Communists, aliens, and other dissenters from questionable government action, or to intervene boldly in state criminal prosecutions.

The Warren Court changed all this. The desegregation decision, *Brown v. Board of Education,* occurred in Warren's first year and ushered in a series of profound reforms. State and federal criminal procedures were modified to protect defendants, including juveniles. Jurisdiction was assumed over the apportionment of state and federal legislative bodies. Religious exercises in public schools were banned. There developed an aggressiveness in protecting the rights of the Negro. In more personal areas, the Court restricted government powers to regulate birth control devices, to inhibit foreign or domestic travel, to censor allegedly obscene literature and films, to deny employment and other benefits to persons deemed "subversive," to discriminate against persons of illegitimate birth, and to strip native-born or naturalized Americans of their citizenship. These results were accompanied by significant growth in the jurisdiction of the federal courts and by development of legal doctrine that together provide a solid basis for further change. In sum, a staggering performance.

The causes of this extraordinary constitutional upheaval were many. Their analysis should provide decades of gainful employment for legal scholars and political scientists. Without in any way wishing to pre-empt the efforts of savants yet unborn, I should like to comment on just a few of the factors which seem relevant.

To start with the negative. In this instance, Mr. Dooley, no mean political scientist, appears to have missed the boat: in making these constitutional changes, the Supreme Court did not follow the "eliction returns." Earl Warren assumed office just months after a new conservative President, and he was that President's first appointee to the Court. The other new figure of importance—William

J. Brennan—also was an Eisenhower appointee. No matter their history, the two new Justices joined New Dealers Hugo Black and William O. Douglas in many libertarian decisions during the 1950's, and several years later, when the fifth vote arrived in the persons first of Arthur Goldberg and then of Abe Fortas, the necessary majority was at hand to revise much of American constitutional law. In doing this the Court broke decisively with a long tradition, most recently exemplified by Justice Felix Frankfurter and Judge Learned Hand. These jurists argued for a passive judiciary which would defer to the executive and legislative branches of government. This argument was based, in part, on the premise that elected officials, unlike federal judges, are responsive to the popular will and thus should be the proximate agents of social change. The Warren Court rejected this cautious philosophy and relied on the obligations it felt under the Bill of Rights to protect racial and political minorities, accused criminals, and other vulnerable groups.

In adopting this activist stance the Court risked retribution at the hands of an aroused Congress and a citizenry angered by what it regarded as the Court's constitutional extravagance. Learned Hand once predicted that judges who are "intransigent" will "be curbed." But the Warren Court was not curbed, although admittedly it was a close thing at times. Professor Kenneth Karst has speculated, wisely I think, that the Court's independence was preserved because it made "the right historical choices." This statement implies that the Court was, in fact, supporting ideas "whose time had come." If this view is correct, an interesting although hardly surprising corollary is that quite diverse currents may coexist within the society. At any given time, the judiciary may be carried by tides different in direction from those which have swept politicians into office. On this issue, Franklin D. Roosevelt and Dwight D. Eisenhower might well have reached rueful accord.

The Court was not, of course, the sole agency at work. The Congress, though often indifferent to civil liberties, responded to its influences by laws against racial and sexual discrimination, and it manifested a new concern for a healthy environment. Congress's decision in 1965 to finance legal services for the poor on a vastly expanded (if still inadequate) level has had particularly broad repercussions. Existing cadres of civil liberties and civil rights lawyers were augmented by a vigorous and idealistic group of young men and women representing the poor. Indeed, this new breed of lawyer, a source of dismay to traditionalists and of delight to others, may prove to be not the least of the Warren Court's heritage. Whatever the complex forces which have shaped the present more liberal and concerned generation, surely the demonstration by the Supreme Court of compassion for the weak and underprivileged must have inspired many young people to view the law as something more than another arm of the Establishment.

The contributors to this volume have themselves handsomely participated in the efforts of the past fifteen years. They frequently have been allied with civil liberties organizations, including of course the ACLU. Supported philanthropically, these organizations provide one of the essential counterweights to the resources of government, and their impact should not be minimized. They serve as the focal points of strategic planning—carrying on litigation, stimulating legislation, participating in lawsuits, and working to prevent legal victories from being dissipated through grudging implementation by the government.

Finally, an often-forgotten but indispensable participant in the effort to reassess constitutional priorities is the individual client himself. In the criminal courts it is said that "the lawyer always goes home," but that is often not true of the client. In the litigation of a test case an individual will often forgo strong contentions special to his case so that the courts will decide a broad legal issue. Many chapters provide examples of such courageous clients—the alien who rejects procedural defenses because he wishes to challenge a law deporting Communists, the traveler denied a passport who rejects a technical defense, the Selective Service registrant who raises novel grounds for resisting induction. All these, and others, are cases in which clients risked their futures in order to establish their principles.

This is a sobering period for those concerned with individual rights. Forces are at work which could corrupt or overrun our free institutions. There are, fortunately, strong countervailing pressures. The courts and the Congress include many men determined to resist encroachments on liberty; the historical and doctrinal weapons for such resistance are available; there are highly motivated lawyers, indefatigable civil liberties organizations, and brave clients ready for battle; above all there are millions of Americans, dedicated to a free society, who fear repression and are determined to oppose it. These favorable omens are reflected in the uninhibited protest that exists all around us. In spite of occasional excesses this is good, because we agree with Robert Kennedy, who said, "It is not enough to allow dissent. We must demand it. For there is much to dissent from."

NORMAN DORSEN

SECTION I

The Right to
the Essentials of Life

THE RIGHT TO
EQUAL EDUCATIONAL
OPPORTUNITY

ROBERT L. CARTER

I

AT A TIME WHEN INCREASED EMPHASIS IS BEING
placed on education as a prerequisite for a growing variety of blue-
collar as well as white-collar employment, it is distressingly evident
that the nation's public school system is not providing the black
underclass with even rudimentary skills in reading, writing, or
arithmetic. The black community views the public school failure
to provide its youth with the necessary educational tools for upward
social and economic mobility as an aspect of the conscious and
callous suppression to which blacks are subjected by the white
majority in this supposedly free and democratic society.

   This widely held conviction helps feed the flames of black discontent and disaffection, bolsters black nationalism, increases black
distrust of white institutions and individuals—all of which, of
course, furthers black-white polarization. Blacks have lost faith in
the efficacy of the law as well, since, according to the law, they are
entitled to the very educational opportunities and advantages they
seek and have thus far been unable to obtain. Although it is clear
under law that educational inequality is prohibited, the law has
been successfully violated, evaded, or frustrated with impunity,

*Robert L. Carter, a practicing lawyer in New York City, is a member of the Board
of Directors of the American Civil Liberties Union, President of the National Committee Against Discrimination in Housing, former General Counsel of the NAACP, and
a participant in numerous civil rights cases. He has written many articles for legal
journals.*

and now apparently with support from the highest offices in government.

The United States Supreme Court's interpretation of the Constitution's guarantee of equal educational opportunity can properly be read as an open-ended proscription against all forms of invidious discrimination which deprive blacks as a group of those educational advantages and opportunities made available at public expense to whites. This approach of the Court is now approximately twenty years old and evolved out of its unsuccessful attempt to make the "separate but equal" doctrine serve the cause of equal treatment.

The "separate but equal" concept predates the Fourteenth Amendment. It had its origin in a decision by the Massachusetts Supreme Court in *Roberts v. City of Boston,* decided in 1849.[1] The doctrine was adopted by the United States Supreme Court in 1896 in *Plessy v. Ferguson,*[2] as properly defining the scope and meaning of the Fourteenth Amendment's equal treatment requirement with respect to black citizens. With that decision apartheid, with its implicit justification for grossly disparate allocation of resources and facilities between whites and blacks, was afforded constitutional sanction on a national scale. A typical example is the per-pupil expenditure for black and white school children for the 1949–1950 school term: Alabama, $130.09 for whites, $92.69 for blacks; Arkansas, $123.60 for whites, $73.03 for blacks; Florida, $196.42 for whites, $136.71 for blacks; Georgia, $145.15 for whites, $79.73 for blacks; Maryland, $217.41 for whites, $198.76 for blacks; Mississippi, $122.93 for whites, $32.55 for blacks; North Carolina, $148.21 for whites, $122.90 for blacks; South Carolina, $154.62 for whites, $79.82 for blacks; District of Columbia, $289.68 for whites, $220.70 for blacks.[3]

Although *Plessy v. Ferguson* involved the validity of racial segregation in railroad cars, and in 1917 the Court explicitly repudiated *Plessy's* application to housing,[4] it was assumed until *Brown v. Board of Education*[5] was decided that "separate but equal" was the appropriate constitutional yardstick in considering claims of educational deprivation based upon race or color.

In 1938 in *Missouri ex rel. Gaines v. Canada,*[6] the United States Supreme Court for the first time sought to place strictures upon the application of the "separate but equal" concept by insisting that equal facilities in fact be provided as a precondition to constitutional sanction of racial segregation.

Gaines made inevitable the United States Supreme Court's decision in *Brown v. Board of Education* in 1954, outlawing racial segregation in the nation's public schools. Sixteen years intervened between the two decisions, but in reformulating the "separate but equal" doctrine by making the threshold requirement the assurance that equal facilities were being provided, the Court laid the basis for the doctrine's ultimate rejection. The certainty of this development is crystal-clear only in retrospect, but part of the legal strategy that underlay *Gaines* was to secure a stone-for-stone, book-for-book "separate but equal" constitutional yardstick in the hope that the maintenance of segregated educational facilities might be rendered so burdensome and expensive as to cause the voluntary abandonment of the practice.

In 1950, with *Sweatt v. Painter*[7] and *McLaurin v. Oklahoma State Regents*,[8] "separate but equal" was virtually abandoned, but the Court refused to accede to the request of the complaining parties to overrule *Plessy v. Ferguson.*

In *Sweatt* the question was whether a recently established law school for blacks was the substantial equivalent of the University of Texas Law School. The question was answered in the negative. "Few students and no one who has practiced law would choose to study in an academic vacuum, removed from the interplay of ideas and the exchange of views with which the law is concerned."[9] Here the Court's commitment to the elimination of constitutional support for segregation was made manifest.

That commitment was even more clearly shown in the *McLaurin* case, decided the same day. McLaurin received the same courses of instruction as his fellow white students, had the same teachers, attended his classes with white students, but he was kept separate and apart from the others pursuant to restrictions imposed. The Court concluded that the University regulations handicapped McLaurin in his pursuit of graduate instruction by inhibiting and impairing his ability to study, to engage in discussion and the exchange of views with fellow students, and "in general, to learn his profession."[10] The conviction that racial restrictions personally interfere with the individual's ability to learn, first articulated in this case, was to become the Court's central thesis four years later in *Brown v. Board of Education.*

In that case, the Court took the final step of formally overruling *Plessy v. Ferguson,* holding that "separate but equal" had no place in the field of education and that racial segregation constituted a denial of equal educational opportunity within the meaning of the Constitution's proscription.

In subsequent holdings, *Brown* was interpreted as requiring not only desegregation in pupil enrollment but desegregation in faculty assignment as well.[11] Moreover, *Brown* became the precedent for the Court's outlawing of enforced racial segregation in virtually all aspects of American life.[12]

Sweatt, McLaurin, and *Brown* struck down specific racial restrictions: the segregated law school, regulations designed to keep black and white students separate and apart on the university campus, and the dual public school system, respectively. Yet there is a common thread that makes these three cases one: a pragmatic attempt to define in real-life terms those practices that deny in fact equality of educational opportunity to blacks and thus must become subject to constitutional prohibition.

Brown was the culmination of this effort. Although a milestone in achievement, *Brown* could not be regarded as the final word— indeed, what the Court had promised in *Gaines* to *Sweatt* through *McLaurin* and to *Brown* was a continuing realism, which would require its appraisal and evaluation of every substantial claim by blacks of educational deprivation, to decide whether and the extent to which such denial was a violation of the Constitution's guarantee of equal education.

But that promise has not been kept. The Court has not moved past *Brown* in its substantive determinations of what constitutes a denial of equal education in its constitutional dimensions; indeed it has not as yet, some sixteen years after *Brown,* been successful in having the dual school system completely abolished throughout the nation.

By the 1963–1964 school term, the eleven states of the old Confederacy had only 1.17 percent of their black children in school with white children.[13] That figure had grown to approximately 25 percent by September 1969, chiefly by virtue of the impact of the United States Civil Rights Act of 1964. The Court has become impatient with the protracted delay and has said that the time for "deliberate speed," the pace enunciated in the *Brown* implementation decree of 1955, is past.[14] What is now required is plans and techniques that promise immediate results.[15]

The fight to eliminate the segregated school in the South is far from being won. It is, of course, doubtful that official school segregation will survive—the mandatory assignment of blacks and whites to schools by race pursuant to law. That much retrenchment is unlikely. What seems certain, however, is that the South will adopt Northern-style school segregation—school assignment to coincide with patterns of residential segregation. In the urban South this will produce virtually total black-white school segregation, as now occurs in the urban North, and *Brown* may become a historic relic.

This outcome, a possibility as long as *de facto* school segregation remains free of constitutional restraint, has become almost a certainty by virtue of President Nixon's policy on *de facto* school segregation announced on March 24, 1970: "De facto racial separation, resulting genuinely from housing patterns, exists in the South as well as the North; in neither area should this condition by itself be the cause for Federal enforcement actions."[16] What Mr. Nixon seems to have overlooked or failed to consider in the formulation of this policy is that racial discrimination created and perpetuates the housing patterns which have been the justification for *de facto* school segregation. In light of the United States Supreme Court decision in *Jones v. Mayer*[16] and the United States Civil Rights Act of 1968, *de facto* segregated housing is unlawful, and hence could hardly give legal support to *de facto* school segregation.

II

Before 1955 the assurances of Northern educators that public schools were offering all children equal access to the same educational advantages and facilities were not seriously challenged. Then almost instantaneously with the *Brown* decision, Northern public school systems came under attack for not affording black children equal educational benefits and for maintaining segregated schools.

In 1955 the New York City Board of Education was prodded into authorizing a study by the Public Education Association to determine whether the quality of education in the predominantly black and Puerto Rican schools in the city equaled that in the predominantly white schools. The study revealed what common sense had long perceived, that the black and Puerto Rican schools were not on a parity with white schools in the city.[17] The study compared the schools on the basis of composite scores made by the pupils of each school on standardized city-wide achievement tests. It was found that in the Puerto Rican and black schools the fourth-grade child was roughly one-half year behind his peer in the predominantly white schools; in the sixth grade he was one and one-half years behind, and in the eighth grade, two and one-half years behind.

Today this is accepted as an accurate profile of the educational gap between whites and blacks in school systems throughout the North and West where black-white school separation exists. This latter phenomenon in the North, known variously as *de facto* school segregation or racial imbalance, is considered adventitious, although it is the inevitable consequence of correlating a neighborhood school-assignment policy with a pattern of housing segregation.

The legal attack on Northern-style black-white school separation has not fared so well. Northern federal courts have given *Brown* a restricted rather than an expansive reading and have followed the path of *Bell v. School City of Gary*.[18] There the court took the view that school separation which is not shown to result from any deliberate or conscious action of school authorities cannot be considered inconsistent with the Fourteenth Amendment's equal education guarantee. Although there are decisions to the contrary, notably *Hobson v. Hansen*,[19] this is the prevailing view, adhered to by the Sixth, Seventh, and Tenth Circuits. In addition, in *Bell*, District Judge George N. Beamer found that evidences of academic disparity adverse to the black public school child threw "little or no light on the quality of instruction, unless there is a corresponding showing of ability to achieve."[20]

Some of the state courts have taken a more advanced view. The New Jersey Supreme Court has held that school authorities are required to eliminate as much black-white school segregation as can be done consistently with sound educational practices.[21] The California Supreme Court seems to be of the same view.[22] In New York, the power of the State Commissioner of Education to order local boards to remove *de facto* segregation has been upheld as an appropriate exercise of the Commissioner's authority to determine educational policy for the state.[23] Illinois and Massachusetts have sought to ban the practice by statute. Currently, the law would appear to be that there is no Fourteenth Amendment compulsion to eliminate *de facto* school segregation; but if school authorities undertake to eliminate *de facto* segregation voluntarily, they run afoul of the law only if their action can be said to be arbitrary and capricious.[24] Thus far the United States Supreme Court has refused to review any case dealing with any aspect of this question.

III

School separation in the North, unlike that in the South, gives the appearance of inevitability and school board innocence and leads courts to conclude that school authorities are not at fault. Other factors that may help explain court acceptance of the *Bell* approach are judicial ignorance concerning possible alternatives to current school assignment policies that produce the separation, and diffidence about intervening in an area that is the appropriate province of the professional educator. Courts are inclined to the mistaken belief that the neighborhood school policy is the only feasible method of assigning pupils to school. A typical reaction is the statement of the court in *Bell:*

> The neighborhood school which serves the students within a prescribed district is a long and well established institution in American public school education. It is almost universally used, particularly in the larger school systems. It has many social, cultural and administrative advantages which are apparent without enumeration. With the use of the neighborhood school districts in any school system with a large and expanding percentage of Negro population, it is almost inevitable that a racial imbalance will result in certain schools.[25]

The argument is completely answered by Judge Irving R. Kaufman in *Taylor v. Board of Education.*[26] There he said:

> The defendant argues, however, that the neighborhood school policy is a reasonable and educationally sound one, and thus that it is not violating the Constitution in adhering to it. But, this argument ignores the essential nature of the plaintiffs' position. They are not attacking the concept of the neighborhood school as an abstract proposition. They are, rather, attacking its application so as to deny opportunities guaranteed to them by the Constitution. . . .
>
>   *   *   *
>
> The neighborhood school policy certainly is not sacrosanct. It is valid only insofar as it is operated within the confines established by the Constitution.

Obviously, the neighborhood school policy can be modified or altered in order to achieve a racial mix, and some school districts have tried various other plans to prevent racial isolation. The Princeton Plan is one such device. Here the child is assigned to school by grade rather than by residence. All children in grades 1 to 3 go to school A; all children in grades 4 to 6 go to school B. Another variation is to take several schools lying in white and black residential areas and pair them for school purposes. Another method is to rezone the schools in order to have them serve mixed rather than black or white areas. Some districts have closed the schools in the black neighborhood and distributed the children among other schools. These remedies work successfully in small or medium-size districts or in large districts with a small black school population. Finally, a proposal that had some currency a few years ago was to establish a public school complex—a school park. Under this proposal all the elementary schools might be in one location, all the junior high schools might be located elsewhere, and all the high schools in a third area. Children would come from all over the district to these school complexes. In large cities where the black school population is predominant or rapidly increasing, the proposal is to establish these complexes so that they will serve the suburban school population as well.

Unfortunately, in *Bell* and cognate cases there was no disposition to examine these rather commonplace alternatives to the neighborhood school, with the result that some very bad law has been developed as regards Northern *de facto* school segregation.

Moreover, the judiciary is probably alarmed about assuming responsibility for a task as vast and as burdensome, and as seemingly imponderable, as eliminating *de facto* school segregation in the face of the demographic and topographic problems which must be surmounted in a school district with a black community of considerable size in terrain expanse and in population.

Effective desegregation in such situations can be accomplished in part through school pairing and rezoning. Large-scale busing, however, would probably have to be undertaken as well. Busing to achieve integration has been loudly condemned, and in New York such action is barred by statute. Although condemnation of busing has been a successful tactic, busing has been a feature of American education for a long time. All school districts bus some children to school. Officials of the United States Department of Health, Education, and Welfare say that desegregation of the South has reduced busing. In short, there was more busing to maintain segregation than is needed for unsegregated schools. Certainly busing school children at public expense will increase if the trend of states giving aid to parochial schools continues.

Yet even when a court is bold enough to order desegregation, as happened in the District of Columbia with Circuit Judge J. Skelly Wright's decree in *Hobson v. Hansen,* the result is the flight of whites from the school system; and in a short space of time the schools may become all black anyway. There the only solution is a metropolitan school organization that combines the District of Columbia and its suburban satellite communities for school purposes.

In all fairness, therefore, it must be conceded that school segregation in the North poses considerably more difficulty for a judge than merely ordering the dismantling of a Southern dual school system. Admittedly, execution of what was court-decreed has been less than successful in those instances as well, but conceptually the solution is simple enough. A decree would merely forbid school assignment on the basis of race and bar the use of policies, practices, and procedures that result in blacks as blacks and whites as whites being assigned to separate schools.

A far more complex assignment, however, is the attempt to give effectiveness to the constitutional guarantee of equal education in a setting where on the surface there is no distinction between blacks and whites as to what is afforded and what is withheld, and where ordering school reorganization requires the development of a school mix, despite patterns of residential segregation and population shifts within the school district. In some cases the public school population is predominantly black, in which case across-the-board integration is no longer feasible within the district itself. The most that can be expected on an intradistrict scale is for the court to require the elimination of as much *de facto* school segregation as is feasible and consistent with sound educational practices. Until and unless district lines are pierced and school assignment is made without reference to residence, *de facto* school segregation will be difficult to eliminate fully in large urban areas with black populations concentrated in a particular section of the community.

For these reasons, equal education has to be given concreteness, specificity, and refinement as educational policy. The contours of equal education as a constitutional requirement and its design as educational policy, practice, or methodology should be virtually the

same. Where educational policy concludes that equal education requires certain specific practices, the courts should make those practices a part of the constitutional dimensions of the equal education
guarantee. Educators have simply failed to tell us what equal education connotes as educational policy, and the courts have been forced
to rely on their own judgment concerning what the equal education
guarantee requires or prohibits.

If equal educational opportunity is a realistic possibility in a
segregated setting, educators should say so and document their conclusion with explanatory professional data. If, as some believe,
equal education means the complete elimination of policies which
result in the racial isolation of black children in the public schools,
educators should give a definitive explanation as to why school
integration is educationally required, as distinguished from being
socially desirable. They should also tell us what forms of school
organization and practices will be needed and suggest methods that
school districts should pursue to reach the desired goal.

In the North, where invidious racial considerations have heretofore influenced educational practices only *sub silentio*, educators
have succeeded in convincing the public that the policies underlying the choice of various forms of school administration are based
upon considerations of educational excellence. In truth these decisions are influenced by a variety of factors, fiscal and political concerns, tradition—and race.

An example, of course, is the neighborhood school policy, which
Northern educators are wont to defend as indispensable for quality
education, it being, in their judgment, one of the best methods for
producing a cooperative school-home relationship conducive to the
educational development of the child.

Yet in our mobile society, that contention will not withstand
even cursory scrutiny. One of the chief consequences of the neighborhood school policy has been that the school reflects the socio-
economic and racial characteristics of the neighborhood it serves.
The result is schools of high and of low quality, with a direct
correlation between the quality of the educational product and the
socio-economic status of the neighborhood served. The neighborhood school policy perpetuates in the classroom the socio-economic
and racial stratification characteristic of the residential patterns of
the community. Therefore, educators who defend and enforce this
policy in our multiracial society, with its increasingly fixed socio-
economic stratification, should be required to spell out with exact-

ness the essential educational ingredients necessary to ensure equal educational opportunity for those attending a school serving a low socio-economic neighborhood as contrasted with a school serving a high socio-economic neighborhood—one serving blacks and one serving whites.

The argument for the neighborhood school policy may have abstract appeal, but the demonstrated operative effect of the policy itself is to provide the most and best in educational resources to affluent whites and the least and worst to poor blacks. Such a result can hardly be supportive of considerations of educational excellence. A Southern judge put his finger squarely on the pulse of the real issue here when he said,

> The system of assigning pupils by "neighborhoods" with "freedom of choice" for both pupils and faculty, superimposed upon an urban population pattern where Negro residents have become concentrated almost entirely in one quadrant of a city of 270,000, is racially discriminatory. This discrimination discourages initiative and makes quality education impossible. The quality of public education should not depend on the economic or racial accident of the neighborhood in which a child's parents have chosen to live—or find they must live—nor on the color of his skin. The neighborhood school concept never *prevented* statutory racial segregation; it may not now be validly used to *perpetuate* segregation.[27]

The school district, another example, is supported on the grounds that decentralized authority is more practical for the administration of what is said to be an essentially local concern. Since a school district's principal benefit will be to the community it serves, it has been regarded as a matter of sound political judgment that the district itself should possess a significant degree of control over the administration and financing of the district's schools. On the shoulders of the local community is left the burden of weighing the benefits of more modern educational facilities against a smaller tax, or the need for imposing a heavier tax levy to keep an inadequate educational plant limping along. Moreover, furtherance of local concern for education, interest, and initiative is said to be the generating force behind the state funding formula that results in wide variations in the financial support of public education from district to district within each state. The degree of variation differs from state to state, but within a state the wealthiest school district may spend as much as five times more per pupil than is expended in the poorest district.

The reality is that a school district's size, its shape, and the quality of education it offers are more often than not determined on a haphazard basis without any acceptable rational underpinning. In the main, the once unstated but now increasingly open determinant is the protection of the interests of the white middle class. Here fiscal and political considerations carry far more weight than does concern for educational excellence for all. There have been some recent sporadic efforts to reduce the number of school districts in a state, but this activity has been ad hoc, without being linked to any state-wide plan to redesign school districts in an attempt to provide a reasonable basis for interdistrict educational equality.

In sum, at present, the implementation of a neighborhood school policy or the size of a school district is determined without a valid or rational educational basis and is not designed to produce equality of educational opportunity, either educationally or constitutionally. Yet courts have a profound reluctance to discount the educator's wisdom. Southern judges have considerably more freedom. They can see that the replacement of the dual school system with a neighborhood school policy may be a mere subterfuge, when the result is as much racial separation as ever.

In addition, the professional educator has fostered the belief that academic disparities evidenced in the predominantly black schools result from causes over which the public school system has no control—socio-economic factors and incidences of family life; that the massive academic failure of the black child is not the responsibility of the school, its methodology, its administration, its personnel; that the black child is uneducable because of background deprivations and disabilities, familial and environmental. This somewhat crude and cruel rationalization, which is closely akin to a concept of genetic inferiority and gives the lie to the protestation that ours is an open society, has now fallen out of fashion. The current thesis is that the educational deprivations of blacks are the product of social-class factors; blacks cannot improve their current depressed socio-economic status without the elimination of their educational deficiencies, and since these are predetermined by class, little hope is held of the black underclass ever achieving equal educational opportunity.

But neither theory presents a true or accurate picture. Public education, in quality and distribution, is the result in great part of political power. Since the dominant and controlling political power is in the hands of the white middle class, it uses this strength to corner for itself a disproportionate share of available educational resources, thereby ensuring the perpetuation of its dominant authority through its progeny. Thus, while the disparities may not be indigenous to class or socio-economic status, that is what the reality is made to appear.

It is true that in view of the powerlessness of the black underclass, this approach also leaves one extremely pessimistic about blacks securing equal educational opportunities in the foreseeable future. There is a great difference, however, in focusing on the privileges and prerogatives of power as a link to educational deprivation, for then one concludes that the evil lies in the maldistribution of educational resources rather than in the innate character of the black poor. The fact that the public school system as it is now organized has evidenced little influence on the child's achievement, independent of background and social class, does not prove that social class determines educational achievement, but rather that social class—specifically, the white middle class—has governed school organization, orientation, and methodology.

IV

The differences between the North and South with respect to equal educational opportunity are largely matters of degree. The South utilized the dual school system as a vehicle to achieve a differential in financial support for the education of blacks and whites. The North has accomplished the same result by use of the neighborhood school, the school-districting process, and the state funding formula. This is not to suggest that officials planned things this way, but that these policies do provide the means for achieving the results reached.

The idea of organizing a school system to serve particular areas within a district, dividing the state into a variety of local districts for school administration, and authorizing these districts to raise funds in their own communities for school purposes, with these efforts being stimulated by supplements from the state treasury, is reasonable enough in the abstract and seems to be entirely neutral as to race. It is only when one looks at the practice in operation that the underlying racism becomes clearly illumined.

In Northern areas the black poor are concentrated more and more in the cities and middle-class whites in the suburbs. The central cities' schools thus have become increasingly black, while suburban school systems remain largely white. The state funding formula, pursuant to which local districts are allowed to levy a tax on real property for school purposes, has meant that wealthy suburban communities are far better able to support a first-rate school system than are the cities. This results in middle-class whites having more adequate educational facilities than can be made available to the black poor.

Nor is the matter solely limited to racial differentiation between city and suburban school systems. The Wyandanch school district in New York with its surrounding communities is an example of black and white school-district separation and fiscal-resource discrimination in the suburbs—a prototype in microcosm of the black-central-city–white-suburban-school picture. Wyandanch is a virtually all-black community and an independent, separate school district, surrounded by affluent white school districts. Although Wyandanch taxes itself at a far higher rate than its surrounding communities are required to do, it cannot, because of its poor tax base, maintain an adequate school system. Except that the school district is almost all black, its manifest inability to fund an adequate school system would have resulted long ago in its abolition and absorption by the surrounding communities. This situation is duplicated in nearly every state in the union.

State power to redistrict for school purposes appears to be absolute.[28] Moreover, where the district lines as drawn create poor districts unable to provide equal educational opportunity, the constitutional mandate would seem to compel the state to redistrict in order to comply with its basic obligations. The constitutional guarantee is addressed to the state and would seem to require that equal educational opportunity have state-wide application. It is not enough that there should be no educational disparity stemming from state misfeasance, malfeasance, or nonfeasance among groups or classes within each local district; the guarantee crosses district lines as well. The state cannot avoid its constitutional obligation by a showing of a reasonable basis for the lines' placement; it must demonstrate a compelling necessity for the present districting in order to save it from condemnation as resulting in an unlawful racial grouping of persons for school purposes.[29]

Obviously there are practical considerations which cannot be disregarded, but within the realm of reasonableness, present district lines must give way to ones more suitably designed to make good the Constitution's promise. Current disinterest in integration as an objective, however, makes unlikely any significant attempts in the near future to challenge the validity of school districting which separates blacks from whites and rich from poor.

Where we are likely to see developments, however, is in attacking the constitutional bases for state school-funding formulas. At present, each state funding formula produces unequal per-pupil financial support for education among various districts within the state. This process and result must be at least constitutionally suspect, if not plainly illegal. Although a knowledgeable buyer may get more for his money than one less informed, the assumption must be that in the public realm, in the absence of proof to the contrary, unequal funds means unequal school facilities. Of course, this is not a complete answer. It may be true that a dollar in Harlem will buy less educationally than a dollar in Scarsdale. But at the very least the Harlem child is entitled to have the same amount of dollars expended for his education as is spent on the education of a child in Westchester. When faced with the problem, a court need not decide at once what the remedy is, or be concerned as to whether a requirement that funding be equalized will produce the same educational result. What it may do is hold the present formula unconstitutional, and allow the legislature time to devise a new funding program in accordance with constitutional standards. If the legislature fails to act within the time allowed, the court should then undertake to devise a remedy of its own. This has been the approach to redistricting for political purposes, and there is little reason to believe that the same method cannot be utilized here. Thus far, however, the cases that have been brought to test the state funding formula have been lost at the trial court and affirmed summarily by the United States Supreme Court.[30] Fortunately, summary affirmance means little more than that the Court does not consider the issue ripe for final adjudication, and is not a decision on the merits.

V

Sixteen years have elapsed since *Brown* was decided. Very few of the litigants involved in *Brown* ever secured the unsegregated education which the Court said they were entitled to. Northern communities, small and large, with or without demographic or topographic barriers to successful integration, have almost universally fiercely resisted school reorganization to eliminate *de facto* segregation or to improve the quality of education in the black schools. At least since 1955, however, when the Public Education Association published its findings about the New York City school system, there has been considerable discussion of the problem, small-scale experiments, and tons of proposals. Nine years after the Public Education Association report, Harlem Youth Opportunities Unlimited (HARYOU) covered much the same ground in its study of predominantly black schools in Harlem.[31]

The feeling is growing that blacks will be educated equally only when they themselves have some say in the educational process. For this reason, community control has gained adherents in the black community. The basic problem with the community control proposals being offered at present is that only limited authority is delegated to the local community and the real power remains, as before, in the hands of the central board of education. Thus, there is little likelihood that the quality of education being offered to black children will show any marked improvement. Yet clearly, the present school organization has failed. Reform of some kind must be undertaken.

Although the chances seem slim, blacks may nonetheless be able to produce better educational results, because an all-pervasive rage surfacing in the black community against the deprivations, limitations, and restrictions imposed on it and against all things white may generate the necessary drive and motivation. It is a somewhat romantic notion to believe that a disadvantaged minority, without full control and authority over the schools their children attend, without power over or control of school financing, will be able, under community control, to make black schools more educationally viable than are segregated schools as now functioning North and South. Yet the politics of the situation leads to the conclusion that this may be the only avenue open.

A great deal of disillusionment is currently being expressed about school integration. The thesis is that integration has failed; that it will not work; that what is needed is compensatory programs for black children in their separate *de jure* or *de facto* school facilities. Whites are supporting the idea of racial separation. Many distinguished Northern white liberals have succumbed to this rationalization, and since separation is what a number of black militants see as the way out, young white radicals are supporting the idea. The adherents of school separation—indeed, of separate so-cieties—are a strange mixture of segregationists, young black mili-tants, not-so-young white liberals, and young white radicals.

Space limitations do not permit an extended analysis of this proposed solution. Suffice it to say that if those who are urging com-pensatory programs were familiar with any experiments along those lines,[32] they would not be so confidently suggesting that approach as a solution. If those who do know that such programs have uni-versally failed are urging them, then, of course, they are engaged in a sinister form of cynicism.

The truth is that integration has not been tried. There has been no great public pressure for integration, north or south. It is true that a long legal campaign to end school segregation began as long ago as 1936. This campaign, however, chiefly involved a few lawyers, the plaintiffs, and their families in the various test cases brought, and others who gave financial and moral support. After *Brown v. Board of Education* was decided, a surprising number of blacks per-sisted, against the will of the white South, in demanding that the dual school system be dismantled. The rate of change has been slow. No one can truthfully say that integration is not a success. Only when the white South accepts integration and commits itself to make it work, and then it does not work, will it be possible to say that integration has failed in the South.

In the North, integration efforts have been resisted by a variety of interest groups—unions, teachers, white parents, administrative personnel. These view changes in the status quo of the public school system as a threat to some vital concern of their own. Thus, fierce resistance takes place—not always sparked by overt racial antipathy or fear, although these surface when the dispute heats up. A factor contributing to the opposition of such groups is that the threat to them seems great, immediate, and ominous whereas the correspond-ing public benefit is only very dimly glimpsed. As a result the pro-posed change is not effectuated, or is so modified as to have virtually no impact whatsoever. Accordingly, it is not correct to say that school integration has failed in the North. A more accurate state-ment is that retention of present *de facto* separation is more palata-ble to the white majority.

If the educational community can come to grips with the basic question, What are the ingredients needed for equality of educa-tional opportunity without sacrifice of educational excellence?—

and the answer has to be more definitive than X number of dollars —then some of this resistance may fade.

It is difficult to conceive of black children obtaining equality of educational opportunity in the absence of school organization that consequentially brings blacks and whites to the same classroom for educational purposes. It is also difficult to conceive of compensatory education in the black schools as a workable remedy. It is quite clear that the public will not pay the cost required. Compensatory education, if seriously undertaken, would mean that more funds would be spent in black schools than in white.

Those who are deeply concerned about the educational plight of the black community must understand that unless the black child is brought into an open school system in which all racial barriers have been removed, equal education for him will remain an empty abstraction. Many complex and complicated proposals for attacking this problem with the black schools left undisturbed have been brought forward, promising that equal educational opportunity or quality education will be secured thereby. If such is really the objective of these proposals, why not open up the whole school system? If compensatory education or remediation is proposed, one would assume that the black child would overcome his educational deficiencies more quickly in a school populated by pupils that are truly representative of the community.

Many white liberals who believe that integration is the remedy for the educational deprivation of the black community tend to define the issue in terms of sentimentality: "helping the poor black child." Our society is too impersonal for such sentiments to be taken seriously. Moreover, school integration is not a gift the white community deigns to bestow on the black community out of the goodness of its heart. Paternalism has no place here. A commitment to equal educational opportunity is one of the basic obligations of this society, an obligation that has thus far been broken with respect to the black community. School integration must be approached, therefore, as a requirement imposed by law.

The black child is educationally deprived, not because of past wrongs or slavery, but because the present society refuses to provide him with a decent education and keeps him consigned to inferior educational facilities. School integration is necessary to correct a present injustice: to remove the barriers that have barred blacks from vindication of their constitutionally guaranteed right to equal education.

NOTES

1. 59 Mass. (5 Cush.) 198 (1849).
2. 163 U.S. 537 (1896).
3. Blose & Jaracy, *Biennial Survey of Education in the United States, 1948–1950*, Table 43, "Statistics of State School Systems, 1949–50" (1952).
4. Buchanan v. Warley, 245 U.S. 60, 81 (1917).
5. 347 U.S. 483 (1954). In its second *Brown* opinion, the Court ordered desegregation effectuated "with all deliberate speed." 349 U.S. 294 (1955).
6. 305 U.S. 337 (1938).
7. 339 U.S. 629 (1950).
8. 339 U.S. 637 (1950).
9. 339 U.S. at 634.
10. 339 U.S. at 641.
11. Rogers v. Paul, 382 U.S. 198 (1965); Bradley v. School Bd., 382 U.S. 103 (1965).
12. *See, e.g.,* Watson v. City of Memphis, 373 U.S. 526 (1963); Johnson v. Virginia, 373 U.S. 61 (1963); Turner v. City of Memphis, 369 U.S. 350 (1962); Burton v. Wilmington Parking Authority, 365 U.S. 715 (1961); State Athletic Comm'n v. Dorsey, 359 U.S. 533 (1959) (mem.).
13. United States v. Jefferson County Bd. of Educ., 372 F.2d 836, 854 *et seq.* (5th Cir. 1966), *aff'd,* 380 F.2d 385 (en banc), *cert. denied,* 389 U.S. 840 (1967); the court provides a comprehensive analysis of the rate of change.
14. Griffin v. County School Bd., 377 U.S. 218 (1964).
15. Alexander v. Holmes County Bd. of Educ., 396 U.S. 19 (1969); Green v. County School Bd., 391 U.S. 430 (1968).
16. 392 U.S. 409 (1968).
17. Public Education Association, *Status of Public School Education of Negro and Puerto Rican Children* (1955).
18. 213 F. Supp. 819 (N.D. Ind.), *aff'd,* 324 F.2d 209 (7th Cir. 1963), *cert. denied,* 377 U.S. 924 (1964); *see also* Deal v. Cincinnati Bd. of Educ., 244 F. Supp. 572 (S.D. Ohio 1965), *aff'd in part,* 369 F.2d 55 (6th Cir. 1966), *cert. denied,* 389 U.S. 847 (1967). *But see* Dowell v. School Bd., 219 F. Supp. 427 (W.D. Okla. 1963) *aff'd in part,* 375 F.2d 158 (10th Cir.), *cert. denied,* 387 U.S. 931 (1967).
19. 260 F. Supp. 401 (D.D.C. 1967), *aff'd sub. nom.* Smuck v. Hobson, 408 F.2d 175 (D.C. Cir. 1969); *see also* Blocker v. Board of Educ., 226 F. Supp. 208 (E.D.N.Y. 1964); Branche v. Board of Educ., 204 F. Supp., 150 (E.D.N.Y. 1962); *cf.* Barksdale v. Springfield School Comm'n, 237 F. Supp. 543 (D. Mass.), *vacated,* 348 F.2d 261 (1st Cir. 1965).
20. 213 F. Supp. at 828.
21. Booker v. Board of Educ., 45 N.J. 161, 212 A.2d 1 (1965).
22. Jackson v. Pasadena City School Dist., 59 Cal. 2d 876, 31 Cal. Rptr. 606, 382 P.2d 878 (1963). Recently, total desegregation of Los Angeles and the use of widespread busing was ordered in Crawford v. Board of Educ., No. 882854 (Super. Ct., Los Angeles Co., Cal., Feb. 11, 1970). Although the decision was based on the Fourteenth Amendment, the California State Board of Education, in March 1970, repealed its directive to local school districts requiring them to act to eliminate *de facto* school segregation.

23. Matter of Vetere v. Allen, 15 N.Y.2d 259, 206 N.E.2d 174, 258 N.Y.S.2d 77, *cert. denied,* 382 U.S. 825 (1965).

24. *See* Matter of Balaban v. Rubin, 14 N.Y.2d 193, 199 N.E.2d 375, 250 N.Y.S.2d 281, *cert. denied,* 379 U.S. 881 (1964).

25. 213 F. Supp. at 829.

26. 191 F. Supp. 181, 195 (S.D.N.Y.), *appeal dismissed,* 288 F.2d 600 (2d Cir. 1961).

27. Swann v. Charlotte-Mecklenberg Bd. of Educ., 300 F. Supp. 1358, 1360 (W.D.N.C. 1969) (emphasis in original). On May 26, 1970, the Court of Appeals for the Fourth Circuit disapproved of much of the busing required at the elementary school level. The case was argued on appeal in the Supreme Court in October 1970.

28. *See, e.g.,* People v. Deatherage, 401 Ill. 25, 81 N.E.2d 581 (1948).

29. *See, e.g.,* McLaughlin v. Florida, 379 U.S. 184 (1964); Loving v. Virginia, 388 U.S. 1 (1967).

30. McInnis v. Ogilvie, 293 F. Supp. 327 (E.D. Ill. 1968), *aff'd,* 394 U.S. 322 (1969); Burruss v. Wilkerson, 90 S.Ct. 812 (1970) (mem.).

31. HARYOU, *Youth in the Ghetto* 161–95 (1964).

32. United States Commission on Civil Rights, *Racial Isolation in the Public Schools* (1967), documents the universal failure of compensatory programs in black schools; *see also* United States Office of Education, *Equality of Educational Opportunity* (1966) (Coleman Report).

THE RIGHT TO
EQUAL EMPLOYMENT
OPPORTUNITY

MICHAEL I. SOVERN

A BEWILDERING VARIETY OF POSSIBLE REMEDIES confronts the victim of employment discrimination based on race, creed, color, or national origin. (Discrimination on the basis of sex is considered elsewhere in this volume.) Since the relevant federal law was fashioned in part to take account of state arrangements, we shall examine state law first.

STATE FAIR EMPLOYMENT PRACTICES LEGISLATION[1]

The thirty-nine state statutes vary considerably in detail, but almost all share a common core that bans specified employment practices and establishes an administrative agency with primary responsibility for enforcing that ban.

Unlawful Discriminatory Practices Proscribed

New York's list of "unlawful discriminatory practices" is, with one major exception, typical. It outlaws discrimination by an employer, not only in hiring and discharge, but also "in compensation

Michael I. Sovern is Dean of the Columbia Law School, former Chairman of the ACLU Committee on Labor, and Director of Training for the NAACP Legal Defense and Education Fund. He is the author of Legal Restraints on Racial Discrimination in Employment and of many articles in legal journals.

or in terms, conditions, or privileges of employment." In other words, employers may not discriminate in any respect against employees or job applicants on racial or religious grounds. They may not, for example, pay discriminatory wage rates, confine blacks to the lowest job classifications, or conduct whites-only training programs.

The statute strikes next at discrimination by employment agencies. An agency may not be influenced by race, creed, color, or national origin "in receiving, classifying, disposing, or otherwise acting upon applications for its services or in referring an applicant or applicants to an employer or employers."

Union discrimination is specifically prohibited too. It is unlawful for a union, because of the race, creed, color, or national origin of any individual, "to exclude or to expel from its membership such individual or to discriminate in any way against any of its members or against any employer or any individual employed by an employer." Unions are thus required to admit to membership and represent without regard to color. They are also implicitly barred from inducing employers to discriminate against job applicants by a clause that makes it an unlawful employment practice "to aid, abet, incite, compel, or coerce the doing of any of the acts forbidden under this article, or to attempt to do so." Since employers are forbidden to discriminate against job applicants, a union that sought to induce such discrimination would violate the statute.

The discriminatory selection of apprentices is dealt with at length. This portion of the statute is unusual: in addition to prohibiting discrimination on racial and religious grounds, it requires registered apprentice-training programs to select trainees on the basis of "their qualifications, as determined by objective criteria which permit review." A major purpose is to outlaw nepotic selection of apprentices. Most states still have only the conventional prohibition of discrimination.

Several practices that traditionally accompany discrimination are also outlawed. Employers and employment agencies are not allowed

> to print or circulate or cause to be printed or circulated any statement, advertisement or publication, or to use any form of application for employment or to make any inquiry in connection with prospective employment, which expresses, directly or indirectly, any limitation, specification or discrimination as to . . . race, creed,

color, [or] national origin . . . or any intent to make any such limitation, specification or discrimination, unless based upon a bona fide occupational qualification.

Rounding out the protections are prohibitions of reprisals against persons who have opposed unlawful employment practices, complained to the antidiscrimination agency, or otherwise assisted in its proceedings.

Virtually every state with an antidiscrimination law outlaws essentially the same conduct New York has proscribed, excepting only the recently added requirement that apprentices be selected on the basis of their qualifications. Dozens of municipalities have also followed suit.

Procedural Arrangements

1. Complaint. To illustrate the procedural arrangements set up to enforce these laws, let us suppose that a black complainant appears at one of the offices of the responsible administrative agency. (The name of that agency varies from state to state: prominent variations include Division of Human Rights, Commission Against Discrimination, Fair Employment Practices Commission, and Civil Rights Commission.) The black complainant reports that when he responded to a particular company's advertisement for a clerk, he was brusquely turned away with the statement that the place had already been filled. His suspicions were aroused because the company did not ask him for an application to be kept on file and he saw no blacks among the company employees visible to him. A member of the agency's staff will thereupon assist in the preparation of a complaint setting forth the complainant's story and claiming discriminatory denial of employment. The complainant will swear that to the best of his knowledge and belief the complaint is true, and sign it.

2. Investigation. In due course an agency representative will be assigned to investigate the matter. He will call on the company and seek to find out what actually happened with respect to the complainant, how the job was filled, and, in general, whether the company's hiring and personnel policies are nondiscriminatory. What happens next will depend on his report.

3. Determination of "Probable Cause." The investigator's report may be exculpating. Any number of circumstances might indicate that the employer was wholly blameless. Consider this combination of facts: the employer's personnel records confirmed the claim that a clerk was hired the day before the complainant applied and showed no other clerical positions filled thereafter; the company's personnel manager maintained that the company does not keep applications for clerical jobs on file because such openings are infrequent; and the investigator, in the course of a walk through the company's premises, personally observed a substantial proportion of black employees, including several engaged in clerical work.

With such a report in hand, the agency official in charge of the case would conclude that the complainant had not been the victim of discrimination. Accordingly, he would dismiss the complaint on the ground that "probable cause" to credit its allegations was lacking.

Some state laws give the complainant the right to administrative review of that dismissal. He may also, if he is so minded, go to court in an effort to reverse the dismissal, but his chances of success, on the facts we have hypothesized, would be nil. Even for complainants with stronger cases, the availability of judicial review of a complaint dismissal means little. The costs of retaining counsel and prosecuting a court action are prohibitive for the ordinary rebuffed complainant. Moreover, the courts normally give considerable weight to administrative determinations, presuming them to be correct unless clearly persuaded to the contrary, and the dismissal of a complaint is no exception to this general rule. The result is that complainants hardly ever seek judicial reversal of a complaint dismissal.

Now let us suppose that the investigation tends to confirm the complainant's suspicion that he was turned away because of his race. Let us suppose, for example, that the employer's personnel records reveal that a clerk was hired the day *after* the complainant applied and not the day before, that those files also contain several applications for clerical positions, whereas the complainant had not been asked to fill one out, and that the investigator's visual check of the composition of the company's work force detects only one black—a janitor. After reviewing this report and perhaps talking with the parties, the agency official in charge would presumably determine, in the language of many of the statutes, "that probable cause exists for crediting the allegations of the complaint."

4. Conciliation. Upon such determination, the agency will usually, and in most states must, attempt to eliminate the discriminatory practice "by conference, conciliation, and persuasion." A successful effort culminates in a conciliation agreement, in which the employer typically makes several promises. In our hypothetical case, the agreement might require the employer to offer the complainant the next job opening he is qualified to fill; to refrain from discriminating in the future; to display commission notices advising employees and job applicants of their right to equal opportunity in employment; and to submit to subsequent investigations aimed at determining whether he has honored his obligations under the agreement and the antidiscrimination law.

Almost every case in which probable cause is found ends in a conciliation agreement. Notwithstanding this fact, the statutes typically say nothing about complainant participation in the negotiations, and many a complainant has been stuck with a conciliation agreement not to his liking. New York recently amended its statute to give complainants an opportunity to object to conciliation agreements. The amendment includes the right to a hearing on such objections, with the qualification that the agency may in its discretion dispense with the hearing. In that event, the complainant is to be treated "as if no complaint had been filed." This becomes intelligible only against the background of New York's unusual election-of-remedies provision, which offers complainants a choice in the first instance between suing in court and having the matter handled by the Division of Human Rights. Once made, the election is binding and the other remedy foreclosed. However, if the Division denies a complainant a hearing on his objections to a conciliation agreement, his right to take the alleged discriminator to court is restored.

5. *Public Hearing.* In the rare case where conference and conciliation seem to be unavailing, a public hearing will be ordered. Neither this order nor even the commencement of the hearing itself precludes further efforts at settlement, and a number of cases are settled at this advanced stage. If the case is not settled, a representative of the agency will present the evidence supporting the charge to an agency tribunal, and the employer will be given an opportunity to rebut the case against him. The complainant may also participate through his own attorney. At this stage, as well as at all earlier points in the processing of the complaint, the agency has the power to subpoena witnesses, books, and papers. Needless to say, the employer is entitled to invoke this power if he needs it to make his defense.

6. *Cease-and-Desist Order*. If, on the basis of the evidence adduced at the hearing, the employer is found to have discriminated in violation of the statute, he will be ordered to "cease and desist." The California statute is typical in allowing wide discretion as to the contents of that order. According to Section 1426 of the California Labor Code, an offender may be required "to cease and desist from such unlawful employment practice and to take such positive action, including (but not limited to) hiring, reinstatement, or upgrading of employees, with or without back pay, or restoration to membership in any respondent labor organization, as, in the judgment of the commission, will effectuate the purposes of this part, and including a requirement for report of the manner of compliance." In effect, the offender will be directed to do essentially what a conciliation agreement would have required of him. However, when an employer resists the agency all the way to a public hearing, he runs a greater risk of being required to pay the complainant the wages he would have earned but for the employer's unlawful discrimination.

7. *Judicial Enforcement*. A cease-and-desist order may not, however, be the end of the matter, for such an order is not self-enforcing. That is to say, if a respondent chooses to ignore it, the agency must go to court to compel compliance. (The respondent, if he prefers, may initiate the judicial proceedings himself. In either event, the ensuing proceedings are the same.) The court will review the record to see whether the agency's findings of facts are supported by "sufficient evidence" and whether it has interpreted the statute correctly. If the court finds these conditions met, it will order the respondent to comply with the agency's order; failure to obey the court's order is then punishable as a contempt of court. Notwithstanding the provision for judicial review in all of the statutes, so few cases get even as far as a cease-and-desist order that occasions for the issuance of court orders are rare.

8. *The Power of Initiation*. Though our hypothetical case began with a complaint from a discrimination victim, the antidiscrimination agencies of many states are not wholly dependent upon such victims to get them moving. Their procedures can also be self-starting—with the agency itself authorized to file its own complaints. And some agencies are authorized to move without a victim if another public official—typically the state attorney general—files a complaint with them.

Title VII of the Civil Rights Act of 1964[2]

Unlawful Employment Practices Proscribed

Title VII includes the whole battery of substantive prohibitions found in the typical state antidiscrimination law. That is to say, it proscribes discrimination on the ground of race, religion, color, or national origin, whether perpetrated by employers, employment agencies, unions, or apprenticeship committees; and it proscribes such discrimination in every aspect of the employment and union relation, including, but not limited to, hiring, compensation, promotion, training, discharge, and union membership. Segregated working conditions are outlawed, as are the common adjuncts to discrimination—classification of employees by race, advertisements which suggest that a racial standard will be applied to applicants, and reprisals against those who invoke the Act or assist in its enforcement. In addition, those barred from discriminating by Title VII must post in appropriate places "a notice to be prepared or approved by the Commission setting forth excerpts from, or summaries of, the pertinent provisions of this title and information pertinent to the filing of a complaint."

A size criterion, however, excludes literally millions of employers from the Act's coverage. To be an employer within the meaning of Title VII, an enterprise must have "twenty-five or more employees for each working day in each of twenty or more calendar weeks in the current or preceding calendar year." Assistant Attorney General (as he then was) Burke Marshall estimated that:

> When Title VII becomes fully effective only 8%—about 260,000 —of the 3,300,000 employers that report to the social security system will be covered. This 8% employ 29 million of the 73 million persons employed in this country.

Governments are also beyond the reach of Title VII. The statute excludes from the definition of employer "the United States . . . or a State or political subdivision thereof." This omission, which renders Title VII inapplicable to another 10 million jobs, is not as significant as it might seem. Though they sometimes disobey, all government bodies are required by the United States Constitution and a variety of other measures to refrain from practicing racial discrimination.

Governments are not only major employers; they also play a significant role as employment agencies. Although the statute declares that the term "employment agency" "shall not include an agency of the United States, or an agency of a State or political subdivision of a State," it then excepts from the exclusion by far the most important of the governmental ventures in employment referral: "the United States Employment Service and the system of State and local employment services receiving Federal assistance." As a result, Title VII can be invoked against state employment services when they fill discriminatory job orders.

Enforcement

Let us, as we did with the state laws, follow the Civil Rights Act's enforcement procedures with a rejected job applicant who believes he has been the victim of racial discrimination. We shall first assume that the alleged discrimination took place in a state without its own antidiscrimination law; as we shall see, the procedure is more complicated when this is not the case.

Title VII has its own administrative agency, the Equal Employment Opportunity Commission, consisting of five members "appointed by the President with the advice and consent of the Senate." A complainant can move the Commission by filing with it a sworn charge claiming that he has been aggrieved by an unlawful employment practice; or a member of the Commission itself may file a charge with it "where he has reasonable cause to believe a violation of this title has occurred (and such charge sets forth the facts upon which it is based)." The Commission must then investigate the charge, and if it determines, "after such investigation, that there is reasonable cause to believe that the charge is true, the Commission shall endeavor to eliminate any such alleged unlawful employment practice by informal methods of conference, conciliation, and persuasion." Like most of the state antidiscrimination agencies, the Commission must treat what goes on in the conciliation process as confidential.

The similarity to state law ends when conciliation fails. If the Commission is "unable to obtain voluntary compliance" within 30 days (plus 30 more if the Commission thinks it can use them fruitfully), the next step is not the holding of a public hearing. Instead, the Commission merely notifies the complainant that it has failed. He may then attempt enforcement on his own: the statute gives him

30 days from receipt of the Commission's notice to commence suit in a federal court if he wishes.

No matter how informative or encouraging the Commission tries to make this particular communication, many victims of discrimination will regard it as the end of the matter. An agency of the United States government has, after all, been unable to make the discriminator give way. How can the complainant expect to do better on his own?

But let us suppose that our complainant has the aid and comfort of a civil rights organization. It provides him with an attorney, and they bring suit in an appropriate federal district court. Though the proceeding is likely to be protracted, it can in the end provide full relief both for the plaintiff and for other employees similarly situated.

Victory has other advantages. The court is given discretion to award "a reasonable attorney's fee" to the prevailing party. The Supreme Court, construing the virtually identical provision in the public accommodations title of the Civil Rights Act of 1964, has held that attorney's fees should "ordinarily" be awarded to prevailing plaintiffs.[3] Victory also allows the Commission to help again. The statute provides: "In any case in which an employer, employment agency, or labor organization fails to comply with an order of a court issued in a civil action brought under subsection (e), the Commission may commence proceedings to compel compliance with such order." In such a case the Commission should normally ask that the offender be held in contempt of court and subjected to punishment until he complies with the court's order. This would be a civil contempt proceeding, tried by the judge without a jury, eventuating in imprisonment of the offender and/or an order requiring him to pay a fixed sum per day until he complies with the court's original decree. The power of the civil contempt sanction has a remarkably taming effect on the contumacious.

Although the Commission's power to help a complainant is severely limited once conciliation has failed, for some complainants the Attorney General will prove a useful ally. He has two relevant grants of power. The statute authorizes him to intervene in a complainant's lawsuit on these terms: "Upon timely application, the court may, in its discretion, permit the Attorney General to intervene in such civil action if he certifies that the case is of general public importance." If the Attorney General is persuaded that the case "is of general public importance," and if the court, "in its discretion," allows him to intervene, the Justice Department will presumably carry the main burden of pressing the lawsuit if the plaintiff wants it that way.

The Attorney General's power to intervene is complemented by authority to sue on his own whenever he "has reasonable cause to believe that any person or group of persons is engaged in a pattern or practice of resistance to the full enjoyment of any of the rights secured by this title, and that the pattern or practice is of such a nature and is intended to deny the full exercise of the rights herein described."

Effect on State Laws

In enacting Title VII, Congress had to take account of the fact that most of the states and dozens of municipalities already had antidiscrimination laws on the books. Since the role left to the states had to be defined not only for Title VII but for other portions of the Civil Rights Act of 1964 as well, Congress included a catchall provision in Title XI, which makes it clear that the Civil Rights Act invalidates only those state laws that are inconsistent with it. In addition, Title VII contains its own general clause on the subject:

> Nothing in this title shall be deemed to exempt or relieve any person from any liability, duty, penalty, or punishment provided by any present or future law of any State or political subdivision of a State, other than any such law which purports to require or permit the doing of any act which would be an unlawful employment practice under this title.

To have stopped with these provisions would have invited confusion and conflict between state and federal enforcement activities. Accordingly, the statute undertakes a more detailed accommodation: in essence it bars action by the federal Commission until a state agency with power to act has had 60 days to dispose of the matter.

THE CIVIL RIGHTS ACT OF 1866

For the black litigant who wishes to bring a lawsuit with a minimum of procedural tangle and a maximum of substantive reach, the Civil Rights Act of 1866 may hold greater promise than the Civil

Rights Act of 1964. If available, the 1866 Act offers a litigant the following advantages: first, he can correct older wrongs because the applicable statutes of limitations may well be measured in years instead of days[4] and because the 1866 law is unencumbered with a recent effective date; second, he can reach smaller enterprises because the 1866 law contains no size cutoff and is based on the Thirteenth Amendment rather than the commerce clause; third, he is probably not limited by Title VII's special provisions concerning seniority, testing, and other matters; fourth, he can obtain swifter relief if, as seems likely, he can sue without waiting for action by the Equal Employment Opportunity Commission or any state fair employment practices commission; and fifth, he can then avoid arguments about what sorts of EEOC actions are prerequisite to his suit. In return for these advantages, the litigant who bypassed the 1964 Act would give up a possibly helpful EEOC investigation, the chance of a successful conciliation, and the prospect of recovering attorney's fees in the event of victory. This means that, for all practical purposes, the 1866 option will be exercised only by complainants supported in their litigation efforts by civil rights organizations.

It may seem a little late in the day to be considering whether the 1866 Act is a fair employment practices law, but the occasion is presented by the Supreme Court's recent decision in *Jones v. Alfred H. Mayer Co.*[5] That decision holds that the Civil Rights Act of 1866 was an open housing law, and much of the Court's analysis seems equally applicable to fair employment.

The portion of the 1866 law before the Court is now contained in 42 U.S.C. §1982. It reads as follows:

> All citizens of the United States shall have the same right, in every State and Territory, as is enjoyed by white citizens thereof to inherit, purchase, lease, sell, hold, and convey real and personal property.

The trial court had dismissed the complaint and the court of appeals had affirmed, holding that the statute protects only against governmental discrimination, not private refusals to sell. The Supreme Court reversed, saying:

> We hold that §1982 bars *all* racial discrimination, private as well as public, in the sale or rental of property, and that the statute, thus construed, is a valid exercise of the power of Congress to enforce the Thirteenth Amendment.

In support of its conclusion, the Court noted: the statute purports to bar all discrimination, not just that perpetrated by government; private injustices against Negroes were among the concerns that led Congress to adopt the 1866 law; and the Thirteenth Amendment empowers Congress to enact laws forbidding racial discrimination because, "surely Congress has the power under the Thirteenth Amendment rationally to determine what are the badges and incidents of slavery" and to outlaw them.

The critical point for students of equal employment opportunity law is that the Civil Rights Act of 1866 also conferred on all citizens the same right as white citizens "to make and enforce contracts." That language now appears in 42 U.S.C. §1981. Applying the analysis utilized in *Jones v. Mayer,* we can fairly conclude that blacks have a protected right to enter into employment contracts, and that anyone refusing to enter into such a contract with a black man because of his race would violate the statute.

That this is not a fanciful extension of *Jones v. Mayer* is strongly suggested by a footnote in which the Court overrules its decision in *Hodges v. United States.* In that footnote, the Court observes that Section 1981 closely parallels Section 1982, the section the Court was construing, and indicates that Section 1981 applies to Negroes who wish "to dispose of their labor by contract."[6]

In advancing the argument that the Civil Rights Act of 1866 affords victims of racial discrimination in employment a right of action, any advocate would have to anticipate the riposte that the very enactment of Title VII in 1964 constitutes strong evidence that the 1866 statute does not reach this subject. For a reply, one need only look to Mr. Justice Harlan's dissenting opinion in *Jones v. Mayer.* He notes that Title VIII of the Civil Rights Act of 1968 contains comprehensive fair housing provisions and goes on to declare:

> I think it particularly unfortunate for the Court to persist in deciding this case on the basis of a highly questionable interpretation of a sweeping, century-old statute which, as the Court acknowledges, see ante, at 415, contains none of the exemptions which the Congress of our own time found it necessary to include in a statute regulating relationships so personal in nature. In effect, this Court, by its construction of §1982, has extended the coverage of federal "fair housing" laws far beyond that which Congress in its wisdom chose to provide in the Civil Rights Act of 1968.

If the Fair Housing Law of 1968 was not sufficient to dissuade the Supreme Court from applying the Civil Rights Act of 1866 to housing discrimination, it would seem to follow that the Fair Employment Law of 1964 should not bar application of the 1866 statute to employment discrimination.

The Supreme Court followed *Jones v. Mayer* in *Sullivan v. Little Hunting Park*,[7] saying "We noted in Jones v. Alfred H. Mayer Co., that the Fair Housing Act of 1968, 82 Stat. 81, in no way impaired the sanction of §1982." The closing paragraph of the *Sullivan* opinion may, however, prove to be a "self-destruct" mechanism. The Court says:

> It is suggested, not by any party but by the dissent, that any relief should await proceedings under the Fair Housing Act of 1968. 82 Stat. 81, 42 U.S.C. (Supp. IV) §3601 et seq. But these suits were commenced on March 16, 1966, two years before that Act was passed. It would be irresponsible judicial administration to dismiss a suit because of an intervening Act which has no possible application to events long preceding its enactment.

In future cases, those who would limit *Jones v. Mayer* will surely urge that it and *Sullivan* apply only to cases arising before the effective date of the 1968 Housing Act. Similarly, those who would avoid application of the principle of these cases to the employment field will maintain that it should not be applied to cases arising after the effective date of Title VII. Whether these arguments will prevail seems likely to depend more upon the composition of the Supreme Court than upon anything we might say about legal theory. Justices Harlan and White were the only dissenters from the 1968 decision in *Jones v. Mayer;* they were joined by Chief Justice Burger in the 1969 decision in *Sullivan.*

Future possibilities of retrenchment notwithstanding, a federal district judge in Ohio quickly adapted *Jones v. Mayer* to employment discrimination and used the Civil Rights Act of 1866 to strike down a union's racist practices.[8]

FEDERAL LABOR LEGISLATION[9]

Under both the National Labor Relations and the Railway Labor Acts, a union selected by the majority of the employees in an appropriate bargaining unit becomes the exclusive representative of all the employees in the unit, not only of those who wish to be represented by that union. All are bound by the actions of the majority's choice, and because the majority's choice is imposed upon everyone in this way, the Supreme Court has consistently held that the statutes implicitly require the union chosen to represent everyone in the unit fairly. The leading case is *Steele v. Louisville & Nashville Railroad,* decided back in the prehistory of equal opportunity law—1944.

Since *Steele,* a worker unfairly represented by the union responsible for bargaining for him has had a right of action in the courts. More recently, the National Labor Relations Board has also undertaken to enforce the duty of fair representation via unfair labor practice proceedings.[10] This means that a victim of union discrimination, instead of having to carry the burden of a lawsuit in the courts, may complain to the General Counsel of the NLRB and let that office prosecute his claim. An unfair labor practice proceeding eventuates, when the charge is well founded, in a cease-and-desist order directing the respondent to fulfill his obligations under the law. Such an order, when enforced by a federal court of appeals, is backed up by the court's contempt powers. Though the Supreme Court has yet to decide whether the Board is correct in using its cease-and-desist powers against unfair representation, it has made clear that the courts will retain their jurisdiction to enforce the duty even if the Board may also do so.[11]

The duty of an employer under the NLRA and the RLA to refrain from racial discrimination against his employees has always been seen as a derivative of the union's duty. It was generally assumed that an employer who wanted to indulge his taste for bigotry was free to do so as far as federal labor legislation was concerned unless a union was implicated. The simplest example of an employer in violation of law was the company that knowingly acquiesced in a union demand that violated the union's duty of fair representation. Thus, an employer who acceded to a union's request that he dismiss a worker because of his race could plainly be ordered to restore the worker to his job and almost certainly could be compelled to pay him lost wages. The simplest example of employer freedom of action under the labor laws was the employer who, without a union in the plant or otherwise on the scene, chose to hire Negroes only in the lowest labor grades and to keep them there. The assumption was that as far as the national labor laws were concerned, such an employer was free to discriminate on the basis of race. The Court of Appeals for the District of Columbia may well have thrown out that assumption in *United Packinghouse Workers v. NLRB.*[12] Judge J. Skelly Wright, writing for the Court of Appeals, admitted that he could find "no cases in which an employer's policy of discrimination as such was alleged to be a violation of the Act." He also acknowledged: "In order to hold that employer racial discrimination violates Section 8(a) (1) it must be found that such discrimination is not merely unjustified, but that it interferes with or restrains discriminated employees from exercising their statutory right to act concertedly for their own aid or protection, as guaranteed by Section 7 of the Act."

Then, in an ingenious reformulation of the issue, he says: "[I]n the context of employer racial discrimination, the question reduces to whether that discrimination inhibits its victims from asserting themselves against their employer to improve their lot." He goes on to answer the question by concluding that racial discrimination does have such an inhibiting effect. He says:

> This effect is twofold: (1) racial discrimination sets up an unjustified clash of interests between groups of workers which tends to reduce the likelihood and the effectiveness of their working in concert to achieve their legitimate goals under the Act; and (2) racial discrimination creates in its victims an apathy or docility which inhibits them from asserting their rights against the perpetrator of the discrimination. *We find that the confluence of these two factors sufficiently deters the exercise of Section 7 rights as to violate Section 8(a) (1).* [Emphasis in original.]

The crucial point is that there is nothing, either in the words of the court's opinion or in the logic of its rationale, that would limit the decision to unionized enterprises.[13] The court itself notes that Section 7 "protects concerted activity by workers to alleviate oppressive working conditions, regardless of whether their activity is channeled through a union, through collective bargaining, or through some other means." It follows from this decision that any employer covered by the NLRA who engages in racial discrimination is vulnerable to a proceeding under that statute. Since the National Labor Relations Board has the cease-and-desist powers that the EEOC lacks, and since, according to *Packinghouse Workers,* the NLRA outlaws racial discrimination by employers as well as unions, the decision effectively converts the NLRA into a comprehensive fair employment practices law.[14]

If the National Labor Relations Act were a brand-new law,

Judge Wright's opinion might have some claim to plausibility, although there would be difficulties with it in any event. But the statute is thirty-four years old. In all that time no one had ever supposed that Congress enacted a fair employment practices law back in 1935, least of all Congress. The decision does not seem likely to survive.

Two Other Federal Remedies

The Fifth and Fourteenth Amendments to the United States Constitution obviously bar job discrimination by governmental bodies. Governments can no more engage in racial discrimination in the labor market than they can in the classroom or the courtroom. But what of private employers and unions? Under what circumstances, if any, do they come under constitutional constraint? Regrettably, the subject is too complex and space too limited to permit discussion here. My thoughts on portions of the subject can be found elsewhere.[15]

Space limitations also force us to pass by the important topic of antidiscrimination provisions in federal contracts. For present purposes, we note only that the federal government requires those from whom it purchases goods and services to promise to foster equal employment opportunity and that federal machinery has been set up to enforce this promise. Once again we must refer the reader elsewhere for details.[16]

The Future

Open questions can be found wherever one looks at the law affecting racial discrimination in employment. We have already asked whether the Civil Rights Act of 1866 and the National Labor Relations Act are comprehensive fair employment laws. Title VII's enforcement has been slowed by preliminary skirmishing over several procedural questions.[17] Numerous bills have been filed asking Congress to give the EEOC cease-and-desist powers. If Congress ultimately chooses to act favorably, what will it do to the private right of action now conferred by Title VII? Destroy it? Convert it to a right to judicial review of EEOC decisions? Preserve it but insist that a complainant make a binding election between his judicial and administrative remedies, in the manner of the New York statute? Or will Congress let the judicial remedy coexist with the administrative one, as seems to be the case with enforcement of the duty of fair representation? Whether it is called preferential treatment, reverse discrimination, or compensation, the issue of special treatment for blacks seems certain to continue to divide us.[18] But the relative importance of this issue, as well as of the whole anti-discrimination effort, will be affected materially by the answer to yet another question, to which we turn now.

To what extent may employers and unions rely on standards which, though formulated in nonracial terms, have the effect of discriminating against blacks? To begin with, we know that deliberate discrimination cannot be immunized by subterfuge. A union that has unlawfully barred blacks from membership may not switch to a system that admits only the relatives of members. An employer that has illegally refused to hire blacks may not switch to a hiring system that gives preference to graduates of X Academy when X Academy is an all-white private school. In both of these instances we can fairly infer that the new standard is intended to continue the old, that the purportedly nonracial criterion is nothing more than a circumlocution. Since the employer and union still intend to discriminate, we have no difficulty in finding their standard illegal.

But suppose that convincing proof of a present intent to discriminate because of race is lacking. Suppose, for example, that a company hires only high school graduates—black or white. Since the proportion of whites holding high school diplomas is higher than that of blacks, this standard puts blacks at a disadvantage. May an employer nonetheless apply it?

Cooper and Sobol have argued brilliantly that any job criterion that adversely affects the employment opportunities of blacks violates fair employment laws unless an adequate business justification for using that criterion is shown.[19] The employer's motive, they maintain, is not determinative. The essence of the Cooper-Sobol thesis is captured in the following brief extracts:

> This shift away from a restrictive focus on the state of mind of the employer is essential to the effective enforcement of fair employment laws, not merely because specific intent is difficult to prove, but because there is frequently no discriminatory intent underlying the adoption of seniority and testing practices, or a wide variety of other

objective and apparently neutral conditions to hire and promotion. These conditions are possibly the most important contemporary obstacles to the employment and promotion of qualified black workers.

* * *

There are two steps to the [Cooper-Sobol] approach: first, a determination of the racial impact of the practice, and second, a determination whether any significant adverse racial impact that exists can be adequately justified. . . .

* * *

The cases and rulings shed some light on the showing of justification that will be required. In *Asbestos Workers Local 53 v. Vogler,* the Fifth Circuit rejected a non-economic justification of nepotism rules—the interest of keeping employment in the family—where, as a result of past racial exclusion, the rule excluded blacks. The court noted that the practice had no trade-related purpose. In *Quarles* and *Local 189,* it was held that the seniority expectations of incumbent white employees are not sufficient to justify the prejudicial impact of seniority rules on blacks, at least where those expectations derived from the prior exclusion of black workers from the seniority unit. . . . The position of every fair employment agency that has considered the testing issue is that test use cannot be justified on the basis of popular conceptions or superficial examination.

* * *

On the other hand, practices having adverse racial impact should be permitted when they serve a significant business purpose that cannot be adequately served by a less prejudicial practice. For example, a bona fide requirement of the ability to type, as measured by an appropriate typing test, is undoubtedly justified regardless of its likely adverse racial impact.[20]

Using this approach, our hypothetical employer could insist on his high school diploma requirement only if he could demonstrate that it correlated significantly with performance of the jobs he needed done. Absent evidence that those with diplomas performed better than dropouts, the employer's refusal to hire dropouts would disadvantage blacks for no good reason. Even if the graduation requirement did correlate with job performance, if some other mode of selection less prejudicial to blacks would work just as well for the employer, his choice of the racially biased criterion could still constitute illegal discrimination, according to Cooper and Sobol.

The ultimate fate of the Cooper-Sobol thesis remains in doubt. The Supreme Court has yet to pass on any aspect of the problem. In the lower courts, the seniority cases tend to support Cooper and

Sobol, as do the cases on nepotism, but the leading case on testing is contra and damaging on diploma requirements as well.[21]

Several years ago, I noted that the black quest for a better life was stimulating a variety of social programs aimed at improving the lot of all the poor and underprivileged, not just the racially disadvantaged. I suggested that "It is one of the Negro's great contributions to American society that his drive for equal opportunity is giving impetus to a social revolution that, measured by the number of people helped, will be far more beneficial to whites than to Negroes." Acceptance of the Cooper-Sobol thesis would take the point further: not only would all employees—black and white—be more fairly treated by a system that dropped job barriers supported by folklore rather than demonstrated utility, but American business too might profit from a system of employee screening governed by rationality rather than superstition.

NOTES

1. This section draws heavily on portions of Chapter 3 of M. Sovern, *Legal Restraints on Racial Discrimination in Employment* (1966). Though the text has been revised to take account of state developments since publication of that book, support for the assertions made here will generally be found there. Since the changes are relatively minor, I bow to our editor's injunction to keep footnotes to a minimum and refer the reader to the book for supporting authority for this section.

2. 78 Stat. 253 (1964), 42 U.S.C. §§2000e *et seq.* (1964). Support for most of the assertions in this section too will be found in Sovern, *supra* note 1.

3. Newman v. Piggie Park Enterprises, 390 U.S. 400 (1968).

4. Title VII's basic limitations period is 90 days, but a number of variations are possible. See §706(d). The applicable period of limitations under the Civil Rights Act of 1866 was discussed in Dobbins v. Local 212, IBEW, 292 F. Supp. 413, 444 (S.D. Ohio 1968), where the court said: "There being no Federal statute of limitations with respect to a Civil Rights Act of 1866 case, the most adaptable State statute governs. *See* Mulligan v. Schlachter, 389 F.2d 231 (6th Cir. 1968). The most applicable Ohio Statute is R.C. of Ohio 2305.09(d)—four years."

5. 392 U.S. 409 (1968).

6. *Id.* at 442 n.78.

7. 396 U.S. 229 (1969).

8. Dobbins v. Local 212, IBEW, 292 F. Supp. 413 (S.D. Ohio 1968); *accord, e.g.,* Clark v. American Marine Corp. 297 F. Supp. 1305 (E.D. La. 1969); Washington v. Baugh Construction Co., 61 CCH Lab. Cas. ¶9346 (W.D. Wash. 1969). *Contra, e.g.,* Harrison v. American Can Co., CCH Lab. Cas. ¶9353 (S.D. Ala. 1969).

9. Except as indicated below, the supporting footnotes for this section can be found in Sovern, *supra* note 1, ch. 6.

10. The Board has been upheld by the Fifth and District of Columbia Circuits. NLRB v. Local 1367, ILA, 368 F.2d 1010 (5th Cir. 1966), *cert. denied,* 389 U.S. 837 (1967); Local 12, United Rubber Workers v. NLRB, 368 F.2d 12 (5th Cir. 1966), *cert. denied,* 389 U.S. 837 (1967); Truck Drivers, Local 568 v. NLRB, 379 F.2d 137 (D.C. Cir. 1967). The Second Circuit, in NLRB v. Miranda Fuel Co., 326 F.2d 172 (2d Cir. 1963), was less hospitable to the Board. For a further discussion of the Second Circuit decision, *see* Sovern, *supra* note 1, at 163 *et seq.*

11. Vaca v. Sipes, 386 U.S. 171 (1967).

12. 416 F.2d 1126, 1135 (D.C. Cir.), *cert. denied,* 90 S.Ct. 216 (1969).

13. As the name of the case suggests, a union was on the scene in *Packinghouse Workers,* but it was not representing anybody unfairly. On the contrary, it tried to get the company to eliminate racially discriminatory practices. This aspect of the case played no part in the portion of the court's opinion discussed in the text.

14. Though the case deals with discrimination against those already on the payroll, other rights conferred on "employees" by the NLRA have regularly been held to extend to those seeking work. The point is developed and authorities collected in Sovern, *supra* note 1, at 152 *et seq.*

15. *See* Sovern, *supra* note 1, at 148–52, 158, 199–200; Sovern, "An Overview of Equal Employment Opportunity," Proceedings of the American Bar Association National Institute on Equal Employment Opportunity, at 1–5 (1969).

16. *See* Sovern, *supra* note 1, ch. 5.

17. Authorities are collected in St. Antoine, "Litigation and Mediation Under Title VII of the Civil Rights Act of 1964," Proceedings of the American Bar Association National Institute on Equal Employment Opportunity (1969).

18. For an excellent treatment of this subject, see Kaplan, "Equal Justice in an Unequal World: Equality for the Negro—The Problem of Special Treatment," 61 *Northwestern University Law Review* 363 (1966).

19. Cooper & Sobol, "Seniority and Testing Under Fair Employment Laws: A General Approach to Objective Criteria of Hiring and Promotion," 82 *Harvard Law Review* 1598 (1969).

20. *Id.* at 1670–73.

21. Griggs v. Duke Power Co., 420 F.2d 1225, CCH Lab. Cas. ¶9379 (4th Cir. 1970), is the testing and diploma requirement case; it collects the leading cases on seniority and nepotism as well.

THE RIGHT TO HOUSING

FRANK I. MICHELMAN

IS THERE "A RIGHT TO HOUSING," OR IS SUCH A right developing?

Most simply and fundamentally, a right to housing might mean a claim upon organized society, on behalf of each individual or household unit, to be assured of access to minimally adequate housing. I shall refer to this as "a right to be housed." Even such a broad statement, of course, leaves open a number of crucial issues. If the statement were accepted as positing a social ideal (it plainly is not accurate as a description of actual practice), further discussion would be required of at least the following questions:

1. How absolute an assurance? At one extreme, we might intend merely an assurance that housing will be available without arbitrary interference or deprivation, and according to the rules which normally govern access to goods. In our present society this perhaps suggests nothing much more than a kind of Horatio Alger guarantee that ability, prudence, industry, and thrift will bring rewards. At the other extreme, we might intend an ironclad assurance that no one, no matter his profligacy or obstinacy, shall ever be deprived of decent shelter. In speaking of "a right to be housed" we would probably have in mind something closer to the latter extreme—an assurance that acceptable housing will be available irrespective of

Frank I. Michelman is Professor of Law at Harvard Law School and a former lawyer in the Department of Justice. He is the author of articles on housing law and constitutional law, and the co-author of a casebook, Government in Urban Areas.

the market returns commanded by one's endowments of talent, influence, or capital, and irrespective even of voluntary choices in one's remote past which have resulted in present inability to pay the true costs of acceptable housing. The principal qualification might be that a person should bear the consequences of unambiguous voluntary choices involving, for example, deliberate and culpable waste of socially provided housing resources.

2. *Access in how inflexible a form?* Again, the question can be stated in terms of extremes. At one extreme, society would fulfill its obligation by tendering a particular housing accommodation on a take-it-or-leave-it basis—a conventional public housing program. At the other extreme, society would simply undertake to amplify the claimant's income to the point where he was autonomously allocating to shelter needs as much as acceptable housing really costs. This would be a fully implemented program of income maintenance. An intermediate undertaking might be to transfer income in a form neither allowing of diversion from the claimant's specific housing needs nor denying him a range of housing choice. This would be a rent supplement program. *A right to be housed* —as distinguished from, say, "a right to life" or "a right to a decent income"—probably envisions something ranging between provision of specific housing in kind and provision of rent supplements.

3. *Adequate by how relative a standard?* Do we have in mind an absolute standard of minimum performance to preserve basic health, privacy, and sanity? Or do we mean something more relative, more emulative, more informed by "equality" impulses? The right-to-be-housed notion itself does not appear to point especially in either direction; but it seems likely that the suggested duality is not a true one, since resort to such words as "minimum" and "basic" will never purge our housing-quality judgments of knowledge about what others in the community or society enjoy.

Is there, then, "a right to be housed" in some sense generally corresponding to the foregoing sketch? The answer may depend on which of our several normative systems we choose to address. Are we asking a question of common morality, of philosophical ethics, or of law? In common morality, it would seem that acknowledgment of a right to be housed is closely linked with acceptance of the welfare state, and that the right is—at least at a rhetorical level—fairly well established. It seems likely, for example, that in declaring the famous ideal of "a decent home and a suitable living environment for every American family"[1] Congress purported to

convey more than a mere Algerism. Yet in formal, systematic, philosophical discussions of social justice (limiting ourselves now to those
proceeding within a "liberal," individualistic, and market-oriented
framework) a right to be housed is much more problematical. In
recent years there has emerged among analysts of justice some interest in "social" or "just" minimums,[2] but the discussion so far remains tentative and general, suggesting no very rigorous approach
to defining the minimum or specifying its contents.

A CONSTITUTIONAL RIGHT TO BE HOUSED?

A constitutional right to be housed is necessarily even more problematical. The perfection of such a right would seem to require,
first, a commanding and coherent ethical theory capable of informing such general constitutional locutions as "due process" and
"equal protection" (since we lack a specific constitutional text on
the subject); second, actual (even if inexplicit) adoption of the
theory by the courts, and especially the Supreme Court; and third,
practical enforcement of the theoretical right in the face of inaction
or resistance on the part of legislative and executive agencies. Since
no such ethical theory seems now available, it is not surprising that
there are few clear signs yet of a legal right to be housed under the
Fourteenth Amendment. If such an ethical argument does appear,
the problems of judicially enforcing the full-blown right may themselves be baffling enough to prevent its outright espousal even by
activist courts.

Nevertheless, it may be possible to detect a halting movement in
the general direction of a significant Fourteenth Amendment right
to be housed. More precisely, there have been two movements
afoot which could one day converge to produce such a right. On
the one hand, a recent process may be traced out whereby the Supreme Court has been reading the Fourteenth Amendment equal
protection clause to require states to protect their citizens against
certain risks of deprivation because of income shortage.[3] On the
other hand, there are signs that the Court is becoming imbued with
(and it is demonstrably accumulating precedents which support)
the idea of housing as a need of outstanding importance, capable of
generating unconventional legal claims. The Court has been persuaded that judicial enforcement of private discrimination in the
sale of homes is "state action" which violates the equal protection

clause;[4] and also that such discrimination, even without any public involvement, is a "badge of slavery" within the ambit of Thirteenth Amendment concern.[5] One may doubt whether discrimination affecting some less "fundamental" commodity would have provoked these bold responses.

The Court has also, according to some interpretations, held in effect that states owe their citizens a positive duty to protect them against private, racial discrimination in the marketing of housing;[6] and again, it seems unlikely that more ordinary needs would have induced such a step. Finally, in the lower courts a remarkable number of breakthroughs in law governing a citizen's standing to challenge the administration of governmental largesse, and his right to procedural indulgence in the course of such administration, appear to have occurred where an interest in housing is at stake. Challenges to the adequacy of urban renewal relocation plans by those being displaced provide the most prominent example. For years litigants were prevented from securing judicial tests of adequacy by various threshold impediments. It was held that neither statutory relocation-planning requirements nor the embodiment of these requirements in contracts between federal and local agencies was intended to confer private rights of enforcement; and that the issue of adequacy was committed to the unreviewable discretion of federal officials. As a result of persistent litigation, courts began to hold, in something like an evolutionary order, that displacees had standing to litigate over the duty of officials to grant them a hearing on the adequacy issue; that officials were required to consider written submissions by displacees in the course of making their decisions; and that those decisions were subject to limited judicial review on the merits.[7]

In the public housing field, old doctrines to the effect that agencies could admit and evict tenants for whatever reason, and without procedural formality, are in process of giving way to requirements that the reasons be substantially related to the purposes of the public housing program and that tenants or applicants be given a fair opportunity to contest adverse decisions.[8] All told, it is clear that "equal access to housing is regarded by the Court as a matter of the most serious social and constitutional concern."[9] Of course, it is a perilous as well as a tempting journey from such a premise to the conclusion that the state's failure to provide adequate housing to those otherwise unable to pay for it should be held a denial by the state of equal protection. The complexities of the argument are a current preoccupation of legal commentators.

The commentaries, and the judicial developments which they scrutinize, suggest that articulation of a fully worked out ethical argument for social assurances of housing may in fact not be indispensable to emergence of the corresponding constitutional right. It is not clear that such ethical arguments exist as would unambiguously condemn poll taxes, skewed legislative apportionments, or refusals to subsidize criminal appeals; and it seems possible that the special judicial solicitude for the interests in voting and criminal defense has been inspired at least as much by pervasive popular attitudes, and ineffable judicial instinct, as by discursive reason or textual exegesis. Yet the Supreme Court recently declared that a legislature's budgetary conservatism in "social welfare" matters— even, perhaps, where the effect is to classify without apparent regard to relative need—is immune to constitutional attack if rationally related to any proper governmental end.[10] Such a doctrine augurs ill for the canonization of housing as a "fundamental right," denial of which can be justified only by "compelling" interests of the state.

A STATUTORY RIGHT TO BE HOUSED?

Lack of a perfected constitutional right to be housed would be immaterial during any period when a like right prevailed by force of statute. But despite the great volume of existing housing-subsidy legislation, it probably cannot now be said that there is a statutory right to be housed. If "a decent home for every American family" is not merely a commitment to freedom of economic opportunity, neither is it yet the declaration of an enforceable legal claim. It remains the statement of a welfare ideal, a general guide to administration and interpretation of the housing statutes—but not an enforceable promise by the government to the public to tax and appropriate as heavily as would be required to satisfy the ideal. Nor, indeed, are the more specific authorizations of the several Housing Acts now being interpreted, or judicially enforced, as such promises. They are understood, rather, as the public talking to itself and its agents—ordering, guiding, legitimating, and to some extent predicting the conduct of public affairs. But when the duly appropriated rent supplement or public housing money runs out, suits do not pry loose more money—despite unappropriated authorizations or unfilled need.

Nevertheless, the panoply of housing acts is having effects on legal doctrine which, in cumulative impact, drift in the general direction of a right to be housed. For one thing, if special judicial sensitivity to housing as a preferred interest is in fact emerging, the apparent lavishing of legislative attention on this need may be a contributing cause. Moreover, the notion of a right to be housed may be functional even though limited in application to resources already dedicated to the purpose by legislative discretion. A most straightforward illustration is the developing law concerning eligibility for housing subsidy, and administrative practices regarding admission and termination.[11] Increasingly it seems that relative inability to afford adequate housing, and willingness not to waste publicly provided housing, will be the only criteria for eligibility. Also, claimants will be guaranteed fair opportunities to contest and receive an impartial judgment concerning these issues. Other public policies, though coherent and not intrinsically unconstitutional—for example, policies opposed to cohabitation by persons not married to one another—will not be permitted to prejudice access to subsidized housing. The distribution of insufficient appropriations among the universe of eligible claimants will, it appears, have to be somehow made random or neutralized as by a first-come-first-served policy.[12] One may suggest that the notion of a right to be housed is implicit in such a set of rules. It could, indeed, be forcefully argued that a tolerance for insufficient appropriations is anomalous within this ascendant system of thought about access to subsidized housing; and it might be surmised that the tolerance will, accordingly, wither away despite possible judicial inability to declare and enforce a right to be housed.

But beyond this surmise, it seems certain that aggressive use will be made of the equal protection clause in an effort to construct out of existing housing-assistance legislation something which verges on a constitutional right to be housed. The argument is, simply, that avoidance of the increase in taxation which would be required for full satisfaction of the legislatively declared need is an insufficient justification for the "discrimination" which results when some but not all members of the needy class receive full assistance. The seeds of such an argument may have been planted by the Supreme Court when it invalidated the use by states of minimum periods of prior residence as a condition of eligibility for public assistance.[13]

Acceptance of this argument would, in theory, leave the state with the choice of either canceling the subsidy programs or funding them fully. Since the former choice seems unlikely, courts would have to proceed in the realization that acceptance of the argument would involve them in ordering the legislative branch either to increase or reallocate the public budget. If past judicial response to that prospect is any guide, frustration awaits those who attempt such litigation. Perhaps a good clue as to how things will go can be gleaned from recent litigation over public assistance programs. The Supreme Court, so far, has turned away equal protection challenges to "percentage reduction" practices which purport to distribute insufficient funds in accordance with relative need,[14] even as it has sometimes insisted that distinctions among applicants be made, if at all, on grounds relevant to need—for example, in rejecting period-of-residency requirements. The result may be that partial funding will be judicially tolerated, but that distribution of the proceeds will have to be correlated with a plausible index of need.

THE RIGHT NOT TO BE TENDERED SUBSTANDARD HOUSING

Suggestion of a right to be adequately housed will immediately suggest to some a duty not to furnish, or place on the market, housing of substandard quality. If a person has a claim on society to be decently housed despite a lack of personal means, it may seem a natural inference that no one is free to take advantage of another's income shortage by inducing him through low rents to accept substandard housing.

At the same time, "negative" duties not to furnish substandard housing may also exist quite independently of "positive" duties to provide adequate housing. Through a tropical flowering of new statutory and common-law conceptions which fairly bewilders, the American legal system is currently breaking away from archaic doctrines which placed the risk of loss and injury from physical defect on tenants, and woodenly insisted that tenants pay the entire agreed rent as long as they inhabit leased premises, despite outrageous disrepair.

Two lines of development and change may be distinguished.

The conventional doctrine that tenants bear the risk of injury from physical defects, in the absence of concealment, fraud, or active negligence by the landlord, is being replaced by statutory and common-law concepts of implied warranties of fitness for use.[15] Also, the conventional doctrine that a tenant whose occupation has been rendered unsafe or otherwise seriously impaired by fault of the landlord must remove in order to be totally or partially excused from rent liability is being replaced by statutes which protect tenants against eviction for justifiable rent withholdings.[16] New public and private remedies now abound in the lawbooks: penal and injunctive enforcements of codes; receiverships designed to accomplish repair out of the revenues and mortgage values of substandard premises; damage recoveries for personal injuries; deductions of tenant-advanced repair costs from future rents; and rent-free occupancy during periods of disrepair.[17]

It is tempting to read this doctrinal revolution—which now verges on acceptance of the breathtakingly simple idea that the very act of placing indecent housing on the market is a tortious affront to the dignity of tenants[18]—as itself firm evidence of the advent in our law of a positive right to be adequately housed. This idea, while not devoid of force or insight, misses some important subtleties. The hypothesized tort of "slumlordism" may indeed be seen as a partial outcropping of an underlying right to be housed. It may as easily be seen as inconsistent with the latter right, in practice and perhaps also in principle. "Adequacy" or "decency" is, after all, a relative notion. Insofar as *shelter* is what is wanted and claimed, it seems undeniable that some shelter—even "substandard," "dilapidated," "unsanitary," or "dangerous" shelter—is better than none. If the effect of introducing sanctions against "slumlordism" is, on the whole, shrinkage and further deterioration of the supply of housing available to persons with low incomes, then it is more accurate to construe such sanctions as vindicating general and abstract values of human decency and dignity than as vindicating the more materialistic right to be housed. There is, in fact, good reason to suspect that shrinkage and deterioration of supply do result from wars on slumlordism, when they are carried on without sufficient commitments to public subsidization of housing suppliers or purchasers.[19] We might, then, say that the *subsidy* programs suggest a right to be housed; but that the array of remedies against standards-violating landlords do not. Yet I think this would be an overly doctrinaire interpretation. The burgeoning concern about landlord "misconduct" should probably be accepted, at least partly, as a somewhat irresponsible, although humanly understandable, reaction by society to its dawning perception that the ideal of a right to be adequately housed is not being realized in practice. It would not be out of character for our society first to react to such a perception by looking about to see if the problem is not simply a result of correctible misconduct on some bad person's part. Here the likely candidates are the landlords. They have been accused, some are being convicted, some are being (rather grudgingly) absolved, and we are learning that the problem is not all, or even mostly, their fault.

A RIGHT TO FREE CHOICE IN HOUSING

Free Choice in Location

Threats to freedom of choice often arise where there is no question of a claimant's ability to afford the housing he would like—for example, through discriminatory refusals to sell or lease. Free choice may also become an issue where the housing in question is publicly provided, because of administrative practices which limit the opportunities of one or another group. Discriminatory assignment to projects, racially deliberate location of new projects, and minimum prior-residency requirements are examples. In short, threats to free choice can continue to arise even if society one day fully recognizes the right to be housed—for example, through a greatly augmented income maintenance or rent supplement program. It is relevant to know, then, how close we are to realization of a right to free choice of housing within one's means—what I shall henceforward call "the right to free choice," as distinguished from "the right to be housed."

The most obvious threat to free choice stems from racial discrimination. There is a clear constitutional right to be free of officially sponsored or supported, racially explicit or racially motivated (*de jure*) discrimination in housing sales, rentals, or occupancy. Also, where governmental complicity is apparent, there seem to be additional protections against being forced (by *de facto* discrimination) into racially segregated housing. These may take the form of prohibitions against the systematic location of subsidized housing so as to create high probabilities of segregated occupancy,[20] or of laws preventing indiscriminate dislocation of persons into a racially closed housing market.[21] In the absence of detectable governmental involvement, protection against discrimination in sales, rentals, and related activities is afforded by "fair housing" and "open occupancy" laws which draw direct and significant support from the Constitution.

Where racial considerations are not evident, governments are nonetheless prevented by the Constitution from indulging in explicit restriction of housing choices on grounds of economic capability—as by "minimum-cost" zoning regulations. Yet all the doctrines so far recited will not fully guarantee a decent freedom of choice for poor or nonwhite households. For insofar as there are some relatively poor persons who would choose a suburban home environment if they could, a promising technique for denying them that choice is to price them out of the market. Even if we assume full implementation of a right to be housed, the level of subsidy is unlikely to be so high as to preclude the pricing-out response— as we know from current difficulties in making an economic success of inexpensive housing in strictly regulated suburbs, even with the aid of various producer subsidies, "leased housing," and rent supplement schemes.

Thus a claim not to have housing choice restricted on account of one's socio-economic status as a practical matter entails a claim to be free of unreasonable land use restrictions; it calls for legal limitations on cost-inflating municipal regulatory powers. Such limitations are plainly in the offing. Not only are they currently a frequent topic of academic discussion, but they are already beginning to appear in legislation.[22] In court, they may be contended for by (1) the same style of equal protection argument which, it was suggested above, may also yield a constitutional right to be housed;[23] or by (2) arguments focused on the political or participatory claims of those who must suffer the consequences of suburban exclusiveness though afforded no voice in the fashioning of the exclusionary regulations; or by (3) appeals to the conflict between such regulations and federal policies calling for provision of subsidized housing outside areas of racial concentration.[24] Courts have occasionally invalidated exclusionary zoning practices because of their "confiscatory" impacts on landowners or because of their tenuous connection with public health, safety, and welfare. But more often, and predictably, the practices survive challenges on these conventional grounds.[25]

A closely related development, which seems fairly likely, would be the imposition by statute, as a condition of public subsidy for major housing developments, of a requirement that the developer provide for a full range of housing types and prices in his development. At least one commentator is prepared to speculate about a constitutional obligation on high-income municipalities to counteract tendencies toward exclusiveness by active promotion of low-cost housing within their boundaries.[26] One reason for resistance to such programs has been a widespread belief that a relatively poor family's immigration into a jurisdiction occasions a net fiscal drain. To the extent that the financing of such governmental services as education and income maintenance is shifted from a municipal to a state or regional tax base, the fiscal effects of intermunicipal migration by poor households are evidently neutralized. Thus legislation which effects such a shift may be seen as related to a right to free choice in housing. Not only does it dissipate a real source of resistance to such migration (and thus of motivation to restrictive land use controls); it also denies what otherwise can serve as a handy disguise for prejudice and so may allow prejudice to be seen and dealt with more effectively.

Free Choice in Use

If it is true that a home is not merely a structure in a physical and social environment, but also the specialized locus of important, personal activities, then a right to "free choice and use" of whatever housing one can afford should encompass a degree of immunity from oppressive rules governing access to and use of such housing. The home is generally understood to be, and is socially valued as, a place for child rearing; for association with chosen intimates; for cultivation and indulgence of specialized—and even unconventional—tastes in art, sex, recreation, diet, and religion. We might, then, expect to see limitations on the degree to which society will allow "ownership" of housing stock to be turned against child rearing or extended into censorship of the private activities and associations of occupants. The emergence of some such limitations can be detected. A legislature may enact that refusal to rent to families because they have young children is unlawful discrimination. A court may hold that such a practice on a landlord's part contravenes "public policy," and thus refuse to award an eviction remedy despite unimpeachable language in the written lease. Various other forms of tenant misconduct asserted by the landlord as grounds for eviction under the lease may be judicially avoided either by unnatural readings of lease language or by invocation of an "unconscionability" or "balance-of-the-equities" doctrine. Somewhat analogously, attempts by homeowners' associations or cooperative or condominium organizations to impose their common morality upon the privacy of a member's home may run afoul of judicial doctrines of "repugnancy to the fee" or "restraint on alienation."

Perhaps as likely as the further development of doctrines such as those mentioned in the preceding paragraph would be the extension of the First and Fourteenth Amendments to cover almost all of the nation's housing stock. In one form or another—below-market-interest-rate loans, FHA guarantees of market-rate loans, supplementation of tenants' rents or owners' mortgage interest, provision of sites through public powers of eminent domain, provision of utilities through government subsidy—a degree of dependence on public powers or funds is likely to overtake almost all housing. At some point, the dependence becomes significant enough to subject the owner effectively to some or all of the obligations imposed on governments by the First and Fourteenth Amendments—including not only those to refrain from undue censorship of tenants' activities but also those pertaining to discrimination and arbitrariness in admission and expulsion practices. The trend is clearly toward such assimilation.[27]

A Right Not to Be Uprooted

If a house becomes a home only through its occupants' settling in and making it so, then a society's recognition of a right to housing must encompass some receptivity to claims not to be involuntarily removed from housing already occupied. Acknowledgment of such claims would reflect sensitivity to the severe inconvenience of moving, including the risk of not finding substitute housing of objectively comparable quality at comparable cost. It would also reflect sensitivity to the trauma of being uprooted—of being torn away from a structure, surroundings, and neighborhood with which one's existence may be interpenetrated in countless important ways. I shall, accordingly, refer to the idea of special claims to retain housing which one has as "a right not to be uprooted."

Evolving anti-eviction safeguards in the constitutional law of public housing are, as we have already seen, ambiguous in their deeper connotations, though they certainly might draw some of their inspiration from a right not to be uprooted. More clearly to the point is the introduction by statute of flexible "sliding" stand-ards of eligibility to occupy subsidized housing, and ways of fixing the amount of rent a household must contribute from its own means, which make it possible for a family to stay put despite its breakthrough to "overincome" status. Also noteworthy is recent Massachusetts legislation which prohibits eviction from public housing except for "good cause"—a rather drastic shift from the pre-existing situation in which local authorities routinely tendered month-to-month leases exposing tenants to eviction without cause on 30 days notice.

The Threat of Eminent Domain

As applied to nonsubsidized housing, a right not to be uprooted must contend with two quite distinct, opposing sets of claims. First, there are the polity's claims to displace housing structures (upon payment of "just compensation" to those whose property is taken) in order to make way for needed public projects such as highways, airports, or city redevelopment. Second, there are the claims of a paramount owner (landlord) to regain possession of his property for altered use or investment.

The claims of eminent domain are unlikely ever to disappear entirely. Payment of compensation—even assuming acceleration of the modern statutory trend to compensate tenants for having up-rooted them as well as owners for their investments—is not directly responsive to a right not to be uprooted, because the injuries do not seem measurable in financial terms. A right not to be uprooted, if taken seriously, would imply deflection or abandonment of the pending public project. At the constitutional level, it would imply resuscitation of the "public use" restriction on eminent domain which most commentators, with reason, now deem moribund.[28] Under some circumstances, however, the equal protection clause is now filling the breach left by the demise of "public use." This is particularly noticeable where the adverse effect of a project is spe-

cially concentrated on a racial minority. One commentator has suggested that it might also come to be so where a project has serious
adverse effects on the housing-choice freedom of the poor; and
there are hints of a more general role for equal protection in eminent domain settings—for example, as a shield for condemnees who
allege that they have not been given the same chance as other nearby
owners to save their homes through participation in a rehabilitation
program.[29]

But more significant than direct limitations on power to uproot
may be the emergence of *procedures* looking toward the consent of
the uprooted, or at least their participation, as a condition of uprooting. While to some extent reflected in statute law, the advent
of these procedures is obviously a response to widespread, and vigorously expressed, popular commitment to a right not to be uprooted.

The statutory manifestation of this trend in the highway programs has assumed a rather modest form as perhaps is fitting when
one considers the great potential for harm to the larger community
from intransigent pockets of resistance to pieces of large-scale transportation networks. Long-standing but vague and ineffective requirements that local preferences be considered in precise route-
planning through urban areas are being reinforced by procedural
requirements focusing on advance notice, publication, and public
hearings. While a more effective background threat of judicial review may result from these procedural innovations, their more
substantial impact may be that appeals to public opinion will become more feasible because of better opportunity for exposure and
publicity. Substantial evidence already exists that energized public
opinion is willing and able to deflect an ill-considered or insensi-
tively evaluated highway or other public project. The new procedures may provide some additional likelihood that public opinion
will be both energized and enlightened.

In the field of urban redevelopment, elaborate publicity and
hearing requirements have existed for some time without providing
satisfaction. Part of the reason has been the failure of governmental
agencies to take the requirements seriously or to treat them as a
channel through which influence might run from the affected public to the agency, as well as vice versa—a failure which the current
rousing of judicial review from its slumber may partially correct.
But in this field, where the external ramifications of a local veto
will often be far less momentous than in the case of a transporta-

tion network, the formal, legal framework for participation by those who stand to be uprooted is not limited to public hearings. Decentralization of authority to take the necessary action is frequently recommended by commentators and supported (somewhat vaguely) by HUD's "workable program" requirement of a "Project Area Committee," and results are forthcoming. In some localities, Model Cities agencies will provide the vehicle while elsewhere other "indigenous," "neighborhood," or "community" groups will emerge or be officially created—sometimes to deal through imaginative contracts with LPA (Local Public Agencies—that is, renewal, redevelopment, and housing authorities), sometimes to accept a portion of the decision-making authority through some type of structural reallocation. This decentralization will frequently place an effective veto on uprooting much closer to the uprooted than has been the case under the conventional city government–LPA dispensation.

The Threat of Private Eviction

When we turn to the conflict between a right not to be uprooted and the claims of landlords to resume control of their properties, discussion becomes a good deal less manageable and orderly (though not less speculative). We here deal with a central element of that body of doctrine known as "landlord-tenant law." It is the case of the "at-will" tenant, or "periodic" tenant (whose tenure is normally supposed to be for indefinite duration or self-renewing for successive short periods, subject to discretionary termination by either party), which presents the strongest challenge to the idea of a right not to be uprooted. That the law has to a degree responded to this case may be taken as an indication that the right enjoys some recognition among us.

Doctrines opposed to retaliatory evictions—against those who call official attention to code violations, or who engage prominently in tenant-organizing or self-help activities—are appearing both in judicial interpretations of constitutional and statutory material and in new legislation expressly addressed to the problem.[30] While these doctrines doubtless are more directly expressive of free speech and right-to-petition values than of a right not to be uprooted, they also imply that society takes particular note of the interest in not being uprooted. It is the risky exposure of this particular interest which is deemed incompatible with free expression, free petition, free

association, and effective enforcement of minimum housing standards.

Also reflecting emergent solicitude for the interest in staying
put are current attacks on the constitutionality of long-established,
summary procedures for evicting tenants who have defaulted in
their rent or refused to depart after notice of termination of a tenancy at will. It is being argued—with some probability of success
—that because such procedures are often so swift and inexorable
as effectively to prevent tenants from raising defenses and counter-
claims based on landlord failures to keep premises in repair, they
violate due process and equal protection rights.[31] Closely related are
attacks—which may be accepted by the Supreme Court this year
and certainly deserve to be—on rules which bar poor tenants from
defending or appealing in eviction cases because they cannot afford
to post bond.[32]

More directly to the point may be various waiting periods written into statutory eviction procedures, which clearly are designed
to protect people against the direct consequences of uprooting without sufficient warning, and which in many cases doubtless have the
additional effect of inducing a landlord to abandon or postpone his
eviction plans considerably beyond the period of firm statutory protection. In a typical pattern, a landlord bent upon eviction may
have to (1) give 30 days written notice in advance to terminate a
tenancy at will; (2) wait an additional 15 to 30 days while his eviction proceeding runs its course from initiation to judgment and
execution; (3) abide by a stay of execution of one to six months
which the judge may grant upon the tenant's showing of difficulty
in locating new quarters. This sort of time cushion is coming to be
regarded as a natural accompaniment of any tenancy. The trend is
indicated by the readiness of some lawyers to challenge, as denials
of equal protection of the laws, statutory procedures which would
dispense with them in certain exceptional cases.

Most directly in point are substantive restrictions, found in
New York "emergency" rent control laws, upon an owner's right
to evict a tenant whose term, whether at will or for a definite period, has expired. An owner may be permitted to evict only when
he can show that he requires the space for his own habitation, or
plans to replace it with more or better housing. Here the right not
to be uprooted (for an indefinite period!) receives explicit recognition and is accorded prevalent weight except as against excep-
tionally weighty counterconsiderations. While it is true that such

laws are found only in a few places, and even then cover only a fraction of the housing stock, it may be anticipated that equal protection arguments will be advanced in attempts to extend their coverage.

THE RIGHT TO OWN ONE'S HOME

Security of tenure is one of the chief attributes distinguishing ownership of housing from the mere occupancy of it through leasing. Two others are (1) command of the capital value of the housing (and particularly the right to short-term or secular appreciation of that value) for such purposes as borrowing and selling, and (2) control over maintenance, renovation, expansion, redesign, and use of the housing and its environs. Perhaps inherent in any combination of indefinite tenure, command of capital, and control over design and use—but also of independent significance—is the status of being an owner. There are convincing signs that the status is valued intrinsically, but it also carries nonpsychic benefits which perhaps reflect its favored position in popular sentiment: income tax deductibility of mortgage interest and real estate taxes, for example; or, somewhat obsoletely, eligibility to vote or stand for public office.[33]

Achievement of ownership status remains, in any event, the surest path to security of tenure and substantial control over use, as well as the only route to command of capital value.[34] It may accordingly make sense to inquire whether there are any signs of "a right to homeownership"—that is, a right to *own* whatever housing one's means (whether or not socially subsidized) give access to, rather than merely occupy it. For the most part, any such right would of course have to be sought in legislation explicitly conferring it.

A statutory right to homeownership must be wedded to a statutory right to be housed; that is, legislating the right to be a homeowner must, if not a mockery, entail provision of the wherewithal. Legislation of this sort now exists; it is, indeed, the modern and fashionable approach to housing subsidy. But any right to homeownership inferred from such legislation would be subject to the same qualifications as those set forth above in discussing a statutory right to be housed. Detection of a right to homeownership in this legislation may, in addition, require some attention of the concept of ownership, insofar as economic factors dictate that most subsidized housing will be in multiple dwellings. A virtually unqualified security of tenure of an apartment-type unit is easily arranged through a cooperative or condominium format. But there will be an irreducible minimum of encumbrance of one's command of the capital value apportionable to one's unit (such as first-refusal rights on the part of other owner-occupants); and, inevitably, a quite substantial impairment of one's right to control. For control over such a densely populated area as an apartment building or complex and its environs simply has to be shared with one's fellows —and indeed, except for matters of interior decor and design, must largely accrue in the form of voting membership in a community of owner-occupants.

THE RIGHT TO EXERCISE CONTROL OVER ONE'S ENVIRONMENT

The right to live in a community and be influential in its affairs may itself be regarded as a valued right associated with the idea of a right to housing. In the preceding discussion, what may be called "a right to control one's environment" has surfaced. We should note that such control may both exist in the absence of ownership and extend well beyond what ownership may connote.

Control in the absence of ownership is now evolving, for example, through "unionization" of the tenantry.[35] Through collective bargaining agreements and "management contracts," the tenants collectively may assume substantial control over environmental factors such as maintenance and use of common areas, and restriction of nuisancelike activities by occupants. They can also influence such critical terms and conditions of occupancy as rent levels, duration of tenure, selection of new tenants, allocation of maintenance and repair burdens, processes of landlord-tenant dispute settlement, and eviction procedures. Thus, the right to control one's environment will in many situations depend significantly on a right to organize, to act in concert, to bargain collectively and be bargained with in good faith. Without overdrawing the implicit analogy to the labor movement, one can already detect a need for legal protections for such "rights" if they are to be made effective, and some response to that need on the part of the legal system. Doctrines opposing retaliatory evictions are a clear illustration, loosely analogous to the prohibition of "discriminatory" termination of employment as an unfair labor practice. Indeed, we are reaching the point where it may be said that there is a generally recognized "right to strike" (that is, withhold rents concertedly) under conditions of egregious housing code violation by landlords. Another echo of labor law history seems to be the emergence of the injunction as a union-busting device,[36] with its suggestion of need for an anti-injunction doctrine analogous to the Norris-La Guardia Act. Further in the future, perhaps, is the possibility of a legal duty on the landlord's part to bargain collectively and in good faith.

One clear departure of the evolution of tenant organizational rights from the evolutionary pattern set by the labor laws pertains to the distinction between private and public establishments. Public employees have always been deemed to enjoy a lesser degree of protection than that conferred on private employees. It seems that the opposite will be the case insofar as tenants are concerned. One reason for the difference may be that in public housing, unlike public employment, there is neither any core economic term of fundamental concern to the taxpayers (analogous to wage levels) to be disputed, nor any grave citizen interest in the avoidance of strikes. Disputes will be limited to maintenance, repairs, and environmental control. Statutes, regulations, and evolving practices are according a good deal of recognition not only to the rights of tenants within a project to organize for influential participation in these matters (even to the point of assuming management responsibilities looking to the eventual transfer of ownership to tenant organizations),[37] but also to be represented on the board of the local housing authority which owns the project. So far there are no analogous doctrines applicable to private owners, except for the legalization of rent strikes where code violations prevail.

Environmental control beyond what ownership connotes refers to the ideas, which now enjoy so much currency, of decentralization and community control of various phases of municipal government. Rather than explore these ideas and their future prospects in this chapter, it seems more fitting to close the circle by remarking that community control by occupants—whether they be unionized tenants, cooperators, or condominium owners—with its implicit "right to live in a community," is not obviously and fully compatible with other aspects of a complex "right to housing." Community control may, and at present does, conflict with both the right to be housed and the right of free choice. The challenge is to devise a satisfying mode of community control which avoids intolerable restrictions on who may become a member of the community. In short, it seems that the truly fundamental issues of civil rights and liberties persist beneath the shifting surface of concern about the various interests which human beings possess.

NOTES

1. Housing Act of 1949, §2; 42 U.S.C. §1441.
2. The work of John Rawls is instinct with such an interest. *See, e.g.,* Rawls, "Distributive Justice: Some Addenda," 13 *Natural Law Forum* 51 (1968); "The Sense of Justice," 72 *Philosophical Review* 281 (1963); *see also* J. Buchanan & G. Tullock, *The Calculus of Consent: Logical Foundations of Constitutional Democracy* 190–97 (1962).
3. Deprivations of voting rights, *e.g.,* Harper v. Virginia Bd. of Elections, 383 U.S. 663 (1966), and of effective opportunity to resist criminal prosecution, *e.g.,* Douglas v. California, 372 U.S. 353 (1963), are pretty clearly within this class. The class, moreover, currently shows signs of expansibility—almost certainly to cover at least some kinds of deprivation of effective opportunity to engage in civil litigation, less certainly to reach deprivations of educational opportunity. *See generally* Michelman, "The Supreme Court 1968 Term—Foreword: On Protecting the Poor Through the Fourteenth Amendment," 83 *Harvard Law Review* 7 (1969); Coons, Clune, & Sugarman, "Educational Opportunity: A Workable Constitutional Test for State Financial Structures," 57 *California Law Review* 305 (1969).
4. Shelley v. Kraemer, 334 U.S. 1 (1948).
5. Jones v. Alfred H. Mayer Co., 392 U.S. 409 (1968).
6. *See* Reitman v. Mulkey, 387 U.S. 369 (1967); Karst & Horowitz, "Reitman v. Mulkey: A Telophase of Substantive Equal Protection," 1967 *Supreme Court Review* 39; Black, "The Supreme Court 1966 Term—Foreword: State Action, Equal Protection, and California's Proposition 14," 81 *Harvard Law Review* 69 (1967).
7. Gart v. Cole, 263 F.2d 247 (2d Cir.), *cert. denied,* 359 U.S. 978 (1959); Powelton Civic Home Owners Ass'n v. HUD, 284 F. Supp. 809 (E.D. Pa. 1968); Western Addition Community Organization v. Weaver, 294 F. Supp. 433 (1968).
8. Vinson v. Greenburgh Housing Authority, 29 A.D.2d 338, 288 N.Y.S.2d 159 (1969); Holmes v. New York Housing Authority, 398 F.2d 262 (2d Cir. 1968). *See also* Thorpe v. Durham Housing Authority, 393 U.S. 268 (1969).
9. Sager, "Tight Little Islands: Exclusionary Zoning, Equal Protection, and the Indigent," 21 *Stanford Law Review* 767, 790 (1969).
10. Dandridge v. Williams, 397 U.S. 471 (1970).
11. *See* Schoshinski, "Public Landlords and Tenants: A Survey of the Developing Law," 1969 *Duke Law Journal* 399, 426–56 (1969); Project on Social Welfare Law, *Housing for the Poor: Rights and Remedies* (1967); *cf.* Goldberg v. Kelly, 397 U.S. 254 (1970).
12. Insofar as such an argument would require appeal to the equal protection clause as well as to the housing subsidy statutes and related administrative promulgations, doubts have been raised by the Supreme Court's broad state-

ment in Dandridge v. Williams, 397 U.S. 471 (1970), that in the area of "economics and social welfare" only a modicum of "rationality" is required to justify statutory classifications. Read more narrowly, however, *Dandridge* perhaps need not preclude resort to equal protection in support of the proposition stated in the text. The justification which chiefly convinced the Court to accept Maryland's imposition of a ceiling on Aid to Families with Dependent Children (AFDC) benefits available to any single family (which discriminates in an obvious way against children in large families) was that this practice tended to avoid inequity between large families on welfare and those, headed by a working member, that survive on the statutory minimum wage. The Maryland practice, that is, could itself be justified by considerations of relative need.

13. Shapiro v. Thompson, 394 U.S. 618 (1969).

14. Rosado v. Wyman, 397 U.S. 397 (1970) (dictum); Lampton v. Bonin, 397 U.S. 663 (1970).

15. *Compare* Bowles v. Mahoney, 202 F.2d 320 (D.C. Cir. 1952), *cert. denied,* 344 U.S. 935 (1953), *with* Saunders v. First National Realty Corp., CCH Pov. L. Rep. ¶11, 434 (D.C. Cir. 1970); Pines v. Perssion, 14 Wis. 2d 590, 111 N.W.2d 409 (1961).

16. *E.g.,* Mass. Gen. Laws ch. 239, §8A.

17. *See generally* P. Dodyk *et al., Cases and Materials on Law and Poverty* 575–633 (1969).

18. *See* Sax & Hiestand, "Slumlordism as a Tort," 65 *Michigan Law Review* 869 (1967).

19. *See, e.g.,* G. Sternlieb, *The Tenement Landlord* (1966).

20. Gautreaux v. Chicago Housing Authority, 296 F. Supp. 907 (N.D. Ill. 1969); Low-Rent Housing Manual §205, §2(g), *implementing* Civil Rights Act of 1964, title VI, 42 U.S.C. §2000d.

21. *Cf.* Norwalk CORE v. Norwalk Redevelopment Agency, 395 F.2d 920 (2d Cir. 1968).

22. Mass. Acts & Resolves 1969, ch. 774.

23. *Cf.* Valtierra v. Housing Authority, 313 F. Supp. 1 (N.D. Cal. 1970), *prob. juris. noted sub. nom.* James v. Valtierra, 398 U.S. 949 (1970), invalidating a statutory requirement of approval by municipal referendum of proposed low-income housing projects, on the ground of invidious discrimination against the poor.

24. *See* Ranjel v. City of Lansing, 293 F. Supp. 301 (W.D. Mich. 1969), *rev'd* 417 F.2d 321 (6th Cir. 1969), *cert. denied,* 397 U.S. 980 (1970).

25. *See* Note, "Large Lot Zoning," 78 *Yale Law Journal* 1418, 1433–37 (1969). *But see In re* Appeal of Girsh, No. 164 (Sup. Ct. Pa., Feb. 13, 1970).

26. *See* Sager, *supra* note 9, at 792.

27. *See* Colon v. Tompkins Square Neighbors, Inc., 294 F. Supp. 134 (S.D.N.Y. 1968). *Compare* Smith v. Holiday Inns, 336 F.2d 630 (6th Cir. 1964), *with* Dorsey v. Stuyvesant Town Corp., 299 N.Y. 512, 87 N.E.2d 541, *cert. denied,* 339 U.S. 981 (1949).

28. Comment, "The Public Use Limitation on Eminent Domain: An Advance Requiem," 58 *Yale Law Journal* 599 (1949). *But see* Talbot v. Romney, Civ. No. 2402 (S.D.N.Y. Aug. 20, 1970), where the court held that it would be "inequitable" and contrary to the purpose of the authorizing statutes to allow urban renewal authorities to evict and demolish in advance of being willing and able to proceed forthwith with redevelopment.

29. *Re:* 815 ½ and 817 Cherry Street, Reading, Nos. 70, 71 (C. P., Berks. Co., Pa., Aug. 22, 1968), *reported at* 3 Clearinghouse Rev. 201 (1969).

30. *See* Edwards v. Habib, 397 F.2d 687 (D.C. Cir. 1968), *cert. denied,* 393 U.S. 1016 (1969). Mass. Gen. Laws ch. 186, §18; ch. 239, §2A.

31. Hutcheson v. Lehtin, Civ. No. 52196 (N.D. Cal. 1969), *reported in* CCH Pov. L. Rep. ¶10,704; *cf.* Sniadach v. Family Fin. Corp., 395 U.S. 337 (1969).

32. Simmons v. Housing Authority, 250 A.2d 527 (Conn. App. Div. 1969), *prob. juris. noted,* 394 U.S. 957 (1969); Sanks v. Georgia, 166 S.E.2d 19 (Ga. 1969), *prob. juris. noted,* 395 U.S. 763 (1969).

33. For signs of the demise of these practices, see Landes v. North Hempstead, 20 N.Y.2d 417, 284 N.Y.S.2d 442, 231 N.E.2d 120 (1967); Kramer v. Union Free School Dist., 395 U.S. 621 (1969).

34. *See* F. & M. Sengstock, "Homeownership: A Goal for All Americans," 46 *Journal of Urban Law* 313, 343–47 (1969).

35. *See generally* Note, "Tenant Unions: Collective Bargaining and the Low Income Tenant," 77 *Yale Law Journal* 1368 (1968).

36. *See* Dorfmann v. Boozer, 414 F.2d 1168 (D.C. Cir. 1969).

37. *E.g.,* the Housing Assistance Administration's "Modernization Program," Low-Rent Management Manual, pt. I, §1.9(2), (3); "Turnkey III Program," HUD Circular, Dec. 17, 1968. *See also* Mass. Gen. Laws ch. 121B., §32.

THE RIGHT TO WELFARE

EDWARD V. SPARER

THE HISTORY OF THE AMERICAN WELFARE SYSTEM traverses more than three hundred years and several cumulative stages, each growing into or coexisting with the next. These stages are represented by the "poor laws," dating from early colonial times; the purely state and local categorical efforts, dating from the early twentieth century (particularly the mother's aid "movement"); the federally funded categorical programs, dating from 1935; and the era of struggle over the "legal rights of the welfare poor," which commenced in 1965 and moved haltingly over the course of five very intense years until 1970, when its first phase was completed. The latter period, and its implications for 1970 and beyond, are the subject of this essay.

The struggle to establish a legal right to an adequate welfare grant, without onerous conditions and with fair administration, for all persons in need of financial assistance began as an offshoot of the now defunct "war on poverty." Two forces have led the struggle, sometimes cooperating, sometimes working independently, never quite sure of their proper relationship to each other and—consequently—weaker in their joint effect. One of these forces is composed of lawyers (funded primarily by the federal government's

Edward V. Sparer is Associate Professor of Law at Pennsylvania Law School, a consultant to many public and private groups serving the poor, former Director of the Legal Services Unit of Mobilization for Youth, and former Director of the Columbia University Center on Social Welfare Policy and Law. He is currently working on a history of public assistance in the United States.

Office of Economic Opportunity); the other is the organized recipients in the various local welfare rights organizations and the National Welfare Rights Organization (NWRO). Organized recipients are not new to the American scene. They existed during the 1930's, and there is some reason to believe they existed during the 1830's and in other periods in less cohesive form. Never before, however, had welfare organization developed among mothers, nor had there been comparable organization on a national scale. And yet, even by its own claims, the organized-recipient movement today numbers only 75,000 out of some 12 million welfare recipients (and, depending upon the definition, some 25 to 50 or more million American poor).

Organized recipients have historical precedents; organized effort by lawyers to represent recipients has none. It is even hard to find an analogy, in all the varied areas of American litigation, to the manner in which welfare litigation sprang into being on a national scale with no prior history, encountered a series of successes on issues where defeat was widely predicted, beneficially affected hundreds of thousands of people, became an area of legal practice with its own complexities, professional fraternity, and law school impact, and within five years reached a rather distinct outline of how far it could develop. If disappointment and discouragement exist within the ranks of welfare lawyers today, it should be recalled that more success was attained than was initially anticipated. It was that very success, plus the pressing social need for major reform, that bred hopes for a still greater success—hopes that national politics and reaction were ultimately to defeat.

The legal strategy, as it emerged over the first few years, consisted of planned assaults against the four major characteristics of the welfare system: (1) the innumerable tests for aid and exclusions from aid, most of which were unrelated to need; (2) procedures which reduced the welfare recipient to a "client," stripped of constitutional and other rights assumed by other citizens and forced into dependency upon the welfare agency's whim; (3) the state and local character of the welfare system, which, among other things, is responsible for the numerous welfare "residence" rules for the continuing major reliance on state and local funding; and (4) the inadequate and often shockingly low amount of the money grant. If the assaults as planned were to succeed, the nature of the American welfare system would be changed, something akin to a "right to live" would gradually emerge, and a better society would result.

THE DEVELOPMENT OF LEGAL RIGHTS TO WELFARE

The Right to Welfare Aid for All Persons in Need of Financial Assistance

Consider the case of an American who is slowly (or perhaps rapidly) starving to death because he is totally without money or other resources. Is he "eligible" for welfare? The answer is that it depends on the state where he lives and the "category" in which he is placed. The federal government, under the Social Security Act of 1935, funds state welfare programs only for needy people who are also blind, or old, or permanently and totally disabled, or members of families with "dependent" children. If the starving American is none of these, he is simply out of luck unless he lives within a state which has a broad "general assistance" program. A few states have such programs; several have none; many aid only a few additional "categories" of needy people. All together, there are many more needy Americans excluded from welfare than deemed eligible for it.

A long-range goal of welfare legal strategy during the 1965–1970 period was to end the categorical nature of the welfare system. Much of this strategy rested upon application of the equal protection clause of the Fourteenth Amendment. Surely the rationality and fairness of the federally supported categories are doubtful. For example, is it not arbitrary to give aid to needy children whose fathers desert them and refuse aid to needy children whose fathers refuse to desert them although they cannot find work? In twenty-five states, the latter children are not eligible for federally supported welfare—Aid to Families with Dependent Children (AFDC); nor would the current Nixon "reform" proposals provide as much aid to such children as the former receive.

Initial legal and organizational strategy, however, was directed against exclusions of needy citizens who fall *within* the federal categories. In particular, state rules excluding needy persons who fall within the federal definition are rife in the AFDC program. Under the federal definition in Section 406(a) of the Social Security Act, a needy child is included (that is, is "dependent") if his father or mother is dead, continuously absent from the home, or incapacitated.[1] Nevertheless state rules of every imaginable sort have excluded many needy, dependent children from AFDC. Some states have excluded children whose mothers worked full time, even though their salaries were less than the state AFDC level. Another state excluded children of a mother deemed able to work though she could not find a job. Other states have required mothers to have a psychiatric examination on demand of the caseworker—or lose AFDC aid. Other rules exclude children who are suspended from school; children whose mothers are under eighteen; children who are sixteen or seventeen years old; children who go to a college instead of a vocational school; children whose mother refuses to file criminal support charges against the deserting father; and so on.

The Department of Health, Education, and Welfare (HEW) has approved programs with all of these exclusions and more. Its interpretation of the Social Security Act is that the federal definition of "dependent child" simply sets the outer bounds for determining which children are eligible for federal funding. The state, according to HEW, is free to *exclude* any dependent children it wishes, subject only to an HEW administrative doctrine called the "equitable treatment" or "condition X" doctrine ("condition X" because it is nowhere stated in the Act but merely inferred by HEW from a variety of statutory provisions).

The "condition X" doctrine holds that the state exclusion must not be "irrational" or "arbitrary" in light of the purposes of the Act.[2] The difficulty, of course, is that HEW has been extremely loath to find state exclusions irrational, and has been somewhat irrational itself about distinguishing valid from invalid rules. For example, in 1961 HEW issued its "Flemming Rule," which prohibited states from denying aid to needy, dependent children who lived in an "unsuitable" home (usually so deemed because the mother acted "immorally" by sleeping with a man who was not her husband). On the other hand, HEW approved several "man-in-the-house" rules which labeled any man the mother sleeps with the "substitute father" of the children and denied aid on the ground that in such situations the children are not "deprived of support or care by reason of the death [or] continued absence from the home" of the father.[3]

King v. Smith was the case which broke the man-in-the-house rule and, quite possibly, most of the other exclusionary devices more narrow than those set forth in the federal Act. At issue in *King* was an Alabama "substitute father" rule of the sort described above. The lower court found that the exclusion of needy children from AFDC aid because their mother was allegedly engaged in sexual relations with a man who was not their father, was not legally responsible for their support, and was not supporting them, violated the equal protection clause.[4] On appeal by Alabama to the Supreme Court the result was affirmed on a statutory ground. The Court, finding it unnecessary to reach the constitutional question, held that under the Social Security Act "destitute children who are legally fatherless cannot be flatly denied federally funded assistance on the transparent fiction that they have a substitute father."[5]

By determining "substitute father" rules inconsistent with the Social Security Act, *King* opened the welfare rolls to over half a million children previously excluded. Additional children have been admitted because of the effect of the case on income computation methods, discussed below. The reasoning of the Court in *King,* however, could have an impact far beyond these exclusions. The Court, after examining the legislative history of the Act, concluded that the Alabama "substitute father" was not a "parent" as that term is used within the Act and that children whose real parent is dead or absent are therefore "dependent" children as that term is used in the Act. The Court then went a step further. Noting that Section 402(a)(10) of the Act requires participating states to furnish aid "with reasonable promptness" to all "eligible" individuals, the Court found:

> The regulation is . . . invalid because it defines "parent" in a manner that is inconsistent with § 406(a) of the Social Security Act. . . . Alabama has breached its federally imposed obligation to furnish "aid to families with dependent children . . . with reasonable promptness to all eligible individuals."[6]

What the Court seems to be saying is that federal definitions are not simply the outer limits for who can get federal funding. The states are not free to exclude anyone from the program so long as they are not being "arbitrary." (Nowhere in its opinion does the Court mention "condition X.") By defining the "dependent children" in the program, the Act also defines the "eligible individuals" referred to in Section 402(a)(10). Accordingly, the states must include *everyone* whom Congress intended to include within the federal definitions and conditions.

If *King* is read as suggested above, virtually all the narrow rules that permeate the state programs may be inconsistent with the Social Security Act. For example, if a state excludes a child because her mother is under sixteen, has not the state excluded a needy, dependent child in violation of its obligation to give aid promptly to all eligible individuals?

Thus far the lower federal and state courts appear to agree with this analysis of *King*. Among the state requirements found invalid by federal district courts have been a California regulation conditioning AFDC aid to needy, dependent children upon passage of a three-month waiting period after desertion,[7] a Connecticut regulation denying aid to needy, dependent children because the mother refuses to name the absent father,[8] and a Pennsylvania regulation reducing assistance to needy children.[9] In addition, a Michigan state court has ruled invalid a regulation denying aid to needy, dependent children where the mother has been convicted of a fraud against the welfare department. Even the dissent in the Connecticut case found that the issue turned on whom *Congress* intended to be eligible, rather than the states. Reason exists, therefore, to believe that not only man-in-the-house rules but the numerous other state rules denying welfare to persons otherwise eligible are on the way out.

But serious obstacles remain. Since the issue turns on congressional intent regarding the excluded class, it is possible to argue that Congress wished the states to have an option with regard to a particular rule. Two federal district courts have found this to be the case with regard to exclusions of children over the age of eighteen who are attending college rather than vocational or high school.[10] HEW rejects the analysis of *King* given above, and continues to maintain that "condition X" is the only relevant test of a state rule which excludes persons included within the federal definition.[11] The Supreme Court, as is made clear in its most recent opinions, is showing great deference to HEW regulations,[12] and may well follow its advice hereafter as to the substance of most issues. As a result, the reasoning in *King* may be so undermined as to leave it without impact beyond the man-in-the-house rules.

Initial legal strategy called for an equal protection attack against exclusions within federal categories, which—with time and success —would lead into an attack against the categories themselves. The *King* case, intended by its planners as the major initial move in the equal protection assault, gave rise instead to a statutory analysis of exclusions within the federal categories that was of no significance to persons who fell outside these categories. Whether *King* will have the broad impact on exclusions within the federal categories that is suggested above is still in doubt.

The Right Not to Be Dependent upon Agency Whim

The charge of antiwelfare politicians is that welfare makes the recipient "dependent." What is meant is that the recipient is dependent upon the welfare check for his material sustenance rather than upon some other source and that, for various reasons, is bad. Of course the recipient is dependent upon the welfare check, but whether that is good or bad depends on whether some better source of income is available. In most cases, no other source—better or worse—is available.

The real problem of welfare dependency is something entirely different. The recipient and applicant traditionally have been dependent on the whim of the caseworker or other departmental representative as to whether they in fact obtain what, according to law, they are entitled to receive. Such whim has been expressed in various forms, and we list merely a few:

(1) Whether an applicant who is clearly eligible for a benefit shall receive it has frequently been considered a matter of agency discretion rather than legal right; (2) certain eligibility requirements have often been so vaguely stated as to make impossible a determination by objective standards; (3) the recipient on the rolls has had no effective mechanism for legal redress if improperly cut off or made subject to illegal demands, other than the "fair hearing" which usually took place months later; (4) the improperly denied applicant has been (and is) similarly at great disadvantage in obtaining relief for long periods of time—far too long for any needy person to be able to maintain his health and that of his children; (5) the recipient has not been protected in his privacy—all facts and circumstances concerning him have been deemed the business of the welfare department—and the recipient's home has hardly been his castle.

To be sure, some of these matters have been subject to HEW regulations limiting welfare department whims. But these regulations were not subject to enforcement by recipients through HEW procedures or, in the eyes of some judges, through the courts.

The leading judicial advance with regard to welfare procedures was achieved in *Goldberg v. Kelly*.[13] At issue was the so-called prior hearing. The Social Security Act had long guaranteed that recipients and applicants be given a "fair hearing" if aid was denied or terminated. The difficulty with this guarantee, among other things, was that it availed a needy mother and children little if the "fair hearing" was granted months after aid was terminated. What were the mother and children to live on while waiting to be vindicated?

To Justice Black, writing in dissent, the due process clause could not afford welfare recipients relief because that clause is relevant only when an individual is deprived "of his own property." Welfare is not the recipient's "property"; it is a "gratuity," a mere "promise of charity." To the five-man majority, however, welfare benefits are "a matter of statutory entitlement for persons qualified to receive them." It "may be realistic today," the Court said, "to regard welfare entitlements as more like 'property' than a 'gratuity.' " Accordingly, it held that constitutional due process applied to the administration of welfare entitlements, the precise nature of the requirements being shaped in part by the nature of the injury suffered. Specifically, because termination of aid pending resolution of a controversy over eligibility may deprive an eligible recipient of the means by which to live, an evidentiary hearing must be afforded *prior* to the termination of benefits.

Goldberg can be a major tool in aiding organized recipients to deal boldly with the welfare departments without fear (or with less fear) of retaliation by cutoff. Other decisions, from various federal and state courts, can also be of profound importance. For example, the California Supreme Court held that the mass "bedchecks" (early-morning home searches for evidence of male friends) engaged in by local welfare agencies violate the recipient's constitutional right to privacy.[14] And a three-judge federal court in New York held that a recipient may not constitutionally be required as a condition of her grant to admit a welfare agent into her home.[15] Successful attacks on man-in-the-house rules, discussed above, have led in some places to the elimination of the more inane type of eligibility question relating to male companionship. Louisiana has even abandoned her regulation governing whom an AFDC mother is allowed to "date." HEW regulations have circumscribed the range of questions that clients may be asked about their financial resources, and the circumstances under which friends, neighbors, and other acquaintances of the recipient may be interrogated about the recipient. And the "blanket waiver"—under which the recipient presumably authorizes the agency to ask anyone anything about him—has been prohibited.

Court decisions have also, at long last, made the federal regulations governing federally funded state welfare plans a body of law which recipients can enforce on their own behalf. However inadequate the federal rules may be, they are nevertheless a prime source of protection. They spell out, among other things, the recipient's rights in application procedures, "fair hearing" procedures, income computation procedures, and uniform treatment requirements. Until recently HEW regarded these procedures as a matter solely between itself and the state welfare agency.

Enforcement of HEW regulations by the agency itself was a rarity. By 1970, however, several cases were before the Supreme Court seeking enforcement of HEW regulations. A court of appeals had concluded in one such case that federal court jurisdiction should not be exercised while HEW was "engaged in a study" of the question.[16] HEW was viewed as having "primary jurisdiction" over enforcement of the Social Security Act and the regulations issued thereunder. Since HEW usually engaged in endless study (or nonstudy) of the statute, the practical effect of this position would be continued nonenforcement. Fortunately, the Supreme Court rejected the doctrine of HEW "primary jurisdiction." The Court said:

> It is . . . peculiarly part of the duty of this tribunal, no less in the welfare field than in other areas of the law, to resolve disputes as to whether federal funds allocated to the States are being expended in consonance with the conditions that Congress has attached to their use.[17]

And when HEW does decide to hold a hearing of its own to determine whether or not a state is conforming to HEW regulations, the Court of Appeals for the District of Columbia has held that organizations of welfare recipients such as the NWRO must be allowed to intervene, call witnesses, and cross-examine state witnesses.[18] By the latter half of 1970, HEW—under criticism from judges, organized welfare recipients, and others—had begun increased enforcement activities.

We have, therefore, the *beginnings* of significant procedural advances in welfare. Eligible applicants must be given aid under the federal Act. Recipients cannot be removed from the rolls without a prior hearing. Some privacy for recipients in the home has been recognized. Not just any kind of question can be asked of recipients. The federal courts are available for enforcement of federal regulations. HEW is active in some enforcement efforts. Organized recipients have the right to intervene in federal-state hearings.

Nevertheless, for every advance, another difficulty remains. Thus, the prior hearing for recipients does not help the applicant[19] who has been unconscionably and illegally delayed—a common occurrence. The 1967 amendments to the Social Security Act, by requiring "home studies" of each AFDC recipient and by linking financial aid to "social rehabilitation,"[20] may have done more to undermine welfare recipient privacy than any of the acts prohibited in such cases as *Parrish* or *James*. The HEW rules may now be enforced in the federal courts, but as of this date HEW appears to be revising its rules so as to blunt the force of the best of them.

Assaulting the State and Local Character of the Welfare System: The "Residency" Tests and Shapiro v. Thompson

Under the old "poor laws," each person was deemed "settled" in a particular location. If he left his place of settlement, he could be forcibly removed and sent back to where he came from. One could gain a new settlement simply by being well-to-do (as evidenced, for example, by paying rent over a certain amount). But if you were poor, you had no right to move. You "belonged"—in typical statutory language—where you originally came from. Under the Social Security Act, as interpreted by HEW, such "settlement" laws were prohibited for the federally funded categorical programs. But Congress explicitly permitted the states to impose *durational* residence tests, if they wished, so that a new resident could be denied aid until he had been a resident for a year before application (AFDC) or five out of the preceding nine years (adult programs).

In *Shapiro v. Thompson*[21] the Supreme Court applied equal protection standards to the welfare residency rules and found them wanting. It did so by ruling that the Constitution protects every citizen's right to interstate travel and movement, that durational residency rules are intended to discourage the exercise of the constitutional right to travel by indigents, that a classification which limits the exercise of a constitutional right can be justified only by the showing of a "compelling" state interest, that no such interest was shown to justify the residency rules, and that therefore the durational residency tests violate the equal protection clause. The particulars in the Court's reasoning, discussed later in this essay, gave great hope that *Shapiro* would have enormous consequences for other welfare rights. By April 1970, as we shall see, the Court—after a significant change in personnel—made it clear that such hope was false. It will suffice to discuss here four narrower questions raised by *Shapiro*.

1. By implication *all* durational residency tests in welfare are unconstitutional now, including those in the general assistance programs (not subject to Social Security Act funding).

2. Subsequent to *Shapiro,* and on its authority, welfare purpose tests have also been found unconstitutional. In New York, for example, a statute barred the granting of AFDC or general assistance aid to anyone who came to New York for the *purpose* of receiving welfare.[22]

3. *Shapiro* is pregnant with implications which militate against continued viability of the state and local financial base of even our partially federally funded welfare programs. The Court said:

> More fundamentally, a State may no more try to fence out those indigents who seek higher welfare benefits than it may fence out indigents generally. Implicit in any such distinction is the notion that indigents who enter a State with the hope of securing higher welfare benefits are somehow less deserving than indigents who do not take this consideration into account. But we do not perceive why a mother who is seeking to make a new life for herself and her children should be regarded as less deserving because she considers, among other factors, the level of a State's public assistance. Surely such a mother is no less deserving than a mother who moves into a particular State in order to take advantage of its better educational facilities.[23]

Do poor persons in fact move because of the lure of higher welfare benefits in another state? Both sides, in *Shapiro,* raked the literature for evidence either way. Despite conflicting claims in the briefs, examination of the sparse primary sources which purport to shed light reveals very little hard evidence. In this writer's own experience, as a lawyer for some one hundred applicants initially denied aid under New York's statute on the ground that they came to New York for the purpose of receiving aid, poor people generally have not moved for such a purpose.

Yet there is no reason to suppose that this situation will continue. Sooner or later, as welfare rights organizations and improved communications systems spread the information to families that are literally starving on the Mississippi, Alabama, Puerto Rico, South Carolina, Georgia, or other state welfare "allowances" that they can at least exist on the New York, New Jersey, or California grants, it is not unreasonable to conclude that poor folk *will* start moving to take advantage of higher-benefit systems. Why shouldn't they? When they do, the separate state and locally funded welfare systems will move into an even greater condition of crisis. In the long run, the constitutional requirements of *Shapiro* will, for better or worse, help collapse this structure and force the issue of a single federal system.

4. *Shapiro* bans *durational* residency tests, but not *residency* tests. The newcomer who does not intend to remain in a state on a more or less indefinite basis is not deemed a "resident." The states—in at least apparent consistency with the holding of *Shapiro*—can bar the nonresident citizen from receiving welfare benefits. The principal group of persons to whom this distinction applies is the migratory workers who move from state to state for the purpose of working in the fields. They often work in the worst of conditions and at times below welfare standards; often they find themselves out of work, with nowhere to go, and ineligible for welfare aid. Why should not the constitutional analysis which was applicable in *Shapiro* to the resident also be applicable to the nonresident migratory worker? If the former's right to travel is chilled by the durational residency test, is not the latter's right to travel infringed even more by the total ban on aid to the nonresident? Is there a compelling state interest in excluding all nonresidents from aid, no matter what their circumstances? If so, it eludes this writer.

The Right to a Minimally Adequate Grant

From the poorest state to the richest, the welfare grant system is absurd and heartbreaking. Mississippi will grant an AFDC family only 28 to 30 percent of what the state determines is necessary for the family to survive. Indeed, the *majority* of states do not grant the AFDC recipient the amount the welfare department determines is necessary for the recipient's survival (known in welfare argot as the "standard of need"). Some states discriminate sharply between AFDC and "adult" (for example, old-age recipients), but there are many states which will not even pay the adult recipient his full need. Nor are the "standards of need" themselves in any way adequate. Though the amount of such standards varies widely from state to state, few equal or exceed the very inadequate federal "anti-poverty line" ($3,335 per annum for an urban family of four, developed on the basis of 1965 costs). No state grant system comes close to meeting the $5,500 which the Federal Bureau of Labor Statistics more recently concluded was necessary for adequate living for a low-income family (more is needed if such items as income taxes are included). Some states, such as New York, calculated a "standard" which assumed that AFDC recipients do not have a "need" to buy newspapers or listen to a radio; if the family included a high school girl, it was concluded that she "needs" only one lipstick roll per year; an unemployed man was calculated as needing fewer razor blades than an employed man, and while all men were assumed to need a suit, belts and suspenders were not budgeted.[24]

Increasing the amount of the money grant, therefore, was and is a prime order of business in the struggle for welfare rights. Four legal strategies have developed.

    1. *False assumptions of income.* A technique used by most state welfare departments to reduce grants has been the promulgation of rules that assume certain income to be available to recipients which in fact is not available. For example, a number of states (in the South and West) followed policies whereby employment was presumed available during certain agricultural seasons, and the AFDC recipient's grant was automatically reduced (or terminated) on the notion that the mother had income during those seasons—whether in fact she had a job or not. Other states would assume—regardless of fact—that "legally responsible" relatives who had agreed to make payments to the family, or were under court order to do so, actually made such payments. And most states that did not have the type of man-in-the-house policy found invalid in *King v. Smith* would reduce the grant of an AFDC mother on the ground that there was a "man assuming the role of a spouse" or a stepfather in the house, even though the man in question was not contributing financially to the children and was not legally bound to contribute. Some states, including New York and Connecticut, even assumed extra income was available to a mother when she had a sister living in the house—regardless, again, of whether the sister had an income, contributed money, or was legally bound to contribute.[25]

Such practices by states accepting federal monies for their welfare programs are now invalid. An HEW rule, apparently invalidating certain of them, effective in 1967 but rarely enforced, was expressly approved by the Supreme Court in *King v. Smith*. Subsequent to *King,* a very clear rule was negotiated that barred assumption of income from "men in the house" and stepfathers (in most cases), but that rule too was unenforced by HEW. Several lawsuits resulted in court decisions upholding the HEW rule against contrary state rules. Nevertheless, enforcement of the HEW rules against contrary practices remains a serious problem.

2. *The "special needs" campaigns.* Many of the more "liberal" welfare states, such as Connecticut, New York, Wisconsin, and California, have long boasted that they had two systems of grants. One was the regular, or "recurring," grant which every family with the same number of people and same income received. The other was the "special" grant for particular needs which a given family might have. New York welfare leaders were especially proud of the special grants system, which provided for home furniture, kitchen supplies, school clothing, and other items. No family in New York need suffer, the social welfare leaders would say, because if it lacks a bed or table or dishtowel or what have you, it need only ask for it. In practice, however, the system was vicious. Few recipients knew of their "special needs" entitlements. Few received them.

In one of the few major examples of close cooperation between organized recipients and welfare lawyers, a series of campaigns were waged to enforce the special needs regulations. These regulations were a natural for such cooperation. Under relevant legal doctrine, eligible applicants could enforce their right to receive the special needs grants. Organizations could easily build themselves by aiding individual recipients. Lawyers could assist in difficult cases. The campaigns worked—for a while. In New York, during 1967 alone, thousands of fair hearing requests were made over "special needs." Most were settled, some for as much as $1,500 (so bad were the furniture and clothing conditions of many recipients). Between May 1965 and June 1968, the average special grant per person in New York City for clothing and furniture alone rose from $24 to $192. And most recipients were still not in the campaign.

The state answer turned out to be quite simple. Those with liberal regulations, such as New York, simply repealed the "special needs" grants, instituted a single "flat grant" system, and rolled back welfare levels generally.

3. *Section 402(a) (23).* Section 402(a) (23) was enacted into law as part of the 1967 amendments to the Social Security Act. It states that

by July 1, 1969, the amounts used by the State to determine the
needs of individuals [i.e., the "standard of need"] will have been
adjusted to reflect fully changes in living costs since such amounts
were established and any maximums that the State imposes on the
amount of aid paid to families will have been proportionally adjusted.

New York welfare recipient lawyers claimed that the elimination of
"special needs" and the general rollback in the welfare standard of
need violated Section 402(a) (23). In April 1970, in *Rosado v.
Wyman*,[26] the Supreme Court agreed. New York was to be given a
short amount of time to readjust its standard upward or lose its
federal subsidy. *Rosado* had the outer attributes of a major welfare
recipient victory; in fact, it was a disaster. It is one thing to force a
state to raise its "standard of need"; it is another to prevent a state
from lowering its actual payment level.

States, as noted earlier, have frequently avoided paying their
"standard of need" by imposing a "maximum" on how much the
state will pay regardless of "standard of need." Often these maximums have been expressed in dollar amounts. For example, the
state standard for Mrs. X may be $100 a month. The maximum may
be $50 a month. Section 402(a) (23) requires that the maximum be
raised "by July 1, 1969," as well as the standard. Thus if the cost of
living had gone up 10 percent "since such amounts were established," the standard must be raised to $110 and the maximum
to $55.

But HEW concluded that states could institute a "percentage
reduction" system to *lower* the amount actually paid, regardless of
Section 402(a) (23). The state was authorized to promulgate a new
regulation under which such persons as Mrs. X would actually be
paid whatever percentage of the standard of need the state wished
to pay. Thus, if the state decided to pay only 20 percent of its
standard, Mrs. X would receive only $22—even though prior to
Section 402(a) (23) she had received $50. Section 402(a) (23), HEW
decreed, applies only to flat dollar maximums (such as the $50 limi-
tation above) and not "percentage reductions" (such as the 20 percent rule above).

Welfare recipient lawyers argued that a "percentage reduction"
system results in a maximum as much as a flat-dollar-maximum
system. A "maximum" is an upper limit; the 20 percent rule in the
example above is an upper limit and therefore invalid. Any other
result, they argued, would subvert the plain meaning and purpose

of the congressional language. But HEW rejected these contentions.

There are answers to HEW. And answers to the answers. The issue need not have arisen in *Rosado*.[27] New York had not created a percentage system and did not rely on the HEW interpretation in question. But the issue was reached in *Rosado,* and the Court agreed with HEW.

To some, the practical lesson from the special needs campaigns and the Section 402(a) (23) litigation is this: If you struggle to get recipients their legal entitlement under the regulations, and struggle to get eligible applicants on the rolls, and win victories against illegal restrictive eligibility rules—the recipients may well be rewarded by a cut in grant levels. Such cuts happened in state after state, and nothing in the Social Security Act appears to prevent it—at least according to the Supreme Court.

4. Equal protection. The fourth major legal strategy for raising grant levels involved the use of the equal protection clause. State welfare agencies use various techniques to reduce grant levels for some persons in need while paying higher grants to others in no greater need. The first of these is the "family maximum," as a result of which small families have their "need" more fully met than large families: in other words, a discrimination in aid based solely on family size is created. Another technique is to pay considerably less to AFDC recipients than to old-age recipients. A third technique, used by New York, is to grant a smaller amount of aid to persons in one part of the state (Nassau and Westchester) than in another (New York City), despite lack of evidence that living costs are different.

The chief problem in attacking these and other grant-reducing classifications is that under traditional equal protection theory (usually articulated in cases involving business regulation) there is a *presumption* in favor of the rationality of state classifications. The Supreme Court has repeatedly held that "A statutory discrimination will not be set aside if any state of facts reasonably may be conceived to justify it."[28] The "state of facts" need not reflect the legislature's actual concern; any rationale that anyone can think up may be enough.

Of course, *some* kind of speculative rationale can be thought up for virtually any discrimination. The "family maximum," for example, is defended on the ground that if welfare families can receive more in aid than the lower-paying jobs in the community (as their "standard of need" might require), heads of such families would lose the incentive to seek employment. This contention is made even though male heads, and many women, are required to seek employment or lose their welfare; even though federal law allows retention of part of the earnings so that such families—if the head is working—will actually get more than by not working; even though, in some states (such as Florida) where the "maximum" on welfare was $85 per month, the family head could not possibly lose an "incentive" to seek work. Paying Nassau and Westchester recipients 7 to 16 percent less than New York City recipients is rationalized on the ground that the latter have a greater "social need" to travel to museums, welfare centers, clinics, beaches, etc.

It is to the credit of welfare lawyers that they were able to make out strong arguments for excepting welfare classifications from the presumption in favor of the rationality of state classifications and for requiring special judicial scrutiny of such classifications. Until the spring of 1970, most of the results were affirmative. Sometimes these paralleled *King v. Smith* by judicial avoidance of the equal protection issue in the process of granting a statutory victory to welfare recipients. Other cases, such as one involving a challenge to a Georgia regulation which prohibited AFDC supplementation of the salaries of mothers employed full-time, and all the lower-court maximum-grant cases, resulted in favorable equal protection decisions[29] without judicial articulation of "special scrutiny" reasoning. In *Shapiro v. Thompson,* the majority opinion made certain "cryptic" comments (as noted by Justice Harlan in dissent) which suggested that plaintiffs' "special scrutiny" theories might soon be accepted by the Supreme Court. Soon after *Shapiro,* in *Rothstein v. Wyman,*[30] a three-judge federal court in New York struck down geographic disparities in welfare payments without a basis in cost of living. The court said as to the constitutional standard:

> It can hardly be doubted that the subsistence level of our indigent and unemployable aged, blind and disabled [children were later joined to the case] involves a more crucial aspect of life and liberty than the right to operate a business on Sunday or to extract gas from subsoil. We believe that with the stakes so high in terms of human misery the equal protection standard to be applied should be stricter than that used upon review of commercial legislation and more nearly approximate that applied to laws affecting fundamental constitutional rights. . . .

In *Dandridge v. Williams*[31] the Supreme Court authoritatively ended all speculation. It upheld the validity under both statute and

Constitution of a Maryland "maximum grant" provision which candidly provided less than the "standard of need" to welfare recipients within the state. The five-man majority, in an opinion of sweeping consequence, rejected a special scrutiny test for "public welfare assistance." To be sure, the Court recognized "the dramatically real factual differences" between welfare cases which involve "the most basic economic needs of impoverished human beings" and the precedents involving the traditional test which "in the main involved state regulation of business or industry." But such a difference affords "no basis for applying a different constitutional standard." Justice Douglas dissented on statutory grounds. Justice Marshall, joined by Justice Brennan, dissented on both statutory and constitutional grounds, noting "the Court's emasculation of the Equal Protection Clause as a constitutional principle applicable to the area of social welfare administration." In short, the possibilities latent in *Shapiro v. Thompson* and the promise of the three-judge decision in *Rothstein v. Wyman* were aborted.

There are serious arguments (best made by Justice Harlan in his *Shapiro* dissent) in favor of "emasculating" the equal protection clause in the social welfare area. It is not our purpose here to make the opposing argument, nor is it our purpose to speculate on how the various personnel changes in the Court subsequent to *Shapiro* affected the *Dandridge* result. But it is appropriate to note that a contrary result in *Dandridge* would have permitted wholesale challenges to the barriers created by state legislatures and Congress to deny welfare assistance to groups of needy people. Distinctions between grant levels of individuals in equal need, whether because of differences in categories or their state of residence, might have been brought down. Traditional divisions between state and federal authority, and between the three branches of government, would doubtless have been altered. The equal protection clause would have become the main vehicle for establishing a constitutional guarantee of human life. In these and other ways, affirmative judicial scrutiny to guarantee equal protection could have led to a different America.

These, then, have been the main legal battles carried on during the first five years of the struggle for a legal right to welfare. They present a very mixed picture. There have been more legal victories than defeats, but the latter have gone to the heart of the effort to change the system. Perhaps the most important effect of the legal struggle is the way it has contributed to the "welfare crisis" all Americans seem to agree we now confront.

Frequently, crisis produces a great legislative change. But the change, if any, that will be produced in the immediate future is quite small. The Nixon Welfare Bill[32] introduces a small federal floor on payments. It fails to raise grants for the overwhelming majority of the welfare poor. Its terms undermine some legal victories, such as those concerning certain man-in-the-house rules. It imposes a stronger emphasis on "work tests" and "work incentives" than we have as yet seen. In short, it too is a mixed bag: some good, much bad, but mostly the same as we have now.

Where Do We Go from Here?

We are participants in a constitutional and human crisis. An increasing segment of the American people will no longer accept what has been and remains acceptable to the rest of the population and to those who exercise the power of government. There are young people who refuse to fight and kill in other lands, despite the legal commands of an elected government. There are blacks, browns, and reds who refuse to tolerate inequality, despite the manner in which certain forms of inequality are protected by the legal process of government. There are American poor, in and out of "welfare," who refuse to tolerate starvation conditions merely because neither Constitution nor statute nor court decision appears to impose upon our government an obligation to protect all of its citizens against starvation. There are also large numbers of Americans, apparently drawn from various classes, who would cast such folk outside the pale of constitutional protection and withdraw all their rights.

It is argued that the Constitution is designed to assure democratic results: the majority governs through the elective process; the minority is guaranteed the right to dissent. Those are the ground rules by which all members of American society must abide. These rules are subject today to increasing challenge. Upon what moral premise must the starving man or woman accept the majority's vote on whether he or she shall live or not? What moral premise requires that the youth accept the majority's vote on whether he must kill other men? What moral premise requires that the black man accept the results of the white majority vote on whether obstacles to his equality shall be removed?

The persuasive argument on such issues has not been moral but pragmatic: If you do not accept these ground rules, the result will be chaos. To which some who suffer under such ground rules, and their sympathizers, reply: We do not prefer the status quo to chaos; only the relatively comfortable see the issue of change in such terms. The ground rules must do more than guarantee the right to persuade the majority; they must guarantee the right to live whatever the majority thinks. The right to live is a *sine qua non* of the social contract.

The welfare recipients' lawyer started his struggle in 1965 not merely as a technician whose function was to help the welfare system conform to what the elected representatives of the majority had decreed it should be. His mission was to utilize the legal process to help change the very nature of the welfare system and, thereby, to change the ground rules of American society. No mere legal technician, he was a grand strategist. No mere advocate of other people's yearnings, he yearned for the change with his clients. And for a brief moment in the 1960's when it appeared that a majority, or at least their elected representatives, were ready to accept some basic change, his mission appeared possible. In 1970, it does not. No more a significant participant in grand change, he appears reduced to what the revolutionist has often accused the lawyer of being—a technical aide who smooths the functioning of an inadequate system and thereby helps perpetuate it. Thus we find among some welfare and other antipoverty lawyers the growing conviction that their profession is but a trade which does more to support the lawyer than it does his impoverished and often hungry client, that their work may be more negative than positive in its social consequence. Drift and anomie set in.

It is painful to abandon the grand strategist's role. It is painful to be defeated in ambitious schemes. It is painful to realize that the struggle for a humane society is long-term, not short-term. It is painful to share the yearning of the dispossessed, presumably speak on their behalf, and observe that one earns a comfortable living in the process (why not abandon role-playing and become one of the dispossessed?). But the real problem is not the lawyer's self-satisfaction. The human and constitutional crisis of America has to do with the situation of the poor, not of the lawyers. The issue for the lawyer is whether he can do useful things to increase the rights of welfare recipients through the legal process. He can.

Welfare Litigation as Part of a Political Campaign

Rather than suffer demobilization from defeats or become giddy from success, the welfare lawyer's job, among others, is to understand the highly political nature of welfare litigation, and to act upon that understanding. This is not simply a matter of evaluating what legal arguments will be acceptable to a particular court at a given time. It is also a matter of seeing litigation as one element among several that may be required to induce a particular change in welfare policy. Some cases—the durational residence cases are an example—are "right" for the time. The lawyer need not do more than engage in well-prepared litigation. Others, however, can succeed only where various nonlitigational efforts have also been made, in order to *make* the time "right."

For a narrow illustration of the point, consider *Goldberg v. Kelly* and the "prior hearing" success. The theory underlying *Goldberg* was first developed in 1965. Although the issue dealt with procedural due process, and was therefore more amenable to courtroom success than some other issues, numerous obstacles stood in the way. Welfare, at the time, was a very novel area to judges, who would approach the area with great caution. Welfare department opposition in many places was extreme. The federal agency, HEW, not only found prior hearings unnecessary for "fairness"; it refused to provide federal matching funds for state payments for the period between an ineligibility determination and a hearing determination (except, where the recipient was successful, on a retroactive basis). Consequently state agencies argued, with some force, that it was unreasonable to require them to make categorical program payments to which HEW would not contribute; the financial burden would be enormous. Yet a legal attack on HEW for not matching such payments might weaken rather than strengthen the recipients' position in the early days of welfare litigation.

Goldberg v. Kelly was the culmination of a number of efforts in what was, in essence, a coordinated political campaign to change the odds. A carefully prepared comment in a very respected law journal laid a scholarly basis for court action. HEW conferences, in which invited "experts" were asked to criticize state fair hearing pro-

cedures, were turned into assaults on HEW's failure either to require or offer federal matching to state prior hearings. The first
effort in a federal courtroom was deliberately made in Mississippi.
Since HEW at the time did not pay attention to "antipoverty" lawyers but was sensitive to civil rights lawyers, the prior hearing issue
was converted into a Southern civil rights issue. Some machinery in
HEW was able to respond, federal matching was offered, the case
was settled, and Mississippi became the first state to hold prior
hearings.

As the "Poor People's Campaign" of the summer of 1968 developed, prior hearings became a campaign demand, in response to the
welfare rights movement. The politics of 1968 was such that the
Johnson administration sought concessions that it might offer to the
Poor People's Campaign. One of these became the welfare prior
hearing. HEW issued a regulation, postponed in its effective date,
requiring such hearings. New litigation was surely influenced by the
fact that the federal agency responsible for welfare now regarded
prior hearings as so significant to "fairness" that it saw fit to require
them. But as national administrators changed, the HEW regulation
was further postponed—with an eye on what the Supreme Court
would do. In the meantime, however, the regulation affected what
the Supreme Court in fact did.

Would *Goldberg* have turned out the way it did without the
development of a general sensitivity to the issue as a result of efforts
on many different fronts? Perhaps, but probably not. It is striking,
when one considers other even more promising issues which lost in
the courts, that far less effort was expended on anything other than
the litigation process. The rule should be: The more difficult and
"political" an issue is, the more a multifaceted campaign should be
carried out, especially at a time, as now, when the court system is
unreceptive to litigation involving social change.

But on precisely what issues can lawyers be of assistance to recipients *today*, what are the connections between those issues and
political strategy generally, and what is the grand strategy for
advancing welfare legal rights?

The Lawyer's Job Is to Provide Technical Aid, and Not to Determine Ground Strategy in Place of the Recipients

Deflating perhaps, but a grand role that strikes more at the heart
of the "welfare system." The task is to help bring into full being that

which did not exist and is struggling now to develop: a constituency which will decide for itself (1) the question we raised earlier, whether legal maneuvers are simply covers for our present inhumane system or whether they are of real value to the poor, and (2) the question we now raise, what the legal maneuvers should be, and how can they be related to an overall strategy.

There are two levels on which such a constituency-building task is carried out by lawyers. The first is with regard to individual clients. It requires an effort to avoid the usual professional role of telling the poor and relatively powerless client what is to be done. Because they know the technical aspect of the subject better than the client, welfare lawyers are prone to tell rather than advise, confine their advice to one option rather than the many that usually exist, shape and control the client's decision although it is made to appear the client is deciding, and generally manipulate and dehumanize in much the same way as the system they are presumably helping the client fight.

The second effort is the central one: to put the lawyers at the service of the organized recipients—the welfare rights movement—so as to help it become a more forceful part of American politics. Individual recipients are not positioned to decide "grand strategy" and the overall use to which lawyers are to be put. The organized movement is. Individual recipients cannot affect national welfare politics. Organized recipients can, if their organizations are strong enough and if they have sufficient support.

Unfortunately, in only a few communities have welfare lawyers aided welfare organization, and in these there has been little sophistication in fulfilling the task. On a national level, there has been only minimal assistance to the National Welfare Rights Organization. There is in 1970, and there will be for at least a few years, a pronounced lack of enthusiasm for such work on the part of the federal government. Since almost all welfare lawyers are government-funded, the financial base for their work probably will shrink in the years immediately ahead.

Helping to build a constituency of welfare recipients who decide legal strategy for themselves is an extraordinarily difficult task. It does not mean organizing by the lawyers, but it does require the closest work with organizers. It does not mean abandoning "test case" litigation, but it does mean assessing the value of such litigation with the organized recipients. It may mean spending more time writing welfare rights manuals and training recipients and organizers in the content of manuals and in the manipulation of grievance procedures. It may mean spending more time helping the organized groups develop alliances with the working poor, or helping the organized AFDC mothers find allies among the unorganized recipients of old-age assistance. It may mean that the national legal centers will put at least part of their staff directly at the service of the national movement. It means finding new financial bases for such work. It may mean that welfare lawyers from around the country will have to volunteer a few weeks a year to serve NWRO, and maybe even pay for their own upkeep while so doing. It may mean that some of the newly sprouting "public interest" law firms, or departments of existing private firms, should also volunteer their time.

What is urged here is that the use of lawyers' time on welfare matters, and the strategy they are to follow, be worked out with the organized recipients—with the ultimate decisions made by the recipients. In other words, the first step in a grand strategy for lawyers in advancing welfare rights is to serve, and thereby help build, an independent rights movement.

Basic Change in the Welfare System Requires New Analysis and Scholarship

Although there will be those who doubt the possibility of changing anything through "analysis and scholarship," as long as we are talking about America as it is we must analyze what we want by way of a welfare system, what other goals are inconsistent with our own goals, and what facts we must find and put before recipient organizations as well as the general public.

At least two issues require the most serious analysis. The first concerns the "work test" and "work incentive" issue. Anglo-American welfare programs throughout their history have been pegged to the "work test" as a means of guaranteeing that able-bodied men or women will not turn to welfare as a substitute for work. At times the "work test" has been used to exclude whole categories of able-bodied people; for example, our categorical system, with the exception of the unemployed parent category, is designed to exclude the able-bodied man and his family. When included in the welfare system, the able-bodied person's willingness to accept an available job—no matter how menial in nature or inadequate in salary—has

been a condition for the welfare grant. The great fear has been that
the poor will lose interest in menial jobs and that without the "work
test" there no longer will be a supply of desperate workers. As we
have seen in *Dandridge v. Williams,* so great has been that fear that
—even with the "work test"—many states have deliberately placed
dollar maximums on welfare to make sure that it was not more
attractive than adequately paying jobs.

Work tests have been brutal in their exclusions and bureaucratic and harsh in their administration. When they are humanely
administered, there has been some reason to believe that the "incentive" to work at certain jobs is *reduced.* Would black mothers agree
to stoop labor in Georgia's fields if adequate welfare grants were
available and not conditioned on their accepting such work?[33]

To all of this, the "welfare liberal" and the "negative income
tax" proponent have worked out what they believe to be a good
answer. Instead of imposing a "work test" for needy, able-bodied
people, why not create a "work incentive." Let us end the system,
the argument goes, wherein every working poor person is "taxed
100 percent" for every dollar he earns. That is, when a poor person
takes a job, let us exempt part of his earnings for the purpose of
determining welfare eligibility. For instance, if the applicant's
family is eligible without work for (say) $2,000 and the applicant
earns $2,000, let him keep 50 percent and deduct only the other
50 percent from his grant. Thus there will be an "incentive" to
work; by working, the person in this example will receive $3,000
annually (instead of $2,000 on welfare or $2,000 solely from his job
without an "incentive" system).

The "work incentive" proposal seems widely attractive. Economists Milton Friedman and James Tobin endorse it. Congress accepted a limited version in 1967 for AFDC recipients (allowing $30
and one-third of remaining income to be retained), and President
Nixon has proposed that the "work incentive" be broadened to 50
percent and be applied to all families with children whose income
falls below his proposed federal floor. Welfare recipients by and
large like the idea; some are even enthusiastic (why should their
job income be "taxed 100 percent"?). The nonwelfare working
poor like it; their total income would be raised. All America seems
united on a good idea; who ever said that the different classes have
different interests?

It is, I suspect, a trap. There are at least four closely related problems: (1) it is extremely expensive to finance a good "work in-centive" *and* an adequate base grant for those who cannot work; (2) as illustrated by President Nixon's proposal, it is the base grant which will be sacrificed in favor of the incentive, thus leaving those who cannot work with an inadequate grant; (3) it pumps most new money to be put into a welfare system into federal subsidy for every sweatshop, every menial job, every poorly paid job in the country; and (4) it thereby conditions survival of the needy poor on their willingness to accept menial jobs, just as effectively as the most harshly administered work test—or perhaps even more effectively.

Thus, when the 1969 White House Conference on Hunger and Malnutrition was considering the NWRO proposal that it support the $5,500 welfare line for all persons in need, Robert Harris, Director of President Johnson's Commission on Income Mainte-nance, was quick to advise the participants what was wrong with the proposal. On the assumption that $5,500 was necessary for decent survival, Harris calculated that to guarantee such income would appear to require $20 billion more in income maintenance programs, a manageable figure (once we abandon warmaking). But, he argued, without either a work test or work incentive, it would cost far more because many persons would not work at lower-paid jobs when they could get $5,500 without such jobs. A 50 percent work incentive on a $5,500 base would cost some $70 billion more, an unmanageable figure, and subsidize persons making up to $11,000 a year. This is surely ridiculous, Harris argued. Naturally his solution was to lower the base grant—even though $5,500 is needed to support a family decently.

We must identify our primary concern. Is it to guarantee that people who cannot or should not work will have enough aid so as to live with minimum decency, or to assure that people who can work will do so regardless of what work they are forced to accept? Suppose a welfare system offered an adequate grant to all those in need (with income below it), and a right to refuse work which paid less than the welfare grant. If, as a result, private business and government were forced to reorganize the economy to ensure that it provided purposeful and well-paying work, would not this be desirable? Are we not producing the opposite result when we subsidize (through the "work incentive") the most pointless and exploitive jobs in the economy while denying decent welfare grants to those who cannot work?

The second and quite different issue concerning which we need more analysis and scholarship is the extent to which the Constitution imposes upon government an obligation to support individuals who cannot survive without such support. Is there a constitutional "right to live"—that is, is there a basis upon which we can fairly interpret the Constitution as implying such a right under modern conditions?

Earlier, we briefly mentioned the equal protection strategy which was moving in that direction and, for the time being, has failed. There probably will not be any major judicial or legislative changes on this matter in the next few years. But the issue is not and must not be dead forever. Legal argument will revive not simply when times change, but also when enough scholarly work has been done to provide the groundwork for forward movement.

For example: Have not even "judicial activists" too readily assumed that the equal protection clause does not impose a governmental obligation to sustain the lives of those who would otherwise perish? Should not the views of such men as Jacobus ten Broek[34] be more vigorously pursued? Is it not time to answer fully the simplistic equation between equal protection "special scrutiny" and the due process abuses of fifty years ago? Even assuming traditional concepts, does not an affirmative duty under the equal protection clause arise when, as a result of government action designed to enrich one group of citizens, other citizens are stripped of the means of survival? Has not this pattern characterized much of government policy in recent decades? Agricultural policy and tenant farmers? Inflation policy and unemployment? Cannot a substantial case be made that there is a direct, causal relationship between affirmative government policy on behalf of the middle class and rich and the substandard condition of the poor? These examples, in my opinion, merely touch the surface of the scholarly work that is needed.

We are not in a period of dramatic advance. By doing what we can: by engaging in scholarship and analysis of where we are going, by holding and expanding the gains we have made, by aiding recipient organization, we can hasten a better time. Too many persons, including a large percentage of welfare lawyers, do not understand that large forward movements are possible only as the expectations of people increase as a result of numerous small struggles, reforms, and increased understanding. Revolutions, legal or otherwise, are not born of despair, defeat, and hopelessness.

NOTES

1. For statistical and other information concerning the federally supported welfare programs, see NCSS Report A-6(10–69), *Program Facts*, published by the Department of Health, Education, and Welfare.

2. *See* Comment, "Welfare's 'Condition X,' " 76 *Yale Law Journal* 1222 (1967).

3. The best general history of the "suitable home" rules and "substitute father" tests is W. Bell, *Aid to Dependent Children* (1965).

4. 277 F. Supp. 31 (M.D. Ala. 1967).

5. 392 U.S. 309, 334 (1968).

6. *Id.* at 333.

7. Damico v. California, 2 CCH Pov. L. Rep. ¶ 10,478, at 11,373 (N.D. Cal. 1969).

8. Doe v. Shapiro, 302 F. Supp. 761, 764 (D. Conn. 1969), *appeal dismissed*, 396 U.S. 488 (1970).

9. Cooper v. Laupheimer, 316 F. Supp. 264 (E.D. Pa. 1970).

10. McClellan v. Shapiro, 315 F. Supp. 484 (D. Conn. 1970); Alexander v. Swank, 314 F. Supp. 1082 (N.D. Ill. 1970).

11. HEW has recently given notice that it intends to codify this position in the Federal Regulations. *See* 35 Fed. Reg. 8766 (June 5, 1970). For a useful analysis, see Comment, "AFDC Eligibility Requirements Unrelated to Need: The Impact of King v. Smith," 118 *University of Pennsylvania Law Review* 1219 (1970).

12. *See, e.g.,* Rosado v. Wyman, 397 U.S. 397 (1970).

13. 397 U.S. 254 (1970). *See generally* on the discretionary whim of administrators, R. O'Neill, *The Price of Dependency* (1970).

14. Parrish v. Civil Service Comm'n, 425 P.2d 223 (Cal. 1967).

15. James v. Goldberg. 303 F. Supp. 935 (S.D.N.Y. 1969), *prob. juris. noted*, 397 U.S. 904 (1970).

16. Rosado v. Wyman, 414 F.2d 170 (2nd Cir. 1969).

17. Rosado v. Wyman, 397 U.S. 397, 422–23 (1970).

18. NWRO v. Finch, 429 F.2d 725 (D.C. Cir. 1970).

19. There is some reason to believe, however, that the federal courts will extend the reasoning of *Goldberg* to grant applications. *See* Barnett v. Lindsay, No. C-328-69 (D. Utah, 1970).

20. " 'Rehabilitation' under H.R. 12080: Acceleration, the Trend Toward Second Class Citizenship for Welfare Clients," in 4 Sparer, *Materials on Public Assistance Law* 277 (1969) (Reginald Heber Smith Program Materials) [hereinafter cited as Sparer Materials].

21. 394 U.S. 618 (1969).

22. Gaddis v. Wyman, 304 F. Supp. 717 (S.D.N.Y. 1969), *aff'd per curiam*, 397 U.S. 49 (1970).

23. 394 U.S. at 631–32.

24. Additional sources concerning the welfare grant system will be found in 3 Sparer Materials, §10. A critique of the federal "poverty line" will be found in Sparer, "The Inadequacy of Present Welfare Grants," also reproduced in §10.

25. *See* materials set forth in "The Sister-in-the-House Rule and Other Assumed Income Regulations," in 1 Sparer Materials, at 166.

26. 397 U.S. 397 (1970).

27. The issue had arisen and been resolved successfully in Jefferson v. Hackney, 304 F. Supp. 1332 (N.D. Tex. 1969), *vacated and remanded,* 397 U.S. 821 (1970). *But see* Lampton v. Bonin, 304 F. Supp. 1384 (E.D. La. 1969), *vacated and remanded,* 397 U.S. 663 (1970).

28. McGowan v. Maryland, 366 U.S. 420, 426 (1961).

29. *E.g.,* Westberry v. Fisher, 309 F. Supp. 12 (D. Me. 1970).

30. 303 F. Supp. 339, 347 (S.D.N.Y. 1969), *vacated and remanded,* 90 S.Ct. 1582 (1970).

31. 397 U.S. 471 (1970).

32. Family Assistance Act of 1970, H.R. 16311, 91st Cong., 1st Sess. (1969).

33. Such required stoop labor was at issue in Anderson v. Burson, 300 F. Supp. 401 (N.D. Ga. 1968). The court upheld the constitutionality of such work tests.

34. J. ten Broek, *Equal Under Law* (1965).

THE RIGHT TO
SPECIAL TREATMENT

GRAHAM HUGHES

THE FIELD OF CIVIL LIBERTIES AND CIVIL RIGHTS
can never escape legal complexities. But its broad moral setting has
traditionally been a comforting one in which we waged battles
against malevolence and struggled to overturn the practices of those
who believed others to be inferior or unworthy of fair and equal
treatment. Recently both the legal and the moral pictures have
clouded over. Practices are called into question which are evidently
not the expression of malevolence but which are justified as redressing past inequalities and imbalances or otherwise promoting
desirable aims and applauded ideals. At the same time they may
appear in other aspects to threaten some traditional expressions of
constitutionally protected values. Such very delicate and complicated moral dilemmas have emerged with any clarity only in the
last few years and they have so far produced only tentative and uncertain responses. One possible position is to assert the constant
duty to interpret constitutional provisions in the light of existing
social needs and so to find a warrant for bold and express patterns
of preferential treatment for disadvantaged groups in the pursuit of
an ideal of adjustment through compensation. On the other side, it
is not difficult to point to practical and moral dangers which might
flow from such a posture and to insist on the importance of con-

*Graham Hughes is Professor of Law at New York University School of Law and
Director of the Law School's Project on Legal Education Opportunity. He is the
author of many articles on legal philosophy, and the editor of* Law, Reason, and
Justice: Essays in Legal Philosophy.

tinuing to look with disfavor on the special treatment of particular groups. So far the law reports offer only the most meager illumination in this troubled area.

At this point some specific examples will serve to concretize the dilemma. A public educational institution, perhaps the graduate school of a state university, may awaken to the fact that it has a lamentably small proportion of blacks among its students. Strenuous efforts to improve this position by attracting to the school black students who meet usual admission requirements fail, probably because there is only a small pool of black students nationally available with such qualifications and they are competed for energetically by some of the most prestigious schools in the country. Accordingly, our school decides to abandon its traditional "color-blind" policy and to accept black students whose qualifications are somewhat below those generally required for admission. This new policy may be announced publicly, or, more probably, it may simply be applied without fanfare. In either event we assume that there is sufficient evidence of the general admission requirements and of the practice of lowering these in the case of black applicants. What would be the result if a white student, rejected by the school, should bring a suit in which he alleged that black students with qualifications less than his had been accepted and that this constituted a denial to him of the equal protection of the law? Could anyone else successfully institute such a suit, or only a white student denied admission in such circumstances?

Somewhat similarly, suppose that a private corporation, in an apparently laudable desire to increase the number of blacks in its employment and in positions of executive responsibility, establishes a hiring practice of giving preference to black applicants when their qualifications are identical with those of white applicants, or even somewhat below, and acts similarly in its internal promotion practices. Could a white applicant, alleging superior qualifications to a preferred black appointee, bring a successful suit under one of the federal or state statutes which prescribe fair employment practices?

In a different context we may suppose that a public housing authority, building a new development, is anxious to make it integrated and to keep it so. Perhaps a statistical projection is made that if available places in the development were filled from those people in the territorial jurisdiction of the authority who are most qualified or deserving of places according to criteria of income, nature of present housing, size of family, etc., then the new development would be filled with approximately 80 percent blacks and 20 percent whites. However, current sociological studies in the public housing field assert that after black occupancy of buildings passes a certain percentage, known as the "tipping point," whites tend to leave the dwellings and the buildings become all black. We may assume that in the area in question the tipping point has been set at 60 percent black. Accordingly the Housing Authority establishes a "benign quota" by which black occupancy is not to rise above 60 percent. After this point is reached, a black applicant is refused and the place allotted to a white applicant who, on generally accepted criteria, leaving out the racial and integration questions, would have been less eligible. Does the rejected black have a remedy against the Housing Authority?[1]

For a final example let us suppose that black students at a state university petition and bring other pressures to bear on the university authorities to set up a black studies program which shall not be open to white students and to provide separate university housing for black students. If the university accedes to these requests, may a white student, denied admission to the black studies program or to the black housing facility, bring a successful suit against the university? Could a black student bring such a suit? Could anyone bring such a suit?

The examples above are not meant to suggest that there is at present in the United States a massive program of preferential treatment in favor of blacks which is posing grave threats to the civil rights of whites. But such practices are clearly in force in some institutions, and the moral and legal dilemmas which they pose have to be confronted. As is so often the case in the United States, most of the moral arguments which can be made on either side will be found to be closely mirrored in the legal arguments as to constitutionality.[2]

A declaration that our master ideal is equality and equal treatment is by no means sufficient to dissolve the problems. For it could be immediately asserted that a society which is sensitively concerned with serving this ideal must be attentive to the past as well as the present and the future. Is a university properly serving the ideal of equality by adopting a color-blind admissions policy when pervasive social injustices have ensured that many young black people are so educationally ill-equipped that they cannot present the qualifications normally required for admission? Does not fidelity to the ideal of equality require that a compensatory allowance be made for this? Indeed, in this educational field a justification could be presented so as to avoid any allegations of unequal treatment. The university might assert that its duty in selecting students for acceptance is to identify those who are most likely to perform well in the context of higher education. In the past certain standard indicia have been used for this purpose which did *de facto* exclude a great number of black applicants. But, it could be argued, these traditional criteria, such as high school grades and performance on standard aptitude tests, can now be shown to be weighted in favor of white middle-class students. If provided with a proper motivation and proper teaching, certain black students are just as likely to do well in the university as certain white students who scored higher on the conventional tests. The university claims to be able to identify these black students by interviews and other procedures. If such an argument is uncontested, the university has now rebutted the charge of unequal treatment (assuming that the interviews were afforded to white students also) and has simply replaced its earlier selection procedures by ones which it claims can more sensitively and accurately identify those students most likely to do well in higher education.

But this is clearly to some extent a factual dispute. In response it could be said that standard tests used by universities for admission purposes do fairly accurately predict those who are most likely to succeed in an academic setting. There is some evidence with respect to aptitude tests used for tracking at the precollege school level that this is so.[3] To assert this is not of course to deny that these tests may be culturally biased or class-biased or (concomitantly) racially biased. Black and poor children may indeed be disposed by environmental factors and family cultural backgrounds to do poorly in these tests. But this does not mean that the tests are likely to be inaccurate as predictors. (Whether it entitles us to call the tests "unfair" is then clearly a more complicated question.) And once the tests are shown to be reasonably accurate (and the most accurate) predictors of academic success, a school or university which wishes to go beyond them to give preference to a black student who has performed less well than a rejected white student will have to move to another justification. This might be that in the selection of students for places in a university, factors other than anticipation of the optimum academic performance are properly relevant. Certainly, many colleges have long been in the habit of according preference to children of alumni or to applicants with a particular regional connection. It would not seem a departure from such a tradition to recognize other reasons as establishing relevant criteria in selection procedures. One such reason might be a public obligation to make reparations to people who had earlier been subjected to disadvantage, which could be viewed as an expression of the ideal of equality through adjustment of a socially unjust situation of unequal opportunity. On a different footing it might be justified in another direction by pointing to the social need to have more black people in positions of responsibility and settings of relative affluence which can generally be reached only through higher education. Such a goal could be thought of both as correcting social injustice and, in a more utilitarian vein, as damping down the fires of discontent and leading to a more harmonious and productive society. Are these proper objectives for a university in its selection of students? Even if they are proper, may they be pursued at the expense of individuals who might be better qualified by criteria relating to the prospect of optimum academic performance? Moving from the moral to the legal question, we are now asking whether a racial classification is permissible in this context, a peculiarly charged context since it involves giving preference to members of one racial group at the expense of members of another. Even if the university's practice were changed somewhat and amounted to giving preference not just to blacks but to all who were classified as disadvantaged, the moral and legal problems would still remain, though they would lose the traditional cloud of suspicion which surrounds racial classifications.

Before pursuing these general considerations further, we can note that the arguments aired above in connection with preferential (or compensatory, or reparative) treatment for one group are not quite appropriate to the "benign quota" example in the housing field. The benign quota is not designed to confer any supererogatory benefit on black people, but rather to curtail their otherwise legitimate claims in furtherance of some other social ideal which, presumably, is considered to be in the interest of society generally and so to benefit both blacks and whites. The benign quota is indeed not designed to benefit any particular group as such, nor is it designed *with the purpose* of inflicting a deprivation on anyone, though the *result* of its imposition may be to deny someone a benefit which he could otherwise claim. Here the complainant will not be a white person who claims that a black person has been unjustifiably preferred to him in pursuit of an ideal of reparation, but rather a black person who claims that a white person has been un-justifiably preferred to him in pursuit of an ideal of integration. Now it is true that when we have spoken traditionally of the evils of *de jure* or *de facto* segregation, we have been most mindful of the alleged harm to blacks, but our black complainant might reasonably urge that he is less interested in the general ideal of integration than in securing for himself and his family decent housing to which he has an otherwise proper claim. This position might be strengthened by the sociological argument that while there is a body of evidence to the effect that segregated educational facilities do acute harm to black children there is no evidence that segregated housing does comparable harm to black people. Indeed the strongest arguments for integrated housing are in terms of its educational impact in breaking down prejudice both in whites and blacks, and it is not easy to see why blacks should have to pay a special price to secure this benefit for everybody. A subtle response here might be that segregated housing breeds *de facto* segregation in schools, but there are others ways of achieving integrated schools than through inte-grated housing and this is perhaps too remote an argument to justify the denial of housing to an individual black. Apart from the generally suspect history of quotas, which always at best tread a narrow line between beneficence and malevolence, there are strong moral arguments against any quota which is expressed in terms of a ceiling or maximum of any racial group. Quotas in terms of a mini-mum of a minority group will be discussed later.

The occasional demands by minority groups for special facilities which are to be closed to the majority present different questions again. In the case of such demands made in educational institutions, with respect to either housing or black studies programs, the justifi-cations may be diverse. They may consist of a general assertion that black people have been so maltreated by the white majority that before we can expect a harmonious integration we must allow them to retreat into isolation for a period during which they can search for self-sufficiency. In the educational field we hear arguments that the value of black studies programs would be diminished if whites were permitted to be present since this would inhibit black students from speaking freely. Such arguments might seem more appropriate in a therapeutic setting which is dedicated to healing a bruised psyche than in an academic context. Again, we are sometimes told that white students are unqualified by their background to partici-pate in black studies programs. If the programs contemplate scholarly activity, it is difficult to see how this could be so, though it may indeed make sense if the programs are primarily conceived as therapeutic. It could be argued that the emotional health of students is a proper concern of universities and that classification by race may be necessary for therapeutic purposes in a medical program, but those who advocate black studies programs would presumably not want to rest on this ground since they rightly present such programs as a suitable scholarly activity in an academic curriculum.

Housing facilities on campus explicitly reserved for a minority group seem equally difficult to defend. Arguments of a therapeutic nature might be repeated here, supported perhaps by the assertion that familiar objections to segregation are less appropriate where a minority, traditionally discriminated against, wishes to withdraw into its own enclave. A black request for separate accommodation, it could be urged, does not rest on an explicit or implicit assertion of superiority and, in view of the small minority of black people in the community at large and their generally depressed socio-economic position, does not have any disadvantageous implications for the white majority. But such a justification would be enormously difficult to translate into any general principle of permission. Should it only apply in communities (municipal or educational) where blacks are in a minority, and should similar privileges be extended to whites where they are in a minority? Would it depend on an investigation of the motives of the separatists so that their request would have to be denied if it should be found that it has any basis in feelings of superiority? If blacks in any community, though in a minority, should ever reach a superior socio-economic position to whites, should such a request then be denied? Rather than trade in such flimsy and shifting criteria, so pervasively open to abuse, it is almost certainly wiser to stick to a flat prohibition of segregation even if in the short run this should lead to hostile responses from black separatists.[4]

The questions briefly rehearsed in the preceding discussion touch on such burning debates in American life that we might expect to find full and ready answers in the law. Such an expectation would perhaps be naive, for the questions are both novel and complex, and the courts will be wise to abstain from quick generalizations.

Put in the broadest terms, state classifications through legislation or other forms of state action must seek to serve an end which is a permissible subject of state action and must be based on a discernible difference which is rationally and reasonably relevant to the pursuit of that end.[5] The modern starting point in the application of these general principles to racial classifications must be the school desegregation cases exemplified by *Brown v. Board of Education.*[6] But *Brown,* though of transcendent importance, is by no means free of ambiguity and certainly does not begin to furnish answers to some of the questions that we have been asking. It is, however, generally agreed that *Brown* cannot reasonably be read as imposing a prohibition on any and every state classification by race. In itself it holds no more than that state-imposed segregation in the field of education is inherently productive of unequal education and is thus constitutionally offensive. It is not even clear from *Brown* itself that all state-imposed segregation is unconstitutional, since it could be argued that in other contexts than that of education no inequality may result as long as fully equal though separate facilities are provided, but this argument is almost certainly now untenable in view of subsequent cases striking down segregation in other public sectors.[7] At the same time there are other, earlier cases in the Supreme Court, which have never been repudiated, and which suggest that in some circumstances racial classifications are permissible even though they involve the infliction of tremendous hardship and deprivation on a minority group. The most notable of these cases are the Japanese-American relocation cases of *Hirabayashi v. United States*[8] and *Korematsu v. United States*[9] in 1943 and 1944, which held that in time of war against Japan it was permissible for the government to enforce evacuation and detention orders against American citizens of Japanese descent living in western parts of the United States. These cases conceded that racial classifications were suspect and particularly so when they imposed such special, onerous burdens, but concluded that "pressing public necessity" justified them in the cases under review.

The most important Supreme Court review of racial classifications in the very recent past has been in the miscegenation case of *McLaughlin v. Florida*[10] in 1964. In one sense a miscegenation statute does not appear to infringe on principles of equal protection, since it applies equally to white or black defendants who marry or cohabit with members of the other race. Historically such laws have been objectionable, since they seemed in fact to reflect the views of the white majority that their purity of race must be preserved from a commingling with blacks. Ought we to view such laws differently if both blacks and whites shared a strong wish to avoid

commingling with each other in marriage or sexual acts? Such moral
deliberation was avoided by the Supreme Court, which was able in
the *McLaughlin* case to strike down the Florida cohabitation statute
by holding that such a racial classification was not necessary for the
accomplishment of a permissible state policy, even assuming for
argument's sake that a ban on racially mixed marriages was a permissible policy to pursue.[11] The language employed by the Court in
the *McLaughlin* case will clearly be of importance in all future
general discussion of this topic, for it designates all racial classifications as constitutionally suspect and holds that, at any rate where
criminal penalties are involved, the classification must not only be
reasonably relevant to the purpose of the statute but must be *necessary* to effect some overriding statutory purpose. The concurring
opinion of Mr. Justice Stewart went so far as to doubt whether any
valid legislative purpose could ever be conceivable which would
make "the color of a person's skin the test of whether his conduct
is a criminal offense." It may be doubted whether such a valid purpose is inconceivable. One writer has posed a hypothetical situation
in which a new and virulently infectious disease may have appeared
which afflicts only members of one racial group.[12] We may imagine
that medical researchers can advance convincing scientific evidence
why members of other racial groups are immune from this disease
and are not carriers of it. If the legislature then enacts a law which
requires members of the afflicted racial group to be vaccinated
against this disease under penalty for noncompliance, it is by no
means obvious that such a statute would be unconstitutional. Indeed, common sense and principles of social morality combine in
leading to the conclusion that our Constitution cannot be so per-
verse as to demand such a holding. At any rate, after *McLaughlin*
the field is clearly open for plausible arguments to the effect that
racial classifications are constitutionally permissible when necessary
for permissible purposes.

Racial designations in record-keeping contexts have explicitly
been held to be permissible by the Supreme Court where they serve
a permissible function and do not have a discriminatory tendency,
though the drawing of a line between situations where such designations are discriminatory and where they are not is a difficult and
delicate matter.[13] Furthermore, in the numerous opinions in state
courts and the lower federal courts in the last decade on the questions of permissible or required steps to combat *de facto* segregation
in schools, there are many dicta and some specific holdings which

can be taken to approve and even to require racial classifications where these are necessary to combat actual patterns of segregation. One of these is the case of *Tometz v. Board of Education*,[14] decided by the Supreme Court of Illinois in 1968. There the Illinois legislature had provided that "As soon as practicable . . . the school board shall change or revise existing attendance units or create new units in a manner which will take into consideration the prevention of segregation and the elimination of separation of children in public schools because of color, race or nationality."[15] The defendants challenged the constitutionality of the provision, alleging that it required race to be considered as a factor in changing or forming school attendance units, which they argued was offensive to the equal protection and due process clauses of the Fourteenth Amendment. The Supreme Court of Illinois pointed out that the question was not whether such action was required of a state but whether it was permissible, and concluded that it was permissible as a reasonable way of combatting the evils of *de facto* segregation, which in the court's view "has a seriously limiting influence on educational opportunity."

In 1969 the Supreme Court of the United States touched lightly on these issues in its decision in *United States v. Montgomery County Board of Education*,[16] a case which originated with a suit in 1964 aimed at breaking down practices of the respondent school board which allegedly promoted segregation. In 1968 the district court had made an order directing that the board must move toward a goal under which, "in each school the ratio of white to Negro faculty members is substantially the same as it is throughout the system," and further directing that for the following school year, "in schools with 12 or more teachers the race of at least one out of every six faculty and staff members was required to be different from the race of the majority of the faculty and staff members at that school." This order was varied somewhat by the court of appeals but reinstated by the Supreme Court, who approved it in an opinion which, perhaps wisely, makes no effort or pretense to examine the boundaries of permissible classification by race in any general, principled fashion. But it must be observed that in both the *Tometz* and the *Montgomery Board* cases, the courts were passing on the constitutionality of measures propounded and designed to combat existing situations of segregation. In the *Montgomery Board* case the segregation arose out of earlier state action and later state inaction, and the order of the district court was designed to combat assignment of teachers which was motivated by racial considerations, so that the remedy could be viewed as essentially a measured corrective to eradicate positive discrimination. There is nothing in these cases or the opinions therein which could be taken clearly to validate a preferential treatment of one racial group even as an interim compensatory technique.

The validation of such preferential treatment may, however, be detected in a federal decision of the District Court of New Jersey in 1969 in *Porcelli v. Titus.*[17] In the events leading to that case the school board had abolished the examination system for selection of suitable candidates for the post of school principal, allegedly in order to appoint to such positions a number of blacks who would not be qualified under the examination system. The plaintiffs were white teachers, who alleged that this action had discriminated against them and who sued under the Civil Rights Act of 1964. The Court found on the record that " 'Race,' in its broadest connotation, played a part in the Board's decision to suspend the promotion lists and abandon the examination system," but went on to find that on a fair reading of the record the new system was designed "not simply to appoint Negroes to promotional positions but to obtain for these positions qualified persons, white or black, whose qualifications were based on an awareness of, and sensitivity to, the problems of educating the Newark school population." On this basis the court found that "there was no intention on the part of the Board to discriminate against white persons."

The *Porcelli* case, which of course is not of great authority in the sense of precedent, does appear to hold that the color of a person's skin can explicitly be made a qualification for a public teaching position without a necessary inference of discrimination. The justifications in the opinion rely to a considerable extent on testimony in the record to the effect that the education of Newark's largely black student body was suffering from the absence in the administration of the schools of black authority figures with whom the pupils could identify. Put in this way blackness becomes a qualification for the position of principal, so that express adversion to color in the evaluation of candidates can be presented as only one way of searching for the best appointee. But this is a dangerous path to tread. Can a private employer expressly make race a factor in his appointments on the ground that his customers identify more with one race than another? Could such procedures ultimately involve us in degrading litigation, with Nazi and South African associations, on whether a person is properly to be classified as white or black? Is whiteness a special qualification for appointment to a principal's post in a predominantly white school? Would this depend on whether white students could identify with a black principal and on whether or not their education would suffer from lack of identification? How reliable are such sociological and psychological arguments, and even if they are reliable, are there not convincing and outweighing moral arguments on the other side?

In the area of employment outside the field of education the law reports offer even less guidance. Here attention for the most part is rightly still focused on practices which discriminate against minorities, particularly in so-called referral unions which operate hiring halls or supply quotas of workers for an employer. In an effort to open up more jobs for minority members the federal administration, under the authority of an executive order forbidding discrimination in federal contract work, promulgated in 1969 the so-called Philadelphia Plan.[18] This requires good-faith efforts to be made to hire a gradually ascending percentage of minority group workers on designated federal projects over a number of years. It is thus an instance of a minimum quota, as opposed to the "benign quota" concept in housing discussed earlier, which is that of a maximum quota. In spite of this, the plan has come under attack from critics who argue that it offends against Title VII of the Civil Rights Act of 1964, which broadly prohibits discriminatory practices in private employment. Litigation is in hand to challenge the plan. There are not as yet any authoritative decisions on the matter, though early in 1970 the Supreme Court denied certiorari to a petition which sought review of a lower-court decision upholding a plan similar to the Philadelphia one.[19]

In the field of housing there are some decisions which on a superficial reading would appear to deny the legitimacy of any quotas based on race. In 1953 in *Banks v. Housing Authority*,[20] the Supreme Court of California struck down a San Francisco Housing Authority plan under which housing was to be allotted to all races in the same proportions as they bore to each other in existing residence patterns. The court said, "It is the individual . . . who is entitled to the equal protection of the laws—not merely a group of individuals, or a body of persons according to their numbers." The Supreme Court denied certiorari in this case. But before too much significance is attached to this decision it must be pointed out that the individual public housing units contemplated by the Housing

Authority would have been segregated, so that the court's opinion can be viewed as a rejection of segregation even when it wears an ameliorative garb. More recent cases have employed language which at the least seems to view classification by race as proper for some purposes in connection with urban housing projects. In the case of *Norwalk CORE v. Norwalk Redevelopment Agency*[21] in the Second Circuit Court of Appeals, a number of black and Puerto Rican plaintiffs brought an action against the redevelopment agency, alleging that in planning and implementing the project the defendants did not assure or attempt to assure relocation for black and Puerto Rican displacees to the same extent as for whites, and arguing that this constituted a denial of the equal protection of the law. Taking the allegations of fact to be true, the court reversed the denial of a remedy in the court below and remanded the case for further proceedings. The court acknowledged that any remedy afforded the plaintiffs might involve classification by race, and went on, "That is something which the Constitution usually forbids, not because it is inevitably an impermissible classification, but because it is one which usually, to our national shame, has been drawn for the purpose of maintaining racial inequality. Where it is drawn for the purpose of achieving equality it will be allowed, and to the extent it is necessary to avoid unequal treatment by race, it will be required." This statement by the court must be read in the light of the nature of the plaintiffs' claim to the effect that "the defendants acted, knowingly and deliberately, so as to compound the problem of racial discrimination in the Norwalk housing market, with the inevitable and intended result that some Negroes and Puerto Ricans would be forced to leave the city altogether."

These cases reiterate a growing theme to the effect that classification by race may be permissible if it is designed to combat segregation or to ensure proper recognition of minority rights. But it will be apparent that a number of issues are still left to be resolved, though more or less tentative guesses as to their disposition might be hazarded. "Minimum quota" requirements, as in the Philadelphia Plan, will probably be approved by the courts; "maximum quotas," as in the benign quota housing possibility, are much more controversial and will probably be disallowed. The patent distinction here is that the minimum quota may be presented as not having a direct exclusionary effect on anyone whereas the maximum quota clearly does have such an effect. A minimum quota of, say, 20 percent blacks to be employed on a certain job could of course be

presented conversely as a maximum quota of 80 percent whites, but
an interpretation of the minimum quota can probably be reached
to avoid such a bald conclusion. This would be to argue that the
intention is to insist that employers must demonstrate a proper
effort to attract black applicants and a readiness to hire them where
they are minimally qualified to do the work, and that quotas are
merely provisional demonstrations of a good-faith discharge of these
obligations. Thus they need not be understood as a requirement to
hire a less qualified black over a more qualified white.[22] Interpreted
this way the quota requirement would not amount to preferential
treatment, but rather to a remedial measure designed to eradicate
previous unequal treatment by some visible and measurable yardstick.

Put in such a way, the validation of the minimum quota of the
Philadelphia Plan type would not contain any explicit or implicit
validation of plainly preferential treatment. It does not seem possible to put up any defense of a maximum quota in these terms. A
further reasonable guess may be that the courts will not approve any
scheme which is baldly stated to be a preferential one justified in
compensatory or reparative terms. But as we have seen, this again
should not be taken to mean that there is no way in which race
might be overtly taken into account in selection procedures in a
variety of contexts, for the justification of compensation or reparation may be abandoned and in its place there may be advanced a
justification in terms of fitness, suitability, or sensitivity for the post
or place. As *Porcelli v. Titus* showed, there is at the least some
possibility that in certain instances the courts may accept such justifications to overcome arguments of denial of equal protection or
infringement of civil rights statutes.[23] To do this is to play with
fire, but perhaps a freezing man has to play such a dangerous game.
The dangers can be somewhat avoided by adding to the fitness or
sensitivity argument a further qualification that again it is only
persuasive where the thrust of the process is to rectify existing racial
imbalance which has adversely affected a particular group. This
seems implicit in the *Porcelli* case.

One thing is abundantly evident. When American constitutional lawyers argue the propriety of some of the procedures discussed here, they are essentially engaging in philosophical debate
about the demands of social justice. Lawyers' debate is not, of
course, quite the same as philosophical discussion, because lawyers
have to talk to each other and endeavor to persuade each other in

the context of principles and decisions which have an authoritative aspect. The philosopher is unfettered by precedent and untrammeled by authority. But in this area, as this discussion has shown, the lawyer is dealing with questions which are not tightly controlled by precise statutory provisions or irrefutable precedents. The guiding constitutional principles allow almost unlimited room for argument and indicate a variety of alternative paths which might be followed.

The most radical arguments for express recognition of the validity of preferential, compensatory schemes are by no means impossible of plausible justification within the corners of constitutional debate. It is easy to understand why those who are impatient with the slow pace of social change might wish to urge such arguments. At the same time we have seen that general declarations of the validity of theories of compensation and preference might lead to the entrenchment of doctrines which could offer great scope in the future for application to unworthy ends. Perhaps the most important question is whether such declarations are really necessary for any practical purpose. We have certainly not yet encountered a situation where a proposed project for redressing injustice to minorities has run into a serious constitutional roadblock. It might be said in response that this is because both government and private institutions are doing so little in this field, and that if massive efforts were made to restructure American society so as to eradicate the worst socio-economic injustices then present interpretations of the Constitution could present substantial difficulties. This may or may not be so, and it is probably profitless for the courts to seek to anticipate such a remote eventuality.

A different question is whether or not the courts should again endeavor to take the lead in this area and to press upon society the moral arguments for compensation and reparation by presenting them as legal duties to be fulfilled. In view of the only qualified success achieved by the courts in the fight for formal equality in the field of school integration, there can be little doubt that such an attempt to press more radical and constitutionally less well grounded doctrines would meet with dismal failure. A society will never be radicalized by its courts but only through political activity. At the moment it appears that any schemes which can realistically be expected to evolve for compensatory practices toward disadvantaged groups will probably be able to pass the test of constitutionality. Further measures await political change.

NOTES

1. A general discussion of benign quotas is Hellerstein, "The Benign Quota, Equal Protection and the Rule in Shelley's Case," 17 *Rutgers Law Review* 531 (1963).

2. Some of the moral and constitutional arguments are discussed in Hughes, "Reparations for Blacks?" 43 *New York University Law Review* 1063 (1968); Kaplan, "Equal Justice in an Unequal World: Equality for the Negro—The Problem of Special Treatment," 61 *Northwestern University Law Review* 363 (1966); Vieira, "Racial Imbalance, Black Separatism, and Permissible Classification by Race," 67 *Michigan Law Review* 1553 (1969).

3. *See* Comment, "Ability Grouping in Public Schools: A Threat to Equal Protection," 1 *Connecticut Law Review* 150 (1968).

4. Apart from general constitutional barriers, such projects may run into a clash with Title VI of the Civil Rights Act of 1964, 42 U.S.C. §2000d, which provides, "No person . . . shall on the ground of race, color or national origin, be excluded from participation in, be denied the benefits of, or be subjected to discrimination under any program or activity receiving Federal financial assistance." During 1969 the United States Department of Health, Education, and Welfare cautioned several colleges that separate black studies programs and separate minority-group housing would violate this provision.

5. *See, e.g.,* Gulf, Colorado & Santa Fé R.R. Co. v. Ellis, 165 U.S. 150, 155 (1897).

6. 347 U.S. 483 (1954).

7. In the period immediately following *Brown,* Supreme Court decisions quickly invalidated segregation on buses, in public parks, on beaches, on golf courses, etc.

8. 320 U.S. 81 (1943).

9. 323 U.S. 214 (1944).

10. 379 U.S. 184 (1964).

11. Three years later the Supreme Court held that restrictions on mixed marriages were generally unconstitutional. Loving v. Virginia, 388 U.S. 1 (1967).

12. Kaplan, *supra* note 2, at 383.

13. See Tancil v. Wools, 379 U.S. 19 (1964).

14. 237 N.E.2d 498 (Ill. 1968).

15. Ill. Rev. Stat., 1967, ch. 122, ¶ 10–21.3.

16. 395 U.S. 225 (1969).

17. 302 F. Supp. 726, 732 (D.N.J. 1969).

18. Issued in pursuance of Exec. Order No. 11246 (1965).

19. Weiner v. Cuyohoga Community College Dist., 19 Ohio St. 2d 35, 249 N.E.2d 907 (1969), *cert. denied,* 396 U.S. 1004 (1970).

20. 260 P.2d 668 (Cal. 1953).

21. 395 F.2d 920, 926, 931–32 (2d Cir. 1968).

22. This argument is made in an opinion of the Attorney General defending the constitutionality of the Philadelphia Plan; Justice Department, Op. Att'y Gen. 9/22/1969, 38 U.S.L.W. 2191 (Sept. 30, 1969).

23. Arguments to this effect are also to be found in an interesting series of opinions in a case where a black appellant challenged the purposeful inclusion of Negroes on a jury. Brooks v. Beto, 366 F.2d 1 (5th Cir. 1966).

THE RIGHT TO
LEGAL SERVICES

JEROME J. SHESTACK

IT IS FITTING THAT ONE OF THE FIRST CHAPTERS in this volume should deal with the right to legal services. Without legal representation, most of the rights we talk about in this book— the right to participate, the right to nondiscrimination, the right to protest, the right to health and welfare—could not be realized. And unrealizable rights are not really rights at all.

Yet when the decade of the sixties began, the right to legal services was not recognized in theory except in capital criminal cases, and in practice, the vast numbers of poor not only lacked legal services but were unaware that such services could help. And the legal profession was content to let this be. True, there were a few dedicated lawyers who struggled to maintain legal aid agencies, but the great majority of the bar remained silent, seemingly oblivious that their profession had any obligation to give continuing meaning to the concept of equal justice. Thus, as late as 1964, all of the legal aid and defender agencies together served less than 5 percent of the poor; 9 cities of over 100,000 had no legal aid at all; in over 100 medium-sized cities the programs were pitiful; and in numerous rural counties there was nothing. The entire 1964 budget for the

Jerome J. Shestack, a practicing lawyer in Philadelphia, is immediate past Chairman of the American Bar Association Section of Individual Rights and Responsibilities, a member of the National Advisory Committee to the Legal Services Program of the Office of Economic Opportunity, and a member of the Executive Committee of the National Legal Aid and Defender Association.

country's legal aid agencies was less than $6 million (contrast that with some $45 million spent last year—a figure still far short of the need).

Ten years later the situation had dramatically changed. As we enter the decade of the seventies, the right to legal services has gained considerable recognition; both the government and the legal profession have taken significant steps to realize that right; and the increased availability of legal services has become instrumental in bringing about major institutional reforms. And yet, there is an ominous trend in the nation which may undo many of the gains of the sixties. More of this later.

Surely, the role of legal services in a progressive democracy deserves considerably more emphasis than it has received from political scientists. The very essence of a democratic society is the concept of equal justice under law. This encompasses not only a just substantive law but equality of access to the processes of law. Denial of legal services is not merely a theoretical defect; it has deep practical ramifications. Lacking effective representation, the poor man sees the law, not as a protector, but as an enemy which evicts him from his flat, victimizes him as a consumer, cancels his welfare payments, binds him to usury, and seizes his children. We know now the unhappy results of the law's failure to meet the just expectations of those it governs. Law loses its stabilizing influence; at best, there is alienation; at worst, unrest and violence.

Thus, the deepest interests of society demand that we address ourselves to the task of providing legal services to those in need of them. Looking back, it is astounding that it has taken us so long to appreciate this.

RIGHTS TO LEGAL SERVICES FOR THE ACCUSED

In discussing the right to legal services, it is simplest to start with criminal prosecutions. Here, the right to counsel is established by the Sixth Amendment to the Constitution. However, for a long time this Amendment was deemed applicable only to *federal* prosecutions, whereas the vast majority of criminal trials take place in *state* courts.

The proposition that the Fourteenth Amendment's guarantee

of due process embodies the assurance of counsel in state criminal trials seems rather clear-cut, but it was not until 1963 that the Supreme Court overruled earlier holdings and proclaimed this principle in the landmark case of *Gideon v. Wainwright*.[1]

"The question is very simple. I requested the Court to appoint me an attorney and the Court refused." This is what Earl Gideon had written to the Supreme Court in support of his claim that a poor man charged with crime is entitled to have counsel. And the Supreme Court agreed. "[R]eason and reflection," Mr. Justice Black said in his clear and forceful style, "require us to recognize that in our adversary system of criminal justice, any person haled into court, who is too poor to hire a lawyer, cannot be assured a fair trial unless counsel is provided for him. . . . The right of one charged with crime to counsel may not be deemed fundamental and essential to fair trials in some countries, but it is in ours."[2]

Gideon's trumpet sounded loud and clear. It called upon the states to provide representation for all persons charged with serious crimes. And two cases which followed, *Escobedo* and *Miranda*,[3] made it plain that the right to counsel begins with the accusatory stage, that is, when an individual is taken into custody and subjected to questioning.

These cases heralded the advent of major changes in the representation of criminals. Before *Gideon,* most defender organizations were voluntary, struggling for funds from charitable sources. In some areas, there was a public defender who drew his salary from the state, and a third system, the mixed defender system, combined financial support from public and private sources. The *Gideon* ruling created a burden that voluntary defender organizations simply could not meet. While there remain some twenty-four voluntary defenders who rely on private contributions for a substantial portion of their budget, the trend now is toward public defender systems. Some of these function on a statewide basis (as in Connecticut, Massachusetts, Minnesota, New Jersey, Colorado, Alaska, and Hawaii); in other states, local or regional defender services operate on a loosely independent basis. More than a hundred public defender offices have been established in the last nine years. Healthy as this response has been, the need is far from being met, and state and local governments have a long way to go before meeting the obligations underscored by *Gideon* and its progeny.

A critical requirement for any defender office is that it be independent in defense of its clients. Recently, the fear has been expressed that this independence may be threatened if the public defender is on the same payroll as the prosecutor and the police department. The fear is not groundless. In the past year, some police departments have exerted severe pressures against legal services lawyers whose clients have charged police officers with discrimination or brutality. Civic organizations supporting legal services organizations handling such suits against the police have been threatened with police boycott, and other pressures have been employed. Legal services lawyers in Philadelphia, Los Angeles, Albuquerque, New Mexico, Baton Rouge, Louisiana, and Camden, New Jersey, have had this experience. Such occurrences give rise to the concern that vigorous defenders on the public payroll may become subject to pressures from ambitious mayors, police chiefs, or prosecutors who see high conviction statistics as the main plank in their political climb.

The dangers appear sufficiently real to require some type of insulation. Such techniques as a public authority to govern the defender organization, court approval for the removal of defender lawyers, a civil service system for defender lawyers, and bar association participation in the administration of the system are insulating possibilities which should be developed. Difficult days lie ahead for the public defender system if its independence is not better secured than at present.

Most small towns and rural areas still cannot afford a public defender system and instead use counsel assigned by the court on a case-by-case basis. Too often, this process has been haphazard, with counsel appointed very soon before trial and assignments rotated among lawyers without reference to experience or competence. Such handling of an assigned counsel system should not be thought of as fulfilling the constitutional obligations in criminal cases.

One improvement which is being experimented with is the "coordinated assigned counsel system" under which a bar association assumes responsibility for obtaining qualified lawyers to defend the indigent accused. A carefully planned and adequately financed assigned counsel system, particularly in small communities, can lead to a high quality of defense. However, over a sustained period such a system is not likely to succeed as a purely voluntary system, and the American Bar Association's Special Committee on Availability of Legal Services recently recommended procedures to strengthen that method, including adequate compensation of assigned counsel and appointment of counsel as soon as possible after arrest and always before preliminary hearing. In the federal courts, an important advance was made by the Criminal Justice Act of 1964, which established modest compensation to lawyers assigned to defend criminal cases in the federal courts. Further amendment is needed to provide, among other things, for bringing all services of counsel within the Act, beginning from the time of the arrest.

For defender services to be effective, states will have to contribute substantially to the funding of programs, and a few states have begun to move in this direction. Perhaps the largest remaining gap lies in the lack of adequate representation for juveniles. In most jurisdictions, such representation is still minimal or nonexistent, although some three years have passed since the Supreme Court first held that juveniles in delinquency proceedings are constitutionally entitled to be represented by counsel.[4]

Inevitably, the quality and quantity of legal services available to the indigent accused of crime will depend on whether the community is willing to provide adequate funds and facilities for that purpose. The prognosis is far from encouraging. The will to provide legal and supporting services to adults or juveniles accused of crime is simply not there. A sensitive observer has pointed out that one of the principal resistances to implementation of the *Gideon* principle is the powerful and largely unconscious dedication which all of us have to the idea of retribution.[5] Regrettably, high officials in our federal and local governments have too often found political advantage in nourishing such attitudes. A mood seems to have been created in the country in which protecting constitutional rights is equated with thwarting law enforcement. Critics of *Escobedo* and *Miranda* proclaim with increasing shrillness that bringing lawyers into criminal proceedings at the start discourages confessions and makes conviction more difficult. Undoubtedly, that is so. One is reminded of Sir James F. Steven's observation that it is easier to sit in the shade and rub red pepper into a poor devil's eyes than to go about in the sun hunting up evidence. But, as Mr. Justice Goldberg pointed out, if a system of criminal justice can work only at the expense of basic individual rights, there is something wrong with that system. It has been said that the quality of a nation's civilization depends on the way it enforces its criminal laws. And there can be no civilized enforcement of criminal law without full legal assistance to the accused.

LEGAL SERVICES FOR CIVIL CASES

There is no specific constitutional provision providing a right to legal services for civil cases, as there is for criminal cases. Yet there is a sound conceptual basis for according a constitutional dimension to such services, at least for civil defendants. A defendant in a civil legal action may lose money or goods, be evicted, lose custody of children, or suffer other disabilities. Such loss may not be ordered by a court without due process of law, and at this stage of constitutional sophistication it seems quite proper to hold that the fundamental fairness embodied in the due process concept is lacking where a defendant cannot afford representation.

The equal protection clause of the Constitution also seems relevant: in *Shelley v. Kraemer*[6] the Supreme Court held that enforcement by a court of *private* racially discriminatory agreements would violate the constitutional requirement of equal protection of the law. From this, it is only a short logical progression to hold that a court order against one who is unrepresented is court enforcement based on distinctions of wealth and similarly runs afoul of the equal protection clause. In *Williams v. Shaffer*,[7] Justice Douglas, dissenting from a denial of certiorari in a case regarding rights of a poor tenant in an eviction proceeding, said:

> We have recognized that the promise of equal justice for all would be an empty phrase for the poor, if the ability to obtain judicial relief were made to turn on the length of a person's purse. It is true that these cases have dealt with criminal proceedings. But the Equal Protection Clause of the Fourteenth Amendment is not limited to criminal prosecutions. Its protections extend as well to civil matters.

Finding a constitutional basis for providing civil legal services for the indigent *plaintiff* is perhaps more difficult unless we are prepared to say that lack of procedural access to the system of justice is per se a denial of equal protection of the law—a proposition for which considerable historical support can be derived[8] and which, in any event, makes a good deal of sense in an adversary system of justice. At the least, the equal protection clause should suffice to dispense with various litigation costs that prove an obstacle to justice for the poor, such as fees for filing, process-serving, witnesses, masters in divorce cases, publication, and transcripts. Recently some courts, particularly in domestic relations matters, have held that

various court costs may not be imposed against the poor, and this
trend will probably grow. While these cases have generally based
their holdings on construction of statutes dealing with court costs,
they have shown an awareness of the constitutional issue. Thus, the
glimmerings of a new constitutional doctrine are there. Underscor-
ing the doctrine is the simple proposition that vindicating legal
rights is so fundamental to our system of democracy that the state
cannot close the system to any person because of poverty. It is hoped
that the next few years will see the maturing of the concept of legal
services as a full-blown right.

Whether or not civil legal services are accorded constitutional
dimension, proper functioning of our system of civil justice requires
that such services be made available to those who cannot afford
them. An adversary system such as ours presupposes that both parties
have like opportunity to present the facts and contentions upon
which the adjudicator passes. Where a party cannot effectively avail
himself of this opportunity, and therefore suffers the consequences
of his failure, the result, as Professor Geoffrey Hazard has pointed
out, is a conflict between the system's pretension and its fulfillment.
Stated another way, lack of legal representation is incompatible with
the ideal of a rule of law which assumes procedural fairness for all
involved in the legal process.

Despite these considerations, the organized bar cannot take
credit for initiating a broad legal services program for the poor. The
impetus came, rather, from the Economic Opportunity Act of 1964,
which created the Office of Economic Opportunity. While the Act
did not initially authorize a program of legal services, in 1964 Sar-
gent Shriver, the Director of OEO, and his advisers approached
American Bar Association officials to sound them out regarding
their support of an OEO-funded legal services program. It would
not have been surprising if the ABA—traditionally dominated by
conservative lawyers—had refused to support the program. Only the
previous year, the ABA had joined with forty-eight state and local
bar associations in opposing the decision in *Brotherhood of Railroad Trainmen v. Virginia,*[9] which upheld the Brotherhood's national program for providing legal services to its members.

To the credit of the ABA, it determined that the program should
be supported and encouraged. Lewis Powell, conservative, Southern, well liked, was then President of the ABA; his advocacy of the
program was undoubtedly a major factor in persuading the House
of Delegates. Vital support also came from Edward Kuhn, then

President-Elect of the ABA, and John Cumiskey and William Mc-
Alpin, chairmen of the principal ABA committees in this field. In
February 1965, the House of Delegates of the ABA adopted a historic resolution directing its officers and committees to cooperate
with OEO in the development of legal services programs for the
poor. The initial successful launching of the program was thereby
assured. Since then, the ABA has worked closely with the OEO
program, vigorously promoting it, defending it, as has often been
necessary, and sharing in the program's policy determinations.

Not all lawyers have been enthusiastic; some bar associations,
particularly in the South, have been hostile; and individual lawyers,
fearful of inroads upon their practice, have even brought lawsuits
charging local programs with unethical solicitation, undue federal
control, and interference with client relationships. The courts have
uniformly rejected such charges and by the end of 1966, the legal
services program was well launched and on solid legal footing.[10]

The OEO-funded legal services program has grown apace and is
now the principal means by which the poor of our nation are provided with legal assistance. By the beginning of 1970, such programs
had been established in forty-nine states and in more than fifty of
the largest cities. There are now some 260 ongoing programs serving
approximately 800 neighborhood law offices and staffed by almost
2,000 lawyers. Almost $47 million was spent on the program in 1969,
and the 1970 budget will be over $50 million.

While there has been a good deal of diversity in the form of the
program, generally a local community-action agency contracts for
conduct of the legal services program with a local legal aid society or
a bar association, or as is most often the case, with a nonprofit corporation organized by the bar association. The board of directors of
the governing association typically draws about one-third of its
members from the poor or representatives of the poor, and the balance from the bar and civic and governmental organizations. Most
of the large urban programs have a central office and a number of
neighborhood offices located in the poverty areas. The programs
utilize full-time staff lawyers but also depend substantially on volunteer lawyers to supplement the staff, and the time of these volunteers
is credited toward the local obligation to provide a percentage of
matching funds. Different means are utilized to reach the rural poor.
In some rural communities, a program providing "circuit-riding"
lawyers has been worked out. Another innovation is the mobile law
office which makes scheduled visits to the small rural areas in the

county. OEO provides broad guidelines, but each program has a considerable amount of leeway in developing its own emphasis.

What have been the objectives of the legal services program and how well have they been carried out? The question has been much argued. Some conceive the legal services program as a federally funded extension of traditional legal aid concerned chiefly with the problems of the individual client. Some see it as giving teeth to that phase of the war against poverty which seeks to give the poor a voice and to stimulate self-help community action. And some see the program principally as a means of bringing about law reform and advancing needed social justice. In fact, the program has partially achieved all three objectives, and the argument might be academic except for its relevance to the future of the program.

In terms of providing legal assistance to individual poor persons, the impact of the program has been substantial. In the fiscal year ending June 30, 1969, some 610,000 clients had been served by the existing programs. The bulk of the problems seem to fall in the family area, followed by housing, consumer, and employment problems. Most of the matters were settled by advice or negotiation, but over 150,000 required court action. The courtroom record of legal services lawyers has been superb. They prevailed on behalf of their clients in 75 to 80 percent of the trials and compiled an even better record on appeals.

Despite these accomplishments, it is obvious that the present program cannot meet the individual needs of the poor. There are about 300,000 lawyers in the United States, or approximately one for every 650 persons. Yet of this number, probably not more than 5,000 lawyers are available to serve the 35 million who fall into the poverty classification—a deplorable ratio of one to every 7,000 persons. This is far below the need. In sixteen California rural communities, for example, it has been estimated that some 850 lawyers are needed to serve the poor, and only about 75 are available. Still, the poor have received more legal services than ever before, and in most major cities a poor person with a really pressing legal problem now has somewhere to go to seek assistance.

The role of legal services lawyers in the community action programs of OEO has been less spectacular. As the war against poverty evolved, one of its strategies included community action programs which were to mobilize the poor themselves in creating new institutions and in making present institutions responsive to the demands of the poor. How this strategy was to be implemented was never made entirely clear. To some, it meant utilizing the poor in assisting the power structure; to others, organizing the power structure; to still others, confronting the power structure. The community action program became embroiled sometimes in city hall politics, sometimes in the disruptions that swept society during the late sixties, and sometimes in the backlash which came in the aftermath of the disruptions. Any program which involves politicizing the poor—for that was certainly one of the potentials of the community action program—risks becoming an object of hostility. In retrospect, many of the lawyers who became involved in community action endeavors were too unaware of the social science implications to give appropriate direction. In any event, the likelihood is that the community action aspects of the OEO program will regrettably phase out under a "benign" if not a more virile form of neglect from Washington.

Nonetheless, in the private sector there have been a variety of community actions in which lawyers have provided assistance, such as in forming self-help groups for cooperative purchasing, merchandising ventures, tenant organizations, and consumer councils. This is an area in which lawyers in private law firms, public interest law firms, and young black lawyers have displayed an interest. For example, the Lawyers' Committee for Civil Rights has formed local committees in some fourteen cities, consisting largely of lawyers from prominent law firms who recognize the obligation of the legal profession to help with urban problems. These committees have played a valuable role in helping organize such community groups. Ultimately, these groups help create the power base the poor need to bring about meaningful change.

It is in the third area, that of law reform, that the legal services program has had its most striking successes and, as a result, faces its greatest dangers. Lawyers have been committed to the philosophy that the American legal system is capable of response to societal needs, and legal services lawyers have tested that hypothesis in the courts by seeking to reform the statutory and regulatory base of the existing order which discriminates against the poor and creates conditions of social injustice.[11] The law reform efforts of the legal services program have generally been made through test cases or class actions, that is, cases which have an impact on large numbers of poor who are not involved in the actual litigation but who would benefit from its outcome.

There are numerous examples of such law reform activities.

Legal services lawyers have brought successful cases to prevent California from reducing medical aid to the indigent, to prohibit landlords from engaging in retaliatory evictions in the District of Columbia, to secure major revisions favorable to tenants in state housing laws in Michigan, and to prevent mistreatment of Mexican farm laborers.

There is no doubt that the welfare law of the United States has changed substantially as a result of the efforts of legal services lawyers. Through a series of successful challenges to the constitutionality of state residency requirements for welfare recipients, the income of the poverty population has been increased by hundreds of millions of dollars. The Supreme Court of the United States also upheld legal services lawyers in striking down the "man-in-the-house" rule which had discouraged new marriages by depriving welfare recipients of payments if an unrelated man resided in the beneficiary's house. Most recently, the Court held that welfare benefits could not be reduced without complying with elements of due process.

So, too, the highly inequitable landlord-and-tenant laws which allow landlords to evict tenants without notice, without reasons, and often in retaliation for invoking municipal codes, have been materially changed in many parts of the country through the work of legal services lawyers.

In the consumer field, law reform has been directed at usury, unfair use of garnishment, unconscionable contracts which deny consumer defenses, and other unfair practices.

The California Rural Legal Assistance program (CRLA), one of the outstanding legal services programs in the nation, has pioneered in such law reform endeavors with dramatic results.[11] In *Ybarra v. Fielder,* the State Director of Agriculture was required to make available to farm workers information regarding the use of injurious pesticides. In *Rivera v. Division of Industrial Welfare,* an order was upheld increasing the minimum wage for 50,000 workers, resulting in benefits of from $15 to $20 million. In *Hernandez v. Hardin,* the United States Department of Agriculture was ordered to institute food programs in nineteen California counties which had refused to sponsor them, for a benefit of approximately $20 million to some 85,000 people. And through a series of class actions against agricultural employers, the toilet and hand-washing facilities made available to California farm workers in 1969 were doubled.

CRLA reports that from July 1, 1968, to June 30, 1969, it represented more than 400,000 different people on more than one occasion in class-type actions for an average of 11,333 persons per salaried attorney, and represented 2,433,000 persons on at least one occasion. A total of $48 million was obtained through these actions, as well as various nonmonetary benefits and protections. The CRLA experience is atypical; it is one of the best of the current programs. But its example is increasingly being emulated.

Not surprisingly, legal services lawyers engaged in law reform activities have stepped on some powerful toes, from grape growers to governors. Legal services programs often challenge sacred cows. Public officials do not like to have to defend their actions; entrenched forces resent having their fairness challenged. Giving the poor rights can be unpopular or made to look unpopular. Spurred by Governor Reagan of California, Senator George Murphy has twice introduced legislation designed to cripple the reform endeavors of legal services lawyers. The second time, in late 1969, in a lax moment in the Senate, the Murphy Amendment slipped through, and its equally pernicious counterpart, introduced in the House by Representatives Albert Quie and Edith Green, might well have passed had it not been for intensive lobbying against the legislation by the Director of OEO and by elements of the organized bar led by Bernard G. Segal, President of the American Bar Association.

Opponents of the law reform activities of the program have argued that legal services lawyers should be limited to the representation of individual clients and should not engage in class-type actions designed to effect reforms in society of which a majority may disapprove. This argument misconceives the lawyer's function. Vigorous, innovative, and independent action on behalf of clients is the lawyer's function in classic terms. Lawyers have always given their clients this kind of representation, challenging statutes, instituting class actions for shareholders, bringing test cases, and otherwise seeking to change existing legal patterns on their clients' behalf. Surely, the poor are entitled to no less.

Moreover, it is unrealistic to limit poverty lawyers to individual representation when the lawyers serving the poor are so few and the poor so many. Given the money, manpower, and time available, and facing the tremendous needs of the poor, the better legal services programs must invariably rely on law reform, class actions, and test cases as a means of maximizing their resources and benefitting large numbers of the poor at the same time.

Beyond even these considerations, those who seek to curb the law reform activities of legal services lawyers seem to me to reveal a startling insensitivity to democratic process. How does one seek redress for institutional grievances? Use of the election machinery is slow and frequently unproductive. The courts, however, often offer an effective forum (and in the case of injunctive relief, a particularly speedy one) in which to seek relief in a manner consistent with our traditions. But if legal access to the courts is to be denied, what alternative remains but the streets? Earl Johnson, a former Director of the OEO Legal Services Program, summed it up simply: "We cannot slam the door of the courthouses in the faces of the poor in fear they may win a lawsuit and then cry out in indignation when they riot over the same grievances."

Law reform thus is not radical or revolutionary; it follows an impeccably conservative legal tradition and one certainly preferable to the alternatives. That these test cases have sometimes brought about dramatic change is not indicative of any unusual or atypical legal process but only of the great defects in our administration of justice which call out for repair.

Recently, sniping against the legal services program has intensified on the local scene, particularly from police chiefs who have resented class suits charging their men with brutality or discrimination. Some police chiefs have threatened to cut off police contributions to United Fund agencies which contribute to legal assistance programs. In Los Angeles, for example, the police department brought severe pressure against the University of Southern California because lawyers associated with its Western Center on Law and Poverty represented plaintiffs in a class action attacking alleged discriminatory and brutal practices by Los Angeles policemen. Such police tactics are alarming as well as shortsighted. Police chiefs should welcome the courts as the forum to resolve charges against police officers who allegedly abuse their authority. Antagonism to the very concept of trying these issues in the courts only arouses community hostility among segments of the population whose cooperation and good will the police need and should have, and gives the impression that the police are above the processes of the law.

Within the past year, attacks on legal services lawyers have increased at such an alarming pace that program lawyers have felt it necessary to form an organization, PLEA (Poverty Lawyers for Effective Advocacy), to protect them from unwarranted attacks. That such an organization should be needed points to a failure on the part of both the federal authorities and the local bar associations to provide sufficient support for the program. Most recently, the National Legal Aid and Defender Association, which has pioneered many of the concepts now accepted in the field, saw fit to establish a special committee to investigate and deal with charges made against legal services agencies.

The attempts to undercut the legal services program will certainly be repeated. As test cases and class actions continue to rock the Establishment boat, the Reagans, the Murphys, the Quies, and others with like philosophies will seize upon such cases as an excuse for shackling the program. The program desperately needs support from the highest levels of government—support that is not now forthcoming. The influential Attorney General of the United States, for example, has displayed no evidence that the legal services program is high on his list of priorities. A desultory administration attitude encourages congressional attack and sustains local sniping.

The battle to preserve the vital law reform and law improvement activities of legal services programs will undoubtedly continue to rage during the next few years. Given the weakness of current political leadership in this area, the key to victory lies in a massive educational effort by the organized bar and the poor themselves concerning the value of such activities. By improving the law, by challenging unjust practices through the courts, by giving the poor a stake in the working of our institutional processes, the legal services program advances the democratic process and reduces the alienation and helplessness that turn people into the streets. It will be tragic if this message is not understood by the American people.

OEO-funded programs have been the heart of the nation's legal services endeavor but not its entirety. The Department of Health, Education, and Welfare now has statutory authority to reimburse state and local public welfare agencies for 75 percent of expenditures to provide legal service to public assistance recipients. The potential of this program is huge. The Department of Housing and Urban Development has also entered this field.

Although these programs have a significant potential, there is little reason to believe that they will receive sustained backing from the top levels of the federal government. OEO itself seems destined for gradual liquidation and absorption into other departments. No one can foretell what that will mean for the legal services program, but the prognosis is not cheerful.

These developments have led some observers to suggest that a new approach to legal services is required. One such suggestion, in which the writer has participated, is to establish a National Justice Foundation, which would be an independent, quasi-public agency modeled after the National Science Foundation or the Communications Satellite Corporation, with public and private representation on its board to consolidate and administer all federally funded legal services programs. An agency that could enjoy a large measure of independence from the congressional, executive, and local harassment which continues to mount seems most appealing, albeit difficult to achieve. Such concepts deserve and undoubtedly will receive increasing attention.

In the private sector, traditional locally funded legal aid associations continue to be significant. Many localities which have been hostile to federally funded programs have at least begun to recognize the obligation to initiate privately funded programs. The National Legal Aid and Defender Association has been particularly helpful in encouraging such new associations.

One of the most encouraging developments of the past three or four years has been the increasing desire of young lawyers to become involved in the problems of the poor. More and more, today's graduates recognize an obligation to become involved in the problems of overriding concern to society—problems of hunger, poverty, overpopulation, housing, education, equal employment. Many have demanded from their law firms the opportunity to devote a portion of their practice to these problems, and leading law firms across the nation have established procedures to permit their young associates and partners to do so. These law firms have realized that if they want to attract and hold the brightest lawyers, they must provide means to permit their young associates and partners to engage in public service activities. In my own law firm, we have long pioneered in this area, giving our associates and partners full credit for such public service to the poor to the same degree as services for paying clients. Some law firms have established ghetto offices to serve the poor; others have established public service divisions to handle *pro bono publico* cases. Whether it has developed out of self-interest or in response to the higher calling of the law, or both, this trend among law firms is a healthy one, fulfilling the higher traditions of the bar and boding well for further development of legal assistance to the poor.

One of the most fruitful of these volunteer programs is that provided by the Lawyers' Committee for Civil Rights Under Law. With the help of Ford Foundation funding, the national Lawyers' Committee has established local counterparts in fourteen cities. These committees enlist the aid of lawyers from major law firms in handling actions designed to bring about institutional reforms to help the poor. Drawing upon the ablest legal talent in their areas and with the backing of prestigious establishment lawyers, the Lawyers' Committee can sometimes effect reforms that elude the government-funded programs.

A recent development of promise is the establishment of public interest law firms to handle law reform and law improvement cases, much in the mode of Ralph Nader's endeavors. There are many young lawyers anxious to join such law firms, but this development has been handicapped by lack of funds. This area certainly would appear to be a productive one for public-minded foundation financing.

The considerable progress of the past decade should not obscure the numerous problems which must be overcome before we can fulfill our obligations to provide legal services to those who cannot afford them. There are too many areas without effective legal services programs, particularly in the South and in rural areas. The case load for lawyers in existing programs is far too heavy, inevitably affecting the quality of the representation. Black lawyers have not yet been sufficiently brought into the programs. Local boards are not as independent of pressure as they should be. There are still too many legal services lawyers who engage in their duties without enthusiasm, idealism, or ability. Much needs to be done to improve legal education in poverty law, especially in its clinical aspects. The concept of group legal services for low- and middle-income groups has still to be developed and to win the approval of the organized bar. The benefits of interdisciplinary efforts with professionals in social services, psychiatry, marriage, and school counseling are still largely unexplored. The possibility of a national legal assistance program akin to the Medicare program needs serious study and development. Too little account has been taken of those who are above the poverty level but whose income is still too low to afford needed legal services. These are only some of the problems.

Formidable as such problems are, they are ones that could be solved if there was a national commitment to do so. Unfortunately, there is not yet such a commitment. What is needed perhaps most of all is an enlightened political leadership which approaches the problem of legal services to the poor, not on the basis of whether it is popular, but on the basis that it is just. In a democracy, equal justice must be considered an absolute and not be subject to the vagaries of pollster statistics. Today, such enlightened leadership is too little in evidence on national, state, or local levels. In its absence, reliance must largely be placed upon the lawyers of this nation to win the support needed for an effective legal services program. The organized bar has not always lived up to its traditions or its obligations. Let us hope that from now on it will begin to do so. I like to think that it *will* do so, and that the legal profession will merit the favorable verdict of history.

History tells us that a nation's progress to social justice is often painful; it is painful today. Part of our progress must be the realization that access to legal services must be more than an expectation; it must be a right. Learned Hand once observed that if democracy is to survive, it must observe one principal commandment: Thou Shalt Not Ration Justice. That commandment is what the right to legal services is all about.

NOTES

1. 372 U.S. 335 (1963).

2. *Id.* at 344.

3. Escobedo v. Illinois, 378 U.S. 478 (1964); Miranda v. Arizona, 384 U.S. 436 (1966); *see also* United States v. Wade, 388 U.S. 218 (1967).

4. *In re* Gault, 387 U.S. 1 (1967).

5. Watson, "On the Low Status of the Criminal Bar: Psychological Contributions of the Law School," 43 *Texas Law Review* 289, 310 (1965).

6. 334 U.S. 1 (1948).

7. 385 U.S. 1037, 1039 (1967).

8. *See, e.g.,* Truax v. Corrigan, 257 U.S. 312, 334 (1921), to the effect that equal access to the civil courts was among the objectives of the Fourteenth Amendment. Section 1 of the Civil Rights Act of 1866, now 42 U.S.C. §1981, specifically provides for equal access to the civil courts. The principal statement made in Congress when the Fourteenth Amendment was introduced was that it was to put the Civil Rights Act beyond the reach of repeal. In addition to the due process and equal protection clauses, the First Amendment right to petition for grievances may also be relevant in developing the constitutional grounding for the right to legal services.

9. 377 U.S. 1 (1964); *see also* United Mine Workers v. Illinois State Bar Ass'n, 389 U.S. 217 (1967).

10. The leading case disposing of such charges arose in a challenge to the Philadelphia legal services program. Judge Raymond Pace Alexander of the

Philadelphia Court of Common Pleas rejected the challenge in a 70-page opinion which has become the landmark decision on this subject. *In re* Community Legal Services, No. 4968, (C.P. Philadelphia Co., Pa., March 1966).

11. In a sense, every lawyer who develops a novel point, creates a precedent, improves on existing procedure, establishes a new practice, or wins an unusual case is engaged in law reform. Perhaps, then, there is no need for this appellation. Yet "law reform" does serve as a handy slogan to remind us that the field of poverty law is new, the inequities in the treatment of the poor many, and the need to establish new doctrines pressing. For a recent excellent analysis of law reform activities, see Robb, "Controversial Cases and the Legal Services Program," 56 *American Bar Association Journal* 329 (1970).

12. The cases in the text that follows are discussed in California Rural Legal Assistance Program, Annual Report (Sept. 1969).

THE RIGHTS OF CONSUMERS

PHILIP G. SCHRAG

"MOM, THERE'S A MAN AT THE DOOR!"

It was a rainy Tuesday in September 1965. Theresa Williams, black, separated from her husband, earning $2,300 a year as a counter waitress, walked across her small apartment in a Bronx housing project. "What do you want?"

"I have a free gift for you," said a male voice.

"I don't want any salesman," she called through the door.

"You don't have to buy anything," he said. "If you just let me show you a sample of carpeting, I have a bottle of perfume for you."

She hesitated for a moment, then opened the door. "I don't have much time," she said.

The salesman explained his "deal": he had high quality wall-to-wall carpeting for sale for only two dollars a square yard. Mrs. Williams' floors were bare, and most of her neighbors' floors were carpeted. She wanted carpeting, but had never been able to afford it. But when the salesman showed her the sample, her hopes sank. It was thin and raggedy; clearly it would wear through in a month or two. She pointed this out.

The salesman reached into his sample case and pulled out a patch of rich, thick material. "Now this is our deluxe carpeting," he said. "It is made of high-quality wool. It costs more, but it will last a lifetime. In fact, we guarantee it for twenty-five years—if it

Philip G. Schrag, formerly Assistant Counsel for the NAACP Legal Defense and Educational Fund in charge of consumer protection litigation, is the Consumer Advocate of the City of New York, and Lecturer in Law at Columbia Law School.

ever wears through or comes up from the floor, my store, the
Quality-Plus Carpet Company, will repair it for free. If you ever
move, we will reinstall it for you. And the best part is this: you
can make the same low weekly payments for this high-grade carpeting that you would for the standard grade." He looked around
Mrs. Williams' living room. "Can you afford eight dollars a week?"
he asked.

"Of course I can afford eight dollars a week," she replied.

The salesman handed her a small bottle of perfume, and began
filling out a contract form. "Just tell me where you work and sign
here," he explained. "We'll put this carpeting down on all your
floors, everything, with free installation, for just eight dollars a
week."

It didn't sound like much. Mrs. Williams signed.

Within a week, the carpeting arrived and was nailed down. It
wasn't the color of the sample, which Mrs. Williams had expected
it to be. In fact, each room was a different color, which surprised
her, but after all, she realized, she hadn't asked him about that. On
close inspection, it didn't seem to be as thick and full as the sample,
but since he'd taken the sample with him, she could not make a
comparison.

Another week passed, and Mrs. Williams received a book of
coupons in the mail from the Liberty Finance Company, in upstate
New York. "Make your payments to us," it instructed. "We bought
your carpet contract from Quality-Plus. Just mail a check or money
order for $32 to us every month, with one of the attached coupons.
Don't be late, because you will have to pay penalty charges, and we
have our ways of collecting." The envelope from Liberty also contained a copy of her contract and several other legal-looking documents, which she threw into a drawer.

The figure of $32 a month startled Mrs. Williams. She rarely
had $32 to spend at one time. The salesman had only said $8 a week.
She looked again at the contract, and for the first time saw the total
price—$1,200. This worried her, and she thought of canceling the
sale, but she knew that with the carpeting already down, the store
would never agree to that.

For a year, she made her payments. Often she was on time;
when she was late, she conscientiously caught up. But the carpeting
began to wear thin, and twice it came up from under the moldings.
Each time, she called Quality-Plus, which promptly sent a man to
repair it without charge.

About fifteen months after the sale, the carpeting began to tear, and Mrs. Williams again called the store. This time, a recording informed her that the number had been disconnected.

Alarmed, she telephoned Liberty Finance. "Oh, yes," said the man at Liberty. "The owner retired and moved to Florida. They've gone out of business."

"But my rug needs repairing. Who will repair it?"

"We suggest you consult the Yellow Pages."

"But who will pay for it?"

"I'm afraid you will," said the man at Liberty. "We're a finance company, not a rug repair shop."

"But they guaranteed it for twenty-five years! I'll just deduct the repair costs from what I owe you."

"I'm afraid that won't do, Mrs. Williams," said the man. "The law obligates you to pay us in full no matter what those salesmen say to you. I'm sorry, because those salesmen will tell a person anything. But it has nothing to do with us. We didn't even know you bought your rug from a door-to-door salesman. You'll just have to keep paying, and if you don't, we know where you work and we can take it out of your wages by garnishment."

Mrs. Williams was angry, and went to a legal aid lawyer. The lawyer's investigation showed that the carpeting was made of nylon, not wool, that it was worth only about $350 and that Liberty's analysis of the law was essentially correct.

"Consumer protection" has recently become a fashionable term, and its meaning has broadened with its popularity. Many of the topics in this book can be dealt with—and have been—under the heading "consumer protection," since it is true that we are all consumers of clean air and water, of municipal services, of education, of civil liberties, and of many other intangibles. Sometimes, we do not pay for these products or services directly; we pay for them through taxes, or by submitting to jury duty, or in other ways. Our rights as consumers of these intangibles are often abridged, and such abridgments are treated in the other chapters of this volume. This chapter is therefore devoted to the more traditional question of the relationship between purchasers of ordinary goods and services, and the producers and distributors of these commodities.

The consumer's central civil right is the right to get his money's worth. In theory, the competitive market system and the law of contracts are designed to ensure that the consumer may have a chance to choose from a variety of offered products, and that once he has chosen, his expectations will be fulfilled. But there are few if any Americans who have never been "taken" by a magazine salesman, a television or automobile repairman, or simply a store clerk who misstated the qualities of his wares. Sometimes, the consumer's expectations are defeated for reasons having nothing to do with a retailer. For example, American manufacturers are now finding the cost of expert supervision over quality control to be so great that they are frequently willing to accept a high rate of defective products; it is cheaper to replace merchandise for those consumers who complain than to ensure that few defective products are distributed. This is true even where the defects pose a hazard to human safety; in 1969, 10 percent of automobile parts tested by the National Safety Bureau failed to comply with federal safety standards. In addition, the high cost of distribution, including promotional advertising, as compared with the cost of materials and manufacture, often makes consumers wonder what their money has gone for. (It is likely, for example, that the door-to-door salesman received at least $200 for selling Mrs. Williams her carpet; this helped inflate the price to $1,200 because it is hard work persuading people to buy things they did not realize they wanted. But if those who buy don't bear the expense of this effort, who will?) Price-fixing conspiracies may also deny buyers their money's worth, but more often limited competition, particularly in low-income areas, produces the same effect though no one is at "fault."

These deficiencies in production and marketing are extremely difficult (if not impossible) to redress by changing the legal rules, in the absence of major reorganization of the economy. But consumers' expectations are also frequently defeated (as were Mrs. Williams') by retailers who lead them to expect far too much, and by rules of law no longer appropriate to the governance of a mass consumer economy, particularly one in which credit plays so large a role.[1]

The frequency with which we are treated to exaggerated or otherwise incorrect statements about products offered us can only be appreciated, I think, by carrying around a pad of paper for a day and noting every instance—in storefront advertising, in newspapers, on television, in conversations with merchants, on coffee shop menus—in which the offerer is not quite telling the truth. We have become so used to exaggerations and half-truths that we are insensitive to them, at least on a conscious level. The absurd statements (for example, that Ajax is "stronger than dirt") and pictorial exaggerations (such as the loading of marbles into a bowl of Campbell's soup to make the vegetables rise to the surface and appear dense) employed on television by major producers are particularly numbing; I think they have played a large role in making us think, in sober moments, that we have no right to expect accuracy from sellers, and to have less than total sympathy for those such as Mrs. Williams who still accept salesmen at their word.[2]

Whether they buy a $1,200 carpet or a can of soup, consumers who make purchases in reliance upon erroneous or exaggerated claims are not without rights. Indeed, the law has worked out quite a sensible set of rules defining precisely the relief to which such buyers are entitled. These rules constitute the law of misrepresentation and the law of warranties. It may seem startling to the millions of housewives who have argued for hours with merchants who refused to take back unacceptable products, but the basic rule is this: whenever a salesman makes a mistake (unless it is plainly a trivial one) in describing merchandise, the customer is entitled to his money back, even if the salesman's error was unintentional.[3] A doctrine known as "puffing" holds that some false statements are so obviously the opinion of the seller that the buyer cannot rely on them as fact. But there are not many recent cases on "puffing," and it can be presumed that when dealing with a commercial seller, an individual buyer these days is entitled to believe the concrete statements made to induce him to buy.

Virtually any such misrepresentation entitles the consumer to a refund, and many different types of falsity are common. For example, sellers may incorrectly describe the qualities of the goods (as when the salesman told Mrs. Williams that the carpeting was wool), or the quantity. They may misrepresent the average lifetime, the uses to which the product can be put, or the identity, location, or qualifications of the manufacturer. Salesmen, particularly those who go door-to-door, have also been known to misrepresent their own authority, connections, or qualifications.

Frequently, false statements are made concerning the existence of bargains or discounts (for example, the perpetual "going out of business" sales), or the reasons for such discounts, or their amounts. The "bait and switch" is a very common technique. The store advertises a bargain, such as $14 sewing machines. The machine is shown to the customer, but the salesman describes only its inadequacies, or it breaks down during the demonstration. Then the customer, having been lured into the store, is shown the much superior, more expensive model.

It makes no difference whether the falsity originated with the seller or was simply passed on by him from the manufacturer to the consumer. Nor does it matter that the buyer could easily have investigated and learned the truth.[4] In any event, the buyer gets his refund. Of course, he must be prepared to return the merchandise, unless it has been destroyed as a result of the seller's fault.[5]

A refund places the buyer in the position he was in before the sale. But if the seller has breached what the Uniform Commercial Code calls a "warranty," the buyer is entitled to even better treatment: he is entitled to damages which will put him in the more desirable position he thought he was in when he had made the sale; that is, he may keep the merchandise and obtain from the merchant an amount of money representing the difference in value between what he got and what he was promised.

"Warranties" in this connection mean far more than the pieces of cardboard with scalloped borders that are often found packaged with new appliances. They include any promises made by the seller. For example, Mrs. Williams received no written statements purporting to be "warranties." But the salesman's statement that the carpeting was made of wool was a warranty that this was true, and his statement that his company would repair the carpet for twenty-five years was a warranty that this was so. Any statement of fact or promise about the goods is a warranty, as is any description of the goods. In fact, if the salesman says nothing but merely shows the consumer a floor sample, he warrants that what the consumer buys will be just like the sample.

The consumer's protection under warranty law goes even further. The law implies that in any sale of goods by a merchant, he warrants that they are "merchantable," which means, essentially, that they work. In other words, a salesman who palms off on a customer a stereo set which does not function or a chest of drawers which falls apart within a week has breached his warranties, even if he never said that it would work or would last a week. Merchandise must be fit for the ordinary purposes for which it is used, and it must also live up to any statements made on the label or container.

Notwithstanding all these rights, consumers are in terrible trouble. The structure of rights, so elegant on paper, is more theoretical than real. The middle-class buyer of a nonfunctioning stereo may be lucky and get a refund; if so, it is probably because the store to which he went wanted his continued business. He would feel sheepish, however, demanding a refund from his grocer because a package of frozen food pictured more quantity and better quality than was actually inside. The low-income consumer is in much greater trouble, because retailers in his neighborhood are much less likely to be interested in good will, so that he will have difficulty obtaining redress in a friendly way when he has been gypped even on a large purchase.

If friendly settlement is impossible (and the 42,000 complaints annually to the New York City Department of Consumer Affairs alone suggest that this is often the case), consumers must look to the courts. This is where the system of consumers' rights breaks down, for despite all their rights to fair dealing, consumers lack the oldest and most fundamental civil liberty: the right to a day in court. The barriers which the legal system has erected to consumer litigation go a long way toward explaining the relative unconcern of merchants and manufacturers with truthful selling and quality merchandise.

The prime barrier is the cost of litigation. The cost of an individual lawsuit is enormous, whatever the suit involves. Experienced lawyers charge from $40 to $100 an hour. Assuming that it takes two hours to interview a client, an hour to write a complaint, two hours to research the law, and two hours to try the case, the simplest litigation would cost each side at least nearly $300 in legal fees alone. But no case is that simple, if it is done well. Each side's lawyer will spend many additional hours tracking down and interviewing friendly witnesses (such as other consumers who bought the same type of merchandise from the same salesman), examining under oath the parties and witnesses on the other side in pretrial discovery proceedings, making and resisting motions for further discovery, and so on. The merchant may try to avoid service of process, or claim that the suit was begun in the wrong court, or engage in any of a thousand dilatory tactics. And of course, when it is all over, he may appeal.[6] On top of legal fees are costs for investigations, expert witnesses (such as a furniture expert to testify that the chest purchased would be expected to fall apart in a week), process servers, court costs, and stenographic services. The result is that litigation over a $50 case may well cost each side more than $1,000. And in the United States, each side pays his own legal fees, regardless of who wins the case.

A "neutral" application of the principle that each side pays its own legal fees would be bad enough. But in most states, consumer contracts may lawfully provide that if the merchant sues the consumer and wins, the consumer pays the merchant's legal fees. Since the merchants' lawyers write the contracts, they do not provide for counsel fees to the prevailing consumer. So in reality, the consumer pays his own lawyer if he wins and both lawyers if he loses.

As Bess Myerson Grant put it in a recent congressional testimony:

> The law of our state and of all states and the nation as well, has often been hypocritical as far as the consumer is concerned. It gives him rights, but then creates economic barriers so high that it is impossible to enforce those rights. It tells him to spend thousands of dollars on a lawsuit to recover hundreds of dollars which he lost in a swindle.

As if this were not enough to keep consumers out of court, the law has special devices for defeating the rights of credit buyers, including most low-income buyers of furniture and appliances. The credit buyer is, after all, in a special position. He has the merchandise at a time when he has delivered only a small part of the price (the down payment) to the merchant. In low-income neighborhoods, it is common that "the payments outlast the goods"; that is, the misrepresentation, or fraud, or breach of warranty may become obvious to the buyer—perhaps because the merchandise disintegrates completely—before the merchant has all his money. The credit purchaser has it in his power, at least temporarily, to effect rough justice. He can throw the costs of misrepresentation upon his creditor by cutting off his payments.

The creditor in such circumstances is armed and dangerous. He may invoke a clause in all his contracts providing that the goods remain his until they are fully paid for, and he may take them back at any time ("repossess them") without first going to court. Creditors will jump-start a partially paid-for car in front of the buyer's house during the night, and drive it off. Repossession of household goods is rarer, since creditors are forbidden to commit breaches of the peace in repossessing, but there have been such cases—the frightened woman, for example, warned not to call her husband at work while a crew disconnected the washing machine in her basement and carried it off on a truck.

Having repossessed the merchandise, the seller may sell it and sue the buyer for the difference between what the buyer owes him and the amount realized by the repossession sale. This will usually be almost as much as the buyer's debt, because repossessed goods do not bring a high price. Of course, the creditor adds to the bill the expenses incurred in the repossession and sale.

Since a given creditor or merchant will have hundreds of collection cases each year, he will benefit from economies of scale not available to consumers. For example, he may be able to hire an attorney on a salary rather than a fee basis. Or he can obtain a "bulk discount" from a collection lawyer. The lawyer, in turn, benefits from the volume in another way. Only a small percentage of consumers who are cheated seek professional help of any sort— 9 percent, according to David Caplovitz' pioneering study, *The Poor Pay More*. Of this number, only a portion see lawyers who try to help them, and of those lawyers, only a small number put up any sort of a fight. The collection lawyer, then, can afford to make some settlement with those few consumers who might make trouble, because he can easily sue the vast majority of consumers without opposition. Ninety-seven percent of the consumers sued in the Civil Court of the City of New York in Manhattan never appear to defend themselves, and therefore lose by default. As a result, their creditor extracts the amount of the judgment from their bank accounts or by garnisheeing their wages.

While these circumstances facilitate use of the courts as a prime means of collecting debts from buyers, other circumstances and legal rules further prevent buyers from having their chance to be heard. Beyond the prohibitive costs of litigation and the doctrine that merchandise may be the seller's until fully paid for are the rules of confession of judgment, wage assignment, and holding in due course. The first of these is fortunately limited to a few states.[7] It permits the buyer to designate the seller's attorney as his lawyer in the event that he stops paying; this lawyer may then appear in court for the buyer and admit that he is withholding his payments for no good reason, so the court will automatically enter a judgment against the buyer. By this device, buyers give up not only their rights to claim such defenses as fraud and breach of warranty, but even the right to notice of a lawsuit against them.

A wage assignment is a document signed by the debtor at the time he obtains credit. It provides that if he stops paying, his creditor may show it to his employer, who is then legally required to pay to the creditor part of the employee's wages every week. If the employee has some reason to stop paying—if, for example, he discovers he has been cheated—the burden is on him to obtain a court order to allow him to tell it to a judge.

A similar device, the prehearing wage garnishment, was held unconstitutional by the Supreme Court in 1969, in a test case brought by the NAACP Legal Defense Fund.[8] The Court held that it deprived wage-earners of their property without prior notice and hearing. By that theory, most creditors' remedies should be unconstitutional, especially wage assignments.

The holder-in-due-course doctrine, used by creditors in forty-five states, is the most widespread and the most surprising of all to consumers, and therefore the most vicious. It has two forms. In one variety, consumers buying on credit sign their names twice, once on a contract and once on a promissory "note." The note contains the phrase "pay to the order of [creditor]," which has no special meaning to consumers but a very special meaning to judges. When sold for cash to a third party, such as a bank or a finance company, the note becomes more unimpeachable than it was in the hands of the store. If the store misrepresented the merchandise, the finance company which paid cash for the note and is suing the buyer for his payments is entitled to say, "That's nothing to us." This hurts the buyer because, for all its difficulties, it is much easier to *defend* a suit by a store on the grounds of misrepresentation or breach of warranty than it is to pay a finance company in full and then spend years trying to sue the store (if it is still in business) in a new litigation. (In addition, a bank or finance company has even more ability to litigate aggressively and efficiently than a store.) Yet that is what is required when the use and resale of a note strips the buyer of his right to defend himself.

Mrs. Williams stumbled over the other version of the doctrine. In some states (even ones which prohibit the use of notes in consumer sales), consumer contracts may contain a clause whereby the buyer agrees to waive, against a finance company or bank buying the contract from the seller, his right to defend himself. In New York, this waiver is effective only if the bank or finance company tells the consumer it has bought his contract, warns him of the waiver, and hears nothing from him for ten days. But the statutorily prescribed warning consists of a single sentence of 125 words:

Notice:
1. If the within statement of your transaction with the seller is not correct in every respect; or

2. if the vehicle or goods described in or in an enclosure with this notice have not been delivered to you by the seller or are not now in your possession; or

3. if the seller has not fully performed all his agreements with you; you must notify the assignee in writing at the address indicated in or in an enclosure with this notice within ten days from the date of the mailing of this notice; otherwise, you will have no right to assert against the assignee any right of action or defense arising out of the sale which you might otherwise have against the seller.

I have never met a consumer who understood and acted upon the warning. Of course, even if Mrs. Williams had understood it, she would not have been able to do anything, since the store did not breach the service warranty until a year after the ten-day warning expired.

Protecting the retail buyer, then, is largely a job of reforming the law of remedies, of improving the consumer's opportunity to confront his abuser. In the 1970's several approaches to this problem will be attempted.

Improving Consumer Representation in Court

Until the late 1960's the lack of contested consumer litigation could be explained in large part by the lack of consumer lawyers. Even consumers who recognized their problems and sought help could not find it. The private bar by and large was not interested or could not afford to get involved, and legal aid societies were over-burdened. The first crack in the system was the emergence of new legal institutions which began to represent consumers; on the front lines, the neighborhood offices of the Office of Economic Opportunity Legal Services Program, staffed by aggressive, issue-oriented beginning lawyers, and for support, institutions such as the National Office for the Rights of the Indigent, the National Consumer Law Center at Boston College, and, until the Nixon Administration's recent decision not to renew its grant, the National Institute for Education in Law and Poverty at Northwestern Law School. Since these offices were not dependent upon fees, they could afford to spend more money, on at least some cases, than the cases involved, and consumer issues began reaching appellate courts. However, it is clear that these offices cannot do the job alone. They do not exist in many areas of the country, particularly in the South. OEO offices in Northern cities are often deluged with housing and welfare litigation, involving more pressing emergencies than consumer disputes. And even where there is an OEO office with adequate resources, such offices may not assist people who do not qualify as "poor"; consumers who earn $4,000 or more a year ($2,500 in some states) still have nowhere to go.

The limitations upon legal services manpower require a mobilization of the private bar to represent the bulk of deceived consumers, but the private bar is unlikely to enter this field unless it is remunerated. The obvious sources of money for the endeavor are the deceiving merchants and manufacturers; if deception is built into the package or advertising, the costs of correcting the deception should fall upon the packager or advertiser. Consumers' attorneys who prevail should be entitled to a counsel fee commensurate with the time they had to spend, and this fee should be included in the court's award. Although the principle of taxing the losing party with counsel fees departs from the usual American rule, there are some precedents for it in the form of statutes (particularly civil rights laws) encouraging litigation in the public interest. Congress extended the principle to consumer protection in the Truth-in-Lending Act, although it remains to be seen whether the courts will award sufficiently high fees to attract the private bar to the cause.

Less Expensive Forums

The overall costs of consumer-dispute resolution might be reduced by removing such disputes from the regular courts and transferring them to other institutions. Small-claims courts were intended to serve this purpose, but many communities have not established them, and in others they have been subverted into collection agencies for creditors.[9] In cities where they work at all, they attempt to enable the consumer to press his claim without a lawyer, informally, without special knowledge of judicial procedure. But the legislators and judges who design these institutions seem unable to imagine a truly informal judicial body; even good small-claims courts tend to impose procedural requirements that boggle the minds of most laymen and are incomprehensible to those of poor education. For example, the would-be small-claims plaintiff in New York must comb city records to determine whether the store that cheated him is Gypsum Furniture or Gypsum Furniture, Inc. An error here could doom his suit.[10] And low-income consumers are as reluctant to go to night court "downtown" as middle-class citizens are to amble through the ghetto after dark. It is to be hoped that truly informal, decentralized "people's courts" will spring up in the next few years.

There has also been some discussion among consumer groups of arbitration as an alternative to litigation. Until arbitration projects are tried and evaluated, it is impossible to know whether this process is really cheaper and more just than litigation; the answer may depend on such details as who performs the arbitration. A serious stumbling block to testing arbitration, however, is distrust of it by consumers and merchants alike; consumers fear that arbitrators will "split the difference" rather than enforce their rights, while merchants are wary that any more accessible institution for conflict resolution will multiply claims made against them. Probably the agreement of merchants in a neighborhood to submit to arbitration will only result from massive pressure on them by local groups.

The Elimination of Short Circuits

It seems likely that confessions of judgment, wage assignments prior to hearing, and the holder-in-due-course doctrine as applied to consumer paper will be abolished by reform legislation or constitutional challenge during the 1970's. All of these devices are methods by which creditors may short-circuit the debtor's constitutional right to notice and adversary hearing before his property is taken from him.[11]

However, it is already plain that elimination of the holder-in-due-course device will lead to a new practice to accomplish the same circumvention of consumers' rights. When they are forbidden to use notes, or to print waiver-of-defenses clauses in their contracts, merchants will refuse to sell on credit, and will insist that consumers borrow money to pay them cash. The salesman will tell Mrs. Williams to go down the street to the small-loan company (or bank, if banks yield to consumer pressure to make loans to low-income borrowers) and obtain a check for $1,200. When the carpeting disintegrates and the store is out of business, the loan company or bank will have an even better claim to be unconcerned than the finance company (which buys the actual contract) does now; all it did was to lend money to the customer—it didn't even ask her what she wanted it for.

Clearly, if abolition of the holder-in-due-course doctrine is to be meaningful, at least some categories of direct-lending institutions will also have to be subjected to whatever claims the consumer may have against the seller of the merchandise which he borrowed money to buy. To start with, banks and loan companies which make loans to more than a fixed small percentage of a merchant's customers might be required to be responsible for the promises the merchant makes.[12]

Class Actions

A promising device to expand the consumer's right to a day in court is the class action, a type of lawsuit in which one consumer sues not only to obtain a small refund for himself but also similar relief for every victim of a merchant's abusive practice. Sometimes the victims are dispersed, and since there is no way of identifying them, class actions are not useful. But on other occasions, where purchases are made on credit or the store keeps delivery receipts, records will be kept of who bought what merchandise at what time, and those injured by abusive practice can be aided if class actions are allowed.

Class actions permit consumers to utilize the same kind of economies of scale that collection attorneys do; they permit a large number of similar transactions to be treated, for the very practical purpose of litigation, as one. A lawyer need be paid only once to try the case, but hundreds or thousands of buyers participate in the judgment. Class actions are also attractive to the private bar, because judges usually allow the prevailing plaintiff's lawyer a generous fee out of the total proceeds, to reward him for helping so many people.

The hitch is that while every state has a law on its books permitting class actions, many states have procedural rules or court decisions which as a practical matter forbid them.[13] Our experience thus far with class actions has not come from consumer cases but rather from antitrust, securities fraud, and civil rights cases; the reason is that these lawsuits are based upon the federal laws or Constitution and are therefore usually initiated in the federal courts, which liberally permit class suits. Misrepresentation and breach of warranty, however, are claims derived from the laws of the states and must therefore be made in the state courts, which treat class suits more suspiciously.

At this writing, the class action is a primary goal of the consumer movement, and the law is in ferment. California and Illinois courts have recently rendered decisions permitting consumers to sue as a class,[41] but the New York Court of Appeals held them to be generally unavailable in that state.[15] Dozens of similar tests have been begun by legal services offices across the country. And half a dozen bills in Congress would permit the federal courts, with their liberal attitude toward the device, to hear consumer disputes where the alleged violation affected interstate commerce. Senator Tydings and Representative Eckhardt have sponsored bills which would permit federal class actions whenever substantial numbers of consumers are victimized by violations of state law.[16]

The Nixon administration opposes these bills, and would permit class actions only after a federal agency has successfully sued the violator. This restriction would subject the injured consumers to the caprices of bureaucratic politics, the shortage of staff in overburdened and underfunded enforcement agencies, and the delays of two successive lawsuits, each of which would be likely to take at least two years. The administration argues that the class action device will be abused, and that fee-hungry lawyers will bring frivolous cases against legitimate industry. But nonmeritorious cases have been rare in the five states that liberally permit consumer class actions, and the device has not been abused by antitrust and securities fraud lawyers, who use it routinely as an effective supplement to government regulatory activities. Class actions are big cases requiring significant investments of time by attorneys who will be compensated only if they win; this fact alone will lead lawyers to accept those cases where consumers have been hurt and to reject borderline cases.

Consumer Self-help

The fastest route to justice for consumers might be avoidance of the judicial process altogether. Organized consumer groups might do more to obtain relief for their members by direct action than by hiring lawyers. Strangely, only Philadelphia has such an organized movement. There, the Consumer's Education and Protection Association (CEPA) will investigate a complainant's grievance and, if it believes it to be valid, will picket the offending merchant or bank in force. It usually succeeds in obtaining a refund. In return for CEPA's help, the complainant is obliged to join the organization and agree to picket for others when called upon. CEPA is constantly expanding its membership and power, and by invoking the First Amendment it has successfully fought off several attacks upon it in the courts.

The Amassing of Countervailing Power

So far, CEPA has limited itself to obtaining individual relief for individual complainants. But such an organization, if sufficiently powerful to lead a successful boycott, might obtain concessions from merchants going beyond individual cases; it might, for example, require a merchant to rewrite his contracts or his advertising, limit his collection techniques, carry higher-quality merchandise, or consent to arbitration. Consumer unions might adopt the model of the labor movement and seek to amass countervailing power to bargain collectively with merchants, or even manufacturers.

Similarly, consumer lawyers who employ sufficiently terrifying legal devices, such as class actions and suits for punitive damages, might be able to obtain the same concessions from merchants by withdrawing or settling proposed litigation. The merchant could settle the suit by entering into a contract with the plaintiff, for the benefit of all the other members of the community and enforceable by any of them.

A New Role for Government

Improvement of consumers' remedies may also come from agencies, which have not been very effective in protecting consumers in the past.[17] A key experiment is now underway in New York City's Department of Consumer Affairs, the first municipal consumer agency. Under the Consumer Protection Law of 1969,[18] all deception in the sale of consumer goods and services is unlawful, including exaggeration, ambiguity, innuendo, and failure to state material facts. The city is empowered to intervene on a consumer's behalf when the law is violated, and to obtain restitution for him, so that he is not relegated to going to court on his own. The law also permits mass restitution actions, in which the city may sue for refunds (as well as its own expenses) on behalf of all its citizens deceived by a particular seller's practice. It remains to be seen whether this power will result in a significant improvement, or whether even a municipal administration will be unable to cope with the volume of consumer abuse which occurs.

If consumers, their organizations, their lawyers, and the agencies designed to protect them become familiar with these legal reforms and devices, and if those measures are effective in deterring abuses by merchants and strengthening consumers who are deceived, they might also be employed to attack some of the larger problems besetting consumers. For example, consumer class actions under the antitrust laws or class suits based on massive violations of manufacturers' warranties[19] might induce producers of goods to be more concerned about the ultimate users. The possibility of mass restitution suits by the government might also affect the behavior of producers.[20] The abuse of consumers is based on an inequality of bargaining power and a parallel inequality of power to press claims; redressing these imbalances must be the major priority for the consumer movement in the seventies.

NOTES

1. Outstanding consumer credit reached $113 billion in 1968, compared with $21 billion as recently as 1950. *Statistical Abstract of the United States* 460 (1969). Over 80% of low-income families buy on time. *See* D. Caplovitz, *The Poor Pay More* 100–101 (2d ed. 1967).

2. For other common examples of everyday falsity, *see generally* S. Margolius, *The Innocent Consumer vs. The Exploiters* (1967). Or watch television.

3. *See, e.g.,* Yorke v. Taylor, 332 Mass. 368, 124 N.E.2d 912 (1955); Dwinnell v. Oftedahl, 235 Minn. 383, 51 N.W.2d 93 (1952); Hammond v. Pennack, 61 N.Y. 145 (1874).

4. Yorke v. Taylor, 332 Mass. 368, 124 N.E.2d 912 (1955).

5. *See* Smith v. Hale, 158 Mass. 178, 33 N.E. 493 (1893).

6. I have elsewhere recorded at some length an autobiographical account of the tactics employed by creditors' attorneys which make consumer cases expensive and keep them from ever being tried. Schrag, "Bleak House 1968: A Report on Consumer Test Litigation," 44 *New York University Law Review* 115 (1969).

7. Pennsylvania, Ohio, Michigan, Illinois, and one or two others. At this writing, the confession-of-judgment rule is being subjected to a powerful constitutional challenge in the United States Supreme Court by lawyers for the Philadelphia OEO Legal Services Program, and will probably be judicially or legislatively abolished by the time this is printed.

8. Sniadach v. Family Finance Corp., 395 U.S. 337 (1969).

9. *See* Comment, "The Persecution and Intimidation of the Low-Income Litigant as Performed by the Small Claims Court in California," 21 *Stanford Law Review* 1657 (1969).

10. For some other examples, see New York City Department of Consumer Affairs, *How to Sue in Small Claims Court in New York City* (1970).

11. *Cf.* Sniadach v. Family Finance Corp., 395 U.S. 337 (1969). The New York

law permitting consumers contractually to waive defenses was repealed in 1970, applicable to contracts signed after February 1971.

12. The first law to regulate this new area is Mass. Acts of 1970, ch. 457, Mass. Gen. Laws, ch. 255, §12(f). And see Littlefield, "Preserving Consumer Defenses: Plugging the Loophole in the New UCCC," 44 *New York University Law Review* 272 (1969).

13. *See generally* Starrs, "The Consumer Class Action, Considerations of Procedure," 49 *Boston University Law Review* 407 (1969).

14. Daar v. Yellow Cab Co., 433 P.2d 732 (1967) (suit to recover taxi overcharges for riders who are identifiable because they pay by coupon); Holstein v. Montgomery Ward, No. 68 C.H. 275 (Sup. Ct., Cook Co. Ill.), 2 CCH Pov. L. Rep. ¶9652, pp. 10784–95 (1969) (suit to collect overcharges for six million revolving-charge customers).

15. Hall v. Coburn Corp., 26 N.Y.2d 396, 259 N.E.2d 720, 311 N.Y.S.2d 281 (1970).

16. *See* S. 3092, 91st Cong., 1st Sess. (1969).

17. *See* American Bar Association, Report of the Commission to Study the Federal Trade Commission (1969).

18. New York City Administrative Code, ch. 64, title A.

19. In Anthony v. General Motors Corp., No. 959058 (Super. Ct., Los Angeles Co., Cal., filed Aug. 12, 1969), a class of thousands of buyers of General Motors three-quarter-ton trucks sued the manufacturer for breach of wheel warranties in the sale of every truck.

20. In 1969, 45 local and state governments settled an antitrust case against several major manufacturers of antibiotics. The settlement with some jurisdictions, including New York City, included the establishment of a large escrow fund on which injured consumers could make refund claims.

THE RIGHT TO
A HABITABLE
ENVIRONMENT

EVA H. HANKS AND JOHN L. HANKS

THE TERM "ENVIRONMENT" IS AN UMBRELLA THAT covers both the complex of physical, chemical, and biological factors acting on an organism or ecological system and the aggregate of political, economic, social, and cultural conditions that influence individual and group behavior. The two definitions are, of course, not unconnected: economic philosophies and cultural attitudes, for example, influence resource and technology decisions which in turn have an impact on the physical environment. Likewise, both natural and man-determined limits of the physical environment set constraints on resource and technology decisions which may influence economic philosophy and cultural attitudes. Because of this connection and because of the diversity of the physical environment, it is difficult to delimit precisely what a right to a healthful and habitable environment might embrace. Nevertheless, it is suggested that to be meaningful such a right should perform two functions. First, it should set limits, similar to those in the Bill of Rights, beyond which even a majority could not tamper with the environment. Examples might include the extermination of an animal species, the destruction of a unique natural phenomenon such as the Grand Canyon or Niagara Falls, or the release of nuclear

Eva H. Hanks is Professor of Law and Associate Dean at Rutgers Law School, and the author of articles dealing with aspects of environmental law.
John L. Hanks is Associate in Law at Columbia Law School, a candidate for doctorates in law and economics at Columbia University, and the author of environmental law articles.

radiation into the environment in quantities imminently dangerous to health and life. Second, such a right should give all interested
parties the opportunity to participate *effectively* in political and
economic decision-making processes which, individually or collectively, have a substantial impact on their environment.

The judge-made common law as a legal mechanism for the protection of the environment can be dismissed at the outset as trivial
in its breadth and ineffective in its application. The historical
common-law remedy for environmental degradation is the private
nuisance (sometimes negligence or trespass) action in which the
plaintiff sues for damages or seeks to enjoin the defendant from
using his property in a way detrimental to the plaintiff's person or
property. The state of the environment testifies to the effectiveness
of the remedy. This is not to say that in isolated instances the nuisance action cannot be used to good effect. But if it is to play a
major role in protecting our environment, it will have to undergo
a metamorphosis.

The obstacles to success along this route are hand-me-downs
from an era when courts (and most everyone else), perhaps appropriately, rendered unquestioning worship unto industrial growth.
That era is coming to an end. If the common law is to grow to
meet present conditions, injuries heretofore nonactionable must be
recognized as actionable. For instance, injuries suffered by all members of the community have traditionally been classified as "public
nuisances," with the result that citizens could not sue in their own
right. To make matters worse, citizens are nearly remediless when
it comes to forcing local officials to bring a public nuisance action.
New concepts of citizen nuisance actions will have to be recognized,
although we may perhaps want to require that the citizen group
first request the proper enforcement official to bring the suit. Joint
tort-feasor concepts will have to be applied to noise and air pollution cases, as is frequently done in water pollution controversies,
to reduce the almost insurmountable burden of showing causation.
The rationale is not new to the law: if four men inflict wounds on
another such that he dies, each is guilty of murder though no
wound by itself would have been fatal. If forty industrial plants
give off noxious fumes which in their totality endanger health and
life, it should be no defense that the fumes from one by itself are
not dangerous.

Another major obstacle to enjoining nuisances is the so-called
balance-of-convenience or balance-of-the-equities doctrine. It rests

on the power of the court to refrain from granting equitable relief when the hardship on the defendant would outweigh the benefit to the plaintiff. The plaintiff is, in such cases, left to his remedy at law for damages. In practical effect, this amounts to a condemnation of private property for a private use by private individuals who do not have the power of eminent domain. Since the Fifth Amendment, as well as similar provisions in state constitutions, permits the taking of private property only for a "public use," it prohibits, by implication, condemnation for "private objects." Not surprisingly, courts have been troubled by the violation of the spirit, albeit not the letter, of the Fifth Amendment. The jurisdictions are about evenly split on the applicability of the doctrine between those who will balance and those who think the doctrine is "improper."[1]

If the doctrine itself is debatable, the ways in which it has been applied are even more so. A recent example is the New York Court of Appeals case of *Boomer v. Atlantic Cement Co.*[2] Ironically enough, the court began by reversing a long history of refusing to apply the doctrine and then held that the defendant should not be enjoined. First, like Pontius Pilate, it washed its hands of the real issues:

> A court performs its essential function when it decides the rights of parties before it. Its decision of private controversies may sometimes greatly affect public issues. Large questions of law are often resolved by the manner in which private litigation is decided. But this is normally an incident to the court's main function to settle controversy. It is a rare exercise of judicial power to use a decision in private litigation as a purposeful mechanism to achieve direct public objectives greatly beyond the rights and interests before the court.

Second, it noted the difficulty of developing adequate pollution control measures. (Will such techniques be developed if the law does not require them?) It concluded that an injunction would close down the relatively new plant at once—a plant worth in excess of $45 million and employing over 300 people. The latter observation indicates the court's willingness to look beyond the consequences of its decision to the immediate parties when to do so suits its purposes. How did it know the plant would be closed down at once? Even if it would, why should it not be closed down? The judicially cognizable damages to the plaintiffs were $185,000, and that sum was not the total damage caused by the plant. Is it reasonable to believe the company would not have installed air pollution control devices to save its $45 million investment? Clearly, what we need is not only a change in the common law but a change in attitudes as well. Until such time, private nuisance actions will not protect us.

CONSTITUTIONAL RIGHTS AND PROTECTIONS

When we look to the United States Constitution, it becomes apparent that the Founding Fathers, surrounded as they were by seemingly unlimited natural abundance, gave scant attention to the right for which we now search. But the Constitution retains its vitality through interpretation in the context of changing conditions. The search, therefore, is not limited to an express statement of a constitutional right to a healthful and habitable environment, but extends to any constitutional language which might reasonably be interpreted as creating such a right. The Fifth, Ninth, and Fourteenth Amendments contain language that could meet this requirement.

A Constitutional Right to a Healthful Environment

The relevant part of the Fifth Amendment states that "No person shall . . . be deprived of life, liberty, or property, without due process of law." The Fourteenth Amendment is to the same effect.

The first question is, What kinds of acts are inhibited by the protection against the deprivation of life or liberty without due process of law? Could it reasonably be said to protect us, for example, against governmental use or approval of use, not absolutely necessary, of 2,4,5-T herbicides (defoliants)? The exposure of the citizenry to unnecessary radiation? The failure of government to stop air pollution? *No court has ever so held,* yet to do so would not unreasonably extend the applicability of the Fifth Amendment beyond cases to which it clearly applies. The government could not constitutionally order that every resident of, say, Kansas City be put before a firing squad, nor for that matter every hundredth or thousandth resident selected at random. If we change the method of execution from the firing squad to slow arsenic poisoning, the result is the same. The jump from these clear cases to a constitutional right to be protected against the hazards to health and life from technology and pollution, inflicted by government or with government approval, is short and obvious.

But although short and obvious, the jump is not without its difficulties. We know that even the constitutional right to life and liberty is not absolute. If it were, the military draft would be unconstitutional. What principle, then, will distinguish between those threats to life and liberty which are unconstitutional and those which are not? Our premise is the supremacy of the individual. Society cannot under "normal" conditions limit the personal freedoms of a few individuals so that the rest of society may benefit. Only under the most compelling and extraordinary circumstances, that is, when the very existence of society itself is endangered, are certain limitations justifiable. Such emergency situations—war, rebellion, epidemics, floods, and the like—are usually temporary and are exceptions to the premised rule. Indeed, the Constitution even permits the cherished writ of habeas corpus to be suspended in times of rebellion or invasion if the public safety so requires.

The pursuit of progress and the general welfare is not considered a ground for restricting the liberty and freedom of some individuals. Thus, if an individual's health or life were more endangered by a government action than that of other individuals, he would be entitled to protection under the due process clauses of the Fifth and Fourteenth Amendments. The spraying of 2,4,5-T near one's home might present such a case. But the nature of environmental and technological threats to health and life will often make it difficult for the individual to prove that his health or life is endangered. The complexity of technology, superior governmental access to information, and the stakes involved (life) all suggest that the plaintiff should not have to prove his case with a preponderance of the evidence. Due process might well require that once the complaining individual has made a prima facie case of threat to health or life, the burden shifts to the government to show otherwise.

In most cases of interest here, however, large segments of society are exposed to health risks, rather than only an individual or a small group of individuals. Air pollution is an example; radiation is another. The social compact theory, in conjunction with judicial deference to administrative discretion, tends to foreclose a substantive constitutional remedy. The rationale of the theory is that each of us surrenders a part of his liberty; as a consequence society in general benefits and all of us share in the benefits. Traffic regulation is an often-cited example; subjection to air pollution and radiation could well be thought of as similarly falling within the confines of the social compact.

Two arguments can be made against substantive judicial review in these kinds of cases. The first is that courts should not substitute their judgment for that of society. If a majority has chosen to shoulder burdens or assume risks in return for certain benefits, neither the courts nor a minority should be permitted to block such decisions. By contrast and as a general proposition, this is not true in cases arising under the Bill of Rights: a majority cannot, except by constitutional amendment, deprive a minority of its guaranteed liberties. But, the argument goes, where the health of a large segment of society is at stake, it might be assumed that society did not treat lightly the issue of imposing such a risk. The societal judgment should therefore be left undisturbed. A second and connected argument is that if the original decision is found to be faulty, society will surely rectify the situation through the legislative or administrative process. Unlike cases where only a part of society is asked to sacrifice its liberty for the greater good, cases where much of society shares both the burdens and benefits presuppose that society will throw off those burdens if in retrospect they prove to outweigh the benefits.

The realities of governmental development during the last half-century substantially undermine the theory of the first argument: "society" simply does not make the decisions with which we are concerned. And it has become clear that administrative agencies do not necessarily represent the "public interest." Further, perhaps because agencies tend to represent narrow economic interests, the benefits and burdens of agency decisions are seldom distributed equally, and those who receive the greater benefits (namely, the industrial captains) control the decision-making processes of government. Not surprisingly, their view of the public good is not necessarily what society's might be. Even if society can be said to make these decisions, it is the unusual case in which the general public has the facts with which to arrive at a rational judgment. More often, those who stand to gain the most are also those who have access to both the facts and the mass media to influence public opinion.

The premise of the second argument is that if a decision is found to be "wrong," society can change it. This, of course, is not true for the run-of-the-mill decision, because society does not participate in the day-to-day governmental decision-making processes. When conditions get bad enough, however, society can usually bring about some changes. Unfortunately, technological impact has now reached dimensions of such magnitude that society may never have the opportunity to reconsider "its" initial decision. The argument that society can revoke social security, minimum wages, Medicare, or the antitrust laws does not apply to many environmental problems. Society may not be able to bring back into existence a dead lake, our genetic pool if mutilated by radiation, or a habitable earth once it begins to cool because of air pollution. In other words, the arguments against judicial review of substantive economic decisions do not necessarily apply to review of substantive environmental-impact decisions. Since the nature of environmental decisions affecting life is of a different order from that of the economic decisions which the courts have rightfully refused to review since the 1930's, it can be argued that the due process clauses of the Fifth and Fourteenth Amendments give a right to a healthful environment that the courts should recognize.

A similar argument can be made under the Ninth Amendment, which provides: "The enumeration in the Constitution, of certain rights, shall not be construed to deny or disparage others retained by the people." One hundred and seventy-five years after the adoption of the Bill of Rights, the Supreme Court interpreted this language for the first time. In *Griswold v. Connecticut,*[3] the Court held unconstitutional a Connecticut statute prohibiting the prescription and use of contraceptive drugs and devices. The Justices took three fundamentally different approaches to arrive at the result. Justices Harlan and White found a right to marital privacy in the due process clause of the Fourteenth Amendment. This approach is similar to the one already discussed with regard to a right to a healthful environment in the Fifth and Fourteenth Amendments. Of interest here are the opinion of the Court, written by Mr. Justice Douglas, and the concurring opinion of Mr. Justice Goldberg.

The opinion of the Court deduced a right of marital privacy from the "penumbra" of several enumerated rights.

[S]pecific guarantees in the Bill of Rights have penumbras, formed by emanations from those guarantees that help give them life and substance. . . . Various guarantees create zones of privacy. The right of association contained in the penumbra of the First Amendment is one. . . . The Third Amendment in its prohibition against the quartering of soldiers "in any house" in time of peace without the consent of the owner is another facet of that privacy. The Fourth Amendment explicitly affirms the "right of the people to be secure in their persons, houses, papers, and effects, against unreasonable searches and seizures." The Fifth Amendment in its Self-Incrimination Clause enables the citizen to create a zone of privacy which government may not force him to surrender to his detriment. The Ninth Amendment provides: "The enumeration in the Constitution, of certain rights, shall not be construed to deny or disparage others retained by the people."[4]

Although it is by no means clear, the Court apparently treated the Ninth Amendment as a rule of construction permitting the development of new rights from values implicit in expressed rights. It can be argued, similarly, that a right to a healthful environment is an implicit premise of the Constitution; all other rights are meaningless without it. But the Constitution also repeatedly gives explicit expression to the values of life and liberty—in the Fifth, Sixth, and Eighth Amendments, as well as in Article I, Section 9, in the context of safeguarding a man's life and liberty in a criminal prosecution. No less is required when the public's life is at stake in an administrative proceeding. The penumbra of these express guarantees would seem to support a claim of a constitutional right to a healthful environment—at least as much as the First, Third, Fourth, and Fifth Amendments supported a claim to a right of marital privacy.

Mr. Justice Goldberg's approach differed significantly from that of the Court. He too treated the Ninth Amendment as a rule of construction. But rather than limit possible new rights to those values implicit in enumerated rights, he would have the courts look to the " 'traditions and [collective] conscience of our people' to determine whether a principle is 'so rooted [there] as to be ranked as fundamental.' " Such rights when found would be incorporated into the "liberty" protected by the due process clauses of the Fifth and Fourteenth Amendments. The test should be met easily. It is difficult to imagine a right more fundamental than the right to life.[5]

The authors are skeptical, nonetheless, that the courts will be willing to recognize a substantive constitutional right even in extreme environmental cases. Economic considerations of the largest scale are involved: Should the manufacturers bear the costs of pollution control? Should we have nuclear power plants? Should the internal combustion engine be replaced? The courts are not well suited to make these kinds of decisions. We do suggest, however, that the Constitution gives procedural rights which, if strictly enforced, may be just as effective as substantive rights. The two most important are the right to have the government meet a burden of proof commensurate to the possible risks whenever it proposes to alter or approve the alteration of the environmental status quo, and the right to effective public participation in the decision-making processes.

Although the individual in America is surrounded by protections to prevent a denial of his life or liberty without due process of law, few protections exist for society as a whole. Administrative agencies are almost immune from judicial review. Provided it has followed proper procedures, an agency will be reversed only in the most flagrant case of abuse of discretion. Yet when the health and life of large segments of society are at issue, due process should require a different standard of review and a different burden of proof. It will not do, for example, to say that a reasonable man could have found that a certain nuclear explosion would not unduly risk the life or health of society. In the light of the consequences should the "reasonable man" prove to be wrong, due process requires proof beyond all doubt that the proposed action is safe. In cases where the impact of a wrong decision would be less extreme, of course, the burden of proof would be less. But due process should require that the standard of review and the burden of proof be appropriate to the consequences.

Deprivation of Property Without Due Process of Law

The arguments for forging an environmental right out of the protection of property found in the Fifth and Fourteenth Amendments, although almost as compelling as those for the protection of life, require a substantially larger intellectual jump. To create an effective environmental right would require that "property" be construed as including not only private property, to which these amendments have historically applied, but public property as well. The trend toward urbanization and industrialization has minimized the importance of privately held real property for most of us. In the housing industry, for example, rental construction starts now exceed nonrental starts. Indeed, for the majority of Americans the most important real property they "own" is that held in common with others, acting through their government: the air we breathe; fishing, bathing, and boating rights on navigable rivers and lakes; the highways and streets; forests, grasslands, wetlands, parks, and beaches; and so on. Increased leisure time and further urbanization will make these commonly held rights even more important than they are today. Policy, if not necessarily history, suggests that publicly held property should receive constitutional protection at least equal to that now accorded privately held property.

If the courts were to create an environmental (public) property right, they would in essence elevate a broad public-trust doctrine to a constitutional principle. No one statement can sum up exactly and definitively what the public trust doctrine is. In some states it is a common-law principle; in others it is a judicial approach to the interpretation of statutory and constitutional provisions dealing with public resources. The doctrine initially applied to submerged lands and navigable waters held in trust for the people, but in some states it has been extended to include park lands. Some courts have referred to it for the proposition that certain public lands cannot be alienated or have their use designation changed. Others, while not denying legislative power to alienate or to convert to a different public use, have treated the doctrine as a mandate to scrutinize all such dealings closely and carefully in order to assure that the public interest is indeed being served. Many cases never mention the public trust doctrine, yet clearly apply its rationale by taking a "closer than normal" look at the procedures used to reach public resources decisions.[6]

Professor Joseph L. Sax in his exhaustive and excellent study of the doctrine concludes: "[P]ublic trust law is not so much a substantive set of standards for dealing with the public domain as it is a technique by which courts may mend perceived imperfections in the legislative and administrative process. The public trust approach . . . is, more than anything else, a medium for democratization."[7] He finds that the underlying principle of the doctrine is that public resources decisions should demonstrably reflect the wishes of the people and that low-visibility decisions arrived at by a few do not meet this criterion. If this is the principle, there is no reason, he argues, why the doctrine should not be extended to other public resources, such as air and the electromagnetic spectrum.

The public trust doctrine "seems to have the breadth and substantive content which might make it useful as a tool of general application for citizens seeking to develop a comprehensive legal approach to resource management decisions."[8] If it were raised to the status of a constitutional principle, the courts need not become embroiled in the substantive legislative and administrative domain of managing the public resources. All courts would, however, be required to review public resources decisions far differently than they do today. Every decision which turned public resources over to private use would be scrutinized closely to assure that special interests were not making off with the public wealth. Every decision which changed the public use designation would be analyzed to make certain that a narrowly oriented agency had not short-circuited the democratic decision-making processes.

Public Participation in Environmental Decisions

It has already been shown that the social compact theory might foreclose a substantive right to life. But even if a right to life were recognized and the public trust doctrine were raised to a constitutional principle, many important environmental decisions would be beyond the reach of the Constitution. The remedy is to bring the reality of administrative agency decision-making into closer harmony with the theory of the social compact: citizens must have a right to effective representative participation in administrative decision-making. To some extent, courts have moved in this direction by giving standing to citizen groups to challenge agency decisions.

The right to participate effectively in governmental decision-making processes would, of course, have implications far beyond environmental matters. Nevertheless, such a right is of particular importance to those concerned with the environment. It is notorious that governmental agencies look with disfavor on "public interest" representatives; the "public interest," in their view, is something to be worked out between the applicant and the agency. Seldom does an agency's bow to public participation rise above the level of lip service: hearings are held *after* the planning has been done, and written complaints are preferred over public hearings.

If the ideal of a democratic republic is to be fulfilled, the courts must respond to the fact that the right to vote no longer guarantees representative government. Perhaps it did when the Constitution was drafted. We were then a population of a mere three million, the central government had limited responsibilities, and many decisions were made at the local town meeting. The development and exercise of the commerce, general welfare, national defense, and taxing and spending powers have enormously increased the size, complexity, and importance of the central government. In turn this has led to a vast proliferation of governmental agencies. A new administration will typically, of course, replace the top-level administrators. But for all practical purposes, the staff-level bureaucracy has tenure. In other words, the operating level of government is to a large degree unresponsive to the vote. This is significant because the great majority of administrative decisions are effectively made by operating-level personnel. Review by top-echelon administrators tends to be perfunctory; and he who too often reverses the decisions of his staff is an ill-advised administrator indeed.

Several constitutional arguments can be pressed for the recognition of a right to participate. The due process clauses of the Fifth and Fourteenth Amendments furnish one basis. Professor Charles A. Reich has suggested that the citizen's need to be heard by his government should be met with a right of public participation founded on the free speech clause of the First Amendment.[9] The First Amendment right "to petition the government for a redress of grievances" may be more directly applicable. Oddly enough, it has been virtually ignored, both in judicial opinions and the legal literature. Yet it hardly seems exhausted by allowing citizens to write to their congressmen.

Aside from due process and First Amendment arguments, a denial of effective citizen participation in agency decision-making may be a denial of equal protection under the Fourteenth Amendment and the due process clause of the Fifth Amendment as it incorporates the concept of equal protection. To the extent that the Federal Communications Commission, for example, allows television broadcasters to participate in its decisions but denies that right to the viewing public, members of that public are denied the equal protection of the laws. Only a warped set of values would treat the interests of the viewing public as inferior to the interests of the broadcasters and hence conclude that the exclusion of the public is not a denial of equal protection.

Finally, an argument can be made under the Ninth Amendment and *Griswold*. Using Justice Goldberg's approach, few rights in a democracy could be more fundamental than the right of the citizen to have some say in his government. Using the "penumbra" approach of the Court, several parts of the Constitution seem to imply such a right: the First Amendment (free speech and the right to petition the government); Article I, Section 2, and the Seventeenth Amendment (election of representatives and senators by the people); Article IV, Section 4 (the "United States shall guarantee to every state in the union a republican form of government"); and the Voting Rights Amendments (Fifteenth—race; Nineteenth—sex; Twenty-third—Washington, D.C.; Twenty-fourth—poll tax). In total, these provisions give operative meaning to the values expressly stated in the Declaration of Independence. But as said earlier, the right to vote is no longer sufficient; agency administrators are for the most part beyond the reach of the vote. A new right must be fashioned to fill the void—a right to effective participation in agency decision-making.

Summary of Constitutional Arguments

It has been argued that we have a constitutional right to a healthful environment—that is, we have a right to life. It has also been recognized that courts may be reluctant to find such a right, primarily because it would involve them in economic decision-making of considerable magnitude. It may be possible, however, to achieve essentially the same results by construing due process to require that governmental agencies meet a burden of proof commensurate with the consequences of an erroneous environmental-impact decision. It has further been suggested that constitutional due process criteria should be applied to public as well as private property. Finally, it has been argued that we have a constitutional right to effective public representation and participation in the decision-making processes of administrative agencies. No contentions have been made as to a right to a "decent environment."[10] A right to procedural due process when the health and life of society are at stake is easily circumscribed, as is a right to participate in administrative proceedings. These are the kinds of rights to which courts have traditionally given protection. A right to a "decent environment" is of a different order. It would confront the courts with the job of defining "decent environment" and thus draw them into the kind of substantive economic review which they have, since the 1930's, properly refused to exercise.

STATUTORY ENVIRONMENTAL PROTECTIONS

The law books are replete with statutes which prohibit the polluting of air and water and other degradations of the environment. It is common knowledge that many of these laws are not enforced. The causes vary: sometimes there are conflicts of interest; sometimes the enforcement agency has been "captured" by the polluting industry; often the funds necessary for proper law enforcement have not been appropriated. But whatever the reason, the laws are not enforced and our environment is deteriorating. Here, too, the concerned citizen usually will not be granted a writ of mandamus to compel enforcement actions. Public opinion may begin to have some effect on how officials perform. Still, to the extent that they remain recalcitrant the courts are not likely to change their position on the mandamus action. In any event, enforcement of pollution statutes will get to the root of the problem about as much as private nuisance actions will: to be effective, pollution and other degradations must be stopped before they begin. This is the approach taken in the National Environmental Policy Act of 1969[11] —unquestionably the most important piece of environmental legislation ever enacted. This Act, signed into law on January 1, 1970, aids citizen groups in the protection of the public interest in a decent environment in three major ways. One, it recognizes a judicially protectable environmental interest. Two, it is a statutory enlargement of the authority and responsibility of federal agencies and departments. Three, it places an affirmative burden on the agencies to develop the environmental record, and injects an ethical value into the decision-making process which favors the ecological status quo.

Standing to Sue

When a citizen group tries to intervene in an administrative proceeding or seeks declaratory or injunctive relief on behalf of a public interest in certain noneconomic—including environmental —values, it is usually met by the argument that it lacks standing. That is, the challenged governmental action is said to affect the group no differently than it affects members of society generally. The group, therefore, is said not to have the requisite interest to be treated as a party. Typically in the past, the argument succeeded. Recently, however, the Supreme Court of the United States in two cases, *Barlow v. Collins*[12] and *Association of Data Processing Service Organizations v. Camp*,[13] has endorsed a trend toward greatly liberalized standing rules. To put these cases into perspective, it will be useful to discuss briefly three lower federal court cases which helped provide the standing breakthrough and which are otherwise relevant to environmental litigation.

In *Scenic Hudson Preservation Conference v. FPC*,[14] the Court of Appeals for the Second Circuit gave standing to three towns and to an association of nonprofit conservation organizations to challenge the issuance of a Federal Power Commission license. The court held that a statute may create new rights or interests and thus give standing to one who would otherwise be barred by the "case or controversy" requirement of the Constitution; that the Federal Power Act created an interest in the conservation of natural resources, the maintenance of natural beauty, and the preservation of historic sites; and that those who had demonstrated a special concern for such values were aggrieved parties and had a right to protect their special interest. An additional finding that the petitioners had a sufficient economic stake to establish their standing detracts somewhat from the importance of the case. Its thrust, nevertheless, was to accept the citizen suit, provided some connection exists between the plaintiff and the challenged administrative action.

In *Office of Communication of the United Church of Christ v. FCC*,[15] the Court of Appeals for the District of Columbia held that members of the viewing public had standing to intervene in a license renewal proceeding in order to enforce policies embodied in the Communications Act of 1934. The court spoke in broad terms of granting "the consuming public" standing to challenge administrative action. The requirement that the plaintiff show some connection to the governmental decision was here put in terms of agency and court discretion to deny standing to those not broadly representative of the public interest, a requirement not inconsistent with the public interest, citizen suit.

The Court of Appeals for the Second Circuit in *Citizens Committee for the Hudson Valley v. Volpe*[16] settled the issue—at least for the Second Circuit—that was left ambiguous in *Scenic Hudson*. The court specifically held that two organizations, an unincorporated citizens committee and the Sierra Club, had standing although admittedly they had no personal economic claim to assert. The plaintiffs were found to be appropriate representatives of the public because:

> They have evidenced the seriousness of their concern with local natural resources by organizing for the purpose of cogently expressing it, and the intensity of their concern is apparent from the considerable expense and effort they have undertaken in order to protect the public interest which they believe is threatened by official action of the federal and state governments. In short, they have proved the genuineness of their concern by demonstrating that they are "willing to shoulder the burdensome and costly processes of intervention" in an administrative proceeding. *United Church of Christ* . . . They have "by their activities and conduct . . . exhibited a special interest in" the preservation of the natural resources of the Hudson Valley. *Scenic Hudson* . . .

Drawing on "environmental language" in the Department of Transportation Act, the Hudson River Basin Compact Act, and a Corps of Engineers regulation, the court held "that the public interest in environmental resources . . . is a legally protected interest affording these plaintiffs, as responsible representatives of the public, standing to obtain judicial review of agency action alleged to be in contravention of that public interest." On the merits, the court held that the Corps of Engineers had exceeded its authority when it issued a fill permit necessary for the construction of the Hudson River Expressway.

Turning now to the decisions in *Data Processing* and *Barlow,* the Supreme Court seems to have adopted a new, two-tier approach to standing problems. The first step is to satisfy the "case or controversy" requirement. To do so, the plaintiff must show "injury in fact, economic or otherwise" (*Data Processing*) or "the personal stake and interest" which imparts the necessary adverseness (*Barlow*). The second step is to determine whether the plaintiff seeks to protect an interest "arguably within the zone of interests to be protected or regulated" by the statute in question. Whether the statute in fact creates a legally protected interest is a question going to the merits and sharply to be distinguished from the standing issue. The Court cited both *Scenic Hudson* and *Church of Christ* for the proposition that the interests protected need not be economic but can reflect aesthetic and conservational values as well.

The tenor of these cases is perhaps more important than the actual holdings. It reflects a willingness to accept the relaxed standing notions that some of the lower federal courts have developed over the last few years and of which *Scenic Hudson, Church of Christ,* and *Hudson Valley* are the most significant examples. If the plaintiff can present one iota of evidence that he or the class he represents was intended by the statute to be protected, he is in court. He can then fully develop and argue the existence of a legally protected interest.

To summarize the position of citizen groups seeking to protect the public interest through judicial review of federal agency decisions: First, the Supreme Court has not definitively settled the question whether associations and other organized groups have standing in their own right. *Hudson Valley* and *Church of Christ* expressly so held, but even in *Church of Christ* the court did not say which of the four plaintiffs (only two were organizational) must be given standing. One reading of *Scenic Hudson* is that it gave standing to a conference (association) of conservation organizations; but that holding is undermined because the court found that one of the member organizations would suffer economic injury and because it sloughed over the fact that the conference itself had not been injured. The Supreme Court in *Data Processing* had an opportunity to settle the issue, but never even discussed the problem. If a "feel" for the cases, however, can substitute for firm holdings, the trend is as common sense would have it: toward giving standing to organizations broadly representative of an injured class.[17]

The second conclusion which can be drawn is that injury in fact suffices to meet the requirements of both the Constitution and the Administrative Procedure Act. No showing need be made that a legal right or legal interest has been infringed. Indeed, the Supreme Court cautions that that issue goes to the merits. One must merely allege that the interest to be protected is "arguably within the zone of interests" protected by the statute. Nor need those interests be economic. Citizen groups should have no difficulty in showing that the interests they assert are arguably within the zone of interests to be protected by the National Environmental Policy Act.

An Environmental Interest

The National Environmental Policy Act creates a judicially protectable interest in the environment of which all of us are the intended beneficiaries. The legislative history leads inevitably to this conclusion. The congressional mood toward our environmental ills, and inferentially, the mood of this legislation, was composed of a sense of shock at the all-pervasive environmental destruction, deterioration, and mismanagement; of urgency in trying to avert a collision course with ecological disaster; and of dedication to a policy which, in the words of the Act, "will encourage productive and enjoyable harmony between man and his environment." In form, the Environmental Policy Act is a statute; in spirit, a constitution.

> A statement of environmental policy is more than a statement of what we believe as a people and as a Nation. It establishes priorities and gives expression to our national goals and aspirations. It serves a constitutional function in that administrators may refer to it for guidance in making decisions which find environmental values in conflict with other values.[18]

It is in this sense that the Act must be read.

Scenic Hudson, Church of Christ, and *Hudson Valley* show a willingness to find a congressional intent to protect large classes of people and to permit appropriate representatives to participate in the decision-making processes of administrative government. The Supreme Court has lent its approval to the trend. The forces which have contributed to this movement are easily identifiable. One is the increasing awareness that administrative agencies do not necessarily operate in the public interest. The other is the general feeling of exclusion and alienation from government which plagues the body politic. Exactly the same forces that have pushed for greatly liberalized standing rules and for the recognition of substantive legal interests in broad classes of persons now push for a recognition of the constitutional character of the Environmental Policy Act. The Act is a broad-gauged and explicit congressional mandate that man has an environmental interest that must be heeded by all federal agencies.

> The Congress authorizes and directs that, to the fullest extent possible . . . the policies, regulations, and public laws of the United States shall be interpreted and administered . . . [§102]
>
> . . . to the end that the Nation may
>
> (1) fulfill the responsibility of each generation as trustee of the environment for succeeding generations; [§101 (b) (1)]
>
> (2) assure for all Americans safe, healthful, productive, and esthetically and culturally pleasing surroundings. [§101 (b) (2)]

In the past, we have often accepted the *non sequitur* that where all are the intended beneficiaries of an interest, none has standing to protect it. The dangers inherent in this philosophy are now apparent. Both logic and experience support the emerging view that an interest so fundamental that all are within the protected class must be permitted its champion. The Environmental Policy Act has created such an interest.

A question of some importance is whether the environmental interest created by the Act includes man-made environments. The legislative history abundantly supports an affirmative answer. To "assure for all Americans safe, healthful, productive, and esthetically and culturally pleasing surroundings" clearly means an obligation of the federal government "to protect and improve the quality of each citizen's surrounding both in regard to the preservation of the natural environment as well as in the planning, design, and construction of manmade structures."[19] Both the natural and the man-made are, in short, "environment" within the purview of the Act.

One subsection requires particular attention:

> The Congress recognizes that each person should enjoy a healthful environment and that each person has a responsibility to contribute to the preservation and enhancement of the environment. [§101(c)]

In the Senate version, each person had a "fundamental and inalienable right to a healthful environment."[20] In conference the language was changed to its present form. The legislative history offers little explanation either of the original language or of the reasons or meaning behind the change. Three interpretations offer themselves. First, Congress might have meant to recognize a right to a healthful environment, but none other. That is, Congress may not have intended to create any other interests in the Act. This construction seems highly unlikely. Congress was not unaware of cases such as *Scenic Hudson;* yet nothing in the legislative history suggests it was bent on reversing a judicial trend. Second, Congress intended to create no special interest beyond the interests it had already created in the rest of the Act. This is the least likely construction. Subsection 101(c) is set apart in a section of its own. It deals exclusively with a "healthful environment" and clearly seems to indicate a special concern with health—that is, with life. This leads to the third interpretation, the one suggested here. Whatever the concern in conference, the section was not stricken from the Act. Life is the primary value. Without it, all other rights are meaningless. It would seem appropriate and entirely in keeping with the spirit of the Act, therefore, to read the language as it was intended in the Senate version. That is to say, aside from the interests created by the remainder of the Act and enforceable in public actions, subsection 101(c) recognizes a "legal right" in every individual to a healthful environment. What does such a right mean? First, anyone suing to enforce it is entitled to his remedy if his right is found to have been abridged. Second, a legal right to a healthful environment could, in certain circumstances, preclude any balancing or weighing of interests during the governmental decision-making process; in some situations no amount of dollars will outweigh the threat to life. Perhaps we already have such a right. However, the Supreme Court has not yet been called upon to expound it. When it is, as it surely will be, prudence may dictate giving the "right to life" a statutory rather than a constitutional basis, at least while its contours are in a stage of development.

The Impact of the Environmental Policy Act on the Jurisdiction of Federal Agencies and Departments

The most difficult problem posed by the Environmental Policy Act is its impact on the existing jurisdiction and responsibility of federal agencies and departments. Sections 102, 103, and 105 are relevant. Section 105 makes the policies of the Act "supplementary" to those in existing authorizations. In Section 102, Congress "authorizes and directs" that the interpretation and administration of all policies, regulations, and laws conform "to the fullest extent possible" to the new national environmental policies established in Section 101, and gives specific directives to help implement these policies. Section 103 directs all agencies of the federal government to review their present statutory authority for the purpose of determining whether "any deficiencies or inconsistencies" exist which "prohibit full compliance" with the purposes of the Act. If so, the agency is to propose to the President measures necessary to create conformity to the Act.

The legislative history shows overwhelmingly that the Environmental Policy Act was intended to have an immediate impact on governmental operations. The clear intention of the Senate was to mandate all federal agencies to consider environmental factors and to increase all jurisdictional authorizations and responsibilities accordingly. Nor did anything happen in conference which warrants a different conclusion. On the contrary—the House conferees retreated from a very restrictive House provision in favor of the present language of Section 102. This was to make it clear that agencies were to comply at once "unless the existing law applicable to such agency's operations expressly prohibits or makes full compliance with one of the directives impossible."[21] Together, then, Sections 102, 103, and 105 give a mandate to all federal agencies to observe the policies of the Act as set forth in Sections 101 and 102, and grant such additional jurisdiction as is needed to implement these policies and to follow the specific directives of Section 102.

Granted that the Environmental Policy Act is jurisdictional, the question remains: What are the limits of the new authority and responsibility of the federal agencies? For example, is the Act applicable to the Atomic Energy Commission when it licenses nuclear power plants? The Corps of Engineers when an applicant seeks a fill or construction permit? The Federal Housing Administration when it insures home mortgages in a subdivision development? The Interstate Commerce Commission when it has been asked to approve the discontinuation of commuter train service? In every one of these cases a potentially detrimental environmental impact exists. In every one there is a causal connection between the governmental action and the environmental impact. If "but for" is the test, virtually every conceivable governmental activity would come within the purview of the Act. Despite its "constitutional" overtones, it could not have been intended to cut quite so wide a swath. Rather, the key concept would seem to be "reasonableness." To take the hypothetical situations posed above: The environmental impact of a nuclear power plant is not exhausted with the disposal of radioactive waste. It seems reasonable to ask the Atomic Energy Commission to trouble itself with the problem of thermal pollution, hardly a peripheral issue, especially in light of the declared goal to "attain the widest range of beneficial uses of the environment without degradation, risk to health or safety, or other undesirable and unintended consequences [§101(b)(3)]." Nor should the Commission be able to ignore the visual pollution an atomic plant might cause. It is not unreasonable to assume that an agency already involved in the siting of power plants should also be charged with assuring "for all Americans safe, healthful, productive, and esthetically pleasing surroundings [§101(b)(2)]."

As for the Corps of Engineers, few cases are imaginable in which the applicability of the Environmental Policy Act is more self-evident. Before it can issue a fill or construction permit, the Corps must consider the effect on navigability. With the passage of the Act, the Corps must act to "preserve important . . . natural aspects of our national heritage [§101(b)(4)]," something which surely includes our navigable rivers, coastal waters, estuaries, marshes, and wetlands.

The case of Federal Housing Administration approval of home mortgage insurance for a subdivision development is just as clear. The FHA sets a number of standards and reviews the developer's plans for compliance. The environmental impact of subdivisions is indisputable and so is their inclusion in the scope of the Environmental Policy Act. As a general proposition, therefore, the FHA is subject to the policies of Section 101 and must abide by the directives set forth in Section 102. Thus, if it were to approve, without more, a development which because of its nature or location constituted a threat to a valuable ecosystem, appropriate citizen groups could intervene to demand compliance with the Act.

On its face, the Interstate Commerce Commission case—approval of the discontinuance of commuter train service—seems a good deal more removed from the reach of the Environmental Policy Act than any of the previous examples. The reason is that the causal chain is so much longer. The next step, after getting a permit to fill an estuary, is to fill it. The destructive environmental impact follows on the heels of the administrative action. The destructive environmental impact of discontinuing commuter train service is a good deal more gradual and attenuated. All of the additional highways, buses, automobiles, parking lots, air pollution, etc. will not appear, dramatically, so many days after the ICC has acted. But appear they will. Interestingly enough, the ICC has not been insensitive to the environmental problems caused by alternatives to mass rail transit. In *New York, New Haven & Hartford R.R., Discontinuance of Trains*,[22] it found that "public convenience and necessity" required continuation of the New York City commuter service. Among other things, the ICC observed that the "undesirable effects of our national, regional, and local roadbuilding programs in the areas of land use, taxation, scenic pleasure, air cleanliness, and safety are all too familiar to most Americans today." It seems, in other words, that environmental concerns are well within the responsibility, authority, and competence of the Commission.

Consequently, the ICC is a clear case for the applicability of the Environmental Policy Act, notwithstanding the less than immediate causal connection between administrative action and detrimental environmental impact.

Cases can be imagined, however, where cause and effect are so far removed from one another that serious questions arise about the reach of the Act. Suppose, for instance, that a conservation group brings suit against the FHA on the theory that the policies of the agency foster single-home ownership; that present construction methods require great amounts of lumber for this type of housing; and that this is an inefficient use of a limited resource, leading to needless deforestation. The group asks that the FHA be ordered to re-evaluate its policies in light of the Environmental Policy Act. The case is clearly distinguishable from that of FHA approval of a particular, environmentally destructive project. Yet a fairly obvious connection exists between the FHA policy and its effect on the nation's forests. It may not, therefore, be unreasonable to force the FHA to rethink what it is doing, and it may not be unreasonable to permit a citizen group to trigger the process in the public interest. The case, in any event, would seem to test the outer limits of the Act's applicability.

Some tentative guidelines emerge to help answer questions about the jurisdiction and responsibility of federal agencies and departments under the Environmental Policy Act. The existence of a review, control, or planning function in the agency raises a presumption for the applicability of the Act. The length of the causal chain between agency action and detrimental environmental impact is a factor to be considered, but it is not decisive. As the potential for serious harm to the ecosystem increases, the remoteness of the causal connection diminishes in importance. "Reasonableness" is a key criterion. Reasonableness, however, means reasonableness in relation to the dimension of the problem—and the problem of our ravaged environment is huge indeed.

The Burden of Developing the Record

The interest created by the Environmental Policy Act may well come to naught if the public interest representatives are to carry the burden of developing the environmental record. Typically, they arrive on the scene late. Even if they participate in the administrative hearings, negotiations and "adjustments" between the agency and the applicant have already taken place. Typically, the applicant has almost every advantage of expertise and financial resources. If the recognition of public interests is to have meaning, the federal agencies must be made to fulfill their responsibility of actively protecting those interests.

> In this case, as in many others, the Commission has claimed to be the representative of the public interest. This role does not permit it to act as an umpire blandly calling balls and strikes for adversaries appearing before it; the right of the public must receive active and affirmative protection at the hands of the Commission.[23]

The Environmental Policy Act has made the obligation imposed by *Scenic Hudson* on the Federal Power Commission one generally applicable to all agencies. The legislative history is clear that the agencies are to approach their new responsibilities as anything but umpires "blandly calling balls and strikes." Rather, they have an affirmative duty to develop the record. They cannot put those performing a public service by seeking to protect the public interest to the task and expense of doing their job for them. They can and should, however, shift some of the burden to the applicant.

Among the alternatives an agency must consider is whether the project should be built at all, any place. In *Udall v. FPC*,[24] Mr. Justice Douglas entertained the heretical suspicion that perhaps we "cannot assume that the [Federal Power] Act commands the immediate construction of as many projects as possible." It is a thought worth pursuing.

Aside from assigning responsibility for the necessary environmental impact studies, there is the question of who has the burden of persuasion, or burden of proof. The overriding principle of the Environmental Policy Act is that all those whose activities affect the environment must show that the ecological impact is compatible with the policies embodied in the Act. Agencies have too often forgotten that an applicant should always have the burden of proving that his proposed actions will be in the public interest.

Finally, the Act meant to put an end to the towering predominance of economic factors in the decision-making process. The new value thrown into the scales is an ecological ethic. Such an ethic rejects much of what we have, until now, called progress in favor of that "productive and enjoyable harmony between man and his environment" which it is our new national policy to nurture into reality.

CONCLUSION

Does our legal system recognize a right to a "habitable environment"? The answer is both yes and no. The Constitution, we have argued, guarantees due process of law when society's health or life is in issue. Due process means that the government has a burden of proof commensurate with the consequences if its decision is erroneous. At least in the federal sphere, a substantive right to life has been accorded recognition by Section 101(c) of the National Environmental Policy Act. However, neither the Constitution, the common law, nor the statutes *guarantee* a "decent" or aesthetically pleasing environment. Common-law nuisance actions give limited protection against injuries to property or person. In isolated cases, they may protect against the grossest sort of aesthetic nuisance. The public trust doctrine, whether elevated to a constitutional principle or vigorously applied as a common-law one, could assure high visibility for public resources decisions. It could not, however, guarantee a decent or pleasant environment.

Aside from the right to life, we have argued for a constitutional right to effective public participation in the decision-making processes of administrative government. The environmental interest created by the National Environmental Policy Act is largely of the same essence. The constitutional right would be a procedural one. It would not assure that the substance of governmental decisions would not lead to a further degradation of the environment; it would assure that all interested parties, including appropriate public representatives, would have the right to share in those decisions. Similarly, the Act, although stating a national policy in favor of a decent environment, does not guarantee it. It does direct agencies to do all that is in their power to maintain and improve our environment. And it gives citizens the right to police the agencies so that they fully and impartially conform to the directives of the Act. If effective public participation does not halt further environmental deterioration, redress will no longer be to the courts but to the Congress. Ultimately, our only redress is ourselves.

NOTES

1. *See generally* 5 R. Powell, *Real Property* §707 (1968); Hanks, "The Law of Water in New Jersey," 22 *Rutgers Law Review* 621, 643–49 (1968).

2. 26 N.Y.2d 219, 257 N.E.2d 870 (1970).

3. 381 U.S. 479 (1965).

4. *Id.* at 484.

5. *See generally* on the Ninth Amendment, B. Patterson, *The Forgotten Ninth Amendment* (1955); Kutner, "The Neglected Ninth Amendment: The 'Other Rights' Retained by the People," 51 *Marquette Law Review* 121 (1968); Redlich, "Are There 'Certain Rights . . . Retained by the People?' " 37 *New York University Law Review* 787 (1962).

6. *See, e.g.,* Texas Eastern Transmission Corp. v. Wildlife Preserves, 48 N.J. 261, 235 A.2d 130 (1966), where the New Jersey Supreme Court held that an owner of private property being used for public purposes had a "lower than normal" burden of proof when attempting to show that a utility was exercising its eminent domain power arbitrarily. The case is discussed in Tarlock, "Recent Natural Resources Case," 8 *Natural Resources Journal* 1 (1968).

7. Sax, "The Public Trust Doctrine in Natural Resources Law: Effective Judicial Intervention," 68 *Michigan Law Review* 471, 509 (1970).

8. *Id.* at 474.

9. Reich, "The Law of the Planned Society," 75 *Yale Law Journal* 1227, 1260–61 (1966).

10. *See, e.g.,* Sive, "The Environment—Is It Protected by the Bill of Rights?" 268 *Civil Liberties* (ACLU April 1970).

11. 83 Stat. 852 (1970). The Act and its legislative history are examined in detail in Hanks and Hanks, "An Environmental Bill of Rights: The Citizen Suit and the National Environmental Policy Act of 1969," 24 *Rutgers Law Review* 230 (1970). The discussion here is a condensation of that article.

12. 397 U.S. 159 (1970). (Cash-rent tenant farmers have standing to challenge a regulation by the Secretary of Agriculture permitting the assignment of certain federal advance payments to secure rent for land used by the tenants.)

13. 397 U.S. 150 (1970). (Sellers of data-processing services have standing to challenge a ruling of the Comptroller of the Currency, allowing national banks to make data-processing services available to other banks and to customers.)

14. 354 F.2d 608 (2d Cir. 1965), *cert. denied,* 384 U.S. 941 (1966).

15. 359 F.2d 994 (D.C. Cir. 1966).

16. 425 F.2d 97 (2d Cir. 1970), *appeal docketed,* 39 U.S.L.W. 3085 (U.S. Sept. 8, 1970) (Nos. 614 & 615).

17. For a thorough discussion of the "public action," see Jaffe, "Standing to Secure Judicial Review: Public Actions," 74 *Harvard Law Review* 1265 (1961); "Standing to Secure Judicial Review: Private Actions," 75 *Harvard Law Review* 255 (1961); "The Citizen as Litigant in Public Actions: The Non-Hohfeldian or Ideological Plaintiff," 116 *University of Pennsylvania Law Review* 1033 (1968).

18. 115 Cong. Rec. 19009 (1969) (remarks of Senator Jackson).

19. S. Rep. No. 91-296, 91st Cong., 1st Sess. 18 (1969).

20. *Id.* at 2. The House bill contained no comparable provision.

21. H.R. Rep. No. 91-765, 91st Cong., 1st Sess. 9–10 (1969).

22. 327 ICC 151 (1966).

23. 354 F.2d at 620.

24. 387 U.S. 428, 449 (1967).

SECTION II

The Right to
Influence Government or
Public Opinion

THE RIGHT
TO VOTE

JAMES C. KIRBY, JR.

IN 1912, POLITICAL SCIENTIST W. J. SHEPARD DELIV-
ered a paper on voting rights, or "suffrage" as he called it, at the
annual meeting of the American Political Science Association.
Shepard identified five conflicting theories of voting rights and
called upon his professional colleagues to meet the need for critical
analysis of the subject.[1]

In 1934, when the same scholar wrote again on the subject for
the *Encyclopaedia of the Social Sciences,* he found that little progress had been made toward development of an intellectually satisfactory theory of voting rights. He could do little more than restate
the various theories he had originally identified. Again he challenged his profession, in much stronger terms, to provide the
necessary scholarship, saying:

> The five theories concerning the suffrage are all mingled in the
> thought of the present time. No single consistent basic concept has
> gained general acceptance. Tangled and confused, this conglomerate
> of ideas offers no satisfactory explanation of the existing institu-
> tional arrangements or any adequate criterion by which proposed
> innovations may be judged. The clarification of the underlying
> theory of the suffrage is one of the important obligations of con-
> temporary political science.[2]

*James C. Kirby, Jr., is Dean of The Ohio State University College of Law, former
Chief Counsel to the United States Senate Judiciary Subcommittee on Constitutional
Amendments, and Executive Director of the Special Committee on Congressional
Ethics, Association of the Bar of the City of New York.*

In 1970, it can be said that Shepard's call for a coherent theory of voting has finally been answered—after the task was taken up by the United States Supreme Court. The decisions of the Court from 1962 to 1970 in the general area of voting rights provide a remarkably clear basis for re-examination of Shepard's five theories and for the development of a single new theory which offers fairly adequate criteria for resolving the issues which are sure to accompany the participatory politics of the future.

EARLIER THEORIES RE-EXAMINED

We can begin with Shepard's summary of the theories which competed in the political thought of 1934:

> The history of the suffrage is connected with five different basic conceptions, or theories, of its nature, most of them not explicitly stated but inherent in the current practise. These are: first, the theory, effective among primitive peoples and in the city-states of antiquity and of the Renaissance, that the suffrage is an attribute or function of citizenship; second, the later feudal theory that the suffrage is a vested privilege, an incident of a particular status, usually connected with the possession of land; third, the theory of the early constitutional regime that the suffrage is an abstract right founded in natural law, a consequence of the social compact and an incident of popular sovereignty; fourth, the theory of modern political science that voting is a function of government, that the voter in casting his ballot performs a public office and that the electorate, like the legislature or the courts, is an organ of government; and fifth, the ethical theory, which is strongly urged at the present time by certain writers, that the suffrage is an important, indeed an essential means for the development of individual character, a condition necessary for the realization of the worth of human personality.[3]

Each of these will be examined briefly to determine its continuing relevance and its relation to current constitutional doctrine.

The Citizenship Theory

The simple theory that voting is an attribute of citizenship has considerable appeal in a full-citizenship society,[4] but it is too broad to explain the contemporary dimensions of voting rights. While there is some support for the proposition that the right to vote for federal officers is a privilege of United States citizenship protected by the Fourteenth Amendment,[5] and Chief Justice Warren has said that the debasement of a citizen's right to vote makes him "that much less a citizen,"[6] it cannot be said that mere citizenship equals voting rights or that all citizens may vote. The widespread disfranchisement of citizens under twenty-one, citizens who are new residents of a constituency, and citizens convicted of crimes should be sufficient to establish the point.

Nonetheless, citizenship is a relevant factor and a proper beginning point in analysis of the current status of voting rights. Under the concept of citizenship inherited from the ancient Greeks and Romans, a citizen generally has the right to exercise all political and civil privileges of the government. Whenever a citizen is denied the right to vote, the justification should be well-founded.

If voting were viewed as an inherent attribute of citizenship, it could be argued that it should be protected on the same basis as citizenship itself. Under the rule of *Afroyim v. Rusk*,[7] citizenship may be lost only by conduct amounting to voluntary relinquishment. Should the most important attribute of citizenship be just as inviolate? Since loss of citizenship cannot be imposed as punishment for crime,[8] it should follow that denial of the franchise is similarly invalid. The citizenship analysis bodes ill for state laws which deprive citizens convicted of felonies of their voting rights, a subject to which we will return in testing other theories.

It is safe to say that a state *may* continue to make citizenship a minimal qualification for voting, even though it is not required to extend the vote to all citizens without restriction. The Court's general statements frequently refer to citizenship as a key ingredient of the constitutional right to vote and indicate that special judicial scrutiny is required of laws which grant the right to vote to "some bona fide residents of requisite age and citizenship"[9] but deny it to others. This lumping of age, residence, and citizenship qualifications may be a clue to the only voting restrictions which can survive logical extension of the emerging constitutional rules.

The citizenship theory suggests an interesting problem. May a state extend the right to vote to aliens? Or could a citizen contend successfully that his personal vote was unlawfully debased and diluted by inclusion of noncitizens? The question is interesting but not viable. Alien voting is not unknown in our history—it flourished briefly in the Midwest in the mid-nineteenth century as an attempt to attract immigrant labor[10]—but it is not likely ever again to be popular with state legislators.

The Vested Privilege Theory

Shepard's identification of this theory with the feudal period possibly should establish its current irrelevance, but just as he could not dismiss it in 1934, neither can we today. Its validity during most of our history is indisputable. Property qualifications for voting in this nation survived long after the Declaration of Independence proclaimed political equality and government by consent. When our government was formed, such qualifications caused more than four-fifths of the adult white male population to be ineligible to vote or hold office, and universal suffrage for adult males was long delayed in the United States because of vestiges of feudal theories of voting. One form of such qualifications, the poll tax, persisted in a few states until 1966. Then it was held unconstitutional under the following rule:

> [A] State violates the Equal Protection Clause of the Fourteenth Amendment whenever it makes the affluence of the voter or payment of any fee an electoral standard. Voter qualifications have no relation to wealth nor to paying or not paying this or any other tax.[11]

The constitutional demise of property and taxpayer qualifications might appear to be complete under such broad reasoning, but there remain a few areas in which property ownership may be relevant.

May ownership of property be made the equivalent of personal residence for purposes of voting qualifications? The Court of Appeals for the Fifth Circuit held in 1965 that Georgia could allow nonresident property owners to vote in the municipal elections of the town of Savannah Beach on the same basis as residents.[12] This may shock some humanistic theorists of voting. The holding could justify the slogan, "One person or one property interest—one vote."

An opposite trend is suggested by the decision of the Supreme Court in *Cipriano v. City of Houma*.[13] There the Court held that the equal protection clause was violated by a Louisiana statute which limited the vote to property taxpayers in elections held to approve issuance of revenue bonds by a municipal utility. The discrimination between property owners and other registered voters was held to be unjustified because all were substantially affected by utility operations and were interested in service and rates.

A case now pending[14] should determine whether property owners may be the exclusive electorate in referenda determining issues in which such voters have more of a separate personal stake. It involves the issuance of revenue bonds which create a lien on taxable property in the electoral district.

Other types of elections in which special voter interest may be a valid voting qualification come to mind, such as referenda on whether paving or street improvements will be made under laws which provide for the assessment of their costs against property owners who benefit therefrom. In our complex system of governmental decision-making, it cannot be said that all property qualifications for voting are dead.

The Natural Rights Theory

Although opinions of the Supreme Court sometimes refer to the "inalienable right"[15] of citizens to participate in the electoral process, such a label is neither warranted from our history nor justified by current constitutional doctrine. So long as any limitations remain upon the right to vote, it can hardly be said to be "inalienable" or "natural." Nonetheless, this theory has strong support and is closely related to the emerging constitutional right to vote.

The idea that all men should vote has struggled fitfully for fulfillment from our national beginnings. It did not take long in our early history for the public to sense that the Constitution permitted electoral systems which fell far short of the ideals which had produced the new nation. The American people moved instinctively and surely toward universal suffrage. A suffrage historian's account of the 1820 Massachusetts constitutional convention recounts a dramatic confrontation which occurred when the Establishment vainly defended property qualifications against the crude natural-rights thinking of the masses:

> The most talented statesmen of the country were present and defended the property test in one way or another. The venerable John Adams was there and painted dire pictures of what would happen if the franchise were extended. Daniel Webster and Joseph Storey gave ample support.
>
> But in spite of all this talent property tests did not stand a

chance. The arguments were attacked sometimes with able retorts, more often with fallacious reasoning, but it made no difference, men had had enough of special privilege and were determined to get rid of discrimination on the basis of property. Men said that they had a natural right to vote, but it only took a few words to ruin that argument utterly. Men said that they should not be governed without their consent but the others pointed to the negroes. Men said that they should not be taxed without being represented, but the others pointed to women. Men said that universal suffrage was a glorious ideal, but the others pointed to minors. Men said that they should be permitted to vote in order to defend their rights, but the others pointed to manifold benefits received from the government even by those who could not vote. Finally men said that they were going to vote anyhow, and the others threw up their hands in despair. The best talent in the country, profound arguments, historical evidence presented by the learned Adams, all the conservative forces of the state, could not stay the onward sweep of suffrage expansion. The only thing that accounts for it is a deep-seated, firm, but more or less unreasoning, conviction that all men should vote. Rude men from rural districts would stand helpless before the intellectual statesmen thundering at them in resounding periods. They would voice a few idle arguments and then vote on the strength of their inbred conviction. The most impressive thing about this entire movement toward broader suffrage is that men came to be filled with a fixed determination that as this country was a democracy all men should have a hand in running it. . . . The political thought of the past twenty years had brought them to a realization that they were part of the government, and now they wanted to get their hands in it.[16]

This instinctive move to broaden suffrage brought liberalization of state constitutions, but no voting reforms occurred at the federal level until the adoption of the Civil War Amendments to the United States Constitution. These amendments were designed to protect the liberties of the newly freed slaves, and civil libertarians were long delayed in sensing their greater potential for broadened suffrage. A century later, when the Fourteenth Amendment came to full flower, the radical thinking which overcame Massachusetts' property tests in 1820 was to gain a new vitality in the constitutional theorizing of the 1960s.

The Government Function Theory

It would seem that such ideas as "government by the people" would require that this theory be an expansive one in determining voting rights, but the opposite is nearer the truth. In Shepard's 1934 article, he described the government function theory as "generally accepted by contemporary political scientists," and then indicated its restrictive potential by describing it:

> The voter does not exercise a natural right when he casts his ballot, but performs a public governmental office. The electorate is not identical with the people, the sovereign authority in the state and the ultimate source of law; it is an organ of government, established, organized and determined by the law, which can, moreover, limit, expand or totally abolish it.[17]

Shepard went on to cite, as examples of justifiable limits on voting, the disfranchisement of criminals, paupers, and the insane and the imposition of educational and taxpaying qualifications—all designed to make the electorate "a more efficient organ of government." Exclusions of paupers and nontaxpayers have since fallen and others of these examples are in jeopardy.

The government function theory has elitist features which are incompatible with current egalitarian theories. The decision of the Supreme Court of California in *Otsuka v. Hite*[18] illustrates its erosion. It held that the state could not deny the vote to a convicted felon whose offense was resistance to the World War II draft for reasons of conscientious objection. The court reasoned that only "compelling state interests" can justify franchise exclusions and concluded that the only crimes for which a state can withhold the vote are those related to the integrity of the electoral process.

The implicit assumption of the government function theory is that certain classes of citizens are unfit to vote and that quality of the electoral process is endangered if they participate. The key to this fallacy is *Carrington v. Rash*,[19] in which the Supreme Court invalidated a Texas law which denied the vote to members of the United States armed forces who moved into the state, regardless of the *bona fides* or duration of their Texas residence and citizenship. In answer to a claim that disfranchisement of military residents was designed to prevent military "takeovers" of some communities, the Court said through Mr. Justice Stewart:

> But if they are in fact residents, with the intention of making Texas their home indefinitely, they, as all other qualified residents, have a right to an equal opportunity for political representation. . . . "Fencing out" from the franchise a sector of the population *because of the way they may vote* is constitutionally impermissible.[20]

The *Carrington* reasoning demolishes the government function theory. The Court is saying, in effect, that our democratic system assumes the risks that eligible citizens may not vote wisely and that the electorate may be an inefficient organ of government. This inherent flaw of democracy must be endured in many ways, and all disfranchisements of adult citizens based on fear of the way people may vote are destined to join poll taxes, property tests, and military exclusions in the trash heap of antidemocratic electoral devices.

The Ethical Theory

The view that voting is a form of personal expression and a means to moral self-realization adds little to the natural rights theory as an analytical tool. It is important, though, for its treatment of voting as a form of personal expression. If it is constitutionally protected as expression—on the same preferred basis as First Amendment rights of speech, religion, press, and assembly—then a constitutional breakthrough of the greatest magnitude has occurred. Recent decisions indicate this to be very close to the truth.

In voting cases, the Court now applies essentially the same "compelling interest" test which it uses in speech, religion, and association cases. The elevation of voting rights to the level of First Amendment rights is illustrated by the Court's mandate that Ohio place George C. Wallace's candidates for presidential elector on the ballot in 1968. The Court held that Ohio's exclusion of all third-party candidates unduly burdened rights of voting and association. The right of a significant political group to have an opportunity to vote for the candidate of their choice was reasoned to be within overlapping rights of individuals to associate for the advancement of political beliefs and their rights as voters to cast votes effectively, both of which were described as ranking "among our most precious freedoms."[21]

Although it overromanticizes voting to claim that it has great individual self-realization values, the Court recognized long ago that the right to vote is a "fundamental right, because preservative of all rights."[22] In a government "by the people," voting should be treated as the highest form of political expression and protected as zealously as the First Amendment's guarantees of other rights of personal expression and association. What Shepard called the "ethical theory" has a much higher claim to legal validity than the phrase connotes.

THE THEORY OF POLITICAL EQUALITY

The long delay in the flowering of the constitutional right to vote was caused largely by the absence of any clear underpinning in the text of the Constitution. In 1904 it could hardly be disputed as sound doctrine when the Supreme Court declared that the Constitution "does not confer the right of suffrage upon anyone."[23] As recently as 1959 Mr. Justice Douglas, in construing the term "right to vote" in Section 2 of the Fourteenth Amendment, reaffirmed that it meant the right "as established by the laws and constitution of the state."[24]

This was undoubtedly the intent of the framers of the Constitution. The only express requirement for popular elections in the original document was that the House of Representatives be elected by the people of the several states, which was accompanied by the provision that voters should have the "Qualifications requisite for Electors of the most numerous Branch of the State Legislature."[25] The President and Vice-President are chosen by electoral colleges composed of electors appointed in each state "in such manner as the Legislature thereof may direct."[26] Senators were chosen by state legislatures until 1913 when the Seventeenth Amendment brought popular election, but, like the provisions on House elections, the Amendment also referred to state law the determination of voting qualifications.

Of state election laws, as such, the original Constitution said nothing more than the quoted reference on House elections. This, and several other provisions, assumed that each state was to have an elected legislature. No other provision required that the new states establish popular elections except possibly the guaranty clause, which directs that "The United States shall guarantee to every State . . . a Republican form of Government."[27] This was the only express indication that state governments were to be representative of the people.

The guaranty clause has fared poorly as a protector of voting rights. The old holding of *Luther v. Borden*[28] that it is enforceable against the states only by Congress and the President is still given lip service by the Court.[29] While Mr. Justice Frankfurter had a point when he accused the Court majority of allowing litigation of guaranty clause claims in other guises in the legislative apportionment cases,[30] and Mr. Justice Douglas would overrule *Luther*,[31] and

other Justices sometimes cite the guaranty clause in their reasoning,[32] it is a dead letter in constitutional litigation. There is no good
reason why the Court should not draw upon the provision in deciding cases which are otherwise justiciable, but the guaranty clause
would still be of little real help in defining voting rights.

No one with a true knowledge of our history can contend that
the framers intended the guaranty clause, or any other, to impose
on the states anything approaching universal suffrage and voter
equality. One constitutional scholar who would treat the clause as
raising justiciable issues can go no farther than to say that it requires
a state legislature to be deemed "unrepublican" unless one house is
apportioned solely on population and the other is no less popularly
representative than the United States Senate or the legislature of
that state at time of its admission to the Union.[33]

The Civil War Amendments added the constitutional text
which was ultimately to free voting rights. It was inevitable that
when the nation resumed the task of reconstruction in the mid-
twentieth century and turned seriously to giving real meaning to the
concept of equality before the law, it would have revolutionary
effects upon laws which perpetuated inequality in political rights.
The equal protection clause as applied under the "one man–one
vote" doctrine has produced a new theory of voting rights which
partakes of both the natural-rights and ethical theories but is best
understood as a new theory of its own, couched in terms of political
equality. The right to vote now flourishes under the simple principle that, except as dictated by necessity, citizens should have equal
voices in the electoral process.

The Supreme Court's precedents offered little hint of the role
which equal protection was destined to play in the flowering of
voting rights. Its origins in the Civil War caused Mr. Justice Miller
to say for the Court in 1873:

> We doubt very much whether any action of a State not directed by
> way of discrimination against the negroes as a class, or on account of
> their race, will ever be held to come within the purview of this pro-
> vision.[34]

The Fifteenth Amendment was adequate to the upsetting of
overt racial discrimination in voting rights[35] and ultimately was to
provide the basis for congressional legislation dealing effectively
with covert and subtle forms of voting discrimination (a statutory
topic beyond the scope of this essay), but the Fourteenth Amend-

ment virtually lay dormant in this area. Indeed, it had little efficacy
in any area and was belittled in 1927 by Mr. Justice Holmes as "the
usual last resort of constitutional arguments."[36] In 1959, the Court
said that the Fourteenth Amendment allowed the states "broad
powers to determine the conditions under which the right of suffrage may be exercised."[37] The Court's customary deference to state
legislative judgments on the subject appeared to be an ample shelter
for most state differentiations in their citizens' rights to vote.

Then came *Baker v. Carr.*[38] Urban voters sued Tennessee election officials upon complaints which were held to state claims for
federal judicial relief because of "dilution and debasement" of
plaintiffs' voting rights by the malapportionment of their state
legislature in favor of rural voters. The majority opinion of Mr.
Justice Brennan held that the Fourteenth Amendment was violated
by Tennessee's laws and indicated that legislative apportionments
generally were to be adjudged under "well developed and familiar"[39] standards of equal protection. Justices Douglas, Clark, and
Stewart each indicated separately that such standards would not
require strict mathematical equality but only that apportionments
be justified upon some rational basis.

If *Baker's* signals had been accurate, and traditional standards
of equal protection had been applied, claims to voter equality
would have rested on a slender reed. Only two years earlier the
Court had summarized the general standard of equal protection:

> Although no precise formula has been developed, the Court has
> held that the Fourteenth Amendment permits the States a wide
> scope of discretion in enacting laws which affect some groups of
> citizens differently than others. The constitutional safeguard is
> offended only if the classification rests on grounds wholly irrelevant
> to the achievement of the State's objective. . . . A statutory dis-
> crimination will not be set aside if any state of facts reasonably may
> be conceived to justify it.[40]

Many understandably thought the relief granted in apportionment cases would be rather mild, because *Baker's* language so
clearly indicated that voter inequalities having rational bases would
be permitted. But they failed to take into account what Dean
Robert B. McKay has aptly called "the two faces of equal protection."[41] Where fundamental civil rights were involved, the Court
had not upheld state discriminations on mere showings of rationality but had applied much higher standards of judicial scrutiny.

Baker's equal protection signals were misleading on the ultimate remedy. When the Court decided the question of permissible apportionments on factors other than population, it launched a bold new doctrine. It went beyond the stricter face of equal protection and contained a new value of its own. By holding that both houses of a state legislature must be apportioned on the basis of population, the Court concluded that no factors based upon economics, geography, or political subdivisions could justify treating people unequally in the selection of their representatives. The Court enthroned a higher rationality than that embodied in any of its equal protection precedents. It properly recognized that other interests can be assigned legal cognizance in a popular democracy only as they serve *people*. If special weight is to be given to interests other than people, it must come through devices other than allowing minorities to control state legislatures.

Chief Justice Warren stated the guiding theories of both representative government and political equality when he said in *Reynolds v. Sims:*

> Legislators are elected by voters, not farms, or cities or economic interests. As long as ours is a representative form of government, and our legislatures are those instruments of government elected directly by and directly representative of the people, the right to elect legislators in a free and unimpaired fashion is a bedrock of our political system. . . . Representative government is in essence self-government through the medium of elected representatives of the people and each and every citizen has an inalienable right to full and effective participation in the political processes of his State's legislative bodies.[42]

The simple mathematical rule of *Reynolds* enabled the Court to clear much of the bramble from the "political thicket"[43] which Mr. Justice Frankfurter had accused it of entering. The result is an arithmetic majoritarianism which, as Robert G. Dixon, Jr., has developed, may defeat real *representation* of pluralistic interests in some circumstances.[44] Dixon identifies several "thorns" and unsettled issues remaining in the apportionment thicket, including: (1) permissible deviations from absolute arithmetic equality, (2) gerrymandering, (3) determining the apportionment base, (4) denial of representation to minority blocs by multimember districts, (5) local governing bodies, and (6) the electoral college system of presidential elections.

The Court has made progress on Dixon's first-listed thorn by refusing to permit a *de minimis* concept to allow any particular range of deviation from the mathematical ideal.[45] Determining the apportionment base, i.e., whether numbers either of persons or of registered voters may be used, has not been too troublesome.[46] The local-government thorn has been cut by the simplistic extension of the "one man–one vote" principle to all popularly elected governmental agencies. In this regard, the Court stated the final word in applying the rule to a junior college district:

> [W]henever a state or local government decides to select persons by popular election to perform governmental functions, the Equal Protection Clause of the 14th Amendment requires that each qualified voter must be given an equal opportunity to participate in that election, and when members of an elected body are chosen from separate districts, each district must be established on a basis which will insure, as far as is practicable, that equal numbers of voters can vote for proportionally equal numbers of officials.[47]

Some thorny brambles remain. The Court has flatly refused to use its powers to remedy the state-law features of the electoral college system,[48] a national counterpart of the Georgia county-unit system which fell early to "one man–one vote."[49] State-unit laws effectively award all of a state's electoral votes to the winner of the barest plurality of its popular votes. This is not the only undemocratic feature of presidential elections, the other being the constitutional weighting of electoral votes among states, and the entire problem can best be settled by constitutional amendment for direct popular election. Nothing else will perfect "one man–one vote" and implement voter equality at the presidential level. (The United States Senate is the only legislative body outside the fold, but its nonpopulation apportionment is immutable. The controlling provision is expressly made unamendable by the Constitution.[50])

The irresistible legislative tendency to gerrymander districts and group voters so as to favor particular parties, candidates, or ethnic groups has not yet been affected by the egalitarian sweep of "one man–one vote."[51] Although *Gomillion v. Lightfoot*[52] pointed the way toward alleviating some racial gerrymandering by upsetting a legislative alteration of municipal boundaries which was designed to fence out black voters, a majority of the Supreme Court refused, in *Wright v. Rockefeller*,[53] to act against congressional districting which quite clearly sought to ghettoize some New York districts into white and nonwhite constituencies. There are countervailing forces at work in this vexing area, and civil libertarians frequently support racially conscious districting which enables the ghetto to be represented by one of its own. The ultimate outcome of this sharp conflict of competing values cannot be predicted.

The multimember district problem is closely related. At-large elections of an entire city's legislative delegation can mean that minority groups or parties are totally disabled from electing a single representative of their choosing. In *Fortson v. Dorsey*,[54] the Court held that such districts were not invalid per se but left open the question of how such districts would be treated upon a showing that they were used to submerge political minorities.

A three-judge federal district court found that this showing had been made with respect to the multimember districts in which Indianapolis voters chose their Indiana state legislators. The at-large elections were found to cause "unjustifiable minimization" of the voting power of ghetto Negroes. The court did not specify single-member districts as the remedy, but it indicated a strong preference by noting the existing evil as "the inability of the Negro voters in the Center Township Ghetto to be assured of the opportunity of voting for prospective legislators of their choice, and the absence of any particular legislator accountable to the described voters for his legislative record."[55]

The only apparent alternative to single-member districts in this situation is the multimember district accompanied by candidate residence requirements. This device was approved by the Supreme Court in *Dusch v. Davis*,[56] and, somewhat surprisingly, there is no requirement that such residence districts be equal in population. In *Dusch*, the Court sustained at-large elections of an eleven-member city council; four could live anywhere in the city, but each of the other seven had to live in a different one of the city's seven boroughs. Thus each borough was guaranteed a resident on the council although their populations varied from about 300 to 38,000. The Court unanimously held that the "one man–one vote" principle was satisfied; it rejected arguments that a councilman elected at large should be treated as representing only the borough of his residence and applauded the plan as "a detente between urban and rural communities that may be important in resolving the complex problems of the modern megalopolis in relation to the city, the suburbia, and the rural countryside."

Presumably, the Court will uphold similar rural-urban "*dé-*

tentes" at the state legislative level. *Dusch's* acceptance of rational malapportionment of legislators' residence districts based upon an accommodation of competing group or geographic interests seems to be at odds with *Reynolds'* insistence that it is people, not trees or acres, which legislators represent. The importance of *Dusch* escaped most apportionment-watchers. It may signal an important retreat from the full egalitarianism of *Reynolds* and foreshadow a return to differentiation according to rational factors other than people in the practice, if not the theory, of legislative apportionment.

In only one other major case has the Supreme Court wavered from full voter equality in testing electoral arrangements. This is *Fortson v. Morris,*[57] in which a 5 to 4 majority of the Court upheld Georgia's election of a governor by its legislature when no candidate received a majority of the popular vote. The fact that this permitted the election of a runner-up in the popular vote was immaterial to the majority which reasoned that a state could permit a legislature to elect its governor in the first instance and could therefore use popular election as a mere nominating process to determine candidates from which the legislature must choose.

As a precedent the Georgia case operates within an extremely narrow area. Its greatest value may be in the eloquent analysis of the constitutional right to vote which it brought from the dissenting Justice Fortas. He first questioned the majority's major premise:

> [I]f the people of Georgia . . . should adopt a constitutional amendment to provide for election of their Governor by the legislature —or for selection of the upper house of their legislature by their Governor . . . I do not believe that the constitutionality of these measures could be cavalierly assumed. Perhaps this Court's voting rights cases could not so easily be nullified. Their meaning and thrust are perhaps deeper than the mechanics of the tally. They are, one may hope, not merely much ado about form. They represent, one has been led to believe, an acknowledgment that the republican form of government guaranteed by the Constitution, read in light of the General Welfare Clause, the guaranties of equal protection of the laws and the privileges and immunities of citizens of the United States, requires something more than an adherence to form.[58]

Fortas found it unnecessary to decide the intriguing hypothetical question of outright legislative election of a governor because he could concede the majority's premise *arguendo* and still disagree with their conclusion. The proposition that a popular-vote loser can be made the electoral winner by majority vote of a legislature was totally at variance with Fortas' view of the underlying voting rights which were at stake. His analysis seems sure to become accepted constitutional doctrine someday and merits further quotation:

> It is not merely the casting of the vote or its mechanical counting that is protected by the Constitution. It is the function—the office —the effect given to the vote, that is protected.
>
> A vote is not an object of art. It is the sacred and most important instrument of democracy and of freedom. In simple terms, the vote is meaningless—it no longer serves the purpose of the democratic society—unless it, taken in the aggregate with the votes of other citizens, results in effecting the will of those citizens provided that they are more numerous than those of differing views. That is the meaning and effect of the great constitutional decisions of this Court.
>
> In short, we must be vigilant to see that our Constitution protects not just the right to cast a vote, but the right to have a vote fully serve its purpose. If the vote cast by all of those who favor a particular candidate exceeds the number cast in favor of a rival, the result is constitutionally protected as a matter of equal protection of the laws from nullification except by the voters themselves. The candidate receiving more votes than any other must receive the office unless he is disqualified on some constitutionally permissible basis or unless, in a runoff or some other type of election, the *people* properly and regularly, by their votes, decide differently.[59]

Equality of votes and voters seems to dictate acceptance of the Fortas view. To permit an outvoted minority to choose a governor because they are joined by a majority of their state's legislators may be supportable under some theory, but it is one which subordinates the concept of political equality and the "one man–one vote" line of cases.

The cases discussed to this point under the equality theory have involved electoral systems and procedures. The final topic, voting qualifications, is more easily analyzed and understood as an area in which equality should be the keystone. The notion that all those subject to a government should participate in choosing its officials has already been shown to be one which has always had an instinctive appeal to the great bulk of the American people. But again, the judicial issues are not so simple. Mr. Justice Marshall, in dissent, in *Hall v. Beals,* is believed to have accurately stated the point to which the Warren Court's decisions have brought the constitutional law of voting qualifications. He said:

> [O]nce a state has determined that a decision is to be made by popular vote, it may exclude persons from the franchise only upon a showing of a compelling interest, and even then only when the exclusion is the least restrictive method of achieving the desired purpose.[60]

Thus, the poll tax qualification,[61] requirements that voters in school board elections be parents or property owners,[62] limiting voting on bond issues to property owners,[63] and exclusion of military residents[64] have all been stricken because of the absence of any showing of compelling state interests. In a prelude to extensions of this rule, the Supreme Court of California held in *Otsuka v. Hite*[65] that disfranchisement of conscientious objectors to the draft served no such interest.

The net result should be appealing to all those who truly believe in democratic self-government. Political equality requires as the ideal that everyone be permitted to vote on an equal basis. We depart from this ideal only for compelling reasons. Some age qualifications are essential, but it may be questioned whether the denial of the vote to citizens over eighteen who are treated as adults for most other purposes serves any compelling state interest.[66] Lengthy residency requirements beyond those necessary for election administration are similarly suspect, and at least two justices are waiting to so hold.[67] Treating convicted felons who have otherwise discharged their debt to society as unfit to vote seems to serve an interest considerably less than compelling.

We are nearing a constitutional rule on voting rights which comes as near political equality as electoral necessities permit. This is possible largely because the Warren Court finally gave true meaning to equal protection in its decisions of the 1960's. Once equality was unleashed it had to be carried this far.

The chain of reasoning now seems indisputable: (1) voting is prescribed by law; (2) laws must satisfy the equal protection clause of the Fourteenth Amendment; (3) equal protection in politics requires that individual people be treated the same in the political process. This higher humanistic rationality is the only course which is really true to basic democratic ideology. It settles our theory of voting and meets the challenges issued by a troubled political scientist in 1912 and 1934.

NOTES

1. Shepard, "The Theory of the Nature of the Suffrage," Proceedings of the American Political Science Association, Ninth Annual Meeting, at 103 (1913).

2. Shepard, *"Suffrage,"* 14 *Encyclopaedia of the Social Sciences* 447, 450 (1934).

3. *Id.* at 447.

4. The Fourteenth Amendment makes all persons born or naturalized in the United States citizens of the United States and of the state where they reside. The term "full citizenship" is therefore warranted despite the presence of decreasing numbers of unnaturalized aliens.

5. Twining v. New Jersey, 211 U.S. 78, 97 (1908) (dictum); United States v. Original Knights of the Ku Klux Klan, 250 F. Supp. 330 (E.D. La. 1965).

6. Reynolds v. Sims, 377 U.S. 533, 567 (1964).

7. 387 U.S. 253 (1967).

8. *Ibid.*

9. Kramer v. Union Free School Dist., 395 U.S. 621, 627 (1969).

10. K. Porter, *A History of Suffrage in the United States* 112–31 (1969 ed.).

11. Harper v. Virginia State Bd. of Elections, 383 U.S. 663, 666 (1966).

12. Glisson v. Mayor and Councilmen of Savannah Beach, 346 F.2d 135 (5th Cir. 1965). See also Spahos v. Mayor and Councilmen of Savannah Beach, 207 F. Supp. 688 (S.D. Ga.), *aff'd per curiam,* 371 U.S. 206 (1962).

13. 395 U.S. 701 (1969).

14. City of Phoenix v. Kolodziejski, 399 U.S. 204 (1970). The Court struck the voting restriction by a 5 to 3 vote.

15. *E.g.,* Reynolds v. Sims, 377 U.S. 533, 565 (1964).

16. Porter, *supra* note 10, at 70–72.

17. Shepard, *supra* note 2, at 449.

18. 51 Cal. Rptr. 284, 414 P.2d 412 (1966).

19. 380 U.S. 89 (1965).

20. *Id.* at 94. Emphasis added.

21. Williams v. Rhodes, 393 U.S. 23, 30 (1968).

22. Yick Wo v. Hopkins, 118 U.S. 356, 370 (1886).

23. Pope v. Williams, 193 U.S. 621, 633 (1904).

24. Lassiter v. Northampton County Bd. of Elections, 360 U.S. 45, 51 (1959).

25. The main provision of Article I, Section 2, that representatives be chosen by "the People of the several States," was the basis of the Supreme Court's holding in Wesberry v. Sanders, 376 U.S. 1 (1964), that congressional districts must satisfy the "one man–one vote" principle.

26. U.S. Const. art. II, §1.

27. *Id.,* art. IV, §4.

28. 48 U.S. (7 How.) 1 (1849).

29. "[T]he Guaranty Clause is not a repository of judicially manageable standards. . . ." Baker v. Carr, 369 U.S. 186, 223 (1962).

30. *Id.* at 297.

31. *Id.* at 242–43.

32. *See, e.g.,* the Fortas dissent quoted on page 189, *infra.*

33. Bonfield, "Baker v. Carr: New Light on the Constitutional Guarantee of Republican Government," 50 *California Law Review* 245 (1962).

34. Slaughter-House Cases, 83 U.S. 36, 81 (1873).

35. *E.g.,* Smith v. Allwright, 321 U.S. 649 (1944); Gomillion v. Lightfoot, 364 U.S. 339 (1960).

36. Buck v. Bell, 274 U.S. 200, 208 (1927).

37. Lassiter v. Northampton County Bd. of Elections, 360 U.S. 45, 51 (1959).

38. 369 U.S. 186 (1962).

39. *Id.* at 226.

40. McGowan v. Maryland, 366 U.S. 420, 425–26 (1961).

41. R. McKay, *Reapportionment: The Law and Politics of Equal Representation* 169–80 (1965).

42. 377 U.S. 533, 562–65 (1964).

43. Frankfurter coined the term "political thicket" in Colegrove v. Green, 328 U.S. 549, 556 (1946), and added the metaphor "mathematical quagmire" in Baker v. Carr, 369 U.S. 186, 268 (dissenting opinion).

44. R. Dixon, *Democratic Representation: Reapportionment in Law and Politics* 436–582 (1968).

45. Kirkpatrick v. Preisler, 394 U.S. 526 (1969).

46. *See* Burns v. Richardson, 384 U.S. 73 (1966).

47. Hadley v. Junior College Dist. of Metropolitan Kansas City, 397 U.S. 50 (1970).

48. Williams v. Virginia State Bd. of Elections, 288 F. Supp. 622 (E.D. Va. 1968), *aff'd,* 393 U.S. 320 (1969); Delaware v. New York, 385 U.S. 895 (1966). For details of the latter action, *see* Pierce, "The Electoral College Goes to Court," *The Reporter,* Oct. 6, 1966, p. 34.

49. Gray v. Sanders, 372 U.S. 368 (1963).

50. The article on the amending procedure concludes: ". . . and Provided . . . that no State, without its Consent, shall be deprived of its equal Suffrage in the Senate." U.S. Const., art. V.

51. Congressional-district gerrymandering favoring a party was challenged in Wells v. Rockefeller, 394 U.S. 542 (1969), but the Court invalidated the districting on other grounds. On remand and after responsive redistricting by the New York legislature, gerrymandering has become the sole issue. Subsequent proceedings could clarify this problem.

52. 364 U.S. 339 (1960).

53. 376 U.S. 52 (1964).

54. 379 U.S. 433 (1965).

55. Chavis v. Whitcomb, 305 F. Supp. 1364, 1386 (S.D. Ind. 1969), *prob. juris. noted,* 397 U.S. 984 (1970).

56. 387 U.S. 112, 117 (1967).

57. 385 U.S. 231 (1966).

58. *Id.* at 249.

59. *Id.* at 250.

60. 396 U.S. 45, 52 (1969) (dissenting opinion).

61. Harper v. Virginia State Bd. of Elections, 383 U.S. 663 (1966).

62. Kramer v. Union Free School Dist., 395 U.S. 621 (1969).

63. Cipriano v. City of Houma, 395 U.S. 701 (1969).

64. Carrington v. Rash, 380 U.S. 89 (1965).

65. 51 Cal. Rptr. 284, 414 P.2d 412 (1966).

66. An issue which may be settled by congressional legislation implementing the equal protection clause under the principle of Katzenbach v. Morgan, 384 U.S. 641 (1966).

67. *See* Hall v. Beals, 396 U.S. 45, 51 (1969) (Marshall and Brennan, JJ., dissenting).

THE RIGHT TO PARTICIPATE

HOWARD I. KALODNER

NO OBSERVER OF THE POLITICAL, SOCIAL, ECONOMIC, and most important, psychological life of the United States as we enter the decade of the seventies can seriously doubt that we are in the midst of a struggle within our boundaries which poses far more of a threat to the survival of our country than any menace, real or imagined, from a foreign nation.

That struggle goes on on many fronts and on a variety of levels —attacks from the political right and the political left; attacks by the young and by the black and brown minorities against the Establishment, and more recently, retributive action by the Establishment. It appears, on the surface at least, that the struggle is both issue-oriented and structure-oriented. Should schools and other service institutions of government be centralized or decentralized; should racial integration be compelled or should racial segregation merely be proscribed; should housing and planning decisions be made by municipal governmental bodies or by bodies chosen by those who live in directly affected areas; should the design and execution of grant programs intended to eliminate or ameliorate poverty be the responsibility of government or of the poor themselves; should university decisions be made by the trustees and administration or by the students and faculty.

Howard I. Kalodner is Professor of Law at New York University School of Law, former Counsel to Mayor John V. Lindsay's Advisory Committee on School Decentralization and the Citizens Committee for School Decentralization, and an editor of materials on urban housing and the legal aspects of public education.

The success of government under law as a principle of governance depends upon voluntary acceptance of that principle by most
of a nation's citizenry, but it also depends, and perhaps more fundamentally, upon a willing acceptance of those institutions of government vested with the authority to enforce existing law and to
change the law. The structuring of new concepts of citizen participation in governmental decision-making, including the possibility of
new units of government, may be a prerequisite to the restoration of
the principle of governance under law.

Discussions of citizen participation and community control begin too often with the movement in the late 1950's and 1960's in the
areas of education, housing, and antipoverty efforts. The proper
perspective would be based on an inquiry into the changing role of
government during the twentieth century. Government has ceased
to be merely the formal mode by which individuals enforce their
private arrangements or the technique through which we protect
against antisocial conduct or invasion from abroad. Government
has become a regulator and at least would-be controller of every
aspect of our economic lives and, moreover, has taken on the task
of defining the areas in which certain minimum standards of well-
being shall be provided. It is obvious that the government established in the eighteenth and nineteenth centuries could not have
undergone these basic changes in function without corresponding
changes in structure.

The first revolution in structure occurred simultaneously with
one of the great changes in function. In the aftermath of the de-
pression of the 1930's, the federal government sought ways to in-
tensify its regulation of the economy, and agencies were created with
considerable regulatory power. Although these agencies had earlier
models, their numbers and breadth of function must be viewed as
a revolution in structure. But their organizational principle did
not comport with the American ideal. They were legislators in all
but the most technical legal sense, but they were not elected by the
people. Their members were appointed by the President, though he
had no veto over their decisions. They bore some analogy to the
federal courts in their composition, but operated without the traditional constraints of judicial bodies.

Procedural safeguards were therefore created to secure for those
affected by agency action a formal mode for influencing, or seeking
to influence, agency decision. That this development was not accompanied by massive public involvement must be due at least in

part to the fact that the influence in Congress of those most directly affected was sufficient to achieve their goals through traditional (though not formal) political means—lobbying, contributions to political parties, and so forth. The procedures adopted—formal hearings in particular—reflect the confidence which those regulated felt in their power to influence results without securing control.

The second revolution in government function, the conversion to a welfare state, began in the same period, but only in the past two decades have its full social and legal implications begun to be recognized. The current demands for citizen participation in government and the creation of new government entities ("community control") in large part represent an effort to fashion new structures in response to this revolution in governmental function.

Of course, other factors reinforce the urgency with which change is being insisted upon by those dependent on the promises of the welfare state: first, the insistence by the blacks that the fulfillment of past promises is long overdue; second, the deterioration of older cities as a result of an inability over the last twenty-five years to maintain necessary capital investment; third, the flight to the suburbs of much of the white middle class, thus depriving the cities of revenues for operating expenses while those costs are rising as a result of the entry of persons needing greater municipal services, as well as the increased recognition by the government that those services are an essential part of governmental operation; fourth, the increasing affluence of the country, which has made the failure to meet its promises of a better life for all of its citizens appear more arbitrary, discriminatory, and unjustifiable.

It is too simplistic to suggest that we are witnessing merely another cycle in the Jeffersonian and Hamiltonian theses, merely another phase in the conflict between power in the people and power in an elitist government.[1] It is also too simplistic to suggest that a "social science idea" underlies the struggle for some fundamental realignment of the ways in which decisions are made or in the bodies which make them.[2]

The purpose of this essay is to inquire into the goals of those who demand restructuring, to analyze alternative routes through which legitimate goals might be achieved, and to consider how far we have gone and speculate on what our next directions will and should be.

The rhetoric of "citizen participation" and "community control" presents an immediate barrier to analysis. It is clear, of course, that the two concepts must embody some notion other than the exercise of the right to vote for President, congressmen, governors, state legislators, mayors, and city councilmen. It should also be clear that although the terms are not synonymous they do represent points along a continuum—a continuum of decision-making. The first revolution referred to above—the revolution in regulation—has provided certain precedents along the early part of this continuum.

For example, government at many levels is required to make its actions public. Such publicity at least provides the necessary basis, though of course not the opportunity, for objection to government action. Lest it be forgotten that this concept of publication of government action remains less than fully executed, "a general philosophy of full agency disclosure" by the federal government required the adoption of a public "right-to-know" law in 1966.[3] Ramsey Clark, then Attorney General, wrote of this statute:

> If the government is to be truly of, by and for the people, the people must know in detail the activities of government. Nothing so diminishes democracy as secrecy. Self-government, the maximum participation of the citizenry in affairs of state, is meaningful only with an informed public. How can we govern ourselves if we know not how we govern? Never was it more important than in our times of mass society, when government affects each individual in so many ways, that the right of the people to know the actions of their government be secure.[4]

But parents in some school systems still do not have access to records maintained by schools on their own children;[5] applicants for public housing find it difficult to determine the precise standards or criteria that leave them on the waiting list while others are accepted,[6] and New York City councilmen had to resort to court to obtain a copy of the New York City Master Plan proposed by the City Planning Commission.[7]

In defining the perimeters of the right to participate, in determining the cutoff point at which the traditional insulated government function will begin and citizen imput terminate, it is well to remember that the struggle for citizen information, let alone participation, has not yet been won.

A second precedent along the continuum of citizen participation may be characterized as consultation, or the right to express one's views *prior* to final governmental determination. The Administrative Procedure Act of 1964 not only contained certain provisions antedating the 1966 Information Act relating to publication but also provisions requiring agency regulations to be published for comment prior to promulgation.[8]

The opportunity to be heard does not, of course, guarantee that what is said will influence governmental action. Political influence, in the broadest sense, or the persuasiveness of evidence or reasoning may from time to time prevail. Large parts of our society accordingly lack confidence in the device of an opportunity to be heard.

Thus in the field of education, in theory boards of education act at public meetings where there is an opportunity for citizen expression. In the field of housing and planning, either state or federal law, or both, require that at least one set of hearings be held prior to significant government action.[9] But until recently, in neither these nor other contexts has the law assured that the opportunity to be heard will come at a time when it might influence decision; the decision is generally taken *prior* to the opportunity to be heard, and the opportunity is therefore a hypocritical indulgence in formalism.[10]

There are many areas of government activity in which there is not even that formal possibility. Two recent cases in the field of housing are suggestive.

In one, a court was requested to order the Secretary of Housing and Urban Development to conduct a hearing at which the plaintiffs would have an opportunity to protest an urban renewal project prior to the Secretary's final judgment that the project was eligible for federal funding under the Urban Renewal Act of 1949. The court rejected the assertion that a formal hearing was required by statute or the Constitution, but it proceeded to say:

> However, the demands of due process do imply that the plaintiffs should be afforded an appropriate procedural opportunity to present their claims to the Secretary. Of course, if that opportunity is to be adequate or meaningful, it must be made available prior to the Secretary's decision to authorize federal funds for the challenged project.[11]

In the second case,[12] the court was asked to enjoin the funding of a middle-income housing project. The court stated that although Title I of the Housing Act of 1949 explicitly required public hearings only prior to the acquisition of property in an urban renewal area, the purpose was to "subject to public discussion and criticism of, as well as participation in the local authority's decision to proceed with projects designed to receive federal funding." From this it followed that any significant change in the plan after the first hearings were held and after land had already been acquired would necessitate another hearing at which affected residents "could challenge the local officials' decision." The plaintiffs failed to secure an injunction, despite the failure to provide a hearing after a plan change, because the court did not regard the change as significant. Nevertheless, the principle established by the decision is important.

Judicial reluctance to demand public hearings where not required by statute of course persists. In a recent New York case[13] the court refused to invalidate an increase in transit fares challenged on the ground, among others, that no public hearings had been held prior to the increase. Although it sustained the increase, the court stated that the

> right to a public hearing . . . cannot cavalierly be dismissed as an ethereal goal or an impalpable principle of law, abstractly appealing only to an inquisitive segment of the public. On the contrary, it goes to the heart of the fundamental fairness which is required of all governmental agencies, officers and employees when dealing with the citizens of the State or their affairs.

A further step along the path of increasing citizen participation is the requirement, sometimes imposed on governments by statute, that citizens affected by governmental action be consulted prior to final decision. Unfortunately, the experience of urban citizens—and not only minority groups—has been that such provisions in the law are diluted or rendered meaningless in practice. Perhaps worse, citizens have discovered that the use of advisory groups has been mere window dressing to provide an air of legitimacy to public action. This experience has characterized the housing field in connection with the citizens' advisory committees which for years were required to be established city-wide as part of a workable program; it has also characterized citizen participation in the administration of educational systems in some large cities. Thus in New York City, prior to the enactment of new legislation, there were local school boards which were to be "advisory only." A study by the Women's City Club of New York concluded:

> There is already some evidence that frustration and a feeling of impotence have been responsible for some resignations from the boards.

> If they are not given what the members can regard as satisfying and
> meaningful functions to perform it will be impossible to continue
> to get citizens of high calibre to be willing to serve.[14]

Perhaps even more revealing is one of the specific recommendations of the Women's City Club: "Communications sent by local
school boards of professional staff offices at headquarters should
always at least be acknowledged."

The Final Report of the Advisory Committee on Decentralization, submitted to the Board of Education of the City of New York
in July 1968, reported that the central suggestion of the chairmen
of the local school boards was that the statutory phrase "in an advisory capacity only" be deleted and the boards "be invested with
real power over personnel, budget, and other matters."[15]

Although it may be unrealistic historically, it is interesting intellectually to consider the chairmen's recommendations. How had
we reached the point at which the opportunity to advise before decisions are made is so sharply distinguished from "real power"?
And, with respect to public-hearing requirements, why do so many
of our citizens regard them as a sham when they have so often been
used in other parts of the society? Does the experience of our welfare
state suggest that government can circumvent the consultative device whenever it is in the hands of those who lack the power to
elect? If this is the case, then to what extent should the defect be
remedied, not by abandonment of the consultative device, but
rather by deeper inquiry into the lack of political power which inhibits its effective exercise?

Any analysis of the political structure of American society might
draw an interesting parallel between the real, as opposed to the
theoretical, power of disadvantaged racial minorities and of students
on university campuses. The parallel in modes of protest and goals
is unmistakable. The university student historically has had no
formal role in the selection of those who govern his conduct and
control his life. Racial minorities have, of course, a formal role
through elections. But the distinction has not been meaningful, at
least not until recent times. Neither group has had a real impact on
the selection of those who control the processes of their respective
governments.

Assuming that a fundamental alteration in political power is
not imminent, there may yet be devices which could strengthen the
consultative role as a vehicle for participation by the politically

powerless. Suppose, for example, that a public officer in receipt of citizen "advice" were required to express in writing his reasons for rejecting or modifying the advice received. Even if we assume a lack of real judicial review, the obligation to meet advice with reason would unquestionably have an impact upon the character of the decisions made. The assumption underlying this conclusion should be made clear: what has prejudiced so many citizens against the advisory or consultative role is not so much that their advice has been rejected as that it has been ignored.

Another test for a somewhat altered form of citizen advisory role is now being undertaken in urban redevelopment through the Project Area Committees which are required for urban renewal areas,[16] through the "widespread citizen participation" provision for neighborhoods receiving federal funds under the Demonstration Cities and Metropolitan Development Act of 1965,[17] and through the requirement of "maximum feasible participation" of tenants in the development and operation of tenant service programs in public housing.[18]

These statutory and administrative provisions appear to contemplate some joint planning between the government and potentially affected citizens. The Department of Housing and Urban Development explains its view of the statutory mandate for widespread citizen participation in Model Cities areas as follows:

> The quality of life in American cities cannot be improved unless people of all classes, races and ethnic groups, and public officials on all levels of government, create processes and mechanisms for assessing problems, developing strategies and planning and implementing corrective actions together.[19]

The difficulty inherent in defining the joint planning arrangement, if this in fact was what HUD contemplated, was made clear in a recent statement by a HUD Model Cities official:

> The residents of the Model Neighborhood are required by Model Cities policy to have access to and capability in decision-making. Any local Model Cities effort which does not afford an effective role to persons affected by the program does not meet Model Cities standards. Any local effort, however, which results in abdication by local government of its administrative and policy-making responsibility also fails to meet program standards.[20]

The political ineffectiveness of the lay citizenry—in planning, housing, education, and other fields—is exacerbated by the fact that decisions on some basic policy issues purport to be matters for expert determination rather than lay judgment. This conflict between technocracy or expertise on the one hand and democracy on the other invites a broad analysis, beyond the scope of this essay. But from our present perspective, it seems plain that the elevation of expert over lay judgment contains a severe threat to citizen participation in decision-making.

In the Economic Opportunity Act of 1964 the Community Action Programs were described as those "developed, conducted, and administered with the maximum feasible participation of residents of the areas and members of the groups served." The Model Cities program rests on a statutory formula which calls for "widespread citizen participation," presumably a step away from the "control" pole of the continuum and back toward the "advisory" pole. The experience under the Community Action Programs is not yet fully documented, but Daniel Moynihan's conclusions about their effectiveness—which he ties to the "maximum feasible participation" standard—were critical to the point of despair:

> Seemingly it comes to this. Over and again, the attempt by official and quasi-official agencies . . . to organize poor communities led first to the radicalization of the middle-class persons who began the effort; next to a certain amount of stirring among the poor, but accompanied by heightened racial antagonism *on the part of the poor* if they happened to be black; next to retaliation from the larger white community; whereupon it would emerge that the community action agency, which had talked so much, been so much in the headlines, promised so much in the way of changes in the fundamentals of things, was powerless. A creature of a Washington bureaucracy, subject to discontinuance without notice.[21]

Moynihan is not wholly explicit as to why the early efforts of the Community Action Programs, resting as they did on a philosophy of maximizing participation of the poor in both planning and execution, were an apparent failure. He says:

> It may be that the poor are never "ready" to assume power in an advanced society: the exercise of power in an effective manner is an ability acquired through apprenticeship and seasoning. Thrust on an individual or a group, the results are often painful to observe, and when what in fact is conveyed is not power, but a kind of playacting at power, the results can be absurd.[22]

This conclusion leaves open at least two critical questions. First, what might be the result if the power conveyed is real, and not a "playacting at power"? Second, if the results of a thrusting of "power" are "painful to observe" when the recipient is inexperienced in power, does the fault lie in the recipient or in a societal failure to prepare? Moreover, is the grant of power, by which Moynihan appears to mean ultimate control, an appropriate beginning point for a change in the locus of governmental decision-making?

It may be that our clearest learning on these and related questions may derive from recent New York legislation calling for the creation of locally elected community school boards in New York City.[23] This law is now being implemented by the election of thirty-one community school boards which will exercise some, but not all, of the power previously held by the appointed central board of education.

As has been true in all the evolutionary stages in shifting power away from central bodies in cities, the shift called for by the New York legislation contains ambiguities which make impossible any simple conclusion about what body has the ultimate "power" to decide any given question. The answer will lie as much in politics as in law. Nevertheless, the development of the New York legislation is instructive to any student of citizen participation and community control.

The very drive toward community control of the schools represented a failure of the techniques of advice and consultation as a mode for citizen participation. If there had ever been serious consideration, by those seeking a systematic change, of the possibility of joint planning and operation of the system, shared by local and central bodies, it is not a matter of public record. Surely this reflects an organic fault in the central body, which could not command even this degree of confidence by its constituency.

The legislature's choice must be characterized primarily as one contemplating a kind of joint power—the central board retains the power to make policies binding the community school boards,[24] and the chancellor (the senior professional officer in the new structure) may make system-wide regulations consistent with such policies, for violations of which he may impose sanctions against community boards.[25]

A second critical aspect of the New York school legislation is

that where the bureaucratic professional interests were most profound—in the hiring, promotion, transfer, and discipline of personnel—the functions of the community school boards are nar-
rowest.[26]

Third, the community control structure was system-wide, suggesting that if, as Moynihan believes, a sociological theory of
alienation from society really underlies theories of community organization and control, then that alienation is felt today by a wide
spectrum of residents, not just by the poor, or the black or other
minorities.

Fourth, the technique of selecting members of the community
school boards appears not to reflect any understanding of the underlying reasons for public demands for changes in the power
structure. The legislation contained at least two significant faults.
First, all persons were required to run district-wide in districts that
had between 75,000 and 100,000 eligible voters. (The district-wide
election was presumably dictated by the selection of the Hare
system of proportional representation, a system so complex that
only the sophisticated can understand it.) Second, the election provisions contained no device to ensure that control of community
boards would rest in persons selected by those most directly affected
by school policy—parents of children currently enrolled in school.[27]
Unfortunately, a recent decision of the Supreme Court may have
foreclosed such a system before it was even attempted.[28]

The result of these two legislative judgments was predictable.
Control of the boards was bound to go to those who were best organized to bring out a disciplined vote. Not surprisingly, the first
round of elections appear to give maximum representation to those
favoring aid to parochial schools and to school-professional groups.[29]

The demand for change in school structure arose from its un-
responsiveness, and the word most frequently heard in three years
of New York debate about school decentralization was "accountability." For example, Dr. Preston Wilcox said the following in
connection with a dispute at a Harlem school:

> But what this experimental program offers is the possibility that, in
> at least one school in one community, the school administrators and
> teachers will be made accountable to the community, and the com-
> munity made obligated to them, in such a way that responsibility
> for successes and failures is shared.[30]

But the only electorate which could hold a school board accountable on a continuing basis was the electorate of parents; in bypassing that electorate the legislature was bound to dilute the effectiveness of structural change in bringing about accountability.[31]
Similarly, a district-wide vote was bound to result in an inability to
identify who was representing whom, a fault which will become
clearer as the new community boards begin to act.

The vote in the community school board elections was markedly
larger than in the elections of Model Cities Committees or the
various poverty agencies under the Community Action Programs.
A turnout of about 14 percent of eligible voters in the school election compares, for example, with the 2 to 5 percent in poverty
agency elections. But the vote could hardly be said to have been im-
pressively large. Those who were most in favor of community control boycotted the elections on the grounds of unfairness in the
electoral system and the failure of the legislation to turn over
plenary powers to the community school boards.[32]

If there is an intellectual fault in all of this, it could be in a too-
ready adoption of new structures to meet problems that may be
endemic to government itself. To deal with the failures of the
electoral process by calling for elections must seem just a little
absurd. To establish structures that are precisely like their larger
counterparts except for a lack of power over basic resource allocation cannot help but raise the question whether the initial difficulties were over something other than size. If existing institutions
were flawed by their failure to be popularly accepted, should it be
assumed that new institutions—identical but smaller—will be more
likely to find that willing acceptance of the exercise of power so
necessary to the functioning of a democracy?

The suggestion of this essay is that recent experiments in the
creation of new levels of government may fail, and that even as they
are pursued, we hope with increasing sensitivity, it is necessary to
understand the possibility of failure.

They may fail because American citizens today actively focus
on particular issues or on persons who have the ability to instill
confidence by their very appearance (mostly on television) regardless of what they say. Thus one could anticipate an uninterested
electorate in an election of a local board to control, for example,
pickup of neighborhood garbage, but a substantial public protest
if such pickups were terminated or curtailed. Since response is

greater to issues than to institutions, it is when institutions refuse or are unable to respond to citizen views on a given issue that they are attacked and demands are heard for reform and restructuring. Moreover, the impatient modern public seldom views seriously promises of future willingness to listen and respond by those who were indifferent in the past.

In short, experience if not logic dictates that increased citizen participation and community control must be defined not only in structural terms—whether it be the election of a community school board or the creation of a "little city hall"—but also in terms of more complex rearrangement of decision-making by new or existing institutions. Such restructuring must permit an interaction between citizen and institutional views so that there is some possibility that the institutional decisions will be accepted by the people who are the intended subjects of official action.

This book is about rights. Not all rights can be secured in the courts. The right to citizen participation must be won largely in the legislatures and in the beflagged offices of executive agencies. Or it may have to be won in the streets.

NOTES

1. *See* M. Sviridoff, *Planning and Participation* 4 (1969).
2. *See* D. Moynihan, *Maximum Feasible Misunderstanding* 167 (1969).
3. 5 U.S.C. §554.
4. Attorney General's Memorandum on the Public Information Section of the Administrative Procedure Act, at iii (1967).
5. *But see* Van Allen v. McCleary, 27 Misc. 2d 81, 211 N.Y.S.2d 501 (Sup. Ct. 1961).
6. This situation may be rectified by §214 of the Housing and Urban Development Act of 1969, P.L. 91–152, 13 U.S. Code Cong. & Ad. News 2490 (1970).
7. Smith v. Elliott, 305 N.Y.S.2d 94 (Sup. Ct. 1969).
8. Administrative Procedure Act §4, 5 U.S.C. §553; *see Bonfield*, "Public Participation in Federal Rulemaking Relating to Public Property, Loans, Grants, Benefits or Contracts," 118 *University of Pennsylvania Law Review* 540, 541 (1970); *see also* Moss v. CAB, 430 F.2d 891 (D.C. Cir. 1970) (negating airline rate schedules promulgated without public notice and hearings).
9. *See, e.g.*, Housing Act of 1949, title I, §105(d), 42 U.S.C. §1455(d); Urban Renewal Handbook, RHA 7206.1, ch. 3 at 1 (HUD 1968).
10. *Cf.* Powelton Civic Home Owners Ass'n v. HUD, 284 F. Supp. 809 (E.D. Pa. 1968).
11. *Id.* at 830–31.

12. Shannon v. HUD, 305 F. Supp. 205 (E.D. Pa. 1969).

13. Glen v. Rockefeller, 307 N.Y.S.2d 46, 53 (Sup. Ct. 1970).

14. Women's City Club of New York, *Performance and Promise* 56 (1966).

15. Advisory Committee on Decentralization, Final Report Submitted to the Board of Education of the City of New York July 1968 (John H. Niemeyer, Chairman), at 29.

16. Urban Renewal Handbook, RHA 7217.1, ch. 5, §2 (HUD, 1969); RHA 7387.1, ch. 1 (1968).

17. §103(a)(2), 42 U.S.C. §3303(a)(2); C.D.A. Letter No. 3 (HUD October 1967), HUD Technical Assistance Bull. No. 3, *Citizen Participation in Model Cities* (1968).

18. Housing Act of 1937 §15(10) *as amended,* 42 U.S.C. §1415(10) (added by the Housing and Urban Development Act of 1968, P.L. 90-448, §204, 82 Stat. 503).

19. HUD Technical Assistance Bull. No. 3, *supra* note 17.

20. Remarks of Mr. Bernard Russell, HUD Assistant Administrator of Model Cities, Proceedings of the National Conference on Advocacy and Pluralistic Planning, January 10 and 11, 1969, at 83 (Mann ed.).

21. Moynihan, *supra* note 2, at 134–35.

22. *Id.* at 136–37.

23. N.Y. Educ. Law art. 52-A (McKinney Supp. 1970).

24. *Id.,* §§2590-g, 2590-e.

25. *Id.,* §§2590-h, 2590-*l.*

26. *Id.,* §2590-j.

27. The system for electing community school board members is set out in *id.,* §2590-c.

28. Hadley v. Junior College Dist., 90 Sup. Ct. 791 (1970).

29. *New York Times,* March 23, 1970, at 1, col. 7; March 24, 1970, at 32, col. 8.

30. Wilcox, "The Controversy Over I.S. 201," *Urban Review* (July 1966).

31. *See* Mayor's Advisory Panel on Decentralization of the New York City Schools ("Bundy Panel"), *Reconnection for Learning, A Community School System for New York City* 17–18 (1967).

32. *New York Times,* March 23, 1970, at 1, col. 7; March 24, 1970, at 32, col. 8.

THE RIGHT TO PROTEST

THOMAS I. EMERSON

IN A DEMOCRATIC SOCIETY THE RIGHT TO PROTEST takes many forms. We are concerned here with protest that is expressed through holding a meeting, marching in a parade, picketing, distributing literature, wearing an emblem, or engaging in similar kinds of demonstration or canvassing. These activities, which may be loosely grouped together as constituting the right of public assembly, have traditionally occupied an important place in our system of freedom of expression. Such forms of communication were well known to our forebears who made the American Revolution. And they have been the stock in trade of numerous social and political movements throughout our history, including those of the abolitionists, the suffragettes, and the labor unions.

The present times are no exception. Civil rights organizations, the black community, the antiwar protesters, the radical youth, and other groups count heavily upon the public assembly to convey their message. Indeed these groups have given this mode of protest a new dimension. They have not only refurbished the old forms but have invented new ones. Today, in addition to a mass meeting, a torch-light parade, or a sit-down, the public assembly may be in the form of a vigil, a shop-in, or a love-in.

The public assembly, in whatever form, is an indispensable

Thomas I. Emerson is Lines Professor of Law at Yale Law School, a former official in the federal government, the author of The System of Freedom of Expression *and other books, and a participant in important free speech cases in the federal courts.*

feature of our system of freedom of expression because it does not depend upon the mass media of communication, which are controlled by the Establishment groups in the society. This form of protest is available to the poor, the underprivileged, and the minorities. It thus helps to preserve some semblance of a "marketplace of ideas" in a system otherwise dominated by the mass media. Moreover, the public assembly has other important characteristics. It brings the speaker face to face with his audience; it provides a dramatic setting in which to communicate an idea; it reveals the depth and intensity with which the participants hold their views; it provides a method for building solidarity within the protesting group. Even more important, the public assembly often tends to have an unsettling effect upon the community, forcing it to face rather than brush aside the issues being called to its attention. All in all, the right of public assembly is a cornerstone of the democratic process.

The principal constitutional support for the right of protest through public assembly is the First Amendment. This provision, it should be noted, guarantees not only the right to freedom of speech and the press but also "the right of the people peaceably to assemble, and to petition the Government for a redress of grievances." The framers were well aware of the special significance of these rights and undoubtedly meant to extend them a high degree of protection. Additional support for the right of public assembly derives from other constitutional provisions, such as the guarantees against arbitrary arrest and detention, and from the whole structure of laws, institutions, and practices which make up the system of freedom of expression. Finally, full realization of the ideal rests upon public understanding and commitment. In this brief survey of the right of public assembly in our society today, however, primary emphasis must be limited to the constitutional protections extended by the First Amendment.

The course of legal decision under the First Amendment has been slow and somewhat wavering. This is due in part to the fact that the Supreme Court's development of First Amendment doctrine did not begin until the end of the second decade of this century. Moreover, most of the issues surrounding the right of public assembly concern matters of local law and order, within the jurisdiction of state and local authorities, and not until 1925 did the Supreme Court hold that the First Amendment was applicable to these areas of government. In the 1930's, however, a series of important cases reached the Supreme Court, mostly involving the Jehovah's Witnesses. Thereafter a scattering of decisions came from the Court, increasing in volume during the period after World War II. By the end of the 1960's a substantial body of law had emerged. Yet the Supreme Court decisions are inconclusive on many points and numerous issues still remain unresolved.[1]

THE CURRENT STATE OF THE LAW

We start from the position that, as a general proposition, the right of protest is guaranteed by the First Amendment. Meetings, parades, demonstrations, leafleting, canvassing, and the like are lawful and entitled to be free from governmental interference. Furthermore, being lawful, such activity is entitled to the same measure of governmental protection against private (nongovernmental) obstruction as is other lawful conduct. Our Constitution extends these protections to the right of protest despite the fact that exercise of the right frequently, in the words of Justice Douglas, "induces a condition of unrest, creates dissatisfaction with conditions as they are, or even stirs people to anger." In a democratic society, as Justice Brennan has emphasized, protest should be "uninhibited, robust, and wide open." Finally, like other First Amendment rights, the right of protest enjoys a preferred status in our constitutional system, and the courts should be alert to maintain, extend, and encourage it.[2]

These, then, are the initial premises with which one begins. The major legal questions that must be explored concern what kind of protest is guaranteed protection under the First Amendment and what limitations, if any, the government may impose upon the conduct thus protected.

Conduct Protected by the First Amendment

The courts, including the Supreme Court, have never addressed themselves in depth to the question of precisely what forms of protest are covered by the First Amendment and hence entitled to whatever protection that constitutional provision affords. Roughly speaking, the conduct protected must be "speech" or "expression" in some guise. Clearly included in this category are all forms of

verbal communication, the distribution of written materials, and
the display of signs and symbols. Equally clearly excluded are the
use of physical force (as in a riot), seizure of property (as in the
occupation of a building), or physical obstruction of a government
operation (as in the destruction of Selective Service files). Some
intermediate areas have been marked out. The Supreme Court has
held that the First Amendment protects the holding of a meeting,
solicitation of members in an organization, and marching with signs
on the Statehouse grounds. Others are not so clear. Although it
had numerous opportunities to do so the Supreme Court successfully avoided deciding whether sitting in at a restaurant or lunch
counter to protest racial discrimination constituted an exercise of
First Amendment rights. But in *Brown v. Louisiana* the prevailing
opinion (subscribed to by three Justices) held that a group of
Negroes who were refused service in a public library on racial
grounds, and remained there "to protest by silent and reproachful
presence," were engaged in conduct covered by the First Amendment. On the other hand, lower federal courts and state courts have
consistently held that prolonged sit-ins, lie-ins, obstruction of en-
trances, and similar conduct are not within the protection of that
provision.[3]

Recently the Supreme Court, in response to claims that certain
conduct was entitled to First Amendment protection as "symbolic
speech," has undertaken to analyze the problem more closely. Originally the Court had accepted without elaboration the proposition
that displaying a red flag, picketing, and saluting the flag constituted the kind of conduct embraced by the First Amendment. Beginning in 1965, however, the Court began to make a distinction
between "pure speech," other kinds of expression ("speech plus"),
and "nonspeech." Thus in *Cox v. Louisiana,* dealing with a state
statute that prohibited obstruction of public passages, the Court
"emphatically reject[ed] the notion . . . that the First and Fourteenth Amendments afford the same kind of freedom to those who
would communicate ideas by conduct such as patrolling, marching,
and picketing on streets and highways, as these amendments afford
to those who communicate ideas by pure speech." This position was
reiterated in several subsequent decisions. Likewise, in *Tinker v.
Des Moines Independent Community School District* the Court referred to the wearing of black armbands in protest of the Vietnam
war as conduct "closely akin" to "pure speech." And in *United
States v. O'Brien,* rejecting a First Amendment defense to prosecu-

tion for burning a draft card, the Court held that the burning involved both "speech" and "nonspeech" elements "combined in the same course of conduct."[4]

The full impact of the Supreme Court's attempt to create two categories of expression embraced by the First Amendment, and to separate the "speech" and "nonspeech" elements in a single course of conduct, depends upon the doctrines it employs for determining the degree of protection afforded covered conduct, a matter discussed below. Nevertheless it is plain that the Court, through this mode of analysis, has drastically narrowed the range of protest for which the First Amendment affords any substantial degree of protection.

The Place of Protest

A second important aspect of First Amendment protection to the right of protest involves the question of where the right may be exercised. The matter is of considerable importance because persons using the public assembly as a means of protest, the mass media normally being unavailable to them, are seeking as large an audience as possible. Denial of access to an audience effectively diminishes the right. Furthermore, the effect of the protest often depends on the location; a march past the White House is far more impressive than one through the side streets of Washington. On the other hand, there clearly must be some limitations. No one would urge that there should be a First Amendment right to enter a private home and deliver a harangue to an unwilling occupant. And the places where people congregate or may be reached by those with a message to deliver are also used for other purposes, in fact may be needed exclusively for another function.

After some hesitation the Supreme Court reached the conclusion that all persons have a constitutional right to use the streets, parks, and similar open places for purposes of public assembly. The position was originally stated by Justice Roberts in *Hague v. CIO,* decided in 1939:

> Wherever the title of streets and parks may rest, they have immemorially been held in trust for the use of the public and, time out of mind, have been used for purposes of assembly, communicating thoughts between citizens, and discussing public questions. Such

use of the streets and public places has, from ancient times, been
a part of the privileges, immunities, rights, and liberties of citizens.[5]

Some years later the Supreme Court seemed to qualify its position. In *Cox v. Louisiana* it upheld a state statute which prohibited
picketing or parading near a courthouse. And in *Adderley v.
Florida* it ruled that a group of students had no constitutional
right to stage a peaceful demonstration on the grounds of the county
jail. Despite some broad language in the opinions, however, the
Court apparently based its limitations upon the particular nature
of the premises involved in the two cases. Shortly afterward, in
the *Logan Valley Plaza* case, the Court reaffirmed the *Hague* stand.
Thus, while regulation of time, place, and manner is permissible,
the basic right to use the streets, parks, and open places for meetings,
parades, and other demonstrations of protest cannot be refused.[6]

With respect to closed public places, such as a school building
or a town hall, the Supreme Court has not yet spoken. There would
seem to be no logical reason why the mere existence of a roof should
make a constitutional difference, and a persuasive argument can
be made that the First Amendment requires the opening of such
public facilities to public assembly, at least where no other facilities
are available. But the courts seem to assume there is no constitutional obligation to make such buildings available. On the other
hand, some courts have held that protesters have a right to distribute antiwar material in a municipal bus terminal or a similar place
where "the primary activity for which it is designed is attended
with noisy crowds and vehicles, some unrest and less than perfect
order."[7]

Closed public places are often devoted to uses inconsistent with
the holding of a public assembly, and hence the opportunity for
use as a place of protest may be limited or totally foreclosed. On
the other hand, if the government does make a public facility available for some public assemblies, such as political meetings by one of
the major parties, it cannot discriminate between different users.[8]

The rules governing the use of publicly owned streets, parks,
and other facilities are also applicable to private (nongovernmental) facilities of a similar nature and serving a similar purpose. Thus
as early as 1946 the Supreme Court ruled in *Marsh v. Alabama*[9]
that a company town could not deny the use of its streets to Jehovah's Witnesses seeking to distribute their literature. And more

recently, in the *Logan Valley Plaza* case, the Court held that picketing on the premises of a privately owned shopping center was protected by the First Amendment. These decisions have wide implications. The fact seems to be that the location for exercise of First Amendment rights does not depend upon whether the property is publicly or privately owned, but upon whether it is dedicated to public use and serves a purpose consistent with exercise of the right to protest.

Extent of Protection

Once it has been decided that the protesting conduct falls within the coverage of the First Amendment (that is, constitutes expression) and takes place in a permissible location, the crucial issue becomes to what extent the conduct is protected by the provisions of the First Amendment. Normally it is not the expression itself that causes injury, but rather some ensuing action which may be induced by the expression. The subsequent action can, of course, be regulated or prohibited without offending the requirements of the First Amendment. The key question, then, is whether the prior expression can be punished or cut off before the conduct has reached the point of action.

The issue may arise at any one of three stages in the communication process. The government may seek to punish expression after it has occurred, through laws prohibiting incitement to riot, breach of the peace, disorderly conduct, and the like. Or it may attempt to halt the communication at the moment it is taking place, as when the police order a speaker to desist or a meeting to disperse. Or it may attempt to prevent the communication from ever being uttered, through requiring a permit in advance or forbidding the expression by a court injunction. Moreover, the ensuing action that is feared from the expression, and which the government seeks to forestall, may be of varying types and threaten different kinds of individual or social interests. Most commonly, the public concern is that the expression will lead to physical violence against person or property, in violation of existing law. Sometimes it is feared that expression of protest will result in some other violation of law, though not one involving violence. And at times restrictions on expression are directed against the possibility of subsequent action that is not itself a violation of any law. These distinctions, however, have never been clearly enunciated in the Court decisions.

The Supreme Court has never finally settled upon the basic test it will use to determine at what point the First Amendment permits expression to be cut off in public assembly cases. Justice Black, usually joined by Justice Douglas, takes the position that expression is entitled to full protection and may not be directly restricted in any way other than by administrative regulation of time, place, and manner. The Court as a whole, while often reaching results consistent with this theory, has always declared that freedom of expression cannot be "absolute." For a period during the 1930's and 1940's the Court appeared to have accepted the "clear and present danger" test in public assembly cases. Under this formula the communication cannot be curbed unless, under circumstances prevailing at the time, it creates a clear and present danger of bringing about some substantial evil that the government has a right to prevent. More recently the Court seems to have dropped the "clear and present danger" test and to rely upon an "incitement" test— whether the communication constitutes a direct incitement to unlawful action. At other times the Court, or some members, have employed an ad hoc balancing test. Under this formula the question is decided by weighing interests in freedom of speech against interests sought to be protected by the restriction. Most recently, in cases where the Court has found the protesting conduct to be "speech plus" or a mixture of "speech" and "nonspeech," it has utilized a loose form of the balancing test. Thus in *United States v. O'Brien,* the draft-card-burning case, it held that "a sufficiently important governmental interest in regulating the nonspeech element can justify incidental limitations on First Amendment freedoms." Often the Supreme Court decisions do not make clear what First Amendment test is being applied.[10]

Apart from the basic test for measuring First Amendment rights the Court has made significant use of other doctrines in deciding public assembly cases. Frequently it has invalidated a restriction on protesting conduct for the reason that the law was too vague and indefinite, or too broad, or allowed administrative officials unfettered discretion. At other times it has insisted that less drastic methods of regulation, ones not affecting First Amendment rights, should be utilized. Undoubtedly much of the legislation now on the books regulating the right of protest, including various forms of breach-of-peace statutes and permit systems, is invalid under the aforementioned doctrines. These decisions have played an important role in narrowing the reach of antiprotest regulation, and in protecting the protest in individual cases. At the same time they have not served to clarify the basic issues, and have indeed tended to retard the development of more fundamental principles.[11]

One additional First Amendment doctrine has an important bearing on the right of protest. The rule against prior restraint holds that, generally speaking, the government may not prohibit communication in advance of its utterance, but may only restrict it through subsequent punishment after it has occurred. This doctrine of prior restraint, if strictly applied, would invalidate any attempt by government authorities to prevent demonstrations or other forms of public assembly from being held, whether through requiring a permit, through court injunction, or in any other way (apart from regulation of time, place, and manner, considered below). But the Supreme Court has made some exceptions to the basic rule against prior restraint, and thus far has not specified what the full scope of its application may be in public assembly cases. The doctrine has been frequently invoked, however, and at least operates to impose an additional burden of justification upon regulations which attempt to restrict protest prior to its occurrence.[12]

The state courts and the lower federal courts, left with little guidance from the Supreme Court, have likewise failed to develop clear-cut principles by which to determine at what point, if any, the First Amendment allows restriction on expression in protest cases. They also have relied heavily upon rules against vagueness, overbreadth, and excessive delegation. There is perhaps some tendency to apply, as the basic doctrine, the "clear and present danger" test.

The actual results reached by the Supreme Court have, on the whole, liberally supported the right of protest. In the first category of cases—those where the countervailing interest is protection against physical violence—there is a dearth of decisions dealing with the situation where violence is feared from the protestors themselves. Cases of this nature have been rare, in part at least because the social interest can usually be adequately vindicated through punishment of the subsequent action, if any ensued. The Court has made clear that the mere presence of large crowds on the streets is not ground for curtailing the protest. And it would appear that the Court would permit only the most inflammatory sort of speech, inciting imminent and serious violence, to be the object of sanction. But the issues have never been fully treated. On the other hand the Court has dealt with a number of cases in which violence might be anticipated from persons opposed to the protest—the so-called

hostile audience cases. With one exception, now probably outmoded, the Court has never approved government action curtailing
protest because of the likelihood of violence from a hostile opposition.[13]

The Court has not had much occasion to deal with the second
category of cases—those where the protest might lead to a violation
of law but one that did not involve physical violence. In the *Julian
Bond* case it held that a militant statement urging resistance to the
draft did not constitute "incitement" and was protected by the First
Amendment.[14] Most likely the Court would allow even greater leeway to expression here than in the violence cases.

Likewise in the third category, where the expression is not expected to induce any violation of law but might lead to some harmful result, the Court has rather consistently upheld the right of
protest. Thus it has invalidated restrictions aimed at preventing
litter on the streets, eliminating annoyance from ringing doorbells,
requiring a license to solicit membership, and forcing disclosure of
the source of leaflets distributed to the public. One important exception to this trend, however, has been introduced recently. The
Court has upheld legislation that restricted forms of protest which
the Court has not considered "pure speech." Thus it has ruled valid
general prohibitions against picketing near a courthouse or at the
entrance to public buildings, and has sanctioned the prohibition
against draft-card-burning. This development, if it continues, could
lead to major limitations on the right of protest.[15]

The state courts and lower federal courts have, in general, followed the Supreme Court. Where they do not, of course, their
decisions are subject to correction in the Supreme Court.

Allocation of Physical Facilities

One further aspect of regulating the right of protest remains to
be considered: the allocation of physical facilities. Many forms of
protest require the use of streets, parks, or other space utilized for
different purposes, produce noise which interferes with other kinds
of activity, or similarly entail physical manifestations which come
into conflict with the use of property for another function. Allocation of facilities between competing uses and between competing
users is essential. Automobile drivers must stay off Pennsylvania
Avenue when a parade is in progress, and two rival groups cannot
march down the avenue at the same time.

The legal doctrines pertinent to cutting off expression that may result in harmful action are not relevant here. The right of protest cannot be preferred to all other uses of the facilities involved. Nor can the allocation be made on the basis of the "clear and present danger" test, the incitement test, or the usual balancing test. Rather the problem is one of traffic controls. The appropriate principle is simply that of fair accommodation between competing interests. This requires regulation of the time, place, and manner, but not the content, of protest, to the extent necessary to adjust the exercise of that right to other uses of the same facilities. The Supreme Court, while never clearly distinguishing traffic controls from other types of restriction, has in effect followed the principle of fair accommodation in resolving such issues.[16]

Administration of Controls

The right of protest does not mean much if it exists only in legal principle while not being achieved in practice. Unfortunately, there are many ways in which the reality does not match the theory. Frequently interference with the right of protest takes plainly illegal forms, as in the case of unwarranted arrests, police brutality against demonstrators, or arbitrary discrimination in the administration of a permit system. At other times it may be accomplished through quasi-legal methods, as where an unconstitutional statute is used or a valid one misused. There are, in theory, remedies available under state or local law to redress these denials of the right to protest. But these remedies are usually protracted, costly, and uncertain. Hence the critical question arises whether other devices are available to meet the problems of administrative breakdown.

There have been three important developments in this direction. One, already mentioned, has been the insistence of the Supreme Court that restrictions on the right of protest meet strict standards against vagueness, overbreadth, and excessive delegation. The other two relate to the operation of permit systems and to supervision by the federal courts.

The Supreme Court has ruled that laws requiring a permit before holding a meeting or demonstration that involves use of the streets or other public places are valid under the First Amendment, at least so long as the permit controls only time, place, and manner. But a permit system is readily open to abuse. Hence the impact of this form of regulation needs to be carefully checked. One way of doing this is to allow those who have been denied a permit to proceed with the meeting or demonstration anyway and to test the validity of the denial if prosecuted for violating the permit law. The Court has sanctioned this procedure where the permit regulation is invalid on its face. But in *Poulos v. New Hampshire* it declined to allow such self-help where the regulation was valid but the permit wrongfully denied; and in *Walker v. City of Birmingham* it reached the same result where the restriction was imposed through an injunction, refusing to consider the validity of the injunction. At the same time, in the *Princess Anne* case, the Court indicated that a permit system, in order to be valid, must contain provisions allowing immediate court review of a permit denial. Just what procedural protections are necessary, however, has not been fully specified.[17]

Developments in federal supervision over state and local authorities have progressed further. An appeal may always be taken to the federal courts from a state or local court decision where a federal constitutional right is involved. But this is usually a time-consuming form of relief. The important thing is to have immediate access to the federal courts as soon as a denial of the federal right has occurred, and the opportunity to take affirmative action in the federal courts to forestall illegal state or local action. The federal Civil Rights Acts make denial of federal constitutional rights by state or local officials a criminal offense, but these provisions have never been invoked in a First Amendment case. On the other hand, civil remedies in the federal courts have been more frequently employed. The federal Civil Rights Acts provide for federal relief by way of injunction, declaratory judgment, or damages, and these remedies are useful in some situations. In the landmark case of *Dombrowski v. Pfister* the Supreme Court extended federal protection substantially by upholding a federal injunction which stopped a criminal prosecution by state authorities where the Court found that the defense to the prosecution in the state courts would "not assure adequate vindication of constitutional rights." Subsequently in *Cameron v. Johnson,* however, the Court somewhat limited the circumstances under which it would apply the *Dombrowski* rule, saying that the "mere possibility of erroneous application of a statute" is not sufficient to justify advance federal intervention. Nevertheless *Dombrowski* has been widely utilized to secure federal protection against the enforcement of invalid state laws or the abuse

of valid ones in prosecutions brought primarily for purposes of
harassment. In general, it may be said, the development of federal
supervision is still in progress.[18]

CURRENT ISSUES AND PROSPECTS

In the decade ahead the right of protest will certainly not diminish
in importance, but most likely will become of increasing significance. There are no signs that the mass media of communication
will be opened to the various groups which now rely heavily upon
the public assembly. Moreover, while our major problems accumu-
late and escalate, the rate of change in our society remains slow;
hence the need for public protest will surely be felt even more
keenly than before. Under these circumstances the social functions
of protest—the warning of grievances deeply felt, the testing of
ideas, the participation in common decisions, the facilitating of
orderly change—will be crucial to peaceful progress. Indeed, support and extension of the right of protest may be the only hope for
avoiding revolutionary violence.

At the same time the right of protest will be under greater pressures than at any time in recent history, even during the McCarthy
era. The turmoil of a changing society is bound to stir forces that
will demand conformity and call for unity. The growing polarization of social and political groups will make more difficult the
toleration of opposing views or the expression of intermediate
views. Efforts to achieve "law and order" as the first (and to some
extent the sole) priority will cut down the willingness to permit
public assemblies that might end in disorder or violence. Thus the
delicate mechanisms for allowing ordered conflict through freedom
of expression, while avoiding physical conflict through violent
action, may be difficult to maintain. If the methods of peaceful protest are forbidden, the new social order will be that of the police
state.

Hence it is imperative in the coming years to strengthen the
right of protest and to adapt it to the new requirements of an
immensely difficult but challenging period. The precise lines of such
a development cannot be predicted. But it is possible to discern, at
least partially, some of the issues that will arise and some of the
solutions that must be considered.

Development of the Doctrinal Basis for the Right of Protest

The Supreme Court, as pointed out above, has failed to develop a consistent or satisfactory doctrinal basis for the constitutional right of protest. The result has been that lower courts, police officials, prosecutors, and other government authorities have been given no clear direction. Likewise persons seeking to exercise their right of protest and the public generally do not have an adequate understanding of the nature of the right, the scope of its limitations, or the underlying principles upon which the law pertaining to it should be administered. There is, in short, grave need for a comprehensive and intelligible set of doctrines that will supply a firm legal foundation for protecting and expanding the right of protest.

The first requirement is an effective definition of the conduct covered by the First Amendment. The Supreme Court's attempt to distinguish between "pure speech," "speech plus," and "nonspeech" is superficial and nonfunctional, and inevitably narrows the area of First Amendment protection. The First Amendment was surely intended to embrace more than simple verbal communication. The very reference to "assembly" and "petition" makes that clear. Likewise the Court's effort to divide a single course of conduct into "speech" and "nonspeech" elements, giving only incidental protection to the speech element, has the same effect of excluding from coverage of the First Amendment conduct that may be an integral part of the communication intended to have protection.

What is needed is a comprehensive definition of "expression" based upon the function the First Amendment is designed to serve. The underlying concept of the First Amendment is that "expression," as distinct from "action," is not in itself normally harmful to society, that the government has adequate powers to protect social interests by controlling "action" without restricting "expression," and that if any system of freedom is to endure, "expression" must be assured special protection. "Expression" in this sense means not only verbal communication but any form of communication and the surrounding conduct necessary to convey the message. All expression includes elements of physical as distinct from verbal activity, and the central question is whether the conduct is predominantly "expression" or "action." Any satisfactory definition of expression as the conduct to be safeguarded under the First Amendment calls for analysis along these lines.

The second requirement is that the Supreme Court settle on a legal principle for determining at what point, if any, the First Amendment allows the government to cut off protesting expression. There is much to be said for acceptance of the "clear and present danger" test as the applicable doctrine. The formula embodies the basic elements that should be taken into account in protecting the social interest at stake while allowing substantial freedom of expression. Yet the "clear and present danger" test has serious defects. It is so vague, and relies so heavily upon the special circumstances of each situation, that the result of its application is difficult to know in advance; and it cuts off expression at the very point where expression begins to be effective. Furthermore, the "clear and present danger" test is of no use in deciding hostile audience cases, since it would confer on the opposition the power to determine whether and how long the speaker may speak. The incitement test, which the Supreme Court now seems to prefer, is even more vague and cuts off expression at an even earlier point. The balancing test, rarely used by the Court in public assembly cases, affords no guidance at all to police, prosecutors, protesters, or others.

We are thus left with the full protection doctrine. Under this test any conduct classified as "expression" rather than "action" could not be "abridged" in any way by government authority. Some leeway is afforded in application of the test through the definitional process. Thus a command by a speaker to his followers to break into City Hall would be considered part of the action. Yet the test remains the most specific of any that have been proposed, is based on the functions meant to be served by the First Amendment, and affords the greatest degree of protection to the right of protest.

There are many who are skeptical of the full protection test, feeling that it does not afford society sufficient assurance of maintaining law and order. It should be remembered, however, that the government still retains full power to control any "action" that takes place, whether arising directly or indirectly out of the expression. Normally this should be sufficient to protect law and order. The alternative is to cut deeply into freedom of protest.

Remedies for Administrative Failure

Clarification of the doctrinal basis for the right of protest would greatly assist the actual achievement of that right in practice. Police officials would have more certain guides in maintaining order, local officials would be limited to considerations of time, place, and manner in granting permits, courts could more effectively enforce and more persuasively expound the rights of the parties, and the general public would more readily know when the constitutional guarantee was being ignored or frustrated. Beyond this point, at least two major legal developments would seem necessary to give assurance that the right of protest amounted to more than an unfulfilled promise.

First, the rights of protesters under permit systems should be more fully protected. The Supreme Court's rule that permit laws must not allow excessive delegation of authority to administrative officials, if fully implemented, would probably require the redrafting, on a narrower and more definite basis, of most such legislation now on the books. In addition the doctrine of prior restraint should be pressed further along the lines suggested in the *Princess Anne* case. Any denial of a permit, which thereby shuts off expression in advance, should be subject to immediate review in the courts with the burden on the government to justify its position. Finally, the limitation on self-help announced in the *Poulos* and *Walker* cases should be relaxed. If a group denied a permit considers the refusal so unjustified that it is willing to run the risk of prosecution for violating the permit law, it should be able to raise as a defense in such prosecution the contention that the permit was illegally withheld. The same rule should apply to a court injunction illegally issued. A proper respect for law and order does not demand that First Amendment rights can be violated and the victim given no opportunity to demonstrate that the violation indeed occurred.[19]

Secondly, the supervisory role of the federal courts should be expanded. For a variety of reasons the federal courts have proved less subject to the pressures of local dominant groups, and more responsive to claims of individual rights, than the state and local courts. They therefore remain, and probably will continue to be, the best institutional device for protecting the right of protest against encroachment by state or local authority. The existing statutory framework permits the federal courts not only to review state and local court decisions but to examine pending judicial and executive actions and to prevent future infringement of rights. The federal courts should accept jurisdiction over any claim that the right of protest is being or is about to be denied in violation of the First Amendment. Experience has shown that the right of protest is frequently not afforded at the local level, and it should be the obligation of the federal government to enforce the federal guarantee. This would not mean that the federal courts would take over the function of the state and local courts, but it would mean that they could require the adherence of local authorities to the demands of the First Amendment.[20]

Of course, full realization of the right to protest will require much more than changes in the legal rules. It can be accomplished only by substantial reform in the practices of the various institutions which determine the legal rights of citizens. Of these the most important is the police. Improved training of the police, limitations upon certain tactics used by the police in handling crowds, the placing of impartial observers at demonstrations, and similar methods are all important. Very likely, more fundamental reforms are necessary. It is doubtful that the right of protest will receive more sympathetic protection at the hands of the police until greater civilian control replaces the growing professionalism of the police, and substantial community control replaces bureaucratic centralization.

The Relation of Peaceful and Violent Protest

A major threat to the constitutional right of protest in the coming decade may arise from the fears generated by violent protest. Most important changes in the power structure of this country have been accompanied by a certain amount of disorder and violence. Yet there seems to be greater apprehension about a serious breakdown of law and order at the present time than for many years past. This situation, which shows no current signs of abating, imposes serious strains upon the system of peaceful protest. Legislatures seek to meet the problem by drastic legislation, executive officials look for a solution in rigorous enforcement of the criminal law, police overreact to signs of possible violence, members of the public become afraid to join in protests, and the whole public atmosphere becomes tense and repressive. Such developments threaten to engulf the whole machinery for protection of the right to dissent.

The remedy, for a democratic society, is certainly not to curtail the right of peaceful protest. No society, at least no open society, can expect to achieve a state of perfect order. Surely no dynamic system of freedom of expression can function without the conflict that it encourages spilling over into some violence or disorder. Furthermore, the remedy in any event would not be to curb the right of peaceful protest. Such a course could only bottle up frustration, conceal the underlying problems, and lead to a greater upheaval. If we are to avoid collapse into a police state, the channels of communication, especially those of the public assembly, must be kept open and functioning.

Where the right of protest is subjected to such pressures, it is essential that special attention be devoted to the separation of peaceful protest, which must be protected, from violent action, which may be punished. In legal terms this calls for rules that will effectively separate "expression" from "action." Thus where a demonstration is primarily peaceful, but is marred by the violence of a small minority, police tactics must be directed toward restraining the violence rather than disrupting the entire assembly. This calls for the development of rules relating to the control of a public assembly while it is in progress, an area of law to which the courts have given little attention. Separation of lawful from unlawful protest also requires that prosecutors, whether in conspiracy cases or others, carefully distinguish between responsibility for the two forms of protest, and that the courts develop rules by which punishment of illegal action does not chill the exercise of legal expression. The public must also be kept aware of the dangers of indiscriminately lumping together all forms of protest, legal and illegal. Only through such measures can the society avoid destruction of legitimate protest in its efforts to deal with the increasing tensions of troublesome times.

Role of the Federal Government in the Tension Between Protest and Order

One of the most significant developments of the last few years has been the entrance of the federal government on the side of state and local authorities in their efforts to uphold law and order against the dangers feared from protest movements. There is nothing novel in the federal government's undertaking to maintain local law and order under special circumstances. The original federal Civil Rights Acts interposed federal authority against infringement of federal constitutional rights growing out of the breakdown of state and local law enforcement. And the Civil Rights Act of 1960 added provisions making it a federal offense to transport explosives in interstate commerce with the knowledge or intent that they will be used to destroy property used for "educational, religious, residential, business, or civic objectives" or to intimidate any person "pursuing such objectives."[21] These provisions were all designed to aid in protecting rights guaranteed by the federal Constitution. In the Civil Rights Act of 1968, however, congressional conservatives included provisions which were intended to serve quite different purposes from the protection of federal rights.

One series of provisions, sometimes called the Federal Riot Act, imposes criminal penalties upon any person who (1) travels in interstate commerce or uses any facility of interstate commerce (such as the telephone or mails), (2) with intent to incite a riot or "to organize, promote, encourage, participate in, or carry on a riot," and (3) then or thereafter "performs or attempts to perform any other overt act" for the purposes specified. The penalty is up to five years imprisonment. The first prosecution brought under these provisions was the famous Chicago Conspiracy case, in which eight diverse leaders of peace, Yippie, and black organizations were charged with conspiracy to cross state lines with the intention of disrupting the Democratic Convention of 1968. Another, and barely noticed, provision of the Civil Rights Act of 1968 makes it a federal offense for anyone, "during or incident to a riot or civil disorder," to injure, intimidate, or interfere with "any person engaged in a business in commerce or affecting commerce." Penalties range up to life imprisonment.[22]

The threat posed by federal legislation of this character is difficult to exaggerate. The Federal Riot Act punishes conduct which may never get beyond the stage of expression, or even much beyond the stage of intent. In a conspiracy case mere agreement would be sufficient to incur the penalties. Quite apart from these constitutional defects, the law would make it unsafe for any person to cross state lines, or telephone across them, in connection with a public assembly to take place in the second state. If violence subsequently happened to occur at the demonstration, such a person would be subject to heavy penalties if a jury (likely to be hostile) found he had had the requisite intent. The second provision would mean that any person who engaged in a demonstration that at some point resulted in injury or interference to almost any business enterprise might find himself vulnerable to federal prosecution. Brought into a conspiracy case under either provision, the protester would find that the statements or actions of any member of the alleged conspiracy would be attributable to him. Through this legislation the federal government could eliminate the leadership and paralyze the rank and file of virtually any political movement that relied upon the right of public assembly.

State and local authorities do not need federal legislation of this kind to help them preserve local law and order. Moreover, the dangers inherent in any legislation which punishes conduct so closely connected with the right of protest are multiplied many times when the federal government brings its enormous power and resources to bear. In this area federal legislation serves no useful purpose and is capable of the gravest harm.

Affirmative Government Promotion of the Right of Protest

Historically the main thrust of legal and other safeguards for individual rights was to restrain the government from interference with the exercise of those rights by private citizens and private groups. As the laissez-faire features of our society disappear, it has become necessary to look more broadly at the state of individual rights to ascertain whether there may be some ways in which governmental powers should be used affirmatively to encourage and expand as well as defend them. In some areas of freedom of expression there is no doubt that positive governmental action is now required to remove obstructions and open up new possibilities. Thus government controls are essential to prevent the mass media of communication from being dominated by a small group and the whole system of free expression distorted. In the years ahead it will be important to explore similar possibilities with regard to the right of protest.

By their very nature those aspects of protest with which we are here concerned seem to demand primarily defense against governmental intrusion rather than affirmative governmental promotion. Meetings, parades, demonstrations, and canvassing are activities which must be organized and carried on by private citizens, not by government. Nevertheless there are some points at which positive governmental action may be important. One of these is the making of governmental facilities available for public assemblies where other facilities are inadequate. Another is in supplying the indirect costs of exercising the right of protest. Thus adequate police protection, by well-trained police officers, is an important obligation of government. Both these forms of government support may become increasingly significant in the years ahead.

Moreover, it is not inconceivable that the government may come to provide some forms of direct subsidy of the right of protest. Until very recent years the notion that government should subsidize criticism of itself would have seemed fantastic. But various developments have begun in this direction. Funds from the Office of Economic Opportunity have not infrequently been used to support organizations or groups that took serious issue with the government on many fronts. Federal aid to education has thus far been substantially divorced from federal control of local educational policy. And various proposals have been advanced for government subsidization of the costs of political campaigns. As these developments proceed, the principles and institutions by which public funds may be allocated to countergroups throughout society should begin to emerge. In this process some subsidization of the right to protest may come to pass. There are great dangers in such a development, but also significant possibilities for expanding and enlivening the system of free expression.

There is one further area in which affirmative government promotion of the right of protest may be anticipated in the years ahead. The existing legal structure for protection of the right of protest, apart from official protection against the use of private force to interfere with expression, relates primarily to the rights of the citizen as against the government. But the individual in our society today often faces restrictions upon his right of protest from private centers of power—corporations, labor unions, professional societies, and many others—which operate as unofficial governments. Official government, broadly speaking, possesses the power to compel such a private organization to recognize the right of its members or other affected persons to protest the policies and practices of the organization. Here also there are the beginnings of governmental intervention to assure some protection. The Labor-Management Reporting and Disclosure Act of 1959 gives every member of a labor organization "the right to meet and assemble freely with other members" and "to express any views, arguments, or opinions."[23] Again there are obvious dangers in government regulation of this kind, and the rights of a member against a private organization are not necessarily the same as the rights of a citizen against his government. But as the power of private associations grows, the need for protection increases. The coming decade may therefore see measures taken to guarantee the right of protest against abridgment by unofficial as well as official power.

NOTES

1. For a more detailed discussion of the right to protest than can be given in this essay, see T. Emerson, *The System of Freedom of Expression* ch. 9 (1970). A collection of legal materials and references may be found in T. Emerson, D. Haber, & N. Dorsen, *Political and Civil Rights in the United States* ch. 4 (3d ed. 1967).

2. The Douglas quotation is from Terminiello v. Chicago, 337 U.S. 1, 4 (1949), and the Brennan quotation from New York Times Co. v. Sullivan, 376 U.S. 254, 270 (1964).

3. De Jonge v. Oregon, 299 U.S. 353 (1937) (meeting); Thomas v. Collins, 323 U.S. 516 (1945) (solicitation); Edwards v. South Carolina, 372 U.S. 229 (1963) (marching); Bell v. Maryland, 378 U.S. 226 (1964), and prior cases (sit-ins); Brown v. Louisiana, 383 U.S. 131 (1966).

4. Stromberg v. California, 283 U.S. 359 (1931) (red flag); Thornhill v. Alabama, 310 U.S. 88 (1940) (picketing); West Virginia Bd. of Educ. v. Barnette, 319 U.S. 624 (1943) (flag salute); Cox v. Louisiana, 379 U.S. 536, 555 (1965). The *Tinker* case is reported at 393 U.S. 503, 505 (1969), and the *O'Brien* case at 391 U.S. 367, 376 (1968). See also Street v. New York, 394 U.S. 576 (1969), in which the Supreme Court declined to pass on the question whether burning an American flag in protest against the shooting of James Meredith constituted "symbolic speech."

5. Hague v. CIO, 307 U.S. 496, 515 (1939).

6. Cox v. Louisiana, 379 U.S. 536, 558 (1965); Adderley v. Florida, 385 U.S. 39 (1966); Amalgamated Food Employees, Local 590 v. Logan Valley Plaza, Inc., 391 U.S. 308, 315 (1968). The Roberts ruling was likewise reaffirmed in Shuttlesworth v. City of Birmingham, 394 U.S. 147, 152 (1969).

7. Wolin v. Port of New York Authority, 392 F.2d 83, 90 (2d Cir.), *cert. denied*, 393 U.S. 940 (1968).

8. Fowler v. Rhode Island, 345 U.S. 67 (1953); Cox v. Louisiana, 379 U.S. 536, 553–58 (1965).

9. Marsh v. Alabama, 326 U.S. 501 (1946).

10. For expression of the Black view see H. Black, *A Constitutional Faith* ch. 3 (1968); Cox v. Louisiana, 379 U.S. 536, 578 (1965). The "clear and present danger" test seems to have been the basis of the decisions in Cantwell v. Connecticut, 310 U.S. 296 (1940); Thomas v. Collins, 323 U.S. 516 (1945); Terminiello v. Chicago, 337 U.S. 1 (1949). The incitement test was used in Feiner v. New York, 340 U.S. 315 (1951); Bond v. Floyd, 385 U.S. 116 (1966); Brandenburg v. Ohio, 395 U.S. 444 (1969). The balancing test was employed in Schneider v. State, 308 U.S. 147 (1939); Street v. New York, 394 U.S. 576 (1969). The *O'Brien* quotation may be found in 391 U.S. 367, 376 (1968).

11. The vagueness, overbreadth, and excessive delegation doctrines have been applied in Hague v. CIO, 307 U.S. 496 (1939); Cantwell v. Connecticut, 310 U.S. 296 (1940); De Jonge v. Oregon, 299 U.S. 353 (1937); Terminiello v. Chicago, 337 U.S. 1 (1949); Edwards v. South Carolina, 372 U.S. 229 (1963); Cox v. Louisiana, 379 U.S. 536 (1965); Kunz v. New York, 340 U.S. 290 (1951); Gregory v. Chicago, 394 U.S. 111 (1969). On the less-drastic-methods rule see De Jonge v. Oregon, *supra*, and Schneider v. State, 308 U.S. 147 (1939); Note, "Less Drastic Means and the First Amendment," 78 *Yale Law Journal* 464 (1969).

12. The doctrine of prior restraint was originally enunciated in Near v. Minnesota, 283 U.S. 697 (1931). It was applied in Lovell v. City of Griffin, 303 U.S.

444 (1938); Thomas v. Collins, 323 U.S. 516 (1945); Kunz v. New York, 340 U.S. 290 (1951). In Carroll v. President and Commissioners of Princess Anne, 393 U.S. 175 (1968), the Court declined to say whether a prior restraint would always be invalid in public assembly cases.

13. On the presence of crowds, see Cox v. Louisiana, 379 U.S. 536 (1965). The point at which the Supreme Court might well cut off speech where violence is feared from the speaker and his supporters is probably indicated by Kasper v. State, 206 Tenn. 434, 326 S.W. 2d 664 (1959), *cert. denied,* 361 U.S. 930 (1960); People v. Epton, 19 N.Y.2d 496, 281 N.Y.S.2d 9, 227 N.E.2d 829 (1967), *cert. denied,* 390 U.S. 29 (1968). The hostile audience cases include Terminiello v. Chicago, 337 U.S. 1 (1949); Kunz v. New York, 340 U.S. 290 (1951); Edwards v. South Carolina, 372 U.S. 229 (1963); Cox v. Louisiana, *supra;* Gregory v. Chicago, 394 U.S. 111 (1969); and the *Princess Anne* case, 393 U.S. 175 (1968). The exception is the *Feiner* case, 340 U.S. 315 (1951).

14. Bond v. Floyd, 385 U.S. 116, 134 (1966).

15. Lovell v. Griffin, 303 U.S. 444 (1938) (littering); Thomas v. Collins, 323 U.S. 516 (1945) (license to solicit); Talley v. California, 362 U.S. 60 (1960) (disclosure). The "pure speech" cases are Cox v. Louisiana, 379 U.S. 536 (1965); United States v. O'Brien, 391 U.S. 367 (1968); Cameron v. Johnson, 390 U.S. 611 (1968). *But cf.* the *Tinker* case, 393 U.S. 503 (1969) (wearing black armbands allowed).

16. See Cox v. New Hampshire, 312 U.S. 569 (1941); Poulos v. New Hampshire, 345 U.S. 395 (1953); Cox v. Louisiana, 379 U.S. 536, 554–55 (1965). Use of sound trucks involves the same principle of accommodation. See Saia v. New York, 334 U.S. 558 (1948); Kovacs v. Cooper, 336 U.S. 77 (1949).

17. Permit systems were first upheld in Cox v. New Hampshire, 312 U.S. 569 (1941). Cases allowing self-help where the permit system is invalid include Kunz v. New York, 340 U.S. 290 (1951); Nietmotko v. Maryland, 340 U.S. 268 (1951); Staub v. City of Baxley, 355 U.S. 313 (1958); Shuttlesworth v. City of Birmingham, 394 U.S. 147 (1969). The denial of self-help under a valid permit system was affirmed in Poulos v. New Hampshire, 345 U.S. 395 (1953), and under an injunction in Walker v. City of Birmingham, 388 U.S. 307 (1967). The requirement of immediate judicial review was indicated in the *Princess Anne* case, 393 U.S. 175, 178–79 (1968), drawing an analogy to procedures required of movie censorship boards in Freedman v. Maryland, 380 U.S. 51 (1965).

18. An action for damages against state authorities for violation of Fourth Amendment rights was sustained in Monroe v. Pape, 365 U.S. 167 (1961). That a declaratory judgment as to the validity of state laws affecting First Amendment rights is ordinarily available was decided in Zwickler v. Koota, 389 U.S. 241 (1967). The decisions on enjoining state criminal prosecutions are Dombrowski v. Pfister, 380 U.S. 479 (1965), and Cameron v. Johnson, 390 U.S. 611 (1968).

19. For discussion of these issues see Monaghan, "First Amendment 'Due Process,'" 83 *Harvard Law Review* 518 (1970); Note, "Defiance of Unlawful Authority," 83 *Harvard Law Review* 626 (1970).

20. For a more elaborate argument to this effect see Bailey, "Enjoining State Criminal Prosecutions Which Abridge First Amendment Freedoms," 3 *Harvard Civil Rights–Civil Liberties Law Review* 67 (1967). See also Note, "The Chilling Effect in Constitutional Law," 69 *Columbia Law Review* 808 (1969).

21. The provision of the Civil Rights Act of 1960 is in 18 U.S.C. §837.

22. 18 U.S.C. §§2101, 245. *See also* 18 U.S.C. §231.

23. The Labor-Management provisions are in 29 U.S.C. §§411–13.

THE RIGHT OF
ASSOCIATION

NATHANIEL L. NATHANSON

IF THIS ESSAY WERE LOOKING ONLY TO THE PAST, a more appropriate title might be "Freedom of Association and the Communist Conspiracy." Ever since *Gitlow v. New York*,[1] sustaining a conviction for the publication and distribution of *The Left Wing Manifesto*, the ideological blueprint for the formation of the American Communist Party, serious concern about internal security, in the sense of insurrection, subversion, disloyalty, and espionage, has been overwhelmingly concentrated upon those suspected of Marxism. Against this background, the decision last term in *Brandenberg v. Ohio*,[2] holding unconstitutional the Ohio Criminal Syndicalism Act as applied to a person identified as a leader and speaker at a Ku Klux Klan organizing rally, comes as a refreshing change of scenery. And finally, as if to signal the end of an era, the Civil Service Commission has recently officially removed from circulation, in compliance with a federal court decision, the requirement that each prospective federal employee sign an affidavit averring that he is not "a Communist or Fascist" and that he does not "advocate" and is not "knowingly a member of any organization that advocates the overthrow of the constitutional form of the Government of the United States or which seeks by force or violence to deny other persons their rights under the Constitution of the United States."[3] Before asking where we go from here, we should

Nathaniel L. Nathanson is Vose Professor of Law at Northwestern University School of Law, co-author of a casebook on administrative law, and author of many articles on constitutional law, administrative law, and related subjects.

pause to look back over the road we have traveled since the defenders of the internal security of the Republic and the defenders
of the Bill of Rights first joined battle in the legislatures, in the
courts, and in public discourse over the significance of the Communist conspiracy and the most appropriate response to it.

THE SMITH ACT AND ITS INTERMITTENT ENFORCEMENT

Professor Zechariah Chafee suggests that the provisions of the Alien
Registration Act of 1940, which came to be "popularly" known as
the Smith Act, were passed in something like a fit of national absent-
mindedness.[4] With disarming candor he tells us: "Not until months
later did I for one realize that this statute contains the most drastic
restrictions on freedom of speech ever enacted in the United States
during peace." But he also notes that a few organizations, including
the American Civil Liberties Union, were not asleep at the switch.
Of course, the originators and active supporters of the statute were
far from absent-minded. Since 1935 they had been drafting and
promoting legislation designed both to prohibit the advocacy of insubordination, disloyalty, mutiny, or refusal of duty in the military
forces and to add several additional grounds for the deportation
of aliens. In the tradition of the A. Mitchell Palmer alien raids of
1919–1920, and comparable proposed legislation, the additional
grounds for deportation were primarily concerned with Communist
affiliation. When "bleeding-heart liberals"—if we may borrow a
phrase from a later era—protested that it was unfair to treat aliens
so harshly for activity which was entirely permissible to citizens,
Representative Smith had a ready answer: Why not subject all
persons, citizens as well as aliens, to substantially the same proscription? The key provision designed for this purpose was the so-called
advocacy clause of the Smith Act, making it a crime "to advocate,
abet, advise or teach the duty, necessity, desirability or propriety of
overthrowing or destroying any Government in the United States
by force or violence." It was also made a crime to organize any "society, group or assembly of persons who teach, advocate or encourage" such overthrow or destruction, or to be a member of such
a group, knowing its purposes. Thus was Congress persuaded to
adopt as Sections 2 and 3 of the Act, with comparatively little attention or opposition, substantially the same kind of "criminal syndicalism" or "anarchy" law that several states had adopted shortly

after World War I, but that had apparently fallen largely into desuetude in subsequent years.

For a while it seemed as though the life of the Smith Act was destined to be about as quiescent as that of its state counterparts. It is interesting to observe that during the war years the only enforcement of the Act was against members of the Socialist Workers Party, an avowedly Trotskyite group. The first full-dress enforcement of the Act against the Communist Party itself (the conspiracy prosecution of Dennis and ten other national leaders of the Party) was begun in 1948, just about the height of the Cold War, and just before President Truman was due to run for re-election. The Supreme Court in *Dennis v. United States*[5] sustained the convictions of all the defendants and the validity of the statute as so applied. Only Justices Black and Douglas dissented, but the majority could not agree on a composite statement of the grounds of decision to serve as the opinion of the Court. Chief Justice Vinson, speaking for himself and three other members of the Court, explicitly approved Judge Learned Hand's reformulation of the "clear and present danger" test in his opinion for the court of appeals, which had also sustained the convictions. Judge Hand had interpreted the test to mean "whether the gravity of the 'evil,' discounted by its improbability, justifies such invasion of free speech as is necessary to avoid the danger." To this abstract statement the Chief Justice added his own assessment of the relevant considerations, summed up in one key sentence: "The formation by petitioners of such a highly organized conspiracy, with rigidly disciplined members subject to call when the leaders, these petitioners, felt that the time had come for action, coupled with the inflammable nature of world conditions, similar uprisings in other countries, and the touch-and-go nature of our relations with countries with whom petitioners were in the very least ideologically attuned, convince us that their convictions were justified on this score." Mr. Justice Frankfurter based his concurrence on a familiar philosophy of judicial review summed up in this sentence: "The demands of free speech in a democratic society as well as the interest in national security are better served by candid and informed weighing of the competing interests, within the confines of the judicial process, than by announcing dogmas too inflexible for the non-Euclidean problems to be solved." Broadly speaking this became known as the balancing test. Mr. Justice Jackson emphasized another aspect of the complicated strands of thinking initiated by Judge Hand—the conspiracy aspects of the case. But he did not explain why a conspiracy to advocate overthrow of the government by force and violence was less entitled to constitutional protection than the advocacy itself. All of the majority opinions de-emphasized imminency of the danger as a significant aspect of the constitutional test.

Dennis was not destined to be the last or even the most significant word about the advocacy and organizing sections of the Smith Act. Up to the present, at any rate, this honor has been reserved for the decision in Yates v. United States,[6] a conspiracy prosecution directed at second-string leaders of the Communist Party in California. Yates was decided after Warren had succeeded Vinson as Chief Justice, and after the fever of the McCarthy era had passed its peak. The convictions of all fourteen defendants were overturned, but Dennis was distinguished rather than overruled. As developed by Mr. Justice Harlan, speaking for the Court, the crucial difference between Dennis and Yates was in the trial judge's instructions to the jury. The essential distinction between the two instructions, according to Mr. Justice Harlan, was that Judge Medina had included in his instructions in Dennis, while the judge in Yates had not, the requirement that there be "teaching and advocacy of action for the accomplishment of overthrowing or destroying organized government by language reasonably and ordinarily calculated to incite persons to such action"; in other words, "those to whom the advocacy is addressed must be urged to do something, now or in the future, rather than merely to believe in something." Mr. Justice Harlan also undertook to give the distinction substance by applying it to the evidence in the particular case in order to determine whether any of the defendants should be subjected to a new trial under proper instructions. With respect to the Party as a whole, he found the record strikingly deficient in proof of advocacy of unlawful or forcible action. Consequently, it was necessary to find evidence implicating the particular defendants with such forbidden advocacy. With respect to five of the defendants he could find nothing to connect them with such advocacy. But with respect to the other nine defendants, there was evidence linking them to a systematic course of teaching of the illegal kind of action condemned by the statute. Apart from mention of sabotage, street fighting, and "moving masses of people in time of crisis," the illegal subjects of instruction were not described. But the proof of the pudding was apparently in the eating. The government understood Mr. Justice Harlan's distinction well enough to decide that even with respect to those nine defendants it did not have sufficient evidence to make another trial worthwhile. Even more important, in practically all other pending cases under the advocacy clause of the Smith Act either the government or the lower courts reached the same conclusion, thus ending its enforcement for the foreseeable future.

Before dismissing the Smith Act we must also consider the history of the enforcement of the so-called membership clause of the statute, which makes it a crime to be a member of, or be affiliated with, any "society, group or assembly of persons, who teach, advocate, or encourage the overthrow or destruction of any . . . government [in the United States] by force or violence . . . knowing the purposes thereof." This is the clause which Professor Chafee characterized as "the most drastic portion" of the Act and as bringing "into our federal criminal law the European principle that a man is known by the company he keeps and that guilt is not personal." The two leading cases under this clause are *Scales v. United States*[7] and *Noto v. United States*,[8] both decided on June 5, 1961. The decision in *Scales*, sustaining a conviction, would have been disheartening, especially in the light of *Yates*, had it not been accompanied by the decision in *Noto*, reversing a similar conviction. In both cases Mr. Justice Harlan again spoke for the Court. In *Scales*, he rejected the contentions that the membership clause was unconstitutional on its face because it violated (1) the Fifth Amendment by imputing guilt to the individual merely on the basis of his associations and sympathies, and (2) the First Amendment by infringing on freedom of political expression and association. Statutory construction was the principal means of arriving at this conclusion. Not only was there implied a requirement of specific individual intent to overthrow the government by unlawful means as speedily as circumstances would permit, but active, rather nominal membership in the association was also required. In our jurisprudence guilt was still personal and the relationship between the individual and the Party's illegal purposes must be sufficiently substantial to satisfy that concept. This required not only active membership in the Party and knowledge of its illegal purposes but also an intention "to contribute to the success of those specifically illegal activities."

Applying these tests, Mr. Justice Harlan concluded that in *Scales* the government had supplied the vital links by testimony describing a Party program for establishing an elaborate underground apparatus in various parts of the country, particularly in certain key industries; participants in the apparatus were apparently committed to the doctrine of violent revolution as a guide to future action. Finally, certain former Party members, in reality agents of the Federal Bureau of Investigation, testified to their dealings with Scales as an official of the Party who helped them to train for participation in this underground apparatus. This was sufficient in *Scales* to make a case for the jury both on the issue of illegal Party advocacy and on the defendant's participation in it. In *Noto,* on the other hand, these vital links were missing. The testimony was long on the teaching of the Communist "classics" but extremely short on the means for carrying them into effect. Apparently it was this insistence on specific proof of present illegal advocacy, attributable to the Party as a whole or to the defendant's immediate group, that was sufficient to discourage the government from further prosecutions under the membership clause, as well as under the advocacy clause.

What then shall we say, in the nature of final evaluation, of the long way around in which the Court has reduced both the membership and advocacy clauses of the Smith Act to relative impotence, compared with what must have been the high hopes of its sponsors and the worst fears of its opponents? In terms of shorthand expression it might be said that the effect of *Dennis, Yates, Scales,* and *Noto* was to assimilate both the advocacy and membership clauses of the Act to a somewhat more particularized version of the general statute making it a crime to conspire "to overthrow, put down, or to destroy by force the Government of the United States ... or to oppose by force the authority thereof, or by force to prevent, hinder, or delay the execution of any law of the United States."[9] On its face, of course, the advocacy clause does not require conspiracy or any kind of group activity. But how would that clause, really applied individually, meet the "clear and present danger" test as formulated by Judge Hand, approved by Chief Justice Vinson, and apparently assumed by Mr. Justice Harlan, speaking for the Court in *Yates, Scales,* and *Noto?* Conceivably, individual and even isolated advocacy of violent overthrow might meet that test in times of great stress and emergency, but then the key element would indeed be the "present danger" rather than "the gravity of the 'evil' discounted by its improbability." One might even wonder how a conscientious judge, strictly applying all the standards of *Dennis, Yates, Scales,* and *Noto* and paying some mind to the requirement of proof beyond a reasonable doubt, could now let a case like *Dennis* go to the jury, assuming that he had exactly that record before him.

The closest the Court has come to giving us a composite picture of the meaning of all these cases is in the all-too-brief *per curiam* opinion in *Brandenberg v. Ohio,* mentioned earlier, holding invalid the Ohio Criminal Syndicalism Statute as applied to the Ku Klux Klan leader. After indicating that reliance upon *Whitney v. California*[10] was misplaced because it had been discredited by later decisions, the Court purported to summarize the effect of those decisions by saying: "These later decisions have fashioned the principle that the constitutional guarantees of free speech and free press do not permit a State to forbid or proscribe advocacy of the use of force or of law violation, except where such advocacy is directed to inciting or producing imminent lawless action and is likely to incite or produce such action."[11] One wonders how seriously we should take the inclusion of the word "imminent," especially since the opinion adds a quotation from *Noto* that "the mere abstract teaching . . . of the moral propriety or even moral necessity for a resort to force and violence, is not the same as preparing a group for violent action and steering it to such action." In other words, does such well-organized group activity make up for a lack of imminent lawless action or does it supply the "lawless action" by its very existence? No wonder that Justices Black and Douglas were in something of a quandary as to whether to join the opinion or to concur specially—a problem which they solved by doing both, at the same time disavowing the "clear and present danger" test and opting instead for Mr. Justice Black's favorite distinction between speech and action. In any event, it is plain that there are plenty of formulas available, and now in good repute, to return to the meaning of the "clear and present danger" test as Holmes and Brandeis understood it, if there is the will to do so.

THE SUBVERSIVE ACTIVITIES CONTROL ACT: AN EXERCISE IN FUTILITY?

Quite unlike the Smith Act, the Subversive Activities Control Act of 1950,[12] also known as the McCarran Act, was probably the most thoroughly debated anti-Communist measure in our history. Basically the Act provided for the identification and registration of

"Communist-action" and "Communist-front" organizations ("Communist-affiliated" organizations were added later); the identification and registration of members of "Communist-action" organizations; and the attachment of various disabilities to membership in such organizations. In its origin a product of the House Committee on Un-American Activities—in fact that Committee's chief claim to fame as a conceiver of legislation—the McCarran Act evolved slowly and painfully from a bill introduced by Representative (later Senator) Mundt, a member of the Committee, on July 26, 1947; it passed through various stages, including one known as the Mundt-Nixon Bill, until finally it was enacted into law on September 23, 1950, when the Senate completed the overriding of President Truman's veto. Meanwhile, the eleven leaders of the Communist Party first indicted under the Smith Act had been found guilty; Alger Hiss had been convicted on two counts of perjury growing out of his confrontation with Whittaker Chambers; Senator McCarthy had blossomed to something like full flower with his attacks upon the "Communist-infested" State Department; Klaus Fuchs had been convicted of espionage and the Rosenbergs had been arrested on similar charges; and most important of all, American soldiers were fighting against Communist aggression in Korea. It was not easy in such times for a congressman to be against anything that was directed against the worldwide Communist conspiracy. No wonder then that some opponents of the McCarran Act, like Senator Humphrey, sought to temper their opposition by supporting a substitute, called the Kilgore Bill, which they said provided a much more realistic and hard-hitting response to the Communist threat. The ultimate result of this tactic was that both were adopted. The Kilgore Bill, providing for the apprehension and detention, in time of war, invasion, or insurrection in aid of a foreign enemy, of each person as to whom there is reasonable ground to believe that he will probably engage in espionage or sabotage, became Title II of the McCarran Act. Title II has still to be enforced or tested in any way. Title I has been embroiled in litigation ever since its adoption.

The anticipated fulcrum for enforcement of the McCarran Act was the compulsory registration of the Communist Party as a Communist-action organization—i.e., an organization which " (i) is substantially directed, dominated or controlled by the foreign government or foreign organization controlling the world Communist movement . . . and (ii) operates primarily to advance the objectives of such world Communist movement." Once the Communist Party was so identified and registered, then other organizations could be identified and required to register as Communist-front organizations. Such an organization is defined as one "which (A) is substantially directed, dominated, or controlled by a Communist-action organization, and (B) is primarily operated for the purpose of giving aid and support to a Communist-action organization, a Communist foreign government, or the world Communist movement." Since neither the Communist Party nor any other organization came forward to register voluntarily under the Act, the government, on November 22, 1950, began the appropriate proceedings before the Subversive Activities Control Board to compel its registration. After lengthy and complicated proceedings before the Board and in the courts, the Supreme Court on June 5, 1961, in a 5 to 4 decision, finally sustained the Board's order declaring the Communist Party a Communist-action organization and ordering it to register.[13]

The arguments before the Court had canvassed the whole panoply of statutory and constitutional issues which had been largely anticipated in the congressional debates. But Mr. Justice Frankfurter, speaking for the Court, characterized most of the constitutional issues as premature. The only significant ones which he disposed of on the merits were (1) that the registration provisions of that statute, taken together with the cumulative consequences of registration, represented a legislative attempt to outlaw the Party by devious means and therefore constituted a bill of attainder forbidden by Article I, Section 9, clause 3 of the Constitution; and (2) that the disclosure provisions of the statute, including particularly the required filing of membership lists, violated the freedoms of expression and association protected by the First Amendment. On the first issue, Mr. Justice Frankfurter found that the Party was neither "outlawed" nor singled out for destruction. The standards for determination were general ones which could be applied to any organization. Even if Congress realized that they would have the effect of singling out the Communist Party and intended them to do just that, the Party could avoid the effect simply by shedding some of the damning characteristics. With respect to the second issue, the disclosure requirements did not violate the First Amendment because they were reasonably related to the characteristics of a "Communist-action organization" as defined in the statute and to the legislative findings regarding the threat of the world Communist movement. This did not mean that compulsory disclosure of asso-

ciation membership was always justified, as had been made plain in
NAACP v. Alabama,[14] where the Court could find no rational relationship between the required disclosure of membership in the
NAACP and the professed objectives of the state with regard to
enforcement of its foreign-corporation registration statute. "But
where the problems of accommodating the exigencies of self-preser-
vation and the values of liberty are as complex and intricate as they
are in the situation described in the findings of Section 2 of the
Subversive Activities Control Act . . . the legislative judgment as to
how that threat may best be met consistently with the safeguarding
of personal freedom is not to be set aside merely because the judgment of judges would, in the first instance, have chosen other
methods."[15]

One of the constitutional issues which Mr. Justice Frankfurter
excluded from decision as premature in the *Communist Party* case
was the question whether the registration and disclosure provisions
of the statute violated the privilege against self-incrimination; this
was, however, the principal ground relied upon by the dissenting
opinions of Chief Justice Warren and Justices Black, Brennan, and
Douglas. In this respect, they partially anticipated the unanimous
decision of the Court, several years later, in *Albertson v. Subversive
Activities Control Board*,[16] holding that an individual who claimed
the privilege could not validly be ordered to register by the Board,
even after the Board had held a hearing and found that he was a
member of the Party. Such a holding was of course foreshadowed by
many decisions holding that admission of Party membership could
not be compelled because it might be used for purposes of prosecution both under the membership clause of the Smith Act and also
under Section 4(a) of the Subversive Activities Control Act itself.
It has also been forecast on several occasions during the debates and
by some commentators.

The decision in *Albertson* still left open the possibility that the
Party might itself be compelled to register and to furnish the list
of its members. This gap was closed by the court of appeals' holding
in *Communist Party v. United States*[17] that the Party could also
plead the privilege on behalf of its members as a defense in criminal
prosecution for its failure to register in accordance with the Board's
order. To have held otherwise would have made nonsense out of
Albertson; so at least the government must have concluded, since it
did not seek review of the court of appeals' decision. This brought

to an inglorious close the seventeen-year attempt to compel the Communist Party to register as a Communist-action organization. The result was to throw the Act back into the lap of Congress to see what, if anything, worth preserving could be salvaged from the wreckage of what had once been the House Un-American Activities Committee's proudest accomplishment. The solution worked out by that Committee, with the cooperation of Senator Dirksen, who was equally determined that the statute and the Board should not lapse into oblivion, was the 1968 amendment eliminating all the provisions for compulsory registration.[18] What remained then was a somewhat bobtailed statute providing for proceedings before the Board which could eventuate in declaratory orders determining whether particular organizations should be characterized as "Communist-action," "Communist-front" or "Communist-infiltrated"; proceedings against individuals charged with membership in Communist-action organizations could result in similar declaratory orders. Such orders would be open to public inspection and would also have some of the same effects as registration under the previous terms of the statute.

The next and perhaps final round of litigation regarding the Subversive Activities Control Act in its attenuated form has apparently been concluded with the refusal of the Supreme Court on April 21, 1970, to review a decision of the Court of Appeals for the District of Columbia in *Boorda v. Subversive Activities Control Board*.[19] The court of appeals treated as controlling those decisions holding that the government may not subject to criminal penalties or to other disabilities a person who knowingly belongs to an organization which advocates overthrow of the government by force or violence, unless it is also shown that the particular member concerned shares the illegal purposes. Assuming then that such innocent membership, in a Communist-action organization was a protected constitutional right, the court of appeals deduced that it was equally protected from the possibly harmful consequences of disclosure, just as membership in the NAACP was protected from disclosure in *NAACP v. Alabama*. The 1961 decision in the *Subversive Activities Control Board* case sustaining the registration provisions was distinguished on the ground that there the order was directed against the Communist Party itself, rather than against an individual member. Since the Party itself could not practicably be required to distinguish between innocent and guilty members, "innocent members were unavoidably caught up in a net designed to disclose the guilty." But the same could not be said with respect to orders separately directed against individual members.

The foregoing distinction, developed by Chief Judge Bazelon for the court of appeals in the *Boorda* case, is a remarkably ingenious way of escaping from the controlling effect of the Supreme Court's 1961 decision. Whatever may be thought of the validity of the distinction, the effect of the denial of certiorari in *Boorda* is clearly to limit the applicability of the statute to the determination of whether particular organizations should be characterized as "Communist-action," "Communist-front" or "Communist-infiltrated." Conceivably the statute and the Board might still be continued for the purpose of making of such determinations, but the strongest argument against it would be the dreary history of the Board thus far in its unrewarding pursuit of any organizations other than the Communist Party itself. In the light of this history it is hard to believe that the Congress of the United States will not now finally realize the folly of a democratic government's attempting to set up an intellectual radar system to warn its citizens against the machinations of those who, in the government's judgment, scheme to subject them, by a gradual poisoning of their minds, to the domination of a foreign dictatorship. Surely the members of Congress will now have the courage to rid themselves of this albatross which the Court has all but slaughtered for them.

TEST OATHS AND LOYALTY-SECURITY PROGRAMS

At the same time that President Truman was doing his best to head off enactment of the Subversive Activities Control Act, his administration was busy implementing the first formal and general loyalty program for government employment, under the aegis of Executive Order No. 9835.[20] Although this order and subsequent similar orders gave rise to many court decisions, few of these were concerned with the substantive, as distinguished from the procedural, aspects of the program. The most fundamental of the procedural questions—the right to fair hearing and especially the right to confront adverse witnesses—is not within our present concern. Rather we must grapple with the more elusive concepts underlying many of the loyalty programs of both state and federal governments. Popularly speaking, these are reflected in such familiar maxims as "a man is known by the company he keeps" and "birds of a feather flock together." Somewhat more legally speaking, we must ask if "guilt by association" is always forbidden. Does "freedom of association" necessarily preclude consideration of certain types of association as bars to various specifically defined employment or professional opportunities? Obviously the propriety of such consideration was a fundamental assumption of the loyalty program initiated by Executive Order 9835, which provided that among the "activities and associations" to be considered in connection with the determination of disloyalty was "Membership in, affiliation with or sympathetic association with any foreign or domestic organization . . . designated by the Attorney General as totalitarian, fascist, communist or subversive." This was the genesis of the Attorney General's List of Subversive Organizations, which was partly a device for giving notice to government employees of those organizations which they would join at their peril.

The philosophy underlying the Attorney General's list was indirectly considered and sustained by the Court in *American Communications Association v. Douds*.[21] There the Court upheld the validity of the non-Communist affidavit provision of the Labor-Management Relations Act, denying the benefits of the Act to unions whose officers refused to execute and file with the Board such an affidavit. In the opinion for the Court by Chief Justice Vinson, challenges based on the First Amendment, the due process clause, and the bill of attainder clause of the Constitution were all rejected. The "clear and present danger" test was irrelevant because the government's interest was "not in preventing the dissemination of Communist doctrine or the holding of particular beliefs because it is feared that unlawful action will result therefrom if free speech is practiced." Rather it was "in protecting the free flow of commerce from what Congress deemed to be substantial evils of conduct that are not the products of speech at all." The regulation was directed at "harmful conduct which Congress has determined is carried on by persons who may be identified by their political affiliations and beliefs." The applicability of the reasoning to similar disqualification from government employment hardly requires elaboration. This was made explicit, for example, in *Adler v. Board of Education*,[22] upholding the New York Feinberg Law, which, much like Executive Order No. 9835, was designed to accomplish the "elimination of subversive persons from the public school system," and provided for its own list of "subversive organizations."

The history of the constitutional law of civil disabilities since *Douds* and *Adler* has been largely one of steady retreat from the generalizations and implications of both opinions. This may be illustrated first by the decision in *United States v. Brown*,[23] striking down as a bill of attainder the provision of the Labor-Management Reporting and Disclosure Act[24] disqualifying from reponsible positions in labor organizations any person "who is or has been [during the past five years] a member of the Communist Party." There the opinion of Chief Justice Warren emphasized not only the identification of the Communist Party by name, rather than by some "objective standard of conduct," but also the inclusion of all members of the Party "without regard to whether there existed any demonstrable relationship between the characteristics of the person involved and the evil Congress sought to eliminate." Since both of these objections were equally applicable to the non-Communist affidavit, one can hardly disagree with the conclusion of the four dissenting Justices that *Douds* was obviously overruled. Similarly, when the Court a year later in *Elfbrandt v. Russell*[25] invalidated a state statute which, through the device of a loyalty oath, subjected to prosecution for perjury and to discharge any public officer who became or remained a member of the Communist Party, Mr. Justice White, speaking for the same four dissenters as in *Brown,* asked how the Court could reach this result without admitting that it was overruling previous cases like *Adler.* Mr. Justice White received his answer, at least in part, in *Keyishian v. Board of Regents*,[26] when the same five-man majority struck down the very statute which had been sustained in *Adler,* including the provision which made membership in the Communist Party prima facie evidence of disqualification from employment in the state educational system. Mr. Justice Brennan, speaking for the Court, explained that "constitutional law has developed since *Adler.*" The governing standard was now that "legislation which sanctions membership unaccompanied by specific intent to further the unlawful goals of the organization or which is not active membership violates constitutional limitations." Apparently "sanctions" in this sentence means "imposes any disqualification or disability." Once the Court had committed itself as explicitly as it had to the meaning of freedom of association as expounded in *Elfbrandt* and *Keyishian,* it is difficult to see how it could have avoided the conclusion in *United States v. Robel,*[27] invalidating the provision of the Subversive Activities Control Act barring members of Communist action organizations from employment in defense facilities. Even the procedure adopted by the State of New York for the determination of subversive organizations forbidden to teachers was comparable to the procedure of the federal statute, and it would hardly bear saying that the defense facilities designated by the Secretary of Defense were *ipso facto* more precious and vulnerable than the state's educational system.

The decision in *Robel* has triggered a reaction in Congress the ultimate result of which is still in doubt. At the instance of its Committee on Internal Security (formerly the House Un-American Activities Committee), the House of Representatives has passed H.R. 14864, which undertakes to provide a statutory framework for personnel security programs both for access to defense facilities so designated by the Secretary of Defense and for disclosure of classified information to employees of government contractors and subcontractors. The same bill also provides legislative authority for a personnel screening program for access to merchant vessels and port facilities comparable to the Port Security Program struck down by the Supreme Court in *Schneider v. Smith*,[28] on the ground that it was not authorized by Congress. Such legislation, if enacted, would not seek to re-establish the absolute ban against employment of Communist Party members invalidated in *Robel*. Rather it would adopt substantially the same flexible standard as embodied at present in Executive Order No. 10865 establishing the security program for access to classified information in industry—namely, that authorization for access will be granted only upon a finding that such authorization is "clearly consistent with the national defense interest." It also explicitly authorizes inquiries into "present or past membership in, or affiliation or association with, any organization, and such other activities, behavior, associations, facts and conditions, past or present, which are relevant to any determination to be made under the provisions of this section." Presumably the administration of the various security programs now in effect continues to play a significant role in the lives of thousands of people deeply involved, either in public or private life, with national defense and classified information. It was revealed during the hearings on H.R. 14864 that over two million people have been cleared under the Industrial Security Program; the likely effect of the bill would apparently be to increase substantially the number of people subject to clearance. For those not immediately concerned, the substance of the standards being applied will probably remain essentially a mystery. It is primarily the absence of any current *cause*

célèbre which supports the belief that the tragic farce of the
J. Robert Oppenheimer security-loyalty trial is not likely to be repeated in the immediate future.[29] Whether that comfortable
assumption will survive a period of stress and anxiety, such as
characterized the height of the McCarthy era, is a subject of concern not so easily dismissed. Intimations of such concern were
reflected in the House debate on H.R. 14864. The ultimate fate
of that bill will itself be some further index of the temper of our
times.

LEGISLATIVE INVESTIGATIONS AND THE RIGHT OF SILENCE

No discussion of freedom of association and internal security could
be complete without some mention of legislative investigations.
Smith Act prosecutions, Subversive Activities Control Board proceedings, loyalty oaths, and loyalty programs flitted somewhat in-
termittently across the security stage, but always in the background
could be heard the beating of the political tomtoms, summoning
the anti-Communist warriors to battle, warning the fugitives of
impending doom. Early in the life of the Un-American Activities
Committee its commitment to the philosophy of exposure for exposure's sake, as well as its determination to dig out and destroy
the cancerous growth of communism, not only in government, but
in every influential area of American life—including, for example,
the movie industry and its writers—was made abundantly and
unabashedly clear. Almost equally early, that philosophy was forthrightly challenged by some witnesses, such as the Hollywood Ten,
who, disdaining reliance upon the privilege against self-incrimination, forthrightly asserted their right of silence with respect to their
beliefs and associations on the basis of the First Amendment. For
many the consequence of such misplaced reliance upon the First
rather than the Fifth Amendment was not only substantial jail
sentences but also years of black-listing from any meaningful use
of their talents in the entire entertainment industry. There was
not even the consolation of an opinion from the Supreme Court,
which for several years consistently denied certiorari, even though
some of the decisions below were by divided courts and the questions presented were obviously of major importance.[30] The result
was that during the height of the McCarthy period, it was hornbook
law that the only way legally to avoid answering the "sixty-four-

dollar question"—"Are you now or have you ever been a member of the Communist Party?"—was to plead the privilege against self-incrimination. Even if the witness was willing to tell all about himself, but could not stomach naming his friends or associates, his only safe refuge was immediate recourse to the Fifth Amendment, lest he be held to have waived his right to invoke it later, once having answered with respect to himself. Only full cooperation could purchase amnesty. Thus was born that unsavory epithet "Fifth Amendment Communist."

Such at least seemed to be the state of the law until the decision in *Watkins v. United States*,[31] reversing a conviction for contempt before the Un-American Activities Committee of a witness who was willing to answer questions about his own involvement with the Communist Party, but not those regarding the previous involvement of others. While the decision in *Watkins* was itself narrowly based on the ground that the defendant had not been afforded fair opportunity to determine the pertinency of the questions to the objectives of the investigation, general observations in Chief Justice Warren's opinion led some optimists to look forward to invalidation of the resolution establishing the Un-American Activities Committee and even to First Amendment protection against inquiry directed into a witness's past or present Communist affiliations. Any such hopes were soon dashed by the 5 to 4 decision in *Barenblatt v. United States*,[32] sustaining the contempt conviction of a witness who had refused to answer questions about his own prior Communist involvement. Mr. Justice Harlan's opinion for the Court rejected both the contention that the mandate of the Committee was invalid because it was too vague and the contention that the First Amendment protected the witness from such compulsory disclosure. Whatever might be the ambiguities of the phrase "un-American activities," it was clear that it was intended to embrace Communist activities; furthermore, in view of the "long and widely accepted view that the tenets of the Communist Party include overthrow of the Government of the United States by force and violence," congressional inquiry was justified by the same principles that underlay the Court's decision upholding state legislation that required public-office holders "to disclaim knowing membership in any organization advocating overthrow of the government by force, which legislation none can avoid seeing was aimed at the membership in the Communist Party." Mr. Justice Harlan did not have to distinguish cases like *Keyishian* and

Robel because they had not yet been decided. The only significant qualification of the *Barenblatt* ruling which has since been made by the Court has been in *Gibson v. Florida Legislative Investigation Committee*,[33] another 5 to 4 decision, reversing the contempt conviction of the President of the Miami branch of the NAACP for refusal to bring to the Committee hearing, or to consult, membership records in responding to questions regarding Communist infiltration of the branch. The opinion by Mr. Justice Goldberg for the Court is significant in its unequivocal holding that freedom of association, and more particularly privacy in the exercise of that freedom, may on occasion be superior to the legislature's investigatory power. The dissenters, Justices Harlan, Clark, Stewart, and White, on the other hand, could not understand why, if membership in the Communist Party was an appropriate subject of investigation, the possibility of Communist infiltration into another organization was not an equally appropriate subject.

A more significant question, for the purposes of our general inquiry, is whether the rule of *Barenblatt* and the principle illustrated by *Robel* and its immediate predecessors can long survive comfortably together in the same intellectual atmosphere. Will it be a sufficient distinction to say that one concerns only inquiry and disclosure, while the other concerns legislatively imposed disqualification from certain ways of making a living? Even though this is clearly a factual difference, it is not so clear that it tends to support the subordination of the First Amendment claim in the former situation and not in the latter. Indeed, realistically viewed, it might well appear that the government's interest in disqualifying Communists from defense facilities and government employment would be considerably stronger than the government's interest in publishing lists of Communists who might then be excluded from various walks of private life by purely private action. To treat the latter governmental interest as controlling would eviscerate the supposedly accepted right to privacy in the exercise of one's freedom of association. The only other way to justify the result in *Barenblatt* is to assume that the government must have some other more vital interest at stake in discovering the extent of Communist influence or infiltration. But if such a presumption is to be indulged on behalf of the Un-American Activities Committee, surely it should be equally applicable to any other legislative investigating committee, including, for example, the Florida Legislative Investigation Committee. Unfortunately this exercise in logic could just as well lead to the destruction of *Gibson,* and perhaps even *Robel,* as to the destruction of *Barenblatt.* At any rate the Court may someday have to face up to the double standard it has applied to congressional and state investigating committees.[34]

BEYOND COMMUNISM: THE INDIGENOUS REVOLUTIONARIES

As we move into the 1970's, it is obvious that the glare of the Red Menace has faded into a faint glow barely perceptible on the horizons of our political life.[35] Even the Un-American Activities Committee, rechristened the Committee on Internal Security and provided with a new charter which pays only incidental attention to communism and other foreign ideologies, looks now to "organizations or groups, whether of foreign or domestic origin . . . which incite or employ acts of force, violence, terrorism or any unlawful means."[36] Similarly it was a concern with the realities of domestic strife, boiling over in city ghettos from Watts to Newark, as well as occasionally erupting on college campuses from Columbia to Berkeley, which found legislative expression in the riot sections of the Civil Rights Act of 1968.[37] The courts too have reflected this change in our preoccupations as demonstrated by two contemporary conspiracy trials. One was the prosecution of five defendants (Dr. Spock, Dr. Coffin, and three others) under Section 12 of the Military Selective Service Act of 1967, for conspiring to "counsel, aid and abet" resistance to the draft.[38] The other was the prosecution of eight—later reduced to seven—defendants, under the riot sections of the Civil Rights Act of 1968, for conspiring to travel in interstate commerce with the intent to incite riots in Chicago during the Democratic Convention of 1968. These defendants, though far removed in apparent philosophy and manner from their predecessors and indeed from each other, find themselves relitigating the same First Amendment issues that were the stock in trade of the Communist defendants of an earlier era.

Both the draft and the riot conspiracy cases provide striking illustrations of the evils attendant upon the use of conspiracy prosecutions for the purpose of discouraging political movements, even assuming that some criminal activity may be originally contemplated or subsequently involved. In the draft cases four of the five defendants were found guilty by the jury. On appeal, the convictions of all were reversed on procedural grounds; two, Coffin and

Goodman, were required to stand trial again if the government chose to prosecute, while two others, Spock and Ferber, were found entitled to acquittal without further proceedings.[39] This conclusion was reached by a majority of the court of appeals after painstaking examination of the record and meticulous application of the principles developed in the Smith Act cases. Applying the requirements of specific illegal intent developed in *Yates, Scales,* and *Noto,* Judge Aldrich, speaking for the majority, was able to find sufficient evidence of such intent in the case of two of the defendants, based on exactly what they said at certain meetings, but not in the cases of the other two. Probably this application of established principles was entirely sound, but it is hard to escape the force of Judge Coffin's dissenting observations that to the general public the results must appear capricious, based as they were on rather obscure and probably adventitious distinctions between the exact statements of the defendants, although they all were committed to the same general objectives and were themselves quite unaware at the time they acted of the significance of the distinctions which the court drew.

The results in the riot conspiracy case thus far, the acquittal of all seven defendants on the conspiracy charges and the conviction of five of them on the individual charges of crossing state lines and doing some other act with the intent to incite a riot, are more difficult to assess without either intense examination of the record or the benefit of an appellate opinion. Nevertheless, the course of the trial itself, even apart from the horseplay of the defendants, indicates how unsuitable the judicial process itself is for the determination of the kind of issues presented by such a conspiracy charge.

Finally, the very circumstances surrounding the initiation of prosecution in the *Spock* case and the riot conspiracy case suggest that such prosecutions, like the prosecutions under the Smith Act, are more likely to reflect political considerations, or at least the prevailing climate of political opinion, than a dispassionate prosecutorial judgment regarding the probability of guilt. This consideration, as well as the apparent artificiality of the results in terms of the realities of the situations, suggests the need for re-examination and reformulation of basic standards if they are to provide a satisfactory guide for future conduct and decision-making. Particularly as applied to relatively formless and open conspiracies like that in *Spock,* the charge of an agreement to persuade others to engage in unlawful conduct by the use of language which might or might not, depending on the exact language and the circumstances, be reasonably calculated to induce such conduct, should be regarded on its face as insufficient to satisfy First Amendment requirements of either precision of imminency. Since under such a charge it is obvious that at the time of the supposed agreement no one can foretell the exact language to be used or the circumstances in which it will be used, the validity of the charge can be determined only by a dubious kind of hindsight based upon the fruition of the alleged conspiracy. In those circumstances the conspiracy charge serves no essential function in protecting public security that could not equally be served by individual prosecutions for the forbidden advocacy or incitement after it has occurred. If this be true, the greater convenience for the prosecution achieved through the conspiracy mechanism seems far outweighed by the possible chilling effect of such essentially "political" trials upon freedom of association and public debate, as well as the danger of discrediting the judicial process itself.

NOTES

1. 268 U.S. 652 (1925).
2. 395 U.S. 444 (1969).
3. *See* Dorsen, "The Life and Death of the Loyalty Oath," *New York Times,* Sunday, Jan. 11, 1970, §E, at 6.
4. Z. Chafee, *Free Speech in the United States* 441–42 (1954 ed.). The Smith Act is now incorporated in 18 U.S.C. §§2385, 2387.
5. 341 U.S. 494, 510–11, 524–25 (1951), *aff'g* 183 F.2d 201 (2d Cir. 1950).
6. 354 U.S. 298 (1957).
7. 367 U.S. 203 (1961).
8. 367 U.S. 290 (1961).
9. 18 U.S.C. §2384.
10. 274 U.S. 357 (1927).
11. 395 U.S. at 447.
12. 50 U.S.C. §§781–94, 811–26.
13. Communist Party v. Subversive Activities Control Bd., 367 U.S. 1 (1961). This decision was preceded by a variety of procedural controversies which substantially prolonged the litigation; these are reflected in Communist Party v. Subversive Activities Control Bd., 351 U.S. 115 (1956), remanding the case to the Board for determination of the reliability of certain witnesses accused of perjury.
14. 357 U.S. 449 (1958).
15. Communist Party v. Subversive Activities Control Bd., 367 U.S. 1, 96–97 (1961).
16. 382 U.S. 70 (1965).

17. 384 F.2d 957 (D.C. Cir. 1967).

18. 50 U.S.C. §§781–94.

19. 421 F.2d 1142 (D.C. Cir. 1969), *cert. denied,* 90 S. Ct. 1365 (1970).

20. 3 C.F.R. 627 (1947 comp.), 12 Fed. Reg. 1935 (1947). The key substantive provision was the establishment of the standard for denial or removal from employment that "on all the evidence, reasonable grounds exist for belief that the person involved is disloyal to the government of the United States." Pt. V. §1. Subsequently this was changed to "on all the evidence there is a reasonable doubt as to the loyalty of the person involved to the Government of the United States." Exec. Order No. 10241, 3 C.F.R. 749 (1951 comp.), 16 Fed. Reg. 3690 (1951).

21. 339 U.S. 382 (1950).

22. 342 U.S. 485 (1952).

23. 381 U.S. 437 (1965).

24. 29 U.S.C. §504.

25. 384 U.S. 11 (1966).

26. 385 U.S. 589 (1967).

27. 389 U.S. 258 (1967).

28. 390 U.S. 17 (1968).

29. See P. Stern, *The Oppenheimer Case: Security or Trial* (1969).

30. United States v. Josephson, 165 F.2d 82 (2d Cir. 1947), *cert. denied,* 333 U.S. 838 (1948); Barsky v. United States, 167 F.2d 241 (D.C. Cir.), *cert. denied,* 334 U.S. 843 (1948); Lawson v. United States, 176 F.2d 49 (D.C. Cir. 1949), *cert. denied,* 339 U.S. 934 (1950) (the *Hollywood Ten Cases*). See J. Cogley, *Report on Blacklisting: I. Movies; II. Radio-Television* (1956).

31. 354 U.S. 178 (1957).

32. 360 U.S. 109 (1959).

33. 372 U.S. 539 (1963).

34. The majority view in *Barenblatt* was reaffirmed by the same majority in Wilkinson v. United States, 365 U.S. 400 (1961), and in Braden v. United States, 365 U.S. 431 (1961). Since then the Un-American Activities Committee was again challenged in litigation still pending in the Northern District of Illinois, in which it is asserted that "the interpretation of section 18 of Rule XI as expressed by the continued conduct of the Subcommittee of the House Un-American Activities Committee attributes a meaning to the rule which renders it unconstitutional, and that this conduct consisted of the exposure of witnesses, including plaintiffs, to public scorn and obloquy and harassment and intimidation of these witnesses without any legislative purpose but rather to chill and deter them and others in the exercise of their first amendment rights." *See* Stamler v. Willis, 371 F.2d 413 (7th Cir. 1966), 415 F.2d 1365 (1969), *cert. denied,* 399 U.S. 929 (1970).

35. For further light on the realities of Communism in America, see D. Shannon, *The Decline of American Communism* (1959).

36. H. Res. 89, *amending* Rule XI of the Rules of the House of Representatives, 115 Cong. Rec. H958 (daily ed. Feb. 18, 1969).

37. 18 U.S.C. §§2101–2; 114 Cong. Rec. 5993 (July 11, 1968). For debates in the House on H.R. 421, the original bill, indicating concern with Stokely Carmichael, Rap Brown, and other leaders of SNCC (Student Non-Violent Coordinating Committee) and similar organizations, see 113 Cong. Rec. 19347–433 (July 19, 1967).

38. 50 U.S.C. App. §462 (a).

39. United States v. Spock, 416 F.2d 165 (1st Cir. 1969).

THE RIGHT TO PUBLISH

HARRY KALVEN, JR.

THERE IS A COMPLEX ANALOGY BETWEEN LIBEL AND obscenity when viewed against the backdrop of the First Amendment that warrants our looking at them together in a single essay. For one thing, they are the problems of free speech the layman is most likely to be familiar with and to have opinions about. In the day-to-day life of publishers, regulations governing libel and obscenity must intrude more frequently than other, more fundamental types of regulation. Moreover, they are both Johnny-come-latelies to the constitutional scene: the first precedent on obscenity does not come from the United States Supreme Court until 1957; the first precedent on libel, not until 1964. The constitutional doctrines about them have been the work entirely of the Warren Court. Finally, to my mind, they share an important characteristic: neither obscenity nor libel can be said in any simple sense to present a clear and present danger of anything, yet there remains a strong momentum for subjecting them both to some degree of control. They provide, therefore, striking examples of the perplexing versatility of free speech problems, and the Supreme Court's responses to them afford a chance to watch at work a contemporary court deeply sensitive to the values involved.

Harry Kalven, Jr., is Professor of Law at Chicago Law School, the director of the Law School's interdisciplinary study of the American jury system, the author of several books on constitutional law, and a participant in litigation involving obscenity and other freedom-of-speech issues.

I

The story of obscenity and the law, which is now an oft-told tale, has a rich history, going back in England to the mid-Victorian era and the enactment of Lord Campbell's Act in 1857, and in America to the impact of that strange figure Anthony Comstock a few years later.[1] It has had its high cultural moments, such as the adjudication of the status of James Joyce's *Ulysses* in 1934, and its judicial heroes, such as Learned Hand, John Woolsey, Curtis Bok, Thurman Arnold, and Jerome Frank.

Our concern here, however, is with the *constitutional dimensions* of the regulation of obscenity and with the effort to square censorship in the name of obscenity with the implications of the First Amendment of the United States Constitution. That story is extraordinary in several respects. Its time span is incredibly short—the Supreme Court does not begin to deal with obscenity until 1956. Its plot is a very busy one: the Court has decided some twenty cases in the intervening decade and a half. As a constitutional matter obscenity has proved difficult for the Court to capture in doctrinal formula; even in so short a span one sees a steady if uneasy evolution. Finally, viewing it for the moment from the standpoint of the Supreme Court as a political institution under the stress of conflicting pressures, it appears that the Court has risked its reputation and prestige quite as much in its dealing with obscenity as it has by its entry into those other famous thickets of school desegregation, reapportionment, and criminal procedure.

The constitutional law of obscenity is, interestingly enough, a child entirely of the Warren Court. That Court's most loyal admirers would not contend that it had been successful in formulating a solution or even in reaching any sort of consensus among the several Justices. Yet even that Court's most ardent critics would admit that it has worked seriously and gallantly at the matter and that the lack of success has been due far more to the nature of the problem than to any shortcomings of judicial technique or philosophy.

Obscenity as a cultural phenomenon is doubtless a rich, colorful, important clue to the values and attitudes of the society. It can pose deep and fascinating issues for a theory of aesthetics. It is, however, of all issues that come before courts of law, the one least suitable to their style, their decorum, their competence, and the one most unnerving to their self-respect. Thus, in a brief filed on behalf of *Playboy* magazine by Thurman Arnold in a Vermont obscenity case, it is said:

> The spectacle of a judge poring over the picture of some nude, trying to ascertain the extent to which she arouses prurient interest, and then attempting to write an opinion which explains the difference between that nude and some other nude has elements of low comedy. Justice is supposed to be a blind Goddess. The task of explaining why the words "sexual relations" are decent and some other word with the same meaning is indecent is not one for which judicial techniques are adapted.[2]

It is abundantly clear that in the decade and a half since obscenity entered constitutional law, we have witnessed a major revolution in community standards for dealing with sex in movies, theater, literature, and the press generally. There has been a candor explosion. And as innumerable popular sociology articles have pointed out to us, the point is not simply that items like *I Am Curious (Yellow), The Story of O,* and *Oh! Calcutta!* are allowed to circulate; it is rather that these items have entered the mainstream of contemporary culture; they circulate at the respectable theaters, movie houses, and bookstores. One cannot but wonder if it may not already be too late to discuss obscenity and the law; obscenity may be obsolete.

Not quite, I suspect. The law is still on the books and the concerns, anxieties, and political dynamite still remain. The regulation of obscenity is a sleeping tiger that could easily be stirred, especially in a country governed according to the whims of a silent majority. We could still experience a crusade for purity that would make the law of obscenity a lively topic again and give genuine importance to the constitutional limits on the regulation of obscenity.

The most striking, and depressing, contemporary evidence of the political potency still lurking in obscenity is to be found in Senate hearings on the nomination of Abe Fortas to the Chief Justiceship during the summer and early fall of 1968.[3] The episode deserves a far fuller treatment than can be attempted here, and its shamefulness transcends the use that was made of obscenity. It is possible, of course, to read it on different levels and to conclude that the senators were not really serious about obscenity but were simply using it as a device to block Fortas much as the hypercritical conflict-of-interest charges were later to be used to block Clement

Haynsworth. Nevertheless, it is arresting that the senators thought obscenity such good ammunition for their purposes.

It is all too easy to criticize the shabbiness of the performance. The senators solemnly receive extended testimony, in salacious detail, from an attorney representing the Citizens for Decent Literature and from a Los Angeles police captain, a specialist in obscenity law enforcement; they listen to a legal analysis from that expert, Senator Strom Thurmond; and then, as the press so gleefully noted, they retire to executive session to view one of those movies Fortas had cleared.[4] It is all too easy to criticize the sheer irrationality of their attack on Justice Fortas, who had not come to the Court until 1965 when the basic structure of obscenity law had been set and who was remembered by students of the problem primarily for casting the deciding vote affirming the 5 to 4 decision *to convict* Ralph Ginzburg. The senators used criteria which would have served also to bar from promotion *all* of the Justices then on the Court, including Harlan, White, and Stewart. But I suspect they knew exactly what they were doing, and the episode is thus a dismal reminder of how much demagogic appeal there still is in being against obscenity.

For our present purposes of a quick survey of the judicial handling of obscenity by the Supreme Court, there are three closely related aspects that it may be profitable to isolate and pursue one at a time:

1. Whether a legal test or definition of the obscene can be worked out.

2. Whether the Court can reach a stable consensus among the nine Justices on any such test.

3. Whether the Court's strategy for squaring the regulation of obscenity with the First Amendment survives today.

The Court has given us two firm points by which to bound the problem. In 1957 in *Butler v. Michigan*,[5] it upset a state statute which sought to prevent the *general* distribution of materials "tending to the corruption of the morals of youth." The Court saw this as an effort "to restrict the adult population to reading only what is fit for children." In a unanimous decision it firmly refused to permit obscenity to be defined so generously. Whatever the possibility of regulating material aimed specifically at children as the target audience, for materials of general distribution obscenity had to be defined with an adult audience in mind; the children were irrelevant. In retrospect this appears to have been a decision of major importance for the conceptualization of the problem, and, we would note, it appears also to be one of the very rare times the Court was to be unanimous in an obscenity case.

The second case from which to take our bearings is *Kingsley Pictures Corp. v. Regents*[6] *in* 1958, which involved a refusal to license a movie version of that obscenity *cause célèbre, Lady Chatterley's Lover.* Again, the Court was unanimous in invalidating, but this time the posture of the appeal yielded six different opinions from the Justices as to just what the fatal flaw in the state's action was. For our purposes the key view is that of Mr. Justice Stewart, who wrote the opinion of the Court. He read the Court below as having barred the movie because it treated adultery "as proper behavior under certain circumstances." In rejecting this position he uttered a gallant dictum on freedom of speech in general:

> This argument misconceives what it is that the Constitution protects. Its guarantee is not confined to the expression of ideas that are conventional or shared by a majority. It protects advocacy of the opinion that adultery may sometimes be proper, no less than advocacy of socialism or the single tax. . . .

He was also making clear that obscenity does not deal with *ideas* in the ordinary sense.[7] Ideas about sexual behavior are like ideas about any other topic. The objection to obscenity is keyed to something more subtle. I suggest it is to the capacity to arouse the imagination, to what might best be called *sexual imagery*.

These two points are sufficient to make it evident that the quest for a test of obscenity will be a most peculiar one. We are concerned, not with competing truths in a marketplace of ideas, but with sexual imagery that will be improper for an audience of adults who are presumably sexually experienced. Starting with the *Roth* case in 1957,[8] the Supreme Court definition has gone through four stages. *Roth* erased any vestiges of common-law notions stemming from *Queen v. Hicklin*[9] in 1868 that the material was to be tested in terms of impact on vulnerable adults or that excerpts could be considered standing alone. The Court keyed its formula to a hitherto little-used English word, "prurient." The test was whether to the average person, applying contemporary community standards, the dominant appeal of the work taken as a whole was to a prurient interest. Although this appeared to be an improvement over many

earlier efforts and had the ring of a technical formula, there was
an awkward circularity in it since a prurient interest might well
be defined as an interest in the obscene. In *Manual Enterprises v.
Day*[10] in 1962, the Court, speaking through Justice Harlan, found it
necessary to add another term to the pruriency test. The case involved the exclusion from the mails of a magazine catering to a
homosexual audience and featuring photographs of nude males. In
a notable instance of employment of neutral principles Justice
Harlan found the male nudes not "more objectionable than the
many portrayals of the female nude that society tolerates." He
found them therefore nonobscene, since whatever their specialized
appeal to pruriency, they lacked "patent offensiveness." Thus the
strange vocabulary of the Court was enriched by adding patency
to pruriency. Then in 1964 in *Jacobellis v. Ohio*,[11] another movie
censorship case, a third term was added to the formula. It was held
necessary that the material be "utterly without redeeming social
importance," and the Court stressed the adverb "utterly." Two
points are worth noting. Both patency and absence of social significance had perhaps been implicit in the original *Roth* formula,
but by a kind of Socratic dialogue the Court was led to elaborate
its central idea. Furthermore, the dialectic had moved steadily in
the direction of narrowing the scope of obscenity. Pruriency and
patency are not enough without an utter lack of social significance.

The terms suggest a metaphysics of their own. It is possible,
apparently, to have valuable inoffensive pruriency. More important, as indicating the narrowness of obscenity concerns, it is possible to have all sorts of materials which are utterly without
redeeming social importance but which are nevertheless beyond
the reach of law because they do not deal with sex. And similarly
with material which is patently offensive. The upshot is that the
Court will tolerate, in the area of materials dealing with sex, criteria such as offensiveness or lack of significance which it would
not tolerate for a moment as predicates for the regulation of other
materials. But when the three criteria are taken together as three
elements each of which must be satisfied, it would appear that the
concession to sex is not so great and that very little material has
been left within the reach of law.

This impression was deepened in 1966, a special date in the
history of obscenity and the law. It was the year the Supreme
Court of the United States met Fanny Hill.[12] The Court was faced
with an interesting dilemma. On the one hand *Fanny Hill* was

perhaps the most celebrated work of pornography in the English language, long prized and studied precisely because of that. If *it* was not obscene, what was left for regulation? On the other hand, it was now 1966, the Justices were men of literacy and taste, and it would be embarrassing for them to take Fanny Hill too seriously. The case seemed to be calling the bluff of the Court's statesmanlike strategy of upholding the *possibility* of obscenity regulation while steadily finding particular items not obscene. The Court gallantly made its choice; it reversed the Massachusetts court's judgment that the book was obscene, accepting for the purposes of argument that court's findings that the book had "some modicum of literary and historical value." And in so doing it restated its original test as now officially three-pronged.

Having reached so much clarity and firmness of direction, the Court in the very next breath—indeed, in virtually the same breath —in another decision handed down the same day, *Ginzburg v. United States,*[13] proceeded to complicate matters again. Apparently the test had not finished evolving. *Ginzburg* involved a criminal prosecution for distribution of the magazine *Eros,* a sophisticated, expensive venture in eroticism. It was not clear whether standing alone the material would have satisfied all three prongs of the test, but this time the prosecution had added evidence of the way in which the magazine had been promoted and marketed. The new rule was that material need not be judged standing alone but could be placed in the context of its advertising. And so judged, the Court held the material obscene. The result was to add a new term of art to the test: "pandering." In effect, the principle was that if a defendant advertised his wares as obscene he would not be heard to deny his advertising. But even this is not quite the formula. Evidence of pandering would be relevant only in what were otherwise, under the three-pronged test, "close cases"; advertising could not alchemize just anything into the obscene.

As far as the test of obscenity for adults goes, this is where matters stand today. The relationship between pandering on the one hand and pruriency, patency, and social significance on the other is complex and the Court's ambivalence is obvious—the two approaches move in opposite directions. Pandering appears designed to make it easy to extend the obscenity net; the threefold test appears designed to shrink it drastically. In any event, as you may have noticed, *Ginzburg* has had a major impact on the marketing customs of the day; now the sure clue to the "dirtiest book" on the shelf is that it will have an utterly blank, dull cover carrying only the title.

The quest for definition shows the Court responding to the dialectic of the cases. The intellectual schema it has erected is impressive. But it is also unfortunately a little ludicrous when one remembers the materials to which it is to be applied.

The formula we have been discussing has been culled from majority opinions, but it gives a misleading impression of the extent of agreement among the justices. The development has been marked by an unprecedented inability of the justices to reach consensus, or at least to abandon announcing their individual views once they have failed to carry the day. The process begins with *Roth* itself, where in addition to the majority opinion of Justice Brennan we are given separate opinions from Chief Justice Warren, Justice Harlan, and Justices Black and Douglas. And it comes to fruition in 1964 in *Jacobellis*. First, there is the "official" position, which repeats the pruriency-patency formula and adds the "utterly without significance" factor to it; but this appears to be the enthusiastic view only of Justices Brennan and Goldberg. Second, there is the position of Justices Douglas and Black adhering to their dissent in *Roth* on the ground that no constitutional regulation of obscenity is possible. Third, there is the endearing position of Justice Stewart which cuts through the elaborate schema the Court has developed and insists the only meaningful test is that of "hard-core pornography." "I shall not today attempt," said the Justice in a memorable passage, "further to define the kinds of material I understand to be embraced within that shorthand description; and perhaps I could never succeed in intelligibly doing so. But I know it when I see it; and the motion picture involved in this case is not that." Fourth, there is the view of Justice Harlan, also stemming from *Roth,* that the tests are different for state and federal regulation; he would apply the *Roth-Day* test to federal regulation but would test state regulation simply under a general standard of reasonableness which would presumably provide the most generous scope for obscenity regulation. Fifth, there is the view of Chief Justice Warren, in which he is joined by Justice Clark. He stresses two points. The "use to which the material is put" should be considered and not simply the material per se, a view that foreshadows the shift in the *Ginzburg* case. Moreover, he is exasperated at the burden the Court has imposed on itself by treating obscenity as a constitutional fact and thus placing itself under pressure to review an endless number of individual cases. He would defer to the judgments of the courts below operating under the *Roth* formula, and not make a *de novo* examination of their findings of obscenity. Two years later in the *Fanny Hill* case, a sixth position becomes evident, that of Justice White who would accept the pruriency-patency test but would *not* add "social importance" as a third independent factor. Thus, while the disagreements are often subtle, it is clear that none of the six positions fully commands the support of more than two Justices!

A further glimpse of the judicial box-score is given in 1967 in the *per curiam* reversal in *Redrup v. New York*.[14] The Court discloses that "two members of the Court hold to one view," a third "to a variant view," others to a somewhat different view, and "another Justice" to still a different formula. A caveat about the practical importance of debating the precise formula is suggested by the further announcement that "Whichever of these constitutional views is brought to bear upon the cases before us, it is clear that the judgments [of obscenity] cannot stand."

This lack of consensus invites speculation that the Court may yet shift away from the *Roth* formula as elaborated; indeed, in *Redrup* it is treated as simply one of the four views described, an equal among equals. *Redrup*, to which some commentators have attached great significance although there is no opinion and only a brief *per curiam* note, offers a clue as to future formulas:

> In none of the cases was there a claim that the statute in question reflected a specific and limited state concern for juveniles. . . . In none was there any suggestion of an assault upon individual privacy by publication in a manner so obtrusive as to make it impossible for an unwilling individual to avoid exposure to it. . . . And in none was there evidence of the sort of "pandering" which the Court found significant in *Ginzburg* v. *United States*. . . . [15]

I would not rush to read this somewhat Delphic dictum as heralding the coming of a new three-pronged formula—juvenile audience, captive audience, pandering—since the Court is so careful to recite the four views, none of which, it might be noted, would dictate this set of results. But certainly the evolution of a legal test for obscenity is still very much in process.

The third aspect of the survey of obscenity and the law relates, it will be recalled, to the constitutional strategy of the Supreme Court in handling the First Amendment. We did not perhaps make

it sufficiently clear in the earlier discussion that in pursuing a definition of obscenity the Court was seeking what might be called the
constitutional definition, that is, the definition of obscenity would
serve to mark the limits of what could be regulated by law consistently with the First Amendment. Indeed one is tempted to
stand matters on their head and say that the chief criterion moving
the Justices to varying positions in defining obscenity has been
their notion of what is constitutionally permissible regulation.

The constitutional foundation for the regulation of obscenity
was laid in the *Roth* case in 1957 at the beginning of the Supreme
Court's engagement with obscenity. The Court appeared to have
found that a strategy for resolving the issue without undue embarrassment had been generated by the general impression at that
time that the test of permissible regulation of communication was
the so-called "clear and present danger" test which had become a
part of popular as well as legal culture. To uphold any regulation
of obscene communications the Court appeared obligated to point
to the substantive evil of which obscenity presented a clear and
present danger. Once the juvenile audience and thematic obscenity were put to one side as *Butler* and *Kingsley* required, there
were not many possibilities of danger left, and the best of them
verged on the ribald. There was little or no evidence that exposure
to obscenity led to antisocial behavior. And while exposing people
against their will to matter they found dirty and repulsive might
well commend itself as a target evil, the awkward fact was that the
law seemed largely concerned not with protecting a captive audience but with protecting a *willing* audience for whom the matter
was presumably attractive. If these dangers would not suffice, the
only other candidate seemed to be the danger of exciting the imagination and stimulating sexual fantasy. The Supreme Court thus
seemed doomed to weighing the danger of stimulating the sexual
fantasies of adults—if the regulation of obscenity had to be measured against the "clear and present danger" test.

In *Roth* the Court, speaking through Justice Brennan, finessed
the dilemma. Utilizing a line of precedent stemming from *Chaplinsky v. New Hampshire*[16] and *Beauharnais v. Illinois,*[17] it held
that the obscene fell into a second-level category of speech[18] that
was per se subject to regulation, and that it was "unnecessary to
consider the issues behind the phrase 'clear and present danger.' "
Thus by placing obscenity in the garbage heap of speech along
with fighting words, the profane, and the libelous, the Court solved

its problem. There was somewhere, *Roth* told us, a kind of communication about sex that was so tawdry and worthless that it could validly be regulated. And the clarity and presence of any danger from it was simply irrelevant.

The question is how this 1957 rationale for the constitutionality of obscenity regulation looks today. There are some difficulties.

In 1964 in *New York Times Co. v. Sullivan*,[19] discussed below, the Court in a libel case did not make any use of the two-level theory that had saved *Roth*, although libel too had been included along with fighting words and the obscene in the original *Chaplinsky* dictum and although the regulation of libel, the *New York Times* case told us, was not in many instances constitutionally valid. The Court might well have been read as abandoning its two-level thesis and thus, perhaps without noticing it, pulling the rug out from under the *Roth* rationale.

Then just last spring in *Stanley v. Georgia*[20] the Court was faced with the unlikely question of whether mere possession of obscenity in one's own home without any intent to distribute it could constitutionally be made a crime. The Court held quite sensibly that it could not, but in its effort to explain why, it appeared, in an opinion by Justice Marshall, to further sabotage the rationale of *Roth* and to leave the constitutional justification for regulation almost as much up in the air as, in other cases, it had left the definition. The State of Georgia, relying on *Roth*, argued neatly that since obscenity was not within the area of protected speech, the state was free to deal with it, subject to limits of *other* constitutional provisions in any way deemed necessary, just as they might deal "with other things thought to be detrimental to the welfare of their citizens." The Court refused to apply *Roth*, stressing that it, unlike the present case, involved "commercial distribution." There is, of course, a point here reminiscent of the thesis that the pimp ought to be punished while the prostitute is let alone, but the working out of this point would require a new rationale for obscenity. Moreover the Court, by emphasizing with some eloquence a man's right to be let alone in his own library, seemed to be in the logical difficulty of asserting that a citizen had an inalienable right to possess obscenity in his library but that no one had the right to supply him with it.

If *Ginzburg*, *Redrup*, and *Stanley* are read together they suggest that the Court, exasperated with its failure to reach consensus under the *Roth* formula, might be ready to embark on a new approach to the whole matter. And as to adults, that new approach would emphasize the unseemly commercialization and the captive-audience aspects of obscenity as the predicate for regulation. Indeed, one might guess that the second point would come to dominate, and that advertising and commercialization would be relevant primarily as they involved thrusting the material upon an unwilling audience.

All this would finally make sense and mark a sensible compromise between that part of the adult population whose sensibilities are offended by confrontation with "obscenity" and that part who are attracted, not offended. However, in making guesses about the future career of obscenity regulation, it would be well to note that these signs of the future were all left by the Warren Court and that we have since moved into the era of the Burger Court, a court that for some time to come will be haunted by Fortas' ghost.

A variety of other issues deserve notice, such as the *scienter* requirement for the distributor, the use of experts, the rules as to permissible prior restraints keyed to obscenity, and the special problems of obscenity on television, but within the compass of this essay we can pause for only a brief comment on two other points.

The first of these points lies somewhat outside the domain of legal circles; it involves what might be called the sociology of the controls of obscenity. To a considerable degree, obscenity has been regulated by informal and extralegal pressures. This process has a long history, going back to Anthony Comstock and the New York Society for the Suppression of Vice. The history includes such bits of Americana as the Watch and Ward Society, the Hays Office, the Legion of Decency, the National Office for Decent Literature, and the Citizens for Decent Literature. The tactics have varied widely from the use of threats of prosecution, blacklisting, and boycotts to simply lobbying for changes in legislation and providing spokesmen in public debate about issues of obscenity. The format of organization also varies widely, ranging from semipublic agencies such as the Rhode Island Commission to Encourage Morality in Youth to organized trade association groups like the Hays Office to church-affiliated groups to women's clubs. At times these campaigns appear to have been effective, especially when they were concentrated in a single community.

The extralegal control of obscenity is not altogether easy to evaluate; the line between coercion and criticism is a subtle one, and principles of free speech require that we extend to those who have a distaste for obscenity a chance too for the robust expression of their views. The extralegal measures have repeatedly shown two vices: they invariably overshoot the legal boundaries and seek to restrict materials that are not obscene, and they are so informal that they provide few procedural safeguards.

Because of the informal nature of these pressures, it has been difficult to subject them to any type of legal control. Perhaps the most important intersection of informal controls of obscenity with the legal system occurred in 1963 when the Supreme Court, in *Bantam Books v. Sullivan*,[21] reviewed the work of the Rhode Island Commission. The Court held unconstitutional the actions of an agency set up by the state to "educate the public" about matters involving obscenity and to recommend prosecutions. The agency had developed lists of disapproved items which it had distributed widely to book and magazine distributors. The Supreme Court saw the arrangement as "in fact a scheme of censorship effectuated by extralegal sanctions." "They acted," said the Court, "as an agency not to advise but to suppress."

So far, we have been talking about the adult audience. However, much of the rhetoric on behalf of obscenity regulation has pleaded the need for protecting children. Despite the *Butler* dictum that children are irrelevant for the regulation of materials for the adult audience, the Court has always left open the possibility that there could be regulation of materials aimed directly at children. Finally, in 1968, in *Ginsberg v. New York*,[22] the Court *upheld* a statute drafted to cover sales to minors of materials somewhat mechanically defined in terms of the three-pronged test as having prurient appeal *for minors,* as being patently offensive *to minors,* and as lacking any social significance *for minors.* It is then abundantly clear that the Court sees the regulation of obscenity very differently when its distribution is aimed at minors. And we are again reminded that the Court may be moving toward a formula in which only the juvenile or the captive audience is relevant and the voluntary adult audience is left free to pursue its own tastes.

If there is further activity on behalf of the juvenile audience, the Court may soon have to confront the neat query posed by Justice Fortas in his interesting dissent in *Ginsberg,* namely, just what are the First Amendment rights of the juvenile audience? Certainly at some point, as he warns, we can overregulate even on behalf of the young.

The second point we shall consider is that there is a possibility of expanding obscenity to cover matters other than sex. The problem centers on whether a concept of "obscene violence" could be developed outlawing the excessive use of the imagery of violence especially when aimed at the juvenile audience. Certainly the three-pronged *Roth* formula suggests analogies, particularly the "utterly without social significance" element.

The key precedent on the matter is *Winters v. New York*,[23] a 1947 case antedating the Court's experience with obscenity. In *Winters* the Court struck down a section of a New York obscenity statute that attempted to prohibit the massing of stories of bloodshed and lust "so as to become vehicles for inciting violent and depraved crimes against the person." The Court found the terms unconstitutionally vague and invalidated the measure on that score, leaving open the possibility of drafting more precise regulation of stimuli to violence. The implication is that the vagueness of obscenity as a term does not offend constitutional criteria because we have had it in the law for over a century, but efforts to create new terms of art unsupported by any traditional gloss will be scrutinized closely. *Winters* is also of interest today because of the firm and full dissent by Justice Frankfurter arguing thoughtfully the case for such regulation and going so far as to draft the preamble for a model statute. Few efforts, however, have been made since *Winters;* in 1968 the Court upset a Dallas movie-licensing scheme which aspired to classify certain movies as "not suitable for young persons" in part because of their portrayal of "brutality, criminal violence, or depravity."[24] The Court, although focusing on the sexual rather than the violence components of the ordinance, invalidated it because it was too vague to give adequate guidance to licensing officials.

In the end, the more one reflects on the idea of obscene violence the more troublesome and futile it seems to be to write it into the law. And one is reminded one more time of how odd and exceptional the concessions are which our constitutional law makes to the regulation of stimuli to sexual fantasy. Sex, it would appear, is different.[25]

II

The second wing of our overview of legal limits on the right to publish moves us to the law of defamation, and somewhat incidentally to its modern complement, protection of the right of privacy. As with obscenity, our perspective is from the vantage point of constitutional law. We are concerned with what the Supreme Court of the United States has had to say about the problem as it has been required to test these forms of regulation of communication against the First Amendment. In brief, as with obscenity, our concern is with *limitations on limitations* on communication.

There are some tantalizing analogies between the constitutional careers of libel and slander. Once again, the constitutional dimension is entirely a product of the Warren Court; the Court's first full confrontation with the law of defamation did not come until 1964, and as with obscenity it was followed by a burst of activity so that the Court has now decided seven cases since 1964. Although the Court appears to have found the problems of defamation more amenable to solution than those of obscenity, there is some sense of evolution of doctrine over the half-dozen-year time span and a sharp sense again of the Justices having to struggle to reach a consensus. Perhaps the last word on such analogies should be given to one of the Court's most distinguished contemporary critics, Justice Black. Dissenting in part in the *Butts* and *Walker* cases[26] in 1966, he observed:

> It strikes me that the Court is getting itself in the same quagmire in the field of libel in which it is now helplessly struggling in the field of obscenity. No one, including this Court, can know what is and what is not constitutionally obscene or libelous under this Court's rulings.

The common law of defamation presents a much older and more formidable, one might even say a more elegant, legal edifice than the common law of obscenity. Arguably, its principal features were decisively settled by cases as far back as *Carr v. Hood* in 1808,[27] *Thorley v. Lord Kerry* in 1812,[28] and *Bromage v. Prosser* in 1825.[29] Although dealing with grievances stemming initially from such homely activities as talebearing and gossip, it became elaborated over time in Anglo-American law into a technical specialty. For present purposes we shall stress six characteristics: (1) Unlike the common law of obscenity, which was thought of as protecting a public interest and was enforced by the state through licensing or criminal sanctions, that of defamation has been conceived as protecting individual interests, since providing redress for private wrongs and the enforcement of its rules was left, in the overwhelming majority of cases, to individual plaintiffs in tort actions. (2) "Individual interests" was identified and conceptualized as the interest in *reputation,* and the law of defamation has thus been devoted to providing monetary remedies for injuries *to individual reputation* caused by the publication of false and damaging statements about plaintiffs. (3) While the gist of the grievance was that the damaging statement was in fact false, unflattering statements were *presumed* to be false so that the burden of proving truth was put upon the defendant. (4) Moreover, in libel and in certain forms of slander the plaintiff, in order to receive substantial money damages, need not show how or to what extent his reputation was in fact damaged; he was entitled to an inference of *general* damages. (5) If the defendant had published the defamatory statement he would be liable even though from his standpoint a mistake or an accident was involved; the law did not care whether he had been intentional and malicious or merely careless or even merely unlucky; he was, as the lawyers put it, strictly liable, a rule strikingly in contrast to most tort law. (6) The jury was assigned a major role in defamation controversies; it had the primary responsibility for determining whether the statement was defamatory and for measuring the general damages.

The law of defamation, then, began with a perception of harm to individuals and only very gradually yielded to any competing perception of the public interest in speech. As Justice Harlan put it in *Butts,* it "originated in soil entirely different from that which nurtured these constitutional values." Nevertheless it did work out over time a complex series of accommodations for the competing interests in speech in the form of a series of *privileges* for false statements about individuals. These ranged from the absolute privilege of high-ranking public officials for statements made while at work, to the qualified privilege for specially useful private communications such as employment or credit references, to privileges for communications in the public sphere. It is this last category of common-law privileges which is of direct interest to us here. These were of two kinds: record libel and fair comment. The record-libel privilege protects statements repeated from official public records so long as they are accurately repeated. Fair comment is a more elusive privilege to characterize. In theory it protects critical expressions of *opinion* if the underlying facts are disclosed. The idea is most clearly seen in the privilege granted the literary critic to be caustic. The idea is most important in the area of criticism of public officials or candidates for public office. Here American law had developed two versions of a privilege to express negative opinions. Under the rule in a majority of states, a distinction was made between fact and opinion, and the opinion was protected only if the facts were stated accurately. Under a minority view, the privilege was broadened to cover erroneous statements of fact if made in good faith.[30] It was, then, this common-law calculus of individual interest in reputation weighed against public interest in speech that the Supreme Court undertook to evaluate against the mandate of the First Amendment, starting with *New York Times Co. v. Sullivan*[31] in 1964.

The constitutional story requires a brief prologue. The Court had had a prior skirmish with libel back in 1952 in *Beauharnais v. Illinois*.[32] There, in a 5 to 4 decision, it had affirmed the conviction of a white supremacist under an Illinois statute prohibiting group libel. In an opinion by Justice Frankfurter the Court avoided any confrontation with the "clear and present danger" test by classifying libel along with "fighting words and the profane" as belonging to a second level of speech. "Libelous utterances," Justice Frankfurter noted, "not being within the area of constitutionally protected speech, it is unnecessary, either for us or for the State courts, to consider the issues behind the phrase 'clear and present danger.' " Five years later in *Roth*, it will be recalled, the Court was again to employ this two-level speech theory to avoid the embarrassment of finding a clear and present danger from obscenity.

Thus, one would have assumed that the common law of defamation raised no free-speech issues of a constitutional dimension for two good reasons. First, as a matter of practice or custom, the law had been on the books for centuries, it had been actively used, and there had been no challenge to it; and second, the answer given in *Beauharnais* would appear to cover any challenge should one be made. But *New York Times Co. v. Sullivan* in 1964 was to upset all such expectations and in the course of so doing possibly herald a revolution in First Amendment analysis.

The case involved a libel action by the police commissioner of Montgomery, Alabama, against *The New York Times* for publishing an editorial advertisement sponsored by a civil rights group criticizing the way Dr. Martin Luther King and student protesters had been treated in Montgomery and asking for funds to continue their efforts. The plaintiff was not actually mentioned by name, but in a strained construction the advertisement was read as applying to his supervision of the police, and there were several very minor inaccuracies in the statement itself. The Alabama court found the allegations defamatory of the police commissioner and held that truth was not a defense since the statement was not *perfectly* true; moreover, there was no privilege of fair comment on a matter of public interest since there were errors in the statement of underlying fact. An Alabama jury awarded general damages of $500,000 and the Alabama Supreme Court affirmed. Alabama had thus been able, without engaging in an outright sham, to exploit the technicalities of libel law to punish *The New York Times,* a symbol of Northern intermeddling in Southern race problems. As a political reality, the case clamored for readjustment. The Supreme Court of the United States, however, could review it only for constitutional errors and not for errors in applying the law of libel; within constitutional limits Alabama, like any other state, was the supreme arbiter of its law of defamation.

In this posture of events the Supreme Court, compelled by the political realities to rescue the *Times* and yet equally compelled by its role to seek high ground in justifying its result, arrived at some very high ground indeed.

This time the Court eschewed the two-level analysis. This suggests either that libel is, on a closer look, very different from obscenity, or that, as we noted above, the two-level test was no longer viable and the rationale for regulating obscenity which was based on it would have to be re-examined when the time came. Instead it found its touchstone in an odd corner: in the fate of the Sedition Act of 1798. Although it had been one of the great ironies of our free-speech history that we had never satisfactorily put to rest the fundamental question whether the Sedition Act *was* constitutional, the Court speaking through Mr. Justice Brennan in effect now held it *unconstitutional,* noting that "the attack upon its validity has carried the day in the court of history." Moreover, in this controversy over the Sedition Act the Court found, as Justice Brennan put it, the clue "to the central meaning of the First Amendment."

This is not the place to re-examine a thesis I put forward enthusiastically at the time, that the Court by positing that the First Amendment had a "central meaning" and by emphasizing the importance of negating seditious libel had put "the theory of the freedom of speech clause right side up for the first time."[33] Other commentators have given the case a less generous reading, and subsequent decisions have left it still unclear whether *New York Times Co. v. Sullivan* will prove to be *the* seminal free speech precedent.[34]

For present purposes it will suffice to note its impact on the law of defamation and to trace its subsequent career in defamation cases.

Coming back to the case at hand, what the Court did was to find the Alabama rule as to fair comment on public officials unconstitutional because in holding the speaker strictly liable for any errors of fact the rule tended to inhibit too seriously criticism of public officials—and thus to resemble too much a rule of seditious libel. The Court did not invalidate the law of defamation in its entirety; it was dealing with that law *only* as it applied to remarks about public officials. Moreover, even in that area it did not eliminate *the possibility* of liability for defamation. The aggrieved official could recover damages under the new constitutional framework if, but only if, he could prove that the remark was made with "actual malice," "that is," said the Court, "with knowledge that it was false or with reckless disregard of whether it was false or not." What the Court had done in effect was to choose between the majority and minority common-law rules as to the level of privilege to be afforded comments on public officials, and to prefer the minority rule. The result, however, was suddenly to give the minority rule constitutional status and to make it by constitutional command the law not only of Alabama but of all the states. To those interested in federal-state relations the exciting consequence was not so much for free speech theory or for defamation law as for the structure of federalism.

The decision left open for future development two kinds of issues. First, questions of *ambit*. How far did judicial review under the First Amendment extend? Was it limited literally to public officials or did it have a more generous sweep? Second, questions going to the *level* of the privilege if the speech was held to require protection. Was all speech that was to be protected constitutionally in this area to be given the same level of protection or would a more subtle calculus of the competing values be required?

These issues were substantially resolved in a series of three cases decided by the Court in 1967, *Time, Inc. v. Hill*,[35] *Curtis Publishing Co. v. Butts*, and *Associated Press v. Walker*. The cases evoked elaborate and interesting opinions, and the complex patterns of positions among the Justices were reminiscent of *Jacobellis* and obscenity. For the present we need only point out the main features:

1. In *Time, Inc. v. Hill* the constitutional protection was extended to the right of privacy.
2. Since in the *Hill* case the plaintiff whose tort remedy was

curtailed on behalf of the countervalues of free speech was neither a public official nor a public figure but simply a private citizen who as a result of being the victim of a crime had become involuntarily and momentarily newsworthy, the strong implication is that the ambit of constitutional protection now extends to anything that is newsworthy, a very generous ambit indeed.

3. The most active and interesting debate among the Justices centered not on the ambit issue, as would have been expected, but on nuances of the level of protection. Three views emerged, keyed to the different status of the aggrieved party in each case: in *New York Times,* a public official; in *Butts* and *Walker,* a football coach and a general, both nationally prominent public figures; and in *Hill,* a private citizen who had become involuntarily newsworthy. In each of these instances *all* of the Justices agreed that the speech was subject to some degree of constitutional protection, that is, it was within the ambit. In the center position were Justices Brennan and White and Chief Justice Warren, holding that the "knowing or reckless disregard" standard of *New York Times* was to be applied in all three situations. At the one extreme were Justices Black and Douglas, who were against any imposition of liability for defamation as they had been against any regulation of obscenity; hence, they would have accorded an absolute privilege in all three situations. At the other extreme was the position elaborated by Justice Harlan, in which he was joined by Justices Fortas, Stewart, and Clark. The Harlan thesis is full of subtlety and interest. He would accord a different level of privilege in each of the three situations in order to achieve the requisite accommodation of the competing interests involved. The strongest privilege to the speaker and the least protection to the subject would be given in the public official case; the weakest privilege to the speaker and the most protection to the subject would be given in the private citizen case; and in between would be the privilege and protection given in the public figure case. He would achieve these levels by using the *New York Times* "reckless disregard" test for the first level; a "gross negligence" test for the middle level; and finally, a simple negligence test to defeat the speaker's privilege in the third situation. Although the Harlan schema is urged with skill and is full of interest, in the end it is the middle position of Justice Brennan that carries the day, although it just barely carries it. *New York Times,* when all the dust has settled, wins across the board and remains a powerful precedent for the future.

That the Court should have devoted so much time and energy and argument to these nuances is perhaps both disturbing and splendid. It may be read as another sign that they now simply cannot agree on anything and we are approaching a day when there will be nine rules of constitutional law on every point. But surely it is better read affirmatively as an indication of the Court's extraordinary concern with and commitment to the values of the First Amendment.

Two further aspects of its general treatment of the defamation-privacy cases are worthy of comment. First, the Court now has command of a new type of problem never before acknowledged in our free speech tradition. The problem arises when discussion of a public issue is interlaced, as it often will be, with statements about individuals which carry a risk of being false in fact. If the aggrieved individual is given an unqualified tort remedy, he will have a power to veto or inhibit the discussion of the public issue. The free speech issue then is how best to accommodate the competing interests, and, as we have seen, the current answer of the Court is in terms of the *New York Times* level of qualified privilege.

Finally, there is the Court's attitude toward falsity. It will not limit the protection of the First Amendment to statements of fact that are true. A realistic theory requires also some tolerance for the false in order to avoid placing the full risks of falsity on the speaker and thereby inhibiting him. Indeed the whole controversy in *New York Times, Hill, Butts,* and *Walker* can be viewed as turning on the question of how to handle the risks of falsity.

Justice Brennan captures the Court's stance toward all this in a great sentence in his *New York Times* opinion, a sentence on which we may end happily our survey of those odd twins, obscenity and libel: "Thus we consider this case against the background of a profound national commitment to the principle that debate on public issues should be uninhibited, robust, and wide open."[36]

NOTES

1. The literature on obscenity and the law has become formidable in recent years. The key article is probably still Lockhart & McClure, "Literature, the Law of Obscenity, and the Constitution," 38 *Minnesota Law Review* 295 (1954).

The English development is reviewed in Alpert, "Judicial Censorship of Obscene Literature," 52 *Harvard Law Review* 40 (1937); N. St. John-Stevas, *Obscenity and the Law* (1956).

The American development can be traced in Kalven, "The Metaphysics of the Law of Obscenity," 1960 *Supreme Court Review* 1; Lockhart & McClure, "Censorship of Obscenity: The Developing Constitutional Standards," 45 *Minnesota Law Review* 5 (1960); Magrath, "The Obscenity Cases: Grapes of Roth," 1966 *Supreme Court Review* 7; Krislov, "From Ginzberg to Ginsberg: The Unhurried Children's Hour in Obscenity Litigation," 1968 *Supreme Court Review* 153; Katz, "Privacy and Pornography; Stanley v. Georgia," 1969 *Supreme Court Review* 203.

Also of major interest on various aspects of the problem are: Henkin, "Morals and the Constitution: The Sin of Obscenity," 63 *Columbia Law Review* 391 (1963); Frank, "Obscenity: Some Problems of Values and the Use of Experts," 41 *Washington Law Review* 631 (1966); Cairns, Paul, & Wishner, "Sex Censorship: The Assumption of Anti-Obscenity Laws and the Empirical Evidence," 46 *Minnesota Law Review* 1009 (1962); J. Paul & M. Schwartz, *Federal Censorship: Obscenity in the Mail* (1961); H. Clor, *Obscenity and the Public Morality* (1969).

And see Katz, "Free Discussion v. Final Decision: Moral and Artistic Controversy Over the *Tropic of Cancer* Trials," 79 *Yale Law Journal* 209 (1969), and the references collected therein.

2. Quoted in Kalven, "The Metaphysics of the Law of Obscenity," 1960 *Supreme Court Review* 1, 43–44.

3. Hearings Before the Senate Comm. on the Judiciary, 90th Cong. 2d Sess., July 11, 12, 16, 17, 18, 19, 20, 22, and 23, 1968; Sept. 13, and 16, 1968, at 283–313, 345–61, 1308–46.

4. "Senator Hart. It makes as much sense to sit around here and look at the movie and conclude we know what persuaded the court to act as it would if we looked at the blackjack that Mallory or the spear or whatever Miranda used. . . . I regret very much the day has arrived when we are here." 1968 Hearings, *supra* note 3, at 1316.

5. 352 U.S. 380 (1957).

6. 360 U.S. 684, 688–89 (1959).

7. The problem of ideas about sexual behavior contrary to community mores is often called the problem of *thematic* obscenity; *see* Kalven, *supra* note 2, at 28–34. *See also* People v. Friede, 133 Misc. 611 (Magis. Ct. N.Y. Co. 1929).

8. Roth v. United States, 354 U.S. 476 (1957).

9. L.R. 3 Q.B. 360 (1868).

10. 370 U.S. 478 (1962).

11. 378 U.S. 184 (1964).

12. A Book Named "John Cleland's Memoirs of a Woman of Pleasure" v. Attorney General of Massachusetts, 383 U.S. 413 (1966).

13. 383 U.S. 463 (1966).

14. 386 U.S. 767 (1967); *see also* Keeney v. New York, 388 U.S. 440 (1967), and the cases following it in the Reports.

15. 386 U.S. at 769.

16. 315 U.S. 568 (1942).

17. 343 U.S. 250 (1952).

18. This so-called two-level speech theory is discussed in Kalven, *supra* note 2, at 9–15; H. Kalven, *The Negro and the First Amendment* 43–50 (1965).

19. 376 U.S. 254 (1964).

20. 394 U.S. 557 (1969).

21. 372 U.S. 58 (1963).
22. 390 U.S. 629 (1968).
23. 333 U.S. 507 (1948).
24. Interstate Circuit, Inc. v. City of Dallas, 390 U.S. 676 (1968).
25. Friends of free speech might well join in saying, *"Vive la différence!"*
26. Curtis Publishing Co. v. Butts and Associated Press v. Walker, 388 U.S. 130, 171 (1967). The two cases were reported together.
27. 1 Campbell 350, 354 (K.B. 1808), establishing principle of fair comment.
28. 4 Taunt. 355, 128 Eng. Rep. 367 (1812), reaffirming the difference between libel and slander.
29. 4 B.&C. 247 (1825), reaffirming the principle of strict liability for defamation.
30. The leading common-law precedent is Coleman v. MacLennan, 78 Kan. 711, 98 P. 281 (1908).
31. 376 U.S. 254 (1964).
32. 343 U.S. 250, 266 (1952).
33. Kalven, "The New York Times Case: A Note on 'The Central Meaning of the First Amendment,' " 1964 *Supreme Court Review* 191, 208.
34. *See* Kalven, "The Reasonable Man and the First Amendment," 1967 *Supreme Court Review* 267; *see also* Pickering v. Board of Educ., 391 U.S. 563 (1968), applying the principle to protect a teacher against dismissal for writing a letter sharply critical of school board policies; Bond v. Floyd, 385 U.S. 116 (1966), using the principle to protect a member of a state legislature from loss of his seat for speech critical of national war policies. *But cf.* Red Lion Broadcasting Co. v. FCC, 395 U.S. 367 (1969), declining to apply the principle to the so-called personal attack rule imposed by the FCC on broadcasters.
35. 385 U.S. 374 (1967).
36. 376 U.S. at 270.

THE RIGHT OF
ACCESS TO
MASS MEDIA

JOHN DE J. PEMBERTON, JR.

It is the right of the viewers and listeners, not the right of
the broadcasters, which is paramount. . . . It is the right
of the public to receive suitable access to social, political,
esthetic, moral, and other ideas and experiences which is
crucial here.[1]

MR. JUSTICE WHITE'S WORDS, RECITED ABOVE, HAVE
already been widely quoted, some of them by Vice-President Spiro
Agnew in his famous November 13, 1969, attack on the networks.
For some, they are merely a restatement of the thought underlying
much of the established First Amendment law protecting freedoms
of speech and the press. For others, they conjure up visions of a
revolutionary new era of people-oriented law in which the First
Amendment guarantees a "right to be heard"—a right of access to
the media of newspapers and broadcasting, even for those "ideas
and experiences" which the media themselves do not choose to air.
To the extent that these words do in fact inspire both sets of interpretations, they may provide the link between the freedoms of
speech and the press which are already protected, and the future
developments of the law, between the attained and the attainable.

Free speech and press, the "first freedoms," are central to the
processes of self-government. But what would work at the time of the
First Amendment's adoption will not necessarily work today. A
speech, a handbill, or even a personal letter might have had an

John de J. Pemberton, Jr., a former professor at Duke Law School and practicing
lawyer in Rochester, Minnesota, served as Executive Director of the American Civil
Liberties Union from 1962 to 1970.

impact on the political process in a predominantly rural nation of thirteen states quite different from what it could have in the United States today. Possibly the biggest difference is that caused by the bombardment of ideas and events which a vast network of mass communications now brings to men's minds. In any event, what is seen and heard on the mass media today is what influences public opinion. Where the Founding Fathers might effectively have protected the political process by keeping government from interfering with what any man wrote or printed or said, the same object can be achieved today, if at all, only by providing such a man's ideas or words access to the mass media.

I

There are many circumstances in which the right to be heard—a right of access to the public's attention—has been protected against suppression exerted by those in authority and sometimes by those in control of the media. In the mid-1930's the Congress of Industrial Organizations sought, through meetings and speeches, to inform workers in Jersey City about their rights under the new Wagner Act. This effort was thwarted by the city's mayor, Frank Hague, who forbade all use of public parks for meetings and speeches. The Supreme Court held Mayor Hague's device to be unconstitutional under the First Amendment. Similarly, in 1940, an Alabama statute which undertook to ban peaceful picketing on the public streets in the course of a labor dispute was held invalid.[2] Municipal license taxes imposed on the door-to-door distribution of religious pamphlets, even when they are being sold, have been struck down as inconsistent with the First Amendment.[3] These cases, and many like them, have established that most public facilities, subject to regulation, serve as media of communications to which every individual is entitled a right of access. The Supreme Court has recognized this right, moreover, in the course of invalidating a federal statute that permitted the Post Office to screen mail coming from abroad that it conceived to be "Communist political propaganda."[4]

Securing this right of access to all *sources* of "ideas and experiences" assures the public of a right to *receive* them through these media. Public demonstrations, sometimes referred to as the "poor man's newspaper," are often the only way those who cannot afford to advertise in newspapers or on television can reach public attention.

It has, moreover, become well established that private ownership of premises such as the streets of a company town or the public areas of a shopping center does not allow the private owner to prevent freedom of speech.[5]

Thus, in one recent incident an organized antiwar group chose streets outside the Port Authority Bus Terminal in New York City to express their views, both because of the large numbers of persons who daily pass through the terminal and because of the concentration of soldiers among them. In early November they decided to take their protest inside the building in order to reach the still greater numbers of people which included those not passing outside on the sidewalk. After two interferences by Port Authority police, they formally requested of the terminal manager permission and protection for "free speech activities in the public areas" of the building, specifying the distribution of handbills, the carrying of placards, the placement of literature tables, and the engaging of passers-by in conversation. Pursuant to Port Authority regulations banning the display and distribution of signs and advertisements "without permission," the manager denied the request. Then the protesters sued for an injunction protecting their claimed right to engage in such activities within carefully prescribed limitations. The Port Authority, a public corporation created by compact between two states, contended that its terminal was an inappropriate place for political expression and that its policy of proscribing all such activity within the building was proper and lawful.

The Court of Appeals for the Second Circuit affirmed a district court order granting the injunction. The court viewed the building, however one described its ownership, as a place dedicated to public use, appropriate for the exercise of First Amendment rights despite the building's purpose—bus transportation—which distinguished it from places traditionally used for meetings and protests: "The privacy and solitude of residents may require that apartment house hallways be insulated from the excitement of volatile exhortations, or the quiet dignity of judicial administration may dictate that courthouse passes be kept free of demonstration. But that is a result based on wisdom and experience. . . . Indeed, the public forum is surely as traditionally a covered meeting hall as a sunlit arena."[6] The court directed that the Port Authority issue new regulations accommodating the interests of the protesters and those of the gen-

eral public in the use of the building, and directed that the protesters be permitted to engage in their proposed activities pending
adoption of such regulations.

This simple right to reach people who attend public meetings or
are present at or pass by a demonstration, a picket line, or a literature table is by no means all that is meant by the "poor man's newspaper." The demonstration itself is often widely reported in the
mass media. When this happens, the audience for its ideas may be
enormously multiplied. Probably the women's suffrage movement
achieved sufficient impact upon public consciousness to affect the
nation's election laws only through such multiplication. News coverage of labor protests profoundly influenced public opinion to
support adoption of the Norris–La Guardia and Wagner Acts. No
public protests influenced a wider audience than the civil rights
demonstrations in Birmingham, Alabama, in 1963, which led to the
adoption of the Civil Rights Act of 1964, or the Selma, Alabama
march of 1965 which gave us the Voting Rights Act of that year.
This multiplication of "ideas and experiences" is really the only
way those who lack direct access to the press and air waves have of
effectively competing with the words of public officials and newsworthy personalities.

There are, however, severe limitations to this method of multiplication. In the case of the Alabama marches, it was only the unwitting cooperation of Police Chief "Bull" Connor and Sheriff Jim
Clarke, each behaving with unconscionable but intensely newsworthy brutality, that turned the demonstrations into the history-
making events they became. Demonstrators have had to learn that
repetition of actions others have used, even to express different ideas
and experiences, dilutes the newsworthiness of their own demonstrations and diminishes the public's attention. In short, the demonstration itself is often what the larger audience learns about, rather
than the ideas and experiences that the demonstrators sought to put
across. Those ideas and experiences may by happenstance get communicated in the course of the news treatment of the demonstration.
But they often do not, and whether they do or not depends upon a
number of circumstances often lying outside the control of those
who are seeking to communicate. With the "poor man's newspaper"
the medium—a demonstration and the reaction to it—is indeed the
message.

The experience of Peter Kiger illustrates part of the problem. A
conscientious objector who had served a prison term for refusing

civilian alternative service, he had leafleted, picketed, and conducted peace vigils constantly to express his opposition to the war in Vietnam. He had made many speeches and his total antiwar activity had reached audiences aggregating in all a few thousand. Efforts he and his colleagues made to call press attention to their activities had proved fruitless. Their demonstrations were common, uneventful, and not newsworthy.

In January 1966 Kiger requested a duplicate of his draft card from his local board for the express purpose of burning it, and the board complied. "Then," in the words of the brief on his behalf in the United States Court of Appeals for the Second Circuit, "Kiger and three colleagues sent out a short press release stating that they would burn their draft cards in the office of the Committee for Non-Violent Action. The next day representatives of every major news medium crowded into a small room to listen to Peter Kiger state his moral opposition to the war and to watch him burn his Notice of Classification. All the media gave the story prominent coverage; the total audience was in the millions."[7]

The preceding August, Congress had hastily amended the selective service law to add four words making it a felony willfully to mutilate or destroy any draft card. As a result Kiger's act, when committed, was defined as a serious crime. Although over twenty-six, he was prosecuted and convicted of this felony. His appeal sought to test the novel theory that his conviction should not stand because his act proved to be the only means by which he could have access to the media, that the governmental interest in protecting the card, when weighed against Kiger's important First Amendment right to communicate ideas and experiences to all who are willing to hear, is too insubstantial to warrant criminal sanction. He could express his views to an audience numbering millions *only* by being seen to commit publicly a severely punishable criminal act.

Kiger's indictment-laden road to access to the media is doubly anomalous. First, if the legal principle unsuccessfully urged on his behalf had been established law when he burned his card, the act would not have been criminal and, for that reason, would not have been successful. Reporters would have no more attended his press conference than they had earlier covered his peace vigils, speeches, and demonstrations.

Second, the criminal act as a device to achieve access to the media is subject to a built-in requirement of escalation. When several draft cards have been publicly destroyed, the fact of destruction becomes less newsworthy. Even though subsequent burners are still seen to be committing crimes—and inviting severe sanctions—they receive increasingly less attention in the media. In order for others to have similar access, their crimes must possess each a novelty distinguishing it from its predecessors. The tendency, of course, is for each to discommode the government, or the general public, more seriously than the last—to invade increasingly more substantial governmental interests than the protection of an easily replaceable piece of paper. The more outrageous the device for gaining newsworthiness, of course, the more news attention will be focused upon the device rather than the message. Kiger's device, therefore, while creditable for achieving his purposes, provides no real solution to the problem of access to the media.

II

With respect to the most widely seen and heard media of communication, television and radio broadcasting, there is an additional body of law protecting rights of access. It was of this body of law that Mr. Justice White was speaking in the *Red Lion* case, in the quotation at the head of this chapter. It does purport to be a people-oriented body of law, oriented to protection of the rights of "viewers and listeners."

It may be significant, however, that the oldest principle of this body of law is really oriented toward congressmen rather than toward people. That principle, the "equal time" requirement, is moreover the only one actually written into statutory law (although its companion, the "fairness doctrine," has since 1959 enjoyed an honorable mention in the same statute).

The equal time requirement appears in Section 315 of the Communications Act, which repeats an identical requirement originally written into the Federal Radio Act of 1927. It provides that whenever a broadcaster permits the use of his facilities by any legally qualified candidate for public office, he shall afford an equal opportunity to use the same facilities to all other candidates for the same office. It becomes operative only on use of broadcast facilities by a candidate; an incumbent who intends to be a candidate to succeed himself or for another office but has not yet announced that candidacy does not invoke its application.[8] Thus officeholders, especially Presidents, Vice Presidents, senators, and representatives, nor-

mally succeed in obtaining extensive exposure on radio and television before any election campaign begins. Only during the
campaign do their broadcast appearances trigger an obligation to
grant their opponents exposure.

Equal opportunity to all legally qualified candidates, moreover,
does not mean that all will be heard. When a candidate has been
sold time, Section 315 only requires that his opponents be given the
right to buy time at the same rates. Nor does Section 315 obligate
any broadcaster to provide any time, either free or paid, to any candidate. If no candidate is put on the air in the first place, no occasion will have arisen to provide equal time to any other. Finally,
Section 315 exempts bona fide newscasts, news interviews, on-the-
spot coverage of news events, and news documentaries from its provisions but adds (and this is the statutory allusion to the fairness doctrine) that this exemption shall not relieve the broadcasters "from
the obligation to afford reasonable opportunity for discussion of
conflicting views on issues of public importance."

Section 315 works well, for congressmen. It encourages maximum exposure of officeholders; broadcasters who are licensees of a
federally regulated resource have an incentive to curry favor with
federally elected officials. But it discourages the exposure of challengers since (1) challengers generally have greater difficulty in
raising campaign funds with which to buy time, and (2) the equal
time obligation of Section 315 makes the provision of free time to
challengers quite burdensome. (The burdensomeness of free time
is felt especially during primaries and other races where more than
two candidates have qualified to compete for the same office. Section
315 requires equal time for all of the candidates, even though the
audience interest in some may be small. When an appearance by a
minor candidate is required, the broadcaster loses not only the
revenue he might otherwise have gained from that time period, but
his profitable audience for subsequent time periods as well.) On the
other hand, the broadcasters and the networks themselves have
taken very little advantage of the exemptions in Section 315, especially those for news interviews and documentaries, to provide a
people-oriented exposure of both major and minor candidates and
their views. During the 1968 presidential primary, for instance, the
ABC network produced a two-candidate "debate" between Senators
Eugene McCarthy and Robert Kennedy in news interview format,
without affording equal time to other candidates, but this initiative
has not been followed on other networks or at other times.

In one presidential campaign, the 1960 one, Section 315 was suspended by an act of Congress to encourage the provision of free time to the two major-party candidates, Senator John Kennedy and Vice-President Richard Nixon, unencumbered by obligations to the several minor candidates. The consequence was a series of television "debates," also in news interview format, carried simultaneously on three networks, which reached the largest audiences in television history. The 1960 suspension was not repealed for the 1964 and 1968 presidential campaigns. In 1970 Congress passed a bill to limit political spending on broadcasting that would have repealed Section 315 as to presidential and vice-presidential candidates in order to pave the way for the grant of free time and the holding of similar debates in future presidential campaigns. On October 12, 1970, President Nixon vetoed the bill.[9]

In short, the provisions of Section 315 purport to be people-oriented: giving fair exposure to candidates for public office would serve a popular interest in effective self-government. But since they do not in fact encourage such fair exposure, since they actually operate to protect the interests of incumbents and well-heeled candidates, they fall far short of the ideal described in Mr. Justice White's important statement.

The fairness doctrine, on the other hand, is truly people-oriented; it does tend to fit Mr. Justice White's prescription of a right in the people "to receive suitable access to social, political, esthetic, moral, and other ideas and experiences." Although it has for eleven years enjoyed the honorable mention in Section 315 which was quoted above, its status is that of a requirement imposed by the Federal Communications Commission as an incidence of the broadcasters' statutory obligation to operate in the public interest. That is, it is an FCC statement of how it will carry out the Communications Act directive that renewals of broadcast licenses "may be granted . . . if the Commission finds that public interest, convenience, and necessity would be served thereby." In essence, the Commission has said that it will make that finding only if a broadcaster has afforded "a reasonable opportunity for the presentation of all responsible positions on matters of . . . importance." "[B]roadcast licensees have an affirmative duty to encourage and implement the broadcast of all sides of controversial public issues over their facilities. . . ."[10]

The fairness doctrine imposes two obligations on broadcasters. First, it affirmatively requires that some discussion of "matters of public importance" must take place; it is unlike the equal time provision, which excuses the broadcaster from any obligation if he allows no candidate the use of his facilities. Second, the fairness doctrine requires the broadcaster to seek out and present, by whatever means may be available to him, someone to be a spokesman for "all responsible positions" in the discussion of such matters. It is not enough for him simply to stand ready, when one side has been aired, to do as much for anyone who comes forth to take the other side or sides.

In particular, the fairness doctrine does not favor those who can afford to buy air time, as does the equal time provision. If one side of a controversial issue is presented on a sponsored program, the broadcaster may try to find a sponsor for the presentation of other "responsible positions." But if he cannot get the other side or sides paid for, his obligation to present them persists; he must air them at his own expense if necessary.

In its general application, the fairness doctrine does not vest rights to air time in particular individuals; it authorizes the broadcasters to choose the spokesmen for all views. For instance, the network broadcasts of the President's annual State of the Union Message (though they may do more) present a partisan view of the issues the President chooses to take up. A right to present the views of the other major party does not vest automatically in the titular leader, or the national chairman, or the national committee of that party. Rather the obligation inheres in the broadcasters (which the networks undertake to discharge for them) to seek out and select the spokesmen who will present the other party's views.

Broadcasters do not differ from other people in preferring a minimum of regulation of their own operations. Moreover, broadcast journalists legitimately fear that any regulation, in the hands of a hostile enforcement body (or one sensitive to the hostility of its congressional overseers), may be used as an instrument of harassment, or in retaliation for unpopular programming. It is a remarkable thing, therefore, that very little hostility to the general principles of the fairness doctrine is expressed within the broadcast industry and that so much of the doctrine as requires responsive presentation to the airing of any one side of a controversial issue is normally carefully observed. (The same unfortunately cannot be said for the broadcasters' acceptance of their affirmative obligation to present discussion of a wide range of controversial issues in the first place.)

Thus, it may be fair to generalize that the fairness doctrine, at least in some aspects, works well. But it works well because broadcasters, at least broadcast journalists, generally want it to. When called upon to enforce it, the FCC has demonstrated a remarkably faint heart. Probably no case better illustrates the difficulties inherent in enforcing a right of access to the mass media than the challenge which the Office of Communication of the United Church of Christ brought to the renewal of the license of station WLBT-TV in Jackson, Mississippi.

The case arose out of complaints that WLBT-TV had failed to provide a fair and balanced presentation of controversial issues affecting Negroes (that is, had failed to conform to the requirements of the fairness doctrine), and had failed to ascertain and fulfill the programming needs and interests of Negroes, who composed nearly half the population of the station's prime service area. In order to bring these complaints into the station's 1965 license renewal proceeding, the OCUCC, joined by individuals and a church from the Jackson area, petitioned the FCC to be allowed to intervene in that proceeding. At the outset that petition presented the FCC with a demand to break precedent. Traditionally only broadcasters and applicants for licenses to broadcast had been allowed to intervene in proceedings for the granting or renewal of licenses; only a broadcaster or a license applicant was thought to have an interest that might be adversely affected by the proceeding, either economically (because the proceeding might result in a loss of a part of the intervener's market) or technologically (because the proceeding might result in some interference with reception of the intervener's signal). The OCUCC and its copetitioners asked the FCC to allow them, as representatives of the listening public for whose benefit broadcasting was required to be regulated, to intervene and be heard in the renewal proceeding.

It was natural for this claim to be resisted. Normally licenses are renewed without a hearing, at considerable saving in time and expense to both the Commission and the licensee. The Commission did resist it and adhered to its traditional practice; it denied the petitioners "standing" to challenge the license renewal. The Court of Appeals for the District of Columbia reversed and directed a hearing. It held that "the Commission must allow standing to one or more of the petitioners as responsible representatives to assert and prove the claims they have urged in their petition."[11] Although representatives of the listening public also must devote much time and money to such an effort, and with considerably less economic incentive than a broadcaster has to do so, the decision greatly increased the possibility that fairness doctrine complaints will be presented forcefully to the FCC.

But when the hearing was ultimately held in the *Church of Christ* case, the FCC's examiner imposed unprecedented burdens of proof on the petitioners and recommended renewal on the strength of station representations and promises of improved performance. A divided Commission granted the renewal and the petitioners appealed once more. The Court of Appeals, in Judge Warren Burger's last opinion written before joining the Supreme Court, four years after the inception of the renewal period, impatiently reversed the Commission. The Court directed the FCC to deny the renewal application and to accept new applications for the Jackson channel.[12]

Not only has the FCC shown little will to enforce the fairness doctrine's requirement that broadcasters present the other side; it has done almost nothing at all to stimulate acceptance of the affirmative obligation to air controversy in the first place. Commissioners Cox and Johnson's analysis of the June 1968 renewal applications of the Oklahoma broadcasters (license periods are so staggered that the renewals in a single state may all be acted upon at one time) amply demonstrates that the FCC routinely renews uncontested licenses despite minimal or no efforts by the licensees to comply with this affirmative obligation.[13] Despite the *Church of Christ* experience, there is no present reason to anticipate that the FCC will change the pattern documented in that analysis. The affirmative obligation is performed, when it is performed, by broadcast journalists who want to perform it, mostly by the more financially secure broadcasters and by them only in intense financial competition with far more rewarding bids to use that broadcast time for entertainment and sports.

A special right of access, that is, a right of reply, is provided under rules adopted by the FCC as a specification of the fairness doctrine requirements in two particular circumstances: personal attacks and political editorials. Although issued under the fairness doctrine rubric, these rules have a particularity which differs significantly; much less is left to broadcaster judgment than in the case of the general application of the doctrine.

In the case of "an attack . . . upon the honesty, character, integrity, or like personal qualities of an identified individual or group" made "during the presentation of views on a controversial issue of public importance," the rules provide that the broadcaster shall promptly notify the person or group attacked, furnish a script or tape of the attack, and offer *the object of the attack* a reasonable opportunity to reply. In the case of an editorial which "(i) endorses or (ii) opposes a legally qualified candidate or candidates" the rules provide that the broadcaster shall promptly notify "(i) the other candidate or candidates or (ii) the candidate opposed in the editorial," furnish a script or tape of the editorial, and offer *the candidate or his spokesman* a reasonable opportunity to reply. Thus, the right-of-reply rules differ from the fairness doctrine in their general application principally because they vest in an identified person or persons a right of access to the broadcaster's facilities. In addition they particularize in some detail the broadcaster's duties when the triggering event, an attack or a political editorial, has occurred.

It was the FCC's application of the principles incorporated in the personal attack rules (although the rules themselves were not promulgated until later) that led to the *Red Lion* case. In this case, the Red Lion Broadcasting Company permitted a sponsored attack over its station upon an author, Fred Cook, who demanded a free opportunity to reply. The broadcaster refused, the FCC ruled that the fairness doctrine required Red Lion to provide it, and the company appealed. The Court of Appeals for the District of Columbia upheld the validity of this application of the fairness doctrine and affirmed the Commission's ruling.

Meanwhile the personal attack and political editorial rules were formalized and adopted in 1967, and the Radio-Television News Directors Association initiated a review of this rule-making in the Court of Appeals for the Seventh Circuit. Contrary to the District of Columbia court's conclusion, the Seventh Circuit Court held the rules unconstitutional. The Supreme Court granted review of both cases and in a single decision upheld the rules and approved the application of the personal attack principle to the Red Lion Broadcasting Company.

In so holding, the Court faced broadcaster arguments that the rules invaded their First Amendment rights. Broadcasting does enjoy protection under the free speech and free press guarantees of that Amendment, and the broadcasters argued that rules specifying what they must carry, on pain of possible license revocation, violated their rights of free speech and press. Moreover, they argued, the obligations of the rules placed a burden on their programming decisions, since if it is held that they have aired a personal attack or a political editorial, subsequent program time and expense must be incurred to comply with the rules. Such a burden, they contended, is inconsistent with rights of free speech and press, and since the rules tend to discourage controversial programming, they operate to defeat the purposes of the fairness doctrine and the Communications Act, as well as of the First Amendment. Finally, they claimed that there was an inherent vagueness in words such as "attack . . . upon the honesty, character, integrity, or like personal qualities" which made the operation of the rules unpredictable, increasing the burden of the rules upon the broadcasters' programming choices and providing an opportunity for capricious enforcement. Both consequences would be inconsistent with the First Amendment. If the First Amendment analysis had been limited to the rights of the broadcasters, these arguments would have prevailed. For each argument the briefs on behalf of the broadcasters cited apposite and landmark precedents, all of continuing vitality. What made the difference was the question, Whose right is paramount? "It is the right of the viewers and listeners, not the right of the broadcasters, which is paramount," the Court answered.[14]

Tracing the history of broadcasting regulation, the Court noted that the existence of regulation was necessary to make communication by broadcasting possible at all. "[O]nly a tiny fraction of those with resources and intelligence can hope to communicate by radio at the same time if intelligible communication is to be had. . . ." Having created the possibility of intelligible radio communication by regulating who might speak on any one frequency at any one place and time, government may require "a licensee to share his frequency with others and to conduct himself as a proxy or fiduciary with obligations to present those views and voices which are representative of his community and which would otherwise, by necessity, be barred from the airwaves." "[A]s far as the First Amendment is concerned those who are licensed stand no better than those to whom licenses are refused."[15]

As for the tendency of the rules to inhibit presentation of controversial public issues, the Court found that the FCC has power to insist on their presentation anyway. "To condition the granting or renewal of licenses on a willingness to present representative community views on controversial issues is consistent with the ends and purposes of those constitutional provisions forbidding the abridgment of freedom of speech and freedom of the press."[16] Finally, the Court found the objection of vagueness was met by the FCC's willingness to forgo imposition of sanctions without warning.

With the decision in *Red Lion,* therefore, it becomes possible to conclude that essentially the entire body of special law of rights of access that is peculiar to the broadcast media enjoys constitutional favor. Its implications for the future growth of a right to be heard are considerable.

III

The future of the right to be heard has been the subject of much recent speculation, some of it quite heated. The notion that the First Amendment will serve, not merely as a shield against government inhibition on content in the media, but as a sword opening an access for individual citizens' "ideas and experiences" into those media, has been pressed with a revolutionary fervor.[17] To these revolutionists, the decision in *Red Lion,* though confined to that special body of law of access peculiar to broadcasting, offers a rationale to undergird the movement of the right of access into all media, a green light for all good things to come.

But considering the fervor with which this revolutionary notion is pressed, it is surprising that the specific proposals put forward to implement it have so far been so modest. Most obviously there has been discussion of importing some elements of broadcasting's right-of-access law into the print media. There have been some independent proposals. But there has not been, as there should be, a great deal of consideration given to legal alternatives available to increase the number and diversity of sources of newspaper and broadcasting content, of owners and operators who control that content.

Of the first of these, no one has seemingly had the courage to propose more than simple right-to-reply legislation. A statute in Nevada provides for it, but there is little evidence of its use so far.[18]

Strangely, no one has yet seriously proposed the imposition of a fairness doctrine on the print media. However, the rationale for doing so has been articulated by a few commentators, especially Professor Jerome Barron.[19] This rationale finds a First Amendment objection to private as well as public censorship or restraint on the flow of ideas from individuals to the public.[20] That objection led the Court in *Red Lion* to find the presence of the fairness doctrine more compatible with the First Amendment than its absence would have been, as applied to the broadcast media.[21] But since an individual metropolitan daily normally has an even tighter throttle on access to its audience than does a licensee of the scarce broadcasting channels, so this argument goes, First Amendment inhibitions on broadcaster censorship should apply with even greater force to newspaper censorship. There are simply more broadcasters than there are metropolitan dailies, in the nation as a whole and in the ordinary metropolitan area.

Of course, the Court did not decide *Red Lion* simply on the basis of this greater compatibility of First Amendment values with the principles of the fairness doctrine. Compatibility it found, in the context of the regulation of a medium of communication whose viability is itself conditioned on the existence of government regulation which prevents chaotic electronic interference by other broadcasters. Comparative scarcity is not essential to the argument, for the essential fact is that the regulatory system is as much responsible for the existence of a broadcasting medium as the Bureau of Engraving is responsible for the existence of United States currency. Since it cannot be established that the newspaper medium is likewise the product of governmental action, its amenability to such regulation as that of the fairness doctrine cannot be rested upon existing precedents, in particular the *Red Lion* case, which deal with the regulation of broadcasting.

What the students of broadcasting regulation have proposed for the print media is a duty to accept ideational advertising.[22] A fifty-year-old decision of an inferior Ohio court is credited with providing some precedent for this; it held that a newspaper was under a duty not to discriminate against one of its potential commercial advertisers.[23] But the proponents claim more than that. A recent federal district court decision ruled that a public high school's student newspaper had a duty to accept a proffered political ad even though it did not discriminate: it refused all political advertising.[24] And a pending action by an Amalgamated Clothing Workers local seeks to compel the metropolitan dailies in Chicago to accept an ad giving its version of a dispute with one of the newspapers' leading commercial advertisers, the Marshall Field Company. Without relying on discrimination, as in the Ohio case, and on the fact of publication by a government agency, as in the student newspaper case, the Amalgamated Clothing Workers' suit claims that an ordinary metropolitan daily, as a business affected by public interest, must accept all advertising proffered that meets minimum, nonideational standards.[25]

The Smothers Brothers' lawsuit against CBS contains another kind of attack on the power of the media themselves to restrain the flow of ideas and experiences to the larger public.[26] Claiming censorship in the networks' application of its standards of acceptability to video tapes submitted for broadcast, this suit asks for damages and an injunction. In particular, the plaintiffs complain that the unorthodox in politics, religion, and social mores was censored by the network. The network, on the other hand, asserts that its differences with the plaintiffs centered on matters of taste.[27] Were the Smothers Brothers to prevail, of course, their victory would not establish that the networks are obliged to air every production that any source may offer them. The claim is only that once a particular producer and a particular kind of program are contracted for, the offering of that producer, when it fits the contract, is not properly subject to censorship by the network on account of the ideas and experiences presented.

The total impact of these implementing proposals, if all are adopted, will be modest indeed. The right of reply, now well entrenched in broadcasting law, looks like a desirable addition to newspaper law, but it will enlarge access to the print media only for those who have become objects of an attack. Ideational advertising is already widely used by those able to raise funds for it; new law on the subject will affect only those having the wherewithal whose ads are now refused. And the Smothers Brothers' claim will enlarge the rights only of those who already have access to the media. All of these remedies will change, but none will radically change, the availability to readers, viewers, and listeners of ideas and experiences not now being aired.

The basic First Amendment concept of protecting the access of all possible *sources* of ideas and experiences to such public attention as each can attain for itself has been underemphasized in the public discussion of access to the mass media. This is the concept that has guided the law of access to public facilities, such as streets, parks, bus terminals, and shopping centers, discussed in Part I above. By contrast, the law of access to the mass media has developed around a narrower concept. The broadest of its concepts is embodied in the fairness doctrine, which is satisfied by the presentation of "all responsible positions" on controversial issues of public importance.

Choosing which positions are responsible enough and what issues are important enough to be aired is left to the judgment of those who operate and manage the medium. As we have seen, reliance on journalists' professionalism tends to make the fairness doctrine work fairly well, as presumably it would without enunciation of the legal principle. But whenever it has been necessary to rely on enforcement machinery, the public interest has been shortchanged.

The basic First Amendment concept is entitled to a try in the mass media too. Instead of imposing a surveillance on the choices made by operators and managers of the media, it would ask essentially whether a greater number of media cannot be made available to other operators and managers. Its emphasis would be on private decision-making as to media content; but it would increase the number of decision-makers.

Present rules of the FCC are designed to increase slightly the number of different operators who may control radio and television stations by limiting the number of stations which any one operator may control. No broadcaster may own more than one AM, one FM, and one TV station in any one market, nor more than seven AM, seven FM, and seven TV stations across the land. These rules tend to prevent a large owner from grabbing up all of the broadcasting channels and tend to leave more remaining ones available to others. But the effect of these rules is not great; a combination of seven very profitable TV stations has provided the economic undergirding for each of three major television networks which dominate all of prime time television broadcasting. Instead of a multitude of private decisions, the choices of only three decision-makers determines the major part of the nation's television fare.

Antitrust law has had some impact on the number of decision-makers who control the content of the mass media. But the focus of antitrust law is upon economic concepts and its preoccupation with such matters as price-fixing and market-sharing has created ambiguity as to whether or not it will foster diversity of decision-makers in the media. A recent antitrust enforcement action against a joint newspaper operating agreement[28] led the Congress to pass the "Newspaper Preservation Act," exempting many such agreements from the antitrust laws; supporters of the Act claimed the exemption was necessary to prevent *reduction* in the number of daily newspapers!

However, the real opportunity for increasing the number of

decision-makers who control the content of the mass media lies in the fast-moving development of newer media which technology has brought on. The principal one of these is cable television, which is now rapidly wiring the television receivers in our major cities to a common source of program origination, and a community antenna, for each neighborhood. Cable now has a capacity for bringing upwards of twenty options to the home viewer who could previously get only three, five, or at the most a dozen television stations off the air. The promise of trebling the present twenty-channel capacity of cable, plus the potential of interconnecting cable systems into diverse local, regional, and national networks, offers a truly great opportunity for achieving diversity in the media. Moreover, the physical and economic similarity of cable broadcasting to the structure of a telephone system suggests by analogy a form of cable service which might introduce still greater diversity. The telephone system is a "common carrier" of communications; it provides the means of communicating but exercises no control over the content of what is communicated. It is legally required to make its means of communication available to all who request the use of them in compliance with uniform conditions as to rates, attachment of equipment, and the avoidance of certain common abuses. Were some or all of the television channels made available by cable to be committed to "common carrier" usage, that is, made available to all producers of television programming who complied with uniform conditions as to rates, equipment, and the avoidance of specific abuses, the number of different sources of television programming would approach a maximum. Common carrier usage might, for instance, permit free political broadcasts sponsored by a party, free educational broadcasts sponsored by a school or museum, free entertainment and sports broadcasts sponsored by commercial advertisers, pay-TV entertainment and sports without commercials, and pay-TV educational broadcasts, all on the same channel, all produced and presented by different lessees of the cable company's facilities. In addition, cable television permits planning for individual receiver access to libraries of film and video tapes designed to afford the viewer access to significant broadcasts at a later time than their original showing. Finally, its technology is likely to become available in the future for a host of other uses, such as facsimile printing for the provision of newspaper, library, and even postal services, computer connection, and shopping and banking services.[29] The

structure of the future cable industry, therefore, is capable of opening access to the mass media for a nearly unlimited number of
sources.

However, it is by no means a necessary result that the growth of
cable television will produce this diversity. The early regulatory
action of the FCC in this field was principally oriented toward protecting the economic viability of on-the-air television broadcasting,
with the result that its rules tended to limit diversity. Although its
latest regulations are differently oriented, the pressure to protect
existing economic interests will always be enormous. Moreover, the
mass media have developed self-consciousness about their power,
and power considerations, independently of economics, would warrant great political pressure against regulatory actions designed to
promote diversity.

Nevertheless, the most promising opportunities for improving
rights of access to the media lie in the developing law that will
govern the structure of new media. Not only does the new technology offer more opportunities for access; experience with broadcasting regulation suggests that structure is more amenable to the
kind of regulation that serves First Amendment interests than is
content. Structure can provide incentives to offer a diversity in content. But the regulation of content, like Section 315's equal time
requirement, may only create counterincentives. Or, like Jackson,
Mississippi's WLBT-TV license renewal, it may just be relatively
ineffective. Moreover, every device for the regulation of content,
even the fairness doctrine, provides the regulator with an opportunity to burden the media manager who has offended important
interests.[30] The regulation of structure is capable of being measured
by more objective standards.

What is missing from today's debate on the right to be heard is a
First Amendment rationale for requiring structural regulation of
the media to promote diversity. The FCC's permissive rules on the
number of stations one operator may control are based only on the
Communications Act; the Commission's reluctance to go further
might be overcome by the thrust of constitutional principles. The
ambiguity of the antitrust laws' economic concepts, as applied to
promoting diversity of sources in the media, might be reduced by
the application of First Amendment concepts. A barrier to the
potential, relatively unregulated burgeoning of concentrations of
control over programming sources in cable television may be found
in the First Amendment. *Red Lion's* expansive reasoning can sup-

port such a constitutional development without running counter to the thrust of traditional First Amendment inhibitions on government interference with content.

No subject could be more important for a democracy than the provision of an effective right to be heard. Any issue confronting self-government in crisis-laden times, whether it be war and peace, population, hunger and famine, protection of the environment, or the justice and effectiveness of law enforcement, is capable of democratic resolution only when every idea and experience can have access to the forums of public debate through the mass media. The greatest opportunity for establishing the right to be heard through the media lies in technological developments. Other devices, such as the fairness doctrine and the right of reply, may have had a salutary impact on the broadcast media, but their effect has been limited and their enforcement presents serious problems. All those concerned for the democratic utility of a right to be heard should therefore focus on the growth of First Amendment law pertaining to structure of the media rather than on the content of any particular program or set of programs.

NOTES

1. Mr. Justice Byron White, speaking for a unanimous Supreme Court in Red Lion Broadcasting Co. v. FCC, 395 U.S. 367, 390 (1969).

2. Hague v. CIO, 307 U.S. 496 (1939); Thornhill v. Alabama, 310 U.S. 88 (1940).

3. Murdock v. Pennsylvania, 319 U.S. 105 (1943).

4. Lamont v. Postmaster General, 381 U.S. 301 (1965).

5. Marsh v. Alabama 326 U.S. 501 (1946); Amalgamated Food Employees, Local 590 v. Logan Valley Plaza, Inc., 391 U.S. 308 (1968).

6. Wolin v. Port of New York Authority, 392 F.2d 83, 89 (2d Cir. 1968), cert. denied, 393 U.S. 940 (1969).

7. United States v. Kiger, 297 F. Supp. 339 (S.D.N.Y. 1969), aff'd, 421 F.2d 1396 (2d Cir. 1970), cert. denied, 90 S. Ct. 1693 (1970); cf. United States v. O'Brien, 391 U.S. 367 (1968), holding the 1966 amendment under which Kiger was prosecuted to be constitutional.

8. McCarthy v. FCC, 390 F.2d 471 (D.C. Cir. 1968).

9. New York Times, Oct. 13, 1970, at 1, col. 1.

10. Editorializing by Broadcast Licensees, 13 F.C.C. 1246, 1250, 1251 (1949).

11. Office of Communication of the United Church of Christ v. FCC, 359 F.2d 994 (D.C. Cir. 1966).

12. Office of Communication of the United Church of Christ v. FCC, 425 F.2d 543 (D.C. Cir. 1969).

13. K. Cox and N. Johnson, *Broadcasting in America and the FCC's License Renewal Process: An Oklahoma Case Study* (FCC, 1968).

14. Red Lion Broadcasting Co. v. FCC, 395 U.S. 367, 390 (1969).

15. *Id.* at 388–89.

16. *Id.* at 394.

17. *See, e.g.,* Barron, "An Emerging First Amendment Right of Access to the Media," 37 *George Washington Law Review* 487 (1969).

18. *See* Donnelly, "The Right to Reply: an Alternative to an Action for Libel," 34 *Virginia Law Review* 867 (1948); Nev. Rev. Stat. §200.570 (1968).

19. Barron, *supra* note 17; *see also* Remarks of Commissioner Kenneth Cox Before the Section on Individual Rights and Responsibilities, ABA Convention, Dallas, Texas, August 1969.

20. *See, e.g.,* Wolin v. Port of New York Authority, 392 F.2d 83 (2d Cir. 1968), *cert. denied,* 393 U.S. 940 (1969); Marsh v. Alabama, 326 U.S. 501 (1946); Amalgamated Food Employees, Local 590 v. Logan Valley Plaza, Inc., 391 U.S. 308 (1968).

21. *See* the Court's footnote 28 in Red Lion Broadcasting Co. v. FCC, 395 U.S. at 401.

22. *See* Barron, *supra* note 17.

23. Uhlman v. Sherman, 22 Ohio N.P.N.S. 225, 31 Ohio Dec. 54 (1919). *But cf.* Bloss v. Federated Publications, 380 Mich. 485, 157 N.W.2d 241 (1968).

24. Zuckert v. Panitz, 299 F. Supp. 102 (S.D.N.Y. 1969).

25. Amalgamated Clothing Workers Union v. Field Enterprises, *dismissed on motion,* N.D. Ill. Dec. 19, 1969, *appeal pending.*

26. Tom Smothers v. Columbia Broadcasting Sys., Inc. (C.D. Cal. 1969). The Smothers also claim antitrust law violations and breach of contract.

27. Lexis, "Saint Thomas and the Dragon," *Playboy,* Aug. 1969, p. 143; Jencks, "Is Taste Obsolete?" Address before the General Conference of CBS Television Network Affiliates, New York, May 20, 1969.

28. Citizen Publishing Co. v. United States, 394 U.S. 131 (1969).

29. *See, e.g.,* the Electronic Industries Association's comments filed Oct. 28, 1969, in FCC Inquiry into Development of Communications Technology, Docket No. 18397, pt. V.

30. Consider, for instance, the number of times in which the relatively powerless, listener-supported FM stations of the Pacifica Foundation, whose programming often offends conventional views and tastes, have been the object of adverse FCC regulatory action.

SECTION III

The Right of
Personal Autonomy

THE RIGHT OF PRIVACY

KENT GREENAWALT

THE TERM "PRIVACY" CONNOTES A VARIETY OF RE-
lated interests. In two excellent treatments of the subject, privacy
has been defined as "the claim of individuals, groups, or institutions
to determine for themselves when, how, and to what extent information about them is communicated to others,"[1] and, more simply, as
"control over knowledge about oneself."[2] Though these definitions
fail to catch the essence of some "right of privacy" claims,[3] they do
serve as an adequate umbrella for the issues discussed in this essay,
which covers primarily searches by the state of home and person, including electronic surveillance as well as more traditional methods,
and more briefly psychological and polygraph testing and the
accumulation of data in computer systems. Other problems also
within these definitions receive attention elsewhere in the volume.
Two of these are the privilege against self-incrimination and the
tort "right of privacy" to be free from undesired uses of one's name
or picture and from the unjustified publication of private information about oneself.

The government frequently needs to obtain information about
individuals that they may not choose to supply. Enforcement of
criminal and certain civil laws would become impossible if the state

*Kent Greenawalt is Professor of Law at Columbia Law School, a former official
in the Agency for International Development, co-author of* The Sectarian College and
the Public Purse, *and a contributor of articles on privacy and other constitutional law
issues to legal journals.*

had to depend solely on the voluntary furnishing of data by possible offenders. However, giving the state unlimited power to obtain information would be destructive of many of the values of a liberal society.[4] Intimate human relationships depend largely on the sense that the participants are free from the observation of others, and that sense is essential to the development of individual points of view and modes of life. Continuing contacts with those looking for damaging information are both highly unpleasant and deeply disturbing to any sense of security. Moreover, the more wide-sweeping the power to gather evidence, the greater the danger that the power will be arbitrarily used to harass those "out of favor" or those against whom particular officials have personal grievances; the greater also the danger that information obtained will fall into inappropriate hands or be misused.

It is the underlying purpose of the relevant constitutional law, statutes, and other legal rules to accommodate the conflict between the government's need for information and the individual's need for privacy. Similar conflicts between private individuals and institutions must also be resolved by the legal order.

THE BASIC LAW OF SEARCH AND SEIZURE

The most important limits on the government's power to search are set by the Fourth Amendment of the federal Constitution. Since the Supreme Court has held that the Fourteenth Amendment made these limits applicable to the states,[5] they set the boundaries for both state and federal authorities. The Fourth Amendment, whose meaning is filled out by judicial decisions, provides:

> The right of the people to be secure in their persons, houses, papers, and effects, against unreasonable searches and seizures, shall not be violated, and no warrants shall issue, but upon probable cause, supported by oath or affirmation, and particularly describing the place to be searched, and the persons or things to be seized.

Protected Areas and Expectations

Traditionally the Fourth Amendment, which safeguards the security of "persons, houses, papers, and effects," was held to protect only certain places against certain types of investigation. It applied to a forcible search of one's person or a search of one's home, but was held not to apply to searches of open fields.[6] Offices, hotel rooms, and automobiles were declared to be constitutionally protected areas, but a visitors' room in a jail was not covered.[7] An investigation was not considered a search within the meaning of the Amendment unless it physically invaded a protected area. Thus the tapping of wires outside a home was not a "search" even if a telephone was located within the home,[8] and it was clear that police officers could gaze across the Hudson River with binoculars into an open window facing the river.

In *Katz v. United States*,[9] a 1967 case involving an electronic listening device placed on the outside of a public telephone booth, the Court eschewed analysis of "physical intrusion" and "constitutionally protected areas" in favor of more flexible concepts. According to the opinion, what an individual "seeks to preserve as private, even in an area accessible to the public, may be constitutionally protected. . . . The Government's activities . . . violated the privacy upon which [Katz] justifiably relied." Human beings often seek privacy in places much more "public" than telephone booths—in open parks, in secluded parts of restaurants, even on crowded streets. It is still unclear whether the novel approach of *Katz*, assuming it is followed, will be applied to such areas or limited to places actually, though momentarily, shut off from the public, such as the telephone booth or a toilet booth. From the perspective of protecting privacy, no such limitation is justified, but the more expansive reading of *Katz* does present serious difficulties of line-drawing. The police and courts would have to decide when privacy is "justifiably relied upon" and when it is not, a rather amorphous test of when the Fourth Amendment comes into play.

Searches With and Without Warrants

The typical search envisaged by the Fourth Amendment is one based on a search warrant, particularly describing the place to be searched and the things to be seized. The theory of requiring a search warrant, emphasized by recent decisions, is simple: before a search can be made the facts to justify it should be carefully evaluated by a neutral and detached magistrate, and the warrant serves as proof to the owner that a search of his premises is authorized.

What happens in actuality has borne scant resemblance to this model. Existing statistics indicate that the vast majority of criminal law searches are carried out incident to arrest, a traditional exception to the search warrant requirement. It is true that when an arrest is made pursuant to an arrest warrant, the subject of the arrest and search still has the benefit of the decision of a neutral magistrate. And even when an arrest is made without a warrant, the "probable cause" standard (sometimes phrased as "reasonable cause") must be met if the subsequent search is to be constitutional. One reason why officers prefer searches incident to arrest is simple convenience, particularly when arrest is without a warrant. But more important, perhaps, the scope of the search is less stringently controlled when the officer need not describe in advance what he is likely to find. Indeed, quite possibly an officer will have probable cause that X is guilty of a crime without having probable cause that any specific kind of evidence will be on his person or premises.

Decisions passing on searches incident to arrest have traced a zigzag course. Most recently in 1969, in *Chimel v. California*,[10] the Court has sharply restricted them. Invalidating a search of the house of an arrested burglary suspect, the Court reasoned that searches incident to arrest should be limited to their special purpose, to assure that the person arrested does not have a dangerous weapon or evidence that he can conceal or destroy. Such searches should not extend beyond the suspect's person and the area within which he might be able to grab a weapon or evidence. The broader searches of premises allowed under earlier cases were rejected as undermining the protection against general and warrantless searches. There are arguments for the earlier position. Under *Chimel*, once someone has been arrested, a policeman may have to stand by to assure that evidence is not destroyed by family or friends while fellow officers seek a search warrant. Moreover, it has been said that once the policemen have entered the premises to make the arrest, the added invasion of privacy involved in a search is comparatively slight. In any event, the present constitutional rule will require much more extensive reliance on search warrants than has been common, but the possibility cannot be discounted that at some future date the Court, particularly one sympathetic to law enforcement, may return to a more flexible approach.

A serious problem with any warrant system is the likelihood that the judge will act as a rubber stamp. Given congested court calendars and the number of criminal offenses in an urban society, the notion that most judges have the time to weigh carefully the merits of a request for a warrant is naive. Nevertheless, the existence of a formal process may still serve as a check on unmerited requests and permit a more solid basis for evaluating the presence or absence of probable cause in subsequent proceedings.

The Court has recognized an exception to the requirement of a search warrant when law enforcement officers have probable cause to search a moving car.[11] Whether such an exception can be extended to ordinary premises in emergency situations is an unresolved issue.

Reasonableness and Probable Cause

Central to the Fourth Amendment is the idea that exploratory searches are not justified; invasion of a person's security is acceptable only if there is a substantial basis for it. Since warrants can be issued only on probable cause, and warrantless searches cannot be sustained on lesser grounds, one essential element of a reasonable search has been that it is based on probable cause. Probable cause thus defines the point at which the individual's interest in privacy gives way to the government's interest in searching. Its elusive meaning is hard to pin down. In a definition often quoted, the Supreme Court stated that a search was justified if "the facts and circumstances within [the officers'] knowledge and of which they had reasonably trustworthy information were sufficient in themselves to warrant a man of reasonable caution in the belief that intoxicating liquor was being transported in the automobile which they stopped and searched."[12] This approach implies two important consequences. If the standard is belief that a fact exists, it suggests that probable cause is present only if the fact is more probable than not, since it would be strange to speak of someone believing something he thinks is less probable than not. Second, the probability demanded by the standard seems fixed, that is, it does not vary depending on the nature of the crime or particular circumstances. It is by no means certain, however, that any definition can be read so literally, and highly respected commentators have rejected a more-probable-than-not standard as too strict.[13]

In reviewing the facts supporting searches, the Supreme Court has been quite demanding. Although hearsay evidence, including informers' tips, can be the basis for probable cause, police officers seeking a warrant must ordinarily support their claim that an informer is reliable and set forth enough of the underlying circumstances so that a magistrate can judge the validity of the informer's conclusions.[14] When a search is based on an informer's tip, a subsequent challenge of it is plainly more difficult if the government can withhold the name of the informer. Yet in a controversial case, the Supreme Court held by one vote that the name of the informer need not ordinarily be given when the validity of an arrest or search is attacked.[15] The majority emphasized that a contrary rule would largely destroy the usefulness of informers, while the dissent stressed that a defendant cannot successfully challenge an informer's reliability if he does not even know his name. Without doubt the rule established also allows law enforcement officers so inclined to fabricate informers when they suspect someone of a crime but lack probable cause for an arrest or search. The conflict here between protecting individual rights and maintaining the usefulness of informers is a very real one, and the circumstances, if any, in which the informer's name must be disclosed will be worked out in future cases. While it seems doubtful that a Court largely composed of Nixon appointees will greatly extend the rights of criminal suspects, the underlying principle of nondisclosure will no doubt be subject to further attack and may at some time in the future be overruled, particularly if the system of law enforcement comes to rely less on informers.

In two "stop-and-frisk" cases,[16] the Supreme Court took a significant step toward a flexible reading of the Fourth Amendment. The essential issue was whether police may stop someone for the purpose of brief questioning and other investigation, and make a limited search of his person, in the absence of probable cause. One way of analyzing the problem is to say that any forcible stop is an arrest and any search is a "search" within the Fourth Amendment, and that no stop can be made without probable cause. The second approach is that such minimal impairment of the ordinary right of free movement does not bring the Fourth Amendment into play, and is, therefore, consistent with the Constitution. The third path, that chosen by an 8 to 1 majority of the Court, is that the Fourth Amendment does govern "stop-and-frisk" but that the requirement of probable cause is not applicable. The Court determined that the individual is protected as much on the street as in his home against unreasonable searches by the police, and that a stop-and-frisk is no "petty indignity," but it held such a limited intrusion is justified in street encounters when an officer reasonably concludes that "criminal activity may be afoot" and has a reasonable fear for his safety. Protecting the safety of the officer requires allowing a limited search for weapons, but no search beyond a patting of the outer clothing is justified if probable cause is lacking.

Despite the criticism of some civil libertarians and the likelihood that the power to stop and frisk will enhance the possibility of police harassment based on unfounded suspicion, it is unlikely that the Court will reverse itself. In an urban setting, there are too frequently situations in which the police have serious reasons, but not probable cause, to suspect criminal activity. For example, if a man is seen running along the sidewalk with a TV set in his hand at two o'clock in the morning, the police will not be able to trace the suspect if they cannot stop him and investigate.

The Court has yet to decide what the police can do if a stop is made and the suspect is totally uncooperative, refusing even to give his name. Probably such a reaction could escalate "reasonable suspicion" into "probable cause," though such a conclusion is arguably inconsistent with the privilege against self-incrimination. The precise differences in the quantum of evidence necessary to make a stop-and-frisk "reasonable" and that required for probable cause are by no means clear, and the lines will have to be worked out on a case-by-case basis. Nor is it now clear whether other limited forms of search, such as requiring persons to be fingerprinted, may also be made on less than probable cause, a question left open by a 1969 decision on fingerprint evidence.[17] It is even possible that the Court will hold in an appropriate case that full-scale searches, say of moving cars, can be made in the absence of probable cause if there is a pressing need for immediate action.

A different theoretical development leading to a similar result would be a reinterpretation of probable cause that would effectively read it out of the Fourth Amendment as an independent requirement. In 1967 the Court overruled an earlier decision and held that the warrant requirement of the Amendment does apply to administrative searches made under municipal fire, health, and housing inspection programs.[18] It acknowledged that such inspections to be effective must be area-wide, and that area-wide administrative searches are thus "reasonable." Therefore, it concluded, probable cause exists for a warrant to search a particular house if it is reasonable to search the area. This case concerns a special problem, but the Court might later choose to generalize the implication that the reasonableness of a search determines whether it is based on probable cause. This would be, of course, a complete switch in the traditional doctrine that probable cause has an independent meaning and that its existence is a necessary element of a reasonable search.

If "reasonableness" is the key concept in evaluating police activity under the Fourth Amendment, the Court might employ a "balancing" approach to search-and-seizure problems. In any particular case, it would weigh such factors as the degree of intrusion, the seriousness of the crime, and the need for quick action to prevent personal injury or the removal or destruction of evidence. Thus it might sustain an arrest and search of a suspected murderer or kidnapper on a quantum of evidence that would be insufficient for the arrest of a prostitute. The "common sense" of a balancing test has great appeal, but there are difficulties. Its application to any particular case would be uncertain, and the flexibility that such a test generally applied would introduce might well undercut the deterrence of unreasonable searches that the present standard achieves.

Where, How, and for What May the Police Search?

The proper extent of searches pursuant to an arrest and during a stop-and-frisk has already been discussed. Given the rationale of recent cases in both these areas, stops or arrests for some crimes should lead to no search whatsoever. There is no reason to suppose, for example, that a suspect arrested for vagrancy or stopped for an ordinary traffic offense has a weapon or is concealing evidence. The logic of the *Chimel* case would dictate that even a limited search in those circumstances is unconstitutional. If this logic is followed, it would discourage the not infrequent police practice of arresting on the pretext of a minor violation in the hope of discovering evidence of some more serious crime.

When a search is made pursuant to a warrant, it must be limited to the area described. It must also be limited in scope to what is reasonable in order to discover the objects described in the warrant. A search for a stolen horse, for example, could not include the shredding of a bedroom mattress. But if the search is for some minute object, say stamps or drugs, the most thorough kind of search is permissible within the described area. Some forms of search, for example stomach-pumping, are so offensive that they are considered unconstitutional independently of the probability that relevant evidence may be obtained,[19] but the Court has sustained the taking of blood samples from drivers suspected of being drunk.[20]

In most jurisdictions the governing statutes prohibit nighttime searches except in special circumstances. They also ordinarily require notice of authority and purpose by the officers undertaking the search. Either in the statutes themselves or by judicial decisions, exceptions have been carved out when notice may create a danger of personal harm or the destruction of evidence. The precise dimensions of the notice requirement as a rule of constitutional law are uncertain, and it is not clear how broadly Congress or a state legislature may authorize law enforcement officials to enter with "no knock."

Until 1967, officers could not search for and seize "mere evidence," such as a bloody shirt, but only contraband and the fruits and instrumentalities of crime. This rule, a vestige of historic property concepts, appeared arbitrary to most critics and spawned some rather strained rulings to bring seized materials within the permitted categories. The Supreme Court has now rejected the "mere evidence" rule[21] and its general re-emergence is very unlikely. An issue not yet faced by the Court, however, is whether mere evidence of a testimonial nature, such as diaries and letters, should be immune from seizure. The protection of such items is arguably related to the protections against self-incrimination and in favor of freedom of speech, and they should perhaps be treated specially.[22]

Enforcement: The Exclusionary Rule and Other Sanctions

Virtually every important case involving the legality of searches and seizures has arisen because a defendant has tried to have the evidence derived from the search excluded from use at his trial. Under existing law, evidence unconstitutionally seized or evidence derived indirectly from such a seizure cannot be used.[23] Debate continues, however, over whether the criminal should go free because the policeman has blundered. The essential arguments for the rule are that the government should not benefit from and be a party to the use of evidence obtained in violation of the Constitution and that exclusion is the only effective deterrent of illegal police action. It is not the only sanction; the individual subjected to an illegal search will often have a right to recover damages for trespass or assault or under a federal civil rights statute,[24] but impecunious police defendants and the prospect of unsympathetic juries are sufficient to render this theoretical protection largely nugatory. Nor are internal disciplinary proceedings or possible criminal penalties likely to be much more effective in most situations, since law enforcement officers and prosecutors do not commonly regard too harshly the activities of those who are overzealous in the fight against crime. While there is need to strengthen other sanctions, for example, by providing liquidated damages and allowing suits against municipalities rather than individual policemen, it would be unrealistic to expect an effective substitute for the exclusionary rule. That is not to say that even it is totally effective. In regard to some kinds of criminals, harassment may be the police goal rather than conviction, and exclusion is a futile sanction. Moreover, even when conviction is the goal, the rule may be circumvented by police who accept perjury as an acceptable adjunct of law enforcement; police who search suspected addicts without probable cause frequently testify that they first saw the suspect drop narcotics on the ground. Another problem with the exclusionary rule is that it can be employed only by a defendant whose own rights have been violated. Thus evidence obtained by an unconstitutional search of A's house may be used against B. Although the courts have been relatively liberal in defining whose rights are violated (for instance, a guest may complain of a search of his host's home), some critics have argued that the use of unconstitutionally seized evidence should not be permitted against anyone.

It was only in 1961 by a narrow majority in *Mapp v. Ohio* that the exclusionary rule was imposed on the states as a matter of federal constitutional law. Though it is now an apparently accepted part of the constitutional law of search and seizure, it is not inconceivable that *Mapp* would be overruled by a Court less sensitive to the rights of criminal suspects. As of now, even the closest violation of the Constitution requires exclusion; a step short of completely overruling *Mapp* would be to hold that evidence clearly seized illegally must be excluded but that evidence obtained because of a reasonable error in judgment is admissible. Needless to say, such a line would not be easy to draw.

Searches by Private Individuals

Private searches are not covered by the Fourth Amendment. However, private individuals, unlike law enforcement officers, are rarely if ever permitted to perform acts of searching that would constitute a trespass or assault in the absence of authorization.[25] Thus a private search of the kind discussed is actionable at civil law. So far the courts have not been willing to exclude such evidence in either criminal or civil proceedings.[26] There is, however, a strong argument that the state should not encourage the gathering of illegal evidence by allowing it to be used advantageously in the courts. Even if this degree of state participation is not sufficient to render the use of such evidence unconstitutional,[27] a statute or judicially developed exclusionary rule would be appropriate to stem some shocking breaches of law by private individuals involved in divorce actions and other private litigation.

ELECTRONIC SURVEILLANCE

The accommodation between individual and government in regard to traditional methods of search has been worked out over hundreds of years, but the advent of sensitive electronic recording and transmitting devices has required much more rapid adjustment in this century. On the one hand, the increasing sophistication and miniaturization of snooping devices create a serious fear that the sense of privacy so essential to membership in a liberal society may be systematically obliterated by the listening ear. On the other hand, law enforcement officials claim that use of such devices is absolutely essential to combat organized crime and is highly valuable in other areas. The applicable legal rules for electronic surveillance have undergone a sweeping transformation in recent years, involving not only new constitutional doctrine but major statutory change at the federal level. Though this is an area still sharply debated and subject to further important developments, the basic guidelines seem set for at least the next few years.

Constitutional Law Principles

When it first passed on evidence acquired by electronic devices, the Supreme Court held in *Olmstead v. United States* that wiretapping is not a "search" within the meaning of the Fourth Amendment and that words cannot be "seized." This decision provoked a classic dissent by Justice Brandeis, who said:

> The makers of our Constitution undertook to secure conditions favorable to the pursuit of happiness. They recognized the significance of man's spiritual nature, of his feelings and of his intellect. They knew that only a part of the pain, pleasure and satisfactions of life are to be found in material things. They sought to protect Americans in their beliefs, their thoughts, their emotions and their sensations. They conferred, as against the Government, the right to be let alone —the most comprehensive of rights and the right most valued by civilized men. To protect that right, every unjustifiable intrusion by the Government upon the privacy of the individual, whatever the means employed, must be deemed a violation of the Fourth Amendment.[28]

The Court later held that electronic listening unaccompanied by physical trespass was not constitutionally prohibited,[29] but it subsequently decided that when physical invasion was present the Fourth Amendment applied.[30] Finally in two 1967 cases, *Berger v. New York*[31] and *Katz v. United States,* the Court shed its earlier "trespass" approach to electronic surveillance. Together these cases indicate that when someone is in an area in which he has a proper expectation of privacy,[32] he is protected against unreasonable government use of electronic devices. Though extending the protection of the Fourth Amendment, the Court did not accept the position advanced by many civil libertarians that the Amendment forbids any electronic eavesdropping because it constitutes a general and exploratory search without prior notice. The Court has said, in effect, that prior notice is not required and that sufficient specificity about the conversations to be overheard and their relation to a particular crime can be obtained to make wiretap and eavesdrop warrants permissible under the Amendment. It has stated that an electronic search will not be sustained without the prior authorization of a neutral judicial officer.

If *Berger* and *Katz* are followed, a constitutional issue of great practical importance is exactly how specific the warrant must be with respect to what will be overheard, and how narrow the time of surveillance must be. Plainly general fishing expeditions against suspected criminal figures, said to be of great value against organized crime, are not permitted, and *Berger* indicates that a two-month authorization is much too long, but the precise lines of permissibility have yet to be drawn.

In cases following *Berger* and *Katz* the Court has required the government to make available to defendants the records of any of their conversations unconstitutionally intercepted, even if the government claims they are not relevant to the case.[33] The theory is that the defendant must be able to make his own investigation of possible relevance. After an official outcry that such a rule might undermine intelligence-gathering, the Court intimated uncertainty in *Giordano v. United States*[34] that all electronic surveillance should be similarly treated. In a more explicit concurring opinion Justice Stewart noted, "the Court has not . . . addressed itself to the standards governing the constitutionality of electronic surveillance relating to the gathering of foreign intelligence information—necessary for the conduct of international affairs, and for the protection of national defense secrets and installations from foreign espionage and sabotage." So long as the general rule remains of disclosure to defendants of all improperly intercepted conversations, the constitutional status of national security interceptions is a matter of considerable significance. Another unresolved question is whether a defendant or some other affected person suffers any deprivation of right if a court chooses not only to disclose to defendants but to make public the fruits of illegal eavesdropping, as did a federal district judge in 1970 with respect to conversations of New Jersey Mafia figures tapped by the FBI over a period of years.

Statutory Law and Executive Practice

A part of the Federal Communications Act passed in 1934 provided that "no person not being authorized by the sender shall intercept any communication and divulge or publish [its] existence, contents . . . or meaning."[35] This language was given an expansive reading to forbid the divulgence of any wiretapping, whether by private individuals or by federal or state law enforcement officers.[36] Despite the broad language of the relevant decisions, the Department of Justice interpreted the Act to bar only interception *and* divulgence, and it did not consider interdepartmental communication to be divulgence. Under this reading a certain amount of wiretapping by federal law enforcement offcers continued, though the evidence obtained was not usable in court. The federal law did

not cover the use of electronic bugging devices.[37] Some states prohibited the use of such devices, but the majority did not. Most
states outlawed some forms of wiretapping, but many allowed at
least some tapping by law enforcement officers. Although divulgence in state courts of wiretap evidence constitutes a federal crime,
the Supreme Court refused to forbid states from admitting such
evidence if they chose.[38]

After three decades in which more than one hundred bills to
regulate wiretapping were unenacted, Congress finally passed new
legislation as a part of the Crime Control and Safe Streets Act of
1968. Title III of the Act represents a comprehensive approach to
the problem of electronic eavesdropping.[39] All private wiretapping,
as under the 1934 Act, is prohibited. So is private bugging with
radio devices. Interception with nonradio devices is forbidden if a
component of the device has passed in interstate commerce, if the
device is used on the premises of a commercial establishment affecting commerce, or if it is used to obtain information about such an
establishment. In short, only "local" use of purely "local" nonradio devices is not covered. Violators may be punished by a maximum fine of $10,000 and maximum imprisonment of five years.
Moreover, evidence obtained by illegal electronic surveillance is
barred from use in federal and state courts, and a civil damage action
is created for the person suffering interception that includes liquidated damages, punitive damages, and an allowance for attorneys'
fees and other costs of litigation. The same criminal penalties
imposed for use are also applicable for those who manufacture, distribute, or advertise devices primarily useful for wiretapping or
bugging. Since few people think the benefits of private electronic
eavesdropping outweigh its harmful effects, these aspects of the
Act are widely approved and not likely to be substantially altered.

Much more controversial is the Act's authorization of limited
law enforcement eavesdropping. With respect to a fairly broad class
of criminal offenses, including for example all drug offenses and
gambling, eavesdropping can be approved by a federal or state court
order, upon an application authorized by the Attorney General or
an Assistant Attorney General or the chief prosecuting officer of a
state or one of its political subdivisions. The particularity required
in the application for an order resembles that underlying traditional
searches, but surveillance can be authorized for up to thirty days,
with a possibility of renewal. Only in certain emergency cases may

electronic surveillance be undertaken without an order. Individuals who are the subject of surveillance must subsequently be served an inventory notifying them of the dates of authorized eavesdropping. Evidence obtained by authorized surveillance is admissible. Unauthorized law enforcement eavesdropping is subject to the same sanctions as private eavesdropping.

It is ironic that legislation authorizing eavesdropping was passed under an administration that had proposed a complete ban and did not want the power given it. The debate over the desirability of wiretapping and bugging will continue. Those in favor of an absolute ban believe that the possibilities of abuse under any scheme that legitimizes eavesdropping outweigh the gains for law enforcement in particular cases.[40] On the heels of frightening disclosures about the Mafia obtained from wiretapping, total prohibition may not now have great public appeal, but the pendulum may swing in that direction if there are highly publicized instances of interceptions of the conversations of innocent persons. It must be kept in mind that the electronic surveillance net catches innocent as well as criminal conversations, and catches the conversations of all those who speak with the subject of the eavesdropping.

Apart from this broad attack, there are narrower grounds for criticizing the present legislation. Even if some eavesdropping is justified, the power should be very narrowly circumscribed, and the Act fails in this regard. Too many persons may obtain orders in too many courts for too many offenses and for too long a time.[41]

Not all kinds of eavesdropping are covered by the Act. It provides:

> Nothing contained in this chapter . . . shall limit the constitutional power of the President to take such measures as he deems necessary to protect the Nation against actual or potential attack or other hostile acts of a foreign power, to obtain foreign intelligence information deemed essential to the security of the United States, or to protect national security information against foreign intelligence activities. Nor shall anything . . . be deemed to limit the constitutional power of the President to take such measures as he deems necessary to protect the United States against the overthrow of the Government by force or other unlawful means, or against any other clear and present danger to the structure or existence of the Government. The contents of any wire or oral communication intercepted by authority of the President in the exercise of the foregoing powers may be received in evidence in any trial hearing, or other proceeding

only where such interception was reasonable, and shall not be otherwise used or disclosed except as is necessary to implement that
power.[42]

An issue of sharp dispute between Attorney General John Mitchell
and his critics is the interpretation of this language and the possibility and extent of any exception in constitutional law to the court
order requirement. The Attorney General has asserted a broad
power to engage in electronic surveillance without court supervision against domestic subversives, such as antiwar activists or the
Black Panthers. Even if the Court ultimately sustains foreign-
intelligence surveillance absent a court order, it is extremely doubtful if it will go as far as the Attorney General. If his position is
correct, any controversial group attacking existing policies and
institutions might be subjected to uninhibited surveillance; the
extreme danger to free political expression is obvious.

"Searches" to Which the Subject "Consents"

Consent to an Ordinary Search

The principles discussed thus far in this essay apply when the
government seeks evidence without the consent of the subject of
the search. A permissible basis for an ordinary search is consent, and
the police often rely on this. Plainly, simple acquiescence when the
police claim the power to enter is not sufficient for consent, but
courts have differed over the degree of intimidation that undermines a claim of consent.[43] There is doubtless some element of implicit coercion whenever the police make a request; one does not
want to appear uncooperative or guilty. Arguably, consent should
not be found unless a person is provided the same kind of explicit
warning required for suspects in custody under *Miranda v. Arizona*,[44] but such an extension does not seem likely in the near
future.

A question on which the Supreme Court has not yet passed, but
one of great importance to welfare recipients and criminals on
parole, is whether a person can effectively be required to waive his
right not to have his person or house searched or entered as a condition of being granted a privilege by the government. The argument for allowing such searches is strongest in regard to the paroled

inmate, who would otherwise still be in jail, but it can be answered that once the state sets a man free it must allow him the essential conditions of freedom. In regard to welfare programs, one federal court has held that a recipient cannot be compelled to open her house to a caseworker in the absence of a warrant, even if it is claimed by the state that home visits are not for the purpose of finding evidence of welfare fraud.[45] This decision is being reviewed by the Supreme Court.

Secret Agents and Informers

Informers and secret agents are historic tools of law enforcement, and it has traditionally been assumed that if one willingly admits them to one's presence, one cannot be heard to complain that they subsequently turn information over to the state. It has made no difference whether they were hired by the government specifically for the purpose of gathering information. Only in 1966 did the Supreme Court intimate that the Fourth Amendment may have any application to informers and secret agents, and it has yet to strike down the testimony of either as unconstitutional.[46] In one case the Court held the testimony of a secret agent valid in a narcotics prosecution when the agent had gone to the premises of the defendant explicitly to purchase narcotics.[47] In another, it upheld the testimony by a friend of James Hoffa about admissions made by Hoffa in his hotel suite, though the Court assumed that the friend had been released from prison and brought to Nashville in order to obtain incriminating evidence against Hoffa.[48] What the Court left open in both cases is how it would treat a government agent not originally a friend of the suspect who insinuates himself into the presence of the suspect under false pretenses. Why it thinks such a situation may be different from that in the *Hoffa* case is not perfectly clear; it is as much an invasion of one's privacy to have a friend surreptitiously turn government agent as it is to have an apparent friend turn out to have been an agent from the beginning.[49] Since the distinction is untenable, it is unlikely that the Court will draw it if the situation left open in these two cases does come before it. That secret agents and informers impair the sense of privacy of those who fear their use cannot be doubted, and lawyers will continue to formulate constitutional arguments to exclude their testimony. If such tactics come to be held in greater abhorrence than they now are, if some of the crimes, such as drug and morals offenses, for which they are most useful cease to be criminal, if alternative investigative methods improve, then such practices may be curtailed under new constitutional doctrine.

Special threats to freedom of expression are created when law enforcement officers infiltrate politically active groups. This technique, used with considerable effectiveness against the Communist Party in this country, is now being employed against radical groups. Of course, a group that believes some of its members may be police "spies" is not likely to engage in candid discussion, and the less hardy of its real members may seek other "safer" political outlets. Even without penetration of private gatherings, police may inhibit radical political action by attending public and semipublic meetings. In January 1970, for example, police officers recorded some of the names and license numbers of persons who attended a speech by Eldridge Cleaver at Iona College in New Rochelle, New York. Many persons interested in attending a talk by a controversial figure may think twice if their attendance is going to find its way into police records. The dangers to a free society are obviously greater if infiltration and close public observation are directed at political action groups than if the Mafia is the target. However, the argument is answerable that groups plotting bombings or other serious violence should not have special immunity from surveillance because they also have a political platform. Regrettably, differentiating groups actually planning violence from those whose rhetoric oustrips their actual intent is by no means easy, and one may doubt whether the police are always likely to exhibit special powers of discernment in this respect.

Participant Monitoring

For a variety of reasons, one party to a conversation may wish to record or transmit it, or simply allow it to be overheard, without the consent of the other participant. The traditional principle has been that the unwitting party simply takes his chance that the other participant is increasing his present or future audience. In 1952, the Supreme Court, in *On Lee v. United States*,[50] upheld the introduction of evidence transmitted by an electronic device carried by a friend of the defendant's who had intentionally engaged the defendant in conversation to elicit incriminating statements. And in *Lopez v. United States*,[51] eleven years later, the Court sustained the use of evidence obtained by a miniature recording device carried on an Internal Revenue agent, who correctly expected the defendant to bribe him. In both cases there were strong dissents to the view that such risks should be borne by the unknowing participant. In *Lopez,* Justice Brennan wrote that each party to a conversation takes the risk of divulgence by the other, a not undue risk,

> for it does no more than compel them to use discretion in choosing their auditors, to make damaging disclosures only to persons whose character and motives may be trusted. But the risk which both *On Lee* and today's decision impose is of a different order. It is the risk that third parties, whether mechanical auditors like the Minifon or human transcribers of mechanical transmissions as in *On Lee*— third parties who cannot be shut out of a conversation as conventional eavesdroppers can be, merely by a lowering of voices, or withdrawing to a private place—may give independent evidence of any conversation. There is only one way to guard against such a risk, and that is to keep one's mouth shut on all occasions.

In arguing that *On Lee* should be overruled, he continued:

> [I]t invokes a fictive sense of waiver wholly incompatible with any meaningful concept of liberty of communication. If a person must always be on his guard against his auditor's having authorized a secret recording of their conversation, he will be no less reluctant to speak freely than if his risk is that a third party is doing the recording. . . . I believe that there is a grave danger of chilling all private, free, and unconstrained communication if secret recordings, turned over to law enforcement officers by one party to a conversation, are competent evidence of any self-incriminating statement the speaker may have made. In a free society, people ought not to have to watch their every word so carefully.

Clearly Justice Brennan overstates his point. Participant monitoring is possible only if one party to the conversation is deceiving the other. Most people do not often communicate confidentially to persons they do not trust. Thus the threat to confidential conversations of allowing participant monitoring is much less severe than the threat of third-party eavesdropping, against which it is impossible to protect by carefully selecting one's conversational partners. Still, there is something to the claim that monitoring does intrude on privacy to a greater degree than an informer unaided by electronic devices, and one can make a good argument that law enforcement monitoring should be subject to court order requirements.[52]

In its last encounter with this problem, the Supreme Court dodged that question.[53] Since it found that a proper order had been issued, it found it unnecessary to decide if such an order was required. In a case restored for reargument during the 1970 term, the Court may clarify whether the principles now applicable to third-party wire-tapping and eavesdropping also apply to recording and transmitting by participants.[54]

Unlike the Federal Communications Act, the Crime Control Act of 1968 does make criminal such monitoring when it is done by a private individual for a tortious or criminal purpose,[55] and a few recent state statutes[56] also protect against some forms of private monitoring. There is a strong need for further criminal and civil sanctions, as well as rules among affected professional groups, against unjustified monitoring.

Surveillance of Employees

Subjection to certain forms of investigation may be an incident of kinds of employment. The use by employers of psychological tests and lie detectors is discussed below, but employers may also use the forms of search already treated. At a plant dealing with sensitive materials, for example, anything workers take home may be examined. A management concerned about breaches of security or trying to prevent simple waste of time may monitor phone conversations of employees. Post office workers know they may be observed by unseen supervisory personnel. Surveillance by employers, whether government or private, is not widely regulated by law, and instances involving it do not commonly come before the courts. But it is significant in judging the overall effect of surveillance on individual privacy; for when employment is conditioned on acceptance of surveillance, acquiescence by employees hardly connotes happy approval. Striking a proper balance between what is justified employer surveillance and what is not may become of increasing concern for legislatures, courts, and administrative tribunals in the coming years. The recent anxiety about airline hijackings suggests that other relationships between private individuals and corporations may give rise to appropriate searches; few would contend that the airlines improperly invade passenger privacy by searching for weapons.

Some Other Threats to Privacy Enhanced by Modern Technology

One's privacy may also be impaired by some other means of gathering information created or significantly enhanced by scientific advances in this century. In different ways, computer technology and polygraph and psychological testing all make it more difficult for affected individuals to control the dissemination of information about themselves. Since none of these threats is easily analogized to traditional searches, framing appropriate legal protections is a complex task.

Computers

At present individuals make a great deal of information about themselves available, in answers to census questions, in income tax returns, in applications for government benefits, in seeking commercial credit, and in a variety of other ways. So long as this information is decentralized, is relatively superficial, and is not easily accessible, individuals are relatively secure. Serious threats to privacy, however, are possible entirely apart from any new technology. When supposedly confidential school records or income tax returns are made available for purposes different from those underlying the acquisition of the information, the lives of individuals affected may be vulnerable to improper scrutiny and a much wider class may fear such scrutiny. When, as disclosed in 1970, the Defense Department maintains files of political associations and incidents containing millions of names, such data is subject to serious misuse, and even its existence is bound to inhibit controversial political activity.

The special threat of computer systems is that they can quickly centralize information and make it readily accessible, and the convenience of assembling data in computer banks may generate its own demand for the acquisition and retention of yet more data.[57] Computer technology, for example, has allowed the Secret Service to compile dossiers of over 50,000 names in their aim to protect the President from persons who may be threatening. Print-outs can provide all the relevant names, and data about those names, in areas where the President plans to visit. Such comprehensiveness and accessibility would be impossible without the computer.

And this pattern of computer compilation and reproduction is being followed by other federal and state agencies for a variety of purposes. The threat to privacy inherent in public officials having such extensive and accessible knowledge about individuals seems particularly dangerous when the relevant information is about non-conformist political beliefs, associations, and activities, which are a main focus of agencies concerned with controlling riots and other disorders, as well as of the Secret Service.

Computers may be used for more than the storing and rapid reproduction of data; bits of information about persons, unimportant in themselves, may be assembled to provide a picture of an individual that is very revealing. Since computers are highly complicated machines that may make errors when there are minor malfunctions, some of these bits may be inaccurate and others may be misleading when removed from their original context. Of course, some of the same aspects of computers that make them "threatening" also make them promising tools in the achievement of social goals. In law enforcement, centralized computers have already given a substantial boost to local police who seek information not obtainable locally. And the centralizing of more general collected data could make government operations more efficient and greatly improve the capabilities of social science.

Much of the controversy over the dangers of computers has arisen in connection with a proposal for a National Data Center.[58] A center might be limited to the accumulation of data in such a manner that it could be used only for statistical or other social scientific studies. But it might serve as the locus for data on particular individuals collected by various agencies and put together in personal "dossiers," or even as the one collecting agent for data, making available to various agencies what they need. Obviously, more serious threats to privacy would be posed if the center had an individual dossier capacity and collected data itself. Proposals for a data center are now in abeyance, in part because its dangerous potentialities are being seriously considered, but the sharing of computers by agencies already presents many of the same threats. Some combinations of technical protections, such as coding, limiting access to portions of files, and purging stale information, and legal safeguards, such as criminal penalties and damage actions for the misappropriation and misuse of data, are needed if the dangers to privacy are to be minimized. Society has already had a taste of what can happen when confidential government information is improperly leaked to other agencies or inaccurate information about one's credit status is widely disseminated. Only careful safeguards will preclude great magnification of these threats. If they are not forestalled, people afraid that what they do will quickly become part of a general and ineradicable record may become very careful to toe the conformist line.

Psychological Tests and Lie Detectors[59]

Certain government agencies, including the Peace Corps, as well as many private enterprises have employed psychological tests to ascertain suitability for particular kinds of jobs. There are three essential criticisms of such tests: they are not reliable; the questions are sometimes embarrassing or too personal—for example, about sexual and religious views; and, most importantly, the tests are designed to produce insights about the individual that he is not consciously revealing. Even if reliability improved and none of the questions were offensive, the third problem would remain, for that is the very nature of a psychological test. Proponents of such tests answer that no one is forced to take them and that the individuals themselves benefit if their unfitness for a kind of employment is ascertained early. In the Peace Corps context, it is much better to have a candidate rejected than to have him break down under stressful conditions. If such tests were widely used by employers, the consent contention would lose its force, for taking a test would in fact be a condition of reasonable employment. If the tests remain as unreliable as they apparently are now, heavy emphasis on them will produce unfair decisions. If they were totally reliable, emotionally unstable individuals greatly in need of the support of ordinary work might be hard put to it to find good jobs, since employers would prefer not to take risks. There may come a distant day when such tests will be widely employed to help individuals find work for which they are psychologically suited, and when society makes a genuine effort to find appropriate jobs for all its members; but in the foreseeable future the use of these tests is likely to do more social harm than social good, except perhaps in connection with jobs that do create a high degree of emotional stress. The balance is much closer when such tests are used, as at schools, to obtain generalizations that will help improvement of the educational process, though the danger of improper disclosure of individual results is serious, and the element of compulsion in the taking of the test is greater than in industry or government.

Polygraph tests are sometimes used in screening employees for high-security positions and in questioning employees if security has been breached. Like psychological testing, lie detectors are not now very trustworthy, though much depends on the expertness of the operator. These tests do not, of course, involve revelations of which the subject is unaware (except insofar as they indicate the truthfulness of his answers), but they do, if they work, force truths out of him that he would prefer not to reveal. The objection to this procedure is much like that which underlies the privilege against self-incrimination, and the use of lie detector tests for a whole group of employees is defensible only when the security interest to be protected is very great. Use in regard to lesser matters may be justified only if a suspect on whom attention has focused requests a test in an effort to clear himself.

In 1970, legislation that with limited exceptions would forbid government use of psychological and polygraph tests on its employees passed the Senate.[60] Similar bills have been proposed before, and it may be expected that this or other legislation will eventually be enacted, and that sometime in the future legislators will also tackle the use of such tests by private enterprises.

One can conceive of a primitive society with little privacy as we know it, or even of small subgroups within this society whose members voluntarily give up a substantial amount of privacy in the interests of a closer unity. But freedom of thought and action, tolerance, and the shared intimacies of love and friendship are difficult to imagine in a complex industrial society if its members generally do not have protection against governmental and private intrusions. The value assigned to privacy and the balance between that and other values is constantly shifting, and it is difficult to predict the accommodations of the future. It is even hard to make accurate comparisons with the past. Certainly the technological threats to privacy have increased, but in an urban and mobile society the possibilities for privacy are also greater, because one's neighbors at any point in time are likely to be rather indifferent to how one is spending one's life. Without suggesting that no reduction in privacy is worth an offsetting gain (perhaps properly used psychological tests, for example, could steer people to more satisfying work), one can conclude that society requires carefully drawn legal measures to protect against the increasing number of intrusions made possible by an advancing technology. Unless the many conflicts between privacy and the need for information are intelligently resolved, they are likely to be resolved inadvertently against privacy.

NOTES

1. A. Westin, *Privacy and Freedom* 7 (1967).
2. Fried, "Privacy," 77 *Yale Law Journal* 475, 483 (1968).
3. In Griswold v. Connecticut, 381 U.S. 479 (1965), the Supreme Court held that a married couple may not be forbidden to use contraceptive devices. The "right of privacy" involved, though affected by the undesirability of snooping in bedrooms, is a right to be free to act in a certain way, not a right to control information. Similar claims have been made that an individual has a "right" to have an abortion and to use drugs.
4. See the discussions in Westin, *supra* note 1, and Fried, *supra* note 2.
5. *See* Mapp v. Ohio, 367 U.S. 643 (1961); Ker v. California, 374 U.S. 23 (1963).
6. Hester v. United States, 265 U.S. 57 (1924).
7. *See* Lanza v. New York, 370 U.S. 139 (1962).
8. Olmstead v. United States, 277 U.S. 438 (1928).
9. 389 U.S. 347, 351–53 (1967). For analysis of this case in the light of some of the problems discussed in this essay, see Kitch, "Katz v. United States: The Limits of the Fourth Amendment," 1968 *Supreme Court Review* 133.
10. 395 U.S. 752 (1969).
11. Carroll v. United States, 267 U.S. 132 (1925).
12. *Id.* at 162.
13. *See* ALI Modle Code of Pre-Arraignment, Tentative Draft No. 1, Commentary to §3.01.
14. *See* Aguilar v. Texas, 378 U.S. 108 (1964); Spinelli v. United States, 394 U.S. 410 (1969).
15. McCray v. Illinois, 386 U.S. 300 (1967). When the identity of the informant would be helpful for a defense to the criminal charge, the government must disclose his name. Roviaro v. United States, 353 U.S. 53 (1957).
16. Terry v. Ohio, 392 U.S. 1 (1968); Sibron v. New York, 392 U.S. 41 (1968).
17. Davis v. Mississippi, 394 U.S. 721 (1969).
18. Camara v. Municipal Court, 387 U.S. 523 (1967). Border searches are assumed not to be restricted by the Fourth Amendment.
19. Rochin v. California, 342 U.S. 165 (1952).
20. Schmerber v. California, 384 U.S. 757 (1966). In this case, the Court also rejected arguments that such searches violate the privilege against self-incrimination.
21. Warden v. Hayden, 387 U.S. 294 (1967).
22. *See* T. Taylor, *Two Studies in Constitutional Interpretation* 68–71 (1969).
23. Mapp v. Ohio, 367 U.S. 643 (1961).
24. *See* Monroe v. Pape, 365 U.S. 167 (1961).

25. If a citizen makes an authorized arrest, he can, one would assume, at least assure himself that the person he arrests does not carry a dangerous weapon.

26. *See* Burdeau v. McDowell, 256 U.S. 465 (1921); Sackler v. Sackler, 15 N.Y.2d 40, 203 N.E.2d 481 (1964).

27. *Cf.* Shelley v. Kraemer, 334 U.S.1 (1948).

28. 277 U.S. 438, 478 (1928).

29. Goldman v. United States, 316 U.S. 129 (1942).

30. Silverman v. United States, 365 U.S. 505 (1961).

31. 388 U.S. 41 (1967).

32. See page 302 for a discussion of this aspect of *Katz.*

33. Alderman v. United States, 394 U.S. 165 (1969).

34. 394 U.S. 310, 314 (1969).

35. §605. This has been amended by the Crime Control Act of 1968, discussed below.

36. Nardone v. United States, 302 U.S. 379 (1937); Benanti v. United States 355 U.S. 96 (1957).

37. In 1966, the Federal Communications Commission issued a regulation prohibiting eavesdropping with radio devices, except when authorized for law enforcement officers by federal or state law. 31 Fed. Reg. 3397 (1966).

38. Schwartz v. Texas, 344 U.S. 199 (1952), *overruled by* Lee v. Florida, 392 U.S. 378 (1968).

39. 18 U.S.C. §§2510–20.

40. My own views are summarized in "Wiretapping and Bugging: Striking a Balance Between Privacy and Law Enforcement," 50 *Judicature* 303 (1967), *also printed in Columbia Law Alumni Bulletin,* Summer 1967, at 4; *Case and Comment,* Sept.–Oct. 1967, at 3.

41. *See* Schwartz, "The Legitimation of Electronic Eavesdropping: The Politics of 'Law and Order,' " 67 *Michigan Law Review* 455 (1969).

42. 18 U.S.C. §2511 (3).

43. *See* Kamisar, "Illegal Searches or Seizures and Contemporaneous Statements," 1961 *University of Illinois Law Forum* 78, 115–19.

44. 384 U.S. 436 (1966).

45. James v. Goldberg, 303 F. Supp. 935, *prob. juris. noted sub. nom.* Wyman v. James 397 U.S. 904 (1970).

46. *But see* Massiah v. United States, 377 U.S. 201 (1964), holding that an informer's eliciting of statements after indictment was a denial of the right to counsel.

47. Lewis v. United States, 385 U.S. 206 (1966).

48. Hoffa v. United States, 385 U.S. 293 (1966).

49. See Kitch, *supra* note 9, at 143–52.

50. 343 U.S. 747 (1952).

51. 373 U.S. 427, 450, 452 (1963).

52. My own views are developed in Greenawalt, "The Consent Problem in Wiretapping and Eavesdropping: Surreptitious Monitoring With the Consent of a Participant in a Conversation," 68 *Columbia Law Review* 189 (1968).

53. Osborn v. United States, 385 U.S. 323 (1966).

54. United States v. White, 405 F.2d. 838 (7th Cir.), *cert. granted,* 394 U.S. 957 (1969), *restored for reargument,* 90 S. Ct. 677 (1970).

55. *See* 18 U.S.C. §2511 (c), (d), which make it clear that the general definition of "intercept" in §2510 (4) does include participant use of monitoring devices and monitoring done with the consent of a participant.

56. *See, e.g.,* Mass. Gen. Laws. ch. 272, §99 B. 4 (Acts of 1968, ch. 738).

57. For an informative, careful, and comprehensive treatment of computers and privacy, see Miller, "Personal Privacy in the Computer Age: The Challenge of a New Technology in an Information-Oriented Society," 67 *Michigan Law Review* 1089 (1969). See also the sources cited there.

58. *Id.* at 1129–40; Note, "Privacy and Efficiency: Proposals for a National Data Center," 82 *Harvard Law Review* 400 (1968).

59. *See generally* Westin, *supra* note 1, at 211–78.

60. S. 782, 91st Cong., 2d Sess. (1970).

THE RIGHT TO
RELIGIOUS LIBERTY

A FORTUITOUS COMBINATION OF CIRCUMSTANCES
explains the launching of the experiment expressed in 1787 in the
promulgation for the new nation of a secular Constitution limiting
the powers and concerns of the government to secular affairs, and
reiterated four years later in a Bill of Rights whose opening words
forbade the government to establish religion or prohibit its free
exercise.[1] Unlike Latin America, which was populated almost exclusively by colonists from the monolithic Catholic states of Spain
and Portugal, the Atlantic Coast between New England and Georgia was largely settled by colonists from England at a time when
the established English church faced grave challenges and religious
pluralism was a reality, *de facto* if not *de jure*. The Englishmen
who came here were Anglicans, Calvinists, Puritans, Baptists,
Quakers, Methodists, and Roman Catholics, to mention but the
major sects. Moreover, notwithstanding the impression given by
elementary-school history textbooks, comparatively few of them
were motivated exclusively or predominantly by religious considerations.

By the time our Constitution was written, the bloody religious
wars that had for centuries plagued Europe were long over and
substantial religious freedom was the rule in England, as of course

*Leo Pfeffer is Professor of Constitutional Law and Chairman of the Department of
Political Science, Long Island University, Special Counsel to the American Jewish
Congress, and a participant in church-state litigation in the United States Supreme
Court. He is the author of* Church, State and Freedom *and other books.*

it was in America. Here, however, freedom of religion was coupled with disestablishment, and by 1787 there was a widespread if not universal consensus that full religious freedom was attainable only in a secular state.

The secular humanism, emanating from Locke and the French Enlightenment, which pervaded American intellectualism during the last quarter of the eighteenth century, was another factor which contributed to church-state separation. So too was the existence of the frontier, where the most practicable church was one in which the only priest was the head of the household and the only source for doctrine or dogma a portable Bible. Indeed, antiestablishmentarianism if not anticlericalism was the common tie that rather curiously bound the pietist Baptist of the backwoods and the intellectual humanist of the seaboard.

These and other factors, some transient, others more or less permanent, constituted the matrix of the American experiment of religious freedom coupled with church-state separation. By and large, the American people have been faithful to the experiment. America has been singularly tolerant of religious diversity and nonconformism, as is indicated by the fact that at last count there were over 250 different religious sects flourishing in this country. In the few instances in which a religious group has been the victim of bias and oppression, the dominant cause was a factor other than religion. The bigotry of the Know-Nothing movement was more anti-Irish than anti-Catholic, as is evidenced by the fact that it does not appear to have encompassed English, French, or German Catholics. Once the Mormons gave up their practice of plural marriages and thus no longer presented a threat to our monogamous social structure, they became a respected part of the American community, and it was the antinationalism of the Jehovah's Witnesses rather than their theology which caused their persecution in the 1940's.

THE FREE EXERCISE OF RELIGION

In this country the Supreme Court is the chief guardian of the people's liberties, and while the Court can be and at least since 1937 has been somewhat ahead of public opinion in tolerance of nonconformism in religion, politics, art, and social patterns, it cannot be too far ahead of the general consensus or it courts disaster.

Hence, the libertarianism of the Court's religious-freedom decisions evidences a general public acceptance of religious diversity and nonconformism. It is unlikely that we are ready yet to elect an avowed atheist to the presidency (although none of the first seven Presidents was a church member before he was elected to the office); nevertheless, there was no significant public dissent and considerable approval, particularly among church spokesmen, of the Court's decision in 1961 that an atheist cannot constitutionally be disqualified from holding any public office.[2]

The most recent decisions of the Court show an ever increasing tolerance toward religious nonconformism. Some of its early decisions expressed a principle that no person, because of his own particular religious beliefs, has a constitutional right to be exempt from the mandate of a valid secular law;[3] and therefore, for example, a Jehovah's Witness child could be expelled from public school for refusing on religious grounds to participate in a flag-saluting exercise.[4] But this decision was shortly thereafter overruled[5] and the principle itself abandoned. The current attitude of the Court is reflected in a 1963 decision holding that a state may not disqualify persons from receiving unemployment insurance benefits by reason of their refusal for religious reasons to work on Saturday,[6] although two years earlier it had held that such persons did not have a constitutional right to be exempt from the operation of compulsory Sunday closing laws.[7]

There is a fundamental difference between the conceptualization of religious freedom in this country and in most other countries. In the latter, the freedom is conceived of as belonging to minority sects or religious groups, often with the qualification that they be officially recognized by the state; it is, in other words, a corporate rather than a personal freedom. In the United States, perhaps by reason of our frontier tradition, religious freedom is oriented toward the individual rather than the sect or group. This is illustrated by a Supreme Court decision in 1963 that a state could not constitutionally punish a woman for a refusal to serve on a jury based upon her individual interpretation of the New Testament's command "Judge not, that ye be not judged."[8] It is illustrated too by the law respecting conscientious objection to military service, which is also a case study in the harmony between the Court and the people, at least as reflected in the acts of their legislative representatives, in the area of tolerance for religious nonconformism, and in the increasing libertarianism of both.

The first Selective Service Law, enacted in 1917, accorded exemption to members of recognized sects whose doctrine and discipline forbid participation in armed combat (such as the Quakers and Mennonites). The second law, adopted in 1940, removed the requirement of membership in a recognized sect, and based the exemption on individual training and belief. In 1948, the law was amended to specify that "religious training and belief" contemplated belief in a Supreme Being, but this was thereafter interpreted by the Supreme Court in the *Seeger* case not to require belief in a personal deity but to mean not very much more than possession of a sincere, deeply held objection to war. The test of religiosity, the Court held, is "whether a given belief that is sincere and meaningful occupies a place in the life of its possessor parallel to that filled by the orthodox belief in God of one who clearly qualifies for the exemption."[9] Moreover, the Court had earlier interpreted the first law to limit the privilege of conscientious objection to citizens so that an alien could be barred from admission to citizenship if he refused to swear that he would bear arms in defense of the country if called upon to do so.[10] In 1946, however, the Supreme Court reversed the decisions and held conscientious objectors to be eligible for naturalization.[11]

The aftermath of some of these decisions indicates the strong commitment to religious liberty on the part of the American people. The 1940 decision upholding expulsion of Jehovah's Witness children for refusal to salute the flag aroused a storm of criticism. Even the American Legion, one of the nation's most nationalistic organizations, could not accept it. The Legion sponsored a bill, enacted by Congress in June 1942 (Public Law No. 623), which, after describing the pledge of allegiance and the flag salute, stated that "civilians will show full respect to the flag when the pledge is given by merely standing at attention, men removing the headdress."

The 1946 decision overruling earlier ones and holding that conscientious objectors to war are not barred from becoming American citizens was not based upon the Constitution but upon an interpretation of the naturalization law enacted by Congress. It would have been a simple matter for Congress to overrule the decision by amending the law to provide expressly that conscientious objectors were barred from acquisition of American citizenship. Congress, during the McCarthy period, did amend the law, surprisingly not to overrule the decision but to reaffirm it.

The *Seeger* decision, which accorded conscientious exemption to draftees whose religious views are quite unorthodox, experienced a similar aftermath. This decision too was not based upon the Constitution but upon an interpretation of the meaning of "Supreme Being" as used in the act of Congress. The decision could easily have been overruled by Congress in an amendment providing that the term was to be interpreted to mean (as it was quite probably originally intended) a deity within the accepted Judeo-Christian tradition. Instead, Congress amended the statute to eliminate entirely the requirement of belief in a Supreme Being but to retain the requirement that objection to war be based on religious training and belief.

For its part, the Court followed up its reading the Supreme Being requirement out of the law by doing the same for the religious-training-and-belief requirement. In the *Seeger* case the applicant struck out the words "training and" in the Selective Service form and put quotation marks around the word "religious" so that the answer read: "I am, by reason of my 'religious' belief, conscientiously opposed to participation in war in any form." In the *Welsh* case,[12] the applicant struck out the words "religious training and," thus clearly if implicitly denying any religious objection to participation in war. The Court held that he nevertheless was entitled to exemption since his strong belief that killing in war was wrong, unethical, and immoral and that his conscience forbade him to take part in such an evil practice was the equivalent of a religious belief.

The aftermath of the Sunday Law decision was analogous. After the Court ruled that Sabbatarians had no constitutional right to exemption, the legislatures in a number of the large industrial states—New York, Massachusetts, Michigan, and Pennsylvania among others—followed the earlier lead of other states—Ohio, Connecticut, Illinois, and others—and amended their laws specifically to exempt Sabbatarians.

The public response to the flag-salute and conscientious objector cases indicates that the national commitment to the free exercise of religion is strong even when such exercise conflicts with interests of national loyalty and security. There is, however, one area of conflict wherein the Court has been considerably less sympathetic to the claim of religious liberty, manifesting here too the national consensus. Where upholding a claim of religious liberty would limit the state's power to protect the welfare of children, the Court has practically always decided in favor of the latter. In 1925, the Court did hold that a state could not constitutionally require that all children be educated in public schools,[13] but that decision did not absolve religiously motivated parents from providing their children with a basic secular education. In one case, the Court refused to upset the conviction under a state compulsory school attendance law of extreme orthodox Jewish parents who asserted that secular instruction of children was forbidden by their faith.[14] In another, the Court disposed similarly of a claim by Amish parents that traditional secular education beyond the age of fourteen violated their religious conscience.[15]

In an earlier case, the Court upheld a state court decision applying an anti-child-labor law against Jehovah's Witnesses who, in conformity with their religious obligations, allowed their children to sell religious pamphlets and literature on the public streets.[16] In another case, the Court refused to review a state court decision which held that although the beliefs of Jehovah's Witnesses did not permit blood transfusions (since they violated the biblical command against eating blood), this fact would not bar a state court from ordering, against the parents' wishes, a transfusion for a sick child whose survival depended upon it.[17]

The Court's concern for the welfare of children when it is confronted with a claim of freedom under the First Amendment is not limited to religion cases. In 1968, the Court refused to apply the liberal standards that it had developed in determining whether a publication was obscene (and hence not entitled to First Amendment protection) so as to bar a state from applying stricter standards to literature sold to children under seventeen.[18] The Court held in that case that even where there is an invasion of protected First Amendment freedoms, the power of the state to control the conduct of children for their welfare reaches beyond the scope of authority over adults.

Earlier the Court had held that fundamental rights of due process, such as notice of charges, right to counsel, and freedom from compulsory self-incrimination, were applicable to juvenile delinquency proceedings.[19] The decision, however, shows clearly that the Court was unconvinced that such proceedings really were in the children's welfare, and that in any event imposition of the due process requirements would not hamper the proceedings to the extent that they were in the interests of the welfare of children. The decision thus was in harmony with the Court's 1943 holding that a Jehovah's Witness child could not be expelled from public school for refusing to salute the flag, and with a 1969 decision that a child could not constitutionally be expelled from public school for wearing a black armband as a symbol of protest against the Vietnam war.[20] However, where the Court has been convinced that a clear conflict exists between traditional constitutional rights and the welfare of children, it has upheld and in all probability will continue to uphold governmental action seeking to protect the children's welfare.

Changes in the personnel of the Supreme Court during the Nixon administration have already begun. Before it is over, it is by no means impossible that a majority of the Court may be Nixon appointees. (Besides Warren and Fortas, Black, Douglas, and Harlan may leave during Nixon's administration even if he serves but one term.) The Nixon Court will certainly be more conservative than its predecessor. Yet it is safe to predict that there will be no substantial change in its treatment of religious nonconformity. The liberal tradition in regard to religion, both within and without the Court, is too well established to be endangered to any significant extent by changes in the composition of the Supreme Court, even assuming the new Justices were inclined in that direction.

There is, however, one particular area wherein a change in Court personnel may effect, if not a change in direction, then at least a slower pace of progress. The Vietnam war has evoked more public opposition than perhaps any other war in American history, and this opposition has manifested itself in an unusually large number of young men being by principle unwilling to participate in it. The traditional pacifist, Quaker, Mennonite, etc. faces no serious problem although the Court has consistently held (and is unlikely to change this holding in the foreseeable future irrespective of changes in Court personnel) that there is no constitutional right to conscientious exemption from military service.[21] Congress has conferred such an exemption for as long as there has been universal military conscription, and, as we have seen, Congress has given no indication of intent to abolish it.

The less conventional religious pacifist is likewise reasonably safe in view of the acceptance by Congress of the Court's liberal interpretation of belief in a Supreme Being in the *Seeger* case. But Congress has not yet reacted to the Court's decision in the *Welsh* case and it is by no means certain that it will accord it a similar sympathetic reception. The Supreme Being requirement was a recent innovation, but the religious belief requirement goes back as long as there has been conscientious exemption. Moreover, the *Seeger* decision was unanimous, whereas the opinion in the *Welsh* case did not command even a majority of the Court and prevailed only because Justice Blackmun took his seat after the case was argued and therefore did not participate in the decision. It is therefore quite possible that Congress may respond to the *Welsh* decision in a manner directly contrary to its response to *Seeger* and state clearly that when it said "religious" it meant religious and not moral or ethical. Nor is it impossible that the Court may reverse itself and hold that this indeed is what the statute means. Should either of these events occur, the Court would be faced squarely with the constitutional issue, avoided in both *Seeger* and *Welsh*, whether the First Amendment establishment clause permits discrimination in favor of religious as against nonreligious objection to war.

In 1961, the Court held unconstitutional a Maryland law which barred from public office persons who would not take an oath that they believed in the existence of God.[22] That decision, coupled with the *Seeger* decision, would seem to point to a trend toward equalization of religious and nonreligious conscience. It is true that, traditionally, conscientious objection to military service has been assumed to mean religious objection; one of the amendments which were to constitute the Bill of Rights and passed the House but not the Senate provided that "no person *religiously* scrupulous shall be compelled to bear arms in person."[23] Nevertheless, under recent decisions interpreting the ban on laws respecting an establishment of religion, the Court could reasonably hold that discrimination against nonreligious objectors to war constituted an establishment of religion. But whether a Court whose personnel is substantially changed by President Nixon would reach such a decision is highly doubtful.

No less doubtful is such a Court's sympathetic treatment of the claim of selective conscientious objection. The present law limits exemption to those opposed to participation in war in any form. A liberal Court could hold that an exemption so limited unconstitutionally discriminates against those whose religious beliefs allow them to participate in a just war; a conservative Court is much less likely to do so.

In *Prince v. Massachusetts*[24] Justice Rutledge, speaking for the Court, expressed doubt that freedom of conscience is entitled to broader protection than freedom of the mind, or that "any of the great liberties insured by the First Article can be given higher place than the others."

All [the Court continued] are interwoven there together. Differences there are, in them and in the modes appropriate for their exercise. But they have unity in the charter's prime place because they have unity in their human sources and functionings. Heart and mind are not identical. Intuitive faith and reasoned judgment are not the same. Spirit is not always thought. But in the everyday business of living, secular or otherwise, these variant aspects of personality find inseparable expression in a thousand ways. They cannot be altogether parted in law more than in life.

Historically this equation of mind and soul may not be entirely true, at least as regards objection to participation in armed combat. Certainly Congress, by excluding exemption because of views which are "essentially political, sociological, or philosophical," rejected the equation. Yet Justice Rutledge may well have anticipated the ethos of the seventies. Certainly, exempting the faithful while conscripting the philosophers smacks of medieval punishment for nonbelief or at least imposition of second-class citizenship on the nonbeliever. In the *Welsh* case the Court went to the verge of adopting Justice Rutledge's equation.

When in 1965 the Court invalidated anticontraception laws,[25] when in 1968 it forbade a state to discriminate against illegitimate children in the right to recover for their mother's wrongful death,[26] and when it holds, as sooner or later it surely will, that the death penalty constitutes impermissible cruel punishment, it has and will apply the enlightenment of the late twentieth rather than the late eighteenth century to the solution of contemporary problems. By that standard, it should hold that rationalists and religionists stand on an equal footing in the application of the draft laws. By the same token it should hold as equals those who object to all wars and those who object to what they in good faith deem to be unjust wars.

Should the Court hold that nonreligious objectors to particular wars are constitutionally entitled to equal treatment with religious objectors to all wars, Congress could respond in either of two ways. It could overcome the effect of the decision by abolishing all conscientious exemption, a measure which though drastic would probably withstand constitutional challenge. Or it could accept the decision (as it accepted the *Seeger* decision) and the risk that the result might well be a *de facto* volunteer army. Although President

Nixon has stated that his goal, after termination of the Vietnam war, is a voluntary army, it seems unlikely that at least so long as the Vietnam war is with us the Supreme Court will compel Congress to choose between a voluntary army or no exemptions for even the most traditional of religious objectors to all wars.

THE ESTABLISHMENT OF RELIGION

Although, as has been indicated, the generation that wrote our Constitution deemed church-state separation and religious freedom to be inseparable, indeed two sides of the same coin, the situation with regard to separation is not quite as clear or as consistent. While the American people have been committed to separation in principle, they have in practice not merely permitted but insisted on public manifestations of religiosity on the part of government and government officials. Thus, of all the Presidents, only Jefferson and Jackson refused to issue proclamations for thanksgiving and prayer and even the former found it politic occasionally to attend religious services held in the Capitol. In the privacy of his notebooks, Madison wrote that congressional chaplaincy was unconstitutional, but as a member of the first Congress, he offered no objection to the employment of a congressional chaplain.

That tension between principle and practice, which in another context was referred to by Gunnar Myrdal as an American dilemma, has been most evident in the arena of education, or more specifically, religion in public education. The era of Jacksonian democracy saw state assumption of responsibility for public education, a development which American Protestantism accepted, if indeed it did not welcome. Although this transfer of responsibility naturally brought with it secularization of the schools, vestiges of their Protestant origin, such as Bible reading and prayer recitation, remained. There can be no doubt that these practices conformed to the wishes of the American people, and even today, eight years after the Supreme Court declared them to be unconstitutional,[27] every survey of public opinion indicates that they are supported by 80 to 90 percent of the population.

If so large a proportion of Americans had favored racial segregation in the public schools, it may be assumed that the Court's 1954 decision in *Brown v. Board of Education*[28] would have long ago been nullified, either by the Court itself through overruling or by the Congress and the state legislatures through constitutional amendment. Paradoxically, the Court's prayer and Bible decisions are today as live and vigorous as ever, notwithstanding sporadic non-compliance. At least three separate efforts to overrule the decision by constitutional amendment were made: the first by Senator James Eastland, the second by Congressman Frank Becker of New York, and the third by Senator Everett Dirksen; all came to naught.[29] The explanation lies in the fact that the American ethos is fundamentally secular, and while the people may like the public and official expression of religiosity, unlike race relations it is not something about which they care deeply or passionately. (The momentary uproar following the first prayer decision was aimed more at the Court than at the decision which evoked it.)

This does not mean the religiosity has disappeared or is likely soon to disappear from the public schools. Aside from the largely rural communities where prayer recitation and devotional Bible reading still take place in the public schools. Christmas observances are to be found, in varying degrees of sectarianism, all over the nation. Nativity scenes and crèches abound in public parks and public school grounds. Occasional protests and even lawsuits by Jews and humanists receive unsympathetic responses from administrative officials and local courts, on the ground that Christmas has now become a national rather than a sectarian holiday.

Despite these practices, which on the whole are marginal (in the large cities Christmas observances generally consist of little more than carol singing), it is unlikely that the Supreme Court will retreat from its forward position in the area of religion in public education. The Court should go further; it should hold unconstitutional even these marginal vestiges of sectarianism in the public schools, for they not only violate the First Amendment but, like racial segregation, although of course to a much lesser degree, they impose a badge of inferiority on those children of minority faiths whose conscience is offended by the practices. The latest Supreme Court decision safeguarding the secularity of public education was in 1968, when the Court held unconstitutional, as a violation of the establishment clause, a religiously motivated Arkansas law forbidding the teaching of the theory of evolution in the public schools.[30] The significance of the case lies not so much in the decision as in the fact that the Court took the case at all, for the statute, enacted in 1928, had long since become a dead-letter law at the time the suit was brought challenging its validity. Inasmuch as the Court had only seven years earlier refused to hear a challenge to a state anti-birth-control statute on the ground that it had become a dead-letter law,[31] its acceptance of the antievolution case can be explained only in terms of its concern for the secularity of the public school system. Notwithstanding changes in the Court's personnel, such concern and the continued secularity of American public education for the indefinite future can reasonably be assumed.

No safe assumption can be made about the second aspect of church-state relations in education, namely, governmental support of parochial schools. The two subjects are closely related, and in a sense American Protestantism has itself to blame for the existence of a Catholic parochial school system. When large-scale immigration from Ireland brought many Catholics to these shores in the 1830's and 1840's, the bishops feared for the preservation of their faith and to ward off the danger of Protestantization decreed the establishment of a Catholic school as an adjunct to every parish church. The new arrivals, however, were eager for Americanization, though not of course for Protestantization, and sent their children into the public schools. Protestant public school authorities and parents, motivated perhaps more by hostility to the aliens than by fervor for their own faith, obdurately refused to remove or even substantially mitigate the Protestant-oriented prayers and Bible readings. The Catholic community thus had no choice but to obey the bishops in order to create havens of safety where their children could find religious freedom and a sense of belonging, and thus evolved the Catholic parochial school system.

Maintenance of an elaborate school system attended by about half the Catholic children in the country has been a heavy burden on the Catholic community, and from the very beginning of the system the Church has demanded governmental financial support. Until very recently, American Protestantism has been equally determined in its opposition, and has succeeded in preventing all but minimal and peripheral governmental financing of parochial schools. This position has been attributed by some Catholic spokesmen to Know-Nothing bigotry, but unjustly so, as is evidenced by the fact that it is mandated by the laws or constitution of practically every state in the Union. It is probable that a substantial majority of Americans do not favor direct governmental support of parochial schools; in New York in 1967, for example, a proposed new constitution which would have removed the barrier to such support was soundly defeated, even in Catholic districts.[32]

Nevertheless, the dramatic ecumenicism which followed Vatican II softened Protestant opposition, at least at the national organizational level, and contributed substantially to the first major breakthrough in the enactment, with the endorsement, by the National Council of Churches of Christ, of the Elementary and Secondary Education Act of 1965, which expressly required inclusion of non-public schools in programs financed with funds authorized by the Act. This was characterized, not only by Catholics but also by many Protestants and Jews as well as governmental authorities, as heralding a new era in church-state relations as these affect governmental support of parochial schools and a recognition of religious groups as partners of public school authorities in providing education for American children. Certainly, adoption of the Act was followed by the passage of laws in various states providing for aid to parochial schools through a variety of devices, such as auxiliary services, financing or purchase of secular instruction, or, at the college level, outright grants for construction of facilities.

This change of attitude on the part of American legislatures (which, as has been suggested, does not necessarily reflect a similar change on the part of the American people) may well bring with it a change of position by the Supreme Court. On the same day in June 1968 that the Court for the first time held that taxpayers could sue to challenge the constitutionality of federal grants to parochial schools,[33] it sustained New York's textbook law.[34] While the decision itself was quite narrow, the language used by the Court can easily be construed to justify far more meaningful governmental support for parochial schools, perhaps even going as far as financing all aspects of parochial school education other than the specifically religious ones. Moreover, of the three dissenters, one has already left the Court and the other two are the oldest members whose service cannot last many more years. With the probably more conservative makeup of new Court personnel, it is reasonable to expect an even more tolerant judicial approach to governmental financing of church-related educational institutions. Hence, notwithstanding the setback at the hands of the New York voters in 1967, advocates of governmental aid to religious schools appear to have substantial grounds for optimism regarding the future of governmental financing of their school systems.

Yet even if these expectations are realized, it is by no means impossible that salvation has arrived too late. While the reports and figures are by no means clear, it is certain that parochial schools are closing down in whole or in part in increasing numbers and that this trend shows no evidence of slowing down, much less being reversed. This is by no means merely the result of consolidating smaller schools into larger ones, although this is part of the explanation. There appears to be a steady decline in the absolute number of Catholic children attending parochial schools (at least at the elementary school level; the figures are not quite so clear at the secondary school level), and a much greater decline when measured in proportion to the increasing Catholic population in the nation.

The standard explanation for this development is financial: with the escalating costs of education, it is simply impossible for the Catholic community to carry the burden alone, and lack of widespread governmental support leaves it with no alternative but retrenchment. (This is almost invariably coupled with the warning that added financial cost to the taxpayer by reason of the transfer of the children to the public schools will be much greater than that entailed by governmental support sufficient to enable the parochial schools to survive.)

Undoubtedly, the explanation is true but it is by no means the whole truth, and its meaning is not quite as simple as the Church assumes. The Irish immigrants and their descendants have not been Protestantized, as the bishops feared they might be, but they have been Americanized. The consequence of this has been the steady decrease, both in absolute figures and in proportion to population, in the number of Catholic girls becoming nuns and sisters (not only do Catholic mothers, like other Americans, practice birth control, but like them they want their daughters to marry and have families), and the parochial school system rests upon large numbers of committed nuns and sisters willing to teach for no more than bare subsistence. Their replacement by lay teachers who have to be paid competitive salaries in a high-income era will require governmental subsidies higher than even a post-Vietnam America may be able to afford, at least in the absence of a much more substantial reduction in governmental expenditures for defense than appears likely for years to come. In addition, America is rapidly coming to expect universal free education beyond the secondary school level, and the ever-increasing cost will in the years ahead of us necessitate consolidation rather than diffusion of educational institutions.

But the dilemma of parochial school education is more profound than is reflected in financial terms. Indeed, it may be suggested, the days of the traditional Catholic parochial school are numbered even

if the Church receives all the governmental support it now seeks.
There are many reasons for this, but perhaps the fundamental one is
that the need which gave rise to it has long ago ceased to exist; the
Protestantization of American Catholics is no longer a threat; on
the contrary, Protestantism may be in greater danger of nonsurvival
in America than Catholicism, although what is more likely—what
with the death of God and the disappearance of saints—is that both
will evolve into a mildly sectarian Ethical Culturism.

Measured by the traditional goals of American Catholicism,
Vatican II is proving to be somewhat of a mixed blessing. Paradoxically, as these goals become more acceptable to non-Catholics they
become less so to Catholics. Liberal Catholics are subjecting the
parochial school system to an exacting scrutiny, and more and more
of them are growing skeptical of both its necessity and its desirability. Moreover, the ecumenicism and enlightenment flowing from
Vatican II have pretty much eliminated the anathema which canon
law had thrust upon the public school system; although the text of
the canon law has not yet been altered, it is no longer a sin or at
least not a serious sin for a Catholic child to attend a public school
even if a seat is available for him in a nearby parochial school.
Finally, in order both to satisfy constitutional requirements for
support out of tax-raised funds and to meet the competition of the
public schools, Catholic parochial schools are rapidly becoming
secularized and their protagonists are vigorously asserting that they
are really nothing but public schools with an hour of religious instruction added. The textbook decision indicates that they may have
succeeded in convincing a majority of the Supreme Court of this,
but thoughtful Catholics are asking that if this is so, why a separate
school system at all? Racial separatism may perhaps be increasingly
a battle standard of the black community, but religious separatism
is rapidly losing favor among Catholics, or at least among young
Catholic parents whose children are reaching school age, and it is of
course these Catholics who will determine the future of parochial
school education.

Does this mean that the parochial school system is on its last legs
and that those who are committed to church-state separation should
abandon the battle? Not at all. It is not dissolution which the system
is facing but metamorphosis. The verified data are sparse, but they
show that most of the parochial schools that are being closed are in
the inner city and cater to a lower-class clientele. What is happening
is that public schools in the cities (not in the suburbs, or at least not

yet) are becoming institutions for the poor and the black just as has happened to public housing and is happening to public hospitals in the inner city. Because the cost of private education is so high, particularly if teachers have to be paid competitive salaries, many parochial schools catering to middle-class and perhaps upper-middle-class whites will have to close unless they receive substantial governmental financing. Because they represent a class with considerable political power, they appear to be increasingly successful in obtaining this financing. This raises the question of the morality of taking money sorely needed for the education of the poor and disadvantaged in order to finance separate and superior education for members of upper classes. Christians may be reminded of Jesus' statement, "For whosoever hath, to him shall be given, and he shall have more abundance: but whosoever hath not, from him shall be taken away even that he hath" (Matthew 13:12). Besides this, do Christian Americans really want an America in which blacks, Puerto Ricans, Mexican-Americans, and poor whites attend public schools (as they live in public housing buildings and are treated for illness in public hospitals) while upper-class whites attend nonpublic schools whose continued existence is made possible only by substantial financing from tax-raised funds?

That the Negro community is aware of and concerned about this development is manifested by the presence, along with such pro-separation organizations as the American Civil Liberties Union and the American Jewish Congress, of branches and officers of the National Association for the Advancement of Colored People, as sponsors and occasionally as plaintiffs in suits challenging laws granting governmental aid to parochial schools as well as in organizations formed to oppose enactment of such legislation. Thoughtful religious leaders—Catholics, Protestants, and Jews—are likewise becoming increasingly troubled. Even those committed to the survival of separate religious schools would not like to see them become a haven for those who are running not to God but away from the Negroes.

The problem has already become so acute that public school administrators, not particularly noted for their willingness to challenge sectarian interests openly, have begun to speak about it in public. According to a report in *The New York Times* of December 7, 1969, Dr. Nathan Brown, Acting Superintendent of Schools in New York City, in an address delivered at an Orthodox Jewish theological seminary, called upon Jewish leaders to keep middle-class youngsters in the school system by de-emphasizing and, in some instances, discouraging enrollment in Jewish day schools. "I deplore," he said, "any action on the part of Jewish parents who escape the city school system for the sole purpose of avoiding racially integrated schools." He referred to what he called the increasing Jewish enrollment in religious and "pseudo-religious" schools in the light of social, ethnic, and class conflicts arising from school reorganization, and expressed the fear that alienation of the Jewish middle class from the system could result in a city of "ghettos surrounded by police protecting one group from another."

The trend toward secularization of religious schools referred to above can only be accelerated by this development. At the meeting at which Dr. Brown spoke, one of the rabbis said, "I would prefer that children would come to our schools because of precommitment to our ideal. But if they don't, I will welcome them anyway and hope they will be committed by the time they are through." But every private institution must cater to its paying clientele; in the long run it is more probable that the school will be secularized than that the children will be sectarianized. Of course, this would not necessarily be so if the school received its major financial support from the government rather than from the parents, but no matter how conservative the Supreme Court may become it is highly unlikely that it will sanction governmental support of private schools which are blatantly religious in their curriculum and practices.

The sum of all this is that, as in many other cases, the provisions of the Bill of Rights reinforce each other. The mandate of the First Amendment that church and state must be separated supports the command of the Fourteenth Amendment that public schools be integrated.

OTHER CHURCH-STATE PROBLEMS

The competing demands of church and state in education present the most serious and pervasive problems under the establishment clause, but other difficult establishment problems have confronted the American people and the Supreme Court in the past and are certain to continue to do so in the coming years. Among these are governmental financing of sectarian welfare agencies, tax exemption for churches, governmental acts of religiosity, Sunday laws, and interreligious adoptions.

As long ago as 1899 the Supreme Court upheld the constitutionality of governmental financing of sectarian hospitals,[35] and it is unlikely that this decision will soon be overruled. Nevertheless, it raises serious problems. In 1946, on the basis of this decision, Congress adopted the Hill-Burton Act under which hundreds of millions of dollars have been appropriated for both public and private hospitals. Initially, the major part of the funds went to public hospitals, but steadily the balance was changed so that today most federal funds go to private hospitals. Of these the majority are sectarian, and most sectarian hospitals are Catholic. Under present Catholic doctrine contraception and abortion, even if therapeutically indicated, are not permissible in Catholic hospitals, with the result that patients needing such treatment (and physicians supplying it) are effectively barred from the institutions. A serious constitutional question is raised by such religiously based exclusionary policy in an institution receiving tax-raised funds. Catholic doctrine forbidding contraception is probably on its last legs, but there does not appear to be any substantial likelihood that the ban on abortion will soon be changed. Hence, the constitutional problem will probably be with us for some time, although it is difficult to justify by standards either of constitutionality or of fairness the taxation of all people to supply hospital services from which some are effectively excluded solely because of religion.

Yet more serious than the constitutional question is the socio-economic problem. Public housing is primarily poor people's housing, and in the large cities at least, poor people are disproportionately Negro or members of other racial minorities. As has been indicated above, the same process threatens to take place in education. In view of the rising costs of hospital care, which even universal health insurance is not likely to meet, duplication of the process in hospitalization appears almost inevitable. Governmental subsidization of private hospitals cannot but accelerate it, making ever more difficult the task of changing an America in which there are two societies, separate but unequal.[36]

Tax exemption for churches is probably safe from successful constitutional attack for many years to come. Only Justice Douglas dissented from the Supreme Court's decision in the *Walz* case[37] upholding the constitutionality of the practice. It is, however, far from secure against legislative limitations. Throughout the centuries accumulation of wealth by churches has been met by governmental counteraction, either by outright seizure (frequently, but by no means always, as part of a revolutionary change in government) or by mortmain or similar restrictive statutes. Seizure of church wealth by government is hardly likely in the United States in the foreseeable future, and mortmain statutes (some of which are still on the books in a few states) are only slightly less unlikely, at least in the immediate future. But opposition to unlimited exemption for churches is being heard with increasing frequency from a heavily taxed public, and legislatures are beginning to take discreet but nevertheless significant exploratory steps. It may take some time, but it would not be rash to predict that the years if not the days of unlimited tax exemption for churches are numbered.[38] Irrespective of constitutionality, supplying churches with services, such as police, fire, and sanitation, which are paid for out of taxes seems not only unfair but violative of religious freedom in that it compels persons to contribute to the support of religions in which they do not believe.

Reference has already been made to the placing of crèches and other religious symbols associated with Christmas on public property. Other acts of governmental religiosity include presidential proclamation of days of prayer and thanksgiving, government-paid chaplains in Congress, the armed forces, and public institutions, the presence of "In God We Trust" on our currency, the inclusion of the words "under God" in the national pledge of allegiance, and the opening of legislative sessions with prayer. Strict separationists consider all these practices inconsistent with at least the spirit of the establishment clause, and from time to time suits challenging them are instituted (some as far-out as one for an injunction forbidding astronauts to recite a prayer or read from the Bible on the moon). None of these suits has been successful, not because the constitutionality of the practices is clear, but more likely because the courts do not consider them of sufficient importance to counter widespread American opinion which unquestionably looks with favor upon these manifestations of governmental religiosity.

It has been suggested above that Supreme Court decisions treating more tolerantly governmental financial aid to religious schools may have come too late to save those schools as religious schools. The same may be said to be true of Sunday laws. In 1961 the Supreme Court upheld their constitutionality on the ground that though religious in origin, they had in the course of time become secular welfare laws.[39] Justice Douglas dissented from this holding, and it may be assumed that judicial attacks on the constitutionality of Sunday laws will continue to be made. These attacks will in all probability be unsuccessful in the Supreme Court, but perhaps for a reason other than the validity of the original decision.

As has been pointed out, the Supreme Court in 1961 dismissed a challenge to a state anti-birth-control law on the ground that the law was no longer enforced and thus had become a dead letter. Some day not too far away, the Court may dispose similarly of an attack on the constitutionality of Sunday laws. Thus, Sunday laws may end not with a bang but with a dismissal for mootness.

Far more serious is the problem of interreligious adoptions. In many states, either by statute or judicial policy, it is the practice when rival couples seek to adopt a child to prefer the couple whose religion is the same as that into which the child was born. In most of these states, however, the preference for religious identity is discretionary and will not be exercised where the welfare of the child would be prejudiced thereby, so that where only one couple seeks to adopt a child the adoption court will not refuse approval solely because of difference in religion between the applicants and the child. In a few states, such as Massachusetts and perhaps New York, the statutes have been interpreted as practically forbidding interreligious adoptions.

In 1955 the Supreme Court, without stating a reason, refused to review a decision by the Massachusetts courts rejecting an application by a Jewish couple to adopt twins born (illegitimately) to a Catholic mother who surrendered them to the couple for adoption.[40] A strong argument can be made that laws forbidding interreligious adoptions violate the establishment clause of the First Amendment.[41] It can be expected that sooner or later the Supreme Court will pass upon the constitutional issues raised by restraints on interreligious adoptions, but in the meantime many children will continue to remain in institutions while couples able and eager to provide them with homes and parental love are barred from doing so.

These are some of the church-state problems facing the nation in the seventies. Because of the Supreme Court's 1968 decision allowing taxpayers to challenge in the courts governmental expenditures for religious purposes or institutions,[42] it is safe to predict that many of them will reach the Supreme Court for final determination of constitutionality. While the Court's language in the textbook decision[43] has caused many, perhaps wishfully, to suggest that church-state separation is dead, plans for interment may be premature. Provisions in the First Amendment other than the establishment clause have faced crises no more severe and have survived; during the McCarthy era responsible constitutional law authorities expressed the view that the free speech clause of the Amendment protects only such expression as a majority of the Congress is willing to tolerate. At the present time the free speech clause is alive and well. A good guess may be made that no part of the First Amendment, not even the establishment clause, is obsolete.

NOTES

1. For a summary of the events and factors leading to the adoption of the religion clauses of the First Amendment, see L. Pfeffer, *Church, State and Freedom* ch. 4 (1967).
2. Torcaso v. Watkins, 367 U.S. 488 (1961).
3. Reynolds v. United States, 98 U.S. 145 (1878).
4. Minersville School Dist. v. Gobitis, 310 U.S. 586 (1940).
5. West Virginia Bd. of Educ. v. Barnette, 319 U.S. 624 (1943).
6. Sherbert v. Verner, 374 U.S. 398 (1963).
7. Braunfeld v. Brown, 366 U.S. 599 (1961).
8. *In re* Jenison, 375 U.S. 14 (1963), *vacating and remanding* 265 Minn. 96, 120 N.W.2d 515 (1963). For disposition on remand, *see* 267 Minn. 136, 125 N.W.2d 588 (1964).
9. United States v. Seeger, 380 U.S. 163, 166 (1965).
10. United States v. Schwimmer, 279 U.S. 644 (1929); United States v. Macintosh, 283 U.S. 605 (1931).
11. Girouard v. United States, 328 U.S. 61 (1946).
12. Welsh v. United States, 90 S. Ct. 1792 (1970).
13. Pierce v. Society of Sisters, 268 U.S. 510 (1925).
14. Donner v. New York, 342 U.S. 884 (1951), *dismissing appeal from* 302 N.Y. 857, 100 N.E. 2d 47.
15. Garber v. Kansas, 389 U.S. 51 (1967).
16. Prince v. Massachusetts, 321 U.S. 158 (1944).
17. People *ex rel.* Wallace v. Labrenz, 411 Ill. 618, 104 N.E.2d 769, *cert. denied*, 344 U.S. 824 (1952).
18. Ginsberg v. New York, 390 U.S. 629 (1968).
19. *In re* Gault, 387 U.S. 1 (1967).
20. Tinker v. Des Moines Independent Community School Dist., 393 U.S. 503 (1969).
21. United States v. Macintosh, 283 U.S. 605 (1931); Hamilton v. Regents of Univ. of California, 293 U.S. 245 (1934).
22. Torcaso v. Watkins, 367 U.S. 488 (1961).
23. 1 Annals of Cong. 766–67.
24. 321 U.S. 158, 164–65 (1944).
25. Griswold v. Connecticut, 381 U.S. 479 (1965).
26. Levy v. Louisiana, 391 U.S. 68 (1968).

27. Engel v. Vitale, 370 U.S. 421 (1962); Abington School Dist. v. Schempp, 374 U.S. 203 (1963).

28. 347 U.S. 483 (1954).

29. For an account of these efforts, see J. Laubach, *School Prayers: Congress, the Courts and the Public* (1969).

30. Epperson v. Arkansas, 393 U.S. 97 (1968).

31. Poe v. Ullman, 367 U.S. 497 (1961).

32. For an account of this "Blaine Amendment" controversy, see R. Morgan, *The Politics of Religious Conflict* ch. 4 (1968). See also J. Pratt, *Religion, Politics and Diversity: The Church-State Theme in New York History* (1967).

33. Flast v. Cohen, 392 U.S. 83 (1968).

34. Board of Educ. v. Allen, 392 U.S. 236 (1968).

35. Bradfield v. Roberts, 175 U.S. 291 (1899).

36. For a general consideration of religion and social welfare, see B. Coughlin, *Church and State in Social Welfare* (1964).

37. Walz v. Tax Comm'n, 90 S. Ct. 1409 (1970).

38. On this subject, *see generally* D. Robertson, *Should Churches Be Taxed* (1968).

39. McGowan v. Maryland, 366 U.S. 420 (1961).

40. Goldman v. Fogarty, 348 U.S. 942 (1955). Both the Massachusetts and the New York statutes have recently been liberalized.

41. *See* Pfeffer, "Religion in the Upbringing of Children," 35 *Boston University Law Review* 333 (1955); Ramsey, "The Legal Imputation of Religion to an Infant in Adoption Proceedings," 34 *New York University Law Review* 649 (1959); *Religion in Adoption and Custody,* Villanova Institute of Church and State Conference Proceedings, 56–114 (1957); Paulsen, "Constitutional Problems of Utilizing a Religious Factor in Adoptions and Placement of Children," in D. Oaks, *The Wall Between Church and State* 117 (1963).

42. Flast v. Cohen, 392 U.S. 83 (1968).

43. Board of Educ. v. Allen, 392 U.S. 236 (1968).

THE RIGHT TO
CONTROL THE USE
OF ONE'S BODY

CHARLES LISTER

LIBERTARIANISM HAS FOR MUCH OF OUR HISTORY
been imprisoned in its English origins. Although we customarily
congratulate ourselves on the uniqueness of our national experience, Americans have been chiefly concerned with precisely those
categories of issues that previously troubled seventeenth- and eighteenth-century Englishmen. We have sought to guarantee appropriate opportunities for participation in the political process, to
prohibit the intermingling of civil and religious authority, and to
prevent injustice in the conduct of judicial proceedings. More
recently, we have deepened, but not appreciably widened, these
commitments by a search for rules to assure evenhandedness in the
allocation of public benefits. I do not mean to belittle the urgency
of these goals: their persistence here, in Stuart England, and in
times and places even more remote is adequate testimony of their
importance. My point is simply that missing is any general conception of limitations upon the reach of governmental interference
with private conduct. In particular, we have not yet formulated,
any more than did Coke or John Wilkes, any systematic denial of
governmental claims to regulate the individual's private use of his
body. It is not that such a denial could not plausibly be drawn from
the Constitution; the difficulty is instead that we have treated the
individual almost exclusively in his public capacities, as a partici-

Charles Lister, who studied law at Oxford on a Rhodes Scholarship, was formerly a
professor at Yale Law School and is now a practicing lawyer in Washington, D.C.

The author wishes to acknowledge gratefully the assistance of Mrs. Harriet Pilpel in
the preparation of this paper, although freeing her from any responsibility for the
views it expresses.

pant in the political process, and so have been content to accept society's authority to enforce majoritarian notions of moral conduct.

There already is evidence that the law, rather breathlessly and more than a little late, will ultimately take a wider view. The impulse for change has come principally from a series of Supreme Court opinions in which the foundations of a constitutional right of privacy were laid. The terms of this emerging doctrine are still largely conjectural. There is every reason to believe that in fact it encompasses several interests, including the right to physical privacy, the right to withhold information, and even the right to a measure of personal autonomy. We have repeatedly been told that privacy is "the most comprehensive of rights and the right most valued by civilized men,"[1] but it is plain that there is agreement neither as to its reach nor as to its constitutional basis. For the moment, we have only an extraordinary series of opinions in which, with stimulating regularity, the Court has unearthed privacy interests in the interstices of the First, Fourth, Fifth, Fourteenth, and even Ninth Amendments.[2] Other providential discoveries presumably await only appropriate litigation. I do not mean that these cases should be distressing: they reflect merely the efforts of discomforted judges, working with greater or lesser artfulness, to fashion rules suitable for the accommodation of newly felt interests.

Several recent cases in the state and lower federal courts may ultimately prove more revealing.[3] They suggest an intermediate premise that promises to limit the occasions for governmental interference with private conduct. The proposition that may be extrapolated from these cases is not, at least as stated, complex: it is that society may properly regulate the behavior of competent adults only if that behavior demonstrably threatens the rights, safety, or interests of others. This maxim, which now is permanently associated with John Stuart Mill, is scarcely novel: it has, in the course of its adventures, been assailed by Stephen, jeered by Holmes, and made the subject of a superb debate among Lord Devlin, H. L. A. Hart, and others. It is not yet widely supported in the cases, and certainly I do not now wish to make as extensive an attack upon government as it implies. I say only that Mill's proposition, despite its breadth and ambiguity, has begun to win acceptance as a coherent solution to the problems created by governmental efforts to regulate the individual's use of his body. It offers what the more general privacy doctrine as yet cannot: an ascertainable standard for the assessment of these difficult issues.

I shall illustrate the usefulness of this standard by an examination of the questions of law and policy that arise from homosexuality, contraception, and abortion. Disparate as these are, they each raise the more general problem of the extent to which society may permissibly regulate the individual's use and control of his body. They reflect, with differing precision and sensitivity, changing accommodations to the demands of traditional morality.

I

Few groups in society are as severely treated as those who are thought to have engaged in homosexual conduct. They are subject in almost every state to criminal prosecution, with the likelihood upon conviction of lengthy terms of imprisonment, followed by the customary civil and social disabilities. Homosexual acts are not made lawful, although the degree of their criminality may be altered, merely because they are performed in private by consenting adults. Perhaps more important, homosexual conduct is penalized by a comprehensive system of noncriminal sanctions. Those who are supposed to have engaged in such conduct are commonly excluded from public employment at all levels of government. These prohibitions reach even the most menial and obscure of positions. Those guilty of homosexual acts are regularly dismissed from the military services, always with a form of discharge that will injure their future opportunities, and are often denied the security clearances essential for employment in many of our largest industries. It is not thought to be necessary for these purposes actually to have been convicted of homosexual activities, nor is it necessary that the alleged acts have occurred recently or even that they be demonstrably representative of an individual's habitual conduct. To put an extreme case, a mature and relatively senior federal employee may be dismissed if it is found, without the procedural and evidentiary protections that would be imperative in a criminal trial, that he was guilty as a teen-ager of isolated homosexual acts.[4] Rumor, speculation, and even fantasies about the physical and other characteristics of homosexuals may be regarded as probative. All homosexuals are not of course dismissed from their jobs, but an injustice is not any the more tolerable merely because it is in practice occasional or discretionary.

These disabilities, severe as they assuredly are, are widely supplemented by less formal methods of punishment. Popular hostility and the rigor of the legal penalties have made profitable the exploitation of homosexuality. As a result, homosexuals must become accustomed to a dreary pattern of physical abuse, extortion, and petty official harassment. Organized crime and even law enforcement officers sometimes participate in these efforts. The consequences are uniformly degrading to the oppressors, their victims, and the law itself.

It should not be supposed that these penalties are applicable only to a small or narrowly defined class of unfortunates. Dr. Alfred Kinsey, whose estimates are still widely regarded as the most reliable of those now available, reported that 4 percent of the adult white males in the United States are exclusively homosexual throughout their lives, that 10 percent are more or less exclusively homosexual for a period of at least three years between the ages of 16 and 65, and that 37 percent have some overt homosexual experience between 16 and 65.[5] Less comprehensive studies from England and Sweden suggest that these estimates may be marginally high, but this evidence perhaps is balanced by later American studies and by reports that homosexuality is significantly more prevalent among the aged than among younger groups. What remains certain, despite relatively minor discrepancies in the empirical evidence and a persistent looseness in labeling, is that a remarkable number of Americans (or Englishmen or Swedes) now engage, or have previously engaged, in overt homosexual acts. Such evidence as now is available suggests that their relative frequency in the population is increasing. These men are evidently distributed widely across every ability level, educational background, and occupational specialty.

At the center of this regulatory system are the statutes which impose criminal penalties upon homosexual conduct. If those statutes were successfully dismantled, so that homosexual acts committed in private by consenting adults were no longer punishable, the employment disabilities and the more oppressive forms of harassment would eventually collapse. Homosexual conduct would not be without important risks, but at least the law would no longer participate in its exploitation. The assumptions upon which these statutes are based are commonly unarticulated, but they seem ultimately to involve either errors of fact concerning the character of homosexuality or unsupported notions that society properly may enforce its moral preconceptions. Let me examine each of these in turn.

The psychiatric literature is by no means free of disagreement, but the prevailing views seem to be the following.[6] First and perhaps most important, homosexuality is not a degenerative disease or even a form of uncleanness. It is a biological and psychological phenomenon that is as "natural" for human beings, and as consistent with their anatomical and psychological potentialities, as heterosexuality. The potentiality for homosexuality is characteristic of every human being, including even judges and legislators, and it is in fact a stage of psychological development through which men and women commonly pass. Although society's repression of homosexuality may precipitate or aggravate personality disorders, homosexuality itself does not cause or even uniformly accompany any particular personality type. Persons who engage, or who have previously engaged, in homosexual acts are frequently not maladjusted in the nonsexual sectors of their personalities. They are often well-adjusted and useful human beings whose nonsexual personality characteristics are indistinguishable from those of heterosexuals. Homosexuals are not more susceptible than heterosexuals to sexual stimulation or otherwise less capable of controlling their sexual drives. Indeed, even if allowance is made for its relative frequency, homosexuality does not result in serious crimes as often as do motives arising from heterosexual relationships. Homosexuals are cheerful and melancholy, generous and miserly, wise and foolish, with the same frequency as heterosexuals. They have simply the misfortune to have had one sector of their personalities develop in a fashion that society, in fear and in ignorance, condemns as degrading or unclean. They are the victims of a social policy that is not needed to protect society and that is in its consequences injurious both to them and to those who participate in their exploitation.

The prevailing psychiatric evidence surely precludes any argument that homosexual acts committed in private by consenting adults threaten the rights, safety, or interests of others. The situation plainly is different if the acts are not in private, if force is used, or if children or other legal incompetents are involved, precisely as it would be in similar cases of heterosexual conduct. As to acts in private between consenting adults, the argument must therefore be that society may permissibly employ the coercion of law to enforce majoritarian understandings of moral conduct. These claims have already been discussed at length by Lord Devlin, Professor Hart, and others, in a debate stimulated by Lord Devlin's contention that an enforced moral code provides cement essential for the preservation of society.[7] There is no need here to rehearse their arguments, except to observe, as has Hart, that Lord Devlin and those who follow him altogether lack evidence for two crucial assertions: there is no reason to believe either that the disappearance of a uniform moral code would ultimately cause the disintegration of society or that the removal of criminal sanctions would encourage sexual behavior that is thought by the community at large to be blameworthy. There is simply no evidence of any association between moral sensibilities and knowledge or fear of the law. The notion that society may enforce morality in order to assure its survival is, as Hart properly charges, utilitarianism without facts.

It is, moreover, important to recognize that Lord Devlin's argument is directly inconsistent with quite fundamental constitutional attitudes. In its simplest form, his thesis is evidently that if a sufficiently large number of citizens abhor the conduct of some smaller number, and if they judge it to be injurious to society, they may properly undertake to make that conduct unlawful. Indeed, one would suppose that it would be, in Lord Devlin's judgment, their obligation so to act. The central point is that the larger group must experience "intolerance, indignation and disgust" at the others' activities.[8] This is no doubt a principle upon which judges and legislators sometimes feel competent to act, but it must be understood to present terrible hazards for the rights and opportunities of minorities. Unsubstantiated fears and prejudices of every description flourish in this country, presumably even among large majorities of our population. It may be assumed that those afflicted with these disabilities suffer indignation and disgust when any member of any unfavored group or class is treated with ordinary fairness. Fortunately, I had supposed that it was now well established, even if it is not always understood, that government may not extend its sanction or approval to any such superstition or prejudice, however widely held.[9] Whatever the force or propriety of Lord Devlin's proposition elsewhere, it should be plain here that government may not attach blame or deny benefits upon the basis of arbitrary or irrational classifications. There are no doubt homosexuals whose conduct warrants punishment, precisely as there are left-handed, or red-haired, or miserly men and women who are blameworthy, but nothing in the characteristics or consequences of homosexuality itself renders punishable all those who engage, or who have previously engaged, in homosexual acts.

Finally, it is pertinent that the existing pattern of legal sanctions against homosexuality encourages the destruction of precisely those values that Lord Devlin professedly is anxious to preserve. Inquiries into sexual conduct are characteristically accompanied by the most indecorous forms of surveillance and investigation. In part, such methods are the consequence of the nature of the information that is sought; in part, they are explained only by the prurience of those who watch and listen. Toilet facilities are kept constantly under observation; private conversations are intercepted and recorded; rumor is assiduously collected; the idle speculations of neighbors and acquaintances are given value; hidden inclinations are stimulated and then punished. Surely it is better that "immorality," particularly if it is to be measured by the shifting prejudices of the fearful and ignorant, should go undetected than that government should participate in acts hostile to its dignity and responsibilities. Government is, as Mr. Justice Brandeis reminded us,[10] above all a teacher, and if government believes that the urgency of its goals justifies the use of any necessary means, however antithetical to the premises of a free society, it must expect that its citizens will shortly prove no less impatient.

For these and other causes, there is reason now to believe that the system of discriminatory rules against homosexuality may soon be dismantled. Britain, after a thorough examination of these issues, has abandoned efforts to punish homosexual acts committed in private by consenting adults. Virtually every major country in the world, with the lamentable exception of the United States, has adopted similar policies. There is no perceptible evidence that society in these countries is any closer to disintegration than our own, or that homosexuality is as a consequence more widely practiced. Even the situation in the United States may now be improving. The American Law Institute urged that sexual acts committed in private by consenting adults should not be the subject of criminal punishment. Illinois, stimulated by this suggestion, no longer punishes all forms of homosexual conduct, and several states have reduced the punishments applicable to many offenses. The City of New York has loosened its restrictions upon the public employment of homosexuals. The courts have taken several hesitant steps toward limitations upon the federal government's employment policies.

These measures are each desirable and important, but they plainly halt well short of any general revision of the law's treatment of homosexuality. Their chief interest is predictive, and consists in their gradual application of Mill's principle that society may regulate private conduct no further than the safety or interests of others demand. They are paralleled by similar developments in a variety of areas loosely involving the individual's use and control of his body. It has, for example, been held that an individual may not be punished by the termination of public employment or other benefits merely because he elects to wear a beard or mustache.[11] The rights of students to select their own clothing and hair lengths have been upheld in several cases.[12] Statutes requiring motorcyclists to wear helmets have been successfully challenged on the explicit basis of Mill's principle.[13] Attacks have been made upon statutes forbidding nudist camps and the use of marijuana.[14] The antiquated state statutes which make criminal virtually all sexual acts except solitary masturbation and "normal" relations between husband and wife are at last being questioned. For example, a federal court in Texas has held that it is impermissible to punish as a crime sodomy committed in private by married couples,[15] and the American Civil Liberties Union has recently requested the New Jersey Supreme Court to declare unconstitutional a 1791 antifornication statute.

The important point is that these and similar developments, diverse and preliminary as they are, represent the earliest stages of a more general assault upon Comstockery. They carry forward the long series of cases in which the Supreme Court has severely restricted the efforts of state and federal authorities to prevent the distribution of materials alleged to be obscene. They are related directly to developments involving human experimentation, the use of drugs, and other questions. At the very center of this assault is Mill's principle, revived after a century and now revised to emphasize the individual's right to control the use of his body. Whatever may be its weaknesses and ambiguities, however much it may assume a passionless rationality of late middle age, Mill's principle at least offers the outlines of a coherent limitation upon government's authority to intervene in the private conduct of its citizens. As such, it promises a suitable complement to the traditional commitments of American libertarianism.

II

Society's efforts to regulate sexual conduct by the direct imposition of criminal penalties fit readily within Mill's principle: sexual activities are already commonly regarded as intensely private, and more important, they threaten the rights or safety of others only in relatively narrow categories of situations. Efforts to regulate sexual conduct indirectly, by restrictions upon the distribution of contraceptive devices and the availability of lawful abortions, raise more complex issues. These issues have recently suffered careful scrutiny from several sources: religious leaders, nutritionists, environmentalists, women's liberationists, and others have each made their distinctive contributions to the discussion of population control and family planning. My purpose is to examine these familiar issues from another perspective and with another goal: I want to assess their implications for a libertarian search for a comprehensive limitation upon government's authority to regulate the individual's use and control of his body. I will deal first with contraception.

The availability both of birth control information and of contraceptive devices has been a frequent subject of legislation. In many states, these statutes have in the past denied citizens rudimentary family-planning assistance, evidently on the premise that unspecified forms of moral disintegration would otherwise follow.[16] Indeed, a series of federal statutes that may be traced into the nineteenth century has survived, purportedly forbidding the importation, mailing, or interstate transportation of contraceptive devices,[17] precisely as other federal statutes have forbidden the transportation of unregistered submachine guns, adulterated butter, and gambling paraphernalia. Not surprisingly, these anticontraceptive statutes were largely ineffective: they sufficed chiefly to limit the dissemination of birth control information to those who, by friendship, income, or other advantage, were able to circumvent or ignore the laws' requirements. Many of these statutory prohibitions were eventually overturned, but it was not until 1965 that the Supreme Court held that they were, at least in some situations, constitutionally impermissible exercises of governmental authority.

Griswold v. Connecticut[18] was the culmination of efforts over many years to obtain a full constitutional review of a Connecticut statute restricting the use of birth control devices. A majority of the Court agreed both that the issues finally raised were justiciable and that the statute must fall, but they were unable to find any collectively persuasive reasons for these results. Mr. Justice Douglas referred to a right of privacy he had discovered among the emanations of several constitutional provisions, but he may ultimately have rejected the statute simply as impermissibly wide. Mr. Justice Goldberg, joined by the Chief Justice and Mr. Justice Brennan, offered a more novel and elaborate constitutional argument. He revived the Ninth Amendment, which long before had been dismissed as mere surplusage, and employed it to widen the protection given by the Fifth and Fourteenth Amendments. Mr. Justice Harlan, building upon a superb dissenting opinion in an earlier case involving the same statute,[19] reasoned that the due process clause of the Fourteenth Amendment includes a right of privacy that, whatever its limitations, at least shields the marital bed from governmental supervision. These views were essentially endorsed by Mr. Justice White's separate opinion. Justices Black and Stewart, in dissent, were each unable to find in the Constitution any notions of privacy that might protect the use of contraceptives by married couples.

The meaning of *Griswold* has since provoked an acrimonious dispute. Despite the ambivalence of Justice Douglas' opinion, many have found in the case the outlines of a broad right of individual and organizational privacy, with origins and limits that have varied with the preconceptions of the discoverer. Others have minimized the repeated references in the opinions to the width of the statute, which might be taken to mean that more artfully drafted legislation would be permissible, and have asserted the existence of broad constitutional restrictions upon government's authority to regulate the sale and distribution of contraceptives. Still others, myself included, see *Griswold* less as an announcement of rights of privacy or autonomy than as a mandate to other judges in other courts to begin to fashion such rights.

Whatever the implications of *Griswold*, it at least seems clear that its opinions collectively include the tools necessary for the protection of contraception from governmental interference. A decision to employ contraceptive devices might be said to threaten the rights or safety of others only under either of two arguments. The first, that contraception prevents the creation of a fetus whose "rights" are thus violated, is remarkably unpersuasive: it presses already attenuated religious assumptions beyond the point of disappearance. Not surprisingly, legislators, who typically are more candid than their defenders, do not resort to this argument. The second, that society will otherwise fall immediately into moral and perhaps economic decline, has each of the deficiencies described in connection with homosexuality. The simple fact is that these statutes, in common with others concerning sexual offenses and abortion, were never intended for the defense of third-party rights or interests, but instead were expected to enforce prevailing notions of moral conduct.

Society's efforts to restrict the availability of lawful abortions raise complex issues that already have provoked popular controversy. There is no need to rehearse these controversies in detail: they have predictably included the declamation of religious and moral predilections, the display of placards, and the reduction of legislators to tears, all in explanation of one or another of the various positions. I want instead to trace briefly the several changes in the law's attitude toward abortion and to examine the most difficult of the legal issues.

The common law's treatment of abortion was a characteristic mixture of precision and ambiguity: it forbade destruction of the fetus after, but not before, it quickened, a moment that might be measured either by whether the mother had detected movement or by whether the fetus was deemed to be reasonably capable of survival outside the womb. It should not be surprising that nineteenth-century legislators came generally to believe that this relatively generous standard was unsatisfactory. Some plainly were troubled by the medical hazards of abortions; others feared the consequences for conventional morality if abortions were freely available in the first months of pregnancy; still others were concerned for the fetus. A series of regulatory statutes followed, many of which are today in force. These statutes commonly forbade abortions throughout pregnancy, with an exception for situations in which the mother's life was thought to be substantially endangered.

More recently, under continuing public pressure and with the stimulation of the Model Penal Code, legislatures have widened the categories of situations in which abortions are lawful. They have begun to authorize abortions in three discrete situations: those in which the mother's physical or mental health might otherwise be seriously impaired, although not necessarily to the point of death; those in which any child is likely to be born with severe physical or mental disabilities; and those in which conception has been the consequence of rape, incest, or other felonious intercourse. Under these statutes, abortion usually must occur in the first months of pregnancy, typically within the first two trimesters. No distinctions are drawn either between married and unmarried mothers or between marital and nonmarital intercourse. Still more recently, public and legislative attention has centered on abortions by request: upon statutes that would, in other words, permit any woman to obtain an abortion at her discretion in the first months of pregnancy. I do not mean to suggest that these reforms have proceeded uniformly: although important progress has been made, they represent in many states our direction and not our present position.

These legislative changes now are being accelerated by judicial review of the more restrictive and ambiguous statutes. State and federal courts throughout the country, including even the Supreme Court, have been asked to hold that these statutes are constitutionally deficient. The methods of attack are several: it is urged that the imposition of restrictions upon the availability of lawful abortions is an impermissible invasion of each woman's constitutional right to control the use of her body, that these statutes are discriminatory in their application, and that their terms are unacceptably vague. Several courts have already approved one or another of these contentions,[20] and there is increasing authority for the general proposition that any such statute, however artfully phrased, is an invasion of individual rights.

These statutes cannot be fully understood from a sketch of their terms alone. Whatever the categories of exceptions they permit, much invariably depends on the machinery provided for their administration. Catholic hospitals, which serve a substantial portion of our population, usually perform no abortions at all; in many public hospitals the categories of exceptions are rigidly construed and the number of abortions informally limited; in hospitals of every description, the background and religious beliefs of the attending physician or his supervisors may be decisive. These are no doubt the predictable consequences of a relatively arbitrary and decentralized process of decision-making, but they have in combination produced a statutory system that is altogether remarkable for its unfairness. The first and most obvious level of discrimination includes those women who, for want of more experienced counsel, select the wrong physician or hospital. The second and more distressing level centers on the patients' financial situations. Studies of lawful abortions in New York City over a twenty-year period indicated that their availability before the law's reform depended importantly upon an ability to pay: there were, for example, nearly eleven times more lawful abortions per thousand live births among patients in proprietary hospitals than among those in the wards of city hospitals.[21] To these must be added the inevitable unfairnesses of any system of local restrictions: the more wealthy patient may elect, as her less fortunate counterpart may not, to visit a jurisdiction that more readily permits lawful abortions. Indeed, we evidently have agents who quite profitably specialize in the arrangement of such travel.

The results are easily imaginable: the more fortunate patients circumvent or ignore the law's restrictions and obtain their abortions with the assistance of modern hospitals and fully qualified physicians; the others must either bear unwanted children or risk the attentions of untrained abortionists. There are in the United States perhaps as many as one million illegal abortions each year.[22] So common and profitable are they that illegal abortions are said to be the third largest source of criminal revenue, following only narcotics and gambling.[23] They carry with them terrible hazards: the incidence of severe infection and other complications is very high, and indeed there is evidence that such abortions are the single most common cause of maternal deaths in many areas of the United States.[24] The simple fact is that abortion statutes do not prevent abortions: they instead offer protection to criminal activity and multiply the medical hazards for those unable to satisfy the law's requirements.

The arguments favoring restrictions upon the availability of lawful abortions are ultimately those that induced nineteenth-century legislators first to adopt them: the medical risks of abortions, the supposed dangers for conventional morality if they were freely available, and the destruction of the fetus. The first two of these may be summarily dismissed. Although abortions were no doubt hazardous in the nineteenth century, they now need be no more dangerous, if conducted by properly trained personnel in appropriate surroundings, than the most common medical and surgical procedures. The medical justification for their prohibition is no better than for tonsillectomies. Indeed, if we were seriously concerned for the mother's safety we would permit all abortions to be conducted by reputable physicians in well-equipped hospitals. The second argument, the notion that these statutes are needed for the preservation of conventional moral standards, altogether lacks factual support. There simply is no evidence of any connection between such statutes and moral sensibilities, and, given the number of unlawful abortions performed each year, it would be remarkable if such evidence were ever to appear. The question therefore turns on the character and relative limits of the rights we wish to attribute to the fetus.

The problem cannot satisfactorily be solved by the oldest and most readily abused of the lawyer's methods, extrapolation from existing rules. It certainly is true that the law already seeks to protect property and other rights that are said to inhere in the unborn, but these are the separate results of a variety of interests and doctrines and not of any general anxiety for the fate of unborn litigants. Any generalization drawn from these situations would be as random as the pressures which created them. If, on the other hand, we attempt to determine at what moment the fetus is sufficiently "human" or "alive" to warrant the law's protection, we plunge immediately into wilderness. The difficulty, as one prominent judge observed, is that "every argument starts from and returns to an ethical or religious assumption."[25] It is at this point that law dissolves into metaphysics. If instead we assume simply that there is human life from the moment of conception, we immediately face a conundrum: How is it lawfully possible to terminate such life involuntarily? One might well answer that it may not be done and that there is indeed an inviolable right to be born.[26] A quite different answer is to announce baldly, as did a recent three-judge federal court, that the mother's interests are "superior" to those of the fetus.[27] In the same fashion, and with rather less hesitation, one might dispose of the father's interests. Yet another answer is to select, as the law traditionally has, a period of weeks or months within which the fetus is given less complete protection, presumably on the basis either that it is not yet human or that it is, in some undefined fashion, human life of a lower order. None of these will readily satisfy those who demand what the Romans called elegance in law.

These are intricate issues, made the more troublesome by the palpable injustices of the situation in many states, but they are more nearly solvable if first placed in perspective. If full acknowledgment is given to the mother's right to control the use and processes of her body, free of interference from any statutory moral code, the question becomes one simply of limits: what constraints, if any, upon the mother's discretion arise from the gradual development of the fetus. Various answers certainly have been given, but the most nearly persuasive is surely that the fetus creates no such limits before it is reasonably capable of a separate existence. Once the fetus is viable, the medical procedure is properly classifiable as inducement of labor, not abortion, and there is wide disagreement as to the kinds and purposes of the constraints that may appropriately be imposed. The important point is, however, that at least until viability the judgment whether to terminate a pregnancy should belong exclusively to the mother. There can be no justification for statutory categories that seek to limit the lawfulness of abortions by the physical or mental circumstances of the mother or fetus; lawful abortions should instead be freely available to every woman at her option.

III

The history of American law consists in no small measure of efforts to enforce morality. These efforts were until recently supported, if not justified, by a system of religious and moral commitments to which most Americans at least nominally adhered. The situation has now altered radically, as we enter a period in which, as one federal judge has observed, "old certainties" are "dissolving" and new ones are as yet "unformed."[28] Many of these ancient certainties, particularly including those which surround the issues discussed here, are plainly irrational, no more deserving of our allegiance than the Emperor Justinian's conviction that homosexuality is a cause of earthquakes.[29] Even if they were not, it is enough that the religious assumptions from which they drew force have lost all meaning: whatever the situation in times and places of religious consensus, there can be no justification, excepting arrant paternalism, for the enforcement of moral standards that have been repudiated by important sectors of the community.

The daily consequences of a statutory moral code are illustrated vividly by the law's treatment of homosexuality, contraception, and abortion. The various statutes designed for their regulation achieve none of their intended ends: they suffice only to promote the most lamentable forms of exploitation and injustice. They squander police and prosecutorial resources in the defense of social policies that cause society only harm. Whatever the expectations of their draftsmen, the products of these statutes are indirect and unwholesome; their ultimate victim is unmistakably the law itself.

The importance of Mill's proposition is that it offers, in a period of shifting moral obligations, a coherent program for the withdrawal of legal sanctions. It sketches the perimeter of an area of human conduct which is, as the Wolfenden Committee urged, "in brief and crude terms, not the law's business."[30] This does not condone or encourage immorality, however defined; it simply gives proper recognition to individual freedom of action and choice. As such, it represents a belated, but entirely suitable, complement to the traditional commitments of libertarianism.

NOTES

1. Olmstead v. United States, 277 U.S. 438, 478 (1928); Griswold v. Connecticut, 381 U.S. 479, 494 (1965).

2. *See, e.g.,* NAACP v. Alabama, 357 U.S. 449 (1958); Katz v. United States, 389 U.S. 347 (1967); Griswold v. Connecticut, 381 U.S. 479 (1965).

3. *See, e.g.,* Finot v. Pasadena City Bd. of Educ., 250 Cal. App. 2d 189, 58 Cal. Rptr. 520 (1967); People v. Belous, 80 Cal. Rptr. 354, 458 P.2d 194 (1969); Norton v. Macy, 417 F.2d 1161 (D.C. Cir. 1969); American Motorcycle Ass'n v. Davids, 11 Mich. Ct. App. 351, 158 N.W.2d 72 (1968).

4. *Cf.* Dew v. Halaby, 317 F.2d 582 (D.C. Cir. 1963).

5. A. Kinsey *et al., Sexual Behavior in the Human Male* 623 (1948). *Compare* Report of the Committee on Homosexual Offences and Prostitution (Wolfenden Report), Cmd. No. 247 at 38 (1957); P. Gebhard, *Sex Offenders* 624–25 (1965).

6. *See generally* H. Ruitenbeck, *The Problem of Homosexuality in Modern Society* (1963); C. Ford & F. Beach, *Patterns of Sexual Behavior* (1951); H. Ellis, *The Psychology of Sex* (1956); I. Rosen, *The Pathology and Treatment of Sexual Deviation* (1964); Bowman & Engle, "A Psychiatric Evaluation of the Laws of Homosexuality," 29 *Temple Law Quarterly* 273 (1955).

7. *See* P. Devlin, *The Enforcement of Morals* (1965); H. L. A. Hart, *Law, Liberty and Morality* (1963); Dworkin, "Lord Devlin and the Enforcement of Morality," 75 *Yale Law Journal* 986 (1966).

8. Devlin, *supra* note 7, at 17. *Cf. id.* at viii–ix.

9. *See, e.g.,* Wieman v. Updegraff, 344 U.S. 183 (1952); Baxtrom v. Herold, 383 U.S. 107 (1966); Pickering v. Bd. of Educ. 391 U.S. 563 (1968).

10. Olmstead v. United States, 277 U.S. 438, 485 (1928).

11. Finot v. Pasadena City Bd. of Educ., 250 Cal. App. 2d. 189, 58 Cal. Rptr. 520 (1967).

12. *See generally* Comment, "A Student's Right to Govern His Personal Appearance," 17 *Journal of Public Law* 151 (1958); Richards v. Thurston, 304 F. Supp. 449 (D. Mass. 1969); Westley v. Rossi, 305 F. Supp. 706 (D. Minn. 1969).

13. American Motorcycle Ass'n v. Davids, 11 Mich. Ct. App. 351, 158 N.W.2d 72 (1968); People v. Fries, 42 Ill. 2d 446, 250 N.E.2d 149 (1969).

14. Roberts v. Clement, 252 F. Supp. 835 (E.D. Tenn. 1966); Comment, "The California Marijuana Possession Statute: An Infringement of the Right of Privacy or Other Peripheral Constitutional Rights?" 19 *Hastings Law Journal* 758 (1968).

15. Buchanan v. Batchelor, 308 F. Supp. 729 (N.D. Tex. 1970); *see also* Cotner v. Henry, 394 F.2d 873 (7th Cir. 1968).

16. A modern listing of such statutes is appended to Note, "Connecticut's Birth Control Law: Reviewing a State Statute under the Fourteenth Amendment," 70 *Yale Law Journal* 322, 333 (1961).

17. 18 U.S.C. §§552, 1461, 1462; 19 U.S.C. §1305.

18. 381 U.S. 479 (1965).

19. Poe v. Ullman, 367 U.S. 497, 522 (1961).

20. *See, e.g.*, United States v. Vuitch, 305 F. Supp. 1032 (D.C. 1969); People v. Belous, 80 Cal. Rptr. 354, 458 P.2d 194 (1969); Babbitz v. McCann, 310 F. Supp. 293 (E.D. Wis. 1970); *cf.* Gleitman v. Cosgrove, 49 N.J. 22, 227 A.2d 689 (1967).

21. Gold, Erhardt, Jacobziner, & Nelson, "Therapeutic Abortions in New York City: A Twenty-Year Review," 55 *American Journal of Public Health* 964 (1965).

22. Kutner, "Due Process of Abortion," 53 *Minnesota Law Review* 1, 10 (1968).

23. D. Lowe, *Abortion and the Law* 77 (1966).

24. Fox, "Abortion Deaths in California," 98 *American Journal of Obstetrics and Gynecology* 645 (1967); Kutner, *supra* note 22, at 9–10, 23.

25. Gleitman v. Cosgrove, 49 N.J. 22, 227 A.2d 689, 709 (1967) (Weintraub, C.J.).

26. *See generally* Drinan, "The Inviolability of the Right to Be Born," 17 *Western Reserve Law Review* 465 (1965).

27. Babbitz v. McCann, 310 F. Supp. 293, 301 (E.D. Wis. 1970).

28. Scott v. Macy, 402 F.3d 644, 649 (D.C. Cir. 1968) (McGowan, J.).

29. *Cf.* Hart, *supra* note 7, at 50.

30. Report of the Committee on Homosexual Offences and Prostitution, *supra* note 5, ¶61.

THE RIGHT TO USE
ALCOHOL AND DRUGS

PETER BARTON HUTT

ENORMOUS PROGRESS IN THE METHODS BY WHICH society controls the abuse of alcohol and dangerous drugs has been achieved in the past few years. Models for an intelligent public approach to these related problems now exist. While full implementation of this reform movement may still be many years away in some jurisdictions, there are definite signs that these models are not just isolated examples but will indeed be implemented on a widespread basis.

The impetus for reform has arisen largely from current attitudes concerning the end points of alcohol and drug abuse—alcoholism and drug dependence. Alcoholism and drug dependence are now almost universally regarded within the medical profession as forms of illness that are properly handled by public health measures. To a physician, an alcoholic or a drug-dependent person requires the same medical attention as any other sick person. Yet society has persisted, at least until recently, in handling these disabilities, and their public manifestations, by punishment rather than by medical treatment.

Most often, this punishment has been in the form of criminal incarceration. Some years ago, it began to take the form of civil incarceration. The particular label attached to punishment is, of

Peter Barton Hutt, a practicing lawyer in Washington, D.C., is a consultant to governmental bodies studying alcohol and drug abuse, the author of many papers on these subjects, and the principal draftsman of the District of Columbia Alcoholic Rehabilitation Act.

course, unimportant. In both situations, the public policy objective has been one of isolation and punishment rather than of treatment and rehabilitation.

This essay reviews some aspects of the recent efforts to change public policy. Although alcohol is, from a pharmacological standpoint, just one of the many dangerous drugs known to man, it is separated out for purposes of this essay because it is the only one that is both socially acceptable and commonly available without significant restrictions. Indeed, with the collapse of prohibition, alcohol became the nation's only legal intoxicant. Because of the special social and legal status enjoyed by alcohol, extensive judicial and legislative reforms have been more easily and rapidly achieved with respect to alcohol abuse and alcoholism than in the comparable areas of drug abuse and drug dependence.

ALCOHOL ABUSE AND ALCOHOLISM

The problem of alcohol abuse, in the form of public drunkenness, has been with us for centuries. While drunkenness accompanied by a public nuisance, or a breach of the peace, was considered criminal under early English common law,[1] mere public intoxication without additional criminal behavior was first made a criminal offense by an English statute of 1606.[2] For over 360 years, in England and America, society has relied basically upon criminal sanctions, rather than upon public health measures, to control intoxication and alcoholism.

In several early cases, decided before 1900, drunken defendants attempted to excuse their criminal action on the ground that they were alcoholics and therefore could not control their conduct. All courts but one rejected this contention, and ruled that only alcoholism which amounted to insanity could provide a defense to a criminal charge.[3] Only in the New Hampshire case of *State v. Pike*[4] did the court rule that an alcoholic defendant could not be held criminally responsible for criminal conduct that was the product of his alcoholism. But the *Pike* decision lay dormant for almost a century, while intoxication and alcoholism problems continued to mount.

Then in early 1966, two United States courts of appeals ruled that a homeless alcoholic cannot be punished for his public intoxication. In the first of those two decisions, *Driver v. Hinnant*,[5] the

United States Court of Appeals for the Fourth Circuit held that the Eighth Amendment to the United States Constitution prohibits such punishment. In the second decision, *Easter v. District of Columbia*,[6] the United States Court of Appeals for the District of Columbia Circuit ruled that common-law traditions, which were also the basis for the *Pike* decision, preclude such punishment. It makes no difference, of course, whether this result is reached by the constitutional approach used in the *Driver* decision, or by the common-law approach of the *Pike* and *Easter* cases. The conclusion is necessarily the same. No longer may the age-old problem of the derelict chronic inebriate be handled by the criminal process. Under these decisions, a new method of confronting this problem must be found.

Fortunately, substantial light had already been shed upon the work that had to be done to replace the present criminal system of handling intoxication and alcoholism. Prior to the *Easter* and *Driver* decisions, the President of the United States had appointed two crime commissions, one to study crime in the District of Columbia and the other to conduct a broad national survey of law enforcement and the administration of justice. These two commissions immediately took up the challenge laid down by the *Easter* and *Driver* decisions and began to search for alternatives to the handling, not just of chronic alcoholics, but of all public inebriates.

The report of the District of Columbia Crime Commission was released to the public in early 1967. This Commission recommended that public intoxication no longer be a criminal offense, and that the routine criminal handling of derelict inebriates be replaced by a modern public health, welfare, and rehabilitation approach to the problem.[7] Under the District of Columbia Crime Commission plan, intoxicated people would be taken immediately to a detoxification center for appropriate medical surveillance, and would then be channeled into a voluntary treatment program.

The report of the United States Crime Commission, which was released to the public a few weeks later, arrived at the very same conclusions and recommendations.[8] It pointed out that the criminal justice system was ineffective in deterring drunkenness or in meeting the problems of the chronic alcoholic offender. It therefore recommended replacement of the criminal system in this area with a comprehensive treatment program under a public health authority.

The two Crime Commission reports were further bolstered in

mid-1967 with the release of the long-awaited Report to the Nation by the Cooperative Commission on the Study of Alcoholism. This report, funded by the National Institute of Mental Health, urged a broad public health approach to the problems of intoxication and alcoholism, replacing the present criminal approach. But it also went much further. It realistically recognized that the substantial rate of drunkenness and alcoholism in this country is rooted in our antiquated moralistic approach to the consumption of alcoholic beverages. The Cooperative Commission concluded that as long as society retains laws that promote the image of alcoholic beverages as exciting and glamorous, alcohol abuse will continue to be as extensive as or even greater than it is at present. The Commission therefore called for basic changes in alcoholic-beverage control laws, in the laws that control drinking by minors, and indeed in the national attitude about these matters. It pointed out that a substantial impact on the problems of drunkenness and alcoholism could be made by promoting a new national attitude toward alcoholic beverages as simply another item in the daily diet.

In 1968, two new federal commissions studying the problem of highway safety highlighted another aspect of the problem of alcoholism. Both the report submitted to the Secretary of Health, Education, and Welfare by his Special Advisory Committee and the report submitted to Congress by the Department of Transportation attributed over 30 percent of our yearly traffic fatalities directly to alcholism. The reports called for a massive commitment to alleviate this problem. Of particular significance, the HEW report pointed out that criminal statutes do not deter alcoholics from drinking and that drivers who have their licenses suspended or revoked may nevertheless continue to drive. The HEW report therefore recommended replacement of the present ineffective punitive approach to alcoholic drivers with a modern therapeutic approach grounded on treatment for the underlying problem.

These developments have made a substantial impact on the federal government. In 1967 and 1968 messages to Congress, the President called for basic changes in the approach to intoxication and alcoholism in this country. He recommended that the states repeal their criminal laws and handle these problems through public health procedures instead. And to help finance these changes, he recommended enactment of federal-funding legislation.

At least partly in response to the presidential messages, Maryland, Hawaii, and the District of Columbia totally revised their laws.[9] It is especially significant that Congress considered the new District of Columbia legislation in depth and enacted it without a single dissenting vote.

Under these new laws, it is no longer a criminal offense to be intoxicated in public. Instead, public intoxication is handled by taking the intoxicated individual to a medical facility rather than to the police precinct. Only intoxication that directly and substantially endangers a citizen may result in an arrest, and even then the offender must first be taken to a detoxification center. The new programs are, of course, just getting under way. In view of the fact that over one-third of the arrests in America in 1966 were for simple public intoxication, these new programs require a fundamental realignment of police philosophy and resources. If properly implemented, the new laws could represent one of the greatest steps forward in the administration of criminal justice in recent years.

In the meantime, the United States Supreme Court had agreed to hear the case of *Powell v. Texas,* which raised basically the same issues as the earlier *Easter* and *Driver* cases. In June 1968, the Court handed down its opinion in *Powell.*[10] In analyzing this case, it is particularly important to keep separate what the Court did, given the particular facts presented to it, and what the Court said in general about the problem of the publicly intoxicated alcoholic.

Five of the nine Justices concluded that alcoholism is a disabling disease and that an alcoholic drinks involuntarily as a result of his illness. Five of the Justices also agreed that a homeless alcoholic, or an alcoholic who for some other reason cannot confine his drunkenness to a private place, cannot constitutionally be convicted for his public intoxication. But because the record showed that Powell had a home and a family, and did not show that Powell was unable to avoid public places when drunk, five members of the Court joined to affirm his conviction.

Thus, the rule that emerges from this case is that, at least for the immediate future, only the homeless, derelict, skid-row alcoholic, or an alcoholic who can show that it is impossible for him to avoid public places when drunk, has a constitutional defense to the charge of public intoxication. In effect, the rationale of the *Easter* and *Driver* decisions—which involved homeless alcoholics— was confirmed. But it seems likely that in the near future, as more knowledge is developed about alcoholism, more effective treatment is made available, and greater numbers of treatment programs and facilities are established, the Court will extend this constitutional protection to all chronic alcoholics. It is not a question of whether it will come, but simply when it will come.

The Court appeared to be adopting, in *Powell,* an interim rule of law. In effect, it handed down a warning to the country that it must begin to meet the problems of public drunkenness and alcoholism on a realistic and humane basis, before revolutionary new legal principles are clearly enunciated and the states are forced to change their practices overnight in a crisis atmosphere.

The logical limits of *Easter, Driver,* and *Powell* have not yet been explored. State cases since *Powell* have divided on the impact of that decision.[11] In *District of Columbia v. Phillips,*[12] however, *Easter* was extended as a potential defense to disorderly conduct. And in *Salzman v. United States,*[13] it was indicated that *Easter* would also be available as a defense for robbery that is a direct product of alcoholism. It seems fair to anticipate that alcoholism will eventually be regarded, along with mental illness, duress, and other similar conditions, as depriving an individual of his capacity to control his conduct, and that therefore it will become generally available as an exculpatory defense to excuse any antisocial behavior it causes.

Congress has also begun to recognize the special problems created by drunkenness and alcoholism. In 1966 and 1967, it enacted general health legislation requiring the states to develop comprehensive health plans for purposes of federal funding.[14] The Department of Health, Education, and Welfare has made it clear that alcoholism is one of the major health problems to be included under those comprehensive health plans. In the 1966 highway safety legislation, and again in the 1968 poverty program legislation,[15] Congress itself included specific references to the major problem of alcoholism.

But it was also obvious that the generalized legislation enacted up to that time was insufficient to meet all the problems raised by the nation's long neglect of alcoholism. As a result, in 1968 the President signed a new law designed specifically to provide additional federal funds to help states underwrite the massive changes necessary to begin handling all intoxication and alcoholism under public health rather than criminal procedures.[16] This law, which was expanded in 1970,[17] is the first federal law in the nation's history dealing specifically with intoxication and alcoholism. It represents a major step forward in our national attitude toward these problems.

In pursuing reform of the laws handling intoxication and alcoholism, it would be a serious mistake to concentrate too heavily upon new federal legislation, or existing federal legislation, and to neglect state and local resources. It is true that substantial funding must eventually come from the federal government; that is an indisputable fact of modern life. But federal funds are meaningless without the state and local statutory framework and detailed planning which are needed to maximize their benefits. State and local jurisdictions must therefore begin to work on new and progressive legislation that will effect the transfer of this entire problem from law enforcement authorities to public health officials. Such legislation must authorize a modern comprehensive program for the prevention, treatment, and control of alcoholism.

The new law passed by Congress for the District of Columbia in 1968 is already available for guidance. Both a Joint Committee of the American Bar Association and the American Medical Association, and the Legislative Drafting Research Fund of Columbia University, have drafted comprehensive model legislation. The National Conference of Commissioners on Uniform State Laws has recently appointed a committee to prepare a uniform act for alcohol abuse and alcoholism, which will review and synthesize the earlier work. In short, there is a wealth of information in this area for anyone who wishes to obtain it. The provisions of these complex new statutes cannot be described here in detail, but the following brief outline should be sufficient to illustrate the general approach.

First, the old public-intoxication law has been repealed. A statute has been substituted which makes drunkenness an offense only when it results in substantial and immediate physical harm to another citizen.

Second, a person found intoxicated in public who has a home and a family to take care of him is escorted promptly to that home, or to a private health facility. If it appears that the inebriate is in medical danger, either he is taken directly to a medical facility or his family is informed that medical help would appear to be required.

Third, an inebriate who has no resources of his own and is thus a public charge is taken to a detoxification center staffed with public health personnel, to receive whatever medical help may be necessary for his acute intoxication. This is a voluntary facility. The individual may be required to remain there for some specified short period of time in order to make certain that he will be able to take care of himself when he leaves. But he has not been arrested, and cannot be detained for a longer period against his will.

Fourth, an inebriate who is taken to a public detoxification center and who has a drinking problem is encouraged to remain for a longer period of time in an inpatient diagnostic center where a complete workup can be prepared on his medical, social, occupational, family, and other personal history. This also is a completely voluntary facility. A genuine offer of meaningful assistance is the only inducement used to persuade an inebriate to make use of it. Never before in our history has any community reached out to these unfortunate people with such an offer.

Fifth, a network of aftercare facilities is established to provide food, shelter, clothing, vocational rehabilitation, job referral, and appropriate treatment as a substitute for simply dumping the unfortunate derelict back onto skid row. Perhaps the most important aspect of this part of the program is the use of residential facilities, such as halfway houses, to provide an entirely new atmosphere that, it is hoped, will reverse the process of degradation that has helped keep the derelicts in their present position. Like the other facilities, these are entirely voluntary.

Sixth, any person arrested for driving while intoxicated, or whose license has been suspended or revoked for that offense, is required to undergo a medical diagnosis for possible alcoholism. If the person is diagnosed as an alcoholic, he is given one of two options. If he agrees to undergo treatment for alcoholism, he is permitted to retain his license. If he refuses treatment, his license is revoked. Thus, treatment for alcoholism will not be compulsory, although it will have an obvious inducement behind it.

It should be apparent from this outline that under the new legal approach, treatment for alcoholism will be provided on an optional rather than a compulsory basis, except for truly dangerous persons. The Crime Commissions, and the majority of treatment experts, have concluded that involuntary civil commitment for alcoholism is as punitive and inhumane as criminal punishment. The history of drunkenness laws has demonstrated that criminal coercion has succeeded only in re-enforcing drinking problems, and indeed in developing an ever-increasing number of alcoholics. Similarly, the history of laws governing treatment for mental illness has demonstrated that civil coercion has greatly hindered the possibility of returning substantial numbers of the mentally ill to productive lives in society. In both areas, therefore, the country is now moving away from coercive treatment toward community-based optional treatment as the only substantial possibility for true rehabilitation.

DRUG ABUSE AND DRUG DEPENDENCE

The abuse of dangerous drugs other than alcohol, and the drug dependence that can result, have also existed throughout recorded history. Perhaps because the intoxication caused by these other drugs is not as noticeable as intoxication due to alcohol consumption, serious law enforcement efforts directed against these drugs did not begin until this century.

The first federal control statute was the Harrison Narcotic Act of 1914,[18] which imposed a tax on the manufacture or importation of any narcotic drug—opium and its derivatives, such as morphine and heroin. Synthetic opiates, having similar addictive capabilities, were brought under control by separate legislation in 1946.[19] Marijuana was placed under the same controls through the Marihuana Tax Act of 1937,[20] and all depressant, stimulant, and hallucinogenic drugs subject to abuse were placed under strict regulation pursuant to the Drug Abuse Control Amendments of 1965.[21]

Congress has responded to mounting concern about drug abuse with statutory amendments providing stronger criminal penalties. In the Narcotic Control Act of 1956, it enacted increased penalties for traffickers in narcotic drugs and marijuana.[22] The Narcotics Manufacturing Act of 1960 both improved controls over the legal supplies of narcotic drugs and increased penalties for illegal production.[23] And in 1968 Congress provided penalties for simple possession of controlled drugs under the Drug Abuse Control Amendments.[24]

This patchwork of legislation has provoked widespread criticism. Virtually everyone agrees that the present criminal laws affecting drug abuse should be repealed and replaced with a comprehensive new statute. At that point, however, the agreement ends. The Comprehensive Drug Abuse Prevention and Control Act of 1970 only synthesizes the prior regulatory controls, without attempting basic reform. It must be anticipated that, as the effectiveness and appropriateness of relying primarily upon the criminal law to control drug abuse is subjected to closer scrutiny, substantial legislative reform will eventually be undertaken. Because of the widely differing views on drug abuse policy, however, it is difficult to anticipate either the timing or the content of future legislation.

The present drive for reform of the handling of drug abuse and drug dependence in this country may be traced to a report made in 1955 by the New York Academy of Medicine urging widespread changes in the control of dangerous drugs, including legalizing the distribution of narcotic drugs to narcotic addicts.[25] At the same time, the American Bar Association Section on Criminal Law was surveying federal and state legislation dealing with narcotics. A Joint Committee of the American Bar Association and the American Medical Association on Narcotic Drugs was formed in 1955. In 1958, it issued an explosive Interim Report recommending an outpatient experimental clinic for the treatment of drug addicts with maintenance doses of narcotics, and in the community rather than on an institutional basis. This report provoked an unprecedented attack by the Federal Bureau of Narcotics in a 186-page pamphlet published in 1959.[26]

The Final Report of the Joint Committee reiterated the dissatisfaction within the legal and medical professions concerning drug-abuse enforcement policies, which tended "to emphasize repression and prohibition to the exclusion of other possible methods of dealing with addicts and the drug traffic." The Joint Committee urged that the role of medicine and public health in dealing with drug addiction and the drug addict be clarified. It opposed indiscriminate distribution of narcotic drugs to addicts, but continued to recommend experimentation with drug maintenance for some addicts in spite of the opposition of the Bureau of Narcotics. Finally, the Committee pointed out that neither compulsory hospitalization of all addicts nor permanent isolation is practicable and, even if feasible, would not be a solution but only a temporizing maneuver —the very antithesis of the medical and scientific approach to the physical and behavioral problems of man.

Undoubtedly spurred on by this report, the President convened an Ad Hoc Panel on Drug Abuse and then a White House Conference on Narcotics and Drug Abuse in 1962. The President's Advisory Commission on Narcotic and Drug Abuse was created in January 1963, and issued its Final Report in November 1963. The Final Report of the Advisory Commission concluded that there had never been a sustained, organized attack upon drug abuse in this country. It made some twenty-five general recommendations, including revision of the federal narcotic laws; recognition that the definition of legitimate medical use of narcotic drugs and medical treatment of drug dependence are primarily to be determined by the medical profession; federal assistance to state and local governments for the establishment, maintenance, and expansion of broad treatment and rehabilitation programs; and enactment of federal treatment legislation.

The District of Columbia and United States Crime Commissions also studied the problems of drug abuse and drug dependence in some detail. The report of the District of Columbia Commission urged comprehensive treatment programs and facilities for drug-dependent persons, on both a voluntary and an involuntary basis. It described several areas where the law should be amended or revised to accomplish this purpose. Similarly, the report of the United States Crime Commission recommended development of a sound regulatory and criminal law approach to dangerous drugs, aimed primarily at reaching the upper echelons of the illicit drug traffic. It recommended clarification of the status of medical treatment of addicts using narcotic drugs, and abolition of all obstacles in the way of medical research in this field. Both Commissions placed primary emphasis for the future upon the development of appropriate treatment and rehabilitation programs and facilities.

In 1966, Congress enacted the Narcotic Addict Rehabilitation Act (NARA)[27] to authorize federal efforts at treatment and rehabilitation. Congress has also provided assistance to the states for treatment and rehabilitation programs using community mental health centers under the Alcoholic and Narcotic Addict Rehabilitation Amendments of 1968,[28] which were expanded in 1970.[29]

NARA provides for civil commitment in lieu of prosecution, sentencing to commitment for treatment, civil commitment of persons not charged with any criminal offense, rehabilitation and post-hospitalization care programs, and assistance to states and localities. In the course of enactment, however, the potential usefulness of NARA was severely limited. For example, a person charged with a crime of violence or with trafficking in narcotic drugs, or one who has been convicted of a felony on two or more occasions, is ineligible for civil commitment in lieu of prosecution or sentencing to commitment for treatment. All treatment under NARA is discretionary with both the judges and the physicians, with the result that there is little pressure or incentive for a truly comprehensive and effective program. It therefore became apparent almost immediately after enactment that NARA would be largely useless without substantial revision, and that has been the experience to date.

In September 1962, the same month as the White House Conference, the Supreme Court underscored the urgency of the problems surrounding the handling of drug abuse and drug dependence by its ruling in *Robinson v. California*,[30] which struck down as unconstitutional on its face a statute making the disease of narcotic addiction criminal. The Court held that California's addiction statute imposed cruel and unusual punishment in violation of the Eighth Amendment. The only disagreement within the Court, moreover, appeared to center upon the narrow question of the meaning of the particular statute involved. No member of the Court dissented from the basic constitutional principle that it is cruel and unusual punishment to impose criminal sanctions upon an addict, who has lost the power of self-control over the use of drugs, for his addiction.

Since *Robinson*, there has been a dispute whether the holding of that case must be restricted to the exact type of statute there involved—covering only the "status" of addiction—or may properly be applied to such "acts" as the trafficking in or possession of narcotics, or even criminal activity undertaken by an addict to support his addiction. Lower courts[31] have generally been reluctant to pursue the logical meaning of *Robinson*.

In the District of Columbia, an attempt was made to broaden the *Durham* "mental disease or defect" rule[32] to include drug dependence. In a series of cases, however, the United States Court of Appeals for the District of Columbia Circuit held that drug addiction, standing alone, was not sufficient to present the issue of mental disease or defect to a jury.[33] The same rule has been adopted in other circuits.[34]

At the same time, separate litigation was begun to test the constitutionality of federal and state marijuana laws, on the ground that such laws irrationally classify marijuana as a narcotic drug in contravention of due process of law, deprive citizens of the right to privacy in the personal use of marijuana, impose unconstitutionally harsh penal sanctions for possession or use of this relatively innocuous drug and violate the equal protection clause by drawing unjustifiable distinctions between marijuana and alcohol. In *Commonwealth v. Weiss*,[35] the court fully upheld a Massachusetts statute and the right of the government to classify marijuana as it did. In *Scott v. United States*,[36] the court acknowledged that there are "many searching questions to be asked about the structure and foundations of existing narcotics laws," but concluded that the record in that case was devoid of a basis on which to resolve those questions.

More recently, probing doubts have again been expressed by the courts about the present handling of drug-dependent persons as criminals. In *Powell v. Texas,* for example, Mr. Justice White, who cast the deciding vote affirming the trial court's conviction of Powell for public intoxication, agreed with the four dissenting Justices that *Robinson* must logically be extended to provide a defense for the use of drugs by an addict, since "punishing an addict for using drugs convicts for addiction under a different name." Perhaps in reliance upon this apparent majority view of the Supreme Court, a panel of the United States Court of Appeals for the District of Columbia Circuit initially held, in *Watson v. United States,*[37] that a mandatory minimum sentence of ten years for possession of narcotics by an addict violated the Eighth Amendment. Two members of the panel concluded that the ten-year mandatory minimum sentence was clearly unconstitutional under the circumstances, and that it was therefore unnecessary to consider whether any other sentence might similarly be unconstitutional. One judge, however, flatly held that no criminal penalty could constitutionally be imposed on a narcotic addict for possession of narcotic drugs for his own personal use. On rehearing *en banc,* the full court held, with two dissents, that these issues need not be faced until it is presented with a fuller record, and it remanded the case for consideration of disposition under NARA.

Once again, although the development of the case law in the field of narcotics has lagged behind the case law in the field of alcoholism, it seems inevitable that the courts will eventually agree that possession of narcotics by an addict for personal use cannot be punished as criminal, and indeed that any activity that is the direct product of addiction is similarly protected from criminal sanctions. The courts will undoubtedly accept this reasoning more readily when the argument is presented in terms of characterizing addiction as simply a further example of involuntary conduct—as was done in *Easter* and *Watson*—and the attempts to force it into the ill-fitting mold of *Durham* or other formulations of the insanity rule are abandoned.

The courts will probably be far more receptive to these arguments once it can be shown that adequate legislation is available both to protect society from dangerous addicts and to provide appropriate and useful treatment and rehabilitation to the addicts themselves. Such legislation is now in the process of development.[38] While the issues have been formulated, their resolution—both in Congress and in state legislatures throughout the country—may take many years.

The law enforcement issues are in particularly sharp focus. There is disagreement, for example, as to whether the medical profession, rather than law enforcement agencies, should determine the proper limits of the use of narcotic drugs in medical practice and the proper methods of treating drug-dependent persons.[39] There are differences about the usefulness and constitutionality of various law enforcement devices, such as preventive detention, wiretapping, no-knock entry, and special sanctions for the professional criminal. There is basic disagreement on both the rationale for criminal penalties—whether possession of marijuana and other "soft" drugs should even be subject to the criminal laws, or in any event should be subject to the same criminal penalty as possession of "hard" narcotics—and the extent to which judges should have wide or narrow discretion in dispensing criminal penalties. These are but a few of the issues that have been raised and must eventually be resolved by legislators before they find their way into the courts.

The public policy issues posed by treatment legislation are just now beginning to emerge, and will perhaps not come into clear focus for some time. There is the fundamental issue whether hard narcotics such as heroin should lawfully be dispensed to addicts, particularly those for whom no other treatment can be found, on a maintenance basis. Even the controls for methadone treatment have not yet been authoritatively delineated. It has been suggested that criminal punishment should never be allowed for a drug-dependent person charged only with possession of dangerous drugs for his own personal use, and that appropriate treatment should be the only approach permitted under those circumstances. Finally, the mode of treatment—whether on a voluntary or an involuntary basis, and whether institutionalized or community-based—must be resolved.

The trend for both mental illness and alcoholism is toward treatment and rehabilitation, and toward use of voluntary and community-based therapy. Acceptance of this approach in the field of drug dependence may well take much longer, because of the widespread and justifiable fear of the present narcotics crime problem. Perhaps only with general recognition of drug maintenance as a rational and indeed humane method of treatment and rehabilitation will modern treatment principles also become fully accepted in the field of drug dependence.

It is only in the past ten years that reform in the handling of alcohol and drug abuse has begun to take shape, and only in the past three years that rudimentary implementation of this reform has been instituted. While substantial progress can be seen, the work has barely begun. Nevertheless, it is clear that the strangle hold of the criminal law upon the problems of intoxication and drug abuse has been broken. Models for new programs are available, and the path is clear for badly needed change. It is only a question of when individual jurisdictions will institute these new reforms—not whether they are possible.

NOTES

1. *See, e.g.,* 19 C.J. *Drunkards* §6 (1920); Moser v. Fulk, 237 N.C. 302, 74 S.E.2d 729 (1953).
2. 4 James I, c.5 (1606).
3. *See, e.g.,* Flanagan v. People, 86 N.Y. 554 (1881).
4. 49 N.H. 399 (1869).
5. 356 F.2d 761 (4th Cir. 1966), *rev'g* 243 F. Supp. 95 (E.D.N.C. 1965).
6. 361 F.2d 50 (D.C. Cir 1966) (en banc), *rev'g* 209 A.2d 625 (D.C. Ct. App. 1965).
7. President's Commission on Crime in the District of Columbia, Report, at 474–503 (1966), *reprinted in* President's Commission on Law Enforcement and Administration of Justice, Task Force Report, *Drunkenness* 68–81 (1967).
8. President's Commission on Law Enforcement and Administration of Justice, Report, *The Challenge of Crime in a Free Society* 233–37 (1967), *reprinted in* President's Commission on Law Enforcement and Administration of Justice, *Task Force Report: Drunkenness* 1–6 (1967).
9. Acts 1968, ch. 146 (1968), Md. Code Ann. art. 2C (Supp. 1969); Hawaii L. 1968, Act 6 (April 18, 1968); District of Columbia Alcoholic Rehabilitation Act of 1967, Pub. # L. 90–452, 82 Stat. 618 (1968). *See* S. Rep. No. 1435, 90th Cong., 2d Sess. (1968).
10. 392 U.S. 514 (1968). The Court earlier had declined to review an alcoholism case, with two Justices dissenting, Budd v. California, 385 U.S. 909 (1966).
11. *Compare* Vick v. State, 453 P.2d 342 (Alaska 1969), *with* State v. Fearon, 283 Minn. 90, 166 N.W.2d 720 (1969).
12. No. DC-855-67 (D.C. Ct. Gen. Sess. Crim., April 26, 1967), *reprinted in* 113 Cong. Rec. 12793 (1967).

13. 405 F.2d 358 (D.C. Cir. 1968).

14. Comprehensive Health Planning and Public Health Services Amendments of 1966, Pub. L. 89-749, 80 Stat. 1180 (1966); Partnership for Health Amendments of 1967, Pub. L. 90-174, 81 Stat. 533 (1967).

15. Highway Safety Act of 1966, Pub. L. 89-564, 80 Stat. 731, 736 (1966); Economic Opportunity Amendments of 1967, Pub. L. 90-222, 81 Stat. 672, 697 (1967).

16. Alcoholic Rehabilitation Act of 1968, Pub. L. 90-574, 82 Stat. 1006-9 (1968).

17. Community Mental Health Centers Amendments of 1970, Pub. L. 91-211, 84 Stat. 54, 57-59, (1970).

18. Pub. L. 63-223, 38 Stat. 785 (1914).

19. Pub. L. 79-320, 60 Stat. 38 (1946).

20. Pub. L. 75-238, 50 Stat. 551 (1937).

21. Pub. L. 89-74, 79 Stat. 226 (1965).

22. Pub. L. 84-728, 70 Stat. 567 (1956).

23. Pub. L. 86-429, 74 Stat. 55 (1960).

24. Pub. L. 90-639, 82 Stat. 1361 (1968).

25. "Report on Drug Addiction," 31 Bulletin of the New York Academy of Medicine 592 (Aug. 1955).

26. Joint Committee of the American Bar Association and the American Medical Association on Narcotic Drugs, Interim and Final Reports, Drug Addiction: Crime or Disease? (1961); Federal Bureau of Narcotics, Comments on Narcotic Drugs (1959).

27. Pub. L. 89-793, 80 Stat. 1438 (1966).

28. Pub. L. 90-574, 82 Stat. 1005, 1009–10 (1968).

29. Community Mental Health Centers Amendments of 1970, Pub. L. 91-211, 84 Stat. 54, 57–59 (1970).

30. 370 U.S. 660 (1962).

31. See, e.g., People v. Nettles, 34 Ill. 2d 52, 213 N.E.2d 536 (1966); In re Carlson, 64 Cal. 2d 70, 48 Cal. Rptr. 875, 410 P.2d 379 (1966).

32. Durham v. United States, 214 F.2d 862 (D.C. Cir. 1954); McDonald v. United States, 312 F.2d 847 (D.C. Cir. 1962); Washington v. United States, 390 F.2d 444 (D.C. Cir. 1967).

33. Horton v. United States, 317 F.2d 595 (D.C. Cir. 1963); Lloyd v. United States, 343 F.2d 242 (D.C. Cir. 1964), cert. denied, 381 U.S. 952 (1965); Castle v. United States, 347 F.2d 492 (D.C. Cir. 1964), cert. denied, 381 U.S. 953 (1965); Green v. United States, 383 F.2d 199 (D.C. Cir. 1967), cert. denied, 390 U.S. 961 (1968).

34. United States v. Freeman, 357 F.2d 606 (2d Cir. 1966); Bailey v. United States, 386 F.2d 1 (5th Cir. 1967), cert. denied, 392 U.S. 946 (1968).

35. No. 28865 (Super. Crim. Ct., Suffolk, Mass., Dec. 20, 1967) (per Tauro, C.J.).

36. 395 F.2d 619 (D.C. Cir. 1968), cert. denied, 393 U.S. 986 (1968).

37. 408 F.2d 1290 (D.C. Cir. 1968), on rehearing en banc, — F.2d — (No. 21,186 July 13, 1970).

38. See, e.g., S. 3071, S. 3246, and S. 3562, 91st Cong., 1st and 2d Sess. (1969 and 1970).

39. Compare Webb v. United States, 249 U.S. 96 (1919), and United States v. Behrman, 258 U.S. 280 (1922), with United States v. Linder, 268 U.S. 5 (1925), and Boyd v. United States, 271 U.S. 104 (1926).

THE RIGHT TO TRAVEL

LEONARD B. BOUDIN

ALTHOUGH THERE IS NO EXPLICIT PROVISION TO
that effect in the Constitution, it has been recognized for many
years that there is a constitutional right to travel inside and outside
the United States—so much so that in 1929 Professor John Hanna
of Columbia Law School regarded the ten-dollar passport fee as a
wrongful interference with the right to travel.[1]

Sir William Blackstone, the legal writer who most influenced
the American colonists, wrote that one of the attributes of personal
liberty under common law was "the power of loco-motion, of changing situation, or moving one's person to whatever place one's in-
clination may direct."[2] Earlier, Chapter Forty-two of Magna Carta
gave every free man the right to leave the realm at his pleasure in
time of peace, thus rescinding the King's order that his political
and religious enemies be confined to the realm.

In this country, the source of the right to travel may be found in
judicial decisions going back to 1849, which predicated it variously
upon the national character of our governmental system, the commerce clause, the privileges and immunities of citizens, and the
right to travel to the seats of government and to petition the government for grievances. Whatever the source of the right, the fact
is that it was generally recognized almost from the beginnings of

*Leonard B. Boudin is General Counsel of the National Emergency Civil Liberties
Committee, Visiting Professor of Law at Harvard Law School, a prolific litigator in
constitutional cases, and the author of articles on the Bill of Rights.*

our nation that American citizens might travel freely from state to state and abroad.

I

Until 1951, the only litigation on the subject involved the efforts of particular states to regulate or impose various burdens upon travel or changes of residence. Invariably these restrictions were struck down by the Supreme Court as unconstitutional. In the famous Passenger Cases of 1849,[3] New York and Massachusetts statutes that imposed taxes upon alien passengers arriving in parts of those states were declared invalid. Several years later, in *Crandall v. Nevada*,[4] the Supreme Court declared unconstitutional a tax upon each person leaving the state by common carrier. The Court viewed all citizens of the United States as members of the same community, entitled to the same right to pass through every part of it without interruption as freely as within their own states.

Then in 1941, in *Edwards v. California*,[5] a unanimous Supreme Court invalidated a California statute directed at the migrant "Okies," making it a misdemeanor knowingly to bring an indigent nonresident into the state. The defendant had brought his wife's brother, a former WPA employee, from California into Texas. Congressman John H. Tolan, Chairman of the Select Committee of the House of Representatives appointed to investigate interstate migration of destitute citizens, appeared in the litigation as *amicus curiae* attacking the legislation of his own state; his contribution is reflected in the majority opinion's reference to "[t]he grave and perplexing social and economic dislocation which this statute reflects." The Court predicated its decision upon California's interference with interstate commerce. Justice Douglas's concurring opinion expressed the view "that the right of persons to move freely from State to State occupies a more protected position in our constitutional system than does the movement of cattle, fruit, steel and coal across state lines." In his view, "The right to move freely from State to State is an incident of *national* citizenship protected by the privileges and immunities clause of the Fourteenth Amendment against state interference."

In contrast to this state interference with travel, there were no federal limitations on the right of American citizens to travel to and from other countries in peacetime. In 1898, a State Department publication was able to state accurately, "In time of peace, a law-abiding American citizen has always been free to leave the country without the permission of the government."⁶ This book was prepared by Gaillard Hunt, the Passport Clerk, and was ordered printed by the Secretary of State. Persons confined in prison or released upon bond pending trial or appeal were exceptions to the general rule.

Early in its history, the passport was issued to facilitate travel, not to control it. Passports were issued not only by the Secretary of State but by state and municipal authorities. Hence, it was said in 1835 that "[t]here is no law of the United States, in any manner regulating the issuing of passports, or directing upon what evidence it may be done, or declaring their legal effect."⁷

This "lack of legal provision on the subject led to gross abuses, and 'the impositions practiced upon the illiterate and unwary by the falsification of worthless passports.' "⁸ The result was the Act of August 18, 1856, which in its original form gave the Secretary of State exclusive power to grant and issue passports to citizens of the United States under rules prescribed by the President.⁹

Since passports were not necessary for lawful travel abroad, the Act was not intended to, and did not, affect the right to travel. Its purpose, on the contrary, was to facilitate travel. Hence the State Department recommended in 1873 that passports be secured because "[c]itizens of the United States visiting foreign countries are liable to serious inconvenience if unprovided with authentic proof of their national character."¹⁰

Congress originally imposed upon the right to travel only one condition—which springs from the very nature of the passport—namely, that the applicant be a citizen or otherwise subject to the jurisdiction of the United States. Consequently, passports were invariably given to citizens as a matter of right. When the issue arose more formally, the right was upheld by Secretary of State Fish and Attorney General Taft, although Attorney General Knox later differed with them.¹¹

Hence, from the beginning Americans exercised the right to travel even with governmental help and certainly without governmental interference. The wartime exceptions merely emphasized the general rule. Thus, in 1861, Secretary of State Seward issued an order that "no person will be allowed to go abroad" or "to land in the United States" without a passport. Passports were also required before one could pass the lines of the Union army.¹² They were denied those who left the country to avoid military duty or those liable for service, unless they gave bond to perform such duty or to provide substitutes. It was not until 1918 that Congress made it unlawful to travel without a passport subsequent to a proclamation of war.[13] In 1941, this restriction was extended to any national emergency.[14] The most recent declaration of national emergency was during the Korean War in 1950,[15] and no President has seen fit to revoke it—however irrational that may appear nearly two decades later. The purpose of those statutes, however, was to establish a form of border control—American border control—and not to screen American citizens by reason of their political views.

II

The Cold War of the late 1940's and early 1950's caused many casualties in our system of civil liberties; these included the government's interference with the right to travel abroad. If the Attorney General of the United States had a list of subversive organizations, whose validity has escaped adjudication as a result of his ingenuity and judicial timidity, so did Mrs. Ruth Shipley, the Director of the Passport Office of the State Department. Mrs. Shipley was a very strong woman who, as Dean Acheson once admitted, could make Secretaries of State quail. Her Index listed 8,000,000 persons who were suspect for political or other reasons. On the grounds that their travel would not be in the best interests of the United States, she denied passports to many persons of eminence, including Congressman Leo Isaacson, Dr. Otto Nathan, the executor of the estate of Albert Einstein, and Dr. Linus Pauling, a Nobel Laureate.[16] Even the author of this essay was told that his travel abroad to represent an American citizen dismissed by UNESCO at the instigation of the State Department was contrary to the best interests of the country.

The State Department argued that it had sole discretion under the Act of 1856, as amended, to issue or deny passports and that it could exercise discretion "in the best interest of the United States." The passage of the Internal Security Act of 1950 gave it another argument, because under that Act, originating in the Mundt-Nixon bill, no member of an organization found by a final order of the Subversive Activities Control Board to be a Communist organization could apply for a passport.[17] Although no organization was thus denominated until 1961,[18] the Department jumped the gun, claiming that it was acting in accordance with the "spirit" of the 1950 Act. It is very difficult to appreciate today that anti-Communist hysteria during the McCarthy period was so pervasive that few persons were prepared to expose themselves publicly by engaging in litigation.

A series of lawsuits was instituted in the early 1950's by American citizens denied passports. One of the first was that of Paul Robeson, the singer, who was probably injured more than any other person by the denial of a passport since he was blacklisted in the United States and was unable to travel abroad, where he could have continued his musical career without interruption. After a lower court sustained the Department of State, the Court of Appeals dismissed Mr. Robeson's appeal as moot on the ground that by the time it was argued his passport by its own terms had expired.[19] The court's conclusion was hardly inescapable. Its position that "no application for renewal or for a new passport is shown to have been made" is unpersuasive since Mr. Robeson was also prevented by the immigration authorities from going to Canada, where a passport was not required. August 1952, however, was too early a date for the courts to face the broad issues presented by the *Robeson* case.

In *Bauer v. Acheson*,[20] the plaintiff emphasized denial of the hearing rather than the substantive right to travel. A three-judge court ordered a hearing stating: (1) there was a constitutional right to travel; (2) its exercise required a passport; and (3) the Secretary had certain (undefined) discretion which could not be exercised arbitrarily. Although this was a welcome ruling, the court might not have allotted any discretion to the Secretary had it been acquainted with passport history.

Shachtman v. Dulles[21] also proceeded on a limited basis—an attack on the Secretary's reliance on the Attorney General's subversive list. The Court of Appeals upheld the complaint because it alleged that the organization was neither "subversive" nor "Communistic" and had sought for nearly six years to demonstrate this to the Attorney General. The court declined to "characterize as invalid, for its own purposes, the listing by the Attorney General," pointing out that he was not a party to the litigation and that the listing was not subject to collateral attack in the passport proceedings.

The court specifically noted, however, that even for denying federal employment, membership in a listed organization was "not enough." Judge Edgerton's concurring opinion went further:

> The premise that a man is not fit to work for the government does not support the conclusion that he is not fit to go to Europe. The Attorney General's list was prepared for screening government employees, not passport applicants.[22]

While much of this and other litigation was going on, the State Department promulgated regulations in 1952 which denied passports to three categories of persons:[23]

> (a) Persons who are members of the Communist Party or who have recently terminated such membership under such circumstances as to warrant the conclusion—not otherwise rebutted by the evidence—that they continue to act in furtherance of the interests and under the discipline of the Communist Party;
>
> (b) Persons, regardless of the formal state of their affiliation with the Communist Party, who engage in activities which support the Communist movement under such circumstances as to warrant the conclusion—not otherwise rebutted by the evidence—that they have engaged in such activities as a result of direction, domination, or control exercised over them by the Communist movement;
>
> (c) Persons, regardless of the formal state of their affiliation with the Communist Party, as to whom there is reason to believe, on the balance of all the evidence, that they are going abroad to engage in activities which will advance the Communist movement for the purpose, knowingly and wilfully of advancing the movement.

The Department created a laborious process. First, imprecise charges, and then a hearing without provision for the confrontation of witnesses. In addition, the regulations provided for review by a nonexistent Board of Passport Appeals (more than a year passed before any such board was constituted with governing rules). Nor could one appeal to the Board without executing an affidavit forswearing Communist Party membership. When ultimately the Board held hearings, they were typical star chamber proceedings in which the passport applicants, confronted with neither evidence nor witnesses, were subjected to cross-examination by the Board.

In a case of considerable importance, Dr. Otto Nathan made the first broad assertion of an absolute right to travel. The Department persisted in its charges despite his execution of a non-Communist affidavit. (Dr. Linus Pauling executed a half-dozen such affidavits to no avail until he received a Nobel Prize.) Dr. Nathan declined to appeal to the Board of Passport Appeals and sued for a passport. Again avoiding the central issue, the district judge directed the Department to give Dr. Nathan a hearing, while declining to state the nature of it.[24] Dr. Nathan instituted contempt proceedings when the Department engaged in further delay, and the district court ordered that he receive a passport forthwith.[25] The government, appealing, applied for a stay of judgment. The Court of Appeals granted a stay upon condition that the Department give Dr. Nathan an immediate "evidentiary hearing"; that the hearing officer make a report based upon the "record" to which Dr. Nathan could file exceptions; and that the Department advise the plaintiff and the court of its final decision in ten days, at which time the court could take further action. The government thereupon capitulated and granted Dr. Nathan a passport.

The decision had significance outside the passport field. The New Deal had elevated "the administrative process," to use Dean James Landis' term, to a high social value, and liberals had made a fetish of protecting administrative action from judicial review. It was the conservatives, led by Congressman Howard Smith, who pursued the contrary course of trying to assure judicial review of agency action, particularly as it affected property rights.[26]

By 1955, a decade of Cold War government had taught the liberals a lesson, and the *Nathan* decision was judicial recognition of it. More recently, the principle of that case has been applied in judicial review of action by the Selective Service System; rarely have courts suddenly turned so critical an eye upon an agency— a scrutiny well justified by the license given this hydra-headed body under General Lewis Hershey.

The Supreme Court eventually resolved the central passport issue in favor of the citizen in *Kent v. Dulles*.[27] Rockwell Kent, the artist, and Dr. Walter Briehl, a West Coast psychiatrist, had been denied passports on grounds of alleged Communist sympathies and affiliations; both declined to execute affidavits forswearing membership in the Communist Party as irrelevant to their right to travel. In a 5 to 4 decision, the Court held that the right to travel was an important attribute of liberty under the due process clause of the Fifth Amendment. Mr. Justice Douglas, writing for the Court, pointed out the importance of travel in the exercise of First Amendment rights. He analyzed the Passport Act of 1926, which gave the Secretary of State the right to issue passports, and noted that "where activities or enjoyment, natural and often necessary to the well-being of an American citizen, such as travel, are involved, we will construe narrowly all delegated powers that curtail or dilute them." In other words, in light of the serious constitutional problems that would have been presented if the governing statute were held to authorize denial of passports on political grounds, the Court interpreted the statute to deny the Secretary such authority.

In speculating on the Court's reasoning in the *Kent* case—especially Justice Frankfurter's decisive vote—weight might well be given to the influence of a companion case, *Dayton v. Dulles*.[28] That case involved charges of espionage which the government had made on the basis of undisclosed evidence. The Supreme Court reversed the denial of a passport, and it seems likely that the procedural infirmities of *Dayton* revealed to the Court all too clearly the potential for arbitrary action that the *Kent* opinion choked off.

It is sad to reflect on the closeness of these decisions, which seemed compelled by elementary civil liberties principles. Since the Court acted, on June 16, 1958, innumerable Americans have traveled who would have been unable to do so earlier, without any indication of danger to the Republic.

The constitutional issue was faced directly in *Aptheker v. Secretary of State*.[29] In 1961, the Supreme Court had upheld the validity of the Internal Security Act of 1950, and the Communist Party was required by a final order to register as a Communist organization.[30] It was no longer necessary for the State Department to rely on the "spirit" of the Act; the registration provisions of the statute had been upheld and what remained were a number of other questions, including the validity of the passport restrictions. But in *Aptheker* the Supreme Court held that the denial of a passport to a person because of membership in an organization required to register as a Communist organization violated the bill of attainder clause and the First Amendment right to freedom of association.

A second important problem in international travel arose when the State Department placed geographic limitations on travel, banning travel to particular areas of the world—China, Albania, North Korea, and later Cuba and North Vietnam. A few of these bans were imposed on the theory that the country of destination was engaged in war and that it would be difficult for the United States to protect its citizens. There were two answers to this: first, citizens have no enforceable right to protection from the government, and, second, the travelers were perfectly happy to waive protection from the speculative dangers.

But the principal reason urged by the government was that it was attempting to place a *cordon sanitaire* upon a country whose policies it disapproved. This was particularly true of China for many years, where even American newspapermen were forbidden to travel. Again, a series of intrepid litigants sought to compel the Secretary of State to validate their passports for travel to China. These included the American writer Waldo Frank, newspaperman William Worthy, and Congressman Charles Porter. Each lost in the Court of Appeals for the District of Columbia, and the Supreme Court declined further review.[31]

Of this group, Mr. Worthy had traveled to China without a passport, and now he sought to renew his passport. When this was denied, he traveled to Cuba, again without State Department permission. By this time the Department of State had imposed very broad restrictions on the right to travel to Cuba following the breach in diplomatic relations. When Mr. Worthy returned to the United States, he was criminally prosecuted on the ground of entry into the United States without a valid passport. The Fifth Circuit Court of Appeals, which was later to make important contributions to civil rights, held that an American citizen had a right to enter the United States with or without a passport as an incident of his citizenship.[32]

In 1962 Louis Zemel, a businessman, wrote the Department of State that he was interested as an American citizen in studying conditions in Cuba, and requested validation of his passport. Mr. Zemel said that he wished to make a trip "to satisfy my curiosity about the state of affairs in Cuba and to make me a better informed citizen." In this assertion, he had an admirable precedent in the issuance on April 15, 1820, of a passport by John Quincy Adams to Luther Bradish, Esq., "being about to visit different foreign countries with a view of gratifying a commendable curiosity and of obtaining useful information."[33]

When the Department refused, Mr. Zemel instituted a lawsuit which ultimately reached the Supreme Court. In an opinion of Chief Justice Warren, the Court held that the Secretary of State, acting under the foreign affairs power of the President, could refuse to validate passports for travel to Cuba.[34] It noted the existing political situation and the government's claim of the danger of subversion of Latin American countries if travel to Cuba were permitted. Separate dissenting opinions were written by Justices Black, Douglas, and Goldberg. Justice Black's principal point was that the President or the Secretary was engaged in lawmaking, which was the exclusive function of the Congress (compare the contemporary challenge to President Nixon's assertion of the power to wage war). Justice Goldberg made a thorough analysis of the historical practices of the Department of State, concluding that there was no precedent for such a ban and that it was not authorized by the Passport Act of 1926 or any other statute.

Supreme Court decisions are not always the last word, except to lawyers. In 1962 and 1963, groups of American students traveled to Cuba. They had passports, but these were not validated for travel to that country. Upon their return, some of the students were charged with separate conspiracies to depart from the United States for Cuba and then to return without validated passports. After an extended trial, Chief Judge Joseph C. Zavatt, in an exhaustive opinion, found them not guilty.[35] He pointed out that the purpose of the Immigration and Nationality Act of 1952 was to create a system of border control, that is, to require proof of citizenship upon crossing American borders, but not to authorize the State Department to impose restriction on the other countries to which the citizen wished to travel. On appeal, the Supreme Court unanimously agreed that the Immigration Act was not intended to authorize the Secretary of State to impose area restrictions.[36]

The Secretary continued, however, to refuse to issue passports to persons who had traveled to so-called proscribed areas. Three lawsuits were thereupon instituted—one by Staughton Lynd, the political scientist who had traveled to North Vietnam, another by Jane Wittman, who had traveled to Cuba, and one by Dick Gregory, who sought a protective order for proposed travel to North Vietnam. Now a decade after the *Frank, Porter,* and *Worthy* cases, a differently composed Court of Appeals held that American citizens had the right to travel to any part of the world without the approval of the Secretary of State.[37] On the other hand, it held that the government had a proprietary interest in the passport and that the passport could not accompany the traveler to proscribed areas. Since the decision was quite unrealistic, as the Department quickly recognized, it soon withdrew any objection to the traveler's carrying his passport with him.

The executive branch has failed to persuade Congress to give it greater authority. Following *Kent v. Dulles,* President Eisenhower sent an emergency message to Congress requesting legislative authority to impose both political and area controls.[38] The

Senate Foreign Relations Committee held extended hearings, examined the State Department representatives, and consistently refused to report out legislation giving the President such power.[39]

Nevertheless, certain problems of international travel remain. Thus, the American who wishes to travel to Cuba continues to meet with difficulties even if he possesses State Department validation for such travel. He must spend hours, sometimes days, in Mexico City going through the bureaucratic machinery at the Mexican internal security agency before he receives a re-entry permit; it is a rare and favored person whom the American Embassy assists in the matter. The traveler without validation must return to the United States via Europe.

Both types of traveler are photographed at the Mexican airport and have their passports marked "*salida a Cuba*." Upon return to the United States, both encounter minor inconveniences with the United States Immigration Department, such as a cursory interrogation (to which they need not respond), brief delays (which they cannot prevent), and a rather more thorough examination of their luggage by customs.

American travelers returning from Cuba or North Vietnam, with or without permission, have found literature and films either confiscated or temporarily withheld for examination by the customs authorities. Other kinds of products are, of course, banned. There is serious constitutional question as to the right of the government to restrict the importation of literature from any country in the world.[40] As the Supreme Court held in *Lamont v. Postmaster General*,[41] we are dealing here less with the right of the foreign publishing company than with the right of the American people to know the facts. Obviously, such a right is interfered with by restrictions on the right of Americans to travel in order to see what they can for themselves rather than rely upon newspaper reports and State Department broadsides. It is an equally serious restriction to prevent American citizens from reading the publications of foreign countries which are brought in by the American traveler.

Another aspect of this problem is represented by our system of controls over the entry of aliens. The government's power to exclude a Belgian Marxist, Dr. Ernest Mandel, is currently being challenged in court by Mandel and a number of American university professors.

This nation also restricts travel to particular countries by our alien residents. Paralleling the area restrictions upon citizens is a set of regulations under the Immigration and Naturalization Act which absolutely ban the travel of resident aliens to restricted areas.[42] Does the government have power to impose any condition whatsoever upon the status of a resident alien? In one of his masterful articles, Louis Boudin argued for the right of the resident alien as against the sovereign's power,[43] making it clear that when an alien is deprived of his resident status because of a wish to travel to a restricted area, an important question as to governmental power is presented.

III

As already pointed out, the earliest right-to-travel cases involved state laws impeding mobility within the United States. After the unanimous *Edwards* decision in 1941 that struck down a California law prohibiting the movement of indigents into the state, for twenty-five years the Supreme Court did not speak on the general question of interstate travel. *New York v. O'Neill,*[44] the one case that arose during this period, involved a maverick travel issue. The Court there refused to invalidate a state law compelling residents to travel to other states to testify in judicial proceedings when they were subpoenaed, reasoning that a citizen has a legal duty to testify and is free to return to his home state afterward.

But in 1966 the Court substantially added to the protection accorded interstate travel. A civil rights case was the vehicle. After a Georgia jury acquitted individuals charged with the murder of Lemuel A. Penn, a black federal official, the federal government indicted a number of individuals under a statute which punishes conspiracies to injure a citizen in the free exercise "of any right or privilege secured to him by the Constitution or laws of the United States."[45] The indictment stated that one of Penn's rights was that of traveling "freely to and from the State of Georgia and the use of highway facilities and other instrumentalities of interstate commerce." The district court dismissed the indictment. On appeal the Supreme Court reversed, holding that Negroes were entitled under the equal protection clause of the Fourteenth Amendment to the exercise of their right to travel and that the statute applied to those interfering with such travel.[46]

The leading case concerning interstate travel followed soon. In

Shapiro v. Thompson the Court struck down as unconstitutional laws of several states and of the District of Columbia imposing one-year residence requirements upon applicants for public assistance.[47] The states had argued that there was a rational basis for the imposition of such restrictions and that they were supported by a federal statute. The Court held that the differentiation based upon length of residence constituted a discrimination which prima facie violated the equal protection clause. Since it interfered with a constitutional right—the right to travel—the test was not rationality but whether there was a "compelling reason" for the differentiation, and this the Court failed to find.

The broad implications of the decision are revealed by the dissent of Chief Justice Warren, in which he pointed out that the same logic might invalidate state residence requirements for voting, tuition-free education, the practice of professions, and occupational licenses. The majority insisted that it was not passing on these matters, saying that such requirements "may promote compelling state interests on the one hand, or, on the other, may not be penalties upon the exercise of the constitutional right of interstate travel."[48]

Historically, residence requirements for professions, licenses, and occupations have been upheld by the courts.[49] The modern trend, however, is different, and follows Professor Walter Gellhorn's expressed skepticism even as to the rationality of such a provision.[50]

On the other hand, residence requirements for voting, even in recent cases, have been upheld by lower courts, and the Supreme Court has refused to review the issue. The arguments with respect to the importance of preventing election fraud are, in my opinion, as specious as those which have been used to support disqualifications of felons and the requirement that signers of nominating petitions must have registered in the preceding election. The argument that only residents have a knowledgeable interest in the issues is doubtful even in municipal elections and certainly is false in regard to national elections. At least as to the latter, one may safely predict that residence requirements for voting will eventually be invalidated. There is also doubt as to the survival of residence requirements for many occupational and professional licenses, including membership in the bar.

Residence requirements as a basis for lower tuition at state universities is a more difficult problem. A dictum in *Shapiro v. Thompson* casts doubt on these provisions:

Appellants' reasoning would logically permit the State to bar new residents from schools, parks, and libraries or deprive them of police and fire protection. Indeed it would permit the State to apportion all benefits and services according to past tax contributions of its citizens. The Equal Protection Clause prohibits such an apportionment of state services.[51]

The case can also be read more narrowly. The California courts have done so and upheld tuition distinctions based on residence, and the Supreme Court summarily dismissed an appeal.[52] These decisions have been explained both on the ground that "denial of low tuition benefits for a period of time would not be a consideration of such importance as to deter travel" and that there is no evidence that residence distinctions in education were "designed to keep people from settling in the state."[53]

Another constitutional issue has arisen in connection with the residence restrictions incorporated in laws legalizing abortion that recently have been enacted in some states. Although anti-abortion statutes have been declared impermissibly vague,[54] no court has yet recognized a general constitutional right to an abortion. Nevertheless, the right of privacy associated with controlling the use of one's body provides the basis for such a ruling. In this light, residence tests for the availability of abortions are vulnerable as restrictions on the right to travel, much as similar residence tests qualifying the constitutional right to vote, and a court has held Hawaii's law invalid on this basis.[55] The fact that most women entering a state to obtain an abortion presumably do not intend to settle permanently should not lead to a different result, although it might be reasonable, at least for a short period after a law authorizing abortions goes into effect, to give priority to residents pending the availability of new facilities.

Additional problems are presented by the decision in *Shapiro v. Thompson*. One is whether the case applies to inhibitions on *intrastate* travel—such as county residence requirements for holding certain state-wide offices. A perceptive student note points out that the answer to this question might depend upon the nature of the right to travel, despite the Court's statement in *Shapiro* that it had "no occasion to ascribe the source of this right to travel interstate to a particular constitutional provision." Does the right derive from the commerce clause, the nature of national citizenship, the privilege and immunities clause, the due process clause of the First Amendment? If it were solely the commerce clause, then the states might well restrict the right to intrastate travel by imposing county residence requirements.[56]

Another problem is whether congressional action could validate residence requirements. While the Court held that such authorization did not exist in *Shapiro,* it also stated that "it follows from what we have said that the provision, insofar as it permits the one-year waiting-period requirement, would be unconstitutional. Congress may not authorize the States to violate the Equal Protection Clause."[57]

New federal legislation also poses problems under the *Kent* and *Shapiro* cases which will require adjudication by the Supreme Court. The Federal Travel Act makes it a crime to travel in interstate or foreign commerce with the intent to carry on any unlawful activity.[58] There is serious question as to whether a statute of this kind is authorized by the commerce clause. For the effect of such a statute is to enforce state penal laws by federal means, perhaps violating the Tenth Amendment and the concepts of federalism which that Amendment signifies. The statute also presents the question whether the lack of uniformity among the various state laws does not violate the equal protection clause. The Travel Act has been upheld in the lower courts, and the Supreme Court has thus far declined to hear the constitutional attacks.[59]

More dramatic, of course, is the Federal Anti-Riot Act, under which the Chicago Eight were prosecuted and under which several Weathermen groups were subsequently indicted. That statute provides that "[w]hoever travels in interstate or foreign commerce or uses any facility of interstate or foreign commerce . . . with intent to incite a riot" or engage in violations of law incident to a riot is guilty of a felony.[60] The statute finds no precedential support in the Mann Act, for example, which involves the transportation of a woman across a state line for purposes of prostitution; there the very act of travel is characterized by the unlawful carrying of the equivalent of contraband.[61] Similarly, cases under the National Labor Relations Act, which involved the transportation of goods deemed regulable under the commerce clause, are of no help. In the Anti-Riot Act situation, we have travel that is characterized by no unlawful activity; moreover, whatever violation of state law occurs is in a state different from the one in which the alleged illegal intent was formed. One constitutional question is whether the temporal and spacial difference between the intention and the violation of state law does not make the federal crime too incorporeal and, indeed, a naked attempt to offer another forum for the punishment of state crime. In addition, of course, a statute of this kind is suspect because it will tend to discourage travel for purposes of exercising one's First Amendment rights in the states of destination. It must be remembered that the line between riot and public meeting is not always clearly defined, and that the statutory definitions offer no comfort to the would-be traveler.

Since Congress has not yet sought to meet the *Kent* and *Aptheker* requirements of a narrowly drawn statute, it seems unlikely that it will do so in the near future. Accordingly, international travel seems reasonably secure from governmental interference in the absence of a declaration of war, after which the executive branch might refuse to issue passports except to a selected few. On the other hand, we can expect increasingly stringent crime prevention laws in which the federal government will attempt to take full advantage of what it regards as its powers under the interstate commerce clause. It is likely that much of this legislation will be held unconstitutional unless there is a marked change in the character of the Supreme Court or in the situation confronting the country domestically.

NOTES

1. Hanna, "Passports—For Revenue Only," *Atlantic Monthly,* Feb. 1929, at 264–68.
2. W. Blackstone, *Commentaries* *134.
3. Smith v. Turner, 48 U.S. (7 How.) 282 (1849).
4. 73 U.S. (6 Wall.) 35 (1867).
5. 314 U.S. 160, 173, 177, 178 (1941) (emphasis in original).
6. United States Department of State, *The American Passport* (1898).
7. Urtetiqui v. D'Arcy, 34 U.S. (9 Pet.) 692, 698 (1835).
8. United States Department of State, *The Department of State: Its History and Functions* 178–79 (1893), quoting in part from 9 Op. Att'y Gen. 352 (1859).
9. 11 Stat. 60 (1856), *now* 22 U.S.C. §211a.
10. General Instructions in Regard to Passports, Sept. 1, 1873, at 54.
11. 3 Moore, *International Law Digest* 920 (1906) (Fish); 15 Op. Att'y Gen. 114 (1876) (Taft); 23 Op. Att'y Gen. 509 (1901) (Knox).
12. United States Department of State, *supra* note 6.
13. 40 Stat. 559 (1918).
14. 55 Stat. 252 (1941), *repealed,* 66 Stat. 280 (1952), *now in the* Immigration and Nationality Act, 8 U.S.C. §1185(b).

15. Proc. No. 2914, 3 C.F.R. 99 (1949–1953 comp.).

16. *See* Comment, "Passport Refusals for Political Reasons: Constitutional Issues and Judicial Review," 61 *Yale Law Journal* 171 (1952); Comment, "'Passport Denied,' State Department Practice and Due Process," 3 *Stanford Law Review* 312 (1951); Boudin, "The Constitutional Right to Travel," 56 *Columbia Law Review* 47 (1956).

17. 50 U.S.C. §785.

18. *See* Communist Party v. Subversive Activities Control Bd., 367 U.S. 1 (1961).

19. Robeson v. Acheson, 198 F.2d 985 (D.C. Cir. 1952).

20. 106 F. Supp. 445 (D.D.C. 1952).

21. 225 F.2d 938 (D.C. Cir. 1955).

22. *Id.* at 944.

23. 22 C.F.R. §§51.135–51.143 (Aug. 28, 1952) (held unauthorized in the *Kent* case), *superseded by* 22 C.F.R. §§51.70–51.104 (1970).

24. Nathan v. Dulles, 129 F. Supp. 951 (D.D.C. 1955).

25. Dulles v. Nathan, 225 F.2d 29 (D.C. Cir. 1955).

26. *See, e.g.,* 5 U.S.C. §§701–706 (Administrative Procedure Act).

27. 357 U.S. 116 (1958).

28. 357 U.S. 144 (1958).

29. 378 U.S. 500 (1964).

30. Communist Party v. Subversive Activities Control Bd., 367 U.S. 1 (1961).

31. Porter v. Herter, 278 F.2d 280 (D.C. Cir.), *cert. denied,* 364 U.S. 837 (1960); Worthy v. Herter, 270 F.2d 905 (D.C. Cir.), *cert. denied,* 361 U.S. 918 (1959); Frank v. Herter, 269 F.2d 245 (D.C. Cir.), *cert. denied,* 361 U.S. 918 (1959).

32. Worthy v. United States, 328 F.2d 386 (5th Cir. 1964).

33. United States Department of State, *supra* note 6, at 10.

34. Zemel v. Rusk, 381 U.S. 1 (1965).

35. United States v. Laub, 253 F. Supp. 433 (E.D.N.Y. 1966).

36. United States v. Laub, 385 U.S. 475 (1967).

37. Lynd v. Rusk, 389 F.2d 940 (D.C. Cir. 1967).

38. H.R. Doc. No. 417, 85th Cong., 2d Sess. (1958).

39. Hearings on Passport Legislation Before the Senate Committee on Foreign Relations, 85th Cong., 2d Sess. (1958).

40. *Cf.* Teague v. Regional Commissioner of Customs, 404 F.2d 441 (2d Cir. 1968).

41. 381 U.S. 301 (1965).

42. 22 C.F.R. 46.3(k) (1970).

43. Boudin, "The Settler Within Our Gates," 26 *New York University Law Review* 226, 451, 634 (1951).

44. 359 U.S. 1 (1959).

45. 18 U.S.C. §241.

46. United States v. Guest, 383 U.S. 745 (1966).

47. 394 U.S. 618 (1969).

48. *Id.* at 638 n. 21.

49. *See* Note, "Residence Requirements after Shapiro v. Thompson," 70 *Columbia Law Review* 134 (1970).

50. W. Gellhorn, *Individual Freedom and Governmental Restraints* 126 (1956).

51. 394 U.S. at 632–33.

52. Kirk v. Board of Regents of the Univ. of California, 78 Cal. Rptr. 260 (Ct. App. 1969), *appeal dismissed,* 396 U.S. 554 (1970).

53. Note, "Shapiro v. Thompson: Travel, Welfare and the Constitution" 44 *New York University Law Review* 989, 1011–12 (1969).

54. *E.g.,* United States v. Vuitch, 305 F. Supp. 1032 (1969), *prob. juris. postponed,* 397 U.S. 1061 (1970); Belous v. California, 80 Cal. Rptr. 354, 458 P.2d 194 (1969), *cert. denied,* 397 U.S. 915 (1970).

55. Johnston v. Hawaii, 456 P.2d 807 (Haw. 1969), *appeal dismissed,* 397 U.S. 336 (1970).

56. *Op. cit. supra* note 49.

57. Shapiro v. Thompson, 394 U.S. 618, 641 (1969).

58. 18 U.S.C. §1952.

59. Marshall v. United States, 355 F.2d 999 (9th Cir.), *cert. denied,* 385 U.S. 815 (1966). *But see* United States v. Fancher, — F. Supp. — (D.S.D. 1969), *appeal dismissed by consent of the parties pursuant to Rule 60,* 398 U.S. 954 (1970).

60. 18 U.S.C. §2101.

61. 18 U.S.C. §§2421–24.

SECTION IV

Rights Against Government Process

THE RIGHTS OF SUSPECTS

ANTHONY G. AMSTERDAM

THERE IS A WIDESPREAD IMPRESSION THAT DECI-
sions of the Supreme Court of the United States during the past
decade have vastly enlarged the rights of criminal suspects and
defendants. That impression is not wholly unfounded, but the
broad form in which it is generally entertained ignores very significant limitations upon what the Supreme Court can do, and what it
has in fact done, to create and enforce such rights. In this essay, I
would like first to consider the limited role of the Supreme Court in
guaranteeing protections for persons suspected or accused of crime;
second, to make some general observations concerning the Court's
performance in that role during recent years; third, to analyze with
more particularity its performance in one much-discussed area—the
treatment of arrested persons by the police; and finally, to draw
some conclusions for the future.

I. The Limited Role of The Supreme Court in Guaranteeing Rights of Criminal Suspects and Defendants

If we are to believe Pär Lagerkvist's *The Sibyl*, the role of the
Pythia, or priestess of the Oracle at Delphi, was of incomparable

*Anthony G. Amsterdam is Professor of Law at Stanford Law School, a consultant
and litigating attorney for the American Civil Liberties Union, the NAACP Legal
Defense and Educational Fund, and numerous other civil rights organizations. He was
a member of the Cox Commission to Study the 1968 Disturbances at Columbia University, and is currently preparing a comprehensive work on criminal procedure.*

grandeur and futility. This young maiden was periodically lashed to a tripod above a noisome abyss, wherein her God dwelt and from which nauseating odors rose and assaulted her. There the God entered her body and soul, so that she thrashed madly and uttered inspired, incomprehensible cries. The cries were interpreted by the corps of professional priests of the Oracle, and their interpretations were, of course, for mere mortals the words of the God.

The Pythia experienced incalculable ecstasy and degradation; she was viewed with utmost reverence and abhorrence; enormous importance attached to her every utterance; but from the practical point of view, what she said didn't matter much.

On its tripod atop the system of American criminal justice, the Supreme Court of the United States performs in remarkably Pythian fashion. Occasional ill-smelling cases are wafted up to it by the fortuities of litigation, evoking its inspired and spasmodic reaction. Neither the records nor the issues presented by these cases give the Court a comprehensive view—or even a reliably representative view—of the doings in the dark pit in which criminal suspects, police, and the functionaries of the criminal courts wrestle with each other in the sightless ooze. It is not surprising, then, that in these cases the Court should be incapable of announcing judgments which respond coherently to the real problems of the pit.

No matter. For the significance of the Court's pronouncements —their power to shake the assembled faithful with awful tremors of exultation and loathing—does not depend upon their correspondence to reality. Once uttered, these pronouncements will be interpreted by arrays of lower appellate courts, trial judges, magistrates, commissioners, and police officials. *Their* interpretation of the Pythia, for all practical purposes, will become the word of the God.

To some extent, this Pythian metaphor describes the Supreme Court's functioning in all the fields of law with which it deals. But the metaphor has special cogency with regard to the field of criminal procedure, and particularly with regard to the subfield that regulates the rights of suspects in their dealings with the police prior to their first court appearance. Let me explain why this is so, and some of the implications of the fact.

First, the Supreme Court—or any other court—lacks the supervisory power over the practices of the police that is possessed by the chief of police or the district attorney. The Court can only review those practices, and thus can only define the rights of suspects subject to them, when the practices become an issue in a lawsuit.

There are several ways in which police practices may become the subject of a lawsuit. An individual who thinks he has been mistreated by the police may file a civil action for damages, or, in limited circumstances, for an injunction, complaining of false arrest, or false imprisonment, or assault, or the violation of his constitutional rights. But such lawsuits (of which I shall say more later on) are very rare—and until recently were so rare as to be insignificant—because the obstacles to their maintenance are formidable. Most persons mistreated by the police are marginal types who are quite happy, once out of police clutches, to let well enough alone. Few have the knowledge or resources to obtain the services of a lawyer. Many lawyers who might otherwise be available to them cannot afford to tangle with the police, because in other cases these lawyers depend upon the good will of the police (say, to protect a divorce client who is being badgered by her estranged husband, or to reduce charges against a criminal client), or upon police testimony (say, in motor vehicle accident cases), or upon more dubious police services (say, referrals).

Juries are not sympathetic to suits against the police; policemen are seldom sufficiently solvent to make verdicts against them worth the trouble to obtain; even fairly solid citizens who sue policemen may have to fear reprisals in the form of traffic tickets, refusals to give needed aid, and that sort of thing. As a result, civil suits seldom bring police practices under judicial scrutiny. And for reasons too obvious to detail, criminal charges against policemen for mistreatment of citizens are rarer even than civil suits.

So, to date, the Supreme Court has had occasion to review police conduct almost exclusively in criminal cases where the defendant is the asserted victim of police misconduct. The way the issue of police misconduct is presented in such cases almost invariably involves the application of "the exclusionary rule" (of which also I shall say more later)—that is, an evidentiary rule which disallows the admission against a criminal defendant, at his trial, of certain kinds of evidence obtained in violation of his rights. This exclusionary rule, whose scope and use to enforce various constitutional guarantees have been considerably expanded by the Supreme Court in the past decade, is today the principal instrument of judicial control of the police and the principal vehicle for announcement by the courts of the rights of suspects in their dealings with the police.

This last point, in itself, has important implications. Certain police practices (for example, the "booking" and "mugging" of suspects and the assorted minor or major indignities that attend station-house detention, ranging from the taking of a suspect's belt and shoelaces to vicious beatings) will virtually never become the subject of judicial scrutiny, because they virtually never produce evidence against the suspect. Since there can arise no exclusionary-rule challenges to these practices, there have been no significant judicial decisions concerning them; and since (as I shall develop shortly) judicial decisions are almost the only source of legal rights of suspects, suspects do not now have legal rights against or in connection with such practices.

Other police practices (for example, refusing arrested suspects the right to use the phone, or detaining them in pigsty cells) may or may not come under judicial consideration, depending on whether they produce evidentiary consequences (such as a confession). Judicial control of these practices and judicial definition of a suspect's rights in connection with them must remain an imprecise, hit-or-miss business for several reasons. Under the exclusionary rule, judicial attention is focused upon an evidentiary product of the practices (say, again, a confession) rather than upon the practices themselves. The confession will ordinarily be a product of several such practices and of other adventitious circumstances (such as the suspect's age and psychological makeup, or the nature of police interrogation); consequently, a judicial ruling admitting or excluding it will seldom give occasion for a clear-cut pronouncement concerning the legality of any one of the underlying practices. Moreover, because these practices are not themselves the focus of the litigation, they will usually be imperfectly explained and explored in the record made before the courts. Courts which come to pass judgment on them may do so half-sightedly; or, realizing this danger, the courts may strive to avoid passing judgment upon practices that they know they do not understand. The result, once again, is that courts are unable to speak clearly concerning any particular or specific rights of a criminal suspect. Still less are they able to develop systematically any comprehensive canon or register of suspects' rights, in the context of the entire range of police practices that affect the suspect.

Second, the Supreme Court of the United States is uniquely unable to take a comprehensive view of the subject of suspects' rights. Its inability is, in part, simply a consequence of its work load. Saddled with a backbreaking docket, properly occupied with other matters of grave national importance, the Court can hear only three or four cases a year involving the treatment of criminal suspects by the police.

But work load is not the Court's only problem. I have said earlier that fortuities determine which criminal cases reach the Supreme Court. Because police practices are ordinarily challengeable only through the exclusionary rule, and because this rule ordinarily comes into play only at trial following a plea of not guilty, police treatment of a suspect is effectively insulated against Supreme Court review in that large percentage of criminal cases (80 to 90 percent of all convictions) that are terminated by a guilty plea.

Guilty pleas may be entered for many reasons in cases that involve serious questions of violations of a suspect's rights in the precourt phases. The arguable violations may have had no evidentiary consequences, or the prosecution may have sufficient evidence for conviction apart from that obtained through the arguable violations. The defendant may be detained pending trial in default of bail on a charge for which a probationary or "time-served" sentence[1] is expectable, so that he will be imprisoned longer awaiting trial on a plea of not guilty than he would on a quick guilty plea. The prosecutor may offer an attractive plea bargain, that is, sentencing consideration for a guilty plea; or the known sentencing practices of the trial judge may promise similar consideration. Obviously, these factors do not operate systematically to send to trial a selection of cases which present the courts with any comprehensive set of issues relative to suspects' rights.

Even among cases tried on a not-guilty plea, most are not appealed, or are not carried through to the level of the Supreme Court of the United States, owing to additional selective factors. Factual findings by the trial judge concerning contested police conduct frequently obscure or entirely obstruct the presentation to appellate courts of issues relating to that conduct. A convicted defendant cannot challenge on appeal any treatment by the police that the trial court, crediting incredible police denials, finds did not occur. (For example, suspects invariably "trip" and strike their heads while entering their cells; they are never shoved against the bars by police.) Or the trial court may admit the police conduct, but credit incredible explanations of it. (For example, the humiliating anal examinations to which certain suspects are routinely subjected in some police stations are invariably justified as "weapons searches" on police testimony that such suspects are known to conceal razor blades between their cheeks.) Or the trial court may admit and resolve against the defendant an issue relating to the legality of police conduct, then sentence him so lightly that an appeal is not worthwhile. (Some trial judges are notorious for imposing light sentences in cases where they have made dubious evidentiary rulings, thereby "buying off" appeals.) In any event, the presentation of a convicted defendant's appeal—still more, the taking of his case to the Supreme Court—depends upon the energy, dedication, and painstaking care of his lawyer, commodities understandably scarce on the part of overworked public defenders or private lawyers conscripted without compensation to represent the indigents who constitute the majority of convicted persons.

For these reasons, the Supreme Court simply never gets to see many sorts of police practices that raise the most pervasive and significant issues of suspects' rights. The cases which do come to the Court are selected by a process that can only be described as capricious insofar as it may be relied upon to present the Court any opportunity for systematic development of a body of legal rights of individuals in the police, or precourt, phases of criminal proceedings. The Court's ability, therefore, to serve as architect of such a body of rights—advisedly to consider and to promulgate a coherent, comprehensive code of suspects' rights—is woefully slight.

Third, the Court is further disabled by the circumstance that almost the only law relating to police practices or to suspects' rights is the law that the Court itself makes by its judicial decisions. Statutes and administrative regulations governing these matters are scarce as hen's teeth. The ubiquitous lack of legislative and executive attention to the problems of police treatment of suspects both forces the Court into the role of lawmaker in this area and makes it virtually impossible for it to play that role effectively.

This point has been largely ignored by the Court's conservative critics. The judicial "activism" that they deplore—usually citing the Court's "handcuffing" of the police—has been the almost inevitable consequence of the failure of other law-making agencies to assume responsibility for regulating police practices. In most areas of constitutional law, the Supreme Court of the United States plays a backstop role, reviewing the ultimate permissibility of dispositions and policies guided in the first instance—and for the major part satisfactorily—by legislative enactments, administrative rules, or local common-law traditions. In the area of controls upon the police, a vast abnegation of responsibility at the level of each of these ordinary sources of legal rule-making has forced the Court to construct *all* the law regulating the day-to-day functioning of the police. Of course the Court has responded by being "activist"; it has had to. And of course its decisions have seemed wildly "liberal," since the only other body of principles operating in the field, against which the Court's principles may be measured, are those under which individual policemen act in the absence of any legal restraint.

The subconstitutional lawlessness that pervades the field of suspects' rights occasions my initial concentration, in this essay, upon the doings of the Supreme Court, and I shall return to larger implications of the point in my concluding section. There I shall state that meaningful development of the rights of suspects in the seventies will require the assumption of responsibility for protecting those rights by administrative processes, and that the Court's role can only be to stimulate or perhaps even to compel such an assumption of responsibility. At this juncture, I want to make a different and more limited point: that the same subconstitutional lawlessness which forces the Court to act also prevents it from acting very effectively in this area.

When the Court reviews the operation of legislation, or of administrative regulations, or of common-law rules governing, for example, criminal trial procedure, its consideration of the constitutional issues raised is informed and greatly assisted by the very fact that it *is* legislation or a regulation or a *rule* of some sort that is in question. Because the rule is articulated in more or less general terms, its contour is more or less visible, its relations and interactions with other rules are more or less perceptible, and some of the judgments and policies that underlie or oppose its acceptance are more or less graspable. But when the Court reviews conduct, such as police conduct, that is essentially ruleless, it is seriously impeded in understanding the nature, purposes, and effects of what it is reviewing. Its view of the questioned conduct is limited to the appearance of the conduct on a particular trial record or records—records which, as I have said earlier, may not even isolate or focus precisely upon that conduct. The Court cannot know whether the conduct before it is idiosyncratic or general, typical or atypical, unconnected or connected with a set of other practices—or if there is some connection, what is the comprehensive shape of the set of practices involved, what are their relations, their justifications, their consequences.

Operating thus darkly, the Court is obviously deprived of the ability to make any coherent response to, or to develop any organized regulation of, the conduct confronting it. Nor can the Court predict or understand the implications of any rule of constitutional law that it may itself project into this well of shadows. If it announces a decision striking down or modifying, for example, some rule of criminal trial practice, it can fairly well foresee what a trial is going to look like following its decision, since the decision will operate within a system governed by other visible and predictable rules. But if it strikes down a police practice, announces a "right" of a criminal suspect in his dealings with the police, God only knows what the result will be. Out there in the formless void, some adjustment will doubtless be made to accommodate the new "right," but what the product of this whole exercise will be remains unfathomable. So, again, the Court is effectively disarmed.

Fourth, if the Supreme Court ventures to announce some constitutional right of a suspect, that "right" filters down to the level of flesh-and-blood suspects only through the refracting layers of lower courts, trial judges, magistrates, and police officials. All pronouncements of the Supreme Court undergo this filtering process, but in few other areas of law are the filters as opaque as in the area of suspects' rights.

Let there be no mistake about it. To a mind-staggering extent—to an extent that conservatives and liberals alike who are not criminal trial lawyers simply cannot conceive—the entire system of criminal justice below the level of the Supreme Court of the United States is solidly massed against the criminal suspect. A few appellate judges, a very few, can throw off the fetters of their middle-class backgrounds—the dimly remembered, friendly face of the school-crossing guard, their fear of a crowd of "toughs," the attitudes engendered, before their elevation to the bench, by years of service as prosecutors or as private lawyers for honest, respectable business clients—and identify with the criminal suspect instead of with the policeman or the putative victim of the suspect's theft, mugging, rape, or murder. Trial judges still more, and magistrates beyond all belief, are functionally and psychologically allied with the police, their co-workers in the unending and scarifying work of bringing criminals to book.

The trial-court judges and magistrates whose attitudes I describe are the human beings that find the "facts" when cases involving suspects' rights go into court (that is, when police treatment of a suspect is not conclusively masked behind a guilty plea or ignored by a defense lawyer too overworked or undercompensated to develop the issues adequately). Their factual findings resolve the inevitable conflict between the testimony of the police and that of the suspect—usually a down-and-outer or a bad type, and often a man with a record. The result is about what one would expect. Even when the cases go to court, a suspect's rights as announced by the Supreme Court are something he has, not something he gets.

But of course, for reasons I have mentioned above, most cases do not go to court. In these cases, the "rights" of the suspect are defined by how the police are willing to treat him. With regard to treatment that has no evidentiary consequences and hence will not be judicially reviewable in exclusionary-rule proceedings, the police have no particular reason to obey the law, even if the Supreme Court has had occasion to announce it. With regard to police practices that may have evidentiary consequences, the police are motivated to obey the law only to the extent that (1) they are more concerned with securing a conviction than with some other police purpose served by disobeying the law (in this connection, it is worth note that police departments almost invariably measure their own efficiency in terms of "clearances by arrest," not by conviction), and that (2) they think they can secure the evidence necessary for conviction within the law.

Police work is hard work; it is righteous work; it is combative work, and competitive. Policemen are undereducated, they are scandalously underpaid, and their personal advancement lies in producing results according to the standards of the police ethic. When they go to the commander's office or to court, their performance according to this ethic is almost always vindicated. Neither their superiors nor the judges whom they know nor the public finds it necessary to impede the performance of their duties with fettering rules respecting rights of suspects. If the Supreme Court finds this necessary, it must be that the Court is out of step. So its decisions—which are difficult to understand anyway—cannot really be taken seriously.

This concludes my observations concerning the Supreme Court's power to guarantee rights of criminal suspects in any other than an unworldly sense. The idealist would conclude from what I have said that the priests surrounding the Pythia are unfaithful to their priesthood. The cynic would conclude that the whole damned system is corrupt. I let such judgments go, and conclude only that

Supreme Court power to enlarge the rights of suspects is very, very
limited.

II. An Overview of Supreme Court Decisions
Announcing Suspects' and Defendants'
Rights in the Past Decade

By what I have said so far, I do not mean to suggest that Supreme
Court decisions respecting suspects' and defendants' rights are unimportant. Like the Pythia's cries, they have vast mystical significance. They state our aspirations. They give a few good priests
something to work with. They give some of the faithful the courage
to carry on, and reason to improve the priesthood instead of tearing
down the temple.

And they have *some* practical significance. With the Pythia
shrieking underground, the priests may pervert the word of the
God but they cannot ignore it entirely, nor entirely silence those
who offer interpretations different from their own. Indeed, fear lest
these alternative explanations gain popular support may cause the
priests to bend a little in their direction.

So it is worth the effort to examine what the Supreme Court has
pronounced concerning suspects' and defendants' rights during the
past decade. In this section, I conduct such an examination for the
purpose of showing that—even in this airy sphere of legal doctrine
—the impression that the Court has vastly expanded such rights
requires qualification in the present, and a guarded prognosis for
the future.

I have three theses here. (1) The Supreme Court has unquestionably expanded the litany of rights of individuals in the criminal
process. It has done so almost exclusively by adding to the register
of constitutional guarantees—the sources or potential seedbeds of
specific rights—which the individual may invoke, and by broaden-
ing the procedural devices through which he may invoke them. But
as regards the substance and the content of the guarantees, the
specific rights vouchsafed in particular situations, the Court has not
been expansive. Its line and style of march have therefore left a lot
of room for back-marching. (2) The Court has avoided announcing
broad and impermeable doctrines protective of criminal suspects
and defendants. It has, indeed, overruled some hoary old doctrines
of this sort. The protective rules that it has announced are flexible,

particularistic, accommodative, and commonsensical. Even in the hands of the Warren Court, these doctrines allowed considerable weight to be given to the interests of law enforcement. In the hands of the Burger Court, they may become instruments for the invariable preference of law enforcement interests over those of the criminal suspect or defendant. (3) The Court has recently displayed a tendency to use a new form of constitutional adjudication in this area: one permitting legislative and perhaps executive retraction of the scope of constitutional rights that it has declared.

First, it is entirely plain that Supreme Court decisions in the late 1950's and the 1960's did add significantly to the rights of criminal suspects and defendants, particularly in state as distinguished from federal criminal trials. These decisions have, in one aspect, a remarkable sameness. Almost invariably, they involve the transposition of basic constitutional guarantees into entirely new areas, that is, the recognition of the applicability of constitutional rights to fields where such rights had not previously been recognized. It is precisely the *wholesale* character of the Court's work—its establishment of whole new stores and stocks of rights in new locations —that has created the impression of rapid and enormous constitutional development favoring the criminal accused, and the attendant public clamor. Neither the development nor the clamor is much concerned with the quality of the merchandise sold at the new locations.

It seems to me that virtually all of the Court's decisions extending individual rights in the criminal process have had this wholesale quality. The most obvious example, of course, is the line of cases in which the Court has "incorporated," one by one, the criminal procedure guarantees of the Bill of Rights into the due process clause of the Fourteenth Amendment, so as to make these guarantees—originally written to govern only federal criminal proceedings —applicable also to state proceedings. The celebrated *Mapp* and *Gideon* cases are milestones in this line, which has now so far progressed that every significant guarantee of the Bill of Rights except the right to bail (whose "incorporation" remains an open question) is vouchsafed to state criminal defendants.[2] Another example is the application of the equal protection clause of the Fourteenth Amendment as a guarantor to poor criminal defendants of the same opportunities to defend, and the same general level of assistance in defending, that a defendant with means can purchase.[3] Still other examples are the application of constitutional criminal procedure guarantees to juvenile delinquency proceedings,[4] the application of criminal search warrant guarantees to "administrative" searches,[5] and the application of the right to counsel beyond the trial stage of criminal proceedings—first to pretrial judicial proceedings[6] and then to precourt police proceedings.[7]

These decisions assuredly do give the criminal defendant, particularly the state criminal defendant, a plethora of new constitutional clauses to invoke. And the Court has also done a lot, within the past decade, to facilitate their invocation. It is only one significant aspect of the "constitutionalizing" or "federalizing" of a defendant's rights—say, by the "incorporation" of a Bill of Rights guarantee such as the right of confrontation—that the substantive law relating to questions of confrontation is governed by the Supreme Court decisions construing the Sixth Amendment. Such decisions may be more liberal than state law rules (for example, a state constitutional guarantee of the right of confrontation, or state common-law hearsay rules) which operate in the same area. To the extent that they are more liberal, the defendant's rights have been enlarged by the "federalizing" exercise. But even where they are not more liberal, his rights have ordinarily been enlarged in several significant ways. Since substantive questions concerning confrontation are now questions of federal law, ancillary issues (such as the vital question of "waiver" of the right) are also governed by federal law; state procedures for trying the substantive and ancillary issues are regulated by federal law; and perhaps most important, claims of error by the state courts in resolving any of these issues may be taken into the federal courts in habeas corpus proceedings following state court conviction and state court appeals.

In all of these matters, the Supreme Court has recently enhanced the ability of state criminal defendants (and of federal criminal defendants as well) to claim the protection of constitutional guarantees: it has announced some very strict standards for "waiver" of the guarantees;[8] it has improved the fairness of procedures for trying issues relative to the guarantees;[9] and it has both broadened the scope of issues raisable, and improved the fairness of procedures for trying the issues, in federal habeas corpus.[10]

When it comes to the *content* of the constitutional guarantees, however, the Court has not been similarly progressive. All the new outlets have been stocked with relatively old merchandise. None of the decisions cited above "incorporating" Bill of Rights guarantees involved any substantive liberalization of what was guaranteed. To the contrary, when the Court incorporated the right to jury trial in *Duncan v. Louisiana,* it plainly hinted at a willingness to cut back on old Sixth Amendment decisions, such as those requiring a twelve-man jury;[11] and when it required a search warrant for administrative searches in *Camara v. Municipal Court,* it substantially watered down the showing needed to obtain a warrant.[12]

In a sense, the Court's equal protection decisions have been even more revealing of its reluctance to push its newly recognized constitutional guarantees very far. The initial application of the equal protection clause to the indigent criminal defendant, in *Griffin v. Illinois,* was accompanied by the sounding pronouncement that "There can be no equal justice where the kind of trial a man gets depends on the amount of money he has."[13] That proposition has implications which would shake the American system of criminal justice to its foundations; but in the fourteen years since *Griffin,* the Court has done nothing with it except to require free transcripts, waiver of filing fees, and appointment of appellate counsel for indigents.[14]

Indeed, a broad survey of the Supreme Court's decisions giving content to the criminal procedure guarantees of the Constitution during the past decade discloses nothing resembling the popularly supposed Mad March to Liberalism. The Court has advanced a little here, retreated a little there, and generally held the line. Take its Fourth Amendment search-and-seizure decisions. Most of those that have recently vindicated defendants' Fourth Amendment claims— requiring a warrant to search a dwelling, insisting that such a warrant cannot be issued on the basis of conclusory, boiler-plate affidavits, disallowing warrantless searches upon equivocal showings of "consent" of the dweller—are rather old stuff: post-*Mapp* reflections in state criminal cases of doctrines long and solidly settled in federal cases.[15] The Court has, it is true, extended Fourth Amendment protections in a few areas. It has overruled the nefarious *Olmstead* case, and thereby subjected wiretapping and electronic eavesdropping to the warrant requirement.[16] It has taken back a good deal of the authorization lent by the *Rabinowitz* case to warrantless searches "incident to arrest."[17] But neither of these developments was very surprising: both *Olmstead* and *Rabinowitz* had been for many years in visible disfavor and bound for overruling.

On the other hand, the Court has delivered some notably regressive Fourth Amendment decisions. It has flatly declined to apply the Amendment as a limitation upon police espionage.[18] In 1967, it disavowed a requirement, which lower courts in increasing numbers had drawn from its earlier decisions, that a defendant who challenged a warrantless arrest be given disclosure, in court, of the name of any confidential informant upon whom the arresting officer had purportedly relied for the "probable cause" necessary to justify such an arrest.[19] In the same year, it sustained a warrantless police "inventory" search, in an opinion which (1) resuscitates the theory—progressively discredited in a series of decisions by the Court since 1950—that warrantless searches may be constitutionally validated if they are, in some broad and vague sense, "reasonable,"[20] and (2) holds, incredibly, that such searches may be "reasonable" even where they are entirely without legal authorization.[21] Another double-header in the same year (1) overrules the antique doctrine forbidding governmental seizure of "mere evidence" of crime, and (2), for the first time in the history of the Court, gives the support of a holding to the proposition (previously announced in some loose dicta) that a dwelling may be searched without a warrant where "exigent circumstances" make it impracticable to obtain one.[22] And in 1969, the Court "dismissed rather quickly" a Fourth Amendment contention whose solidity and importance it seems not to have appreciated in the least: the contention that one cotenant's constitutional right against warrantless search of his property cannot be abrogated by the consent of another cotenant.[23]

The Court's Fifth Amendment decisions demonstrate the same quality of holding the line. Its application of the privilege against self-incrimination to protect the suspect in the police station, in its celebrated *Miranda* decision,[24] does confirm a broad extension of the privilege—although one that is not so newfangled as many appear to believe.[25] (I shall say more about *Miranda* in the following section.) On the other hand, the Court in *Schmerber v. California*[26] sustained involuntary blood-taking against Fifth Amendment objection, limiting the privilege to "testimonial" extractions in accordance with the theories of John Henry Wigmore, archenemy of the amendment.[27] And unless I misread the implications of a 1964 decision of the Court, its extension of the Fifth Amendment to the states was accompanied by the quiet subversion of an ancient and therefore unquestioned tenet of the jurisprudence of self-incrimination: that the privilege entirely insulates a suspect from being required to give incriminating responses; it does not merely shield him from the incriminating *use* of those responses.[28]

Second, the Court has eschewed the announcement of broad and inflexible rules protective of the criminal suspect, and has instead developed conceptions of the relevant constitutional guarantees that apply them flexibly and particularistically to the circumstances of individual cases. It has taken what the Justices doubtless believe to be a common-sense, nondoctrinaire approach to the Fourth and Fifth Amendments. I have already mentioned cases that provide several instances of this approach: the holdings which require a warrant for administrative searches but permit the relatively indiscriminate issuance of such warrants;[29] which require warrants for electronic surveillance but do not find that the dragnet nature of such surveillance per se precludes the drafting of warrants sufficiently specific to meet constitutional standards;[30] which insist upon a warrant as the precondition of valid search of a dwelling, *unless* there is no time to obtain one;[31] which refuse to find that any class of objects is, as such, constitutionally immune against search or seizure, so long as the search and seizure are made under a warrant or otherwise reasonably;[32] and which permit the extraction of incriminating information from a suspect but protect him against its incriminating use.[33] Other examples of this style of constitutional jurisprudence are also notable: the subjection of police "stop-and-frisk" practice to constitutional restraint, but its release from the exacting restraint of a requirement of "probable cause";[34] some, but limited, expansions of the notions of "standing" and "taint" in connection with challenges to unconstitutionally obtained evidence.[35] But perhaps the most striking example of the style is the *Schmerber* case,[36] whose archetypal character deserves a further word.

Schmerber, as I have said, involves the involuntary extraction of blood from a criminal suspect for purposes of chemical analysis. In dealing with this practice, the Court first holds that blood-taking falls outside the ambit of the Fifth Amendment, because blood is not a "testimonial" communication. Blood-taking is, however, a "search" or "seizure," subject to Fourth Amendment restraints. This choice to apply the Fourth rather than the Fifth Amendment is critical: it implies constitutional regulation of blood-taking instead of its prohibition; for whereas the Fifth Amendment entirely precludes incriminating extractions without regard to their circumstances or manner, the effect of the Fourth Amendment is merely to insist that the circumstances and manner of the extraction be reasonable.

Coming to the question what is "reasonable" in this connection, the Court again takes a flexible approach. It first points out that searches *into* the body are more intrusive than searches *of* the body and therefore require greater justification. (This notion that the Fourth Amendment requires increasing degrees of justification for increasing degrees of intrusiveness of searches and seizures lays the foundation for the Court's subsequent validation of stop-and-frisk without probable cause in the *Terry* and *Sibron* cases.[37]) Thus, while warrantless search of an accused's pockets incident to his arrest is permissible,[38] searches that breach the body wall of an arrested person may ordinarily be made only with a warrant. *However,* warrants need not be obtained if there is no time to get one,[39] as where the dissolution of blood alcohol is imminent. So the taking of Schmerber's blood without a warrant was reasonable. But, says the Court, such a taking must be reasonable in manner as well as in justification. Body searches that involve undue pain, danger of infection, or embarrassment may, for those reasons, violate the Fourth Amendment. In Schmerber's case, the blood-taking met these requirements, since it was done by medical personnel in a medical environment. *Schmerber,* I suggest, represents a studiedly practical, flexible, common-sense, nondogmatic approach to problems of suspects' rights; and it typifies the Court's approach during the past decade.

Third, in a related, very recent development, the Court has begun to couch its constitutional holdings in terms that permit— indeed, invite—legislative or executive retraction of the rights declared in the holdings. The reasons for this development are unclear and may be several. It is consistent with the practical mode of adjudication just described to recognize and hence to solicit legislative or responsible executive resolution of particular problems regarding suspects' rights. The Court may well be feeling, and attempting to remedy, the difficulties that a long-time subconstitutional lawlessness has posed for its own lawmaking in this area (see Part I, above). Probably, also, the Court is simply tired of its role as solitary lawmaker and is asking for some help. Its suspects' rights decisions have been greeted by considerable popular decrial; such decrial counsels caution but provides little guidance; by inviting legislation into the area, the Court may be attempting to sound out the strength and direction of public feeling and to reduce it to a form that does provide guidance.

But whatever its reasons, the Court plainly has taken lately to issuing invitations for legislatures, and perhaps for executive policy-makers, to curb some of its decisions. In its first serious attempt at contitutional regulation of electronic surveillance, a 1967 decision,[40] the Court took the approach—unprecedented in the area of suspects' rights but long used and useful in other constitutional areas as a means of passing the buck back to the legislature—of reviewing the facial constitutionality of a New York surveillance statute. The Court's criticism of that statute pointed the way to congressional authorization of wiretapping and electronic eavesdropping, under defined procedures, in Title III of the Omnibus Crime Control and Safe Streets Act of 1968.[41] Previously, in *Miranda v. Arizona,* the Court had announced a set of procedures that were to be required in the taking of suspects' confessions by the police, *"unless* other fully effective means are devised to inform accused persons of their right of silence and to assure a continuous opportunity to exercise it."[42] This invitation too was taken up—and apparently abused—by Congress in the 1968 Act, which purports to replace the *Miranda* procedures in federal criminal cases with another means of protecting the right of silence: namely, the traditional pre-*Miranda* inquiry into the voluntariness of confessions.[43] (It remains to be seen whether this congressional dodge will satisfy the Court.) Once again, in 1969, while condemning arrests without probable cause for the purpose of fingerprinting suspects, the Court suggested that the Fourth Amendment might well tolerate "narrowly circumscribed procedures for obtaining, during the course of a criminal investigation, the fingerprints of individuals for whom there is no probable cause to arrest."[44] Not unexpectedly, Senator McClellan has recently put a responsive bill in the hopper.[45]

The three points that I have made in this section imply a lugubrious prognosis for the advancement of suspects' and defendants' rights by judicial decisions in the near future. The advances of the recent past have been engineered through a wholesaling process that has created more the possibility of rights (and the appearance of rights) than actual rights. Such a line of advance would plainly have peaked out in the 1970's, even without any change in Supreme Court personnel. This is so because the Court, by 1969, had just about run out of big new constitutional guarantees to proclaim (excepting, again, the bail right). Further advance would require a different approach—the giving of expansive content to the guarantees—and the Court has shown no consistent disposition in that direction.

But of course, an added effect of the Court's wholesaling in the field of suspects' rights has been, by creating the appearance of enormous constitutional development, to arouse a reaction against "coddling criminals" and a consequent demand for Justices who are "strict constructionists." Mr. Nixon obviously feels this demand keenly, and has told us that he intends to fill the Burger Court with Justices of the sort. It is they who will assume the work of giving content to the guarantees pronounced by the Warren Court. These guarantees are for the most part undeveloped, and where developed, are not very liberally developed. If the Warren Court's few liberal decisions dealing with the content of the guarantees had been more doctrinal and less particularistic, they might have confronted the new Justices, the "strict constructionists," with something of a dilemma: the choice of evils between overruling past decisions (that is, the liberal decisions) or following them to liberal results. But the Warren Court's development of a highly particularistic and accommodative approach to deciding cases under the guarantees leaves the "strict constructionists" ample room to reach conservative substantive results consistent with the jurisprudential conservatism of *stare decisis*.

Even as applied by the Warren Court, these flexible and particularistic approaches frequently preferred the asserted interests of law enforcement to those of individuals suspected of crime. Probably no pragmatic calculus, in our time, could do otherwise. In the hands of the Justices whom Mr. Nixon appoints, the doctrines will surely tend to prefer law enforcement interests in an increased number and range of situations—perhaps (but I hope not) invariably. The impact of the legislation that the Court has latterly invited into the area is likely to support that tendency.

III. SUPREME COURT DECISIONS AND THE RIGHTS OF THE SUSPECT IN THE STATION HOUSE

It will be useful now to focus briefly upon one particular area of a suspect's rights: those relating to his treatment by the police following arrest and prior to his first court appearance. It is in this area that the Supreme Court has handed down the decisions, particularly the *Miranda* decision, that have gone furthest in protecting the suspect—indefensibly far, in the view of many critics of the Court. But, for reasons that emerge from what I have said in the two preceding parts, I conclude: (1) that the Court neither has succeeded nor can succeed in providing adequate protections for the suspect in the station house; (2) that its protective decisions are quite justified, so far as they go; but (3) that they do not go far enough, and, for failure to go far enough, may be self-defeating.

First, the Court has been seriously engaged in the business of protecting arrested persons from abusive conduct by the police for about thirty-five years.[46] During this time, all of its relevant decisions have come in the context of questions raised by the exclusionary rule: that is, questions relating to the admissibility of evidence obtained by the police from the suspect during the post-arrest, precourt period.[47] Until a year or so ago, all of its cases concerned the admissibility of confessions.[48] During the past few years, the Court has also dealt with the admissibility of fingerprint evidence and lineup or "showup" identifications.[49]

As I said in Part I above, such exclusionary rule decisions cannot serve—and the Court's decisions have not served—to establish any comprehensive set of suspects' rights following arrest, or even clearly to define particular rights of suspects in connection with their post-arrest processing by the police. Coherent regulation of police processing of arrested persons would involve consideration of such matters as "booking" and "mugging" practices, record-keeping incidental to arrest and to these practices, the confiscation of personal effects of the arrestee, the conditions and duration of his detention, the circumstances and limitations of the permissible use of force against him, his access to means of communication, the availability of medical treatment, and his treatment under special circumstances (inebriation, for example). The Court has never dealt distinctly with any of these matters. So far as its decisions are concerned, it is impossible to define a suspect's rights in any of these regards. Most of the relevant police practices have never been discussed by the Court. Those that have been were discussed only in terms of their products—ordinarily, confessions. The simplest questions regarding specific rights of suspects in the station house therefore remain unresolved. For example, even after *Miranda,* one cannot say that an arrested person has a right to phone a lawyer. One can only say that if the police obtain a confession from him after he has been refused the chance to call a lawyer (and if he can prove it), his confession will be inadmissible in evidence. Obviously, then, the Court's decisions do and must fall very far short of giving the suspect adequate protections, or "rights," following arrest.

Second, consideration of the course of the Court's confession decisions is comprehensible in the context of the institutional realities that I described in Part I. Prior to Supreme Court announcement of a federal constitutional rule excluding involuntary confessions from evidence in state criminal cases, there had been a common-law evidentiary rule that purported to exclude such confessions. Administration of this rule was in the hands of state court judges; and in view of their usual attitudes regarding persons charged with crime, it was not surprising that they sustained the admission into evidence of confessions obtained under some pretty shocking circumstances. *Brown v. Mississippi*,[50] which reached the Supreme Court in 1936, was a horror case: the defendants had been so badly treated by the police that one of them appeared in court still bearing on his neck the rope marks that resulted when he was strung up to obtain his "voluntary" confession. This was a bit too strong for the Justices, who consequently held that the *Brown* defendants had been denied due process of law.

Admittedly, there was no very obvious theoretical ground for this holding. The Fifth Amendment to the Constitution forbade compulsory self-incrimination; but that Amendment applied only to federal criminal proceedings; its "incorporation" into the due process clause of the Fourteenth Amendment, and the more general principle requiring that state courts exclude evidence obtained in violation of the Constitution, were of a much later era. It was far from evident, in 1936, why the due process clause required anything more of state criminal proceedings than a regular and fair trial, giving the defendant a regular and fair opportunity to contest his guilt under state evidentiary rules, including the rule which the Supreme Court of Mississippi held allowed admission of the *Brown* confessions.

Yet the Supreme Court of the United States must have perceived that beneath the regularity of its forms the *Brown* trial was a pious charade. The defendants were plainly going to be found guilty if their confessions were admitted into evidence; their guilt was established, not by the trial, but by hanging them up and whipping them until they confessed; and this whole procedure was "revolting to the sense of justice."[51] So the convictions were reversed.

What followed was dictated less by the logic of *Brown* than by the refusal of the state courts to honor *Brown*. Once the Supreme Court had rendered its decision that a coerced confession was federally inadmissible, it obviously had some interest in seeing to it that the decision and the Court were not tweaked by the nose.

During the years after *Brown,* the state courts generally persisted in admitting confessions extracted by third-degree practices; the Court obviously saw that its *Brown* decision was being treated uncharitably, and it reversed these convictions as well. In numerous cases, the defendant told a credible story of physical abuse by the police, but the trial judge discredited it. Since the Supreme Court does not admit to reviewing findings of credibility, it discovered other bases for reversal in the uncontested facts of those cases. Thus, *Brown* was extended from cases involving admitted physical brutality to those admittedly involving prolonged "grilling," mob intimidation, etc.

As the chain of reversals lengthened, the lower courts responded by invariably finding all the relevant facts against the defendants. No longer could they risk admitting confessions concededly extracted by brutality or other coercive pressures, so they found that the pressures did not exist. Time and again, cases came before the Supreme Court in which the defendant testified that he had been abused in the police station, the police denied it, and the trial court believed the police. *Brown* was palpably being evaded in at least some of these cases, and there was little that the Supreme Court could do about it.

In 1943, it found a device for dealing with this problem, at least in federal criminal cases. The defendants in *McNabb v. United States*[52] were subjected to a prolonged postarrest detention and interrogation, as a result of which they confessed. The Court, without reaching the question whether the confessions were involuntary, held them inadmissible. For, it said, the protracted detentions violated the command of a federal statute that arrested persons be promptly taken before a magistrate. The purpose of this procedural requirement was said to be to check "resort to those reprehensible practices known as the 'third degree' ";[53] and since the Court had ample power, in a federal criminal case, to fashion exclusionary rules on nonconstitutional grounds, it held that confessions obtained during detention in violation of the statute should not be received in evidence.

Actually, both the Court's construction of the statute and its statement of the statute's purposes were questionable. But the kind of detention it conveniently found that the statute forbade was indeed the spawning ground of the third degree; experience had shown that such detention created conditions in which coercive police practices were both likely to occur and almost impossible for a defendant to prove to the satisfaction of a trial judge; and the Court in *McNabb* decided, once and for all, to put the question of admissibility of confessions, in federal criminal cases, beyond the reach of trial court resolution of the inevitable swearing contest between the suspect and the police.

The lower federal judges did not take *McNabb* at its word. They could not believe that the Supreme Court had meant to hold a confession inadmissible on the sole ground that it had been made during prolonged detention. So they insisted that, to support exclusion, a defendant must show a causal connection between the detention and his confession. The demanded causal connection usually amounted to a showing of coercion; thus, *McNabb* was effectively nullified. After some equivocation, the Supreme Court finally enforced *NcNabb* according to its terms and purposes. In its *Mallory* decision[54] in 1957, it declared crisply and definitively that any confession made during a period of unnecessary delay in taking an arrested person before a magistrate was *eo ipso* inadmissible in a federal criminal trial.

But the *McNabb-Mallory* rule did not solve the major problem: state criminal cases. It could not be applied in state cases, for two reasons. There was no ostensible provision of federal law forbidding prolonged postarrest detention of suspects by state officers. And in any event, there was no general principle requiring the state courts to exclude evidence obtained in violation of federal law; to the contrary, *Wolf v. Colorado*[55] permitted them to use such evidence. Yet as the Court continued to wrestle with state confession cases, presenting monotonous swearing contests between police and defendants, and monotonous resolutions of those contests by state trial judges in favor of the police, the need for something like a *McNabb-Mallory* rule to govern state cases was apparent.

In the early 1960's, doctrinal developments in nonconfession cases gave the Court a handle on the problem. *Wolf* was overruled in *Mapp v. Ohio*,[56] which required the state courts to exclude evidence obtained by unconstitutional searches and seizures. *Gideon v. Wainwright*[57] held the Sixth Amendment right to counsel applicable to the states. It now remained only to hold that the right to counsel applied in the station house, and that evidence—that is, confessions—obtained in violation of that right fell within the exclusionary rule. The Court took both steps in 1964, in *Escobedo v. Illinois.*[58]

The effect of *Escobedo* must be considered in the light of an almost contemporaneous decision, *Wong Sun v. United States*.[59] The *Wong Sun* case held that confessions taken from a suspect following his illegal arrest were the products of the arrest, and hence inadmissible under the Fourth Amendment exclusionary rule. It is standard Fourth Amendment doctrine that an arrest is legal only upon "probable cause." Hence, if a suspect was taken into custody without probable cause, his subsequent confession would be excluded from evidence by *Wong Sun* and *Mapp*. On the other hand, *Escobedo* announced that the suspect's right to counsel attached at that point in a criminal investigation when the investigation "has begun to focus on a particular suspect, the suspect has been taken into custody," and he is interrogated.[60] In any case of "probable cause" for arrest, the investigation will have "begun to focus on a particular suspect"; so the combined effect of *Escobedo* and *Wong Sun* was much like that of *McNabb-Mallory:* it made confessions obtained from uncounseled suspects in the station house *eo ipso* inadmissible, without the need to resolve factual questions of "voluntariness."

The questions were yet to be resolved whether the right to counsel in the station house implied a right of the suspect to be *warned* that he could have a lawyer, whether the right included a right to *appointed* counsel for indigent suspects, and under what circumstances the right could be waived. *Miranda v. Arizona* resolved these questions. It answered the first two in the affirmative, and it laid down strict standards governing waiver, including the presumption that a suspect long detained and questioned without counsel had not waived counsel. *Miranda* also provided a more solid theoretical basis for *Escobedo*. Adverting to the privilege against self-incrimination—also recently "incorporated"[61]—as the suspect's right most needful of protection in the station house, it explained that the right to counsel given by *Escobedo* was a necessary safeguard of the privilege. In subsequent decisions, the Court has recognized that station-house lineups and other identification confrontations pose many of the same problems as do confessions—basically, the dangers of unprovably unfair police practices that assure conviction at trial—and it has guaranteed the right to counsel at such confrontations.[62]

If my analysis of this thirty-five-year process is correct, what the Supreme Court has done is to recognize, after long and exasperating experience, that the right vouchsafed to suspects by *Brown v. Mississippi* is essentially worthless if it is left to vindication by state trial judges upon the testimony of policemen. No experienced criminal lawyer could doubt that judgment. *Miranda's* insistence that the suspect have a lawyer in the station house is plainly necessary, as the Court says, "unless other fully effective means are devised to [protect his] . . . right of silence."[63] And the only fully effective means that comes to mind is a shakeup of the police forces and the trial benches of the fifty states.

Third, however, *Miranda* does not go far enough. Although its standards governing waiver of the right to counsel are strict, it does permit findings of waiver to be made. Those findings will be made by the same old trial judges, following the same old swearing contest. As a result, *Miranda* will likely go the way of *Brown,* unless the Supreme Court is prepared to enforce to the hilt its hint in *Miranda* that "the fact of lengthy interrogation or incommunicado incarceration before a statement is made . . . is inconsistent with any notion of [waiver.]"[64]

Probably, the Court will not enforce this principle. In the Omnibus Crime Control and Safe Streets Act of 1968, Congress has purported to overrule *Miranda* in its application to federal cases.[65] The statute is of doubtful constitutionality, but it expresses a feeling-tone that the Justices are not likely to ignore when federal or state cases involving the application, and particularly the extension, of *Miranda* come before them. Mr. Nixon's "strict constructionists," in any event, would not likely extend *Miranda* by a nail's breadth, even though for want of that nail the kingdom should be lost.

IV. PROTECTION OF SUSPECTS' RIGHTS IN THE SEVENTIES

So we cannot rely upon the Supreme Court in the 1970's to provide adequate definition and protection of the rights of suspects. That job is beyond the power of the Court in the best of times, and present times are not the best. If the job is to be done, it must be done by others. But by whom?

I think that it must be done, and that sooner or later it will be done, by local legislators, executives, the police command structure, and citizens in their communities. In the light of past performance—or rather, nonperformance—by all of these persons, this may seem a vain hope. Yet several recent developments suggest that it is not altogether vain.

Three developments in particular seem to me the most significant of the 1960's in their implications for the future evolution of suspects' rights: (1) the emergence of widespread and more or less organized community concern with regulation of the police, and a recognition by local politicians and the police bureaucracy of a need to respond to this concern; (2) the articulation of models for such regulation that emphasize policy formulation through an administrative process involving citizen participation; and (3) the assumption by a few courts of a new and more affirmative role in the regulatory process.

First, the police are in deep trouble in many communities, and deeply aware of it. No amount of good that emerges from our black ghettos is likely ever to redeem the misery which our society has inflicted upon the millions of citizens it has penned into them. But it is nonetheless true that, in many ways, the ghettos are the most vital part of contemporary American society: the source of movements and institutions that may redeem us all in the end. One such movement is community-wide, organized, and effective concern with controlling the police.

The inhabitants of a black ghetto, unlike those of a white or middle-class neighborhood, are able to identify with the criminal suspect instead of with the police. They know it is highly possible, at any time, that the police will treat any one of them as a suspect —a possibility that simply never occurs to most white or middle-class people. As a result, they are concerned with the way the police treat suspects.

Of course, there are other reasons why the ghetto-dweller is uniquely concerned with the police. The policeman in the ghetto is one of the few points of contact between its people and the larger society, all of whose oppressions he comes to symbolize. His symbolic role makes his integration into the community peculiarly difficult, and shapes community demands for regulation of the police in ways that reflect something other and more than the community's judgment concerning the proper ways in which suspects should be treated.

Nevertheless, the ghettos have begun to advance in the process of making their concern for regulation of the police effective. Community spokesmen and local politicians have articulated specific demands for changes in police policies and practices, behind which community support can be mustered. And the police—sometimes with and sometimes without prodding from city hall—have learned that it makes sense to listen to the demands. In riot situations, and increasingly in less catastrophic ones, police officials have discovered the vital truth of the old cliché that the police need citizen cooperation; and they have also discovered that in order to get it, they may have to behave in ways that the community approves.

I would not contend, certainly, that progress in the systematic control of the police by an informed citizenry has been enormous. The police have sometimes ignored and sometimes quickly forgotten the lessons they might have learned in moments of community turmoil. The demands of the black ghettos have frequently been too limited, concerning only, for example, the assignment of black patrolmen to their area, or the appointment of black command personnel. And black community pressures have often engendered offsetting, repressive pressures from the white community. But the beginnings of community arousal and its effective mobilization have been made.

Second, institutional models have been proposed—and in high places—that would regularize and improve a process of citizen control over police practices. Both the National Crime Commission and the National Commission on Civil Disorders have recommended the greatly increased use of formal policy-formulation and rule-making procedures by police departments.[66] They have urged, for example, the promulgation of written departmental directives governing "such matters, among others, as the issuance of orders to citizens regarding their movements or activities, the handling of minor disputes, the safeguarding of the rights of free speech and free assembly, the selection and use of investigative methods . . . the decision whether or not to arrest in specific situations involving specific crimes,"[67] and "the circumstances under which the various forms of physical force—including lethal force—can and should be applied."[68] Regulations of this sort would provide what the courts have never been able to supply: comprehensive and coherent definition of the rights of suspects, together with procedures for assuring that they are respected.

Even if there were no citizen participation in the formulation of these regulations, their enunciation would mark a significant advance in suspects' rights. They would bring the major issues up to visibility, and would subject police resolution of those issues to correction by political and (to a lesser extent) judicial process. Also, it is likely that police administrators themselves would resolve the issues in a fashion more considerate of individual rights, when designing rules of general application posted for public scrutiny, than do individual policemen in their unguided, invisible, and adrenaline-stimulated treatment of particular suspects.

But in addition, direct involvement of citizens in the rule-making process appears to be practicable.[69] Experience in the planning and operation of OEO programs, Model Cities programs, and an increasingly broad range of other service programs points the way. These experiences have not always been happy ones, but they have accustomed ghetto communities to the notion of popular participation in administrative decision-making, and have developed some useful procedures (and warned us about some useless ones) for participation. The burgeoning of OEO Legal Services offices and other lawyers' groups available to represent community interests adds measurably to communities' capacity to demand, and effectively to fulfill, a role in administrative processes.

Recognition that police policy-formulation *is* an administrative process suggests the applicability to it of administrative procedures found serviceable in other contexts. Such procedures may be established by legislation or executive order, or put into effect by the police themselves. (Even in a time when the temper of many legislatures is repressive, legislators who would not want to "handcuff the police" by substantive legislation may be persuaded of the desirability, from the standpoint of efficient law enforcement, of regularizing the procedures for police self-management.) The procedures might involve citizen participation in varying forms. Citizens' advisory committees could be consulted at the drafting stage of new police regulations. Proposed drafts of the regulations could be promulgated for study and comment by interested persons, or for discussion at public hearings, prior to final promulgation. Or the regulations could be formulated by task forces that include community and police representatives.

Third, the courts may have a role in stimulating this administrative process and reviewing its products. Judicial review of administrative rule-making in other areas is commonplace, and suggestions have lately been made that the courts review police regulations in the same fashion that they review those of other agencies.[70] Review of this sort would reach a far broader range of issues than those which courts have heretofore considered under the exclusionary rule. And greater judicial sensitivity to individual rights can be expected in the review of general police policies than has heretofore been found in exclusionary rule cases, where judicial disapproval of police practices entailed "setting the criminal free."

More important even than judicial review of the substance of police policies may be the role of courts in assuring that the policy-making process gets started and is carried out by fair procedures that assure the citizen an effective voice. One offshoot of the civil rights struggles of the sixties has been the increasing use of federal injunctive actions to curb unconstitutional police practices.[71] In some of these cases, the courts have gone beyond mere restraint of the challenged practices, and have issued orders that require affirmative action by the police, such as protection of civil rights demonstrators.[72] In a very few cases, the courts have required police formulation and implementation of rules adequate to protect citizens against abuse.[73]

These cases lay the technical foundation for the next step—admittedly a big one—that I hope to see the courts take. That is a recognition of the right of representative citizens to sue for a court order requiring their police departments to undertake and fairly to pursue administrative procedures for the promulgation of regulations governing all police practices that affect the citizen. I think there is a solid legal basis for judicial recognition of such a right.

Due process of law comports the command that public agencies —particularly an agency, such as the police, which possesses broad and virtually monopolistic powers to use force and restraint upon the citizenry—act according to uniform, visible, and regular rules of law.[74] When the extraordinary powers of the police are used unrestrainedly—that is, in the absence of such rules—they are used arbitrarily in a constitutional sense, in violation of due process. Such ruleless police actions may also violate standards established by state law for all administrative action. So, both the federal and the state courts may be authorized and obliged to require the police to make rules governing, among other things, suspects' rights.

It is probably true of judges, as of legislators, that some who would refuse to "handcuff the police" by substantive rules of their own making would nevertheless be willing to insist that the police make rules of self-governance through fair administrative procedures. It is to be hoped that in many communities police departments can be persuaded to embark upon this course without legislative or judicial intervention. In any event, whether voluntary, legislatively required, or court-ordered, the process of police rule-making seems to me the most promising source of future development of suspects' rights.

The product of that process will be better or worse depending upon the extent to which enlightened citizens, through intelligent use of the process, demand civilized standards of police behavior. At the moment, the ghettos are far behind other communities in making this demand. Perhaps it is a *credo quia absurdum,* but I believe that eventually the rest of us will learn to follow the ghettos' lead.

NOTES

1. A "time-served" sentence is common for many minor offenses. The judge sentences the defendant to a period of imprisonment equivalent to the time he has spent in jail prior to conviction, credits the preconviction time against this sentence, and so releases the defendant forthwith.

2. *See* Mapp v. Ohio, 367 U.S. 643 (1961), and Ker v. California, 374 U.S. 23 (1963) (Fourth Amendment right against unreasonable searches and seizures); Robinson v. California, 370 U.S. 660 (1962) (Eighth Amendment right against cruel and unusual punishment); Gideon v. Wainwright, 372 U.S. 335 (1963) (Sixth Amendment right to counsel); Malloy v. Hogan, 378 U.S. 1 (1964) (Fifth Amendment privilege against self-incrimination); Pointer v. Texas, 380 U.S. 400 (1965) (Sixth Amendment right of confrontation); Klopfer v. North Carolina, 386 U.S. 213 (1967) (Sixth Amendment right to speedy trial); Washington v. Texas, 388 U.S. 14 (1967) (Sixth Amendment right of compulsory process); Duncan v. Louisiana, 391 U.S. 145 (1968) (Sixth Amendment right of jury trial); Benton v. Maryland, 395 U.S. 784 (1969) (Fifth Amendment right against double jeopardy). The Court has not considered in recent years the applicability to state criminal proceedings of the Eighth Amendment right to bail. Apart from the bail right, the only still "unincorporated" criminal-procedure guarantee of the Bill of Rights is the Fifth Amendment right to prosecution by indictment, a guarantee which (for reasons too complex and tangential to develop here) is probably not worth the trouble to "incorporate," even from the defendant's point of view.

3. *See* the line of cases from Griffin v. Illinois, 351 U.S. 12 (1956), through Williams v. Oklahoma City, 395 U.S. 458 (1969), dealing with the rights of indigents to state-paid transcripts; and the extension of the principle in Douglas v. California, 372 U.S. 353 (1963), to require appointed counsel for indigents on appeal.

4. *In re* Gault, 387 U.S. 1 (1967).

5. Camara v. Municipal Court, 387 U.S. 523 (1967); See v. City of Seattle, 387 U.S. 541 (1967).

6. Hamilton v. Alabama, 368 U.S. 52 (1961); White v. Maryland, 373 U.S. 59 (1963).

7. Massiah v. United States, 377 U.S. 201 (1964); Escobedo v. Illinois, 378 U.S. 478 (1964); United States v. Wade, 388 U.S. 218 (1967).

8. *E.g.,* Carnley v. Cochran, 369 U.S. 506 (1962); Brookhart v. Janis, 384 U.S. 1 (1966); Miranda v. Arizona, 384 U.S. 436 (1966); Swenson v. Bosler, 386 U.S. 258 (1967).

9. *E.g.,* Jackson v. Denno, 378 U.S. 368 (1964); Simmons v. United States, 390 U.S. 377 (1968); Alderman v. United States, 394 U.S. 165 (1969); *cf.* Burgett v. Texas, 389 U.S. 109 (1967); Harrison v. United States, 392 U.S. 219 (1968).

10. Townsend v. Sain, 372 U.S. 293 (1963); Fay v. Noia, 372 U.S. 391 (1963); Sanders v. United States, 373 U.S. 1 (1963); Peyton v. Rowe, 391 U.S. 54 (1968); Carafas v. LaVallee, 391 U.S. 234 (1968). The Court has similarly broadened postconviction remedies for federal convicts. Sanders v. United States, *supra;* Kaufman v. United States, 394 U.S. 217 (1969).

11. 391 U.S. 145, 158–9, n. 30 (1968). True to these hints, the Court has since overruled its long-standing Sixth Amendment decisions requiring a twelve-man jury. Williams v. Florida, 399 U.S. 78 (1970).

12. 387 U.S. 523, 534–39 (1967).

13. 351 U.S. 12, 19 (1956).

14. *See* note 3 *supra.* Since this text was written, the Court has also rendered a decision, rather narrowly drafted, applying the equal protection clause to prohibit the jailing of indigents in default of payment of fines that they cannot afford to pay, where the incarceration exceeds the maximum period of imprisonment authorized by law for the offense. Williams v. Illinois, 399 U.S. 235 (1970).

15. *Compare* Stoner v. California, 376 U.S. 483 (1964), *with* Johnson v. United States, 333 U.S. 10 (1948); *compare* Aguilar v. Texas, 378 U.S. 108 (1964), *with* Nathanson v. United States, 290 U.S. 41 (1933); *compare* Bumper v. North Carolina, 391 U.S. 543 (1968), *with* Amos v. United States, 255 U.S. 313 (1921).

16. Katz v. United States, 389 U.S. 347 (1967), *overruling* Olmstead v. United States, 277 U.S. 438 (1928). In so doing, it is significant that the Court did not accept the argument, urged by the more liberal opponents of wiretapping and eavesdropping, that application of the warrant requirement to these practices would constitutionally invalidate them altogether, because no sufficiently specific warrant could be drawn delimiting the "things to be seized" by the electronic monitor.

17. Chimel v. California, 395 U.S. 752 (1969), *overruling* United States v. Rabinowitz, 339 U.S. 56 (1950).

18. Lewis v. United States, 385 U.S. 206 (1966); Hoffa v. United States, 385 U.S. 293 (1966).

19. McCray v. Illinois, 386 U.S. 300 (1967).

20. Concerning the significance of the choice between two inconsistent but long coexistent theories of the Fourth Amendment—the warrant theory and the "general reasonableness" theory—*see* A. Amsterdam, B. Segal, and M. Miller, *Trial Manual for the Defense of Criminal Cases* §229 (1967).

21. Cooper v. California, 386 U.S. 58 (1967).

22. Warden v. Hayden, 387 U.S. 294 (1967).

23. Frazier v. Cupp, 394 U.S. 731, 740 (1969).

24. Miranda v. Arizona, 384 U.S. 436 (1966).

25. *See* Bram v. United States, 168 U.S. 532 (1897).

26. 384 U.S. 757 (1966).

27. The Court stopped somewhat short of constitutionalizing Wigmore, *see* footnote 7 of the *Schmerber* opinion; *and see* Amsterdam, Segal, and Miller, *supra* note 20, §232.

28. *See* Murphy v. Waterfront Comm'n, 378 U.S. 52 (1964).

29. *See* notes 5, 12 *supra.*

30. *See* note 16 *supra.*

31. *See* notes 15, 22 *supra.*

32. *See* note 22 *supra.*

33. *See* note 28 *supra.*

34. Terry v. Ohio, 392 U.S. 1 (1968); Sibron v. New York, 392 U.S. 40 (1968).

35. Jones v. United States, 362 U.S. 257 (1960); Wong Sun v. United States, 371 U.S. 471 (1963); Alderman v. United States, 394 U.S. 165 (1969).

36. Schmerber v. California, 384 U.S. 757 (1966).

37. Note 34 *supra.*

38. Note 17 *supra.*

39. *Cf.* Warden v. Hayden, 387 U.S. 294 (1967).

40. Berger v. New York, 388 U.S. 41 (1967).

41. 18 U.S.C. §§ 2510–20.

42. Miranda v. Arizona, 384 U.S. 436, 444 (1966). Emphasis added.

43. 18 U.S.C. §3501.

44. Davis v. Mississippi, 394 U.S. 721, 728 (1969).

45. S. 2997, 91st Cong., 1st Sess. (1969).

46. This area has been the subject of sustained attention by the Court since 1936, the date of the Court's first decision holding a coerced confession inadmissible in a state criminal trial: Brown v. Mississippi, 297 U.S. 278 (1936). The Court had earlier dealt with the admissibility of confessions in a few federal criminal cases, particularly Bram v. United States, 168 U.S. 532 (1897), and Ziang Sung Wan v. United States, 266 U.S. 1 (1924), but such cases were rare and involved no systematic consideration of the problems of postarrest treatment of suspects by the police.

47. I put aside decisions in a few cases involving prosecutions of police officers under the federal civil rights statutes: Screws v. United States, 325 U.S. 91 (1945); Williams v. United States, 341 U.S. 97 (1951); United States v. Price, 383 U.S. 787 (1966). These are extreme cases factually, and hence not very informative.

48. *See* the review in Ritz, "Twenty-Five Years of State Criminal Confession Cases in the U.S. Supreme Court," 19 *Washington and Lee Law Review* 35 (1962).

49. Davis v. Mississippi, 394 U.S. 721 (1969); United States v. Wade, 388 U.S. 218 (1967); Foster v. California, 394 U.S. 440 (1969).

50. 297 U.S. 278 (1936).

51. *Id.* at 286.

52. 318 U.S. 332 (1943).

53. *Id.* at 344.

54. Mallory v. United States, 354 U.S. 449 (1957). By the time of *Mallory,* the statutory provision that had supported *McNabb* had been translated into Rule 5(a) of the Federal Rules of Criminal Procedure, requiring that an arrested person be taken before a committing officer "without unnecessary delay."

55. 338 U.S. 25 (1949). *Wolf* apparently assumed that unreasonable searches and seizures by state officers violated the due process clause of the Fourteenth Amendment, but held that the state courts were not therefore required to exclude evidence obtained by such searches and seizures.

56. 367 U.S. 643 (1961).

57. 372 U.S. 335 (1963).

58. 378 U.S. 478 (1964).

59. 371 U.S. 471 (1963).

60. 378 U.S. at 490–91.

61. Malloy v. Hogan, 378 U.S. 1 (1964).

62. *See* note 49 *supra.*

63. 384 U.S. at 444.

64. *Id.* at 476.

65. *See* note 43 *supra.* The statute also purports to overrule *Mallory.*

66. President's Commission on Law Enforcement and Administration of Justice, Report, *The Challenge of Crime in a Free Society* 103–6 (G.P.O. ed. 1967); National Advisory Commission on Civil Disorders, Report, at 164–65 (G.P.O. ed. 1968).

67. President's Commission on Law Enforcement and Administration of Justice, *supra* note 66, at 104.

68. National Advisory Commission on Civil Disorders, *supra* note 66, at 165.

69. *See* President's Commission on Law Enforcement and Administration of Justice, *Task Force Report: The Police* 33–35 (1967).

70. *Id.* at 32–33; *cf.* K. Davis, *Discretionary Justice: A Preliminary Inquiry* (1969).

71. *See* Note, "The Federal Injunction as a Remedy for Unconstitutional Police Conduct," 78 *Yale Law Journal* 143 (1968); *e.g.,* Lankford v. Gelston, 364 F.2d 197 (4th Cir. 1966); *NAACP* v. Thompson, 357 F.2d 831 (5th Cir.) *cert. denied,* 385 U.S. 820 (1966).

72. *E.g.,* Williams v. Wallace, 240 F. Supp. 100 (M.D. Ala. 1965); Cottonreader v. Johnson, 252 F. Supp. 492 (M.D. Ala. 1966).

73. Hicks v. Knight, 10 Race Rel. L. Rep. 1504 (E.D. La. 1965); Cunningham v. Grenada Municipal Separate School Dist., and United States v. City of Grenada, 11 Race Rel. L. Rep. 1776, 1782–83 (N.D. Miss. 1966).

74. *See* Landman v. Peyton, 370 F.2d 135, 139–41 (4th Cir.), *cert. denied,* 385 U.S. 881 (1966). Jackson v. Bishop, 268 F. Supp. 804, 815–16 (E.D. Ark. 1967), *vacated on other grounds,* 404 F.2d 571 (8th Cir. 1968); Holt v. Sarver, 309 F. Supp. 362 (E.D. Ark. 1970).

THE RIGHTS OF
CRIMINAL DEFENDANTS

DANIEL A. REZNECK

NO PERIOD OF OUR HISTORY SINCE THE ADOPTION of the Bill of Rights can equal the last decade in the scope, rapidity, and intensity of the changes in the law of criminal procedure. The rights of criminal defendants in both federal and state courts have been greatly enlarged. At the same time, public concern over crime in the United States has led to controversy over some of these procedural changes, which has tended to obscure their nature and significance.

Many of the changes are the result of decisions by the United States Supreme Court, and the Supreme Court has been the focus of the public debate. But it has not been alone in finding abuses and inadequacies in practices of our criminal courts. A number of state courts have also been in the forefront of procedural change, and lower federal courts have in many instances anticipated and even gone further than the Supreme Court decisions.

Moreover, there have also been major legislative reforms, such as the federal Criminal Justice Act of 1964, providing legal and other assistance to indigent defendants, and the federal Bail Reform Act of 1966, facilitating the availability of pretrial release. Important changes in procedural codes and rules have been enacted, most notably the 1966 amendments to the Federal Rules of Criminal Procedure.

Daniel A. Rezneck is a practicing lawyer in Washington, D.C., Adjunct Professor of Law at Georgetown Law School, and a former Assistant United States Attorney. He is a frequent contributor to legal periodicals on criminal law issues.

The reforms of recent years are manifestly a response to "felt necessities" and are not an ephemeral phenomenon. Procedural overhaul of the criminal law reflects a broad consensus among lawyers and judges which has transcended their differences as to detail and degree. The various proposals of the American Bar Association's Project on Standards for Criminal Justice attest to an innovative spirit in the profession and an acceptance of the need for continued improvements in the administration of criminal justice.

We seem to stand at a watershed in the movement for procedural reform. The basic patterns of the last decade are now clear. Some of these trends have evidently reached their climax, while others are emerging. It is possible to discern the outlines of some future changes and developments.

Three themes have been dominant in recent years: (1) the steady "federalization" of criminal procedure by the imposition of federal constitutional guarantees on the states through the due process and equal protection clauses of the Fourteenth Amendment; (2) judicial concern with the fairness of such pretrial law-enforcement practices as search and seizure, interrogation, and identification of suspects; and (3) an effort to enhance the reliability of the criminal trial as a means for determining guilt or innocence.

The process of incorporating the criminal law guarantees of the federal Bill of Rights into the Fourteenth Amendment and thereby applying them to the states is now virtually complete. That course began over thirty years ago, but it was greatly accelerated after the decision in *Mapp v. Ohio*,[1] imposing on the states the federal exclusionary rule for evidence seized in violation of the Fourth Amendment. Now almost every one of the constitutional rights of criminal defendants in federal courts is protected to the same extent against state abridgment, including the right to fair notice of the charges; the right to a speedy and public trial by jury with the assistance of counsel; the privilege against self-incrimination; the right to confront and cross-examine accusers and witnesses; and the freedom from unreasonable searches and seizures, cruel and unusual punishment, and double jeopardy. Of all those constitutional guarantees applicable in federal courts, it appears that only the right to indictment by a grand jury in a felony case will escape the reach of the "incorporation" theory.[2]

Along with the incorporation of the specific provisions of the federal Bill of Rights into the due process clause of the Fourteenth Amendment has come an enhanced role for the equal protection clause in the development of the law of criminal procedure. The states have been required by principles of equal protection to accord indigent criminal defendants the same opportunity to appeal and to obtain a trial transcript which would be available to a defendant with funds. Thus criminal procedure—once almost entirely determined in the state courts by state law—is now permeated by federal law, and criminal defendants can look to the federal Constitution for many of their rights.

This engrafting of federal constitutional guarantees onto state criminal procedures has been accompanied by the expansion of federal remedies for state violations of federal constitutional rights. The most important development has been enlarged federal-court review of state practices through postconviction proceedings such as habeas corpus. This in turn has induced many states to enlarge their own remedies for violations of federal constitutional rights, in order to diminish federal-court supervision. As a result criminal defendants in both state and federal courts not only have the full range of federal constitutional rights but more effective means of vindicating them.

The second major trend of recent years—judicial regulation of various law enforcement practices by declaring certain evidence illegally obtained and proscribing its use at trial—has given rise to many of the controversies over criminal defendants' rights. These decisions have brought the courts into conflict with federal and state law enforcement officials and substantial segments of public opinion.

It is probable that there will now be a pause in the rate of procedural change with respect to these matters. The courts have historically drawn back from continuing confrontations with the other branches of government, especially when popular opinion strongly supported the need for executive and legislative action. The potential impact of court decisions on existing law enforcement practices is so great that it will take time for the courts to evaluate the effects, the bar to assimilate the new doctrines, and law enforcement agencies to adjust to changed rules and devise alternative practices. Moreover, constitutional guidelines for search and seizure, interrogation, and identification of suspects have now been established. Although multifarious issues remain for decision, they primarily require explication and application of prior doctrine.

Much of the emphasis in recent years has been on improving

the accuracy and fairness of the trial process. The most important constitutional development was the decision that criminal defendants in all serious cases in both state and federal courts are entitled to receive the effective assistance of counsel.[3] There is no longer any question that the fact-finding, guilt-determining process at trial cannot function properly without the aid of defense counsel. The rights of defendants have also been advanced by new constitutional limitations on the use of out-of-court statements not subjected to cross-examination before the trier of fact, and by prohibition of adverse comment on a defendant's exercise of his right not to testify. In these respects the criminal trial has become a more reliable method of determining guilt.

Now attention has begun to shift to other aspects of criminal procedure. Major segments of the criminal justice system are still characterized by a minimum of defined standards and a maximum of discretion for governmental officials, with attendant dangers of arbitrariness and injustice.

This essay will consider three such components of the system: pretrial discovery, guilty plea procedures, and sentencing practices. The search for standards and the limitation of official discretion in these areas are likely to be the principal outlets for procedural reform in the next decade. Procedural changes here may transform the administration of criminal justice as much as did the developments of the last decade.

PRETRIAL DISCOVERY

Pretrial discovery by the defense of evidence and information in the possession of the prosecution has been limited in this country. Discovery has generally been available only in the discretion of courts and prosecutors. A comprehensive study of pretrial discovery in criminal cases concludes that "in most jurisdictions, the defendant has few if any rights to obtain information prior to trial regarding the prosecution's case against him or other relevant issues."[4]

Even states which provide extensive discovery in civil cases as of right have not done the same in criminal cases. This anomaly resulted from factors once thought to be peculiarly compelling in criminal cases: the danger that defendants might tamper with the prosecution's witnesses or fabricate evidence; the belief that defendants already had such advantages over the prosecution as the presumption of innocence and the requirement of proof beyond a reasonable doubt; and the assumption that discovery in a criminal case was necessarily a one-way street because of the privilege against self-incrimination.

These attitudes are now changing. The Supreme Court has described

> the growing realization that disclosure, rather than suppression, of relevant materials ordinarily promotes the proper administration of criminal justice. . . . [There is an] expanding body of materials, judicial and otherwise, favoring disclosure in criminal cases analogous to the civil practice.[5]

Recent developments point to a significant enlargement of the rights of criminal defendants to pretrial discovery. The 1966 amendments to the Federal Rules of Criminal Procedure expanded the discovery available in the federal courts. Several state courts have exercised their rule-making powers to do the same. The National Crime Commission favored freer discovery in criminal cases.[6] The American Bar Association's Project on Minimum Standards for Criminal Justice has proposed more extensive rights of criminal discovery than those now in effect anywhere in the United States.[7]

Several considerations account for the favorable attitude toward criminal discovery. There is awareness of the inequality of pretrial investigative resources between prosecution and defense in most criminal cases. The prosecution has available a force of trained investigators and can utilize state-supported expert witnesses and laboratory facilities. It also has legal powers to obtain information before trial through the grand jury process and search-and-seizure warrants. The defense frequently consists of appointed counsel, inexperienced in the criminal law and lacking investigative or expert services.

It is also recognized that the operation of our criminal justice system requires that the defense should have the full opportunity to contest the prosecution case, an object which can be accomplished only by intensive pretrial preparation. Discovery by the defense has therefore come to be regarded as an essential aspect of the accusatorial method of criminal justice.

As the Supreme Court has said:

> In our adversary system for determining guilt or innocence, it is rarely justifiable for the prosecution to have exclusive access to a

storehouse of relevant fact. Exceptions to this are justifiable only by the clearest and most compelling considerations.[8]

It is plain, however, that the trend toward freer discovery would not have its present momentum if it did not also further interests transcending those of the criminal defendant. It has become apparent that discovery also serves objectives of the courts and the prosecution. As in civil cases, discovery can increase the efficiency and reduce the time of trials by narrowing and focusing the issues, enabling counsel to prepare their cases more effectively, bringing about stipulations as to undisputed matters, and facilitating cross-examination.

Moreover, discovery makes possible a better-informed decision by defense counsel whether to advise a defendant to plead guilty. Prosecutors have always found it useful in securing guilty pleas to let the defendant know when he is confronted with an overwhelming case. In view of the judicial insistence that guilty pleas must be intelligent and genuinely voluntary,[9] freer pretrial disclosure will not only help to secure guilty pleas but may be essential to assure that such pleas are valid.

The recent proliferation of new constitutional and other procedural rights, combined with the increasing resort of prisoners to postconviction remedies, has also led courts and prosecutors to seek new methods of securing finality in the criminal process. Pretrial discovery contributes to that goal by enabling defense counsel to identify, raise, and fully litigate many legal issues, especially constitutional questions, in advance of trial. A fully developed factual record on these issues can obviate the need for extended postconviction proceedings.

Freer pretrial discovery thus is a logical outgrowth of other developments in criminal procedure. Defense lawyers, prosecutors, and judges, each for their own disparate reasons, now join to favor pretrial discovery. This assures that the criminal justice system will continue to progress toward enlarged discovery.

The constitutional underpinnings of discovery in criminal cases, although as yet imperfectly recognized, are fundamental and pervasive. Considerations of due process and equal protection, as well as some of the specific guarantees of the Bill of Rights, underlie many discovery issues. So far the Supreme Court has grounded only one aspect of discovery on a constitutional basis: the duty of the prosecution to disclose exculpatory or favorable evidence to the defense. In the leading case of *Brady v. Maryland,* the Supreme Court stated:

> We now hold that the suppression by the prosecution of evidence favorable to an accused upon request violates due process where the evidence is material either to guilt or to punishment, irrespective of the good faith or bad faith of the prosecution.[10]

Brady was only the initial step in the evolution of the constitutional law of discovery. It has given rise to many complex questions, such as the time when disclosure must be made, what matters must be disclosed, and the respective functions of prosecutor, judge, and defense lawyer in implementing the *Brady* duty. While most of the *Brady* questions are as yet unanswered, its implications are far-reaching and the doctrine has great potential for expansion.

Moreover, *Brady* does not exhaust the relevant constitutional mandates. In view of the disparity of resources between the prosecution and the defense in most cases and the further disparities between indigent and affluent defendants, due process and equal protection considerations permeate many problems of criminal discovery. The requirements of due process may ultimately extend beyond disclosure merely of exculpatory information in the possession of the prosecution. That is the most compelling case for disclosure, but the disparity in investigative resources may be overcome in many criminal cases only by requiring the prosecution to disclose all of its evidence and information relevant to the case.

Furthermore, with respect to the indigent defendant who cannot afford proper pretrial investigation or the marshaling of necessary expert testimony, the principles of equal protection may require the state to take certain affirmative steps to overcome this inequality. Some jurisdictions, by statute, rule, or judicial decision, have made efforts toward that end. The federal Criminal Justice Act, for example, provides for court appointment and compensation of experts to assist the defense. Another means of implementing the mandate of equal protection may be for the states to make the public investigative and scientific facilities and resources available to the defense as well as the prosecution. This notion of a distinterested inquiry into the facts has analogues in the civil law system of pretrial judicial inquiry. Such tempering of the traditional adversary system is justifiable to further the search for truth, the primary objective of the criminal trial process.

Other constitutional guarantees may be recognized as a predicate for discovery. A defendant's right to confront and cross-examine his accusers and to receive the assistance of counsel, now protected by the Sixth and Fourteenth Amendments in both federal and state courts, may require giving the defense pretrial access, or at least access at trial, to matters heretofore inaccessible to discovery in many jurisdictions. For instance, effective cross-examination of prosecution witnesses may necessitate access by the defense to their pretrial statements to law enforcement officials and to their grand jury testimony. Such access precludes surprise at trial and makes possible one of the most potent forms of impeachment—confronting a witness with contradictions in his prior statements or testimony. The vigor of cross-examination is in direct proportion to the opportunity of the defense to anticipate prosecution testimony and prepare lines of possible impeachment.

As the trend to freer discovery accelerates, the need to resolve many discovery issues on constitutional considerations will be avoided through the exercise of courts' rule-making and supervisory authority. The 1966 amendments to the Federal Rules of Criminal Procedure, comparable developments in the states, and the recent ABA discovery proposals indicate an emerging consensus on matters such as a defendant's right to discover his own statements and to have access to the reports and tests of expert medical and scientific witnesses.[11] This consensus may eventually encompass such controverted points as access to names of prosecution witnesses, subject to the prosecution's right to obtain protective orders denying or delaying disclosure on a sufficient showing of danger or necessity.

Enlargement of the frontiers of discovery will bring other issues to the fore. The move to equalize criminal and civil discovery highlights the problem of mutuality of discovery in criminal cases. The terrain of the prosecution's right to discovery from the defense has scarcely been explored thus far. Rights of mutual discovery are being accorded in some jurisdictions. Under the Federal Rules of Criminal Procedure, the defendant's right to obtain maximum discovery is conditioned on his willingness to make certain pretrial disclosures about his own case to the prosecution. In a number of states the prosecution has been granted independent rights of discovery, including notification by the defense of its intent to rely on claims of insanity, alibi, or self-defense at trial; in some instances, the defense must disclose its own witnesses. The ABA's recent discovery proposals would authorize compelling a defendant to submit to various forms of pretrial disclosure to the prosecution, such as furnishing fingerprints, handwriting examplars, and other physical samples, standing in a lineup, speaking for identification purposes, posing for photographs, and submitting to medical examinations.

These developments raise fundamental issues. On the one hand there is the constitutional privilege against self-incrimination and the tradition of our accusatorial system that the defendant is entitled to put the prosecution to its proof without any help from him. On the other side is the doctrine that the constitutional privilege against self-incrimination protects only against compelled communications of a testimonial nature and the belief that the exigencies of law enforcement justify subjecting a defendant to identification procedures, at least under judicial control and conditions designed to guarantee fairness. Determining where to strike the balance between these competing values and how far discovery in criminal cases can and should become a two-way street will be a major undertaking.

GUILTY PLEAS

Although much attention has been given to improvements in criminal trial procedures, the trial is not the most important part of the criminal justice system. The overwhelming majority of all defendants still plead guilty without trial.[12] The role of the guilty plea process in the administration of criminal justice has only recently received emphasis. In the past this process has been highly informal and has reflected a widespread judicial indulgence in legal fictions to avoid hard problems.

Now the movement for improved procedures and clearer standards has begun to focus on the rights of those who plead guilty. Courts are now approaching the guilty plea process with a view to protecting rights long accepted in theory but imperfectly implemented in practice.

The Supreme Court has attempted to infuse procedural content into the acceptance of guilty pleas. The Court has held that a plea of guilty in either a state or a federal court, to be constitutionally valid, must be "truly voluntary"[13] and genuinely informed and intelligent.

The Court has approached the problems of the guilty plea through its rule-making powers for the federal courts and constitutional adjudications binding the state courts. Under Rule 11 of the Federal Rules of Criminal Procedure a federal court may not accept a guilty plea "without first addressing the defendant personally and determining that the plea is made voluntarily with understanding of the nature of the charge and the consequences of the plea." This is not to be done in conclusory fashion. The defendant must be informed of the essential elements of the offense with which he is charged. He must be told the consequences of pleading guilty—the range of penal and other sentencing alternatives to which he will be exposed and the fact that he will give up his right to a trial and the constitutional rights he would have at trial. Moreover, the court must also determine that there is a "factual basis" for the plea, so that the defendant is not in the position of pleading guilty to a charge which has no evidentiary support.[14]

Essentially the same requirements now govern the validity of guilty pleas in state courts under the due process clause of the Fourteenth Amendment.[15] Observance of these procedures must affirmatively appear on the court record; there is no presumption of regularity or compliance.

These safeguards against improvident guilty pleas are a substantial advance over the slipshod practices which have frequently prevailed. The case reports reflect numerous instances of defendants who were marched into court for summary plea proceedings based on ritualistic incantations by judge, prosecutor, and defendant, without exploration of the real circumstances surrounding the plea. All too often such procedures have resulted in efforts by prisoners to overturn their guilty pleas and prolonged litigation over the facts of the original plea. The new procedures should impart greater orderliness and finality to the guilty plea process.

These reforms, however, by no means solve all the problems of the guilty plea. Instead, the heightened realism with which the courts now approach guilty pleas will force them to confront aspects of the process which have been overlooked, ignored, or rationalized away.

The concern for assuring that guilty pleas are "truly voluntary" will require a re-examination of the circumstances leading up to the plea, especially of so-called "plea bargaining." Plea bargaining is not a simple or unitary concept. It covers a number of disparate situations, including negotiations over sentencing and reduction and dropping of charges. Sometimes it takes place between prosecution and defense without judicial involvement. Judges sometimes participate at various points and in various ways.

There is disagreement as to plea bargaining in both principle and practice. The adjectives commonly applied to it are "informal," "off-the-record," and "invisible." To some, these qualities are the sources of its utility, to others its principal weaknesses.[16] Some have regarded plea bargaining as inherently coercive and therefore unconstitutional on the ground that it induces defendants to forgo their trial rights in the expectation either of leniency after plea or a heavier sentence after conviction at trial. Others regard plea bargaining as a primary method of relieving congestion in overburdened courts and attribute other positive values to it, such as facilitating rehabilitation of the guilty, minimizing the harm from long prison sentences, and encouraging cooperation with law enforcement officials.

In other contexts the Supreme Court has held that procedures which penalize or burden the assertion of constitutional rights are constitutionally suspect.[17] To the extent that a defendant is likely to receive more lenient treatment by pleading guilty than he would after conviction at trial, it is more difficult for him to exercise his right to a trial. To the extent that there is, in fact, a disparity in sentencing those who plead guilty and those convicted after trial, the decision to plead guilty can never be as completely free as if no disparity could result from a decision one way or the other.

Nevertheless, the Supreme Court has clearly indicated that no per se rule of constitutional invalidity will be applied to plea bargaining.[18] The relationship to plea bargaining of the "truly voluntary" test for the validity of guilty pleas will be dealt with on a case-by-case basis, as the courts have treated the validity of out-of-court confessions. There they have considered the issue of voluntariness in the context of the totality of surrounding circumstances and have fashioned procedures such as the *Miranda* rules to protect the defendant's freedom of choice. They have not ruled out extrajudicial confessions altogether. The same will be true of plea bargaining. The courts will evaluate concrete aspects of plea bargaining and try to build in safeguards against improvident guilty pleas.

One such aspect is the practice of some prosecutors of maximizing their negotiating positions by charging more serious offenses than the evidence warrants or by proliferating counts against a defendant. The National Crime Commission noted the dangers to the negotiating process posed by this practice, and the Supreme Court has indicated that it may affect the integrity of a guilty plea.[19] Equal protection considerations are also relevant to the prosecution's conduct of plea bargaining. If bargaining concessions are offered by the prosecution without standards defined in advance or articulated reasons, the negotiating process can lead to widely different results for similarly situated defendants.

The importance of the participation of defense counsel in the plea-bargaining process can scarcely be exaggerated. In view of the overwhelming number of guilty pleas, plea bargaining is as critical a stage in the criminal proceeding as the trial. It is difficult to see how a defendant can ever be protected in the process without the aid of counsel. The availability of maximum pretrial discovery also is integrally related to the bargaining process. A genuinely informed decision to plead guilty requires knowledge by the defense of the strength of the prosecution's case in order to assess the relative merits of pleading or standing trial.

Another crucial aspect of plea bargaining is the proper role of the court: whether a judge should participate actively in the negotiations and try to bring about a plea by committing himself to a particular sentencing disposition; whether this creates such danger to a truly voluntary decision by the defendant that a judge should remain entirely aloof from the negotiations; or whether he should take some intermediate position, such as indicating approval of the terms of the plea bargain in advance without a commitment to a particular disposition.[20]

Increasing the visibility of plea bargaining by opening up the bargain on the court record at the time of plea is a potentially important safeguard which should be tested in practice. The procedure in many courts of having the defendant recite that he is pleading guilty solely because he is guilty and for no other reason obscures the reasons for the plea. Full disclosure of the bargain and the considerations leading the defendant to accept it provides a basis for careful judicial inquiry at the time of plea and an informed determination of its voluntariness. All these matters, and many others as well, will have to be resolved in the process of scrutinizing plea bargaining.

SENTENCING

Perhaps the most significant reforms are likely to occur in the procedures for sentencing convicted defendants. There is an exigent need for changes in sentencing practices. Little has been done thus far to formulate standards and assure procedural regularity.

Yet sentencing is the most critical stage of the proceeding for most defendants, especially since so many plead guilty. And sentencing has a close relationship to the success of the correctional system. Whether fair sentencing procedures are employed may influence the attitude of a convicted offender toward the legal system and affect his capacity and motivation for rehabilitation. Many critics of the enlargment of defendants' rights in pretrial and trial procedures nevertheless are concerned over the failings of the correctional system. Thus, there is greater receptivity to change in the dispositional phase of the criminal proceedings.

Trial judges have had almost complete discretion in sentencing within the statutory limits. Sentencing has lacked most of the procedural restraints that govern official action at other stages in the criminal case. The adversary system for testing the facts relevant to sentencing has had little scope. Judges have not generally been required to disclose to the defense the information they rely on to sentence, or to articulate any reasons for their sentences. Definitive standards and criteria for sentencing have not been promulgated. Disparity in sentencing by different judges, and between different types of defendants by the same judge, is a notorious fact of the criminal justice system. Appellate court review of trial court sentencing has been infrequent and is absent in many jurisdictions. Standards for such review are undeveloped.

Although judicial freedom from procedural restrictions at sentencing is rationalized by the desirability of dispensing "individualized justice" to convicted offenders, the judge's "individualized justice" may be arbitrary fiat to the defendant. The point at which judicial discretion turns into "a license for arbitrary procedure"[21] is often so fine as to be nearly invisible. In view of the seriousness of the sentencing decision, infusion of procedural regularity to make sentencing conform to principles of due process, equal protection, and fair treatment is necessary.

A number of methods are available to limit discretion and guard against arbitrariness. Among the most important is a larger role for the adversary system, principally through enhanced disclosure of sentencing information to the defense. The value of adversary procedures and freer discovery extends to sentencing as well as to the pretrial and trial stages of the case. There are too many flaws in the conventional sentencing model: sentencing on the basis of information communicated privately to the judge by a supposedly expert staff of probation officers, without disclosure of the presentence report or investigation to the defense for fear of drying up the probation officer's confidential sources of information.

The dangers of inaccuracy and bias in information used to sentence are at least as great in presentence investigations as in any other form of ex parte inquiry. It is unthinkable that decisions on guilt and innocence should be made in the manner of sentencing decisions. Reliance on information untested by an adversary proceeding for a decision of such magnitude is an invitation to error and arbitrariness. Disclosure to the defense of detrimental information in a presentence report and the opportunity to meet it are a minimal requirement of fair procedure and should be recognized as an element of due process.

The constitutional foundations of this principle have already been laid down. The Supreme Court has held that due process considerations require disclosure to the defense of staff reports relied on by a juvenile court judge in deciding whether to transfer a juvenile accused of crime for trial as an adult. In *Kent v. United States,* the Court stated:

> There is no irrebuttable presumption of accuracy attached to staff reports. . . . While the Juvenile Court judge may, of course, receive *ex parte* analyses and recommendations from his staff, he may not, for purposes of a decision on waiver, receive and rely upon secret information, whether emanating from his staff or otherwise. The Juvenile Court is governed in this respect by the established principles which control courts and quasi-judicial agencies of the Government.[22]

This principle is manifestly relevant to the disclosure of presentence information, although the Supreme Court has not yet revaluated the issue of defense access to presentence reports as a constitutional matter. The trend toward enhanced disclosure of presentence reports in both federal and state courts should receive impetus from the emerging constitutional doctrine reflected in *Kent.* Disclosure of presentence reports was not made mandatory in the 1966 amendments to the Federal Rules of Criminal Procedure, but the framers of the rules urged judges to disclose such information freely to the defense, and many federal judges will ordinarily do so.[23] There is strong support for establishing rights of disclosure by statute, decision, or rule of court.[24]

A second useful technique in regularizing sentencing is to require the judge to state on the record the reasons for the particular sentence he imposes. The need to give reasons is a check on arbitrariness, since the process of articulation obliges the judge to focus on the factors relevant to sentencing, to separate out permissible from impermissible considerations, and to try to justify the fairness and rationality of the result. Moreover, if appellate review of sentences is adopted as a further safeguard, a statement of reasons is indispensable to meaningful review.

Considerations of constitutional due process also support this method of imparting regularity to sentencing. In its decision in *Kent v. United States*,[25] discussed above, the Supreme Court stressed the importance of a statement of reasons in a just procedural system. The Court applied this principle to one aspect of sentencing in *North Carolina v. Pearce*.[26] It there held, as a requirement of due process, that when a judge gives a more severe sentence to a defendant after a conviction on retrial than had originally been imposed, "the reasons for his doing so must affirmatively appear." These reasons must be based upon "objective information" concerning the defendant's "identifiable conduct" after his first sentencing. Although the *Pearce* requirements were specifically designed to protect the right of a defendant to seek a retrial without fear of retaliation by the sentencing judge, the principle of giving reasons is capable of application to all sentencing.[27]

A widely discussed reform is appellate review of sentencing. Such review occurs as of right in Great Britain and in some of our states. It is not, however, the practice in most states or in the federal courts except in extremely limited circumstances.[28]

Appellate review, although not a panacea for abuses in sentencing, can make substantial contributions to greater procedural regularity. The existence of a right to appellate review is a check on arbitrariness at the trial court level, since sentencing judges will know that their sentences must pass the scrutiny of a higher court. Appellate courts can also ensure trial court compliance with other procedural requirements at the sentencing level, such as disclosure of presentence information and a statement of reasons. A sentence

not imposed in compliance with applicable procedural requirements would be vacated by the reviewing court and sent back for
resentencing.

The fashioning of standards for appellate court review of the
substance of sentencing decisions is more difficult. Legislative specification of appropriate criteria for sentencing is one way to determine reviewing standards, but such criteria are likely to be so
general as to give relatively little guidance to either senencing or
reviewing courts in specific cases.

The Constitution may provide certain standards or criteria for
appellate review. It is constitutionally impermissible for a sentencing judge to give weight to some considerations. In *North Carolina
v. Pearce,* for example, the Supreme Court invalidated a more
severe sentence which the trial judge imposed because the defendant
had successfully appealed and obtained a new trial. Likewise, for a
trial court to impose a heavier sentence on a defendant for exercising his right to a trial instead of pleading guilty is a denial of due
process of law and an unconstitutional burden on the defendant's
rights to and at trial.[29] The availability of judicial review to
prevent this kind of arbitrary trial-court action would also help to
maintain the fairness and integrity of guilty plea procedures. By
protecting defendants against retaliation for exercising their trial
rights, such review can guard against improvident guilty pleas.

The requirements of equal protection provide additional constitutional standards for review of sentencing. Grossly disparate
sentences between defendants who appear, on the record on which
the sentencing court acted, to be similarly situated, or equal sentences to defendants differently situated, may be subject to challenge on grounds of denial of equal protection. It should be noted,
however, that if reviewing courts are given power to increase as well
as reduce sentences on appeal,[30] equal protection considerations
could also lead to raising sentences in particular cases to achieve
uniformity among similarly situated defendants or to create disparity among differently situated offenders.

In general, constitutional provisions provide governing standards for appellate review of sentencing only in egregious and
clear-cut cases. To review sentencing in the ordinary case, appellate
courts will have to fashion standards through case-by-case adjudication. Appellate courts are likely to move cautiously, mindful of
the potential conflict between defined standards and the concept of
individualized justice for each offender. On the other hand, the

development of such standards is not impossible, any more than it is in appellate review of administrative agencies, where decision-making is confided in the first instance to presumed experts. Appellate courts will have before them the same record on which the trial court acted, including presentence reports. If the presentence information is disclosed to the defense and reasons are given at the sentencing level, the appellate courts will also have the advantages of the functioning of the adversary system and the benefit of the sentencing judge's deliberations to assist them.

The capacity of trial courts to improve the sentencing process should not be underestimated. Although the availability of appellate review would help to develop more discerning sentencing criteria, trial courts in many jurisdictions have recognized the magnitude of the sentencing problems and taken measures on their own to deal with them. In some courts, sentencing panels and councils have been set up to make sentencing judgments collective or to afford the sentencing judge the advice of colleagues. Sentencing institutes are also coming into wider use, providing opportunity for judges to exchange views on sentencing, promulgate sentencing criteria, and become acquainted with developments in penology and correction.

From the standpoint of fair procedures, the dispositional phase has too long been the weakest link in the criminal process. Improvement in sentencing is an essential adjunct to other reforms which have enhanced the quality of many pretrial and trial procedures in this country.

NOTES

1. 367 U.S. 643 (1961).

2. See the lecture by Justice Brennan—an accurate prophecy of things to come—"The Bill of Rights and the States," 36 *New York University Law Review* 761 (1961).

3. Gideon v. Wainwright, 372 U.S. 335 (1963).

4. ABA Project on Minimum Standards for Criminal Justice, *Standards Relating to Discovery and Procedure Before Trial* 25 (Tent. Draft 1969) [hereinafter cited as ABA, *Discovery Standards*].

5. Dennis v. United States, 384 U.S. 855, 870–71 (1966) (footnote omitted). Many of these materials are collected in ABA, *Discovery Standards, supra* note 4, and in the Supreme Court Advisory Committee's Note to amended Fed. R. Crim. p. 16.

6. President's Commission on Law Enforcement and Administration of Justice, Report, *The Challenge of Crime in a Free Society* 139 (G.P.O. ed. 1967) [hereinafter cited as National Crime Commission Report].

7. *See* ABA, *Discovery Standards, supra* note 4, at 1.

8. Dennis v. United States, 384 U.S. 855, 873 (1966) (footnote omitted).

9. *See* the succeeding section of this chapter, pp. 441–44 *infra*.

10. 373 U.S. 83, 87 (1963).

11. *See, e.g.,* Fed. R. Crim. P. 16; ABA, *Discovery Standards, supra* note 4, at 13.

12. McCarthy v. United States, 394 U.S. 459, 463 n.7 (1969); D. Newman, *Conviction: The Determination of Guilt or Innocence Without Trial* 3 (1966).

13. McCarthy v. United States, 394 U.S. 459, 465 (1969); Boykin v. Alabama, 395 U.S. 238 (1969).

14. McCarthy v. United States, 394 U.S. 459 (1969).

15. Boykin v. Alabama, 395 U.S. 238 (1969).

16. For various points of view on plea bargaining, see the reviews of D. Newman, *Conviction: The Determination of Guilt or Innocence Without Trial* (1966), *reviewed,* Taylor, 76 *Yale Law Journal* 598 (1967), Specter, *id.* at 604, Weinberg and Babcock, *id.* at 612; ABA Project of Minimum Standards for Criminal Justice, *Standards Relating to Pleas of Guilty* 60–78 (Approved Draft 1968) [hereinafter cited as ABA, *Guilty Plea Standards*]; Note, "Unconstitutionality of Plea Bargaining," 83 *Harvard Law Review* 1387 (1970).

17. Jackson v. United States, 390 U.S. 570 (1968).

18. Brady v. United States, 397 U.S. 742 (1970).

19. National Crime Commission Report, *supra* note 6, at 135; Brady v. United States, 397 U.S. 742, 751 n. 8 (1970).

20. *See* ABA, *Guilty Plea Standards, supra* note 16, at 71–77 and Supp. at 1–5.

21. Kent v. United States, 383 U.S. 541, 553 (1966).

22. *Id.* at 563.

23. Supreme Court Advisory Committee Note to amended Fed. R. Crim. P. 32.

24. *See* ABA Project for Standards for Criminal Justice, *Standards Relating to Sentencing Alternatives and Procedures* 210–24 (Approved Draft 1968) [hereinafter cited as ABA, *Sentencing Standards*].

25. 383 U.S. at 554.

26. 395 U.S. 711, 725–26 (1969).

27. *See* ABA, *Sentencing Standards, supra* note 24, at 269–71.

28. ABA Project on Standards for Criminal Justice, *Standards Relating to Appellate Review of Sentences* 6, 13–15 (Approved Draft 1968) [hereinafter cited as ABA, *Appellate Review of Sentences Standards*].

29. *See* Scott v. United States, 419 F.2d 264, 274 (D.C. Cir. 1969).

30. *See* ABA, *Appellate Review of Sentences Standards, supra* note 28, Supp. at 1–5.

THE RIGHTS OF PRISONERS

PHILIP J. HIRSCHKOP

IN 1910, WINSTON CHURCHILL STATED THAT "THE mood and temper of the public with regard to the treatment of crime and criminals is one of the most unfailing tests of the civilization of any country." Earlier, Fedor Dostoevsky had advanced the same idea, saying that "the degree of civilization in a society can be judged by entering its prisons." More recently, Chief Justice Warren E. Burger called for a comprehensive and profound examination into our penal system from beginning to end.[1] When such an examination is made, it will find depravity and sadism.

Were our society to be judged by Dostoevsky's standards, we would be found no more civilized than the Czarist Russian society of the nineteenth century that condemned him to life exile in a Siberian labor camp. This is not principally because of the physical tortures, although these are as imaginative, varied, and brutal in some of our state prisons as anywhere else. It is because of the utter despair of life and contempt for law and society that our so-called correctional institutions engender in their inmates, the psychological consequences of which are indescribable.[2]

The rights of prisoners cannot be appreciated without an understanding of the nature of prisons. American prison systems were innovations of the New World. The original colonies had no peni-

Philip J. Hirschkop is a practicing lawyer in Alexandria, Virginia, a member of the ACLU Board of Directors, a participant in a number of civil liberites cases, and Adjunct Professor at Georgetown Law Center. He is co-author of a leading study of prison conditions.

tentiaries, but rather gaols to detain people for trial or to hold occasional debtors. Felons were punished by being branded, maimed, pilloried, burned, or simply executed. Indeed, the reformers of that day posed incarceration as a progressive alternative to inhuman physical abuses.

Thus, prisons as we know them today were founded, not as a step forward from physical brutality, but rather as an alternative to it.[3] It was a nineteenth-century alternative that has not progressed very much. Prisoners in the stocks had no rights. The transfer of a system of punishment from brutality to incarceration added nothing to prisoners' rights. While certain physical punishments have been slowly abandoned, major concepts remain static. Despite some progressive programs, such as the federal work-release program in the Prisoner Rehabilitation Act of 1965,[4] public and judicial attitudes toward prisoners have, until recently, prevented expansion of the few "privileges" afforded prisoners into meaningful "rights." The courts have maintained a "hands-off" policy, which has enabled prisoners to secure only those rights which jailers allow, and a sharp dichotomy has grown between the developing standards of decency in society and outmoded state concepts of penology.

When penitentiaries were founded, "[t]he object of prosecution and punishment [was] to *prevent* crime, as well as to vindicate public justice."[5] But for many centuries, the fundamental idea underlying criminal law was one of vengeance.[6] It was this idea that motivated the pillorying, water tortures, rack, whip, and other punishments of the eighteenth and nineteenth centuries.

The usefulness of most jails is very much in question in light of their record of failure as reflected most dramatically by the tremendous rate of recidivism and growing crime indexes all over the country. It is accordingly understandable that jails themselves are becoming outmoded, and incarceration being replaced by work or education release or similar programs in federal and a growing number of state prison systems. Forward-looking theories, such as those advanced by Karl Menninger in *The Crime of Punishment,* indicate that prisoners should be treated for the social ills of crime just as patients are treated by doctors for their physical ills. The counsel to the Federal Bureau of Prisons, Eugene N. Barken, has stated that "a court which imposes terms of imprisonment not knowing what kind of treatment and facilities await the defendant, is the same as a physician who prescribes not knowing the makeup or consequences of the drug."[7]

As important as the philosophy are the physical facilities themselves. In the United States, over one-third of the prisons are seventy-five years old or older. Most of them lack modern plumbing, modern security systems, modern hygiene, modern culinary equipment, etc. When a prisoner enters most prisons, a twentieth-century man arrives in an eighteenth-century setting; the context itself inhibits the exercise or development of individual rights.

Only with the abandonment of the concepts of retribution and deterrence in favor of modern theories of rehabilitation will physical punishments be abandoned in our prisons and rights of prisoners be allowed to emerge. Only in the last couple of decades has the theory of rehabilitation received any judicial recognition. In 1949, the Supreme Court stated that "[r]etribution is no longer the dominant objective of the criminal law. Reformation and rehabilitation of offenders have become important goals of criminal jurisprudence."[8] The Court took cognizance also of the modern penological idea that the punishment should fit the offender and not merely the crime, and thus be meted out with regard to the past life and habits of a particular offender. There should also be individualized sentences that distinguish between, for example, first and repeated offenders. Chief Justice Burger recently underscored the new stress on education and correction: "The administration of criminal justice in a civilized country must embrace the idea of rehabilitation and training of the guilty person as well as the protection of society."

Despite the developing law, major abuses in prisons continue. Despite the handful of victories granting to prisoners substantial rights compared to those (if any) they held a decade ago, the whole structure of prison administration and the laxity of most courts allow wide abuses.

Practically speaking, the prisoners' lot has improved only with respect to the cruder physical punishments. Thus, when a man arrives at his place of incarceration, he will more than likely find himself in a mixture of felons and misdemeanants, of juveniles and adults, and of those already convicted and those awaiting trial. He will find himself subjected to homosexual attacks and induced to use drugs. Within days or weeks, a prisoner will feel the utter hopelessness of the situation and the complete power that the individual guard has over his health and life. Prisoners in many state prisons will learn that they may only have a set number of sheets of paper and can mail letters only on certain days. They will learn that in most instances everything they write, whether it be to courts or otherwise, is read by a guard or a prison administrator. They will also learn that they can no longer get various publications, or take courses, or conduct business, or do the things that they have been trained to do all their lives and that would be essential for proper rehabilitation.

Prisoners also learn that if they complain they will be transferred to a punitive segregation unit (often without reasons given), where they will probably lose their opportunity for an early parole and very likely lose "good time," thereby extending their prison term. Moreover, in punitive segregation prisoners may not write to anyone, sometimes not even courts; they are not allowed to take showers, are often forced to sleep on cement floors, are sometimes held in cells at subfreezing temperatures with little or no clothes, and are often put on reduced rations leading to severe hunger pains and weight loss.

Finally, prisoners learn that not only does the superintendent have complete discretion over their lives for the term of their imprisonment, but indeed the individual guard has the same power. Punishment is frequently based on the uninvestigated complaint of a guard, often one with little formal education or penal or psychological training.

When a judge sentences a man to prison, he knows that the man is normally eligible for parole after serving one-fourth of his term and that he receives ten days "good time" for each twenty days served. If a defendant is given a twelve-year sentence, the judge anticipates that the man will be eligible for parole after three years. If parole is not granted, the judge knows that if the defendant comports with prison rules he will automatically accrue four years "good time" and be released after eight years. In effect, the judge is giving a three-to-eight-year sentence. Unfortunately, a prison superintendent may thwart the outcome of this careful procedure by a single administrative decision with none of the stringent procedural safeguards that due process demands. When the courts defer to administrative discretion, it is usually untrained guards to whom they delegate the final word on reasonable prison practices. This is the central evil—the unreviewed administrative discretion granted to the poorly trained personnel who deal directly with prisoners. The existence of this evil necessarily leads to denial of access to the courts. Prison becomes a closed society in which the cruelest inhumanities exist unexposed.

Development of the Law

There are very few broad legal guidelines to determine the rights of prisoners. Happily, a prisoner is no longer regarded as a "slave of the state," as it was expressed in the past by various courts. The Supreme Court recognized in 1948 that while lawful incarceration must necessarily end or limit many privileges and rights,[9] a prisoner should not be stripped of any rights other than those which would be detrimental to the administration and discipline of the institution or the program established for him. Only a few years before that, another federal court recognized that "[a] prisoner retains all rights of an ordinary citizen except those expressly, or by necessary implication, taken from him by law."[10] Or, as succinctly stated by the Supreme Court of California: "A convicted felon, although civilly dead . . . is nevertheless a 'person' entitled to the protection of the Fourteenth Amendment."[11]

Despite these noble judicial words, there has been great reluctance to surrender to prisoners any of their rights—including the right to communicate; the right to be free from cruel and unusual physical and emotional punishments; the right to due process in internal prison proceedings; the right to adequate medical treatment; the right to an environment that does not impair health; the right to political freedom; and the right to be free from religious and racial discrimination.

The "Hands-Off" Policy

While theoretically a prisoner retains many of the rights mentioned above, in practice they are often lost. A chief reason is that there is a long-standing policy of the courts not to interfere in prison administration and discipline at any level.[12] Alternatively, it is often stated that there must be a clear abuse of discretion before the courts will act.[13]

The traditional judicial response to petitions alleging maltreatment of prisoners and denial of basic human rights has been to disaffirm jurisdiction on the grounds that the "internal affairs" of state prisons are beyond the scope of the court's jurisdiction.[14] This "hands-off" doctrine[15] is a product of judicial deference to putative administrative expertise and has prevented significant inquiry into the administration of penal institutions. The doctrine is not a rule of law but a policy of judicial abstention. Courts usually justify this noninterference on the basis of separation of powers—administration of prisons viewed as an executive function; allocation of state and federal power (states retain the power to proscribe an act as criminal and to set the punishment); cost (improved penal procedures are expensive and courts cannot appropriate funds); and fear that judicial lack of expertise in penology will create disciplinary problems.[16]

Reluctance to protect the constitutionally derived basic human rights of prisoners is an abdication of judicial responsibility; it operates to strengthen the status quo and isolates penal systems from public scrutiny. Court refusal to hear complaints impedes the development of standards for circumspect prison administration. It legitimates intolerable conditions and undercuts the efforts of concerned citizens to correct such conditions. It effectively places prison officials in an invulnerable position with absolute power. Probably the greatest single step that can be made in the administration of prisons is to have the courts meet their obligations with respect to the Constitution and the rights of prisoners and no longer hide behind the hands-off doctrine.

Despite the traditional reluctance of the courts to interfere with the internal administration of prisons, some inroads have been made during the last several years. Realizing the tremendous power of superintendents and guards to add years of punishment to a prisoner's sentence, a New York court stated, "[I]t seems quite obvious that any *further* restraint *in excess* of that permitted by the judgment or constitutional guarantees should be subject to inquiry."[17] This touches the core of the deficiencies in the hands-off doctrine.

It was not until the mid-1960's that a series of decisions weakened this doctrine and perhaps signaled its demise. A few courts began not only to recognize due process rights of prisoners but to apply the Eighth Amendment standard of cruel and unusual punishment to extend judicial protection to inmates.

Thus, in 1966 a federal district court in California declared it cruel and unusual punishment to hold a man in a strip cell without furniture, adequate light, or ventilation while denying him food and health care. The court rejected the hands-off doctrine because prison authorities had "abandoned elemental concepts of decency by permitting conditions to prevail of a shocking and debased nature."[18]

In the next few years, other lower federal courts released men from solitary confinement and struck down the use of corporal punishment. In one case, the hands-off doctrine was rejected because conditions in solitary violated the Eighth Amendment in that they "could only serve to destroy completely the spirit and undermine the sanity of the prisoner."[19] In another case, concern was expressed that "[c]orporal punishment is easily subject to abuse in the hands of the sadistic and unscrupulous" and that "[w]here power to punish is granted persons in lower levels of administrative authority, there is an inherent and natural difficulty in enforcing the limitations of that power." That court went further to find that the use of the strap in this day is "unusual and . . . cruel."[20] Taken together, these decisions signal a new approach to the Eighth Amendment in prison cases. The courts took an important step in seeking the advice of national penological experts such as James V. Bennett, former Director of the Federal Bureau of Prisons, and Fred T. Wilkenson, the Director of the Missouri Division of Corrections. Further, they took judicial notice of established guidelines, such as the directives of the United States Bureau of Prisons, the American Correctional Association Manual of Correctional Standards, and the report of the President's Commission on Corrections.

During the period that these cases were being decided, the United States Supreme Court handed down two major decisions seriously weakening the hands-off doctrine. In 1966, the Court summarily affirmed a lower-court decision which held that the Fourteenth Amendment protected prisoners.[21] In 1969, the Court held:

> There is no doubt that discipline and administration of state detention facilities are state functions. They are subject to federal authority only where paramount federal constitutional and statutory rights supervene. It is clear, however, that in instances where state regulations applicable to inmates of prison facilities conflict with such rights, the regulations may be invalidated.[22]

What is apparent from these decisions is that the courts have finally taken to heart the old doctrine:

> Time works changes, brings into existence new conditions and purposes. Therefore a principle to be vital must be capable of wider application than the mischief which gave it birth.[23]

The principle embodied in these words stands as an open invitation to judicial activism, a mandate ordering judicial cognizance of the problems and applications of contemporary knowledge. Accordingly, lower courts have followed the Supreme Court in eschewing the hands-off policy in prison cases. A federal court in Arkansas decided: "However constitutionally tolerable the Arkansas system may have been in former years, it simply will not do today as a Twentieth Century goes into his [sic] eighth decade."[24] Going even further, federal courts in New York and Rhode Island not only found various jail conditions unconstitutional but adopted specific standards of due process to meet these deprivations.[25]

PRISONERS' RIGHTS

Due Process

Probably the most important question of legal rights hinges now around the question of due process for prisoners. This is especially true in the treatment of prisoners who have been placed in punitive segregation, given punitive transfers, denied "good time," or had the length of their sentence altered because of alleged prison infractions. Until recent years, this area had been virtually undeveloped, much as juvenile rights remained fallow for so long. Several opinions have paved the way for what will one day be a code of prisoner rights. These rights will probably have to be imposed on prison administrators reluctant to give up their despotic powers over the lives and welfare of inmates.

The importance of due process for prisoners was recognized by a federal court in Arkansas, which stated that "a theoretical right of access to the Courts is hardly actual and adequate if its exercise is likely to produce reprisals, physical or otherwise, from Penitentiary personnel."[26] In that case, the court ruled that a prisoner must be given advance notice of the character of a prohibited act and the punishment which that particular conduct will incur. Soon thereafter, a New York court ruled that a prisoner should be given advance notice of the charges against him for infractions of jail rules.[27]

In a case leading to a judicial breakthrough in the setting of standards of due process, an Alabama court held that prisoners may not be denied fundamental rights out of deference to internal prison policy. It explicitly stated: "[T]he Due Process and Equal Protection Clauses of the Fourteenth Amendment follow [persons] into prison and protect them there from unconstitutional action on the part of prison authorities carried out under color of state law."[28] Subsequently, two federal appellate courts extended due process rights to transfers of people from one mode of custody to another.[29]

Even more recently, two courts extended the due process rights of prisoners still further. In a New York case,[30] Judge Constance Baker Motley held that prior to any administrative punitive action a prisoner must be given written copies of charges against him; a record of any hearing; the right to cross-examine his accusers and call witnesses in his own behalf; the right to retain counsel or to appoint a counsel substitute; and a decision in writing briefly setting forth the evidence upon which it is based, the reasons for the decision, and the legal basis for the punishment imposed. Judge Motley also specified a maximum period a man may spend in solitary confinement.

In a Rhode Island case,[31] Judge Raymond J. Pettine, after lengthy consultation with counsel and a canvass of the prison population, ordered the adoption of various regulations concerning classification of prisoners and transfers for punitive reasons. The net effect will be to prevent prison administrators from buying off the rights of their wards by threatened transfer to punitive segregation or denial of other rights. These two cases are apparently the precursors of a number of excellent decisions recently rendered giving strong indication of this trend in prison rights.[32] It is to be hoped that these decisions have signaled an end to the right-privilege distinction which in the past has impeded judicial protection of prisoners.[33]

While most of the cases above apply to the release of prisoners from punitive segregation, there is no logical reason, as some courts have already indicated,[34] for the same analysis not to apply to forfeiture of "good time."

Freedom from Cruel and Unusual Punishment and Abusive Treatment

Despite the emerging theories of probation and work and education programs, the use of physical punishments still flourishes in prisons. Thus, as late as twenty years ago, Virginia still used a form of the rack. In Arkansas, recent disclosures show the use of barbaric forms of torture, including an electrical charging device known as the "Tucker Phone" in which one wire led from an hand-cranked telephone was attached to the genital organs of an inmate and another wire led to his big toe. The instrument was then cranked, sending electrical charges into the body of the inmate. Hypodermic needles were pushed under fingernails; lighted ends of burning cigarettes were placed on bodies; and beatings were administered without just cause, with fists, knotted ropes, brass knuckles, canes, hoe handles, pick or ax handles, clubs, trace chains, rubber hoses, "bull hides," *ad nauseum*. Disclosure of these conditions caused the district court in Arkansas to declare the whole system unconstitutional.[35] Similarly, a state court in Pennsylvania recently declared unconstitutional, as cruel and unusual punishment, incarceration of untried inmates in Holmsburg Prison, because the conditions there were "an affront to the dignity of man."[36]

In Spartanburg, South Carolina, solitary confinement consisted until recently of locking a man in a cement structure with no ventilation where he was chained immobile and fed one cracker a day. In other prisons men are held for long periods in cells with neither natural or artificial light. A Tennessee court recently declared that holding men nude in inadequately lighted or ventilated cells and forcing them to sleep on cement floors with no means to maintain personal cleanliness was cruel and unusual punishment.[37] Thus, despite developing concepts of penology, archaic physical punishments persist.

Even if all the whips and torture devices and physical beatings were to be successfully proscribed tomorrow, physical abuse would only be mitigated. It would not be ended, because of the continuing lack of physical care by prison authorities[38] and, above all, the psychological tortures imposed on prisoners. Locked incommunicado for years in "strip" cells or solitary confinement, subjected to the constant fear of beatings or loss of "good time" without any reason or explanation, prisoners know far worse agony than most physical beating can cause.

The most obvious avenue for judicial restriction of physical abuse in penal institutions would seem to be the constitutional ban on cruel and unusual punishments. Owing to judicial timidity, however, this mandate has never been fully utilized as a vehicle for reform. Its promised assurance of a humane government has remained a sterile promise for prisoners. Courts have refused relief in case after case that reveal seemingly endless instances of official cruelty.

Nevertheless, several decisions have applied more understanding tests. Subjecting a prisoner to the demonstrated risk of loss of sanity for any offense in prison is plainly cruel and unusual punishment as judged by present standards of decency.[39] In another case the judge followed standards of the Supreme Court that cruel and unusual punishment should be tested against the "evolving standards of decency that mark the progress of a maturing society," and found that the confinement to punitive segregation was so disproportionate to the offense committed as to amount to cruel and unusual punishment.[40]

Communications

It has been a long-established policy that prison officials are entitled to censor all mail.[41] But the Supreme Court in 1941 introduced a major exception to this rule: that censors could not interfere with mail to courts in which a prisoner was seeking legal redress.[42] This principle was given fuller vitality in other opinions holding the court mail from a prisoner may not be delayed any longer than required for sorting and must be delivered without censorship of any kind.[43] Some courts have extended the right of communication to contact with public officials; to government officials involved in the problems of incarceration; to groups such as the American Civil Liberties Union;[44] and to counsel.[45]

Despite these rulings, few judges have recognized the right of prisoners to have the tools, in the form of legal materials, to seek judicial relief.[46] Thus, a number of states have expressly prohibited the acquisition of law books in prison libraries. Some states do not allow law books in cells; others do not allow individual prisoners to own law books.[47] Some courts have made inroads here, citing need for prison reform and urging use of law students to render legal assistance.[48] Even in states that authorize prison law libraries or permit prisoners to own books, it is rare to find volumes dealing with civil (as opposed to criminal) problems.

Fortunately, many of these censorship issues that exist in state prison systems have been resolved in the federal system, where regulations require law libraries and free correspondence by prisoners. A recent major decision may be the harbinger of judicial intervention against most state censorship of inmate mail.[49]

Medical Treatment

Another major area of concern is medical treatment. In the overwhelming majority of prisons, there are no full-time doctors. Moreover, many prison doctors are unqualified to treat the illnesses they are examining. Some doctors, seeing large numbers of prisoners for relatively short periods, exhibit a hard attitude that all prisoners are malingers. Despite recent inroads in other areas, there has been virtually no progress here. Almost all cases hold that medical treatment of prisoners is an internal matter with which the courts will not interfere. One of the few cases to the contrary held that while "The hands-off doctrine operates reasonably to the extent that it prevents judicial review of deprivations which are necessary or reasonable concomitants of imprisonment. Deprivation of reasonable medical care and of reasonable access to the courts are not among such concomitants, however. Prisoners are entitled to medical care and to access to the courts."[50]

Nondiscrimination

Many federal and state courts have held that prisoners may be denied freedom to worship together and to have certain religious materials. A few courts have held to the contrary.[51]

While the case law concerns several religions, the major area of litigation involves Black Muslims. The restriction of rights to the Muslims involves the determination by prison administrators that it is not a true religion. Furthermore, they say that even if it were a religion the Muslims would cause trouble if allowed to practice it; there is evidence also that racial prejudices against black people have played a role. Oddly enough, many administrators feel that the Muslims are model prisoners, not taking part in homosexual activities, and disciplining themselves within the restrictions of prison rules. Despite this, prison authorities continue to deny them many basic rights, including the right to hold services, to receive their official newspaper, *Muhammad Speaks,* to listen to broadcasts of Elijah Muhammad, and to receive the Koran.[52] One decision ruled that the Black Muslims met the test of religion in having a belief in a Supreme Being,[53] and the trend now is to grant the Muslims the right to worship in the absence of a particularized showing that prison administrators need to curb religious practices generally.

Another frequently litigated practice is racial segregation in prisons, which has been declared unconstitutional in a number of cases. While it remains fairly widespread, it is being quickly overcome through litigation in many states.[54]

Other Rights

There are other areas of difficulty. One concerns the right to be free from involuntary servitude or cruel and unusual punishment as a result of coerced hard labor. The courts have rejected this argument and held that hard labor, as a penalty for crime, is expressly permitted by the Thirteenth Amendment and not prohibited by the Eighth.[55]

Another widespread practice is the denial to prisoners of citizenship or voting rights during and after incarceration. While there have been some legislative inroads into these disabilities, they still remain a serious problem.[56]

Prisoners have also been prevented from filing civil suits or participating in civil litigation, especially involving business and domestic relations. Here there has been progress. The Supreme Court has ruled that prisoners may sue under the Federal Tort Claims Act.[57] Other courts have held that prisoners may recover both punitive and exemplary damages for denial of their rights by prison authorities while in prison; and that where a prisoner complained of denial of his rights, the court had a duty to appoint counsel where it was necessary for an indigent prisoner to receive fair consideration.[58]

Prisoners are also denied any kind of consortium or conjugal visitation of wives. While it may be premature to expect recognition of these personal rights, there should be an immediate end to other barbaric rules, such as those that permit wives to obtain divorces and remarry without notice to the prisoner or without a chance for the prisoner to fully participate in the litigation, and others that enable children to be adopted without the consent of an imprisoned father.

FUTURE RIGHTS

Many immediate changes can be made to secure wider rights for prisoners and to enforce those that are now recognized. First, all censorship restrictions with regard to courts, public officials, and social action groups must be lifted if the cloak of secrecy surrounding punishments inflicted on prisoners is to be parted. Furthermore, there should be administrative review, according to fair procedures, of all punitive decisions. Thus, "good time" should not be taken from a prisoner or a man transferred to segregation unless he is given written charges, a chance to confront and examine his accusers, a chance to have some type of representation at a hearing, and a report of the hearing, including the findings and reasons of an impartial body. In addition, all special courts for prisoners who commit crimes in prison should be abandoned and prisoners should be subject to the regular judicial process.

There are other rights to which prisoners are entitled which go far beyond the problems of censorship and legal remedies. Some courts are now starting to speak of rights of rehabilitation, rights of privacy, and rights of freedom of thought. Many other potential improvements for prison systems are being explored, including psychiatric services and psychological testing for prisoners; conjugal visiting privileges; separation of hardened criminals from misdemeanants and minors; case workers to work with prisoners; better paid, recruited, and trained guards and administrative personnel; an administrative review board to review the actions of prison supervisory personnel; and work and educational release programs.

While many of the above are now merely considered privileges, some of them will be enunciated as rights and enforced within the near future. Probably the most basic is the right to treatment or rehabilitation. Acknowledging that a sociological theory may ripen into constitutional law, one court recently considered whether the Constitution required a program of rehabilitation, but concluded that it was not yet an enforceable right.[59]

There has also been some recognition of a right to privacy and to be free in one's person. It was recently held that inmates "ought at least to be able to fall asleep at night without fear of having their throats cut before morning and that the state has failed to discharge a constitutional duty in taking steps to enable them to do so."[60]

The most far-reaching of the recent opinions indicated that prisoners should not only have freedom from physical punishments and degrading situations, but should also have freedom to think and express themselves as they see fit, on both political and religious matters. The judge in that case went on to find cruel and unusual punishment of the prisoner because of "1) severe physical deprivations, i.e., loss of energy giving food and loss of exercise, 2) needless degradation, 3) loss of work opportunities of a rehabilitative nature, 4) loss of money which might have been earned by working, 5) loss of schooling and training opportunities, 6) loss of self improvement through reading books of one's own choice, and 7) great mental anguish."[61]

CONCLUSION

The need to extend rights of prisoners has been best put in perspective by a recent ruling:

> That penal as well as judicial authorities respond to constitutional duties is vastly important to society as well as the prisoner. Treatment that degrades the inmate, invades his privacy, and frustrates the ability to choose pursuits through which he can manifest himself and gain self-respect erodes the very foundations upon which he can prepare for a socially useful life.[62]

The ultimate result of the physical brutality and denial of proper procedures is that prisoners lose hope for themselves and respect for the legal system. Combined with physical brutality and arbitrary procedures, this makes prison life unbearable. Probation, work and education release, and other rehabilitative programs will not work unless prisoners have the mental attitude to be able to benefit from them. Before such programs can be successful, we will have to adopt Karl Menninger's view that crime is an illness, and give treatment as we would for any illness.

Since the states have failed to administer prisons properly, the courts must exercise their authority in protecting the constitutional rights of citizens. The federal courts must establish minimum standards of due process. They have every right, reason, and obligation to impose various proven standards as minimum standards.[63] Until that is done, each prisoner subject to the whim of a guard is no better off than the prisoner in Kafka's *The Trial,* who found "it is an essential part of justice dispensed here that you should be condemned not only in innocence but also in ignorance."[64]

While that philosophy prevails, rehabilitation is impossible and recidivism must flourish.

NOTES

1. Burger, "No Man is an Island," 56 *American Bar Association Journal* 325 (1970).

2. *See* Hirschkop & Millemann, "The Unconstitutionality of Prison Life," 55 *Virginia Law Review* 795 (1969).

3. For a historical discussion of incarceration, see S. Rubin *et al.*, *The Law of Criminal Correction* (1963).

4. Pub. L. 89–176, 79 Stat. 674 (1965).

5. Blyew v. United States, 80 U.S. (13 Wall.) 581, 600 (1871) (Bradley, J., dissenting) (emphasis in the original).

6. Howard v. State, 28 Ariz. 433, 237 P. 203 (1925). For further discussion, see K. Menninger, *The Crime of Punishment* (1969).

7. H. Perlman & T. Allington, eds., *The Tasks of Penology* 104 (1969); *see also* the milestone publication on the overall effect of prisons on prisoners, D. Glaser, *The Effectiveness of a Prison and Parole System* (1964).

8. Williams v. New York, 337 U.S. 241, 248 (1949); *see also* Trop v. Dulles, 356 U.S. 86, 111 (1958) (Brennan, J., concurring).

9. Price v. Johnston, 334 U.S. 266, 285 (1948).

10. Coffin v. Reichard, 143 F.2d 443, 445 (6th Cir. 1944).

11. *In re* Jones, 57 Cal. 2d 860, 862, 22 Cal. Rptr. 478, 479, 372 P.2d 310, 312 (1962).

12. *E.g.*, Price v. Johnston, 334 U.S. 266 (1948); Tabor v. Hardwick, 224 F.2d 526 (5th Cir. 1955), *cert. denied*, 350 U.S. 971 (1956).

13. Walker v. Blackwell, 360 F.2d 66 (5th Cir. 1966).

14. For a discussion of judicial treatment of prisoners' complaints prior to 1963, see Note, "Beyond the Ken of the Courts: A Critique of Judicial Refusal to Review the Complaints of Convicts," 72 *Yale Law Journal* 506 (1963); Note, "Constitutional Rights of Prisoners: The Developing Law," 110 *University of Pennsylvania Law Review* 985 (1962).

15. Fritch, *Civil Rights of Prisoners* 31 (1961), appears to be the source of the phrase "hands-off doctrine."

16. *See, e.g.*, McCloskey v. Maryland, 337 F.2d 72, 74 (4th Cir. 1964); Haines v. Kerner, 427 F.2d 71 (7th Cir. 1970).

17. People *ex rel.* Brown v. Johnston, 9 N.Y.2d 482, 485, 215 N.Y.S.2d 44, 45, 174 N.E.2d 725, 726 (1961) (emphasis by the court).

18. Jordan v. Fitzharris, 257 F. Supp. 674, 680 (N.D. Cal. 1966).

19. Wright v. McMann, 387 F.2d 519, 526 (2nd Cir. 1967).

20. Jackson v. Bishop, 404 F.2d 571, 579, 580 (8th Cir. 1968).

21. Washington v. Lee, 263 F. Supp. 327 (M.D. Ala. 1966) (3-judge court), *aff'd per curiam*, 390 U.S. 333 (1968).

22. Johnson v. Avery, 393 U.S. 483, 486 (1969).

23. Weems v. United States, 217 U.S. 349, 373 (1910).

24. Holt v. Sarver, 309 F. Supp. 362, 381 (E.D. Ark. 1970).

25. Sostre v. Rockefeller, 312 F. Supp. 863 (S.D.N.Y. 1970); Morris v. Travisono, 310 F. Supp. 857 (D.R.I. 1970). For an excellent discussion of this problem see Jacob, "Prison Discipline and Inmate Rights," 5 *Harvard Civil Rights–Civil Liberties Law Review* 227 (1970).

26. Talley v. Stephen, 247 F. Supp. 683, 690 (E.D. Ark. 1965).

27. *Cf.* Wright v. McMann, 257 F. Supp. 739, 745 (N.D.N.Y. 1966), *rev'd on*

other grounds, 387 F.2d 519 (2nd Cir. 1967). A later district court opinion in this case adopted specific procedural guidelines. Wright v. McMann, No. 66 (N.D.N.Y. July 31, 1970).

28. Washington v. Lee, 263 F. Supp. 327, 331 (M.D. Ala. 1966), *aff'd per curiam,* 390 U.S. 333 (1968).

29. Shone v. Main, 406 F.2d 844 (1st Cir.), *vacated as moot,* 396 U.S. 6 (1969); United States *ex rel.* Schuster v. Herold, 410 F.2d 1071 (2nd Cir.), *cert. denied,* 396 U.S. 847 (1969).

30. *See* Sostre v. Rockefeller, 312 F. Supp. 863 (S.D.N.Y. 1970).

31. Morris v. Travisono, 310 F. Supp. 857 (D.R.I. 1970).

32. *E.g.,* Wright v. McMann, *supra* note 27, which apparently follows the guidelines of Sostre v. Rockefeller, 312 F. Supp. 863 (S.D.N.Y. 1970); Nolan v. Scafati, No. 7538 (1st Cir. Aug. 14, 1970) (indicating that some assurances of elemental fairness are essential in prison administration); Carothers v. Follette, No. 68 Civ. 3927 (S.D.N.Y. July 15, 1970) (forbidding certain punishments "until procedures are adopted which meet rudimentary standards of due process").

33. *See* Van Alstyne, "The Demise of the Right-Privilege Distinction in Constitutional Law," 81 *Harvard Law Review,* 1439 (1968).

34. *E.g.,* Outten v. Peyton, No. 12,141 (4th Cir. Dec. 3, 1969).

35. Holt v. Sarver, 309 F. Supp. 362 (E.D. Ark. 1970).

36. Bryant v. Hendricks, 7 Criminal Law Reporter 2463 (Phila. Ct. Common Pleas Aug. 11, 1970).

37. Hancock v. Avery, 301 F. Supp. 786 (M.D. Tenn. 1969).

38. *See* Davis, "Sexual Assaults in Philadelphia System and Sheriff's Van," *Trans-Action* (Dec. 1968).

39. *See Ex parte* Medley, 134 U.S. 160, 167–70 (1890).

40. Sostre v. Rockefeller, 312 F. Supp. 863 (S.D.N.Y. 1970).

41. *E.g.,* Ortega v. Ragen, 216 F.2d 561 (7th Cir. 1954), *cert. denied,* 349 U.S. 940 (1955).

42. *Ex parte* Hull, 312 U.S. 546 (1941); *see also* Lee v. Tahash, 352 F.2d 970 (8th Cir. 1965).

43. *E.g.,* Coleman v. Peyton, 362 F.2d 905 (4th Cir.), *cert. denied,* 385 U.S. 905 (1966).

44. Nolan v. Scafati, No. 7538 (1st Cir. Aug. 14, 1970); Burns v. Swenson, (8th Cir. Aug. 31, 1970).

45. Sostre v. Rockefeller, 312 F. Supp. 863 (S.D.N.Y. 1970); *see also* the thoughtful dissenting opinion of Judge Keating in Brabson v. Wilkins, 19 N.Y.2d 433, 437, 227 N.E.2d 383, 385, 280 N.Y.S.2d 561, 564 (1967); McDonough v. Director, 7 Criminal Law Reporter 2429 (4th Cir. Aug. 5, 1970).

46. *See generally* 48 *The Prison Journal,* No. 1, at 22, 23 (1968); Note, "The Right of Expression in Prison," 40 *Southern California Law Review* 407 (1967); Robinson v. Birzgallis, 311 F. Supp. 908 (W.D. Mich. 1970).

47. However a recent three-judge federal district court opinion sets availability of legal materials as clear right, Gilmore v. Lynch, 8 Criminal Law Reporter 2028 (N.D. Cal. Sept. 2, 1970).

48. United States v. Simpson, No. 23,352 (D.C. Cir. Oct. 1, 1970).

49. Palmigiano v. Travisono, (D.R.I. Aug. 24, 1970).

50. Edwards v. Duncan, 355 F.2d 993, 994 (4th Cir. 1966).

51. *See, e.g.,* Sostre v. McGinnis, 334 F.2d 906 (2nd Cir.), *cert. denied,* 379 U.S. 893 (1964); Long v. Parker, 390 F.2d 816 (3rd Cir. 1968); Barnett v. Rodgers, 410 F.2d 995 (D.C. Cir. 1969).

52. A recent class action has granted broad relief to Muslims in this area.

Northern v. Nelson, C-69 279 (N.D. Cal. July 8, 1970). *But see* Gittlemaeker v. Prasse, 428 F.2d 1 (3rd Cir. 1970).

53. Fullwood v. Clemmer, 206 F. Supp. 370 (D.D.C. 1962).

54. Washington v. Lee, 263 F. Supp. 327 (M.D. Ala. 1966), *aff'd per curiam,* 390 U.S. 333 (1968); Wilson v. Kelley, 294 F. Supp. 1005 (N.D. Ga.), *aff'd per curiam,* 393 U.S. 266 (1968); Mason v. Peyton, No. 5611–R (E.D. Va. Oct. 16, 1969).

55. United States v. Reynolds, 235 U.S. 133 (1914); Draper v. Rhay, 315 F.2d 193 (9th Cir.), *cert. denied,* 375 U.S. 915 (1963).

56. *See, e.g.,* Green v. Board of Elections, 380 F.2d 445 (2nd Cir. 1967), *cert. denied,* 389 U.S. 1048 (1968).

57. United States v. Muniz, 374 U.S. 150 (1963).

58. Sostre v. Rockefeller, 312 F. Supp. 863 (S.D.N.Y. 1970); Hudson v. Hardy, 412 F.2d 1091 (D.C. Cir. 1968).

59. Holt v. Sarver, 309 F. Supp. 362 (E.D. Ark. 1970); *see also* United States *ex rel.* Schuster v. Herold, 410 F.2d 1071, 1091 (2d Cir.), *cert. denied,* 396 U.S. 847 (1969).

60. Holt v. Sarver, 309 F. Supp. 362 (E.D. Ark. 1970).

61. Sostre v. Rockefeller, 312 F. Supp. 863, 885 (S.D.N.Y. 1970).

62. Barnett v. Rodgers, 410 F.2d 995, 1002 (D.C. Cir. 1969).

63. *See* American Correctional Association, *Manual of Correctional Standards* (3d ed. 1966); American Law Institute, *Model Penal Code* §304.7 (Proposed Official Draft 1962); President's Commission on Law Enforcement and Administration of Justice, *Task Force Report: Corrections* 85 (1967).

64. F. Kafka, *The Trial* 62 (Modern Library ed. 1964).

THE RIGHTS OF
JUVENILES

DANIEL A. REZNECK

THE SUPREME COURT'S DECISIONS ON THE RIGHTS
of juveniles have initiated far-reaching changes in the law.[1] Many
courts have had to revaluate long-established practices and procedures in juvenile cases. Some have gone beyond the specific mandates of the Supreme Court in according new procedural protections
to juveniles. Others have still fallen short of what the Constitution
requires.

A number of states have comprehensively overhauled their
juvenile court acts to take account of the new judicial doctrines.
Several model codes of juvenile court procedure have been proposed to reflect the best current thought in the field.[2] The output
of legal commentary on juvenile rights is voluminous.[3]

The direction of the Supreme Court decisions is unmistakably
toward according juveniles accused of delinquency many of the
procedural rights of adults charged with crime. But the Court has
repeatedly emphasized that it recognizes differences between juvenile and criminal proceedings and does not wish to turn juvenile
cases into replicas of adult criminal prosecutions.[4] The Court has
not held that an accused juvenile is entitled to all the procedural
guarantees of an adult.

Significantly, the Court has not based any of its decisions on the
equal protection clause of the Fourteenth Amendment. Although

Daniel A. Rezneck is a practicing lawyer in Washington, D.C., Adjunct Professor of
Law at Georgetown Law School, and a former Assistant United States Attorney. He
is a frequent contributor to legal periodicals on criminal law issues.

it has considered disparities in a state's treatment of juveniles and adults relevant, it has not held procedural disparities to be impermissible per se. Instead the Court has decided these cases under the due process clause, applying the test of whether a particular procedural right is one of the "essentials of due process and fair treatment" in a juvenile proceeding. In effect, the Court has employed the technique of "selective incorporation" of the procedural rights of adults in determining the rights of juveniles—the same method it has used to impose various criminal law guarantees of the Bill of Rights on the states through the Fourteenth Amendment.

The Court has proceeded cautiously along the path of "incorporation." It has sought to accommodate the philosophy of individualized treatment and rehabilitation which has animated the juvenile court movement in this country. It has upheld claims of constitutional right for juveniles only if satisfied that the asserted right is essential to the fairness and reliability of the juvenile court process and that its allowance would not significantly interfere with the juvenile court's attainment of its objectives.

The Court has thus far dealt only with one of the three stages of the juvenile proceeding—the adjudicative, or trial phase. It has not determined the rights applicable in the pretrial and dispositional phases. These stages of the juvenile process differ in certain respects from the adult criminal process, notably in the recent development of new techniques for adjusting juvenile cases without trial through consent decrees and pretrial conferences, and in the wider range of dispositional alternatives available, at least in theory, to the juvenile courts. These differences may justify greater procedural informality and flexibility in the pretrial and dispositional stages of the juvenile proceeding.

Moreover, the Court's decisions have all concerned the rights of juveniles accused of delinquent conduct constituting a crime if committed by an adult; in each case the dual threat of confinement in a state institution and stigmatization as a "juvenile deliquent" was present. Such cases are the most compelling for application of procedural guarantees derived from the criminal law—they are "comparable in seriousness to a felony prosecution."[5]

Many juvenile cases, however, do not have these characteristics. The Court has not yet decided what procedural rights are necessary or appropriate in a juvenile case not involving the charge of criminal conduct, such as "truancy" or "incorrigibility"; or in a case not carrying the potential stigma of a "delinquency" adjudication, such as a proceeding to declare a juvenile "in need of supervision," a new legal status some states have created to cover juveniles whose conduct does not violate state criminal statutes; or in a case not leading to confinement in an institution with penal features, such as a proceeding to declare a child "neglected" or "dependent" and place him in a foster home. Juvenile courts ordinarily exercise broad jurisdiction over noncriminal conduct and adjudicate matters of status and living conditions in addition to identifiable unlawful acts. It is therefore unlikely that the Supreme Court will subject the juvenile courts altogether to strict procedures drawn from the criminal law.

The Court has thus far held five procedural guarantees of the criminal law binding on juvenile courts in delinquency proceedings based on alleged violation of criminal statutes. It has decided that:

1. A juvenile charged with delinquency, and his parents or guardian, must be given written notice of the specific charge or factual allegations against him at the earliest practicable time in advance of any hearing to adjudicate the merits of the charge. Such notice must in any event be afforded sufficiently in advance of the hearing to permit preparation.

2. Before an adjudicative hearing may be held, the juvenile and his parents must be notified that he has a right to be represented by counsel retained by them, or if they are unable to afford a lawyer, that counsel will be appointed for him.

3. The privilege against self-incrimination is applicable in such a hearing, and the juvenile must be advised that he does not have to testify or make a statement.

4. Absent a valid confession adequate to support a determination of delinquency, an adjudication at an adjudicative hearing must be based on the sworn testimony of witnesses who are available for confrontation and cross-examination.[6]

5. The evidence must prove beyond a reasonable doubt that the juvenile has committed the offense charged.[7]

In addition, the Court has held that before a juvenile may be transferred from juvenile court to adult criminal court for prosecution as an adult, the juvenile court must afford him a hearing, at which he has the right to the effective assistance of counsel. His counsel is entitled to receive access to all records and reports which the juvenile court considers in making its transfer decision, and the court is required to state on the record its reasons for ordering a transfer.[8]

This essay will consider some unresolved questions of constitutional rights in a delinquency proceeding. In accordance with the Supreme Court's differentiation of juvenile proceedings into three phases, the discussion will be divided into three parts: adjudicative, pre-judicial, and dispositional.

The Adjudicative Stage

Fair Notice

The Court's requirement of fair notice in advance of the adjudicative hearing has important implications. Although pleading with the technicality of a criminal indictment may not be required, a constitutionally sufficient petition will have to indicate both the factual and the legal basis on which an adjudication of delinquency is sought. If the claim of delinquency rests on a criminal law violation, the specific statute must be cited. No defendant in a civil or criminal case can adequately prepare a defense without knowing the rule of law invoked against him; this is especially true with respect to criminal violations, since the same conduct frequently may violate more than one statute. This principle of fair notice should also govern when the conduct charged does not involve a criminal law violation, such as truancy, incorrigibility, or being "beyond control."

It follows that if the factual or legal basis of the alleged delinquency has not been indicated in the petition, an adjudication of delinquency cannot stand, even if the evidence adduced at the hearing is sufficient to support it. It is also essential to know what was actually decided in the delinquency proceeding in order to determine whether there was compliance with the requirement of fair notice. This will require juvenile court judges to specify their factual findings and legal conclusions in adjudicating a case without a jury, and to delineate the legal and factual issues if the case is tried to a jury. Moreover, if the right to appeal or to obtain judicial review by some other method is recognized, identification of what was decided in the juvenile court will be indispensable to meaningful review.

Furthermore, the reach of the principle of fair notice is not limited to giving notice of the charges before adjudication. It also requires that the statute on which the charges are based must give fair notice of the proscribed conduct. A criminal conviction cannot be based on a statutory standard too vague to be intelligible. The rule should be the same for an adjudication of delinquency.

This problem is acute in juvenile courts because of statutes defining delinquency to include "truancy," "beyond control," "incorrigibility," and "habitually involved in immoral matters." These categories invite a subjective judgment, especially if the court is authorized to convict merely by finding the juvenile "involved" in delinquency whether or not he has committed any specific act. If juvenile court statutes continue to attach the stigma of delinquency and the threat of confinement to a juvenile engaged in noncriminal conduct, they will face challenge on grounds of unconstitutional vagueness.

The Right to Counsel

The right to counsel in the adjudicative stage should require that the juvenile be given the opportunity for counsel when he first appears before the court for an initial hearing after a petition has been filed. This is consistent with the settled rule in criminal prosecutions that any proceeding at which a defendant is called upon to plead is a "critical stage" of the proceeding and he is entitled to counsel.[9] The initial hearing in a juvenile proceeding is likewise a "critical stage" if the juvenile is called on to admit or deny involvement.

Simply informing the juvenile and his parents at the initial hearing of the right to counsel is no guarantee that it will be exercised. The question arises whether the juvenile must affirmatively assert his right, or whether counsel should be provided unless the juvenile and his parents affirmatively waive it. Due process should require that counsel be appointed automatically and the juvenile be afforded opportunity to consult a lawyer before deciding how to plead. It is difficult to see how a juvenile can validly waive the right to counsel, and with it a meaningful hearing on the merits, without the prior advice of counsel. There is therefore an exigent need for the states to make adequate provision for the representation of juveniles by counsel competent in such cases.

Confrontation and Cross-examination

Although it has been urged that juvenile courts should have wider latitude in receiving evidence than adult criminal courts, there is no justification for any material departure in the adjudicative stage from the rules of evidence in criminal cases. These rules have evolved from the experience of centuries as the best method for determining guilt and innocence. Moreover, some of the most important evidentiary principles, including the hearsay rule, have a constitutional basis in the right of confrontation and cross-examination.

This constitutional dimension is decisive for the proper resolution of one of the most serious evidentiary problems in juvenile courts: whether the trier of fact may rely at the adjudicative hearing on social studies and other investigative reports on the juvenile which have been compiled by the court staff. Such reports often contain hearsay several times removed from anyone's personal knowledge. Moreover, they frequently assert facts relating to the juvenile's character and prior involvements with the law which would not be admissible at a criminal trial. Due process should prevent the trier of fact from considering such materials during adjudication and from basing a finding of delinquency on them.

In any event, whatever materials or facts are relied on by the trier of fact must be disclosed to the juvenile and his counsel. The practice of some juvenile courts of relying on undisclosed information as a basis for decision conflicts with principles of due process controlling all judicial and quasi-judicial bodies.[10]

The Trier of Fact

A much debated question in juvenile cases is the right to trial by jury. Some believe that a jury trial introduces undue formality and interferes with the rehabilitative objectives of the juvenile court by heightening the juvenile's sense that he is an adversary of the court and society. It has also been argued that trial by jury allows the intrusion of members of the public and impairs the confidentiality of juvenile proceedings designed to protect the juvenile from exposure of his misconduct to the community.

In juvenile delinquency proceedings based on alleged violations of the criminal law, however, the constitutional case for jury trial is as strong as in adult criminal trials. Recent studies attest to the efficacy of the jury as a fact-finder.[11] Juvenile court judges have not demonstrated superiority over the jury in determining whether a violation of the criminal law has been committed. The judge's special competency should lie in the selection among dispositional alternatives and the formulation of a plan of individualized treatment. The issues in a delinquency trial charging a criminal law violation are the same as in a criminal trial of the same offense. The jury functions of weighing the evidence, evaluating the credibility of witnesses, and finding the facts are not different or more difficult in determining whether a juvenile committed a criminal act than in determining whether an adult did. Other values of the jury system—as a bulwark against possible judicial arbitrariness, as assurance that each case will receive careful individual attention, and as a means of enforcing the criminal law in accord with current community standards—are as applicable for juveniles as for adults.

Objections based on the asserted "formality" of jury trials miss the point that trial by jury is not a matter of form but of substance. The product of long historical experience, it expresses the judgment of our legal system as to the best method of adjudicating criminal charges. Formality or solemnity is desirable in a matter of such consequence. A jury trial is no real threat to the confidentiality of juvenile proceedings or to the chance of rehabilitating the juvenile without public stigma: if a jury trial would be detrimental to an accused juvenile for these reasons, he and his counsel can waive it.

The right to jury trial need not include every offense, however petty, that may lead to an adjudication of delinquency. Petty offenses are not triable by jury as of right in adult criminal courts. Moreover, since the jury trial would be derived from the constitutional right applicable in criminal cases, there is no necessity to apply it to delinquency charges not based on violation of the criminal law.

However the question of the constitutional right to jury trial is resolved, other aspects of the mode of trial in juvenile cases require revaluation. There is a widespread practice in juvenile courts of intermingling investigative, accusatory, and adjudicative functions. Where a jury trial is not guaranteed, the constitutional problems created by such intermingling of functions are at a maximum. In many communities the juvenile court participates in the investigation of juvenile cases through its official arm, the probation officer; in the decision to bring charges by issuing arrest warrants and approving the filing of delinquency petitions; and then in adjudication by finding the facts and determining delinquency.

This intermingling violates an elementary principle of due process in any case, criminal or civil: the right to a fair trial by an impartial trier of fact. The Supreme Court has held that a judge who participates in the accusatory phase of a criminal case cannot sit as a trial judge in the same case.[12] The principle that the trier of fact must be independent of the investigative and accusatory process is established in administrative law.[13] Participation by the juvenile court in investigative and accusatory functions creates the danger of prejudgment in adjudication and leads to the court deciding on the correctness of its own actions. It also gives the court ex parte access to the facts, resulting in denial of the rights of confrontation, cross-examination, and effective assistance of counsel.

A change in the method of trying cases in many juvenile courts seems constitutionally required. The governing principle must be separation of fact-finding from the investigative and accusatory functions.

Judicial Review

The Supreme Court manifestly contemplates judicial review of juvenile proceedings. Although this does not necessarily connote a right of appeal, some mode of review must be available either by appeal or by collateral proceedings such as habeas corpus. One of the purposes of the Court's decisions is to limit the discretion of juvenile courts and transform them into a system functioning with procedural regularity under defined standards. Judicial review is the primary means of preventing a juvenile code from becoming a "license for arbitrary procedure."[14]

If the availability of judicial review is recognized, it follows that some record of the proceedings must be kept, preferably a stenographic transcript or other verbatim recording. And the juvenile court must indicate on the record what it decided and why. Meaningful review requires no less.

THE PRE-JUDICIAL STAGE

Prevailing practices of arrest, detention, interrogation, and identification of suspected juvenile offenders are all subject now to increasing constitutional scrutiny. Just as the rights of adult criminal defendants have received enhanced judicial protection, so will the rights of juveniles.

Arrest, Search, and Seizure

The Fourth Amendment guarantee of the right of the people to be free from unreasonable searches and seizures is clearly applicable to juveniles. Since the Fourth Amendment right is not limited to the criminal law or criminal cases, the label affixed to juvenile proceedings, whether "civil," "criminal," "quasi-criminal," or "*parens patriae*," is irrelevant. The Supreme Court has held that "civil" searches not directed at securing evidence of crime, such as fire and health inspections, are governed by the Fourth Amendment; the Amendment is a bulwark of individual privacy against officials, however benevolent.[15]

Whether the Fourth Amendment protects juveniles in the same way as it does adults is a more difficult question. There is no reason to differentiate juveniles arrested for criminal law violations from adults with respect to the "probable cause" requirement of the Fourth Amendment. An arrest on suspicion or solely for investigation of a crime is as objectionable for a juvenile as for an adult.

But in categories of juvenile court jurisdiction not involving criminal law violations, such as truancy, incorrigibilty, neglect, or dependency, a "probable cause" standard is inappropriate. The Court's decisions on "civil" searches indicate that the probable resolution will be to deny officials the right to arrest, search, and seize juveniles without reasonable grounds, but permit the grounds to be adapted to the exigencies of particular situations. Reason to believe that a juvenile is within a category of noncriminal juvenile court jurisdiction and that it is necessary for his own welfare to take him into custody is likely to be the constitutional standard.

Detention

Prehearing detention of juveniles presents some of the most troubling issues in the juvenile court process. Widespread abuses have arisen in many states from broad and unregulated powers of detention over juveniles: routine detention regardless of whether the welfare of the juvenile or the community safety would be endangered from releasing him; the use of detention for shock effect on alleged delinquents; the absence of articulated standards for determining when to detain; detention without judicial determination of need or probable cause; and overcrowding of detention facilities, often leading to the confinement of juveniles in adult jails.[16]

Denial to juveniles of bail pending adjudicative hearing and of a prompt detention hearing has generally been based on the labeling of juvenile proceedings as noncriminal. The Supreme Court's rejection of such labeling as a basis for determining the procedural rights of juveniles raises the question of the constitutional right to bail, especially when the charge is violation of a criminal statute. Due process will not permit an absolute power to detain a juvenile for any offense, however minor, without a showing of necessity for detention to safeguard either the juvenile or the public safety.

Recognition that the power to detain a juvenile cannot be absolute does not necessarily require his admission to bail in its traditional form, that is, the posting of a monetary bond. The evils of the bail bond system in this country have been convincingly documented.[17] A constitutionally valid right of prehearing release for juveniles may encompass various conditions limiting his freedom of movement, similar to those authorized under the federal Bail Reform Act of 1966. As one court has phrased it, the "substantial equivalent of bail" may be an adequate substitute for bail itself.[18] It is also possible that the welfare of the juvenile can sometimes be better served by his detention in a juvenile facility than by releasing him, at least if no other community facilities are immediately available. If this can be demonstrated, prehearing detention may be justifiable.

As a concomitant to the right of prehearing release, there should be a prompt detention hearing. Any decision to detain must ultimately be a judicial determination, based on defined standards as applied to the facts of the individual case. Prehearing detention is a matter of such consequence to the juvenile that due process must also afford him the opportunity to be heard meaningfully on the decision to detain, that is, through counsel. In any case based on an alleged criminal law violation, this should include a determination of probable cause that he committed the offense charged.[19]

Interrogation and Identification

The constitutional prohibition against involuntary confessions is fully applicable in juvenile delinquency proceedings. Indeed, the requirement of voluntariness should be more strictly applied to juvenile confessions because of the factors of immaturity and doubt as to the reliability of such confessions.

It also seems clear that the requirements of *Miranda v. Arizona*[20] apply to "custodial interrogation" of juveniles in the pre-judicial stage. Although purportedly reserving the point, the Supreme Court in *In re Gault* virtually held *Miranda* applicable.[21] If the *Miranda* rights, including that of counsel, are necessary to prevent erosion of an adult's privilege against self-incrimination, they are even more essential in the case of a juvenile. Further, at the time a juvenile is interrogated about a serious crime, he faces possible transfer for criminal trial as an adult. The peril of self-incrimination, not just as a juvenile delinquent but as an adult charged with crime, is real and substantial.

The more basic question is whether the *Miranda* requirements must be applied even more strictly and supplemented for juveniles. It may be that a juvenile, at least a child under sixteen, cannot validly waive his right to counsel without first receiving the advice of counsel. The *Miranda* inquiry whether interrogation was "custodial" seems irrelevant for a juvenile—any official interrogation can generate the pressures to answer at which *Miranda* was aimed. And the presence of a parent or guardian during interrogation of a juvenile may be held necessary to prevent overreaching.

Those who believe that legitimate rehabilitative and law enforcement objectives would be impeded by imposing the *Miranda* requirements have a relatively easy solution. That is to immunize the juvenile from the use of his statements, and any evidence obtained therefrom, in subsequent proceedings either to adjudicate him a delinquent or convict him as an adult. This would render the *Miranda* rules inapplicable by removing the factor which created them: the need to protect against compelled self-incrimination. The use of statements and other evidence obtained without compliance with *Miranda* would then be limited to the informal adjustment and disposition of cases without an adjudication of delinquency and the possibility of confinement. This would enable juvenile confessions to be utilized as a rehabilitative technique while at the same time protecting the values and purposes of the privilege against self-incrimination.

The *Miranda* rules should apply equally to interrogation at the intake point of the juvenile court, where the juvenile first comes into contact with juvenile court personnel. Moreover, the role of counsel at intake is crucial for other reasons. A lawyer can have an important impact at intake because of the dispositions of the case potentially available at that time, including informal adjustment without the commencement of a delinquency proceeding. The intake stage is another critical stage of the proceeding for a juvenile, comparable to the decision whether to transfer him for trial as an adult. The right of counsel is an indispensable adjunct to decision-making of this consequence.

The right to counsel should be recognized in other procedures in juvenile court as it has been in adult criminal cases. The assistance of counsel at a lineup or showup conducted for identification purposes is particularly important. The Supreme Court has held that counsel at this stage is necessary to guarantee the fairness of eyewitness identifications and thus enhance the reliability of the guilt-determining process at trial.[22] These considerations apply with the same force in juvenile cases. Likewise, the due process requirements for all forms of identification of suspects are essential to assure fair treatment to juveniles.[23]

THE DISPOSITIONAL STAGE

The juvenile court movement has assumed that a specialized court with *sui generis* procedures could provide individualized treatment and rehabilitation rather than punishment for juvenile offenders. The validity of this assumption and the attainment of these objectives largely depend on the effectiveness of the dispositional stage, which presents distinctive problems of procedure and individual rights.

Procedures

Once an adjudication of delinquency has been made in accordance with due process standards, the need for observance of procedures derived from the criminal law substantially evaporates. The principles of due process apply to the dispositional stage, but their content can be defined to reflect the characteristics of the disposition of a juvenile case.

The essence is a fair hearing, at which the juvenile is given an opportunity to be heard meaningfully through counsel on the appropriate disposition of his case. Since the range of dispositional alternatives open to the juvenile court is wide in most states and the outcome is so crucial for the future life of the juvenile, a summary or ex parte proceeding would be intolerable. Counsel must be given the opportunity to present the juvenile's side and explore dispositional alternatives with the court.[24]

A fair hearing at this stage also requires disclosure of the social reports and other investigative materials relied on by the court for disposition. This is indispensable if counsel is to participate effectively in the dispositional decision. Although the Supreme Court has held that there is no constitutional right to cross-examine the witnesses who have supplied information for the presentence report in a criminal proceeding,[25] this doctrine should not control the procedural development of the dispositional phase of the juvenile proceeding. If the juvenile statute requires further findings to support a juvenile's confinement after an adjudication of delinquency, it is clear from the *Kent* decision that the court cannot rely on secret materials in making the findings.

Even if additional findings are not a prerequisite, disclosure of the basic information relied on for the disposition is necessary to implement the right to be heard. In view of the complexity of devising an adequate treatment plan for a juvenile, there must be full and accurate development of the facts about his personality, history, family background, and the available community facilities. Reliability in the fact-finding that leads to disposition is as important as in the adjudicative phase. Reliance on undisclosed information, without opportunity for the juvenile and his counsel to meet it, is as objectionable in disposition as in adjudication.

The Right to Treatment

One of the most significant implications of the *Gault* decision is that courts may have a supervisory function to perform with respect to the treatment of adjudicated delinquents. The Court expressed doubt whether juveniles in fact receive individualized treatment and rehabilitation from the juvenile court system. It called attention to cases which indicate that since treatment is the essential *quid pro quo*, "a juvenile may challenge the validity of his custody on the ground that he is not in fact receiving any special treatment."[26]

The most exigent cases for judicial intervention are presented by the practice in some states of committing or transferring juveniles committed as delinquents to adult penal institutions, where they may be confined together with adult felons. This practice is inconsistent with the juvenile court's professed objective of special treatment rather than punishment. Such confinement cannot be lawfully justified without granting the juvenile all the constitutional guarantees of adults charged with crime.

When a juvenile is confined in a juvenile institution, judicial processes should also be available to test whether he is receiving adequate treatment. A committed juvenile has a statutory right to treatment in some jurisdictions, and he may be held to have a constitutional right to it as a condition of his confinement. The concept of a "right to treatment" is emerging in other areas of the law; in particular, it has been held applicable to the mentally ill.[27]

The effectuation of this right for juveniles can be accomplished only by an assault on a nation-wide problem: the poverty of community resources devoted to realization of the rehabilitative goals of juvenile courts. The specialized juvenile court system and procedures can ultimately be validated only if treatment is afforded in fact and not merely promised.

NOTES

1. The Court has thus far rendered three major decisions: Kent v. United States, 383 U.S. 541 (1966); *In re* Gault, 387 U.S. 1 (1967); and *In re* Winship, 397 U.S. 358 (1970).

2. *E.g.,* National Conference of Commissioners on Uniform State Laws, *Uniform Juvenile Court Act* (1968); National Council on Crime and Delinquency, *Model Rules for Juvenile Courts* (1969); Children's Bureau, Social Rehabilitative Service, United States Department of Health, Education, and Welfare, *Legislative Guides for Drafting Family and Juvenile Court Acts* (1969).

3. *E.g.,* Dorsen & Rezneck, "In re Gault and the Future of Juvenile Law," 1 *Family Law Quarterly,* No. 4, at 1 (Dec. 1967); Ketcham, "Guidelines from *Gault:* Revolutionary Requirements and Reappraisal," 53 *Virginia Law Review* 1700 (1967); Paulsen, "The Constitutional Domestication of the Juvenile Court," 1967 *Supreme Court Review* 233. For the most recent decisions, see the section on Juvenile Law in the CCH Poverty Law Reporter.

4. *In re* Winship, 397 U.S. 358, 359 (1970); *In re* Gault, 387 U.S. 1, 30 1967); Kent v. United States, 383 U.S. 541, 555 (1966).

5. *In re* Gault, 387 U.S. 1, 36 (1967).

6. These four rights were established in *id.* at 33, 41, 55, 56, respectively.

7. *In re* Winship, 397 U.S. 358, 368 (1970).

8. Kent v. United States, 383 U.S. 541, 554, 557 (1966). Although ostensibly an interpretation of the District of Columbia Juvenile Court Act, the *Kent*

decision rests on "constitutional principles relating to due process and the assistance of counsel." *Id.* at 557 (footnote omitted).

9. White v. Maryland, 373 U.S. 59 (1963); Hamilton v. Alabama, 368 U.S. 52 (1961).

10. Kent v. United States, 383 U.S. 541, 563 (1966).

11. *See generally* H. Kalven & H. Zeisel, *The American Jury* (1966).

12. *In re* Murchison, 349 U.S. 133, 136–37 (1955).

13. Administrative Procedure Act, §5(c), 5 U.S.C. §554; Amos Treat & Co. v. SEC, 306 F.2d 260, 266–67 (D.C. Cir. 1962).

14. Kent v. United States, 383 U.S. 541, 553, 561 (1966); *see also In re* Gault, 387 U.S. 1, 73–74 (1967) (opinion of Harlan, J.).

15. Camara v. Municipal Court, 387 U.S. 523 (1967); See v. City of Seattle, 387 U.S. 541 (1967).

16. *See* President's Commission on Law Enforcement and Administration of Criminal Justice, *Task Force Report: Juvenile Delinquency and Youth Crime* 13, 19, 36–37 (1967) [hereinafter cited as National Crime Commission, Task Force].

17. *E.g.,* D. Freed & P. Wald, *Bail in the United States* (1964).

18. *Cf.* Fulwood v. Stone, 394 F.2d 939, 943–44 (D.C. Cir. 1967).

19. Cooley v. Stone, 414 F.2d 1213 (D.C. Cir. 1969).

20. 384 U.S. 436 (1966).

21. 387 U.S. 1, 55–56 (1967).

22. United States v. Wade, 388 U.S. 218 (1967).

23. *Cf.* Stovall v. Denno, 388 U.S. 293 (1967).

24. *See* National Crime Commission, Task Force, *supra* note 16, at 33.

25. Williams v. New York, 337 U.S. 241 (1949).

26. 387 U.S. at 22–23 n. 30.

27. Rouse v. Cameron, 373 F.2d 451 (D.C. Cir. 1966); *see generally* Note, "The Nascent Right to Treatment," 53 *Virginia Law Review* 1134 (1967).

THE RIGHTS OF
MENTAL PATIENTS

BRUCE J. ENNIS

IDENTIFYING THE CONSTITUTIONAL PROBLEMS IN-
herent in civil commitment of the mentally ill requires no particular expertise. If you substitute "crime" for "mental illness" and
"defendant" for "patient" you will find that virtually every important right guaranteed to the criminal is denied to the patient.

Although there are three times as many mental patients as there
are prisoners, the Supreme Court seems to be unaware of their
existence. Not once in the past twenty-five years has the Court considered the procedural or substantive rights of a civil mental patient.

Lower-court judges, most of whom reached intellectual maturity
shortly after 1924, when the English edition of Freud's *General
Introduction to Psychoanalysis* first appeared in this country, are
aware that there are things about the human mind which laymen
do not know. Intrigued by the promise and awed by the mystery
of psychiatry, they consider it the better part of discretion to leave
the patients to the doctors.

Consequently, the rights of mental patients are even less clearly
defined than the rights of juveniles or welfare recipients. In the legal
framework, involuntary patients occupy a no man's land between
the criminal law and the civil law, and they receive the protections
of neither. The rhetoric of institutional psychiatry encourages this
ambiguity. Although these patients are confined because they are

*Bruce J. Ennis is a staff attorney of the New York Civil Liberties Union and
Director of its Mental Illness Litigating Project. He is the author of a forthcoming
book on mental illness and the law.*

"dangerous" or a "nuisance" to others, their confinement is, ostensibly, for their own welfare. The right to counsel, the privilege against self-incrimination, these and other important rights are thought inappropriate because the "purpose" of commitment is not punishment but treatment. Society is ambivalent about warehousing its recalcitrant teen-agers and its doddering grandparents under the guise of psychiatric care, and that ambivalence is reflected in the law. Faced with judicial indifference and societal ambivalence, the mental patient cannot say with confidence what rights he has or is likely soon to have. Nor can I. Accordingly, this essay must intend a more modest goal than others in this book. The most that can be expected in so brief a survey of so vast a problem is a summary of selected issues, followed by a catalogue of others.

Summary of Selected Issues

The Standards for Involuntary Commitment: Danger and Welfare

Mental patients can be committed if they are dangerous to themselves or others (essentially a "police power" concept), or, even if they are not dangerous, for their own welfare (essentially a *parens patriae* concept). The "welfare" standard, but not the "danger" standard, assumes that the prospective patient lacks the insight or capacity to make a responsible decision concerning hospitalization. Analytically, suicidal patients would fall within the *parens patriae* concept. But they are routinely committed whether or not they are capable of weighing the merits and demerits of suicide. Indeed, they are committed whether or not they are mentally ill. In some states (Tennessee, for example) the "capacity" test is explicitly set forth in the statute. In others (New York, for example) it is not, but is so routinely relied upon in psychiatric reports as to carry the force of statute.

Danger. Deeply rooted in every society is the belief that the mentally ill, as a class, are much more dangerous than the mentally healthy. Madness and danger are served up together like ham and eggs. Much has been written about the reasons for that belief. We fear what we don't understand, and it is difficult to understand irrational or unconventional behavior. With a mental patient, we don't know what to expect next, so we play it safe and expect the worst. And we are almost always wrong.

The myth that mental patients are more dangerous than the average member of society is not based on empirical evidence and is therefore not likely to be destroyed by empirical evidence, but the evidence is there, nonetheless. An important New York study of 5,000 released patients showed that patients with no prior record of arrest committed less than one-twelfth the number of crimes committed by the average member of society, and that the rate for serious crimes was even lower.[1] Other studies reach the same conclusion.

This is not to suggest that mental illness and danger are mutually exclusive concepts. Some mental patients are dangerous, some are not. The important point is that a diagnosis of mental illness tells us nothing about whether the person so diagnosed is or is not dangerous. Psychiatrists know this, but judges don't. Accordingly, even in states where danger is a prerequisite to commitment, thousands of persons are committed without any "proof" that they are dangerous. The psychiatrist says they are mentally ill, and the judge then assumes they are dangerous. In effect, the prospective patient is presumed to be dangerous until he proves he is not. This is preventive detention at its worst.

Moreover, it is becoming increasingly clear that psychiatrists cannot tell us which patients are likely to be dangerous and which are not, even when they try. Professor Dershowitz of Harvard Law School has been studying this problem for several years. Three points emerge from his research: (1) psychiatric predictions are wrong much more often than they are right; (2) psychiatrists are less accurate in their predictions than other professionals, less accurate than psychologists and social workers, for example; (3) psychiatrists are particularly prone to overprediction.[2] The psychiatric rule of thumb seems to be: When in doubt, commit. Take any group of allegedly dangerous patients. If you set them free, a few will commit dangerous acts. But most of them, certainly more than 90 percent of them, will not.

Psychiatrists overpredict dangerous behavior for a very good reason. If a psychiatrist incorrectly predicts nondanger, his error will be brought to his attention by an outraged community. But if he incorrectly predicts danger, the patient will be confined, with no opportunity to show the psychiatrist he was wrong. Because psychiatric predictions are in large part self-fulfilling, it is difficult to

assess their reliability. That is why studies such as Operation Baxstrom, infrequent as they are, deserve special attention. In New
York, if a convict becomes mentally ill while serving his sentence,
he is transferred to Dannemora, a maximum-security hospital run
by the Department of Corrections. When his sentence expires, the
state must either release him, which it rarely does, keep him in
Dannemora, or transfer him to a *civil* hospital. Before 1966, the
choice between Dannemora or a civil hospital was made by state
psychiatrists. If they thought the patient was dangerous, he would
be kept in Dannemora. Otherwise, he would be transferred to a
civil hospital. In 1966, the Supreme Court changed all that. In
Baxstrom v. Herold[3] it ruled that a time-expired prisoner must be
transferred to a civil hospital unless he receives substantially all
the procedural protections he would receive as a civilian, including
jury trial.

New York simply didn't have the facilities to give all those
patients jury trials. So, in a matter of months, nearly 1,000 Dannemora patients whom psychiatrists considered too dangerous for
low-security civil hospitals were transferred to civil hospitals nonetheless. The results probably did not surprise Professor Dershowitz,
but they astonished the psychiatric profession. To use an analogy
coined by Professor Grant Morris, the so-called dangerous patients
turned out to be purer than Ivory Snow. They were, in fact, 99.54
percent *non*dangerous.[4]

After one year the Department of Mental Hygiene reported
that "there have been no significant problems with the patients. All
have been absorbed into the general patient population, many
reside on open wards, over 200 have been released, and only seven
have been certified as too dangerous for a civil hospital."

In statistical terms, Operation Baxstrom tells us that psychiatric predictions of dangerous behavior are incredibly inaccurate.
In human terms, it tells us that but for a Supreme Court decision,
nearly 1,000 human beings would have lived much of their lives
behind bars, without grounds privileges, without home visits, without even the limited amenities available to civil patients, all because a few psychiatrists, in their considered opinion, thought they
were dangerous and no one asked for proof.

Compounding the problems inherent in the "danger" standard
is the almost universal ambiguity surrounding that concept. Do we
mean only danger to persons, or is danger to property enough? Do
we mean only physical injury, or is self-neglect or verbal abuse

enough? Do we mean only imminent danger, or are we willing to lock up people who might be dangerous next month, or next year? With the exception of California, no state statute even begins to spell out answers to these questions. Committing psychiatrists answer them daily, each in his own way, and based on his own value preference for a safe society or a free society. Because predictions of dangerous behavior are so grossly unreliable, and because "danger" is, at best, an elusive concept, perhaps we should authorize involuntary confinement, if at all, only if the necessity for confinement is proved "beyond a reasonable doubt."[5]

California's new Mental Hygiene Law,[6] which became effective July 1, 1969, is a sensible step toward placing substantive limits on preventive detention. The California Law specifies the type of danger (physical harm), the degree of danger (substantial), and the time period within which to gauge the danger (imminent). It requires also a recent overt act, threat, or attempt as a basis for a prediction of future dangerousness, thereby approximating the Supreme Court's insistence that predictions of future harm must be based on "evidence of past conduct pointing to probable consequences."[7] If the California patient behaves himself while in custody, he cannot be held for more than 31 or 107 days, respectively, because he is thought to be dangerous to himself or to others.

Welfare. Preventive detention is only one of the social functions which state mental hospitals serve. By all estimates, most involuntary patients are hospitalized, not because they are dangerous, but because someone else believes they need psychiatric care and believes they are unable to recognize that need. Although the "capacity" test has much superficial appeal, in practice it serves as little more than a semantic justification for doing what the decision-maker thinks *should* be done. It is almost inconceivable that a psychiatrist or judge would say to an individual, "I really think you need to be hospitalized," and then go on to say, impugning his own expertise, "nevertheless, I think you have made a responsible decision to refuse treatment, and I am therefore going to let you go your way."

There is an even more fundamental objection to the "capacity" test. It assumes not only that the decision-maker will respect the prospective patient's choice, if that choice is reasonable, even though it differs from his own, but also that the decision-maker's choice will *itself* be reasonable and based on something other than his own personal preferences and beliefs. It will not. Some psy-

chiatrists value liberty more than health; others disagree. Some
consider the convenience of the family or the community as important as the wishes of the prospective patient; others disagree.
Some believe that hospitalization is therapeutic for almost anyone
with a mental problem. Others will tell you that hospitalization is
itself a traumatic and psychologically disturbing experience and
antitherapeutic in virtually every case.[8] If we think there is any
medical standard against which we can evaluate the reasonableness
of the decision-maker's recommendation of hospitalization, we are
wrong.

The Right to Adequate Psychiatric Treatment

It would be difficult to find a concept that has produced so
much commentary and so little change as the "right to treatment."[9]
The theory is simple: If the justification for confinement is a supposed need for treatment, the patient must either be treated or be
released. To date, even though no state maintains even the minimum ratio of physicians to patients which the American Psychiatric
Association, a conservative organization, says is essential to adequate treatment,[10] not one patient has been ordered released because of inadequate treatment. Judges are understandably reluctant to enforce the right to treatment. If they did, state hospitals
would be emptied. There are two ways to improve the unspeakably
deplorable conditions in state mental hospitals: improve the facilities or reduce the number of patients. The first is unrealistic. Legislatures have known for years that their hospitals offer nothing
more than food and shelter for the majority of the patients. Mental
hygiene budgets, though totally inadequate, are already enormous.
New York's Department of Mental Hygiene, for example, is the
largest state government agency in the United States. Furthermore,
there are nearly three-quarters of a million hospitalized patients
and more than 3 million persons receiving outpatient services, but
fewer than 23,000 psychiatrists in the entire United States.[11]

The second alternative—reducing patient populations—is somewhat more realistic. In New York, to choose one example, the average patient population has declined from 90,000 to 65,000 in the
last ten years. Many patients in state hospitals do not really need
psychiatric care. By narrowing the standards for admission to exclude geriatrics, for example, the patient population can be drastically reduced. Perhaps a more effective method, which has yet to

be tried, would be to place an absolute or presumptive time limit on confinement. If the patient had not been "cured" in that period of time, it would be presumed that he was not treatable, and he would be released. The concept of a deadline finds some slight support in *Robinson v. California*,[12] which precludes punishment based on the "status" of being mentally ill.

Medical Commitment Followed by an Opportunity for Judicial Review

A small but growing list of states authorize involuntary hospitalization, even in nonemergency situations, based on a certificate of mental illness signed by two physicians. The principal objection to "medical" commitment is that it authorizes a deprivation of liberty without a prior opportunity for a judicial hearing. Several state courts have held that two-physician commitments are unconstitutional.[13] And two very recent Supreme Court decisions offer a powerful analogy. In one, the Court ruled that an alleged debtor could not even temporarily be deprived of the "use" of his wages without "notice and a prior hearing."[14] And in the other, the Court ruled that welfare benefits could not be terminated without giving the recipient a prior opportunity for a hearing.[15] In neither case was the right to full-scale judicial review considered sufficient. If, except in an emergency, property cannot constitutionally be taken without a prior opportunity to be heard, can less be said for liberty?

Proponents of medical commitment argue that prospective patients should be spared the stigma and trauma of being tried and convicted of being sick. This argument sounds more impressive than it is. Medical commitment creates just as much stigma as judicial commitment. To the patient's neighbors, and to prospective employers, it matters little that it was not a court but only two physicians who thought he was crazy. More important, not even the most vigorous proponents of medical commitment would urge the abolition of prompt judicial *review*. At such review the patient will be tried and, perhaps, convicted of being sick. If the patient wants a trial, he will get a trial. The only question is when he should be tried, and the stigma-and-trauma argument is irrelevant to the resolution of that question.

On the other hand, there are several strong policy reasons in favor of prior judicial hearings. The first is that courts and psychiatrists frequently disagree. In New York, for example, between one-third and one-half of the "two-physician" patients who do request judicial review are promptly discharged.[16] Most of them are administratively discharged because the hospital knows it would be futile to oppose release. Even when the hospital is sufficiently sure of its opinion to go to trial, between 10 and 20 percent of the patients are discharged by the court.

It is also important to note that confined patients are subject to disabilities not imposed on prospective patients. Generally, judicial review of medical commitment is not automatic. The patient must affirmatively request review. Once confined, the patient is immediately subjected to tranquilizing medication and, in some cases, shock therapy, both of which have the undisputed effect of decreasing his initiative and will to resist. The confined patient cannot shop around to find lawyers, psychiatrists, or witnesses who might help him.

Many prospective patients have, at best, tenuous ties with the community. If those ties are severed, even for a few days, it is common for them to lose their part-time jobs and their transient hotel rooms. That fact is often of crucial significance at the hearing. Frequently the hearing turns, not on whether the person is mentally ill (there are many mildly mentally ill persons who do not require hospitalization), but on whether he has some place to live, or some form of support, if he is discharged. Courts are understandably reluctant to discharge a patient who will have no place to sleep but an alley. It is therefore of vital importance that the hearing be held *before* the individual's ties with the community are severed. Related to this point is the again understandable judicial reluctance to change the status quo—whether from "civilian" to "patient" or from "patient" to "civilian." It is one thing if a judge is confronted with an individual dressed in civilian clothes and is asked to make that individual a patient. It is quite a different thing if a judge is confronted with an individual who is already a patient dressed, as they frequently are, in hospital robe and slippers, and is asked to make that patient a civilian.

Incompetence to Stand Trial

To be charged with both crime and mental illness is to be twice cursed. The doctrine of incompetence to stand trial, developed in the eighteenth century,[17] was based on the humanitarian principle that no defendant should be *forced* to trial if his mental condition precluded an effective defense. The doctrine made sense at that time, when punishments were likely to be as severe as lawyers were to be scarce. But today, to commit a man for twenty years because he painted zebra stripes on his horse,[18] or for fifty-nine years because he allegedly stole a horse and buggy worth $125,[19] and is incompetent to prove his innocence of those grave charges, makes no sense.[20] It makes even less sense if a court-appointed attorney thinks he can gain an acquittal without any assistance from his incompetent client. A recent study financed by the National Institute of Mental Health concluded that "a defendant is much better served from every point of view if he is returned to trial, except in the rare exception of the death penalty."[21]

There are situations when it is to the defendant's advantage to postpone trial. But it is increasingly common for prosecutors to initiate incompetency proceedings over the defendant's objection. If successful, the prosecution gains the results of a criminal conviction (indefinite commitment) while denying to the defendant the procedural protections of a criminal trial (jury trial, proof beyond a reasonable doubt, etc.). The improper use of incompetency proceedings as a dispositional alternative to criminal trials could be curbed if judges would accept a simple proposition: that the Sixth Amendment right to a speedy trial protects both competent and incompetent defendants.[22] Memories fade, witnesses die, and documents are lost whether the defendant is competent or not. Perhaps it is unfair to try an incompetent defendant; it is equally unfair to hold a presumably innocent man under criminal auspices for the rest of his life simply because he is incompetent to prove his innocence. To avoid that all too common result, we should require that after one year the criminal proceedings against an incompetent defendant must be dropped, and that further confinement, if any, must be under civil auspices.

Discrimination Against Former Mental Patients

Mental illness is reversible, but its social consequences are not. If two physicians say a man is crazy, they will be believed. But if they later say he has recovered and is as well as any of us, they will not. In the job market it is probably better to be an ex-felon ("he paid his debt") than an ex-patient. "Have you ever been hospitalized for a nervous or mental condition?" "Have you ever received psychiatric treatment?" "Have you been disqualified for military service for psychiatric reasons?" These and similar questions appear on college application forms, on driver's license forms, on applications for employment as a mailman, a teacher, a sanitation worker, on virtually every piece of paper that stands between the former patient and a better life. The presumption of continuing illness implicit in each of these questions is a heavy burden to bear, an almost impossible burden to bear, and to make it worse, the presumption is all too often conclusive and irrebuttable. An affirmative answer to any of these questions results in automatic rejection, *regardless of the applicant's current mental condition.*

Consider what it must be like to apply for a job and be told that your present mental condition is irrelevant; that letters from private psychiatrists attesting to your current (and future) mental stability will not even be considered; that you will be rejected because in the past, perhaps twenty years ago, you were mentally ill.[23] Per se discrimination against former mental patients raises substantial questions of equal protection (can they be treated differently from former "physical" patients, or from all others who, like them, are at present mentally competent?), of procedural due process (can they be denied employment without being afforded at least an opportunity to establish their present mental stability?), and of cruel and unusual punishment (can they be denied employment because of a no longer existing "status" which they had no power to control?).

This is new ground. Case law on the rights of former patients is almost nonexistent. New York has, by statute, attempted to prohibit per se discrimination,[24] but the statute is too narrowly drawn to be of much assistance. "It requires no argument to show that the right to work for a living in the common occupations of the community is of the very essence of the personal freedom and opportunity that it was the purpose of the [Fourteenth] Amendment to secure."[25] Former patients will have to start from there.

CATALOGUE OF OTHER ISSUES

The following catalogue, though far from exhaustive, illustrates the range of other important and unresolved constitutional issues which can arise in almost every commitment or retention proceeding.

Knowing Waiver

In several states, the patient will not receive a judicial hearing on the propriety of his commitment or retention, or on the necessity for the appointment of a committee to manage his property, unless he affirmatively requests a hearing. His silence or inaction is deemed to constitute a waiver. If he were charged with crime or delinquency or narcotics addiction, the court would require an affirmative and a "knowing, competent and intelligent" waiver which, arguably, means he must first have conferred with counsel.[26] The policy reasons which led to those rulings would seem to apply with even greater vigor to persons alleged to be mentally ill.

The Privilege Against Self-incrimination

Although unusual behavior frequently initiates the commitment process, most patients are committed primarily because of what they say rather than because of what they do. If they did not tell the doctor they heard voices or were being followed by the CIA, there would not be enough "evidence" to commit. *In re Gault*[27] held that "no person shall be 'compelled' to be a witness against himself *when he is threatened with deprivation of his liberty.*" If, as the Court hinted in *Gault,* it is the consequence of the proceeding, not its "purpose," which triggers constitutional rights, the privilege should be applicable in a mental commitment proceeding.[28]

Counsel

As of 1966, forty-two jurisdictions authorized retained or appointed counsel in commitment proceedings. There is growing, though belated, recognition that appointed counsel is a constitutional right.[29] The proper role for the attorney, however, has yet to be resolved.[30] Is he an advocate, a guardian, or an information-gatherer for the court? Should he oppose commitment when he believes his client would be better off in the hospital? Rather than prejudge the issue before the court, thereby depriving the prospective patient of a meaningful hearing, the attorney should do everything he can to achieve his client's expressed wishes. And he should not worry that he might, to his client's disadvantage, win. If the necessity for hospitalization cannot be shown even in the face of vigorous opposition, then it is probably safe to say that the prospective patient is not sufficiently disturbed to justify involuntary commitment.

It is equally important that legal representation not stop at the hospital door. Confined patients often lose their apartments, their welfare checks, and their children. The anxiety the patient experiences over the prospect of finding himself homeless and destitute upon discharge exacerbates his emotional difficulties and impedes recovery. The need for legal services *within* the hospital is enormous. It is a need we have not even begun to meet.

Less Drastic Alternatives

Probably the greatest opportunity for reform lurks in the respected doctrine of the "least drastic alternative." As the Supreme Court ruled in *Shelton v. Tucker,* "even though the governmental purpose be legitimate and substantial, that purpose cannot be pursued by means that broadly stifle fundamental personal liberties when the end can be more narrowly achieved. The breadth of legislative abridgment must be viewed in the light of *less drastic means* for achieving the same basic purpose."[31]

Simply stated, even if a person requires psychiatric treatment, full-time hospitalization should be unconstitutional if there are less drastic alternatives, for example day treatment or night treatment, or even outpatient treatment, which would suffice. The first step is to persuade the courts that the person or persons recommending full-time hospitalization must bear the burden of proving there are no less drastic *existing* alternatives. Two cases from the District of Columbia Circuit are helpful in that regard.[32] The second step is to persuade the courts that if less drastic alternatives would suffice but simply do not exist, the state will either have to create them or leave the prospective patient alone. It should be stressed to the courts that the creation of noninstitutional services would not cost the state more money—it would cost less. In recent studies conducted in New York City and Denver, for example, prospective patients who would otherwise have been hospitalized were randomly assigned to two groups. The first group was admitted and received institutional services; the second group was not admitted and received day treatment or treatment in the community. Two-year follow-up studies showed that the outpatient group responded more favorably to treatment than the inpatient group, and cost the state only half as much money.[33]

Involuntary Servitude

A few cases,[34] and numerous authorities,[35] recognize that "cost-saving" as opposed to "therapeutic" labor is unconstitutional under the Thirteenth Amendment. But it is extraordinarily difficult to prove that a given type of work is *not* therapeutic.[36] It is clear, however, from the enormous disparity between the per diem cost of private psychiatric hospitalization and the cost of state hospitalization that state mental patients perform a tremendous amount of cost-saving labor. If a given type of labor *is* therapeutic, we would expect to find patients in private facilities performing that type of labor. Conversely, labor which is not generally performed in private facilities should be presumed, by statute, to be cost-saving rather than therapeutic. Also, an effective statute should place on the *hospital* the burden of proving the therapeutic value of all labor.

There are, of course, other important constitutional questions. Can patients be forced to pay the costs of involuntary hospitalization? Can they be denied the right to vote? Are they entitled to automatic periodic review of their mental condition? Can the state be forced to pay for "independent" psychiatric opinion? Can patients be medicated even though medication is against their religious beliefs? Can they be photographed and fingerprinted against their will and even though their identities are known? Can they exchange uncensored communications with attorneys?

All the questions raised in this essay are now in litigation; all of them remain to be resolved. For now, it is more true than false to say that mental patients have no rights.

NOTES

1. Brill & Malzberg, Statistical Report Based on the Arrest Record of 5354 Male Ex-Patients Released from New York State Mental Hospitals During the Period 1946–1948 (unpublished); Ennis, "Mental Illness," *1969–1970 Annual Survey of American Law* 29, 45–48.

2. *E.g.,* Dershowitz, "The Psychiatrist's Power in Civil Commitment: A Knife That Cuts Both Ways," *Psychology Today,* Feb. 1969, at 47.

3. 383 U.S. 107 (1966).

4. Morris, "The Confusion of Confinement Syndrome: An Analysis of the Confinement of Mentally Ill Criminals and Ex-Criminals by the Department of Correction of the State of New York," 17 *Buffalo Law Review* 651, 672 (1968).

5. *Cf. In Re* Winship, 397 U.S. 358 (1970); *see* Bazelon, "Implementing the Right to Treatment," 36 *University of Chicago Law Review* 742, 748–49 (1969).

6. The Lanterman-Petris-Short Act, especially §§5260, 5264, 5300.

7. Minnesota *ex rel.* Pearson v. Probate Court, 309 U.S. 270, 274 (1940).

8. *E.g.,* the articles in *Mental Hygiene,* Jan. 1969, at 5 and 65.

9. For comprehensive recent analysis of this burgeoning area of the law, see "A Symposium: The Right to Treatment," 57 *Georgetown Law Journal* 673 (1969); "Symposium," 36 *University of Chicago Law Review* 742 (1969); *see also* Comment, "The Nascent Right to Treatment," 53 *Virginia Law Review* 1134 (1967).

10. Birnbaum, "Some Comments on the Right to Treatment," 13 *Archives of General Psychiatry* 34 (1965).

11. R.S. Rock, *Hospitalization and Discharge of the Mentally Ill* 1 (1968); Hunt, "Crisis in Psychoanalysis," *Playboy,* Oct. 1969, at 108.

12. 370 U.S. 660 (1962).

13. *E.g.,* State *ex rel.* Fuller v. Mullinax, 364 Mo. 858, 269 S.W.2d 72 (1954); *In re* Lambert, 134 Cal. 626, 66 P. 851 (1901).

14. Sniadach v. Family Fin. Corp. 395 U.S. 337 (1969).

15. Goldberg v. Kelly, 397 U.S. 254 (1970).

16. Greenland, "Appealing Against Commitment to Mental Hospitals in the United Kingdom, Canada, and the U.S.: An International Review," 126 *American Journal of Psychiatry* 538, 541 (1969).

17. Frith's Case, 22 Howell's State Trials 307 (Old Bailey, 1790); 4 W. Blackstone, *Commentaries* *25.

18. Chayet, "Legal Neglect of the Mentally Ill," 125 *American Journal of Psychiatry* 97, 98 (1968).

19. Association of the Bar of the City of New York, *Mental Illness, Due Process and the Criminal Defendant* 72 n. 1 (1968).

20. *E.g.,* Foote, "A Comment On Pre-Trial Commitment of Criminal Defendants," 108 *University of Pennsylvania Law Review* 832 (1960).

21. McGarry, "Demonstration and Research in Competency for Trial and Mental Illness: Review and Preview," 49 *Boston University Law Review* 46, 55 (1969).

22. *E.g.,* Williams v. United States, 250 F.2d 19 (D.C. Cir. 1957); Wells, *by* Gillig v. Attorney General of the United States, 201 F.2d 506 (10th Cir. 1953); *see also* Foote, *supra* note 20.

23. *See* Cohen *et al.* v. Leary, No. 02715 (Sup. Ct. N.Y. County, 1970); Velazquez v. Hoberman, No. 10664 (Sup. Ct. N.Y. County, 1970).

24. N.Y. Mental Hygiene Law §70(5).

25. Truax v. Raich, 239 U.S. 33, 41 (1915); Schware v. Board of Bar, Examiners, 353 U.S. 232, 238–39 (1957).

26. *E.g.,* Johnson v. Zerbst, 304 U.S. 458, 464 (1938) (criminal defendant); *In re* Gault, 387 U.S. 1, 34 (1967) (juvenile and mother); Heryford v. Parker, 396 F.2d 393, 396 (10th Cir. 1968) (mentally deficient child and mother); State *ex rel.* Byrnes v. Goldman, 59 Misc. 2d 570, 302 N.Y.S. 2d 926 (Sup. Ct. 1969) (unrepresented infant narcotics addict).

27. 387 U.S. 1, 50 (1967).

28. *See* Ennis, *supra* note 1, at 33–37.

29. *E.g.,* Heryford v. Parker, 396 F.2d 393 (10th Cir. 1968); *see also* Draft Act Governing Hospitalization of the Mentally Ill §9(f), *reprinted in* Lindman & McIntyre, *The Mentally Disabled and the Law* 402 (1961).

30. *E.g.,* Cohen, "The Function of the Attorney and the Commitment of the Mentally Ill," 44 *Texas Law Review* 424 (1966).

31. 364 U.S. 479, 488 (1960) (emphasis added).

32. Lake v. Cameron, 364 F.2d 657 (D.C. Cir. 1966); Covington v. Harris, 419 F.2d 617 (D.C. Cir. 1969).

33. Wilder, Levin, & Zwerling, "A Two-Year Follow-up Evaluation of Acute Psychotic Patients Treated in a Day Hospital," 122 *American Journal of Psychiatry* 1095 (1966); Langsley, "Family Crisis Therapy," 7 *Family Process* 145 (1968).

34. *E.g.,* Jobson v. Henne, 355 F.2d 129 (2d Cir. 1966); Stone v. City of Paducah, 120 Ky. 322, 86 S.W. 531 (1905).

35. *E.g.,* Bartlett, "Institutional Peonage—Our Exploitation of Mental Patients, 214 *Atlantic Monthly,* July 1964, at 116–19; T. Szasz, *Law, Liberty and Psychiatry* 63, 189 (1963); Goldman & Ross, "Our Forgotten Mental Patients —Who Are They?" *Parade,* Nov. 1956, at 18.

36. *E.g.,* Krieger v. New York, 54 Misc. 2d 583, 283 N.Y.S2d 86 (Ct. Cl. 1966).

THE RIGHTS OF
SELECTIVE SERVICE
REGISTRANTS

MICHAEL E. TIGAR

On the Wall in Chalk is Written:
They want war.
He who wrote it
Has already fallen.[1]

THERE ARE FEW WHO WILL DEFEND THE SYSTEM OF
conscription which, in shreds and patches, shambled into the
1970's. Tinkers and tinkerers are hard at work, and here and there
the voice of one who recognizes the Selective Service System for
what it has become: an instrument of repression, a means by which
the executive branch can mobilize or demobilize the country at will
by adjusting monthly calls, a sprawling network of local boards
each chasing its own version of the national interest, and collectively armed with life-and-death power over 37 million or more
American men.

Now and again over the years of its life, the American Civil
Liberties Union has led important attacks on the more obviously
offensive manifestations of the System's power, focusing on denials
of fair hearing, curtailment of free speech, and failure to respect
rights of conscience. As 1970 began, the Union successfully concluded, by a unanimous Supreme Court decision in one of its cases,
a two-year battle to invalidate the regulations under which local
boards had been stripping registrants of their draft exemptions and
deferments and ordering them to report for induction ahead of

Michael E. Tigar is Acting Professor of Law at the University of California, Los
Angeles, former Editor in Chief of the Selective Service Law Reporter, and a participant in draft and other constitutional litigation.

schedule. This entirely discretionary power to be judge, jury, prosecutor, and executioner's accomplice had been used in case after case to punish registrants for dissentient behavior.[2]

In its fiftieth year, a substantial portion of the Union's effort and volunteer lawyer time is invested in draft law cases, pressing other claims that the System falls short of elementary constitutional decencies.

FROM OUT OF THE PAGES OF HISTORY

"At common law," as lawyers say, there was conscription, but only of "rogues, vagabonds and sturdy beggers," no doubt a means of rounding up those who had been driven off the land in seventeenth-century England but who would not or could not find employment in the cities.[3] But this is not a very honorable beginning, and so the institution of conscription in America is said by its apologists to be derived from the colonial militia. Any modern discussion of the constitutional basis of compulsory military service must begin by laying this rumor to rest.[4]

The colonies, and later the new states of the American Union, had militia units in which every able-bodied male was obligated to train once a year or so and to serve if the colony or state was in danger. The Constitution recognized these institutional arrangements, and gave the Congress the power to provide for calling the militia into national service. Congress was also given the power to raise armies, and stringent control over military expenditure. To one who reads the words the framers of the Constitution wrote, it seems clear that a system of compulsory military service directed by the executive branch and administered on a national basis was not contemplated. If there was to be compulsion, the states would do the compelling. The national standing army, which the framers thought would be small, was to be a volunteer force. The early Congresses not only recognized this constitutional plan but defeated attempt after attempt to institute a federally administered system of conscription. As the young Daniel Webster thundered during a debate on such a proposal in 1814:

> Is this, sir, consistent with the character of a free government? Is this civil liberty? Is this the real character of our Constitution? No, sir, indeed it is not. . . . The people of this country have not

established for themselves such a fabric of despotism. They have not purchased at a vast expense of their own treasure and their own blood a Magna Carta to be slaves. Where is it written in the Constitution . . . that you may take children from their parents, and parents from their children, and compel them to fight the battles of any war in which the folly or the wickedness of government may engage it?[5]

In 1863, the Congress did vote for conscription, and a constitutional challenge to the new system was briefly successful by a 4 to 3 vote of the Pennsylvania Supreme Court, the decision being overturned, again 4 to 3, when a new justice took his seat.[6] Conscription was reinstituted during the First World War, in substantially its present form, and the opposition to it brought on a series of prosecutions against the political opponents of the draft. These and related prosecutions of dissenters were among the events which brought the ACLU into being, and contributed to stifling public discussion at a time when it was most needed. As Zechariah Chafee has written:

[T]ens of thousands among those "forward-looking men and women" to whom President Wilson had appealed in earlier years were bewildered and depressed and silenced by the negation of freedom in the twenty-year sentences requested by his legal subordinates from complacent judges. So we had plenty of patriotism and very little criticism, except of the slowness of munition production. Wrong courses were followed like the despatch of troops to Archangel in 1918, which fatally alienated Russia from Wilson's aims for a peaceful Europe. Harmful facts like the secret treaties were concealed while they could have been cured, only to bob up later and wreck everything.[7]

World War II brought conscription again. Then, briefly in 1947 and 1948, Selective Service was scheduled for liquidation. The enactment in 1948, after bitter debate, of a peacetime draft is perhaps the most significant political event of the postwar period. Whatever may be the occasion during time of war to activate executive powers which otherwise lie unexercised, the justification in time of peace for bypassing the constitutional scheme of rules for the raising and control of armies seemed, to opponents of the 1948 Act, attenuated at best. Also, the conscription system for which Congress provided in 1948, which exists in 1970 with few major changes, studiedly disregarded the principles of fair hearing which had been guaranteed to those subject to other federal regulatory agencies. Finally, the system of conscription posed a clear danger to political and religious freedom. These three issues are still the subject of debate. They are considered below.

PROCEDURAL HORRIBLES—GENERAL HERSHEY'S CABINET

When 1970 opened, General Lewis B. Hershey had been replaced as Director of Selective Service, but the System he built and shaped lives on. Some basic decisions about the System's structure are, of course, made by the Congress. Congress has decided that we shall have conscription. It has decreed that women are exempt from the draft, though there is little rational basis for such a distinction. Congress has also determined that aliens are liable for service to almost the same extent as citizens. An alien, once registered, may leave the United States, and so long as he remains outside he will be exempt. Diplomatic and consular officials and tourists are exempt. But every alien admitted for permanent residence, and any alien who remains here for more than a year, is draft-eligible. The latter group can escape liability only by renouncing all opportunity ever to obtain American citizenship. The rationale for including aliens is, no doubt, the xenophobic philosophy which has pervaded most American legislation in the field of immigration, but it is worth noting that few if any other countries require aliens to serve.

More abhorrent to many is our extension of conscription to those, such as residents of Puerto Rico, who are in our possessions, territories, "commonwealths," or (less charitably) colonies, even though these persons do not have the full right of participation in American government. In the case of Puerto Rico, as eminent legal scholars there have contended, the imposition of conscription is the more onerous because there has been no self-determination by the Puerto Rican people on the issue and our claim of sufficient sovereignty over the island to impose conscription into the American armed forces is tenuous at best.

Congressional decision about the System aside, the machinery of conscription is a grotesque perversion of the image of justice. There are about 4,100 local Selective Service boards, each consisting of three or more members. The statistical portrait of the typical board member depicts a man, white, middle-aged, middle-class.[8] These members serve without pay. They are not required, as a condition of being nominated by their respective governors and approved by the President (really by the Director of Selective Service), to know anything about the law they administer.[9] This "law" is not really entitled to the name: it consists of a forty-page statute riddled with inconsistencies, bad draftsmanship, and dormant provisions. To this is added the Selective Service Regulations, another couple of hundred pages, and then four or five hundred pages of memorandums and advisory bulletins from the Director of Selective Service. In addition, the board must apply provisions of several lengthy Army regulations, totaling scores of printed pages. As a means of countering the institutional pressures which ensure that board members are largely innocent of this body of knowledge, the System established by rule that the registrant is presumed available for military service (1-A) unless he proves otherwise. Fair? Maybe, except the System has never published an index to its glut of regulatory material, or even a simple handbook (such as you get with your income tax forms) summarizing the law. A lawyer might be able to figure a way through the maze, except that few are trained to do so, and the Selective Service regulations forbid representation by counsel when the registrant appears before his local board. From the local board's decision there is, true, an appeal, but the appeal is to another board of volunteers with the same qualifications, who may decide hundreds of cases *each hour* they meet. Beyond this lies another, national board, but the registrant in most cases has no right to appeal to this body, and in any case, it keeps no records of its deliberations, if any, and gives no reasons, if it has any, for its decisions.

Add to these facts the local board's discretion to refuse to hear witnesses offered by the registrant on his behalf, and its power— under the regulations—to listen to witnesses whom the registrant cannot cross-examine.

How can the System get away with ignoring the procedural guarantees which are generally thought essential to a fair decision, and which are observed by almost every other federal agency—the Federal Communications Commission, the Interstate Commerce Commission, the Federal Power Commission, and so on? The answer lies in the creation of the System's essential features in time of war and total national mobilization. During the World Wars, the System operated with scant regard for individual rights in the interest of processing as many men as possible into the armed services. Many procedures were built into the law which disregard basic rights. In addition, the courts long took the view that no error, no matter how plain, committed by the Selective Service was subject to judicial review and correction. Not until 1946, when the shooting had stopped, did the Supreme Court decide that some limited judicial review of Selective Service decisions was available.

Even then, in *Estep v. United States*,[10] the Court was willing to give great deference to the decisions of the System, as it had been willing to do in considering other executive decisions with unprecedentedly great impact upon individual liberty. The Japanese Relocation Cases,[11] justifying the removal from their homes of tens of thousands of American citizens of Japanese descent, and tens of thousands of aliens against whom there was not the slightest suspicion, are an egregious instance of that deference. So it was that the procedures the System followed received little authoritative critical examination.

In the wartime mold, the peacetime conscription bill was cast. And the Selective Service System, with largely the same personnel as had administered wartime conscription, simply went back in 1948 to business-as-before.

Of late, however, four lines of attack have been begun against the denial of procedural rights in the System. First, legislative pressure, through open hearings before congressional committees, has been brought upon the Congress and the President.[12] The result of this pressure is uncertain. In April 1970, the President moved to restrict occupational deferments, and asked the Congress to end the mandatory undergraduate student deferment. He also pledged that the administration would move toward "reducing draft calls to zero." The student deferment was earnestly debated in the Ninetieth Congress, as legislators considered renewal of the conscription law. In the end, there was not enough congressional resolve to abolish the badge of privilege represented by deferment of college students. But the Congress did, in 1967, contribute to abolition of the deferment for graduate students, and attempted to ensure that once a registrant graduated he would be prime draft material. This legislation no doubt heightened college students' sense of awareness of foreign and military policy issues, and, together with the escalation of the Indochina war, contributed to an explosion of protest on the campuses. But all of the proposed changes amount at best to tinkering. Even the proposal to reduce draft calls to zero does not speak of abolishing or seriously reforming conscription. Selective Service would still be with us, ready to get back to business-as-usual to raise a force of conscripts. The

President does, of course, have the power to work substantial change in the system and may be induced to do so by the pressures generated in the course of legislative hearings in 1971 (when the present conscription law expires). Among these regulatory changes might be provision for informing registrants of their rights under the System.

A second line of attack has been through provision of legal and counseling services to registrants by individuals and organizations. While the System actively discourages the effective participation of lawyers, a lawyer or counselor can materially assist a registrant by informing him of his rights and choices within the System. An informed registrant, in turn, may be more able to enforce local-board compliance with applicable regulations. This movement to provide legal services has received impetus from the publication of guides to the draft law.[13] It has also been aided by the participation of national organizations such as the American Civil Liberties Union, the Emergency Civil Liberties Committee, the National Lawyers Guild, and the Central Committee for Conscientious Objectors. Regrettably, however, the provision of advice and assistance to registrants has not yet effectively reached the ghettos and *barrios*.

Third, constitutional arguments have been advanced against the denial of procedural rights by the System. Why, after all, should it be permitted to send a man to war without a meaningful hearing, when it is not permitted to expel a student,[14] disbar a lawyer,[15] fire a civil servant,[16] or terminate a welfare recipient's benefits without such a hearing?[17] Selective Service answers that the statute presumes a registrant to be available for service, and that it merely determines when and where and if he will fulfill this obligation.

This contention is arrant nonsense. For one thing, the peacetime conscription system is not directed at total mobilization, and Selective Service has acknowledged that deferring registrants from service is as important a task as providing manpower to the standing military forces.[18] A fair hearing seems appropriate in carrying out this task. Too, the System's view rests upon the idea that deferments and exemptions are "personal privileges," revocable at the will of any local board or Selective Service official, without any basis in reason and without a hearing of any sort. This view that governmental benefits are "privileges," shared by welfare administrators, public employers, and others of like mind, has been discredited. It may be conceded that the Congress could make everyone liable to service, and that deferments are in that sense "privileges."

But having established the privilege, the Congress may not, consistently with constitutional command, deprive anyone of it without a fair hearing to determine whether the deprival is appropriate and meets the legislative criteria. Nor may entitlement to any such privilege be conditioned upon giving up a right, such as the right to free speech, which the Constitution guarantees.[19]

A fourth ground of procedural attack is by use of developing doctrines of delegation of legislative power. Many will recall that during the administration of Franklin D. Roosevelt, broad-gauge social programs were enacted by the Congress and placed in the hands of administrators to be carried out. After a series of rebuffs from the Supreme Court, the changing composition of that body led to development of the principle that the Congress might validly delegate great power to an administrative agency, subject to no guideline for action but "the public interest, convenience, and necessity." This "old law" of delegation is systematized in Supreme Court decisions approving these grants of power.[20]

The "new law" of delegation does not address the proposition that Congress can delegate great power in general terms. Rather, it rests upon two crucial premises. First, a delegation of power over personal liberties must be made with greater precision than a delegation of general regulatory power. Second, the Court will carefully scrutinize every administrator's claim of power over personal liberties to ensure that the Congress has in fact given him the power he claims to have. In one leading case, *Kent v. Dulles*,[21] the Secretary of State claimed to have authority to deny passports based on political affiliations. The court looked at the history of the legislation granting the Secretary the power to regulate the freedom to travel, and determined that the Congress had not given him authority to restrict that freedom based upon such grounds.

In another case, *Greene v. McElroy*,[22] the security clearance of an aeronautical engineer had been revoked without a hearing, effectively depriving him of his livelihood in his chosen profession. The Court considered, but did not decide, the constitutional question whether the due process clause compelled a full hearing. The Court held only that due process guarantees—confrontation of one's accusers, cross-examination, notice of charges—are so important that it would not presume that Congress intended to dispense with them. Unless the Department of Defense is given a clear, unmistakable command by the Congress to jettison these important guarantees of fairness, it may not do so. (Of course, if such a command were issued, its constitutionality would have to be considered.)

The rationale of *Kent* and *Greene* extends to Selective Service cases. True, the Selective Service Act expressly excludes draft board proceedings from the procedural requirements of the Administrative Procedure Act, which provides a full arsenal of procedural rights. However, this authorization should not be considered a congressional approval of the Selective Service System's abandoning all attempts to ensure the fairness of its decision-making process. Counsel at appearances before local boards is not forbidden by the Act, nor are the rights of cross-examination, confrontation, notice of the grounds upon which the board decides, and so on. Without explicit legislative authorization for denying these rights, given the serious constitutional issues raised by their denial, the System should be held not empowered to deny them.

This theory was applied by the Supreme Court in *Gutknecht v. United States*,[23] an American Civil Liberties Union case argued by the author and decided January 19, 1970. Under the "delinquency" regulations of the Selective Service System, local draft boards were given the power to take away the deferment or exemption of any registrant, classify him 1-A (available for combatant military service), and order him for induction out of the normal order of call. This broad-ranging power had been used since 1967, at the urging of the Director of Selective Service General Hershey, to punish registrants who engaged in protests against the draft and against American military action in Vietnam. This use of power by the local boards, without procedural safeguards, raised serious free speech and due process questions. But the Supreme Court invalidated the delinquency regulations, not on an expressly constitutional basis, but on the basis of *Kent* and *Greene*:

> In *Kent v. Dulles,* 357 U.S. 116, 128–129, we refused to impute to Congress the grant of "unbridled discretion" to the Secretary of State to issue or withhold a passport from a citizen "for any substantive reason he may choose." *Id.,* at 128. Where the liberties of the citizen are involved, we said that "we will construe narrowly all delegated powers that curtail or dilute them." *Id.,* at 129. The Director of Selective Service described the "delinquency" regulations as designed "to prevent, wherever possible, prosecutions for minor infraction of rules" during the selective service processing. We search the Act in vain for any clues that Congress desired the Act to have punitive sanctions apart from the criminal prosecu-

tions specifically authorized. Nor do we read it as granting personal privileges which may be forfeited for transgressions which affront the local board. If federal or state laws are violated by registrants, they can be prosecuted. If induction is to be substituted for these prosecutions, a vast rewriting of the Act is needed. Standards would be needed by which the legality of a declaration of "delinquency" could be judged. And the regulations, when written, would be subject to the customary inquiries as to infirmities on their face or in their application, including the question whether they were used to penalize or punish the free exercise of constitutional rights.[24]

The new doctrine of delegation may, one can see, provide a principled alternative ground for decision of cases raising constitutional issues. As such, it is a powerful legal weapon not only in draft cases, and not only in litigation about due process, but in cases raising questions of freedom of speech, press, assembly, and religion and of other freedoms as well.

Now it may be objected that the Selective Service System cannot function if it must give a hearing to every registrant every time it changes a classification. This objection has some merit. A thoroughgoing reform of the Selectice Service System in order to ensure that it gave at least as much due process as, say, the Federal Communications Commission would be expensive and would create a massive federal bureaucracy. It may, that is, be impossible to operate a fair system of compulsory military service except at prohibitive cost. If that is so, then abolition of conscription seems the only principled alternative.

CONSCRIPTION AND CONSCIENCE

Conflicts between conscience and the commands of government trace a long path in the history of conscription. The colonial militias apparently excused men whose religious affiliation with a pacifist church precluded their serving. The Civil War draft act provided that any man could avoid service on payment of a bounty. The World War I draft act excused members of historic "peace churches" who believed in the tenets of their faiths.[25] The World War II law made provision for conscientious objectors, not by reference to the creeds of particular churches, but by describing the sort of *individual* belief which would qualify a registrant to do alternative service instead of military duty. The statutory standard has been amended since, and today a conscientious objector is defined as one who, by reason of religious training and belief, is conscientiously opposed to participation in war in any form. A religious belief is defined to exclude essentially political, philosophical, or sociological beliefs and a "merely personal moral code." One who meets these standards is classified 1-A-O, and if inducted, is ordered to perform military service in a noncombatant capacity.

One who meets all the requirements for a 1-A-O classification and is further opposed even to noncombatant service in the military is to be classified 1-O and assigned, if called, to civilian alternative service.[26]

The hostility by local boards to conscientious-objector applicants, and board members' abysmal ignorance of the criteria for conscientious-objector status, have been documented.[27] In the arena of litigation, however, two principal issues are the focus of concern: the statutory definition of religion and the problem of objection to particular wars.

The statutory standard, "religious training and belief," has been held unconstitutional by two distinguished courts, once on the theory that it discriminates against sincere nontheist objectors,[28] and once on the theory that it is an establishment of religion.[29] The Supreme Court has, however, declined to face the constitutional issue head-on.

The Supreme Court held long ago that "The law knows no heresy, and is committed to the support of no dogma, the establishment of no sect."[30] This basic principle has been the subject of continuing debate as to its function and limits. The Supreme Court has held that not all governmental recognition, in legislative enactment and in the bestowal of benefits, of differences between "religious" and "nonreligious" activity amounts to an establishment of religion. The Court in the 1969 term upheld a municipality's legislative program of broad tax exemption for church-related property, saying that the exemption represented neither hostility to nor sponsorship of religious associations, but was part of a statutory scheme designed to promote a number of institutions which served purposes the community thought important.[31] Of course, in the field of Selective Service, the government (as Mr. Justice Blackmun observed when he was a circuit judge) is "demanding" and not "bestowing," and the consequences to a registrant's life and liberty of a refusal to exempt him as a conscientious objector are both obvious and serious.[32] And, unlike New York's tax-exemption statute, the Selective Service law singles out religion for special treatment.

Under these circumstances, it is not difficult to wonder, as Judge Wyzanski wondered in *United States v. Sisson*,[33] whether limitation of the conscientious-objector exemption to religious believers is a special preference or sponsorship extended by government in violation of the prohibition against establishment of religion.

What other explanation may rationally be advanced for saying that a young atheist whose deepest ethical convictions prevent his participation in war is to serve in the armed forces or go to jail, while a registrant who believes the same thing and calls his source of belief "God" is exempted from such a choice? To be sure, it is sometimes said that the conscientious-objector exemption is a matter of legislative grace and that since Congress need not have exempted anybody, it may create an exemption upon the terms and conditions it wishes. This sort of argument was advanced and rejected in an analogous context in *Sherbert v. Verner*.[34] Mrs. Sherbert, a Seventh-Day Adventist, was ruled ineligible for unemployment benefits by the State of South Carolina because she was unavailable for Saturday work. The state contended that since unemployment benefits were a benefit or privilege voluntarily extended by it, that they might be conditioned in any manner the state saw fit. The Court held, "It is too late in the day to doubt that the liberties of religion and expression may be infringed by the denial or placing of conditions upon a benefit or privilege," and struck down the prohibition on Mrs. Verner's receiving compensation. So in the field of Selective Service, whether or not there is a constitutional right to be a conscientious objector (a question considered below), there is surely a right not to have the exemption administered upon a basis which prefers one religious faith over another, or religionists in the orthodox mold over persons whose beliefs are conventionally described as nonreligious, "ethical," "humanistic," or "philosophical."

Another objection raised to recognition of "nonreligious" objection is that one cannot tell whether such persons are sincere in their beliefs. This argument is fatuous: there is no reason to suppose that detecting a sincere "ethical" belief is any more difficult than detecting a sincere "religious" belief.

The Supreme Court has up to now avoided decision of these

serious constitutional questions by giving the broadest possible interpretation to the "religious training and belief" portion of the statutory definition. In *United States v. Seeger*,[35] the Court held that the standard must be interpreted to comport with "the ever-broadening understanding of the modern religious community." The Court went on to quote from the writings of contemporary theologians and philosophers, including Paul Tillich, John A. T. Robinson, and David Saville Muzzey. No doubt this broad interpretation of the statutory language was induced by consideration of the constitutional questions raised by a narrow, exclusive definition of religion. Indeed, Justice Douglas remarked in his concurring opinion that the statute had been stretched beyond its literal terms "in the candid service of avoiding a serious constitutional doubt." In the 1969 term, in *Welsh v. United States,* the Court stretched the *Seeger* rationale still further, though over the protest of Justices White and Stewart and Chief Justice Burger, and with Justice Harlan grudgingly concurring in the result while listing a series of constitutional issues which the Court's plurality opinion ducks.[36]

A related question is that raised by religious objection to a particular war, or "selective" conscientious objection. Of course, much of the controversy in this field misses the point entirely, for there are many registrants whose local boards believe, or who may themselves believe, that they are objectors to particular wars when in reality they fall within the statutory definition. That a man would have fought in World War II is not necessarily a disqualification, for example. The question asked is "Are you a conscientious objector," not "Would you have been one?" Today's wars are different from World War II in that increased danger of nuclear annihilation accompanies them, and in that they pose great risks to civilian populations. A registrant should more properly be asked, "Is there any war in which you can imagine your country being involved in which you could conscientiously participate?" And even if the answer is "yes," the registrant may not be disqualified. A man need not be a pacifist to be a conscientious objector. If he is willing to use force in defense of himself, of his family when in immediate physical danger, or even, the Supreme Court has held, of his church and its members, he may still be a conscientious objector.[37] That is, a registrant might well distinguish between a situation in which he was asked to fight a foreign war as a part of an army, and a situation in which he would take up arms to defend his home against an invasion of our shores.

But if by no stretch of the statutory language can a registrant escape the appellation "selective objector," as where he objects to participation in the war in Vietnam but would not object to participation in an American intervention in Israel, one must make a constitutional argument similar to that used in discussing the statutory standard of "religious training and belief." Let me suggest two alternative analytical approaches to this problem.

One approach is to begin by asking, Is there a constitutional right to be a conscientious objector? If there is such a right, it is analytically a right to refuse to perform a governmental command, because of an overriding religious conviction, to enter the armed forces. This right cannot logically be limited to those who say they will refuse service in all wars, since the determination of whether such a right will be recognized turns upon the relative interests of the state and the potential draftee with respect to each military conflict in which the right of conscientious objection is asserted. The argument runs as follows: The free exercise clause of the First Amendment protects a man from assaults upon his deeply held beliefs, in the form of commands by the government, to perform in ways inconsistent with those beliefs. If a man's deeply held religious beliefs would be offended by service in the armed forces, what justification is there for compelling him either to serve or to go to jail? Perhaps when the nation is in imminent danger, or in a time of total national mobilization, one might reasonably put men to such a choice. But absent such a state of things, the right of free exercise ought arguably to be protected.

This principle is not novel. Courts have recognized that a religious belief inconsistent with governmental command may at times be a basis for disobedience of that command. In California, a tribe of Indians used peyote, a hallucinogenic drug, in religious rituals. The California Supreme Court held that the tribe members could not be prosecuted under the narcotics laws applicable to the generality of citizens, for the Indians' conduct was protected by the constitutional guarantee of free exercise of religion.[38] And while the Supreme Court did in the last century uphold, in the face of a constitutional free-exercise challenge by Mormons, laws prohibiting polygamy,[39] the Court recognized the principle contended for here: Absent some compelling, overriding governmental interest, a claim of free exercise must be honored. (It goes almost without saying that in defining "religion" for purposes of delimiting the scope of the free exercise guarantee, there may be no discrimination in favor of more orthodox beliefs and against those which are less traditional.)

Therefore, if there is a constitutional right to be a conscientious objector, there is a constitutional case for selective objection, in the sense that the availability of the right will turn on whether there is, in a particular conflict, a countervailing governmental interest sufficiently strong to defeat it. More than this, however, if there is a First Amendment right to refuse military service on religious grounds, that right may be exercised at the option of the holder of it, and claimed or not claimed depending upon the dictates of his conscience with respect to the acceptability of particular wars.

Even if there is no First Amendment right to be a conscientious objector, there is still a constitutional case for selective objection. Congress cannot, as we saw above, discriminatorily grant a benefit or a privilege. The present conscientious-objector exemption, if construed or applied to deny claims of selective objection, establishes such a discrimination. Members of the Society of Friends, the Church of the Brethren, and other pacifist sects, and those registrants whose individual beliefs lead them to oppose participation in all wars, are preferred under such a test, while those whose religious training and belief leads them to distinguish "just" from "unjust" wars are the victims of it. Among the "just war" pacifists are many Catholics, whose theology from the time of Saint Augustine has taught that only wars which meet certain tests of objective and techniques of warfare may be regarded as having divine approval.

The argument against selective objection is, therefore, that one may not, in establishing the conscientious-objector exemption, prefer some faiths over others, and give official sanction to those whose source of spiritual guidance teaches abhorrence of all wars and those who believe just as deeply that only some wars are permissible.

Ought We to Conscript?

The serious questions of national policy near the surface of the debate over ending conscription do not admit of easy answers. The objection most often voiced to ending conscription is fear of a "volunteer" army composed of the poor, the black, and the brown, and harnessed to the will of its highly trained and politically conservative officer corps.

It bears noting that we already have an officer corps which is largely professional, certainly at the higher ranks, and that we suffer from its political influence. On the other hand, one should note that the existence of a cheap and easily expansible conscript force is one element of the presidential power to involve the country in a series of military actions designed to crush revolutionary movements in the Third World.

The overriding issue of military policy at this moment is not the draft but the employment of American forces in Indochina, Latin America, and all over the world in propping up reactionary regimes. Our large standing army gives the President "flexibility" to accomplish these interventions. Ending conscription would arguably require scaling down military activity, if the same level of military expenditure is to be maintained, for a high enough wage would have to be paid to attract men into a volunteer force.

Earlier, I argued that the Constitution must be twisted out of recognition to find authority for a national system of conscription. Upon the basis of these constitutional considerations, litigants in ACLU-sponsored cases have urged that the system of conscription is unconstitutional. As an alternative, it has been urged that whereas conscription may be permissible in time of total mobilization or national emergency, the system of forced military service entails such a severe restriction on the personal liberty of millions of young men that in time of nominal peace it is constitutionally interdicted. Raising an army may be a permissible goal, but in pursuing it Congress is bound to follow the course which impinges to the least possible extent upon protected freedoms.[40] As the ACLU said in its most recent policy statement:

> The present Selective Service law as presently administered and in present circumstances is a violation of civil liberties and constitutional guarantees. . . .
>
> Military conscription is a severe infringement of individual liberties, at best the resort of a nation facing an imminent threat. It must rest upon the interests of national security, what James Madison called "the impulse of self-preservation." ACLU believes that government has a duty to prove to the public that so drastic a step as conscription is required today. No such showing has been made.

Instead, conscription has become a habit of mind for the nation, winning a lazy acceptance from adults beyond its reach, but creating havoc and hostility from young men whose lives it disrupts and too often takes. It is shameful for a free nation to continue for thirty years a form of involuntary servitude without regular and conclusive showings of its necessity.

In the past, ACLU appraisals of the draft have challenged the government to accept the burden of proof and have invited wide public debate on the conscription issue. The Union's determination that the present law is a violation of civil liberties makes clear that, in its view, proof is lacking to justify the contraventions of due process and the infringements of individual rights that characterize the present Selective Service system.

There is another argument to be made here. A conscript soldier makes very little money in comparison to what he could command on the labor market. He serves, by definition, against his will. The cavalier and unsupported assertion in one ill-considered Supreme Court case arising during a time of national hysteria over World War I, that there is no merit in the claim that conscription is involuntary servitude, should be re-examined. Economists of both liberal and conservative persuasions have recognized that conscription in effect imposes a tax on the young men who serve at less than the market rate of pay.[41] The "tax" in question, viewed more properly as forced labor, offends a basic American principle against the imposition of such service except as conviction for crime.

In brief compass, one can only suggest arguments, ideas, and judgments which more detailed reflection might permit one to accept, validate, and act upon. Enough has been said, I hope, to suggest that the institution of conscription poses a daily and dangerous threat to the formal guarantees of freedom and fairness which the Constitution makes to the generality of citizens.

NOTES

1. Brecht, *Selected Poems* (Hays trans. 1947).
2. Gutknecht v. United States, 396 U.S. 295 (1970).
3. Selective Service Law Reporter, Practice Manual ¶2 [hereinafter cited as Practice Manual].
4. Practice Manual ¶¶2, 2302–3; *see also* Friedman, "Conscription and the

Constitution: The Original Understanding," 67 *Michigan Law Review* 1493 (1969).

5. *Quoted in* Friedman, *supra* note 4, at 1542–43.

6. Practice Manual ¶2303.

7. Z. Chafee, *Free Speech in the United States* 561–62 (1942).

8. *See* National Advisory Commission on Selective Service, *In Pursuit of Equity: Who Serves When Not All Serve?* 19 (1967); J. Davis & K. Dolbeare, *Little Groups of Neighbors: The Selective Service System* (1968); Tigar & Zweben, "Selective Service: Some Certain Problems and Some Tentative Answers," 37 *George Washington Law Review* 510 (1969).

9. Practice Manual ¶42 describes the qualifications and duties of local board members.

10. 327 U.S. 114 (1946).

11. Hirabayashi v. United States, 320 U.S. 81 (1943); Korematsu v. United States, 323 U.S. 214 (1944).

12. In October and November 1969, extensive hearings were held on the fairness of Selective Service procedures by Senator Edward Kennedy's Subcommittee on Administrative Practice and Procedure, Senate Committee on the Judiciary. The Committee report and transcript are now available.

13. *The Selective Service Law Reporter,* a guide for lawyers, counselors, and others, is the most thorough of these publications. It is available from the Public Law Education Institute, 1346 Connecticut Avenue N.W., Washington, D.C. The Central Committee for Conscientious Objectors publishes an excellent guide, the *Handbook for Conscientious Objectors,* now in its tenth edition and available for $1.00 from CCCO, 2016 Walnut Street, Philadelphia, Pennsylvania. See also A. Tatum & J. Tuchinsky, *Guide to the Draft,* a Beacon paperback.

14. "Symposium: Student Rights and Campus Rules," 54 *California Law Review* 1 (1966).

15. *In re* Ruffalo, 390 U.S. 544 (1968).

16. Scott v. Macy, 349 F.2d 182 (D.C. Cir. 1965).

17. Goldberg v. Kelly, 397 U.S. 254 (1970).

18. *See* Tigar & Zweben, *supra* note 8, at 528–29.

19. *See* O'Neil, "Unconstitutional Conditions: Welfare Benefits with Strings Attached," 54 *California Law Review* 443 (1966).

20. L. Jaffe, *Judicial Control of Administrative Action* 28–73 (1965).

21. 357 U.S. 116 (1958).

22. 360 U.S. 474 (1959).

23. 396 U.S. 295 (1970).

24. *Id.* at 307–8 (footnote omitted).

25. The history is traced in United States v. Seeger, 380 U.S. 163 (1965).

26. See the discussion in the CCCO *Handbook for Conscientious Objectors, supra* note 13.

27. Davis & Dolbeare, *supra* note 8.

28. United States v. Seeger, 326 F.2d 846 (2d Cir. 1964), *aff'd,* 380 U.S. 163 (1965).

29. United States v. Sisson, 297 F. Supp. 902 (D. Mass. 1969), *appeal dismissed,* 399 U.S. 267 (1970).

30. Watson v. Jones, 80 U.S. (13 Wall.) 679, 728 (1871).

31. Walz v Tax Comm'n, 90 S. Ct. 1409 (1970).

32. *In re* Weitzman, 38 U.S.L.W. 2550 (8th Cir. April 4, 1970).

33. 297 F. Supp. 902 (D. Mass. 1969), *appeal dismissed,* 399 U.S. 267 (1970).

34. 374 U.S. 398, 404 (1963).

35. 380 U.S. 160, 188 (1965).

36. 398 U.S. 333 (1970).

37. *See* Sicurella v. United States, 348 U.S. 385 (1955).

38. People v. Woody, 61 Cal. 2d 716, 40 Cal. Rptr. 69, 394 P.2d 813 (1964).

39. Reynolds v. United States, 98 U.S. 145 (1878). *See* Comment, 56 *California Law Review* 100 (1968).

40. *See* Schneider v. New Jersey, 308 U.S. 147 (1939); United States v. Robel, 389 U.S. 258 (1967).

41. Tigar & Zweben, *supra* note 8, at 534.

SECTION V

The Rights of
Particular Groups

THE RIGHTS OF
WOMEN

PAULI MURRAY

I

ALTHOUGH A HALF-CENTURY HAS ELAPSED SINCE American women won a protracted struggle for the right to vote, they continue to occupy a subordinate status in society comparable in many respects to that of a racial minority. Numerous sex-based inequalities rooted in law and custom perpetuate lingering assumptions that in areas not associated with childbearing and motherhood, women are incapable of assuming full responsibility for themselves as adult citizens, and that, like children, they require the special protection or restraint of the laws. Moreover, there is a persistent tendency to define all women in relation to their biological function and to treat them as sex objects rather than as persons. The fact that many of these assumptions and the practices upon which they are based are being successfully challenged does not make more palatable to a growing radical feminist movement in 1970 the vestiges of discriminatory distinctions based upon sex. Particularly when they are embedded in the law, these distinctions reinforce a pervasive bias against women which prevents them from assuming their rightful place in the community as equals with men.[1]

Pauli Murray is Professor of American Studies at Brandeis University, a member of the ACLU Board of Directors, and a former consultant to the Equal Employment Opportunity Commission. She is the co-author of a leading study of employment discrimination against women.

A classic example of the continuing effect of traditional inequality is found in the jury laws of many states. At the beginning
of World War II, twenty-four states still excluded women from
jury service. As late as 1966, Alabama, Mississippi, and South Carolina provided that only males were eligible to serve as jurors, and
did not abandon this policy until a federal court ruled in the landmark decision *White v. Crook*[2] that the Fourteenth Amendment
prohibits sex discrimination as well as racial discrimination in jury
service.

Although women are now eligible to serve on all federal and
state juries, approximately half of the states continue to make sex
distinctions in their jury laws. Many of these statutes provide that
women may claim exemption from jury duty solely on the basis of
sex. The Supreme Court held in 1961 that a Florida law providing
that women not be called to serve as jurors unless they register with
the clerk of the court their desire to serve did not violate the Fourteenth Amendment.[3] This classification on a purely biological basis
perpetuates the myth that the woman's place is in the home and
that women are not expected to participate in public affairs. Jury
officials frequently seize upon the exemption to discourage women
from serving on juries. Employers often permit male employees to
be absent for jury service without loss of pay, while denying this
privilege to female employees on the ground that they are not required by law to serve on juries and consequently can take time
off only at their own expense. The practical effect of a blanket
exemption of more than half the adult population is almost to
nullify the jury laws with respect to women and to impair the
constitutional standard that juries should represent a fair cross
section of the community.

Examples of sex-based discriminatory criminal statutes include
those which impose heavier penalties upon female than male offenders for the same offense,[4] or which penalize a female prostitute
but not her male customer. When such statutes are enacted by
predominantly male legislatures and upheld by predominantly
male judges, they raise an inference of bias inherent in attitudes of
male supremacy.

In most states abortion is a criminal offense unless it is necessary
to save the life of the mother. These criminal-abortion statutes have
become a primary target of feminist protest, which asserts that they
violate a woman's right to control her own reproductive processes
in deciding whether she shall have a child. Such a decision, it is

urged, should rest entirely with the woman and her physician without the intervention of the state. Consequently, earlier campaigns to liberalize abortion statutes are giving way to demands for outright repeal of existing legislation and widespread attacks through the courts upon the constitutionality of abortion laws. In March 1970, Hawaii became the first state to repeal all criminal penalties for abortions approved by licensed physicians and performed in a licensed hospital on women who have resided in the state for at least ninety days. Although the residence requirement may be open to constitutional objection, Hawaii's action is expected to have an impact upon other state legislatures where similar proposals are now pending. More recently, New York and Alaska adopted similar legislation leaving decisions on abortion solely to the woman and her physician. New York imposes no residency requirement, while Alaska requires that the woman be domiciled within the state for thirty days. Moreover, in view of the invalidation of local abortion statutes by federal courts in the District of Columbia and Wisconsin and by the California Supreme Court, ultimately the issue of constitutionality will probably be determined by the Supreme Court of the United States.

Laws which permit females to reach a majority or to marry without parental consent at an earlier age than males, though apparently favorable to women, actually strengthen the traditional view that the primary goal of womanhood is marriage and therefore women should be encouraged to marry early and have children, while men are expected to prepare themselves for broader social pursuits. The "protective" aspect of continuing legal distinctions based upon sex is inconsistent with the increasingly significant role of women in the national economy. Nearly half of all women 18 to 64 years of age are in the labor force. More than one in three workers (37 percent) is female, and approximately three-fifths of all working women are married and living with their husbands. Yet in some states married women are still subjected to legal restrictions in matters of contractual capacity, the right to convey real property, and the right to establish a legal domicile. In a few states a married woman but not a married man must apply for court approval before she can engage in an independent business. Only four states recognize a married woman's right to acquire a separate domicile from her husband for all purposes, even when the couple live apart through business necessity or by mutual agreement. Many jurisdictions permit a husband in a personal-injury action to sue for loss of his wife's services and conjugal association, or loss of consortium, while denying the wife a reciprocal right of recovery.

The sex-based discriminatory laws which have aroused the widest controversy in recent years are those state statutes which restrict women's employment opportunities and which will be considered later. Here, it should be pointed out that the leading precedent for the validity of legal distinctions based upon sex is a 1908 Supreme Court decision in *Muller v. Oregon*,[5] which upheld an Oregon maximum-hours law applicable to women only. Three years earlier, in *Lochner v. New York*,[6] the Court had struck down a similar statute in New York which covered male employees in bakeries on the ground that it was an arbitrary interference with the liberty of the individual to contract with respect to his labor and thus in conflict with the Fourteenth Amendment. Faced with the logic of *Lochner,* the Court found it necessary to harmonize the result reached in *Muller* with the equal protection clause of the Fourteenth Amendment by promulgating the doctrine that "sex is a valid basis for classification."

The constitutionality of the Oregon statute rested upon two grounds: (1) differential legislation was justified by the differences between the sexes in physical structure, physical strength, "the self-reliance which enables one to assert full rights, and in the capacity to maintain the struggle for subsistence"; and (2) some protective legislation was necessary for women in order "to secure a real equality of right" and "to compensate for some of the burdens which rest upon [them]."

The *Muller* decision reflected an era when women were politically disfranchised, represented only about 18 percent of the labor force, lacked the protection of strong unionization or federal labor standards legislation, and were particularly vulnerable to extreme forms of exploitation. It also reflected the traditional view of male dominance through the Court's paternalistic observation that woman is so constituted that she would continue to depend upon and look to man for protection even if all statutory restrictions were removed and she stood on an absolutely equal plane with him.

The sweeping language of the *Muller* decision served to strengthen sex bias. The case has been cited in support of court rulings which upheld the exclusion of women from jury service, discriminatory treatment in licensing occupations, and the barring of women from a state-supported college. Although, in upholding the Fair Labor Standards Act in 1940, the Supreme Court abandoned the original basis for differential treatment of men and women, the *Muller* case has not been overruled. It remains an effective roadblock to the full equality of women, and by reducing the ability of women to earn money, it helps keep them in exactly the dependent position which is used to justify differential legislation. Further, as we shall see, it now appears to be in direct conflict with the present national policy to promote equal employment opportunity without regard to sex. By treating *all* women as a class, the rationale of the decision ignores individual differences, capacities, and economic interests. Whatever may have been the justification for the legal protection of women workers in 1908, the doctrine that "sex is a valid basis for classification," like the racial "separate but equal" doctrine, has produced discriminatory results which overshadow any continuing utility. In the light of changed conditions and attitudes, *Muller* should be re-examined and discarded.

As we have observed in the case of racial discrimination, legal distinctions based upon sex tend to reinforce and to perpetuate inequalities which do not have the sanction of law. Similarly, official segregation of the sexes serves the function of maintaining the privileged position of the dominant male group. Some state universities have segregated or excluded women students on the ground of sex. As recently as February 1970, a three-judge federal court in *Kirstein v. The Rector and Visitors of the University of Virginia*[7] held that the exclusion of women from the University of Virginia at Charlottesville violated their constitutional rights under the equal protection clause of the Fourteenth Amendment, but dismissed as "moot" an action to desegregate all male and female public institutions of higher learning in Virginia. The Department of Justice in 1969 acquiesced in two court-approved plans which sought to achieve desegregation of the races by segregation of the sexes in public schools, and this technique is beginning to be discussed more widely in the South.

Occasionally by statute but more frequently by custom, women are excluded from eating places, taverns, clubs, and bars traditionally used by males for social and business or professional purposes. In these instances women are denied freedom of action and opportunities to participate with their male colleagues in matters of mutual business or professional interest. More important, perhaps, is that as in cases of racial discrimination, women are humiliated and made to feel inferior when they are denied service in places of public accommodation, however thinly disguised as "clubs" these may be. Similarly, single women are often denied rental of apartments by landlords applying a double standard vaguely related to morals.

It is generally known that women face formidable barriers to advancement in politics, government, industry, business, and the academic and other male-dominated professions. During the decade 1959–1969 women lost ground in elective positions. A study of women in public service released by the Republican National Committee in November 1969 showed that representation of women in the national Congress dropped from 17 to 11, in state elective posts from 41 to 30, and in state legislatures from 347 to 305. The Women's Bureau of the Department of Labor estimated that in 1959, 18,000 women held elective county posts. The Republican National Committee found by actual count only 3,862 women holding these positions in 1969.

Women in the professions in the United States compare unfavorably with their counterparts in other countries. In 1964, only 8 percent of the scientists, 6 percent of the physicians, 3 percent of the lawyers, and 1 percent of the engineers in the United States were women. In Denmark, 50 percent of all lawyers are women; in the Soviet Union, 36 percent; in Germany, 33 percent; in France, 14 percent; and in Sweden, 6.1 percent. Women represent 32 percent of the pharmacists in the Soviet Union. They constitute 85 percent of the dentists in Finland and 24.4 percent of the dentists in Sweden.

American women have also lost ground in the academic professions. In 1940, 28 percent of college faculty members were women. By 1960 the percentage had dropped to 22 percent. Although women constitute two-fifths of the faculties of teacher's colleges, they represent only one-tenth of the faculties of prestigious private universities. Dr. Alice Rossi of Goucher College has reported a study of 188 graduate departments of sociology across the country during the school year 1968–1969 which showed that while 30 percent of all doctoral candidates and 37 percent of all master's candidates were women, only 14 percent of full-time assistant professors, 9 percent of full-time associate professors, 4 percent of full-time full professors, and 1 percent of department chairmen were women. Dr. Rossi made it clear that sex and not marital responsibility makes the greatest difference to career advancement. She included data from a study by L. R. Harmon which covered men and women holding Ph.D.'s in the social sciences who have spent twenty years in academe.[8] Harmon showed that while 90 percent of the men had reached full professorships, only 53 percent of the single women and 41 percent of the married women had achieved this rank. Other data reveal that 88 percent of women college teachers earn less than $10,000 a year as compared with 55 percent of the male professors earning a similar salary.

Women have begun to challenge the discriminatory practices of institutions of higher education. On February 6, 1970, the Women's Equity Action League (WEAL) filed a formal complaint with the Secretary of Labor requesting that the Office of Federal Contract Compliance institute an immediate compliance review for all universities and colleges receiving federal contracts. The complaint, filed under the provisions of Executive Order 11246 as amended by Executive Order No. 11375, which forbids sex discrimination by government contractors, charged that universities and colleges discriminate by using quotas for women in admission to graduate and undergraduate programs, in scholarship and financial assistance, in the hiring of women for their faculties, in paying women faculty members less than their male counterparts, and by promoting women far more slowly than men. By October 1970, WEAL had filed similar complaints against more than 200 colleges and universities.

Despite the all too evident facts of sex discrimination and the almost universal concern for individual human rights since World War II, sex discrimination in the United States has not received the serious attention given to other areas of injustice and remains relatively immune from general public condemnation. The moral issue is blunted all too often by resort to ridicule or by emphasis upon sex differences as justification for unequal treatment. It was not too long ago, of course, that racial differences were cited to justify racial discrimination.

It is not generally perceived that race bias and sex bias produce similar results in their victims: frustration of emotional growth, a negative self-concept, apathy, pervasive hostility, and social waste. Alienation of the sexes growing out of resentment against discriminatory treatment, while less visible than violent racial tensions, may be just as corrosive of healthy human relationships, particularly in view of the intimacy between the sexes and their obvious interdependence. The high rate of divorce and broken homes and the more extreme manifestations of the new feminism tend to support this view. Furthermore, since discrimination against women affects more than half the population, cutting across all stratifications of race or economic and social class, there is a growing view that such massive domestic problems as poverty and racism cannot be resolved unless and until sex-based discrimination is eliminated.

II

In the job market especially, women are victims of the relentless operation of stereotypes based upon sex and contradictions in American values. During the 1960's employment discrimination became a major issue for resurgent militant feminism which recognizes the relationship between economic dependency and inferior status. Unlike those subtle manifestations of sexism which are difficult to combat, discrimination in employment can be measured—in losses in family income, in poverty and unemployment, and in the under-utilization of individual talents.

The initiation of a national legislative policy of equal employment opportunity in the 1960's has created a climate of opinion and a forum in which women can expose and challenge long-standing grievances against economic exploitation. Since the firm establishment of an enforceable right not to be discriminated against in employment will help to weaken barriers against women in other areas and will act as powerful leverage in their thrust toward full legal and social emancipation, the remainder of this discussion will focus upon some of the significant developments in this field.

All available data indicate that women work for the same reason as men—economic necessity—and are a permanent and growing sector of the labor force.[9] Yet the female wage earner is still looked upon primarily as a woman, wife, and mother and only secondarily as a wage-earner. This attitude persists even though women were the responsible heads of 5,273,000 or 11 percent of all families in the United States in 1968, and in 22 percent of all husband-wife families the wife's earnings contributed two-fifths or more of the total annual family income.

On the one hand, we lay great stress upon the need for productive capacity and upon the right of the individual to develop in accordance with potential, and billions of dollars are spent encouraging youth to further their education. On the other hand, these heavy investments in human potential are partially canceled out by employment barriers which discourage women from the full use of their abilities. Many young women do not go on to graduate study because they cannot hope for placement commensurate with their training. With few exceptions, business and industry generally will not consider women with graduate degrees for employment.

American society is also child-centered and cherishes the ideal of motherhood. It values the woman for her capacity to produce children but denies her the right to ensure that her children will be properly fed, clothed, housed, and educated. As a wage-earner, she is made to realize that the esteem she has been accorded relates largely to her biological function. Job discrimination which blocks her development not only diminishes her feeling of self-worth as a person; it also deprives her children proportionately even though she may be the chief breadwinner of her family.

The same stereotyped thinking also works against the single woman who, in many instances, may be professionally trained through graduate school and who may be responsible not only for her own support but also for elderly dependents. One result of these contradictions is that while there is a severe labor shortage at middle management and professional levels, in 1965 more than 20 percent of all employed women with four years of college training were working in nonprofessional positions and 7 percent of women with five or more years of college were working in similar unskilled and semiskilled jobs.

Dramatic breakthroughs of a few women in fields formerly closed to them may obscure the fact that, as a group, their gains are illusory.[10] The income gap between male and female workers has widened to the same degree and over the same period as the income gap between white and black workers. In 1955, the median annual earnings of female workers who were employed full time the year round were 64 percent of those of full-time male workers. By 1966 their median income was only 58 percent of that of their male counterparts.

A study of the employment of women in the federal government issued by the United States Civil Service Commission showed that on October 31, 1968, women constituted 34 percent of the full-time white-collar workers in federal employment but were concentrated in the lower-paying jobs. They represented 67 percent or more of the white-collar employees in each of the four lowest grades, but 2.7 percent or less in each of the top four grades. The same situation prevails in private industry. The Equal Employment Opportunity Commission's first nation-wide survey of employment patterns in American industry, based upon official reports for 1966, revealed that sex discrimination continues to prevent women from reaching jobs at managerial and professional levels. EEO-1 data indicated that women account for more than two-fifths of all white-collar jobs, but hold only one of ten managerial positions and one of seven professional jobs. Conversely, they fill nearly 45 percent of the lower-paying service jobs. Other studies show that a woman high school graduate earns less than a male worker who has not completed eight years of education. In 1968, less than 2 percent of all women workers earned over $10,000. The unemployment rate for women was 4.8 percent, compared with 2.9 percent for men. Among families headed by women, poverty was three and a half times as frequent as among husband-wife families.

Negro women are frequently victimized by both race and sex discrimination. Their situation is aggravated by the fact that a higher proportion of black women work than their white counterparts, their contribution to family income is proportionately greater, their families are larger, their median earnings are less, and they are more vulnerable to unemployment and poverty than white women. Studies made in 1967 showed that women were the responsible heads of 27 percent of all Negro families in the central cities and that in about half of these families headed by women, the annual income was below the poverty level. The Negro woman's plight makes it clear that unless employment policies directed against discrimination include both race and sex, a significant segment of the black community will be exposed to the constant threat of poverty.

Prior to the 1960's public action against discriminatory employment practices was limited to traditional bases such as race, color, religion, or national origin. Except for minimum wage legislation and equal pay laws in some states, the general issue of sex discrimination in employment was ignored. During the past decade, however, significant steps have been taken to remedy this neglect. On the whole, progress at the state level has been spotty and has lagged behind measures prohibiting other types of bias. For example, at least 28 jurisdictions had legislated against age discrimination in employment by the end of mid-1970, but only 25 of the 40 jurisdictions with fair employment practices acts to which the Equal Employment Opportunity Commission defers cases had extended full coverage to sex-based discrimination.

The most extensive state activity has been the adoption of equal pay laws. Forty jurisdictions now prohibit discrimination between males and females in the rate of compensation for equal work. A few jurisdictions without equal pay laws deal with the subject in their fair employment practices legislation. The typical equal pay law is administered by the state's labor officer or agency and provides a complaint procedure and for recovery of unpaid wages in a civil suit. A few of these laws provide only criminal penalties for violation—a notoriously ineffective enforcement tool.

During the Kennedy and Johnson administrations the federal government assumed leadership for developing a comprehensive national policy to ensure wider employment opportunities for women. A factor which gave impetus to this development was the creation in 1961 of the President's Commission on the Status of Women, headed by the late Mrs. Eleanor Roosevelt. Following the Commission's report and recommendations submitted in October 1963 and supplemented by the reports of its various advisory committees,[11] President Kennedy established by executive order the Interdepartmental Committee and Citizens' Advisory Council on the Status of Women as continuing bodies to facilitate the implementation of the Commission's recommendations. Similar commissions were set up in all of the states.

The United States Civil Service Commission at President Kennedy's direction prescribed a policy of nondiscrimination in federal employment in 1963. The Fair Labor Standards Act was amended by the Equal Pay Act of 1963. Title VII of the Civil Rights Act of 1964 was amended during the House debate to include sex as a prohibited ground of discrimination in employment. In October 1967 President Johnson, prodded by the National Organization for Women (NOW) and other women's groups, added "sex" to the federal government's formal nondiscrimination policy in federal employment, employment by federal contractors and subcontractors, and employment under federally assisted construction contracts. President Nixon extended this policy in 1969 to military establishments and civil service positions within the government of the District of Columbia and the legislative and judicial branches of the national government.[12] Compliance reviews and affirmative-action procedures now include sex in the implementation of governmental policy.

In addition to specific policies against discrimination because of sex, women (as well as men) may invoke several federal statutes in seeking broader employment opportunities. The Age Discrimination in Employment Act of 1967, administered by the Department of Labor, prohibits discrimination in the hiring, discharge, terms, and conditions of employment of any individual 40 years of age but under 65. It is enforceable under provisions of the Fair Labor Standards Act, and aggrieved individuals may institute civil suits under appropriate procedures. The value of this law to women workers becomes evident when it is recalled that in March 1968, the median age of all women in the labor force was 40 and that nearly three-fifths (58.9 percent) of all women workers were 35 years of age and over. It would also appear that applications of the Railway Labor Act and the National Labor Relations Act to cases of racial discrimination under Supreme Court rulings can be extended to comparable situations involving discrimination because of sex.

The Equal Pay Act of 1963 and the sex provisions of Title VII of the Civil Rights Act of 1964 are the two most important federal statutes directly affecting the rights of women since the adoption of the Nineteenth Amendment. If vigorously enforced, this legislation can effect unprecedented changes in the economic position of women. Already it has stimulated the enactment of similar laws by an increasing number of states.

As an amendment to the Fair Labor Standards Act, the Equal Pay Act prohibits all employers covered by FLSA from paying wage differentials based upon sex "for equal work on jobs the performance of which requires equal skill, effort, responsibility, and which are performed under similar working conditions." Exceptions to this prohibition are "where such payment is made pursuant to (i) a seniority system; (ii) a merit system; (iii) a system which measures earnings by quantity or quality of production; or (iv) a differential based on any other factor other than sex." An employer is also barred from reducing the wages of any employee in order to comply with the Act. Labor unions are forbidden to cause or attempt to cause an employer to discriminate against an employee in violation of the Act. Criminal penalties are provided for willful violation.

Administered by the Wage-Hour Division of the Department of Labor, the equal pay amendments authorize the Secretary of Labor to bring suits to enjoin violations and recover unpaid wages. Recovery may also be sought through employee actions. The overall effectiveness of this legislation is limited by the number of exceptions permitted and the exemptions from coverage by FLSA. Executive, administrative, or professional employees, including those employed as academic or administrative personnel or as teachers in elementary schools, are among the groups of workers excluded. Despite these limitations, the impact of the statute can be greatly increased if its provisions are applied to harmonize with the broader statutory scheme of Title VII and are interpreted to prohibit wage differentials which are the result of prior discrimination based upon sex.[13]

The sex provisions of Title VII stand as a historic milestone in the legal recognition of the rights of women, despite many efforts to devalue their importance by references to their peculiar origin and lack of legislative history.[14] Their significance can be measured by the fact that during the first four years of EEOC's administration of the statute, sex-based discrimination was involved in 27 percent of the approximately 24,000 charges assigned for investigation—more than 7,600 charges. The most severe limitation of the law is that EEOC has no enforcement power and can seek only voluntary compliance. Aggrieved persons under certain procedures may sue in the federal district courts to enforce their rights under the Act. The law also provides for the appointment of counsel, the commencement of suits without payment of fees, costs, or security, and the award of attorney's fees to the prevailing party in the discretion of the court.

Title VII prohibits sex-based discrimination by employers, labor organizations, and employment agencies except in those certain cases in which sex is a bona fide occupational qualification reasonably necessary to the operation of a particular business or enterprise. The rights protected extend to classified advertising and other methods of recruitment, hiring, discharge, compensation, terms and conditions of employment, job classification, job referral, union membership, participation in apprenticeship training, on-the-job training, and other employment practices. It should be kept in mind that while discrimination against women was the chief reason for including the sex provisions of Title VII, the Act also protects male employees in those instances in which they have suffered discriminatory treatment because of their sex. A notable example is the Commission's ruling on flight-cabin attendants in the airline cases. EEOC has issued findings of probable cause in several other situations involving charges by male employees of discrimination.[15]

The Equal Employment Opportunity Commission has moved gradually toward a liberal interpretation of the sex provisions of

Title VII, and while its views are not binding on the courts, which ultimately will determine the scope and effect of the statute, some of the lower federal courts have adopted EEOC's position. As of April 1970, the Supreme Court had not considered the merits of any case involving issues of sex-based discrimination under Title VII but had consented to review a decision involving discrimination against a mother of preschool-age children.

A sampling of Commission rulings will illustrate the variety of situations which raise issues of sex bias. EEOC has ruled that it is an unlawful employment practice for an employer to maintain separate job classifications, lines of progression, seniority lists, or wage rates based on sex. An employer may categorize jobs as heavy, medium, or light so long as all three categories are open to both male and female employees. Employer-imposed restrictions upon the job opportunities of married women or women with small children are unlawful. Nor may an employer bar the employment of women because of marriage or having reached a specified age when similar restrictions are not applied to male workers. Thus, airline companies which terminate the employment of stewardesses upon marriage or upon reaching the age of 32 or 33 have been held to violate Title VII.

The Commission has held that a difference in compulsory or voluntary retirement age based on sex is unlawful, but interprets this rule so as to permit a gradual adjustment of existing plans for earlier optional retirement for women. It has stated that, as a general rule, pregnant employees are entitled to maternity leave with the right to reinstatement in the same or a similar job and pay and with no loss of employment benefits. It has also declared that, generally, an employer may not discriminate between males and females in medical, hospital, life, and accident insurance coverage.[16]

Litigation in the federal courts to date has centered upon controversies arising out of the application of Title VII to the rights of working mothers with small children, the bona fide occupational qualification (BFOQ) exception, classified advertising, and state labor laws regulating the employment of women.

The case of *Phillips v. Martin Marietta Corporation*,[17] now pending before the Supreme Court, demonstrates the potentially adverse effect of a narrow judicial construction of Title VII upon working mothers, who constitute an important segment of the labor force. The Fifth Circuit Court of Appeals upheld a company policy against hiring women with children of preschool age as not in violation of Title VII. Announcing the "sex plus" rule, the court declared that

> [w]hen another criterion of employment is added to one of the classi-fications listed in the Act, there is no longer apparent discrimina-tion based solely on . . . sex. . . . The discrimination was based on a two-pronged qualification, i.e., a woman with pre-school age children. Ida Phillips was not refused employment because she was a woman or because she had pre-school age children. It was the coalescence of these two elements that denied her the position she desired.

Chief Judge Brown, in an opinion joined by two other judges, dissented from a decision denying a rehearing of the *Phillips* case before the full court.[18] Noting that in March 1967 there were 10.6 million working mothers in the labor force with children under 18 years of age and that of the total number of working mothers 4.1 million (38.9 percent) had children under 6 years of age and 2.1 million (20.7 percent) had children under 3, he de-clared that mothers, working mothers, and mothers of preschool-age children were the specific object of governmental solicitude, and that it was incongruous to suppose that Congress had intended to legislate sex equality "by a statutory structure enabling the em-ployer to deny employment to those who need it most through the simple expedient of adding to sex a non-statutory factor." More-over, he pointed out, the rule was in conflict with the policy of the administration to encourage unemployed women on public assist-ance who have children to enter the labor market by providing for the establishment of child-care centers to enable them to accept offers of employment. "If 'sex plus' stands," he declared, "the Act is dead." The Supreme Court has granted certiorari and will review the decision.

A second area of controversy is the BFOQ exception.[19] EEOC has declared that this exception must be narrowly construed and that the principle of nondiscrimination requires that individuals be considered on the basis of individual capacities and not on the basis of characteristics attributed to a group. Thus, while EEOC will consider sex as a BFOQ in such obvious situations as a female saleswoman or model for women's clothing, a woman attendant for a female restroom, an actor or actress, or in the entertainment field where sex appeal is a factor, the Commission maintains that there are few jobs which cannot be performed by both sexes.

The Commission will not accept the BFOQ defense where an

employment policy is based upon stereotyped assumptions about women in general, such as the comparative turnover rates or absenteeism of women employees, male aggressiveness in salesmanship, and female digital dexterity, or upon preferences of employers, co-workers, clients, or customers. Nor may an employer use BFOQ as a defense for refusal to hire qualified women because the job involves heavy-weight lifting, travel or work with men, work late at night, or work in isolated job locations. In specific instances, EEOC has rejected the BFOQ defense to an employer's refusal to employ a female as a lifeguard, a purser on a passenger ship, a courier guard on a security truck, or a pilot on a commercial airline solely because of sex. It has also ruled that sex is not a BFOQ for the position of flight-cabin attendant on airlines, and that the duties of such an attendant—whether a purser, hostess, steward, or stewardess—can be performed satisfactorily by both sexes.

Several federal courts have adopted the Commission's approach. For example, in *Weeks v. Southern Bell Telephone & Telegraph Co.*,[20] the Fifth Circuit Court of Appeals rejected an employer's defense that its refusal to assign a woman employee to a job as switchman was based on the requirements of the job to lift in excess of 30 pounds and perform other strenuous activity, and that the job also involved emergency calls at all hours of the night and working alone during late night hours. The court held that, in order to rely upon the BFOQ exception to Title VII, the employer has the burden of proving that all or substantially all women would be unable to perform safely and efficiently the duties of the job involved. It declared that Title VII rejects paternalism which denies a woman the power to decide whether or not to take on unromantic tasks. Said the court:

> Men have always had the right to determine whether the incremental increase in remuneration for strenuous, dangerous, obnoxious, boring or unromantic tasks is worth the candle. The promise of Title VII is that women are now to be on an equal footing. We cannot conclude that by including the bona fide occupational qualification exception Congress intended to renege on that promise.

The issue of advertising in sex-segregated "Help Wanted" newspaper columns is also being tested through court action. Title VII makes it unlawful to advertise employment opportunities indicating a preference, limitation, specification, or discrimination based on sex except in instances where sex is a BFOQ for the advertised employment. The prohibition applies to employers, labor unions, and employment agencies but not to newspapers acting as publishers. On August 1968, EEOC issued a guideline ruling that the placement of ads in columns classified by publishers on the basis of sex, such as columns headed "Male" and "Female," would be considered an expression of the prohibited conduct. Subsequent to the EEOC ruling, a similar policy was adopted by New York City, and all major newspapers in that city discontinued as of December 1, 1968, the use of sex-segregated columns unless the jobs involved a BFOQ. The EEOC ruling was challenged by the American Newspaper Publishers Association and the Washington *Evening Star* in a suit to enjoin issuance of the guideline. Although a preliminary injunction was denied and the guideline became effective on January 24, 1969, trial of the issue was still pending in early 1970 and there has been no judicial determination of the application of Title VII to sex-segregated "Help Wanted" columns.[21]

The most controversial issue arising out of the administration of the sex provisions of Title VII is the impact of the federal statute on the state "protective" labor laws applicable to women only.[22] The enactment of Title VII has brought to a head the controversy over the validity of these laws, which has grown in intensity as women have entered the labor force in large numbers and sought to climb the economic ladder. Two issues are involved: (1) the conflict between the broad purpose of the federal statute to promote equal employment opportunities without regard to sex and those state laws and regulations the effect of which is to restrict employment opportunities for women; and (2) whether restrictive laws applicable to all women as a class violate equal protection rights guaranteed by the Fourteenth Amendment to the Constitution.

State regulations which apply to women workers fall roughly into two categories: (1) laws which confer benefits upon women, such as minimum wages, premium pay for overtime, rest periods, and physical facilities; and (2) laws and regulations which prohibit the employment of women in certain occupations or under certain conditions (such as, bartending or mining), or which restrict their employment with respect to hours, lifting of weights, or night work. The first category of laws presents little difficulty, for an employer can comply with both the state and federal statutes by extending benefits conferred upon female workers to male employees. EEOC has ruled in accordance with this principle.

Laws and regulations in the second category present more complex issues. Eleven jurisdictions prescribe the maximum weight which women employees may lift or carry. These limitations vary from 15 to 50 pounds. Eighteen states and Puerto Rico prohibit or regulate night work for adult women in certain industries or occupations. Twenty-six states prohibit the employment of women in certain specified occupations or under certain working conditions considered hazardous to health or safety. Thirty-eight states and the District of Columbia regulate the number of hours daily and weekly that women may work in one or more industries. In 3 of the 38 states, both men and women in some industries are covered by hours laws; in the others, only women.

The controversy arises between those who support the continuation of these laws as necessary to protect a large number of women in unorganized and low-paying jobs who have no other shield against exploitation, and women workers who assert that these laws are used to perpetuate economic discrimination based on sex. The real issue is not the social value of enlightened labor standards for health and safety but the evil effects of standards applied to one sex only. By restricting all women as a class irrespective of their varying capacities and economic interests, male workers are given a preferred position in industry. After wrestling with this issue for several years, on August 19, 1969, EEOC issued a guideline which declared unequivocally that the state laws and regulations which prohibit or limit the employment of women, "although originally promulgated for the purpose of protecting females have ceased to be relevant to our technology or the expanding role of female workers in our economy. The Commission has found that such laws and regulations do not take into account the capacities, preferences, and abilities of individual females and tend to discriminate rather than protect. Accordingly, the Commission has concluded that such laws and regulations conflict with Title VII of the Civil Rights Act of 1964 and will not be considered as a defense to an otherwise unlawful employment practice or as a basis for the application of the bona fide occupational qualification."

While judicial pronouncements on this issue are still too few to indicate a decisive trend, scattered decisions support the Commission's view and several courts have expressed doubts about the continuing validity of the state labor laws. Federal district courts in California, Oregon, and Illinois have held that state hours laws which limit the number of hours women may work (and weight-lifting limitations where the issue was raised) violate Title VII and are superseded by the federal statute by virtue of the supremacy clause in the Constitution. A similar result was reached with respect to a Chicago ordinance which prohibited the employment of women as barmaids.[23] The Wyoming Supreme Court held in 1968 that the state law forbidding employment of women as bartenders in that state was repealed by implication in the subsequently enacted state Fair Employment Practices Act.[24]

Several states have moved to modify their policies in accordance with the EEOC ruling. The Attorneys General of Michigan, Oklahoma, Pennsylvania, South Dakota, and Massachusetts have issued opinions in 1969 finding that their state protective statutes are void to the extent that they are in conflict with Title VII or, as in the case of Pennsylvania, with the state fair employment practices law, which is in harmony with the federal statute. The Attorney General of North Dakota has declared that prosecution under that state's law regulating the hours of working women may now be precluded by Title VII. The Ohio Industrial Relations Director announced on September 4, 1969, that his office would suspend prosecutions for violation of Ohio's protective labor statutes until the state legislature conformed these laws with Title VII and the EEOC Guideline on Sex Discrimination. Several states have either repealed or modified their hours legislation applicable to women workers.

Although in some actions women plaintiffs under Title VII have attempted to raise the broader constitutional issue of the conflict between state protective legislation and the equal protection clause of the Fourteenth Amendment, the lower courts, feeling bound by the *Muller* decision, have avoided ruling on this question. If the Supreme Court should hold that Title VII supersedes conflicting state statutes, this would have the practical effect of overruling *Muller* by implication.

III

The foregoing developments constitute the beginnings of a broad attack against sex discrimination, but much remains to be done if the promise of the 1960's is to be fulfilled. Basic to any meaningful change in the position of women in the United States is the awakening of public consciousness to the realization that discrimination because of sex is as morally indefensible and harmful to the nation as racial discrimination and should be similarly outlawed. Remaining legal inequities based upon sex must be vigorously challenged, and existing remedies against sex bias must be seized upon and fully utilized.

The right of women to nondiscrimination should be expressed in all federal, state, and local policies directed against discrimination generally. Several riders to the Omnibus Postsecondary Education Bill (H.R. 16098) now pending in Congress and introduced by Congresswoman Edith Green illustrate this principle. The riders would amend the Civil Rights Act of 1964 to add a sex provision to Title VI which prohibits discrimination in federally assisted programs; remove the exemption of educational institutions from Title VII; amend the Fair Labor Standards Act to remove from the equal pay provisions the present exclusion of executive, administrative, or professional employees, including those employed as academic administrative personnel or teachers in elementary and secondary schools; and amend the 1957 Civil Rights Act to add "sex" to the jurisdiction of the United States Commission on Civil Rights. The extensive hearings held on Section 805 of HR 16098 during the summer of 1970 revealed hard data showing massive discrimination against women in many areas.

In addition to these proposals, the 1964 Civil Rights Act should be further amended to include sex provisions in Title II, covering places of public accommodation, and in Title IV, dealing with desegregation of public schools. Proposed amendments to Title VII to give EEOC adequate enforcement powers are of special interest to women, since in the absence of coverage by state fair employment practices laws women must look largely to the federal statute to enforce their right to equal employment opportunity.

All state civil rights laws relating to housing, education, and fair employment practices should include sex provisions. Sex discrimination in employment by state, county, or municipal governments should be specifically outlawed. Similar prohibitions should apply to educational institutions as to both admissions and employment practices. State jury laws should be revised to apply equally to men and women and should include exemptions or excuses from jury service based upon objective standards and available to both sexes. Similarly, all state protective laws regulating the employment of women should be re-examined with a view toward redrafting these statutes so as to preserve social gains and extend labor standards for health and safety to all workers. Civil rights and civil liberties groups can perform a useful public service in this field by preparing a model state labor standards bill to be introduced in the various state legislatures.

A national system of day-care centers to assist working mothers and working fathers in maintaining stable employment is of vital importance to the advancement of women in job training and career opportunities. Current surveys conducted by federal agencies of child-care arrangements of working mothers show that of the 12.3 million children under 14 included in the survey, only 2 percent were in group care, such as day-care centers, nursery schools, and after-school centers. Federal-state programs to facilitate the development of day-care services need to be implemented and expanded. Overtime work should be made voluntary for all workers, male and female, so that working parents have a choice in determining how best to fulfill their family obligations. National and state legislation should be enacted to promote the extension of social insurance to include cash maternity benefits as a protection against loss of earnings because of disability before and after childbirth. Income tax provisions should be revised to raise the limit on income under which deductions for child-care services are allowed. The Fair Labor Standards Act should be extended to cover workers in domestic service and agricultural employees.

Overarching all legislative proposals to remove sex-based inequities, however, is the intensely controversial issue of a constitutional guarantee of equality of the sexes. First proposed in 1923, the Equal Rights Amendment resurfaced in 1970 as the foremost political demand of the women's rights/liberation movement. The House of Representatives on August 10, 1970, by a vote of 352 to 15, adopted H.J. Resolution 264, which provides:

> Equality of rights under the law shall not be denied or abridged by the United States or by any State on account of sex. Congress and the several States shall have power, within their respective jurisdictions, to enforce this article by appropriate legislation.

Extensive Senate hearings on the companion text (S.J. Resolution 61) were held in May and September 1970.

Professor Thomas I. Emerson of Yale Law School outlined the conceptual framework of equal rights as a constitutional theory before the Senate Judiciary Committee. He declared:

> The basic premise of the Equal Rights Amendment is that sex should not be a factor in determining the legal rights of women, or

of men. . . . Sex is an inadmissible category by which to determine
the right to a minimum wage, the custody of children, the obligation to refrain from taking the life of another, and so on. . . . The
fundamental legal principle underlying the Equal Rights Amendment, then, is that the law must deal with the individual attributes
of a particular person, not with a vast overclassification based upon
the irrelevant factor of sex.[25]

According to Professor Emerson, this basic principle would not
apply to the one type of situation (which rarely occurs) in which
the law may focus upon a characteristic unique to one sex, such as
the payment of medical costs of childbearing, which applies only
to women, or a law relating to sperm banks, applicable only to
men. "Such legislation cannot be said to deny equal rights to the
other sex. There is no basis here for seeking or achieving equality."
In sum, says Professor Emerson, "unless the difference is one that
is characteristic of *all* women and *no* men, or *all* men and *no* women,
it is not the sex factor but the individual factor which should be
determinative."

Advocates of the amendment point out that the doctrine which
permits "reasonable" classifications under the Fourteenth Amendment, particularly as applied to sex, has made the constitutional
status of women ambiguous and has permitted discriminatory distinctions in the law. They assert that women want equal rights and
responsibilities with men as full citizens and do not want special
privileges and restrictions under the law. On the other hand, opponents attack the Amendment on traditional grounds: that it would
endanger protective laws for women; that it would subject women
to compulsory military service; and that it would create legal
chaos. This last objection, significantly, is identical to the argument
advanced against the adoption of the Woman's Suffrage Amendment more than fifty years ago.

Underlying the constitutional arguments is the less articulated
but omnipresent issue of political power. Militant feminists have
rallied behind the Equal Rights Amendment in a symbolic effort
to challenge male dominance of societal structures. That their bid
to share power in accordance with their numbers in the population
has been something less than successful was dramatized by the fate
of the Equal Rights Amendment in the Senate. Although it was
sponsored by 82 senators at the beginning of the 91st Congress, on
October 13, 1970, the Senate adopted two additions designed to
kill the House-passed Amendment. The Ervin amendment would

exempt women from military service on grounds of sex, thus negating the principle of equality. The Baker amendment would add the controversial issue of separation of church and state by permitting "nonpartisan prayers" in public schools, thus overturning the Supreme Court ruling that such prayers in public schools are unconstitutional.

Senator Birch Bayh, in an effort at compromise, brought forth a substitute proposal on October 14, 1970, which appears to be of dubious value. It reads:

> Neither the United States nor any State shall, on account of sex, deny to any person within its jurisdiction the equal protection of the laws.

On its face the language of the proposal, borrowed intact from the Fourteenth Amendment, appears unobjectionable. Advocates of the Equal Rights Amendment, however, justifiably point out that the language is deceptive and that the substitute proposal is wholly unacceptable on both constitutional grounds and policy considerations. They assert that the concept of equal rights is unequivocal and differs from the concept of equal protection as applied to women, a concession which Senator Bayh admits in "recognizing the need for a flexible standard in cases where differential treatment under the law may be justified." It hardly seems worth the effort involved to add to the Constitution an amendment which merely inherits the judicial history of the Fourteenth Amendment as applied to sex and which the Equal Rights Amendment was designed to overcome. Moreover, the substitute proposal might have the effect of freezing into the Constitution legal distinctions based upon the irrelevant factor of sex.

It is now abundantly clear, as the struggle for equal rights for women moves toward 1971, that the achievement of this goal rests ultimately upon the organized power of feminists and their male allies to make this goal one of the nation's priorities and to effect those fundamental political changes necessary to its realization.

NOTES

1. *See generally* on sex discrimination, L. Kanowitz, *Women and the Law: The Unfinished Revolution* (1969); Murphy & Ross, "Keeping Woman in Her Place: The Legal Basis for Sex Discrimination," in *With Justice for Some*

(1970); Siedenberg, "The Submissive Majority: Modern Trends in the Law Concerning Women's Rights," 55 *Cornell Law Review* 262 (1970).

2. 251 F. Supp. 401 (M.D. Ala. 1966).

3. Hoyt v. Florida, 368 U.S. 57 (1961).

4. *See, e.g.,* Commonwealth v. Daniels, 430 Pa. 642, 243 A.2d 400 (1968); United States *ex rel.* Robinson v. York, 281 F. Supp. 8 (D. Conn. 1968).

5. 208 U.S. 412, 422, 423 (1908).

6. 198 U.S. 45 (1905).

7. Civil No. 220–69–R (E.D. Va., Feb. 6, 1970).

8. See E. Lewis, *Developing Women's Potential* (1968); Rossi, "Status of Women in Graduate Departments of Sociology, 1968–1969," *American Sociologist,* Feb. 1970, at 1–12.

9. Publications of the Department of Labor's Women's Bureau, particularly the *1969 Handbook on Women Workers,* provide useful statistical information.

10. *See* C. Bird, *Born Female* (1968), ch. 5, "The Loophole Women."

11. The Commission report and summaries of the Committee reports have been published as M. Mead & F. Kaplan, *American Women* (1965), and are also available in full from the United States Government Printing Office.

12. Exec. Orders Nos. 11246, 11375, 11478.

13. *See, e.g.,* Schultz v. Victoria National Bank, — F.2d — (5th Cir. 1969).

14. *See generally* on the 1964 Act, Murray & Eastwood, "Jane Crow & The Law: Sex Discrimination and Title VII," 34 *George Washington Law Review* 232 (1965); Note, "Classifications on The Basis of Sex and The 1964 Civil Rights Act," 50 *Iowa Law Review* 778 (1965); Note, "Sex Discrimination in Employment under Title VII of The Civil Rights Act of 1964," 21 *Vanderbilt Law Review* 484 (1967); Miller, "Sex Discrimination and Title VII of the Civil Rights Act of 1964," 51 *Minnesota Law Review* 877 (1967).

15. *But see* Diaz v. Pan American World Airways, Inc., 62 Lab. Cas. ¶9434 (S.D. Fla. 1970).

16. See Pressman, "Sex Discrimination and Fringe Benefits Under Title VII of the Civil Rights Act of 1964," CCH Employment Practices Guide, New Developments §8004 (1969), for a discussion of the problems in this area.

17. 411 F.2d 1, 3–4 (5th Cir. 1969), *cert. granted,* 397 U.S. 960 (1970).

18. 416 F.2d 1257 (5th Cir. 1969).

19. Comment, "A Women's Place: Diminishing Justification for Sex Discrimination in Employment," 42 *Southern California Law Review* 183 (1969).

20. 408 F.2d 228, 236 (5th Cir. 1969); *see also* Cheatwood v. South Central Bell Tel. & Tel. Co., 303 F. Supp. 754 (M.D. Ala. 1969); Bowe v. Colgate-Palmolive Co., 416 F.2d 711 (7th Cir. 1969).

21. One federal district court has rejected the argument that newspapers are subject to the prohibition against discriminatory advertising when they publish sex-segregated help-wanted columns because they are acting as "employment agencies" for prospective employers and employees. See Brush v. San Francisco Newspaper Printing Co., 63 Lab. Cas. ¶9470 (N.D. Cal. 1970).

22. United States Department of Labor, Women's Bureau, *Summary of State Labor Laws for Women* (1969); Oldham, "Sex Discrimination and State Labor Laws," 44 *Denver Law Journal* 344 (1967); Ross, "Sex Discrimination and 'Protective' Labor Legislation," Hearings on the Equal Rights Amendment (S.J. Res. 61) before the Subcomm. on Constitutional Amendments of the Senate Comm. on the Judiciary, 91st Cong. 2d Sess., May 5, 6, and 7, 1970, at 392.

23. Rosenfeld v. Southern Pacific Co., 293 F. Supp. 1219 (C.D. Cal. 1968); Richards v. Griffith Rubber Mills, 300 F. Supp. 338 (D. Ore. 1969); Caterpillar Tractor Co. v. Grabiec and Illinois Bell Telephone Co. v. Grabiec, 63 Lab. Cas.

¶9522 (S.D. Ill. 1970); *But see* Mengelkock v. Industrial Welfare Commission, 284 F. Supp. 950 (C.D. Cal.), *vacated,* 393 U.S. 83 (1968); Krauss v. Sacramento Inn, 63 Lab. Cas. ¶9468 E.D. Cal. 1970).

24. Longacre v. State, 448 P.2d 832 (Wyo. 1968); see also Mating Game, Inc. v. California, No. C954160 (Super. Ct. Los Angeles County 1969).

25. 116 Cong. Rec. S 17646 (daily ed. Oct. 9, 1970). See also the testimony before the Senate Judiciary Committee in favor of the Amendment by Professor Norman Dorsen (*id.* S 17648), Professor Leo Kanowitz (*id.* S 17642), and Mrs. Marguerite Rawalt, and the testimony against the Amendment by Professors Paul A. Freund and Philip B. Kurland.

THE RIGHTS OF
TEACHERS
AND PROFESSORS

WILLIAM W. VAN ALSTYNE

IN 1926, A YOUNG TENNESSEE SCHOOLTEACHER, John Thomas Scopes, was convicted and fined $100 for having violated a criminal statute in that "he did teach in the public schools . . . a certain theory that denied the story of the divine creation of man, as taught in the Bible, and did teach instead thereof that man had descended from a lower order of animals." On appeal to the state supreme court, counsel for Scopes (including Clarence Darrow and Arthur Garfield Hays) contended that the statute offended the religious establishment clause of the state constitution, and that it violated the Fourteenth Amendment to the federal Constitution in that it abridged the civil liberty of John Scopes to teach the subject of biology freely, according to his own best professional understanding. The Tennessee Supreme Court flatly rejected both arguments. It observed that Scopes was a *public* schoolteacher, that the law did not affect his teaching or his freedom of speech as a private citizen, and that it had no application to private schools and to private teachers, who were wholly at liberty to utilize their property, their professional skills, and their freedom of contract to provide for whatever latitude of teaching freedom seemed to them most agreeable. Conceding that the state was constitutionally restricted from unlimited control over such *private*

William W. Van Alstyne is Professor of Law at Duke Law School, former General Counsel to the American Association of University Professors, and current chairman of its standing committee on academic freedom and tenure. He has written many articles on academic freedom and other aspects of constitutional law.

arrangements (the United States Supreme Court had recently held as much in invalidating state laws forbidding the teaching of German in any school to children below the eighth grade and forbidding parents to enroll their children in parochial schools[1]), the Tennessee court held that the Fourteenth Amendment had no application whatever to the state's relations with its own employees.[2]

Had the Tennessee court noticed a paragraph in an opinion of the Supreme Court of the United States issued only six months earlier, however, it might not have treated Scopes's claim quite so lightly. The problem before the Supreme Court, although wholly different in its facts—it concerned the regulation of trucks on public highways—raised a constitutional issue very similar to the issue in the Scopes case. In the trucking case, the Supreme Court assumed that no one had a constitutional right to force a state to construct public roads, and also that the plaintiff trucking company would have had no recourse had it been unable to haul goods at all for lack of such roads. The Court then considered whether this fact implied that the state could attach any conditions it wished to the use of its roads—on the claim that whatever use it permitted would be a mere "privilege" that it was entirely free to withhold. The Court concluded that the proprietary position of the state did not immunize it from the Fourteenth Amendment:

> If the state may compel the surrender of one constitutional right as a condition of its favor, it may, in like manner, compel a surrender of all. It is inconceivable that guaranties embedded in the Constitution of the United States may thus be manipulated out of existence.[3]

In 1968, forty-one years after the celebrated "monkey trial," and after a long series of cases applying this doctrine of unconstitutional conditions, the Supreme Court had occasion to correct the Tennessee court which had abandoned the rights of teachers under the Constitution in 1927. Reviewing a nearly identical Arkansas statute forbidding the teaching of a theory that mankind ascended or descended from a lower order of animals and forbidding the use of any textbook teaching such a theory in the public schools, the Court concluded that the statute was unconstitutional in that it concerned an establishment of religion foreclosed to the state by the due process clause of the Fourteenth Amendment.[4]

In essence, the Constitution had assimilated the simple truth of Alexander Hamilton's observation, "A power over a man's subsistence amounts to a power over his will."[5] That sort of power must yield to the Bill of Rights. As a consequence, teachers and professors are not bereft of constitutional protection against governmental threats of dismissal on grounds otherwise violative of their substantive constitutional rights. Rather:

> To state that a person does not have a constitutional right to government employment is only to say that he must comply with *reasonable,* lawful, *and nondiscriminatory* terms laid down by the proper authorities.[6]

In the particular determination of what constitutes "reasonable" conditions, moreover, the trend of the last decade has been increasingly to resolve doubtful cases in favor of the teacher because of additional considerations of public interest identified with his professional security. It is outrageous enough that political conformity not justified by compelling exigencies of the moment or by the unique nature of a particular public office should be laid upon any group of employees, private or public, by threats to their jobs, but the public consequences may be doubly unfortunate if such conditions can be imposed on teachers.[7]

SUBSTANTIVE RIGHTS

The drive of the judicial process has, as a consequence, severely cut back the use of political litmus tests for teaching eligibility and the tendency of school boards and legislatures to police the extramural political utterances and private lives of teachers through threats to their jobs. Specifically, political disclaimer oaths, bans on membership in feared or hated political organizations or unions, discharge for extramural criticism, and dismissal or revocation of teaching certificates for private behavior not specifically shown to affect the teacher's professional competency, his intramural working relationships, or his classroom integrity, gradually have been rolled back by judicial decree.[8]

Indeed, as to political matters, it can be argued that not even active and knowing membership, including some degree of personal sympathy even for illegal objectives of the group, is sufficient basis for a teacher's dismissal, short of some concrete act in furtherance of an illegal objective inconsistent with one's lawful obligations as a teacher. As for oaths, in all likelihood the state may go no further than to require that one be willing to affirm a general commitment to uphold the Constitution and faithfully perform the duties of the position one holds.[9] Moreover, while neither the First nor the Fifth Amendment entitles a teacher to withhold information when his competence or professional integrity is drawn into question by his employer on the basis of reasonably specific and creditable allegations of impropriety related to his job, information elicited under such circumstances by a public employer may not be utilized for purposes of criminal prosecution, and vague fishing expeditions on mere suspicion are not permissible.

The areas which remain most in controversy are those respecting the degree of protected extramural utterances, especially those critical of the school or university itself, and the degree of a teacher's freedom within his own classroom. A review of two recent Supreme Court decisions may indicate the dimensions of the problems.

In *Pickering v. Board of Education*,[10] the Supreme Court reversed the determination of a county board of education which concluded, after conducting a full hearing, that the newspaper publication of a local teacher's letter criticizing the way the board had handled proposals to raise new revenue for schools, and factually false in certain respects, was per se sufficiently harmful to the operation of the schools as to warrant the teacher's dismissal. The board also took the position that the teacher, by virtue of his public employment, "has a duty of loyalty to support his superiors in attaining the generally accepted goals of education and that, *if he must speak out publicly, he should do so factually and accurately, commensurate with his education and experience.*" In this respect, the board seemed to stand on high ground. Even the 1940 Statement of Principles of Academic Freedom and Tenure, promulgated by the American Association of University Professors and endorsed by more than three score national educational associations, appears to lay this degree of constraint at least upon those who teach at the college level:

> As a man of learning and an educational officer, he [the college or university teacher] should remember that the public may judge his profession and his institution by his utterances. Hence he should at *all* times be accurate, should exercise appropriate restraint, should show respect for the opinions of others, and should make every effort to indicate that he is not an institutional spokesman.[11]

Nonetheless, the Supreme Court disagreed with the board's dismissal of Martin Pickering, on constitutional grounds: in the absence of specific evidence that the operation of the schools had in fact been adversely affected as a consequence of Pickering's letter, a factually unsupported presumption of harm per se could not be used to override the teacher's First Amendment freedom of speech. As to the board's claim that the teacher owed it a duty of loyalty to avoid public disparagement of the board's judgment on the operation of the schools, the Court observed:

> [T]he question whether a school system requires additional funds is a matter of legitimate public concern on which the judgment of the school administration, including the School Board, cannot, in a society that leaves such questions to popular vote, be taken as conclusive. . . . Teachers are, as a class, the members of a community most likely to have informed and definite opinions as to how funds allotted to the operation of the schools should be spent. Accordingly, it is essential that they be able to speak out freely on such questions without fear of retaliatory dismissal.[12]

Thus, even granting that accuracy and moderation may be desirable standards for a teacher to cultivate when moved to dissent, where the issue is not so intimately associated with the teacher's customary duties that his particular statements will tend to carry some remarkable public influence, and where he does not seek to trade upon his employment relation or to represent that he speaks other than as a private citizen (Pickering signed his letter only with his name), the board may not insist upon the same exacting standards of accuracy and professionalism to which the teacher can be held within the employment relationship itself. In such circumstances, a threat to a teacher's livelihood is constitutionally incompatible with the First Amendment protection of free and unhindered debate on matters of public importance.

The *Pickering* decision marks an extremely important step in the substantive rights of teachers, even while undertaking a careful balancing and weighing of competing interests permitting other distinctions to be made as additional cases arise.[13] Even now, for instance, dicta in *Pickering* quite clearly indicate that a teacher may not publicly ventilate whatever he desires to draw to public attention, however deeply felt his need to do so, with indifference to certain enforceable constraints specifically associated with his position as employee. It may be well to note certain facts which were *not* involved in *Pickering,* to indicate the difference their presence might make in the outcome of other cases:

1. None of the information publicized in his letter drew from anything that Martin Pickering learned solely as a consequence of his employment. Had it done so, the result might have been different: the extramural release of information acquired under specific conditions of confidentiality might provide a sufficient basis for dismissal on the claim that the ability of a teacher's administrative superiors and colleagues to exhibit a degree of frankness essential to the operation of the school would be impaired if they were forced to operate under the risk that every memorandum, proposal, policy, or conversation could become a subject of instant public notice. Should it make a difference, however, if the information release pertained to a subject that was being falsely represented to the public by the school authorities, or if it involved an undisclosed policy of the school that was illegal, or even if neither of these, it was clearly a matter reasonably subject to the influence of public judgment respecting the operation of the school?

Pickering is itself so heavily qualified by the Court that no answer can confidently be forecast, nor do recent developments in companion areas of the law (for example, administrative law and libel) uniformly point in one direction. The First Amendment may require, however, that if the institution seeks to act against the teacher under these circumstances, it may do so only pursuant to clear and specific rules respecting confidentiality, and that such rules must be of narrow compass and substantial justification.[14] Possibly the outcome may even be made to depend upon the retrospective public importance of the disclosure itself, that is, whether it truthfully brought to light a matter of serious institutional impropriety which would have gone unattended but for the breach of confidence—assuming of course that the employee had first attempted to raise the issue intramurally by whatever means the institution provided.[15] A willingness to vindicate the employee's freedom to speak out at least under these circumstances may serve the public interest to an extent that outweighs whatever marginal tendency the results may have to inhibit utter frankness in the normal operation of the school.

2. The criticism of board policy explicit in Pickering's letter transcended any purely work-related grievance of his own and sought no premature advantage of public leverage in the redress

of a personal complaint. Thus, it not only served a central function of the First Amendment in that it bore directly on an issue currently before the electorate (consideration of a proposed tax increase for educational purposes), but its publication could not be criticized as tending to undermine established procedures for the orderly and efficient review of individual, work-related complaints. The point may be instructive in two regards. The avoidance of disruption to intramural efficiency may well support an employment requirement that teachers forbear from ignoring established channels for the review and redress of work-related grievances and institutional policy, and similarly to forbear from bringing outside pressure to bear upon the operation of those institutional processes. Simultaneously, however, the failure of an institution to provide adequate internal mechanisms for the fair and orderly review of an employee's request to be heard on work-related matters, at least as they may reflect on the overall quality or policies of the school in which there is a substantial public interest, may entitle him to bring the matter to public attention without unreasonable apprehension that by doing so he will imperil his job. Specifically, the public interest to be served in protecting a teacher's freedom to speak in protest, and his own right to petition for redress of grievances, must be weighed against the adequacy of institutional channels in determining whether efficiency in administration fairly requires greater circumspectness in his public utterances.

3. The *Pickering* case did not involve the public ventilation of differences of opinion between Pickering and anyone with whom he was *closely* associated as a working colleague or subordinate. Indeed, the Court explicitly left open the possibility that a teacher could be terminated for publishing a letter so critical of those in immediate supervisory contact with him that, whatever its truth, it would necessarily lead to such intolerable personal relations in the future, impairing the efficient operation of the school, as to require that one or the other employee be transferred or terminated. The point is plain enough. Just as one who would "rather be right than be President" must also be prepared to give up his post in the President's cabinet as the price of publicly airing any differences he may have with the President, so teachers in equivalent positions of personal discretion and loyalty cannot expect that even the First Amendment will secure their position against the loss of personal confidence which may follow from the public ventilation of every difference in opinion or policy judgment they may have with their

superiors. Nevertheless, as schools and universities have grown in size, specialization of employment functions and impersonal working relations render it doubtful whether this consideration will properly apply to many situations or to many employees.

4. Perhaps the most troublesome qualification of this seminal case results from the Court's great stress upon the fact that while some of the statements in Pickering's letter were not wholly accurate, the letter was entirely without public impact ("greeted . . . with massive apathy and total disbelief"), the inaccuracies were matters of trivial detail, and the author was, at worst, merely careless without either knowingly or recklessly misrepresenting anything. At the same time, the Court did imply that were a teacher's public statements made with knowledge of their falsehood or with cavalier disregard for their truth or falsehood, their publication might "call into question his fitness to perform his duties in the classroom," *even assuming they still had no effect and were not concerned with a subject within his special competence.*

As a logical exercise, the Court's concession is not without appeal: a person who is reckless with the truth in any respect may indeed invite some question about the degree of care and preparation he employs in his professional calling. As a matter of common experience, however, the proposition is almost certainly unsound: teachers, like others, may sometimes be foolish in making statements outside the area of their particular discipline even while preserving the most rigorous personal standards within it. Beyond this, moreover, if one must fear that even extramural utterances on political matters wholly unrelated to his work can be seized upon as a pretext to bring his entire professional competence and standing into question, the result must surely chill freedom of speech and gravely disadvantage those who teach against the greater freedom of other private citizens. In addition, elemental considerations of political realism remind one that even reckless inaccuracy in extramural expression is unlikely to occasion any inquiry into a teacher's classroom competence *unless the point of the expression happens to be offensive to those with power to press the inquisition.* Precisely because the Court's suggested standard is too susceptible to abuse and misapplication for purposes of retaliatory dismissal, it should not be allowed at all.

Whatever the shortcomings of the *Pickering* decision, it nonetheless does settle the protected boundaries of a teacher's freedom of extramural expression in reasonably good fashion as a firm first step.

Unfortunately, the same cannot be said of the only noteworthy decision to date respecting the scope of academic freedom within the classroom itself: the teacher's prerogative to teach his subject according to his own best professional understanding. In *Epperson v. Arkansas*[16] the Supreme Court discerned no reason for a statutory prohibition on the consideration of evolutionary theory in any state-supported educational institution other than the legislature's desire to accommodate distinctly religious interests, and it declared the statute to be in violation of the religious establishment clause of the First Amendment. The decision is not entirely satisfactory even on its own terms, as the Court has seldom upset a law because of misgivings about the motives of those who enacted it, and has instead sustained it if it can be said to serve any possible permissible objective.[17] And, as Mr. Justice Black observed in his concurring opinion, the prohibition may have been adopted merely to remove a subject of endless disruptive controversy from further consideration within the public schools.

More importantly, the decision did not at all rely upon any constitutional claim of the individual biology teacher to some personal degree of academic freedom in the presentation of the subject she had been employed to teach. On the contrary, at several points individual Justices broadly implied that there may be no constitutional support at all for such a claim in the face of the power of the state to designate the content of state-supported curricula. Thus, Mr. Justice Black declared:

> I am . . . not ready to hold that a person hired to teach school children takes with him into the classroom a constitutional right to teach sociological, economic, political, or religious subjects that the school's managers do not want discussed. . . . I question whether . . . "academic freedom" permits a teacher to breach his contractual agreement to teach only the subjects designated by the school authorities who hired him. . . . [I]t is doubtful that, sitting in Washington, [this Court] can successfully supervise and censor the curriculum of every public school in every hamlet and city in the United States. I doubt that our wisdom is so nearly infallible.[18]

The difficulty is not stated with complete fairness when presented in such broad terms. One may readily concede that among the contending preferences of teachers, students, parents, and the members of an elected board of education, the necessity that curricular decisions must ultimately rest somewhere devolves the logical choice upon the more democratically accountable board or, as a general recourse, upon the legislature. They, at least, are subject to the orderly and formal check of the electoral process as well as to the informal influences of various groups (PTA's, student organizations, professional education associations, teacher unions), and subject also to the admonitions of the federal Constitution—such as the establishment clause of the First Amendment. It is also true that the school classroom and, albeit to a distinctly lesser extent, the university classroom are not at all free and voluntary forums in which the remunerated teacher may appropriately assert the same full measure of his own freedom of speech that he has a citizen's right to pursue in private life. Attendance of students is compelled by law, and they constitute a wholly captive audience neither free to depart if offended by or in disagreement with the teacher's utterances, nor even genuinely free to offer dissenting views as against the presumed authority of the teacher, armed with his command of sanctions over classroom decorum, the awarding of grades, and the dispensing of personal recommendations. The teacher is indeed remunerated for his hired service, employed for a specific task, and insulated within his classroom even from the immediate competition of different views held by others equally steeped in the same academic discipline. Far from freedom of speech licensing the teacher or professor to use his classroom service deliberately to proselytize for a cause or knowingly to emphasize only that selection of data best conforming to his own personal biases, it is widely recognized that such a practice furnishes precisely the just occasion to question his fitness to teach.

If this is so with repect to the individual teacher or professor, surely it is no less so when the prescription for biased treatment of the subject, or the mandate to use the classroom as an instrument of ideological proselytism, is fashioned instead by a legislature or a school board—one that so rigidly determines the exact and pre-selected details of each course that in fact it employs the teacher as a mere mechanical instrument of its impermissible design. For instance, it may be relatively unimportant that Henry Steele Commager's high school text on American history is purchased in bulk and prescribed as the basic text in high school civics rather than a similar text by Jones or Smith—unless, of course, its particular selection *plus* detailed proscriptions on any classroom reference to other texts, or to other impressions and other historical ideas, cumulatively combine to describe a process of unfree education and academic indoctrination.

Indeed, it may be seen that arbitrary restrictions on alternative sources of information or opinion, not resulting from understandable budgetary constraints or from the fact that time itself is a scarce resource and rations what teachers and students can see or study, are precisely what the First Amendment disallows. Against school board selections of only certain theories to be advanced and others forbidden to be examined or mentioned at all, a mere taxpayer should have standing to contest his compelled financial support for the propagation of ideas to which he is opposed.[19] Against state law dictation that a student be disciplined for consulting any source of education other than those arbitrarily prescribed, clearly the student could succeed on a First Amendment claim.[20] Nor may teachers or professors be made to endure similarly arbitrary restrictions on the course of their own inquiries or *upon their own communicated classroom references.* One may not, as a condition of his employment, be made an implement of governmental practices which themselves violate the First Amendment. Concurring in *Epperson,* Mr. Justice Stewart more nearly recognized that there were indeed important First Amendment issues involved beyond the valid but limited reach of the religious establishment clause:

> It is one thing for a State to determine that "the subject of higher mathematics, or astronomy, or biology" shall or shall not be included in its public school curriculum. It is quite another thing for a State to make it a criminal offense for a public school teacher so much as to mention the very existence of an entire system of respected human thought. That kind of criminal law, I think, would clearly impinge upon the guarantees of free communication contained in the First Amendment. . . .[21]

In one of the last of the political litmus-test cases, the Court appropriately recalled the rhetoric of Judge Learned Hand:

> The Nation's future depends upon leaders trained through wide exposure to that robust exchange of ideas which discovers truth "out of a multitude of tongues, [rather] than through any kind of authoritative selection."[22]

Within the classrooms where the nation's future leaders are trained, no robust exchange at all would be possible if the state were constitutionally free to select just one view of any given subject and forbid its teachers to avoid mention or consideration of any other. Consistently with the constitutional sense of Judge Hand's declaration, therefore, it must follow that no teacher or professor may be subjected to dismissal for refusing to yield to such an authoritarian demand. It is a pity that the Court declined the opportunity, in *Epperson,* to reaffirm the point.[23]

PRETERMINATION PROCEDURAL DUE PROCESS

"The history of liberty," Mr. Justice Frankfurter once observed "has largely been the history of observance of procedural safeguards."[24] The point is especially well taken with respect to teachers.

Suppose, for instance, that a public school teacher on annual contract simply fails to receive any notice that his teaching contract is being renewed for the coming year. Or suppose that an assistant professor in a state college receives notice that his three-year contract is not being renewed and, upon inquiry to learn the reason, is advised that it is contrary to institutional practice to provide a statement of reasons. Or suppose that a full professor in a state whose legislature has neither adopted a tenure system nor even delegated authority to the state regents to provide for one receives notice in midyear that his service will terminate the following June. In each case, the teacher may believe that one of the reasons significantly contributing to his termination involves a standard forbidden by the Bill of Rights—possibly retaliation for a protected extramural utterance, a disfavored political affiliation, or something similar. Alternatively, he may have vague suspicions about the factors contributing to the decision—perhaps false gossip about his private life or groundless rumors about his teaching, which he is convinced are utterly without foundation. Or again, he may be genuinely puzzled as to why he was let go. In the absence of procedural safeguards antecedent to the effective date of his termination, it is surely clear that the substantive protection he was thought to enjoy may be altogether lost.

If he has extraordinary fortitude, a teacher in these straits may retain private counsel to file suit, alleging that the action taken against him was based on certain constitutionally prohibited grounds. Then, he may hope to invoke the court's assistance to ascertain more definitely the reasons and evidence leading to his termination, and thereafter attempt to prove at his own expense that some substantive constitutional or statutory right of his was infringed. On that basis, he may hope eventually to recover damages, to be reinstated by court order, or at least to secure the useful judicial declaration that the institutional rather than he was at fault. In view of the practical difficulties, however, it is not surprising that there have been vastly fewer such cases than, for instance, the annual cascade of investigative reports by the American Association of University Professors have found to have merit in point of fact.

Faculty members are not litigious by nature; the costs of formal controversy are high and usually must be borne personally; the burden of proof falls upon the plaintiff-teacher and is often exceedingly difficult to carry; and the ordinary case may not reach judgment for months or even years after the plaintiff has been separated from his job. In addition, there is a practical recognition that the extralegal hazards of such litigation are themselves great: to sue and to lose is to establish a public record against oneself as a teacher and further to prejudice one's chances for employment or advancement. To sue and to win will ordinarily not make it possible actually to resume teaching at the institution in most instances, and it will almost certainly spread upon the public record whatever evidence of the plaintiff's shortcomings the defending institution can muster—thereby warning off other institutions which may be wary of seemingly irascible professors who sue their employer and launder their linen in public.

Without question, therefore, the effective protection of the substantive constitutional rights of teachers and professors may critically depend upon the availability of pretermination procedural due process. Post-termination judicial remedies for teachers, like postsuspension remedies for students[25] or posteviction remedies for tenants,[26] are often simply too little and too late. Indeed, the analogy to these other areas of remedial concern has been perceived by the courts, and gradually a separate right to pretermination procedural due process has received constitutional recognition.

The source of a teacher's constitutional right to due process may be found in several places. The most obvious is in the procedural implication of each and every substantive constitutional right which government is forbidden to deny or to abridge even when it acts as an employer. For instance, to the extent that the First Amendment has been held to forbid a public institution to terminate a teacher because of some extramural utterance, and to the extent that post-termination judicial proceedings are inadequate as a deterrent or corrective of the violation, the First Amendment should imply the right to a pretermination hearing (or at least to some efficacious intramural or administrative review) sufficient to assure the timely protection of freedom of speech. Similarly, to the extent that the equal protection clause protects a teacher from termination on grounds that are "patently arbitrary or discriminatory," adequate protection from such a denial of rights requires a degree and form of pretermination procedural due process essential to determine and to abate the substantive violation. If the courts continue to declare that the teacher has a substantive freedom from discriminatory termination and nevertheless deny him the minimum of procedural due process essential to the effective and timely vindication of that freedom, the law will in effect be cynically nullified.[27]

Moreover, rights established by statute, administrative order, or the common law may also imply a constitutional entitlement to whatever form of procedural due process is essential to their protection. Where the state has chosen to protect one's status beyond the minimum required by the Bill of Rights (for example, by providing that teaching contracts shall be renewed or continued except on certain specified grounds such as incompetence, medical disability, or insubordination), one's statutory right to continued employment may imply an entitlement to whatever degree of procedural due process is essential to ensure the protection of that right:

> [Appellant] is entitled to have procedural due process observed in the protection of these substantive rights even though substantive due process would not compel the rights to be given.[28]

A third basis for an independent constitutional requirement for procedural due process may exist when the proposed action of the government would do more than terminate the individual and would, in addition, inflict an injury on some aspect of his personal liberty of which he may not be deprived without due process. Thus, where termination would be accompanied by institutional conduct injurious to the teacher's personal standing apart from the loss of his job (for instance, dismissal on published grounds of racial bigotry), protection of his personal reputation entitles the individual to the observance of procedural due process as a precondition to governmental deprivation of that aspect of his personal liberty.[29]

In an entirely complementary fashion, where the government induces private persons to establish a dependency subject only to a given number of express and implied risks which the individual assumes, a subsequent decision to terminate him on grounds other than these will harm him beyond the loss of his job as such; it will leave him far worse off than if he had not been induced by the government in the first instance. Thus, in an analogous situation of the government's terminating an existing relationship with a contractor, Judge Warren Burger said in 1964 that this "places the latter in a different posture from one initially seeking government contracts and can carry with it grave economic consequences." He went on:

> Thus to say that there is no "right" to government contracts does not resolve the question of justiciability. Of course there is no such *right*; but that cannot mean that the government can act arbitrarily, either substantively *or procedurally,* against a person or that such person is not entitled to challenge the processes and the evidence *before* he is officially declared ineligible. . . .[30]

Finally, an independent right to procedural due process may be found in the accumulating judicial recognition that one's status in the public sector is itself a form of "liberty" or "property" which, though subject to forfeiture like any other aspect of liberty (say, for commission of a crime), nonetheless is an interest not to be divested without adequate procedural safeguards to minimize unreasonable risks or error or prejudice.[31] Since 1961, for instance, the federal courts have held that a student receiving a state-subsidized education for which he performs no productive service in return (maintenance of grades and observance of rules are continuing conditions of attendance, but hardly the bargained-for economic exchange of a contract) may not be dismissed absent a high degree of pretermination procedural due process. As one court observed:

> Whether the interest involved be described as a right or a privilege, the fact remains that it is an interest of almost incalculable value, especially to those students who have already enrolled in the institution and begun the pursuit of their college training. Private interests are to be evaluated under the due process clause of the Fourteenth Amendment, not in terms of labels or fictions, but in terms of their true significance and worth.[32]

Although there is no equivalent case-law support developing the *extent* of predetermination procedural due process for teachers, "the protection to be afforded . . . can hardly be less than that afforded a student, and probably should be greater."[33]

It has been essential to stress these preliminary points on the just procedural claims of teachers because of the paucity of cases. Practically all of the successful litigation by teachers has been limited solely to establishing protection from certain *grounds* of termination—nonrenewal, nonrehiring, or nonhiring. However, because the postinjury judicial processes are plainly inadequate to prevent the use of such grounds in fact, the elaboration of procedural due process for teachers is critical in the evolving law of teachers' rights.

While the Supreme Court has not yet held unequivocally that either a tenured professor or a probationary public school teacher is entitled to any degree of constitutionally compelled pretermination procedural due process, it appears reasonably certain that the proposition will be recognized. In 1956, the Court loosed a dictim in reversing the summary termination of a tenured public university professor, noting that there had been no orderly inquiry into his continuing fitness or competence to hold his job and declaring that "the summary dismissal of appellant violates due process of law."[34] In 1970, the same case was cited by the Court for the proposition that "*procedural* due process must be afforded" one who is sought to be discharged from public employment.[35] The central thesis appears nearly to have won the day, and the critical issue remains only to determine the extent and form of procedural due process on a case-by-case basis.

In the elaboration of pretermination procedural due process for teachers, two principal considerations should be borne in mind. The first is that the right to procedural due process does not contemplate a single, frozen, stylized method of trial-type procedure irrespective of the subject in controversy or the gravity of the outcome. The second consideration, a corollary to the first, is that the particular degree and form of procedural due process constitutionally required in a given situation is determined by means of a rough and ready judicial cost-benefit analysis which weighs the predicament of the individual against the costs to society in having to move only with ponderous formality. While certain requirements are fairly characteristic of most constitutionally compelled proceedings (for example, notice and, to a lesser extent, an opportunity to be heard), the configuration of nearly all other procedural rights is determined by a complex of particular cost-benefit concerns. A rather full panoply of particular procedural rights might, for instance, be thought to include all of the following:

1. Terminal action may not be taken other than pursuant to regularly established rules or standards which have been made available to the employee and which are reasonably precise and clear;

2. Proceedings to terminate the employee must be preceded by furnishing specific notice of charges providing a statement of facts sufficient to warrant the action contemplated. Adequate time must be provided to enable the employee to prepare for the ensuing hearing, and a list of witnesses plus access to other evidence proposed to be introduced at the hearing must be made available to him on request.

3. The hearing must be held before an impartial trier of fact, the outcome of the hearing must be determined solely on the basis of material placed in evidence in the course of the hearing, and a record must be made of the proceedings.

4. The employee may be represented by counsel present during the proceedings, and notice must be provided that counsel will be furnished upon request in the event the employee is unable to retain counsel.

5. The employee is entitled to know the evidence offered against him, to confront adverse witnesses, to conduct cross-examination either personally or through counsel, to offer evidence and witnesses in his own behalf, and to testify in his own behalf or to decline to do so within the privilege against self-incrimination.

6. A decision adverse to the teacher may be subject to appeal on briefs and oral argument, based on the record, with the scope of review *de novo* on alleged errors of law (such as whether the rule was incorrectly interpreted) and limited on findings of fact to determine whether they are supported by substantial evidence in the record considered as a whole.

In fact, however, there is probably no instance of teacher termination which would activate all of these possible procedural rights as a matter of constitutional law, and the particular combination of any two or more of them will vary in an extraordinary fashion depending upon a number of considerations:

"Due process" is an elusive concept. Its exact boundaries are undefinable, and its content varies according to specific factual contexts. . . . Whether the Constitution requires that a particular right obtain in a specific proceeding depends upon a complexity of factors. The nature of the alleged right involved, the nature of the proceeding, and the possible burden on that proceeding, are all considerations which must be taken into account.[36]

The degree of pretermination procedural due process to which a public employee is entitled may be most heavily influenced by the degree of hardship to the employee. Where the hardship may be great, the need for procedural safeguards against the risks of error and prejudice are correspondingly high.

In *Greene v. McElroy*,[37] for instance, the Court noted that revocation of a security clearance (without a full hearing) had effectively prevented an aeronautical engineer from pursuing his long-established career not only with the private manufacturer who discharged him solely as a consequence of the government's action—because his access to classified information, foreclosed by the government's action, was essential to his job—but in virtually all other jobs at his skill level. As a result of the government's action, Greene was forced to take other work elsewhere, at a greatly reduced skill level and at one-fourth his former pay. Considerably troubled by constitutional considerations, the Supreme Court held that the security-clearance revocation based on unavailable statements by unidentified informants (depriving the employee of "the traditional procedural safeguards of confrontation and cross-examination") was not authorized by federal statute. The case is especially instructive, since the Court was obliged to weigh against the employee's need for information the government's interest, not only in national security, but in the protection of confidential sources which might be unwilling to provide information should disclosure of their names and testimony be required.

The *Greene* case is to be contrasted with the 5-to-4 decision three years later in *Cafeteria Workers v. McElroy*,[38] upholding exclusion of a short-order cook from the cafeteria of a gun factory upon the commandant's unilateral decision, without notice or hearing of any kind, that the employee failed to meet security requirements. Noting that the employee had already secured equivalent employment elsewhere, that the exclusion had not affected equivalent employment opportunities in general, and that the basis of the decision implied little stigma ("the Superintendent may have simply thought that Rachel Brawner was garrulous, or careless with her identification badge"), a slim majority held that neither notice nor an opportunity to be heard was constitutionally required.

The great weight of the "hardship" factor in the rationing of procedural due process is also illustrated in several recent Supreme Court decisions outside the employment field. In *Goldberg v.*

Kelly,[39] the Court held unconstitutional the termination of welfare benefits prior to an evidentiary hearing which was otherwise elaborately provided for following termination. The Court noted that the effect of termination had critical consequences to the person left totally destitute and that, even weighed against the high costs to government (loss of money to recipients who would be judgment-proof against recovery of payments illegally received, administrative burdens and costs of providing a hearing, etc.) procedural due process would therefore require "timely and adequate notice detailing the reasons for a proposed termination, and an effective opportunity to defend by confronting any adverse witnesses and by presenting his own arguments and evidence orally."

In *Sniadach v. Family Finance Corp.*,[40] the Court held that requirements of procedural due process would require notice and an opportunity to be heard in court by a wage-earner *prior* to the freezing of one-half of her wages attached by an alleged creditor, although the wages thus attached were simply to be held by the employer subject to the order of the court following later full trial of the creditor's claim. The hardship to the wage-earner in the loss of even one-half of her means of support, plus the coercive effect of the freeze to force a settlement without contesting the creditor's claim in an ensuing hearing, were grave enough consequences to require notice and an opportunity to be heard in court in advance.

In *Jenkins v. McKeithen*,[41] a state criminal investigatory commission without any prosecuting or formal sanctioning power of its own, but with authority to express an official opinion as to who might be guilty of criminal misconduct, was required "to afford a person being investigated the right to confront and cross-examine the witnesses against him, subject only to traditional limitations of those rights," as well as to present his own position personally and through witnesses. The consequences of public stigma to a person under investigation was enough virtually by itself to activate fair substantial procedural rights on behalf of the individual.[42]

From these cases, it can be seen that the hardships to the individual, which partly measure the degree of antecedent procedural due process to which he is entitled, necessarily embrace not only the loss of his job at one institution, but the probable impact on his opportunities elsewhere and the larger repercussions to his reputation as well.

In the teaching field, moreover, there are significant public interests allied with the teacher's interests which further tip the balance in favor of pretermination procedural safeguards. It is, in fact, a false view of the matter to suppose that the proper balance is merely one of weighing the needs of the individual against the needs of society—which nearly always assures from the outset that the individual will weigh more lightly.[43] While the Supreme Court has not as yet given a separate constitutional status to academic freedom as such, it has nevertheless repeatedly emphasized that the protection of individual teachers is critical to protect the public interest in teaching, research, investigation, publication, and education itself, and that procedural due process for teachers is critical to the *public* stake in intellectual pluralism and the advancement of knowledge.[44] As a consequence, the balance to be struck in apportioning requirements of procedural due process is not one of choosing between the needs and rights of the individual and those of the state, but between certain proper concerns of the state and certain substantial public interests directly served by protecting those who teach from arbitrary decisions.

We may therefore reasonably expect that constitutionally compelled pretermination procedural rights of teachers will follow with at least as much generosity as in the case of other public employees. A federal district court recently held that a 59-year-old university maintenance mechanic with fourteen years of service could not be dismissed for allegedly assaulting his supervisor and threatening others without "advance written notice [of specific charges] with the opportunity to respond either in writing or by an informal appearance," even though he was otherwise assured of an elaborate *post-termination* process of administrative review.[45] One may readily suppose that pretermination notice and opportunity to be heard are at least equally required procedural requisites for professors at the same university. Equally, a federal court of appeals has recently held that a part-time attending physician may not be dismissed from a municipal hospital and stigmatized by an allegation of racism, in the absence of a "full hearing" preceded by a reasonably precise and specific written statement of reasons for the proposed action.[46] Termination of a teacher in similar circumstances must surely require at least the same extent of pretermination procedural due process.

Within the past year, at least four federal court decisions have fulfilled specific prophecies of professorial right to pretermination procedural due process. They have done so, moreover, even where the teachers were merely probationary appointees, early in their careers, on short-term contracts, and where termination occurred simply from notice of nonrenewal furnished well in advance of end of the term.

In *Roth v. Board of Regents*[47] an assistant professor on a one-year contract, without tenure, and in his first year of teaching was notified by the state university president five months in advance of the end of the academic year that his employment contract would not be renewed. In spite of the teacher's youth, his slight dependency on his job in the very first year, the absence of any published ground stigmatizing his reputation or character, the absence of evidence specifically indicating grave personal hardship in finding employment elsewhere, the fact that the contract was only one year and was simply not renewed (rather than being terminated during the term), the obvious need of the institution to reserve discretion in judging the performance and excellence of probationary appointees before committing itself to tenure, and the institution's concern that the ordeal of elaborate procedures in mere nonrenewal cases might well force upon it a system of instant tenure with the cost to society of insulating mediocrity, the court nonetheless concluded that pretermination procedural due process would require at least (1) a statement of the reasons why the university intended not to retain the teacher, to be furnished upon his request; and (2) notice of a hearing at which he might respond to the stated reasons, to be provided upon his request. In connection with the hearing, the court said that:

> the professor must have a reasonable opportunity to submit evidence relevant to the stated reasons. The burden of going forward and the burden of proof rests with the professor. Only if he makes a reasonable showing that the stated reasons are wholly inappropriate as a basis for decision or that they are wholly without basis in fact would the university administration become obliged to show that the stated reasons are not inappropriate or that they have a basis in fact.[48]

Within three weeks of *Roth,* a federal district court in Alabama[49] held that several instructors given notice of nonrenewal well before the expiration of their second one-year contracts had "not been accorded procedural due process" and were entitled to "formal notice and specification of the charges and a hearing" before termination by nonrenewal could become effective. Almost simultaneously, the Wisconsin federal district court that decided the *Roth* case also reinstated several tenured and nontenured state university professors who were suspended with full pay but excluded from the campus, where the suspension was for the reason that the teachers' continuing presence during highly disruptive campus events was thought to pose an immediate danger. No notice was furnished explaining in what way their presence was believed to contribute to the danger, however, nor was any preliminary hearing provided prior to the suspension, nor was a hearing assured at the earliest practical time following such interim suspension, assuming that emergency circumstances made even a preliminary prior hearing impractical.[50]

More instructive than the fact that the courts in these cases specifically based the result on the teachers' constitutional right to procedural due process, or the fact that each represents an extension of the form of that due process beyond anything hitherto recognized in comparable circumstances in any other court, is the particular weighing process which was observed. In *Roth*, by far the most elaborate of the three cases, the court noted the following items which weighed in favor of the claim for notice, statement of reasons on request, and an opportunity for hearing:

1. Of 442 non-tenured teachers at the university, only four were given notice that contracts would not be offered them for 1969–1970. Thus, the technical consideration that the employee was merely on a one-year contract and altogether lacked tenure simply was not conclusive of the real situation. Where customary practice indicates that continued employment is ordinarily to be expected and nonrenewal is as extraordinary as here (less than 1 percent of probationary employees), the alleged need of the university employer for complete freedom of summary termination will be tested according to the reality of the situation rather than the legal form. The point for public school teachers on annual contract, where, however, nonrenewal is equally exceptional, is a valuable one. Indeed, where nonrenewal is otherwise a relatively rare event, the administrative burden of furnishing a written statement of reasons and an opportunity to be heard on request cannot be seen as onerous. Similarly, the very fact that nonrenewal may be *known* to be a rare event in the practices of the particular institution makes the fact of nonrenewal in a given case a much more severe judgment than otherwise and one which is correspondingly likely to affect a teacher's opportunities elsewhere. As a consequence one has a greater entitlement to a fuller measure of pretermination procedural due process.

2. The nonrenewal occurred during political controversy on

campus; indeed, the terminated teacher separately alleged that the decision not to renew was in retaliation for expressions he claimed were protected by the First Amendment. The Court was quick to discern that the theoretical constitutional protection of such a substantive right could readily be subverted in the absence of some minimal pretermination procedure: "Substantive constitutional protection for a university professor against non-retention is useless without procedural safeguards." Thus, the prophylactic value of pretermination procedures under the circumstances was reasonably essential to protect not merely the teacher's economic and reputational interests but his substantive constitutional interests as well.

3. The job impact on the teacher in his prospects for relocating elsewhere was more substantial than in the *Cafeteria Workers* case (involving exclusion from one place of a short-order cook), the public interest in his protection greater (given the public benefits flowing from the protection of academic freedom); the custom of authoritarian operation of universities is nowhere near as firm or habitual as that of military installations; and the governmental reasons for acting and for withholding the basis so to act (national security) are without qualitative counterpart on behalf of the university.[51]

There is, moreover, substantial educational support for this emerging judicial view that the reasonable protection of institutional discretion to evaluate its probationary academic staff does not require the perpetuation of summary and unreviewable powers of nonrenewal or termination. In the majority of colleges and universities, the authority to make these decisions is delegated in the first instance to the senior faculty of each department. Even so, the American Association of University Professors, which tends to draw a high proportion of its members from the senior ranks and which is very much influenced by considerations of quality control, has recently proposed procedural standards virtually equivalent to those set down in the *Roth* case.[52] As courts may appropriately defer in otherwise doubtful cases to the judgment of those closest to the firing line of education, professional recommendations such as these may themselves contribute to the formation of the constitutional norm.

In any case, it is becoming evident that teachers and professors do have a claim of constitutional right to pretermination procedural due process, whatever the fullness of time may determine to be its particular requirements in each set of circumstances.

NOTES

1. Meyer v. Nebraska, 262 U.S. 390 (1922); Pierce v. Society of Sisters, 268 U.S. 510 (1925).

2. Scopes v. State, 154 Tenn. 105, 109–10, 289 S.W. 363, 364–65 (1927). The court nevertheless reversed Scopes's conviction on other grounds—that the judge had levied the $100 fine, rather than the jury as specified by the state constitution.

3. Frost Trucking Co. v. Railroad Comm'n, 271 U.S. 583, 594 (1926); *see also* Justice Holmes dissenting in United States *ex rel*. Milwaukee Publishing Co. v. Burleson, 255 U.S. 407, 437 (1921): "The United States may give up the Post Office when it sees fit, but while it carries it on the use of the mails is almost as much a part of free speech as the right to use our tongues. . . ."

4. Epperson v. Arkansas, 393 U.S. 97 (1968).

5. *The Federalist* No. 79 (Hamilton).

6. Slochower v. Board of Higher Educ., 350 U.S. 551, 555 (1956) (emphasis added). The reference to "nondiscriminatory" terms of public employment, incidentally, discloses a second principal textual source of substantive constitutional protection: the equal protection clause of the Fourteenth Amendment. *See also* Trister v. University of Mississippi, 420 F.2d 499 (5th Cir. 1969); Johnson v. Branch, 364 F.2d 177 (4th Cir. 1966), *cert. denied*, 385 U.S. 1003 (1967).

7. Wieman v. Updegraff, 344 U.S. 183, 196–97 (1952) (Frankfurter, J., concurring).

8. *See, e.g.*, Keyishian v. Board of Regents, 385 U.S. 589 (1967); Baggett v. Bullitt, 377 U.S. 360 (1964) (disclaimer oaths and affidavits); Morrison v. State Bd. of Educ., 82 Cal. Rptr. 175, 461 P.2d 361 (Cal. 1969) (revocation of teacher's life diploma reversed in spite of evidence of private homosexual conduct not shown to involve students or to affect teacher's work); Finot v. Pasadena Bd. of Educ., 250 Cal. App. 2d 189, 58 Cal. Rptr. 520 (1968) (teacher may not be transferred for sporting a well-trimmed beard in defiance of principal's ban). *See generally* "Developments in the Law: Academic Freedom," 81 *Harvard Law Review* 1045 (1968).

9. *See* Ohlson v. Phillips, 304 F. Supp. 1152 (D. Colo. 1969), *aff'd per curiam*, 397 U.S. 317 (1970).

10. 391 U.S. 563, 568–69 (1968).

11. Republished in AAUP Policy Document and Reports, at 3–4 (Spring, 1969) (emphasis added). But see 1965 Committee, "A Statement on Extramural Utterances," *id*. at 11: "Extramural utterances rarely bear upon the faculty member's fitness for his position."

12. 391 U.S. at 571–72. *See also* Dickey v. Alabama State Bd. of Educ., 273 F. Supp. 613 (M.D. Ala. 1967), *determination of appeal postponed*, 394 F.2d 490 (5th Cir. 1968).

13. For recent applications of *Pickering*, see Brukiewa v. Police Comm'r, 263 257 Md. 36,263 A.2d 210 (1970); McGee v. Richmond Unified School Dist., 306 F. Supp. 1152 (N.D. Cal. 1969).

14. *See* Meehan v. Macy, 392 F.2d 822 (D.C. Cir. 1968), *modified on reconsideration* (in light of *Pickering*), No. 20,812 (D.C. Cir., Aug. 23, 1968).

15. *Cf.* Parrish v. Civil Serv. Comm'n, 425 P.2d 223, 57 Cal. Rptr. 623 (1967); Lefcourt v. Legal Aid Soc'y, 38 U.S.L.W. 2633 (S.D.N.Y., June 2, 1970).

16. 393 U.S. 97 (1968).

17. *See, e.g.,* United States v. O'Brien, 391 U.S. 367 (1968) (draft-card burning punishable).

18. Epperson v. Arkansas, 393 U.S. at 113–14 (concurring opinion).

19. *See* Lathrop v. Donohue, 367 U.S. 820, 873 (1961) (Black, J., dissenting).

20. *See* Tinker v. Des Moines Independent Community School Dist., 393 U.S. 503, 511 (1969).

21. 393 U.S. at 116.

22. Keyishian v. Board of Regents, 385 U.S. 589, 603 (1968).

23. Two federal courts have recently extended constitutional protection to a teacher's classroom assignments and discussion. Keefe v. Geanakos, 418 F.2d 359 (1st Cir. 1970); Vought v. Van Buren Pub. Schools, 306 F. Supp. 1388 (E.D. Mich., 1969).
38 U.S.L.W. 2034 (E.D. Mich., 1969).

24. McNabb v. United States, 318 U.S. 332, 347 (1943).

25. Dixon v. Alabama Bd. of Educ., 294 F.2d 150 (5th Cir.), *cert. denied,* 368 U.S. 930 (1961) (public university students may not be indefinitely suspended in the absence of pretermination procedural due process).

26. Thorpe v. Housing Authority, 386 U.S. 670 (1967) (per curiam).

27. Cafeteria Workers v. McElroy, 367 U.S. 886, 900 (1961) (Brennan, J., dissenting).

28. United States *ex rel.* Smith v. Baldi, 192 F.2d 540, 544 (3d Cir. 1951), *aff'd,* 344 U.S. 561 (1953). *See also* Goldberg v. Kelly, 397 U.S. 254 (1970); Joint Anti-Fascist Refugee Comm. v. McGrath, 341 U.S. 123, 185 (1951) (concurring opinion); Greene v. McElroy, 360 U.S. 474 (1959).

29. *See* Birnbaum v. Trussell, 371 F.2d 672, 678 (2d Cir. 1966). *See also* K. Davis, *Administrative Law: Cases, Text, Problems* 154–55 (1965).

30. Gonzalez v. Freeman, 334 F.2d 570, 574 (D.C. Cir. 1964) (emphasis added).

31. *See* Reich, "Individual Rights and Social Welfare: The Emerging Legal Issues," 74 *Yale Law Journal* 1245, 1255 (1965), favorably noted by Mr. Justice Brennan in Goldberg v. Kelly, 397 U.S. 254, 262 n. 8 (1970); Reich, "The New Property," 73 *Yale Law Journal* 733 (1964). *See also* "Developments in the Law: Academic Freedom," 81 *Harvard Law Review* 1045, 1081 (1968).

32. Knight v. State Bd. of Educ., 200 F. Supp. 174, 178 (M.D. Tenn. 1961).

33. Lafferty v. Carter, 310 F. Supp. 465, 470 (W.D. Wis. 1970).

34. Slochower v. Board of Higher Educ., 350 U.S. 551, 559 (1956).

35. Goldberg v. Kelly, 397 U.S. 254, 262–63 (1970) (emphasis added).

36. Hannah v. Larche, 363 U.S. 420, 442 (1960); *see also id.* at 487–88 (Frankfurter, J., concurring).

37. 360 U.S. 474 (1958).

38. 367 U.S. 886 (1961).

39. 397 U.S. 254 (1970).

40. 395 U.S. 337 (1969).

41. 395 U.S. 411, 429 (1969).

42. *But cf.* Hannah v. Larche, 363 U.S. 420 (1960).

43. *See especially* Mr. Justice Black's dissenting opinion in Barenblatt v. United States, 360 U.S. 109, 134, 144 (1959).

44. See Keyishian v. Board of Regents, 385 U.S. 589, 603 (1968); Sweezy v. New Hampshire, 354 U.S. 234, 250, 261–63 (1957) (concurring opinion); Wieman v. Updegraff, 344 U.S. 183, 196–98 (1953); Shelton v. Tucker, 364 U.S. 479, 487 (1960).

45. Olson v. Regents of Univ. of Minnesota, 301 F. Supp. 1356, 1361 (D. Minn. 1969).
46. Birnbaum v. Trussell, 371 F.2d 672, 679 (2d Cir. 1966).
47. 310 F. Supp. 972 (W.D. Wis. 1970).
48. *Id.* at 980. *But see* Nelson v. County of Los Angeles, 362 U.S. 1, 16 (1960).
49. Fluker v. Alabama Bd. of Educ., Civil No. 3034-N (M.D. Ala. March 31, 1970).
50. Lafferty v. Carter, 310 F. Supp. 465 (W.D. Wis. 1970).
51. The reasoning and basic procedural guarantees developed in *Roth* were applied four days later by the same court in behalf of two public school teachers whose annual contracts had not been renewed. Gouge v. Joint School Dist. No. 1, 310 F. Supp. 984 (W.D. Wis. 1970).
52. *See* Report of Committee A on Academic Freedom and Tenure, "Procedural Standards in the Renewal or Nonrenewal of Faculty Appointments," 56 *AAUP Bulletin* 21 (Spring, 1970).

THE RIGHTS OF
STUDENTS

ROY LUCAS

ON ANY GIVEN SCHOOL DAY IN THE 1970'S OVER SIXTY
million students will be trained and contained in an American
educational institution. Sixty-three percent will be in elementary
schools, 25 percent in high schools, and 12 percent in some form
of college. These students will constitute over one-fourth of the
entire American population. Their rights vis-à-vis over one million school officials are the subject of this essay.

The concept of rights and power for students is as old as the
Western university itself. Indeed, before 1706 the Chancellor's
Court at the University of Oxford adjudicated fifty-three volumes
of cases, the majority of which involved conflicts between students
and University authorities.[1] Students then "were reputed a litigious
race, but . . . they were on guard against the lawyers they employed."

An 1886 Pennsylvania decision involving private Dickinson
College is one of the earliest leading cases. The institution's president charged one John Hill with "singing, hooting and throwing
stones" during a disturbance. Hill denied the accusation before
the faculty, and left the meeting when it appeared that his denial
was sufficient. The faculty, however, relying on secondhand rumors, continued its meeting and ordered Hill expelled.

*Roy Lucas is President of the James Madison Constitutional Law Institute, Editor in
Chief of the College Law Bulletin, and the author of a forthcoming book,* Toward a
Democratic University: The Rights of Students and Faculty.

Hill then took his case to court, arguing that the entire manner of proceeding had been improper. The court agreed with Hill and ruled that he had a right to be notified of the specific charges and of the evidence against him, to confront and question his accusers as well as call witnesses on his own behalf, and to be presumed innocent.[2] The law school cases around the turn of the century also required a minimum of fair procedure before an institution could dismiss a student.[3]

In the mid-1920's, however, the tide of judicial sympathy shifted. Courts ruled that both public and private colleges could expel students with no hearing, without notice of charges or reason, and with no opportunity to present a defense. Among the most celebrated cases were expulsions for not being "a typical Syracuse girl," for smoking off campus, for suggesting that administrators made passes at coeds, and for permitting guests to drink alcohol at one's home off campus.

More recently, and in particular since 1960, courts have reassessed the myriad questions of student rights. Both in high schools and colleges these rights have visibly expanded. There is, indeed, a virtual movement afoot to widen student rights by systematic litigation. Someday, students may even claim the same rights that are taken for granted by other citizens. The principal concern of the remainder of this essay will be the customary, constitutional, fiduciary, and contractual rights of American students in the coming decades.

CUSTOMARY RIGHTS OF STUDENTS

It was custom, as the Masters of 1280 assured Bishop Sutton of Lincoln . . . which gave them the right to inquire into the delinquencies of scholars, and which gave the Chancellor jurisdiction to try them. . . .

—C. E. Mallett

Custom and practice have long sanctioned the plenary authority of school and university officials over students. Only within the last decade, however, has practice begun to embrace the concept of substantial rights for students. The most persuasive, relevant sources of practice have been statements issued by relatively impartial organizations involved in the educational process. The first such document, the Joint Statement on Rights and Freedoms of Students, was drafted and endorsed by representatives from leading organizations.[4] The principles of the Joint Statement have been echoed in subsequent documents such as A Statement on the Rights and Responsibilities of University Students, prepared by the Section on Individual Rights and Responsibilities of the American Bar Association, a Proposed Model Code of Student Rights, Responsibilities and Conduct, prepared by the Committee on Student Rights and Responsibilities of the ABA Law Students' Division, and an influential proposed code with commentaries prepared by faculty and students in a seminar at the New York University School of Law, entitled Student Conduct and Discipline Proceedings in a University Setting.

While these codes differ somewhat on both major and minor issues, they share several characteristics. First, they agree that higher educational opportunity is so important that it should be a carefully protected right, not to be taken away except for weighty reasons, and then only in accordance with careful procedural safeguards.

Second, they agree that students should to a large extent have the same civil rights as citizens, namely, freedom of speech, press, assembly, association, and religion, and freedom from invidious discrimination.

Third, each of the statements sets out a code of fair procedures in disciplinary hearings. These procedures constitute a form of "academic due process" for students, similar to the hearing procedures which have long prevailed in matters of faculty discipline.

These new standards may have greater practical effect than an entire series of Supreme Court decisions. Student governing bodies, disciplinary study committees, and students charged with offenses can point to the standards as something recognized by professional educators to be model codes and minimum concepts of fairness. College officials are more likely to accept codes recommended by their counterparts than applicable court decisions issued from a foreign frame of reference. Moreover, when a court must decide a question of student rights, the Joint Statement can be used as evidence that due process concepts are not figments of a legalistic imagination but rather procedures which have already been accepted as wise by professional men in the field of education. Several courts have already taken this approach, and there has been a wealth of scholarly commentary in this area.[5]

Student Expression and Assembly

Students, like other citizens, speak and listen, distribute leaflets, publish newspapers, march, and demonstrate. Similarly, educational officials, like other authorities, may attempt to silence speech, ban speakers, prohibit leaflets, censor newspapers, and punish marches and demonstrations. This combination of attitudinal currents running in opposite directions can create clashes over the scope of a student's right to speak and protest. Three such cases have been considered by the Supreme Court during this century, and many others by lower courts.

The celebrated *Flag Salute Case*[6] was the first to mark the bounds within which student expression would be protected by the First Amendment. Students who were Jehovah's Witnesses had been expelled from West Virginia public schools for refusing to salute the American flag. They did so on the ground that it was inconsistent with their religious beliefs to acknowledge the symbolism of the flag. In holding that it was a violation of the First Amendment to require the flag salute, the Court stated as a basic principle:

> [C]ensorship or suppression of expression of opinion is tolerated by our Constitution only when the expression presents a *clear and present danger* of action of a kind the State is empowered to prevent and punish.

The Court thus established that educational authorities—principals, deans, boards of education, etc.—must make a showing of "clear and present danger" posed by a student's expression before curtailing action can be taken. This standard derives, of course, from the important role of expression—even nonverbal expression —in a free society, the special need to preserve free inquiry in the educational setting, and the tightly limited area allowed for government intrusion into speech. Where some threat of disruption or violence is involved, it will be important to establish whether it was the expression itself or adverse reaction thereto which triggered the conflict. If school authorities have less drastic means available to avoid disruption than those that were actually used, this will be relevant to the constitutional decision.

Student-discipline controversies are complicated by the varieties of student expression. These have included not only refusal to salute the flag, but the wearing of armbands, buttons, and hair styles to express a point of view, as well as leaflets, guest speakers, newspapers, demonstrations, and sit-ins. There has been considerable litigation here, more than in all other areas of student rights combined.

Recently, *Tinker v. Des Moines Independent Community School District*[7] came before the Supreme Court in an appeal by students who had worn black armbands to protest the war in Vietnam. Although the students had done no more than engage in peaceful protest, they were ordered by school authorities to remove their armbands. The Supreme Court found that the students' First Amendment rights had been violated. This was so because no action of the students had created any material and substantial interference with appropriate requirements of school discipline. A majority of Justices, however, made no mention of the "clear and present danger" test. Since *Tinker,* at least seven lower federal courts have stepped back from a "clear and present danger" test, and the Supreme Court will accordingly have further opportunities to amplify its position on student expression.[8]

A second area of student expression has been the right to hear speakers with varying points of view. Despite a considerable volume of litigation on this point, educational authorities persist in attempting to exclude speakers whose views might provoke criticism of the institution. Four three-judge federal courts, two United States courts of appeal, and the highest courts of New York and California have struck down various officially imposed restrictions on invitations to speakers and the right of speakers to use facilities at the college or school where invited.[9]

The principle to be drawn from these decisions is that only a limited number of formal restrictions can be imposed. Student organizations may be required to reserve a room for the speaker at a reasonable time, but the controversial nature of a given speaker is not relevant. Nonetheless, experience shows that college officials will not always be swayed by the weight of judicial authority. Further litigation, therefore, may well focus, not only on testing bans on speakers, but on recovering attorneys' fees, and compensatory and punitive damages for First Amendment violations.

The student press has been a further focus of free-expression litigation. Two issues are important here: one, freedom from censorship, and two, the access of varying viewpoints to a student press financed by public funds.

Dickey v. Alabama Board of Education[10] is the landmark case on censorship. A college student-newspaper editor, Gary Dickey, refused to obey a rule that prohibited criticism of the Alabama legislature in the paper. When ordered not to print a particular editorial (defending the concept of academic freedom) he instead printed the word CENSORED across the page. Expulsion was followed by a federal court action for reinstatement, in which Dickey prevailed. The district court found that a student-newspaper editor had a First Amendment right at least to criticize state officials. A college rule prohibiting such criticism could not be justified.

If the *Dickey* decision is construed broadly, it will stand as a bar to many forms of censorship. While it left open several questions, it was the first clear-cut judicial declaration to the effect that campus newspaper censorship was taboo. One unresolved issue is whether minority-viewpoint students, who are compelled to pay student fees supporting a paper, may demand either equal space, or a partial refund, when the paper consistently advocates positions they deplore. Although such cases are not easily manageable, these students may have substantial claims on both counts. Another obvious problem is the student editor who himself attempts to impose a regime of censorship upon the paper. His subordinates, under the principles of the *Dickey* case, will probably be held to possess First Amendment freedom from editorial censorship as well.

Two final touchy questions are those of libel and obscenity— what standards apply? At the college level the general law of libel and obscenity would seem appropriate. College papers theoretically reach a mature, educated audience. However, in high school and below, standards of obscenity may be tightened by judges who fear adverse impact on immature minds. Empirical verification of such impact is yet another question.

The second question, access to the student press by people with viewpoints not otherwise represented, was presented in *Zucker v. Panitz*,[11] and *Avins v. Rutgers University*.[12]

Zucker held that a publicly financed high school paper, which accepted commercial advertising, must on the same terms accept paid antiwar advertisements proposed by students. To do otherwise, the court held, was to exclude particular ideas from a public forum without sufficient justification.[13] By contrast, *Avins* held that a potential contributor to a law review could not insist that his article be printed after it was rejected for justifiable reasons, which might include jurisprudential outlook. *Avins* differed from

Zucker in two respects. First, *Avins* was asking for a remedy which involved many more factors than the simple question of printing or not printing an ad. Law reviews receive large numbers of articles, and can print only a few. Second, the reasons for rejecting Avins' article were not clearly impermissible. His argument, that constitutional questions should hinge on legislative history or framers' "intent," had been mooted at length many times before. With twenty articles on twenty new topics to choose from, the *Rutgers Law Review* might reasonably reject his work.

On different facts the *Avins* case might have gone the other way, particularly if one hypothesizes a law review inviting a contribution, reserving space for it, and deciding against the article because of overt political pressure.

Reports from the United States Student Press Association indicate that hundreds of censorship incidents occur each year at American colleges. The same must be true below the college level. If such censorship is to be stopped, interested parties must ensure that the student press develops financial and corporate autonomy. The access problem, moreover, can be resolved by division of authority among editors, guest columns, and conscious efforts to invite and print critical responses to earlier material.

Demonstrations, sit-ins, and other types of "speech plus" are the final areas of student expression and assembly, as well as the most visible and often the most effective. Despite the *Flag Salute Case,* a number of cases concerning college disciplinary actions indicate that college authorities have somewhat greater leeway here to promulgate narrowly drawn rules with respect to time, place, notice, and number of participants. On the other hand, when the simple question was presented whether a college could require that all student demonstrations be approved in advance by the administration, the simple answer was no.[14] A federal district court ruled that such a requirement was "on its face a prior restraint on the right to freedom of speech and the right to assemble."[15]

Building takeovers, acts of violence, and sit-downs, however, have met with marked judicial hostility. Cases from Louisiana, New York, Colorado, West Virginia, and Missouri have emphatically stated that the First Amendment protects only the peaceful demonstration in a setting where students have a clear right to be in the first place. Yet the fact that a student is arrested during a demonstration has been held insufficient evidence of disruptive conduct.[16] The college must establish that there is "substantial evidence" of actual disruption by the student. Mere participation in a peaceful demonstration is fully protected by the First Amendment.[17]

Nonetheless, participants in seriously disruptive demonstrations are not always without recourse. One circuit has held that disciplinary action must be based upon clear and narrowly drawn college rules.[18] A regulation against "misconduct," without further elucidation, cannot support disciplinary action. Since the vast majority of colleges have such hopelessly vague and sweeping regulations, this defense may be crucial in the future.

STUDENT PRIVACY

While the majority of lawsuits by students have involved First Amendment claims, often coupled with due process issues, the majority of complaints made by students to organizations such as the National Student Association are against administrative and police searches of student dormitories, personal belongings, and the like. Invariably, the search is made without a warrant or any pretense of emergency. In nonacademic society, both for criminal searches and administrative inspections, a warrant is generally required. Indeed, the Fourth Amendment's language is not limited in terms to searches for evidence of crime. Its history points to an all-inclusive concern for individual privacy.

The concern for student privacy has three foci: one, that educational officials not be clothed with third-party power to consent to searches of student rooms and lockers; two, that officials be required to obtain warrants before searching; and three, that illegally seized evidence be inadmissible in criminal or administrative (disciplinary) proceedings.

Although present case law is unfavorable, ample theoretical justification exists for each of these results. Recent Supreme Court explanations of the Fourth Amendment completely undermine the justification for allowing warrantless searches, and considerable scholarly commentary favors application of the warrant requirement to lockers and dormitories in an educational setting.[19]

In a recent federal case Alabama police officers were informed by reliable sources that certain students possessed marijuana in their dormitory rooms at Troy State University. They held two morning conferences with university officials and other students, made up a list of rooms they desired to search, and went to the campus. Accompanied by the dean of men, they searched a student's room without his consent. No effort was made to obtain a search warrant. The police acted instead in reliance upon a campus rule which stated:

> The college reserves the right to enter rooms for inspection purposes. If the administration deems it necessary the room may be searched and the occupant required to open his personal baggage and any other personal material which is sealed.

The search uncovered traces of marijuana in the proverbial matchbox. Thereupon the university expelled the student, and public authorities brought criminal charges against him. He challenged the search as being in violation of rights protected by the Fourth Amendment—for bootleggers, pickpockets, and, he argued, students as well. In *Moore v. Student Affairs Committee of Troy State University*,[20] the federal district court upheld the search and the college rule as applied to justify the expulsion. The court ruled that the student's interest in privacy is subordinate to "reasonable exercise[s] of the college's supervisory duty." Not being a tenant, but one with or subject to a "special relationship" to the college, the student was bound by "[a] reasonable right of inspection" thought "necessary to the institution's performance of" the duty to "operate the school *as an educational institution*" (court's emphasis). This right of inspection, the court went on to say, could justifiably be exercised upon "a reasonable belief . . . that a student is using a dormitory room for a purpose which is illegal or which would otherwise seriously interfere with campus discipline." Even assuming a full Fourth Amendment right in disciplinary proceedings, the search was nonetheless valid because "conducted by a superior charged with a responsibility of maintaining discipline and order or of maintaining security."

In more than one respect, the *Moore* case falls short of implementing even the most elementary features of the Fourth Amendment as applied in recent years by the Supreme Court.

While the facts of the *Moore* case itself are not the most favorable to a claim of privacy, those are not the typical invasions that occur from day to day in a dormitory. As the Supreme Court had stated in criminal *and* administrative cases:

The basic purpose of this Amendment, as recognized in countless decisions of this Court, is to safeguard the privacy and security of individuals against arbitrary invasions by governmental officials.[21]

The college rule at issue in *Moore* allowed inspection when "the administration deems it necessary." *Moore,* however, neither cited nor acknowledged the existence of the Supreme Court's decisions applying the Fourth Amendment in the administrative area, although they had been law for almost a year. Even in a wiretapping case,[22] the Court emphasized that a phone booth, which is far more public than a dormitory room, was not subject to unreasonable search because "the Fourth Amendment protects people, not places. . . . Wherever a man may be, he is entitled to know that he will remain free from unreasonable searches and seizures." *Moore* quite inappropriately adds an exception—that students are not people and dormitory rooms are not protected places.

Nowhere in the court's opinion is there an intimation that search warrants hold the place accorded them by the Supreme Court. Again, in the administrative cases overlooked by the Court in *Moore,* the need for an impartial magistrate emerges. In *Camara v. Municipal Court:*

> When the right of privacy must reasonably yield to the right of search is, as a rule, to be decided by a judicial officer, not by a . . . government enforcement agent.[23]

The *Moore* decision sought to justify a standard of "reasonable cause to believe" *as interpreted by college officials* because of "the special necessities of the student-college relationship and because college disciplinary proceedings are not criminal proceedings in the constitutional sense."[24] One cannot quarrel with the standard itself, but the fact that it is implemented by college officials rather than a neutral magistrate is an all-important difference.

We might ask what "special necessities" there are which do not exist in the inspector–houseowner, fire warden–businessman, and police–suspect cases? The Court mentions none. Fire prevention is at least as important as searching students' rooms for marijuana. Searches for general housing code violations are probably more crucial to society than rummaging through dormitory rooms. Certainly, searches for evidence of major crimes are more important. Yet, the search warrant requirement prevails in each of these cases, except in emergencies. Why should the student be stripped of his privacy? Special necessities of higher education may exist in a class-

room or research laboratory, but dormitories are hardly different
from apartment buildings, until they are made so by an overbear-
ing concern for the private lives of their occupants. If the students
lived off campus, they would presumably be free from unconsented
and unwarranted searches. The accident, or even requirement, of
living in a dormitory has scant relation to classroom activities and
can hardly be viewed as a central element of unique educational
concern.

A final weakness in the *Moore* decision is its acceptance of the
University's desire to retain master keys for search purposes. The
Court found it "settled law" that "the Fourth Amendment does
not prohibit reasonable searches . . . conducted by a *superior*
charged with a responsibility of maintaining *discipline* and *order*
or . . . security."[25] In support of this surprising conclusion the
opinion cited four federal criminal cases and gave no indication
that a contrary position might be tenable. Two of the cases cited,
United States v. Grisby[26] and *United States v. Miller*,[27] involved
the search of *military* personnel on *military* grounds pursuant to
military law. *Grisby* grew out of the search of a corporal's quarters,
specifically authorized by a superior military officer, and based
upon probable cause that evidence of theft would be found. Not
only was *Miller* strictly a military case, but the search was incident
to a lawful arrest and therefore lawful on that independent ground.

If the *Moore* decision meant that a dormitory in the educational
setting of intellectual freedom was to be treated as if it were a
military barracks, such a novel and frightening assumption should
have been overtly articulated. Instead the Court previously laid
special emphasis on the role of the "school as an *educational institution*." Covertly, to be sure, this role was found to justify a regime
analogous to military law, a result which would please only the
most authoritarian college administrator. In light of the fact that
the Constitution itself leaves military law up to Congress, and
largely outside the civilized framework of the Bill of Rights,
neither *Grisby* nor *Miller* deserved citation, much less conclusive
weight.

Without unduly elaborating the contrary decisions, we might
note that in 1955, the Fifth Circuit held that a married couple had
no authority to consent to the search of their own garage when it
was occupied by the woman's mother.[28] Certainly a homeowner
should have a greater interest in clearing stolen property from a

garage than a college would have in dormitory rooms that were never even used by the administration.

The decisions contrary to *Moore* reflect a sensitive recognition that fictions of control, possession, ownership, and agency do not repeal the Fourth Amendment.[29] By the same token, fictions about the need for "law and order" on the campus and in the dormitory should not cause one to lose sight of the higher law and justice embodied in the United States Constitution. What has been said about the *Moore* decision applies with equal force to other cases involving search of student lockers, consent by roommates, and the like.

The Student's Personal Autonomy

Educational institutions are said to exist primarily to educate the minds of young people. Nonetheless, educators from high school to college have shown inordinate interest in the length of student hair, their mode of dress, and other aspects of what can be denominated as personal autonomy. Many educators are wielding barbers' shears to trim the locks of anyone who resembles Charles Evans Hughes, Albert Einstein, or Ringo Starr.

The earliest lower-court decisions upheld the concept of school power to control student dress, and one case sustained a high school rule outlawing the use of talcum powder.[30] In one instance, however, high school students were vindicated for refusing to wear graduation gowns which reeked of fumigants.[31] The latter case would seem close to a nineteenth-century California decision that a sheriff may not sever the plaited queue of a Chinese accused,[32] a practice then viewed as cruel and unusual punishment because of its religious implications. A shorn Chinese, by tradition, would be barred from life after death.

The year 1969 saw a judicial turnabout. Leading federal judges, one after another, found varying grounds to reinstate students suspended for having long hair, in belated recognition that this mode of personal expression does not interfere with schoolwork. By the middle of 1970, twelve federal district courts[33] and the United States Courts of Appeals for the First and Seventh Circuits[34] had recognized hair style as a protected constitutional right, subject to abridgment only upon a showing of compelling justification.

Such justification might be gross uncleanliness, but not the adverse reaction of intolerant contemporaries. In a few districts, however, long-haired students may still be unable to obtain judicial relief.

Beyond the question of hair, beards, and talcum powder are more fundamental problems of the student's dignity and autonomy. The unresolved issue which most clearly stands out is the suspension or expulsion of girls, both married and single, who become pregnant. To exclude these girls from educational opportunity is a discrimination which has no basis other than the psychological reaction of other students and school staff to conduct which a decreasing minority decries as "immoral." This is a cruel response to a situation in which the unwed girl needs education and sympathy more than ever before. A few courts are beginning to recognize that there is no reason to exclude pregnant girls from school, and this trend is likely to continue.[35]

The Student and Academic Due Process

The student's right to a full, fair, and impartial hearing prior to suspension for a semester or more is a further consideration of special interest. In this sphere the Supreme Court has not spoken. However, the principles approved in *Dixon v. Alabama Board of Education*[36] have been widely followed at both the college and the high school level. In *Dixon* the Fifth Circuit set out the following guidelines:

> [T]he student should be given the names of the witnesses against him and an oral or written report on the facts to which each witness testifies. He should also be given the opportunity to present to the Board, or at least to an administrative official of the college, his own defense against the charges and to produce either oral testimony or written affidavits of witnesses in his behalf. If the hearing is not before the Board directly, the results and findings of the hearing should be presented in a report open to the student's inspection. If these rudimentary elements of fair play are followed in a case of misconduct of this particular type, we feel that the requirements of due process of law will have been fulfilled.

This much has now been *universally* accepted in subsequent litigation. Controversy continues, however, over temporary suspension, the rights of confrontation and cross-examination, the right to utilize retained counsel, and the elimination of inherent bias from the judging body.

Dixon seemed to imply that the hearing must *precede* disciplinary action. This subsequently became the explicit holding of a Wisconsin case.[37]

Dixon realized that facts might be "easily colored by the point of view of the witnesses," but nonetheless implied that an opportunity to confront and question those witnesses might not be required. *Esteban v. Central Missouri State College*[38] went on to hold that confrontation and cross-examination by the student were required in order to ensure that evidence would not go unchallenged.

On the right to utilize retained counsel, *Dixon* was silent, but it has since been held that the right is constitutionally mandated.[39]

Bias in the disciplinary panel was not at issue in *Dixon,* and remains a troublesome question. One case stated that bias could be presumed from a disciplinary committee member's prior involvement in viewing or investigating the facts.[40] This has been the rule generally in administrative proceedings. Other courts, however, particularly the Sixth Circuit,[41] passed with little comment over bias which would have been striking if, for example, the Securities and Exchange Commission had been the adjudicating body.

Many of these administrative due process questions have been resolved by the Supreme Court's 1970 decision in *Goldberg v. Kelly.*[42] That case held that the rights to have notice, retain counsel, present argument, confront and cross-examine witnesses, and demand a reasoned decision were required in hearings *prior to* termination of welfare benefits. Termination of the opportunity to attend school would also seem a penalty requiring similar ingredients of procedural due process.

Finally, there are other procedural due process rights which may come into play through future litigation. In particular, the privilege against compulsory self-incrimination has been given full scope in other administrative areas, such as a noted disbarment case.[43] Where student conduct might also have been of a potentially incriminatory character, this Fifth Amendment right may be invoked at the disciplinary hearing. One student case has recognized the right; another has refused to do so.[44]

Student Rights at Private Institutions

Much of what has gone before may apply only to students in public, fully tax-supported institutions. The full panoply of students' *constitutional* rights may not apply in "private" institutions at all. There is ample legal theory to the contrary, but courts have faced this issue in circumstances which led them to reach an adverse conclusion.

"Public" institutions must adhere to constitutional norms because officials are clothed with the power of the state government doing the business of the state "under color of state law." But officials at "private" institutions are often neither subsidized, appointed, nor controlled by government.

The epitome of "privateness" would be a small kindergarten, fully supported by private donations and fees, and conducted in the home of its sole "teacher." Could one lightly maintain that the student at such a kindergarten could claim that the Fourteenth Amendment governed each and every act of his teacher? Hardly. The relationship there must be governed by the principles of private law, not public law.

At the other end of the spectrum, however, is the more typical "private" college. It is a mammoth corporation. Its buildings were made possible largely by low-interest government loans. Students there receive many scholarships, loans, and research grants directly from the state and federal governments. Faculty also receive government grants, and may often claim the protection of a state tenure law. State accrediting agencies require certain standards of this university. State regents have a power of "visitation." Government subsidies may even account for one-third to one-half of its annual operating budget. It may save tens of thousands, even millions of dollars annually because of government tax exemptions and free municipal services. Degrees from this college are recognized by state and federal governments for a variety of purposes. It does the same job as the state university. Must it live up to the minimum standards of the Constitution? Perhaps.

Ultimately, the question is one of degree. Recent decisions by federal courts have been divided on applying First and Fourteenth Amendment standards to large private universities.[45] Scholarly commentary and earlier federal decisions have leaned in the other direction, particularly where racial discrimination was involved.[46]

While federal courts have no monopoly on virtue, their role in enforcing federal constitutional rights, aided by life tenure which the founders considered a meaningful safeguard, has been of no small significance. Litigants will thus continue to seek a federal forum in student cases, and to do so must allege infringement of federal constitutional rights. They should stress each and every aspect of government involvement.

Students also should assert state claims which may be cognizable under the federal court's so-called pendent jurisdiction. The state claims can be cast in the language of contractual and fiduciary relationships. Students may contend that they lack equal bargaining power; hence the contract must be construed in their favor. Similarly, they may assert that they are the beneficiaries of a trust relationship which requires the utmost in fair treatment.[47] Neither of these theories has the comprehensive, unified character of the Bill of Rights. Nevertheless, they may be of use in special situations where a private university attempts to justify particularly unfair actions on the basis of a sweeping college catalogue provision.

CONCLUSION

Social critics frequently remark that the level of civilization in a given society is measured by how well it treats its aged, its poor, its ethnic minorities, its women, prisoners, mental patients, and other underprivileged groups. One might add students to this list. Students' rights vis-à-vis the administrators of educational institutions are weaker today than at the dawn of the medieval Western university. The corporate university or school board grants students no voting power. The gains of students have come from court decrees, negotiations of undue length, and the use of force. Future increases are most likely to come about in the same way.

Although this essay has outlined the relevant legal theory in some of the most important spheres of student rights, it should be recognized that courts are ill-equipped to deal with large-scale denials of citizens' rights, including those of students. Moreover, students generally have neither adequate funds nor sufficient legal talent available to aid them in other than a hit-and-miss fashion. Changes must come about by the organized, well-planned action of students themselves and of their supporters. These changes can take place in only one college and one school at a time.

The coming decades are likely to see great changes in students' rights with a potentially significant impact on education at all levels. As these changes transpire, many courts will be called upon to enforce particular constitutional, statutory, fiduciary, and contractual rights of individual students. Perhaps it is true, as Judge Learned Hand wrote, that "[l]iberty lies in the hearts of men and women; when it dies there, no constitution, no law, no court can save it; no constitution, no law, no court can even do much to help it."[48] Yet courts can hasten or delay the death of liberty. They can offer moral leadership in a stagnant society, or they can choose to sit pat. One lesson of the *School Desegregation Cases,* from the "deliberate speed" of 1954 to "immediate desegregation" in 1969, is that courts can make a large difference if only they will.

NOTES

1. *Registers of the Chancellor's Court, discussed in* 1 C. Mallet, *A History of the University of Oxford: The Mediaeval University* 48 (1924).

2. Commonwealth *ex rel.* Hill v. McCauley, 3 Pa. County Ct. 77 (Cumberland County 1887).

3. *See, e.g.,* Baltimore Univ. v. Colton, 98 Md. 623, 57 A. 14 (1904).

4. These included the American Association of University Professors, the United States National Student Association, the Association of American Colleges, the National Association of Student Personnel Administrators, and the National Association of Women Deans and Counselors.

5. *See, e.g.,* Wright, "The Constitution on the Campus," 22 *Vanderbilt Law Review* 1027 (1969); Goldstein, "The Scope and Sources of School Board Authority: A Nonconstitutional Analysis," 117 *University of Pennsylvania Law Review* 373 (1969); Van Alstyne, "The Student as University Resident," 45 *Denver Law Journal* 582 (1968).

6. West Virginia Bd. of Educ. v. Barnette, 319 U.S. 624, 633 (1943), *overruling* Minersville School Dist. v. Gobitis, 310 U.S. 586 (1940). Emphasis added.

7. 393 U.S. 503 (1969).

8. *See, e.g.,* Butts v. Dallas Independent School Dist., 306 F. Supp. 488 (N.D. Tex. 1969), for an extreme example.

9. *See, e.g.,* Brooks v. Auburn Univ., 412 F.2d 1171 (5th Cir. 1969).

10. 273 F. Supp. 613 (M.D. Ala. 1967), *vacated as moot,* 402 F.2d 515 (5th Cir. 1968) (student transferred to another institution). *See also* Vought v. Van Buren Pub. Schools, 306 F. Supp. 1388 (E.D. Mich. 1969); Antonelli v. Hammond, 308 F. Supp. 1329 (D. Mass. 1970).

11. 299 F. Supp. 102 (S.D.N.Y. 1969). *See also* Lee v. Board of Regents, 306 F. Supp. 1097 (W.D. Wis. 1969).

12. 385 F.2d 151 (3d Cir. 1967), *cert. denied,* 390 U.S. 920 (1968).

13. A lower state court decision in New York, however, ruled that for a student newspaper to criticize religion was a violation of the establishment clause. Panarella v. Birenbaum, 60 Misc. 2d 95, 302 N.Y.S.2d 427 (Sup. Ct. 1969). The case is almost surely in error, and has been appealed.

14. Hammond v. South Carolina State College, 272 F. Supp. 947 (D.S.C. 1967).

15. *Id.* at 948. However, the requirement that university officials be "notified" forty-eight hours in advance was sustained in Powe v. Miles, 407 F.2d 73, 84 (2d Cir. 1968).

16. Wong v. Hayakawa, No. 50983 (N.D. Cal. April 24, 1969) (unreported).

17. Saunders v. VPI, 417 F.2d 1127 (4th Cir. 1969); Scoggin v. Lincoln Univ., 291 F. Supp. 161 (W.D. Mo. 1968).

18. Soglin v. Kauffman, 418 F.2d 163 (7th Cir. 1969); *contra,* Esteban v. Central Missouri State College, 415 F.2d 1077 (8th Cir. 1969), *cert. denied,* 398 U.S. 965 (1970). *See generally* Note, "Uncertainty in College Disciplinary Regulations," 29 *Ohio State Law Journal* 1023 (1968).

19. Notes, 17 *Kansas Law Review* 512 (1969); 3 *Georgia Law Review* 426 (1969); 4 *University of San Francisco Law Review* 49 (1969); 9 *Santa Clara Lawyer* 143 (1968).

20. 284 F. Supp. 725, 729–31 (M.D. Ala. 1968).

21. Camara v. Municipal Court, 387 U.S. 523, 528 (1967).

22. Katz v. United States, 389 U.S. 347, 351, 359 (1967).

23. 387 U.S. at 529, *quoting* Johnson v. United States, 333 U.S. 10, 14 (1948).

24. 284 F. Supp. at 730.

25. *Ibid.* (emphasis added).

26. 335 F.2d 652 (4th Cir. 1964).

27. 261 F. Supp. 442 (D. Del. 1966).

28. Holzhey v. United States, 223 F.2d 823 (5th Cir. 1955).

29. We might also recall the Supreme Court cases disallowing consent to searches by hotel clerks, Stoner v. California, 376 U.S. 483 (1964), and landlords, Chapman v. United States, 365 U.S. 610 (1961), neither of which was cited by the Court in *Moore.*

30. Pugsley v. Sellmeyer, 158 Ark. 247, 250 S.W. 538 (1923).

31. Valentine v. Independent School Dist., 187 Iowa 555, 174 N.W. 334 (1919).

32. Ho Ah Kow v. Nunan, 12 Fed. Cas. 252 (No. 6546) (C.C.D. Cal. 1879).

33. *See, e.g.,* Richards v. Thurston, 304 F. Supp. 449 (D. Mass. 1969), *aff'd,* 424 F.2d 1281 (1st Cir. 1970).

34. Breen v. Kahl, 419 F.2d 1034 (7th Cir. 1969), *cert. denied,* 398 U.S. 937 (1970.) *See generally* Note, 42 *Southern California Law Review* 126 (1969); Note, 17 *Journal of Public Law* 151 (1968); Comment, 20 *Alabama Law Review* 104 (1967).

35. The authorities are reviewed extensively in Goldstein, *supra* note 5.

36. 294 F.2d 150, 159 (5th Cir.), *cert. denied,* 368 U.S. 510 (1961).

37. Stricklin v. Regents of Univ. of Wisconsin, 297 F. Supp. 416 (W.D. Wis. 1969), *appeal dismissed as moot,* 420 F.2d 1257 (7th Cir. 1970).

38. 415 F.2d 1077 (8th Cir. 1969), *cert. denied,* 398 U.S. 965 (1970).

39. French v. Bashful, 303 F. Supp. 1333 (E.D. La. 1969).

40. Wasson v. Trowbridge, 382 F.2d 807 (2d Cir. 1967).

41. *See* Jones v. State Bd. of Educ., 407 F.2d 834 (6th Cir. 1969), *cert. dismissed,* 397 U.S. 31 (1970).

42. 397 U.S. 254 (1970).

43. Spevack v. Klein, 385 U.S. 511 (1967).

44. *See* Goldwyn v. Allen, 54 Misc. 2d 94, 281 N.Y.S.2d 899 (Sup. Ct. 1967); Furutani v. Ewigleben, 297 F. Supp. 1163 (N.D. Cal. 1969).

45. *Compare* Coleman v. Wagner College, — F.2d —, No. 34869 (2d Cir. June 22, 1970); Powe v. Miles, 407 F.2d 73 (2d Cir. 1968), *and* Browns v. Mitchell, 409 F.2d 593 (10th Cir. 1969), *with* Brown v. Strickler, 422 F.2d 1000 (6th Cir. 1970).

46. *See generally* Friendly, "The Dartmouth College Case and the Public-Private Penumbra," 12 *Texas Quarterly*, No. 2, at 9 (1969); Note, "Student Due Process in the Private University: The State Action Doctrine," 20 *Syracuse Law Review* 911 (1969).

47. For an extensive examination of the fiduciary approach, see Goldman, "The University and the Liberty of Its Students—a Fiduciary Theory," 54 *Kentucky Law Journal* 643 (1969).

48. L. Hand, *The Spirit of Liberty* 144 (I. Dilliard ed. 1959).

THE RIGHTS OF
UNIONS AND
UNION MEMBERS

CLYDE W. SUMMERS

CONSCIENTIOUS OBJECTORS, POLITICAL DISSENTERS, and labor unions—these were the bruised and embattled groups when the American Civil Liberties Union was born. Unions were seen as a part of the workers' age-long struggle to be free, an expression of the demand for manhood, and an instrument of industrial democracy. Therefore, protection of the rights of labor unions and the civil liberties of union members became the central concern of the ACLU in the 1920's. Sweeping injunctions were condemned as denying the right of assembly and the right to strike; legal restrictions on union organizers and pickets were opposed as curbing freedom of speech; and the prosecutions of union leaders on flimsy evidence was challenged for denial of a fair trial.

These battles of the 1920's have now been largely won; in most parts of the country, unions have become accepted parts of the established system. Although remnants of the old issues remain, the basic framework for defining the rights of unions and their members has changed fundamentally. The dominant issues today are of a wholly different order, and are much less susceptible to satisfying answers.

Today, the rights of unions and their members, and the diffi-

Clyde W. Summers is Garver Professor of Law at Yale Law School, a member of the National Academy of Arbitrators and the International Society of Labor Law and Social Legislation, and former Chairman of the New York Governor's Commission on Improper Union-Management Practices. He has written many articles on labor law.

cult problems they present, have three marked characteristics which sharply distinguish them from traditional civil liberties issues. First, the significant rights are not defined in constitutional but in statutory terms; reliance is placed not upon the judicial shield but upon the legislative sword. The rights of unions are affirmatively enforced by the National Labor Relations Act of 1935, and the "Bill of Rights" for union members is statutorily defined in the Labor-Management Reporting and Disclosure Act of 1959. The crucial civil liberties questions concern not what the Constitution commands but whether the statutes are adequate; and answers cannot be sought in legal or historical analysis but must be sought in moral and practical judgment.

Second, the protection of these rights guards primarily against private action, not public action; exercise of these rights is to be free from encroachments by economic power as well as governmental power. The union's right to organize runs not only against legal restraints but also against employer action; the union member's speech on behalf of his union is not punishable by the private economic sanction of discharge; and his speech criticizing union officers is not punishable by the private sanction of expulsion from the union. The difficult civil liberties questions concern not what rights unions and union members should have against government, but what rights they should have against individuals and private groups.

Third, legal recognition of unions and establishment of collective bargaining create a system of industrial government with a whole range of new civil liberties questions as to the rights of the individual within that system. What rights shall he have to equal treatment under the governing rules of the collective agreement? What freedom shall he have to dissent from union policies? What voice shall he have in choosing union officers? And what constitutes due process in union trial procedures? Although these questions seem to be simple analogues of traditional civil liberties issues, they have an important added dimension. Protection of these individual rights requires encroachment on the freedom of collective bargaining and the rights of unions to self-government. The rights of the individual are gained only at the expense of curtailing the rights of unions.

Because of these three characteristics, the civil liberties issues confronted here are precursors of problems which must be of central concern in the future—the protection of personal freedom

within institutions of private power. Labor law provides an illu-
minating example of the problems of reconciling individual rights
with collective power, and the effort to design, through deliberate
legislative and administrative action, methods of increasing personal freedom within the institutional structures. The rights placed
in issue range from freedom of assembly to procedural due process,
and the devices relied upon range from detailed legal intervention
to reliance on countervailing power. The controlling legal rules
which have evolved are too complex to describe in detail, and the
issues too numerous to probe meaningfully within the limits of
this essay. The most that can be done here is to sketch an outline
which will give some glimpse of the nature and complexity of the
problems.

FREEDOM OF ASSOCIATION AND THE RIGHT TO ORGANIZE

The right to form and join unions has long been recognized as a
part of freedom of assembly protected against governmental restraints by the First Amendment.[1] Although an aura of doubt has
surrounded the question whether this constitutional protection
extended equally to public employees, these doubts have now been
largely dispelled by decisions of lower federal courts which have
invalidated state laws prohibiting policemen and firemen from
joining a national union[2] and which have upheld suits brought
under the Civil Rights Act of 1871 by teachers who were discharged
for joining the American Federation of Teachers.[3] "Union membership is protected by the right of association under the First and
Fourteenth Amendments," the courts agreed.[4] Public employment
could not be conditioned on the surrender of this constitutional
right, nor does the state interest in preventing strikes justify destroying the employees' right of association in a labor union.

The constitutional right of association, however, protects little
more than the union's shell of existence; it does not guarantee the
union any freedom to function as a labor organization.[5] As the
courts explicitly acknowledged in the public employee cases, the
right of association does not include the right of the union to strike
or picket, to act as a collective bargaining representative, or even
to make binding collective agreements. If unions seek to act as
bargaining representatives, then the Constitution guarantees no

freedom from legal controls over their internal affairs. Unions may be barred from statutory rights and procedures because the members have elected officers who refuse to sign non-Communist affidavits;[6] or barred from collecting dues because officers have once been convicted of a crime;[7] and unions may be prohibited from acting as bargaining representatives because supervisors have been admitted to membership.[8] Statutory provisions now regulate the amount of union dues and the procedures for assessing them; the purposes for which union monies may be spent and the form of financial accounting to the members; and the qualifications of union officers along with the manner of electing them. None of these statutory restrictions has been seriously challenged as violating the constitutional right of association. The basic values which underlie this and other constitutional rights have, of course, been given weight in designing the statutes, but this only emphasizes that the rights are shaped more by statutory judgments than by constitutional prohibitions.

Statutory recognition of the right of association was expressed by words of near-constitutional majesty in Section 7 of the Wagner Act:

> Employees shall have the right to self-organization, to form, join, or assist labor organizations, to bargain collectively through representatives of their own choosing, and to engage in other concerted activities for the purpose of collective bargaining or other mutual aid and protection.

These words, implemented by Section 8, proscribing unfair labor practices, affirmatively protected not only the union's right to exist but its right to function as a bargaining representative. Employees were protected against employer discrimination for joining unions or engaging in organizational activities; unions were protected against employer domination or control; employers were required to recognize the majority union as the representative of their employees; and the right to strike or picket was protected against hostile employer action. None of these rights are absolutes—some of the limitations will be sketched in later sections—but the crucial point here is that the statutory right of association goes far beyond the constitutional right; the statute provides the substance to fill the constitutional shell.

The right of association is commonly expressed as one belonging to the union, but the first word of Section 7 reminds us that this is an individual right belonging basically to "employees" and only derivatively to the union. This distinction becomes critical when the desires of the union and the individual clash, for as an individual right, the right to associate includes the right not to associate. Any doubts as to the nature of the rights created by Section 7 were dispelled in 1947 when the Taft-Hartley Act made explicit the negative right by adding to Section 7 the words, "and shall have the right to refrain from any or all such activities," and Sections 8(b)(1) and 8(b)(2) were added protecting Section 7 rights from union action.

The individual's right not to associate, however, is far from absolute, for it is qualified in certain respects by the union's collective power. Two limitations cut directly into the individual's freedom of association. First, and most fundamental, Section 9 of the National Labor Relations Act provides that the union selected by the majority of the employees in a bargaining unit shall be the exclusive representative of all employees in the unit. Although the individual is not required by law to join the majority union, he cannot bargain for himself or through any other union; he is compelled to accept the majority union as his representative.[9] Because Section 9 cuts so deeply into freedom of association, it spawns a wide range of issues which require weighing the rights of the individual against the needs of the union and the collective bargaining process.

Union security clauses cut even more directly into freedom of association, but the cut is not so deep because of the accommodation made in Taft-Hartley between the individual's right and the majority union's need. Under Section 8(a)(3) the individual cannot be required to join the union, obey union rules, or participate in union affairs, but he can be required to tender to the union regular dues and initiation fees. His right not to associate is reduced only to the extent that he can be required to contribute financially to the majority union. This meets the union's primary need for financial support of its bargaining function by requiring all those whom the union represents to share the costs of that representation.[10]

Freedom of association is the core of statutory protection for the rights of unions and individual employees; much of what follows is an elaboration of that basic statutory right. Freedom of association, however, runs against other rights and interests of both employers and unions; because of this, the recurring problem is reconciling or accommodating the competing claims.

Union organizing drives frequently trigger a battle of words, or more than words, to influence employees in the exercise of their right of association. If the employer remains neutral, free speech issues remain simple, even though two unions are locked in bitter struggle.[11] Virulent campaign literature can raise constitutional questions as to reach of libel actions to curb such speech, but the Supreme Court has declared that the standards enunciated in *New York Times Co. v. Sullivan*[12] should be applied because the policy of the National Labor Relations Act is to encourage free debate in labor disputes.[13] Damages can be recovered "only for defamatory statements published with knowledge of their falsity or with reckless disregard of whether they are true or false," and actual damages must be proved.

When the employer enters the contest, however, seeking to persuade the employees not to join or vote for the union, a wholly new dimension is added, for he occupies a special position of power over the employees whose right of association is at stake. He controls their employment, and he also controls the workplace where organizing activities are normally most convenient and effective. This raises two distinct, though related, problems. To what extent does his position of economic control affect his freedom to speak to his employees? To what extent can he use his control to exclude union organizational activities from the workplace?

Employer Freedom of Speech—Persuasion and Job Control

The employer clearly has a constitutional right to make known to his employees facts and opinions which will influence their decision concerning union representation.[14] He has a major stake in that decision; but what is more important, the employees are entitled to know all points of view in order to exercise fully their freedom of association. The employer, however, has no constitutional right to use his control over their jobs as an instrument of coercion, and the National Labor Relations Act affirmatively protects the employee's freedom of choice from employer economic restraint and coercion. The employer may inform but he may not threaten; or in the words of Section 8(c), "The expressing of any views . . . shall not constitute or be evidence of an unfair labor practice . . . if such expression contains no threat of reprisal or force or promise of benefit."

The line between protected speech and prohibited coercion is much easier to articulate than to apply in concrete cases. Because the employer controls his employees' livelihood, his words which on their face are an appeal to reason may carry an unspoken coercive thrust, and that thrust may be blunted little, if at all, by his disavowals of an intent to retaliate. Probing the employer's unspoken purpose and the employees' nearly unconscious response is nearly impossible in a legal proceeding. More important, use of such subtle considerations raises serious questions when the issue at stake is determination of the limits of freedom of speech.

The solution of the National Labor Relations Board has been to look almost entirely at the face value of the words used. Even so, the line is difficult to draw, for the employer may "predict" that if the union wins, strikes for higher wages will compel him to move his plant to an area where wages are lower;[15] he may "inform" the employees about other plants which have closed because they could not afford union wages;[16] or he may "report" to his employees that customers have stated that if the plant becomes unionized, they will rely on other suppliers.[17] Neither the Board nor the appellate courts have been able to draw a clear line between "thinly veiled threats of reprisals" and statements of "harsh economic facts" beyond the employer's control.[18] The difficulty in drawing the line is inherent in the problem of balancing freedom of speech and freedom of association in the economic context of the employer-employee relationship. An uncertain line, however, surely seems preferable to no line at all, for the employer should neither be wholly silenced nor wholly unrestrained. A balance must be struck, and that which has been struck does not allow either freedom to override the other entirely.

Free Speech and Valid Elections

Quite different questions are raised by the Board's decision that a noncoercive speech, though not an unfair labor practice, may invalidate a representative election. The Board insists that the wording of Section 8(a) does not alter the Board's responsibility for conducting elections under conditions which "enable employees to register a free and untrammeled choice for or against a bargaining representative." Thus the Board held that although it was not an unfair labor practice for an employer to call employees into the office in small groups and read them a speech disparaging the union officials and urging the employees to vote against the union, the election should be set aside because the conduct was "so glaring that it is almost certain to have impaired employees' freedom of choice."[19] Similarly, an anti-union "captive audience" speech within twenty-four hours before an election, by its "last minute timing would interfere with that sober and thoughtful choice which a free election is designed to reflect."[20]

Carrying its logic another long step, the Board invalidated an election because the employer attacked the union for "race-mixing." The employees could be given "a temperate, factually correct statement" of the union's position on integration because it was germane to the employees' choice, but neither the employer nor the union could "deliberately seek to overstress and exacerbate racial feelings by irrelevant and inflammatory appeals."[21] Further, misrepresentation of material facts by either the employer or the union, if made so shortly before an election that the other cannot effectively reply, will cause the election to be set aside.[22]

The Board's rationale is that employees are entitled to know all relevant facts and opinions so that they can intelligently exercise their freedom of choice; but those facts and opinions cannot be expressed under such conditions, at such times, or in such form as to "make impossible a sober, reasoned and informed choice." However sweetly reasonable one finds the Board's logic, it proceeds from different premises than the Supreme Court's declaration in *Linn v. Plant Guards,* that "free debate on issues dividing labor and management '. . . should be uninhibited, robust and wide-open and . . . may well include vehement, caustic, and sometimes unpleasantly sharp attacks.' "[23] The Board has thus plunged deeply into policing both the tenor and the truth of pre-election statements, unwilling to rely upon the open market of discussion. Underneath is an assumption, both provocative and challenging, that in the private institutional structure, the marketplace is so constricted and controlled that open discussion is not enough, that the underlying values of free speech call for safeguards to protect informed and reasoned choice. This raises not only serious constitutional issues, as yet untested, but also more fundamental issues of broader concern as to how the purposes of free speech can be achieved when the channels of communication are limited and truth may not catch up with falsehood.

Union Free Speech—Right of Access[24]

When the unions seek to use the employer's workplace as a forum for persuading employees to join, freedom of speech and freedom of association combine, but they run against another important interest—the employer's property right in the premises, which normally includes the right to control access to and activities on the premises. On both sides, these rights may be of fundamental practical importance. The employer's premises may be the most effective place for the union to reach employees, but organizing activities can seriously impede or disrupt the employer's business.

The efforts to accommodate these competing interests have thus far led to few clearly settled rules and no solidly settled principles. Variant combinations of circumstances have produced a complex of cases which are not always consistent, but through these cases have seemed to run two minimal union rights. First, for employees—as contrasted with outside organizers—the employer's premises are a natural and appropriate place to persuade other employees to join or not join unions; the employer can prohibit employees from engaging in union solicitation during nonworking time, such as lunch hour and rest breaks, only when he can show that such prohibition is necessary to maintain production or discipline. Second, the union has a right to reasonable access to the employees; the employer cannot exclude outside organizers or enforce a broad no-solicitation rule if other practical channels of communication are not available.[25]

The minimal right of reasonable access is now being supplanted by a principle of equal access to channels of communication. The Supreme Court has suggested that a crucial consideration is "whether the employer's conduct to any considerable degree created an imbalance in the opportunities for organizational communication." The employer's no-solicitation rules are valid if the union's "opportunities for effectively reaching the employees with a pro-union message . . . are at least as great as the employer's ability to promote the legally authorized expression of his anti-union views."[26] Although union solicitation can be prohibited on the selling floor of a department store, if the employer makes anti-union speeches to his employees on company property, the union must be given an equal opportunity to make pro-union speeches in order to correct the "glaring imbalance in opportunities for organizational communications."[27] Also, the goal of "encouraging an informed electorate" justifies requiring an employer to provide the union with the names and addresses of all employees so as to ensure the union an equal opportunity to reach the employees through the mails.[28]

The underlying rationale is much like that used by the Board to invalidate elections. The fundamental right at stake is the employees' freedom of association, and the rights of the employer and the union are to be tailored so as to promote the employees' making a fully informed, thoughtful, and sober choice, free from distortions and imbalances of advocacy. The rationale here, however, does not lead to confining or censoring speech in the name of freedom of association, for when the union seeks equal opportunity to communicate with the employees, freedom of association is furthered by enlarging freedom of speech within the institutional structure. The principle of equal access does encroach on the employer's property rights, but he is still able to control organizational activities so far as necessary in practical terms to carry on his business. Basic personal freedoms are protected and promoted by relatively minor limitations on economic power.

THE RIGHT TO STRIKE AND THE RIGHT TO PICKET

Despite the passionate assertions of many unionists and civil libertarians that there is a constitutional right to strike, the path of the law has not led in that direction. The Thirteenth Amendment prohibits involuntary servitude, and this protects a person who refuses individually to work; but it does not protect groups of employees who refuse in concert to work.[29]

However, as collective bargaining has extended to public employees, denial of their right to strike has become a civil liberties issue, if not a constitutional one. One argument is that since other employees have the right to strike, denial of this right to public employees is discriminatory, particularly as to those public employees who are not performing critical services. A second argument is that the right to strike cannot be barred unless some substitute such as arbitration is provided for determining terms and conditions of employment. The premise is that confining an employee to individual bargaining is a violation of his civil liberties, even when that employer is the government. These arguments have thus far gained neither judicial nor legislative acceptance.

Statutory protection of the right to strike in the private sector is stated in the unqualified words of Section 7, that "Employees shall have the right . . . to engage in other concerted activities for the purposes of collective bargaining or other mutual aid or protection." But the statute then chops away that right with qualifications. Strikes creating "national emergencies" can be and are prohibited for eighty days.[30] Strikes to capture work jurisdiction from another union,[31] or to enforce demands which are not mandatory subjects of bargaining, are unfair labor practices;[32] and ingenious forms of partial strike action such as the "hiccup" and "checkerboard" strikes make the strikers vulnerable to discharge.[33] Strikes against secondary employers or refusal to work on "unfair" materials brings down upon the union the legal wrath of injunctions, suits for damages, and unfair labor practice orders.[34]

Even though the strike is entirely legal, it is only thinly protected against employer economic action. The employer cannot flatly discharge those who strike, but he can hire replacements to continue operations and then refuse to take back the strikers who have been replaced.[35] Where potential replacements are available, the right to strike is only an open door to unemployment.

The right to strike is primarily a union right almost wholly submerging the individual. The very presence of a majority union strips minority groups of employees of the right to strike on their own; Section 9(a) makes the majority union the exclusive representative not only for bargaining but for deciding on concerted activities. Thus, strikes called by minority groups to protest delays in negotiations,[36] racial discrimination by the employer,[37] or the inadequacy of the employer's "final offer"[38] without first obtaining the sanction of the majority union have been held not protected by Section 7. The orderly process of bargaining, it is said, requires that employees make their demands through the union and be bound by its decision as to whether or not to strike.[39]

The union may also deprive employees of their right not to strike. Union members who cross picket lines to work during a strike may not only be expelled from the union, but they may also be fined and then sued by the union for the amount of the fine. The individual's right is overridden by the union's need for control over its members so as to strengthen its ability to make the strike effective.[40] The individual must find his freedom by avoiding becoming a member of the union or resigning his membership prior to the strike. Under a valid union security agreement, this is legally possible but scarcely practical, except for the most cautious and well-informed employees.

The right to picket, as contrasted with the right to strike, has constitutional roots, though of uncertain vitality. In 1940, in *Thornhill v. Alabama*,[41] the Supreme Court struck down a statute prohibiting all picketing with the declaration, "the dissemination of information concerning the facts of a labor dispute must be regarded as within that area of free discussion that is guaranteed by the Constitution." Peaceful picketing was constitutionally protected as the workingman's means of communication. For four years the picketing–free speech doctrine flowered,[42] though with visible fragility,[43] but within ten years it had shriveled to little more than a barren stalk.[44] Finally, in 1957, in *Teamsters Union v. Vogt*,[45] this doctrine was ceremoniously buried by the Court, which summarized the intervening decisions as holding that states, in enforcing a valid public policy, "could constitutionally enjoin peaceful picketing aimed at preventing effectuation of that policy." The state policy of protecting employees' freedom of association justified enjoining organizational picketing which had as its purpose to coerce the employer to put pressure on his employees to join the union.

Despite these later decisions, the doctrine that picketing is specially protected as a form of speech is not entirely dead. In 1964, in the *Washington Apple Case*,[46] the Supreme Court narrowly construed the Section 8(b)(4) prohibitions on consumer picketing at a secondary site. The Court stated that because of a "concern that a broad ban against peaceful picketing might collide with the guarantees of the First Amendment," picketing will not be outlawed "unless there is the clearest indication in the legislative history that Congress intended to do so as regards the particular ends of the picketing under review." With this presumption in favor of picketing, the Court refused to read a not so ambiguous proviso as prohibiting a union from picketing a supermarket if the signs induced customers only to stop buying apples packed by employees who were on strike. Constitutional protection of picketing was explicitly reaffirmed in 1968. In *Amalgamated Food Employees, Local 590 v. Logan Valley Plaza, Inc.*,[47] the Court held that picketing in the parking lot and on the sidewalk of a shopping plaza could not be enjoined as trespassing. Although privately owned, the shopping plaza was open to the general public and an appropriate place for the exercise of First Amendment rights. The state might limit picketing because of its purpose or the manner in which it was conducted, but a general ban on all picketing violates the First Amendment. We are now back to *Thornhill v. Alabama,* though with little likelihood that the Court will repeat the cycle. The constitutional value in picketing will be more important in shaping the interpretation of statutes than in striking them down.

The right to picket, like the right to strike, is statutorily protected by Section 7, for it is a "concerted activity . . . for mutual aid and protection," but it is subject to even more extensive and complex restrictions. Section 8(b)(4) regulating secondary boycotts severely limits the use of picketing to persuade employees of secondary employers to refuse to work, and prohibits much, though not all, use of picketing to persuade customers of secondary employers to refuse to trade. Section 8(b)(7) curtails the use of even primary picketing to persuade employees to join the union.

The statutory protection and the statutory limitations seem to proceed from the premise that picketing, like a strike, is an instrument of economic pressure. However, where the purpose of picketing is to persuade customers not to trade, the free speech element of the customer's right to know is added, and it is at this point that any intelligible rationale of the statute, at least as it is now interpreted, disappears. In secondary consumer picketing, the consumer's right to know is balanced against the businessman's interest in trading with a struck employer. Only by the grace of the Supreme Court is the consumer's right to know given any weight, and then only to the extent of permitting product picketing. In organizational picketing, the consumer's right to know is balanced against the employees' freedom of association, for the ultimate object of the union's pressure is not the employer but the employees. The union, by inducing consumers not to trade, undermines the employees' job security and encourages them to join the union to preserve their jobs. Here, the Board decisions have given overriding weight to the consumers' right to know, for it has read the extremely ambiguous words of Section 8(b)(7)(C) as permitting a union to engage in unlimited "informational" picketing advising the public, including consumers, that the employees are not members of the union, even though the purpose of the picketing is to force the employees to accept the union as their representative.[48] Such inconsistent and unrationalized accommodations of competing interests invite statutory or decisional reconsideration. The problem of picketing and free speech is neither dead nor resolved; we may only be beginning to understand its difficulty.

FREEDOM OF UNION POLITICAL ACTION

When Congress passed the Taft-Hartley Act in 1947, the Federal Corrupt Practices Act was amended to prohibit unions from making any "contribution or expenditure in connection with any election for federal office." This paralleled earlier restrictions on national banks and corporations. Two lines of argument were used to support these restrictions on use of union funds. First, the pooling of political funds by centers of private power unduly influences elections, makes elected officials compliant, and distorts the democratic process by submerging individual voters and making their voices ineffective. Second, dissenting union members should not be compelled to contribute to political causes with which they disagree as a price of participating in the government of their bargaining representative. Countering these arguments, it was urged that these restrictions deprive unions of their freedom of speech, a right which belongs as much to associations as to individuals. Viability of the election process requires that all channels of communication remain open and that the views of every group be known; pooling of funds is necessary if views are to be communicated to large audiences and political activity to be effective. If minorities need protection against the use of union funds for political speech-making, ways can be found without denying the majority their First Amendment rights.

The constitutional issues raised by this statute are of the first magnitude;[49] but after more than twenty years, they are still unresolved and are likely to remain so. In *United States v. CIO*,[50] the Supreme Court dismissed an indictment of union officers for distributing a union newspaper urging all union members to vote for certain candidates. The Court interpreted the statute as not reaching communications addressed solely to union members and not delivered to the public at large. In *United States v. UAW-CIO*,[51] the union was charged with having paid for television broadcasts urging the election of certain candidates for office. When the case came to the Court on a demurrer to the indictment, the Court held that the conduct charged violated the statute, but refused to rule on the constitutionality of the statute until after a full trial and conviction. The case was sent back for trial and the jury rendered a verdict of not guilty, ending the case.[52] No other cases have resulted in conviction, so no other cases have come to the Court.

Unions have adjusted their political fund-raising to avoid the statute. Since the statute applies only to expenditures out of general dues of the union membership, unions have created special funds for federal elections which are raised by soliciting voluntary contributions. General dues money is then used for other political purposes. Unions have not sought to raise new test cases, and violations are kept at low visibility. The problems of proof and the serious constitutional problems have created understandable reluctance to prosecute. Both unions and prosecutors seem content to leave the constitutional issues untested.

The Court, however, has confronted and answered the question whether, apart from this statute, an individual can be compelled to contribute to union political activities. In *International Ass'n of Machinists v. Street*,[53] individual employees on a railroad sued to enjoin enforcement of a union shop agreement because a substantial part of the money they were compelled to pay to hold their jobs was used to finance campaigns of candidates whom they opposed and to promote political causes with which they disagreed. The Court skirted the constitutional issue by taking the path of statutory construction. The primary concern of Congress in permitting the union shop was to protect the union from "free riders," but there was "a congressional concern over possible impingements on the interests of individual dissenters from union policies." The accommodation of these interests was to be achieved by permitting unions to compel all employees to share the costs of negotiating and administering collective agreements, but not permitting unions to force employees, over their objections, to support political causes which they oppose.

The restriction on political expenditures in *Machinists v. Street* is far more than that under the Corrupt Practices Act, for it reaches far beyond support of candidates in elections and includes all kinds of "political activities" advocating any "political cause." It thus apparently reaches lobbying for safety legislation, issuing brochures on tax policy, holding antiwar rallies, and publishing articles on abortion reform. Indeed, it might include almost all expenditures other than those "germane to collective bargaining."

Devising a remedy to accommodate both union and individual interests required even more judicial inventiveness than interpreting the statute. Restraining collection of all funds from those who objected to political expenditures would allow them to escape paying their share of the costs of collective bargaining; prohibiting all expenditures for disputed political purposes would prevent the majority from stating its views on political issues "which might be offensive to the First Amendment." The solution devised by the Court was to allow an individual who protested political expenditures to recover from the union that portion of his money which the union had expended for the protested purposes. The employee could object generally to all political expenditures, and the burden was on the union, which had the facts and records in its possession, to prove the proportion of dues used for political expenditures.[54]

The Court suggested that the union could budget in advance the proportion of dues to be used for political purposes and then have a simple procedure for dissenters being excused from paying this amount. The Court even pointed to the English device of establishing separate political funds and then allowing members to contract out of contributing the portion of dues going to the political fund by signing a simple form. Such internal arrangements, the Court said, would avoid prolonged and expensive litigation. Unions, however, did not rush to set up such internal arrangements which would simplify their conforming to these decisions. On the contrary, unions have largely ignored these decisions, and for the very reason the Court suggested. Litigation is prolonged and expensive, and few individuals can afford the cost of enforcing their rights, particularly against the union whose treasury is fed by their compulsory dues.

FAIR REPRESENTATION—UNION DUTY AND INDIVIDUAL RIGHTS

The basic structural principle of exclusive representation gives the majority union the power to bind individuals who are not members of the union to terms and conditions of employment which they do not want, and which may be worse than they might obtain by individual bargaining. Such regulatory power requires restraints. In *Steele v. Louisville & Nashville Railway*,[55] a union of railroad workers had negotiated a collective agreement which placed Negro employees at the bottom of the seniority list and had the effect of ultimately eliminating them from their jobs. The Supreme Court, in holding this agreement unlawful, declared:

> Congress . . . did not intend to confer plenary power upon the union to sacrifice, for the benefit of its members, rights of the minority of the craft, without imposing on it any duty to protect the minority. . . . So long as a labor union assumes to act as the statutory representative of a craft, it cannot rightly refuse to perform the duty, which is inseparable from the power of representation conferred upon it . . . to represent non-union or minority union members of the craft without hostile discrimination, fairly, impartially, and in good faith.

The union's duty of fair representation circumscribes all exercise of its bargaining power. Arbitrary discrimination against individuals or groups on bases other than race is equally prohibited,[56] and that discrimination may be found in dismissals, denial of vacations, or lower rates of pay.[57] Even the use of union bargaining power arbitrarily to injure employees outside the bargaining unit may be prohibited.[58]

Although the right to fair representation is stated in broadest terms, the effective protection given is quite restricted. *First,* the standard of fairness is vague, if not illusory, particularly when applied to the making of a new agreement. The *Steele* case recognized that the collective agreement could not establish identical terms for all employees, and that the union must be able to make variations based on "relevant differences." It went on to say that "discriminations based on race were obviously irrelevant and insidious." Later cases have not clarified or raised the standard, but rather have emphasized that the union, in negotiating an agreement, must be allowed "[a] wide range of reasonableness . . . subject always to complete good faith and honesty of purpose in the exercise of its discretion."[59] The result is that courts have been reluctant to intervene except in cases of racial discrimination. This is nearly inevitable, for the union, in negotiating agreements, represents a wide range of groups whose interests compete or conflict, and a process of exchange, compromise, and surrender is necessary to reach an agreement. The courts cannot weigh too closely the allocation of benefits among employees without disrupting the process.[60] *Second,* the legal remedies have little practical value, for the litigation is prolonged and expensive, and can be deliberately made even more so by the union.[61] Remedies are now available before the National

Labor Relations Board,[62] but their practical value is yet to be proved.

The Union's duty of fair representation extends beyond the making of the collective agreement to its administration;[63] indeed, the union's duty in processing grievances potentially has more practical substance than its duty in negotiating contracts because the individual's rights have more specific content. General practices such as the union's refusing to process grievances of Negroes,[64] acquiescing in racially discriminatory applications of contract provisions,[65] or charging nonmembers for carrying grievances to arbitration[66] clearly violate the duty of fair representation. More important, in practical terms, the union's settlement of any individual's grievance without his consent raises potential problems of fair representation.

The element which gives substance and specific content to the union's duty to process grievances is the collective agreement which creates legally enforceable contract rights in the individual employee.[67] Where the collective agreement requires enforcement only through the grievance procedure and arbitration, the individual must look to that procedure for enforcement of his rights.[68] However, if the union refuses to process the grievance or settles it without the individual's consent, then the individual can sue both the employer and the union to enforce his rights upon a showing that the union, in handling his grievance, has violated its duty of fair representation.[69]

The standard of fairness is again described with unilluminating adjectives, used in the alternative; the union violates its duty if its refusal to process the grievance is "arbitrary," "discriminatory," or "in bad faith." These words, however, take on more definite meaning here because the right at stake is the individual's contract right created by the collective agreement, and the union's duty to represent is the duty to enforce that right through the grievance procedure. The collective agreement, therefore, provides a standard for measuring the union's duty, and the "fairness" of a grievance settlement can be judged by whether it is consistent with the express and implied terms of the collective agreement. The courts need not substitute their judgment for that of the union as to what terms should be included in the collective agreement, but need insist only that the union settle grievances in accordance with general rules as established by the collective agreement.

Although the union's duty in grievance handling has not been elaborated by the courts or the Board, protection of the individual employee within the collective structure would seem to require the following: (1) Grievances cannot be settled on bases which are contrary to the clear terms of the collective agreement, for the essence of arbitrariness is failure to follow established rules and standards; (2) ambiguous contract provisions must be consistently interpreted and enforced, for settlement of similar grievances on different terms is discriminatory; (3) settlement of even doubtful grievances for improper motives such as personal hostility, political opposition, or racial prejudice constitutes bad-faith representation; (4) the union, as exclusive representative, has a fiduciary obligation to use reasonable care and diligence in investigating and processing grievances and determining their merit.

The problem here is the one pervading labor law—the accommodation of collective power and individual rights. The courts cannot effectively oversee the union's negotiation of an agreement without invading deeply the freedom of the union to represent employees in ordering terms and conditions of employment. However, this very freedom of the union to establish the governing rules heavily obligates the union to follow those rules, and this is an obligation which the courts can enforce without invading the union's function. By insisting on evenhanded application of general rules, the courts can give the individual significant protection against the abusive use of power or the arbitrariness of vagrant discretion.

THE RIGHT TO A DEMOCRATIC UNION

Just as the Wagner Act of 1935 sought to further freedom of association by affirmatively protecting the rights of employees to form and join unions, the Landrum-Griffin Act of 1959 sought to enlarge the democratic process by affirmatively protecting the rights of members within those unions.[70] These two basic statutes, both of near-constitutional quality in expressing basic rights, are closely linked in a relation of tension and mutual support.

The Landrum-Griffin Act trespasses directly on freedom of association, for it penetrates deeply into the union's processes of self-governance, imposing on the union and its members democratic standards and procedures of decision-making. This invasion of freedom of association is in part a response to the Wagner Act's own limitations on the individual's full freedom of association. The individual is compelled to accept the majority union as his representative; he is not free to act individually nor to be represented by a union of his own choosing. Moreover, the majority union, through its collective agreement, makes the rules governing his employment, and through its grievance procedure interprets and enforces those governing rules. Because the individual is compulsorily associated with the union and subservient to its governing power, the law is called upon to protect the rights of the individual within the union. In the words of the Senate Committee on Labor in recommending regulation of union elections:

> The Government which gives unions this power has an obligation to insure that officials who wield it are responsive to the desires of the men and women whom they represent.[71]

From another perspective, legal protection of democratic rights within the union grows from the same roots as legal protection of freedom of association and expresses the same values. Unions have historically been considered instruments through which workers can gain a voice in determining terms and conditions of employment. One of the fundamental purposes of the Wagner Act in affirmatively protecting freedom of association was to strengthen the process of industrial democracy. Unions serve the purpose fully, however, only if they are internally democratic, for the worker gains no voice in his industrial government unless he has a voice in the union which speaks for him. Legal prescription of union democracy thus fulfills the purpose of protecting freedom of association.

Moreover, statutory protection of the democratic process helps limit government intervention in union affairs, for it gives union members tools to change union policies and correct abuses from within. It does not destroy union autonomy, because the members remain free to decide all substantive policies; on the contrary, protection of the democratic process reinforces the principle of union self-government because it adds legitimacy and acceptability to the union's policy decisions, thereby reducing the demands for substantive controls. The Landrum-Griffin Act, seeking to preserve maximum union autonomy, further limited government intervention by safeguarding only basic democratic rights and enforcing only minimum democratic standards, leaving unions free within these quite wide limits to design their own structures of government.

The nature of the union's power over the individual, and the function of the union in providing a form of industrial democracy, led almost inevitably to stating the statutory standards of internal democracy for unions in terms of those required of other instruments of government. The rights of individuals to be protected are expressed in terms analogous to those of a citizen in a democracy. Indeed, Title I is entitled "Bill of Rights of Members of Labor Organizations," and protects, among other things, equal rights for members, rights of speech and assembly, the right to sue, and the right to a fair trial within the union. Title II gives union members the right to an accounting for union funds; Title III protects local self-government against overreaching control by national unions; Title IV protects the election process; and Title V imposes a fiduciary responsibility on union officers.

The broad sweep of Landrum-Griffin precludes even a cursory description of the rights of a member within his union, for those rights are nearly as manifold and complex as the rights of a citizen in a democratic government. The citizenship analogy, however, is more appealing than precise, for unions differ structurally and institutionally from government; definitions of constitutional rights cannot be borrowed uncritically to apply to unions. The difficult question, and the one ultimately of general importance, is how individual rights must be specially shaped to protect the democratic process within private institutions. The purpose here, therefore, is not to catalogue the rights created by the statute, but rather to illustrate how the statute shaped democratic rights to fit the union structure.

The core of the democratic process is the right of the individual to participate in decision-making, and in a union the irreducible minimum for exercise of this right is union membership—the analogy here between the right to membership and the right to vote is quite obvious. Even so, statutory protection of this elementary right vacillates, for Landrum-Griffin gives no protection of the right to join, but gives extensive protection against expulsion.[72] The Civil Rights Act of 1964 prohibits unions from excluding workers because of race, color, religion, sex, or national origin, but individuals may still be excluded for any other reason and thereby denied the franchise. In contrast, no member can be expelled, suspended, or fined except upon written charges and after a full and fair hearing; and the statute puts limits on the reasons for which a member can be expelled. Thus, he cannot be expelled for publicly urging adoption of "right to work" laws which the union opposes as a threat to its survival,[73] for bringing suit in court to enjoin the union from submitting a dispute to arbitration as required by a collective agreement,[74] or for filing unfair labor practice charges against the union without first attempting to obtain correction through internal union appeals.[75] The member cannot be compelled to choose between his right of franchise within the union and exercise of other basic rights outside the union.

Protection of the right to participate requires that the right to vote be linked to the union's decision-making process. In most governmental structures the link is normally through election of representatives, but in unions many decisions are made in membership meetings. In unions, therefore, protection of elections is not enough; the right to vote must extend to the right to require that membership meetings be called,[76] that motions which are in order at a meeting be entertained and put to a vote,[77] and that order be maintained so that a member who seeks to speak can be heard.[78] The statute regulates elections in detail, but fails to provide any explicit protection of these rights; it has been left to the courts to find them implicit in other basic rights, and some courts have refused to do so.[79] The union is largely free to decide which decisions are to be made through direct democracy and which through representative democracy and the special forms each of those may take. This very freedom of the union requires that legal protections be flexible enough to fit the particular process used by the union so as to make the right of participation a practical reality.

The "Bill of Rights" of Title I affirms the union members' freedom of speech, and though this statutory protection against union restraints was intended to be closely analogous to the constitutional guarantee against governmental restraints, the special character of union structures requires special safeguards against union restraints.[80] In *Salzhandler v. Caputo*,[81] a union member distributed a leaflet accusing a union officer of mishandling union funds. The member was charged with libeling an officer, tried before a trial board consisting of union officers, found guilty, and barred from participating in union affairs. The court rejected the argument that just as constitutionally protected speech did not include defamatory statements, so the statutorily protected speech did not protect the libeling of union officers. The analogy was not appropriate, said the court, for union tribunals, unlike courts, could not be relied upon for the kind of impartial review necessary to protect union members' freedom of speech. Trial boards, made up as they are of union officers or members rather than judges, were groups "to which the delicate problems of truth and falsehood, privilege and 'fair comment' were not familiar," and their procedures were "peculiarly unsuited for drawing the fine line between criticism and defamation." The values of free expression of opinions and the right of members to criticize union management would be seriously undermined if members spoke at the peril of having their statements found libelous by such tribunals. The basic rights of union members must be substantively defined so as to achieve effective practical protection within the working structures and procedures of the union.

Fair and honest elections are obviously basic to the democratic process in unions as well as government, and the governmental analogy provides some useful mechanical guides: elections must be held at reasonable periodic intervals, each member shall have one vote, voting shall be by secret ballot, candidates have the right to have observers at the polls, and the ballots must be preserved for one year.[82] However, fairness in union elections, if it is to have practical reality, requires regulations going far beyond any yet known in government elections. The institutional structure of unions gives incumbent officers almost insuperable advantage over challengers who would unseat them. The incumbents have opportunities to contact union members, control the channels of communication within the union including the union newspaper, and create an administrative bureaucracy which can serve as a ready-made political organization.

Title IV of the statute recognizes this practical advantage of the incumbent and attempts to give the opposition some measure of equality at least during the election campaign period. The union is required "to comply with all reasonable requests of any candidate to distribute . . . at the candidate's expense, campaign literature . . . to all members in good standing," and is further required not to discriminate against any candidate with respect to the use of membership lists or distribution of campaign literature. This guarantees the opposition a substantial opportunity to get its views before the voters, and at least "equal time" during the campaign. "Equal access" to the membership list, however, does not give practical equality; a list of the members and their addresses may be the only way a challenger can know who the potential voters are and solicit their support, especially where union members are widely scattered; the incumbents have little need for such lists, for they can develop their lines of contact during their term of office. More realistic equality would be achieved here by applying the rule in government elections which gives open access to voting lists.[83]

The advantages of incumbents is further reduced by the statutory provision prohibiting the use of union dues money "to promote the candidacy of any person" in a union election. This bars open use of the union treasury or administrative machinery for vote-getting and bars blatant use of the union newspaper for campaign propaganda. It does not, however, reach more subtle devices; and more importantly, it does nothing to offset the advantages built up by the incumbent during his term of office.[84] Rather than silencing the union newspaper, which blanks out the challenger, practical equality would be better served by requiring the newspaper to serve as a forum, open equally to all candidates to make themselves and their views known to the members.

The courts, in applying the statute, have displayed a remarkable combination of perceptiveness and obtuseness toward the need to protect the election process from undue advantages by the incumbents. The Supreme Court invalidated a union rule which limited eligibility for major elective office to members who had held other elective offices, because in practice it was not possible to win an elective office without the blessing of the incumbent administration;[85] but a district court refused to invalidate a union rule which required members working throughout the State of Nevada to vote in person in Reno, the headquarters of the union where the officers were permanently located.[86] The Supreme Court in one case declared that even though a valid election had been held subsequent to an invalid election, a new supervised election should be held because the incumbents could use "their inherent advantage over rank and file challengers" so that unfairness in the first election would infect the second;[87] but in another case, the Court strained the language of the statute to hold that federal courts could not give pre-election remedies compelling a union to correct violations before the first election was held.[88]

Underlying the problem of providing fair and open elections is the pervasive character of union political structures as one-party oligarchies. Unions, with rare exceptions, lack two-party systems with continuing organized opposition to the administration. The special problem of protecting the democratic process in unions is one of making the union leadership responsive to the desires of the members through a one-party political system. The initial moving force for making union leaders responsive is making them aware of the members' dissatisfaction with union policy. This plays not only on their fear of being replaced but also on their pride in pleasing the members, and their responsiveness depends on the forcefulness with which the democratic process registers dissatisfaction. Heavy criticism of a union officer may not lead to his defeat but still lead to his changing his ways; although a union president is re-elected, his policies will be influenced by the size of the vote for the opposition. Within the one-party bureaucracy there are almost always ambitious potential leaders watching for evidence that incumbent officers have become vulnerable to an election challenge; and even completely secure officers want and seek to win the approval of as many members as possible.

Freedom of speech must be broadly protected to encourage full expression of dissatisfaction, and the election process must be carefully protected to obtain accurate measurement of the extent of the dissatisfaction. The legal validity of an election, for example, ought not to depend upon whether it has correctly determined the winning candidate but whether it has accurately measured the margin of victory. Because the one-party structure impedes formation of new majorities and handicaps opposition candidates, the democratic rights of a member within his union must go beyond those of a citizen within his government and be specially tailored to penetrate the one-party structure if union policies are to be responsive to the desires of the membership.

Conclusion

The National Labor Relations Act and the Labor-Management Reporting and Disclosure Act have shaped and given legal content to a system of industrial relations through which workers can have a voice in decisions governing their terms and conditions of employment. Together, these statutes provide a constitution-like structure for private industrial government, and the basic premise of those statutes is that industrial government shall be democratic. The central core of the Wagner Act was protection of freedom of association in forming and joining unions; and the central core of the Landrum-Griffin Act was protection of the democratic process within those unions. There was thus created a whole new structure of individual rights which might be termed civil liberties within private institutions. These rights, though secondary within the constitutional or legal hierarchy, may be primary in terms of practical importance to individuals subject to the institutions of private power.

This characterization of the rights created by our basic labor legislation immediately suggests that perhaps other legislation should also protect individual rights and democratic processes within other institutions of private power. Our society is increasingly dominated by large organizations such as corporations, trade associations, professional societies, universities, foundations, and political parties which have varying forms and degrees of control over individuals who come within their institutional sphere. However, neither the Wagner Act nor the Landrum-Griffin Act has provided any significant impetus for protecting democratic rights within these other institutions. Labor legislation cannot, of course, serve as a prototype, for the rights must be defined to fit the special needs and structures of each institution; indeed, the character of some of these institutions may be such that larger democratic values would be better served by legal protection of only some or even none of the democratic rights within the institution. What is remarkable, if not disturbing, is that such extensive protection of the democratic process in industrial institutions has generated so little serious consideration as to how and in what degree individual rights should be protected within other institutions of private power.

Emphasis on the nature of the rights protected by our basic labor legislation obscures our limited commitment to those rights, for the protection in fact provided is far less than the general description of those rights suggests. First, large numbers of workers are not protected by these statutes, and this includes those, such as farm workers and employees in small enterprises, who most sorely need the protection. Second, employees in unorganized establishments have no protection of employment rights against arbitrary action by the employer, much less any avenue for democratic participation. Third, even where the laws are applicable, the legal remedies are not adequate to give effective protection. When vindication of democratic rights is through private suits, individuals or small groups are pitted in litigation battles against the collective institutions whose legal and financial resources are often overwhelming. When vindication is through the National Labor Relations Board, the remedies are too little and far too late. Indeed, much of the lack of organization is due to lack of adequate remedies to protect the right to organize. When vindication of union members' rights to fair elections is through the Secretary of Labor, prosecution is slow and too often halfhearted. In short, protection of democratic rights within our industrial government is broad and comprehensive, but in fact it protects only a portion of workers and with only partially adequate remedies.

NOTES

1. Thomas v. Collins, 323 U.S. 516 (1945).
2. Atkins v. City of Charlotte, 296 F. Supp. 1068 (W.D.N.C. 1969).
3. McLaughlin v. Tilendis, 398 F.2d 287 (7th Cir. 1968).
4. AFSCME v. Woodward, 406 F.2d 137, 139 (8th Cir. 1969).
5. Freedom of association includes the right of unions to provide legal assistance to members injured on the job and to refer such members to approved lawyers. Brotherhood of R.R. Trainmen v. Virginia ex rel. Virginia State Bar, 377 U.S. 1 (1964).
6. American Communications Ass'n v. Douds, 339 U.S. 382 (1950).
7. DeVeau v. Braisted, 363 U.S. 144 (1960).
8. International Ass'n of Machinists v. NLRB, 311 U.S. 72 (1940).
9. J. I. Case Co. v. NLRB, 321 U.S. 332 (1944).
10. NLRB v. General Motors Corp., 373 U.S. 734 (1963).
11. See generally Bok, "The Regulation of Campaign Tactics in Representation Elections Under the National Labor Relations Act," 78 Harvard Law Review 38 (1964); Christensen, "Free Speech, Propaganda and the NLRA," 38 New York University Law Review 243 (1963).
12. 376 U.S. 254 (1964).
13. Linn v. United Plant Guard Workers of America, Local 114, 383 U.S. 53 (1966). Any state remedy for defamation which was more restrictive on speech in union organizing campaigns would be in conflict with the federal statutory policy and therefore invalid.
14. NLRB v. Virginia Elec. & Power Co., 314 U.S. 469 (1944).
15. Mallory & Co. v. NLRB, 389 F.2d 704 (7th Cir. 1967).
16. NLRB v. Collins & Aikman Corp., 338 F.2d 743 (5th Cir. 1964).
17. Union Carbide Corp. v. NLRB, 310 F.2d 844 (6th Cir. 1962).
18. See, e.g., the majority and dissenting opinions in Morse Instrument Co. v. NLRB, 388 F.2d 1 (6th Cir. 1967); and NLRB v. Golub Corp. 388 F.2d 921 (2d Cir. 1967).
19. General Shoe Corp., 77 N.L.R.B. 124 (1948).
20. Peerless Plywood Co., 107 N.L.R.B. 427 (1953).
21. Sewell Mfg. Co., 138 N.L.R.B. 66 (1962); Archer Laundry Co., 150 N.L.R.B. 1427 (1965); Comment, "Employee Choice and Some Problems of Race and Remedies in Representation Campaigns," 72 Yale Law Journal 1243 (1963).
22. Steel Equipment Co., 140 N.L.R.B. 1158 (1963); Hollywood Ceramics Co., 140 N.L.R.B. 221 (1962).
23. 383 U.S. 53, 62 (1966).

24. *See generally* Gould, "The Question of Union Activity on Company Property," 18 *Vanderbilt Law Review* 73 (1964).

25. Republic Aviation Corp. v. NLRB, 324 U.S. 793 (1945); NLRB v. Babcock & Wilcox Co., 351 U.S. 105 (1956); Comment, "No-Solicitation and No-Distribution Rules: Presumptive Validity and Discrimination," 112 *University of Pennsylvania Law Review* 1049 (1964).

26. NLRB v. United Steelworkers of America, 357 U.S. 357, 364 (1958).

27. May Dep't Stores Co., 136 N.L.R.B. 797 (1962).

28. NLRB v. Wyman-Gordon Co., 394 U.S. 759 (1969).

29. Dorchy v. Kansas, 272 U.S. 306 (1926).

30. United Steelworkers of America v. United States, 361 U.S. 39 (1959).

31. NLRB v. Radio & Television Broadcast Engineers, Local 1212, IBEW, 364 U.S. 573 (1961).

32. *See* NLRB v. Wooster Div. of Borg-Warner Corp., 356 U.S. 342 (1958); Local 189, Amalgamated Meat Cutters of North America v. Jewel Tea Co., 381 U.S. 676 (1965).

33. International Union, UAW (AFL) v. Wisconsin Employment Relations Bd., 336 U.S. 245 (1949); NLRB v. Blades Mfg. Co., 344 F.2d 998 (8th Cir. 1965).

34. Local 1976, United Bhd. of Carpenters v. NLRB, 357 U.S. 93 (1958).

35. NLRB v. Mackay Radio & Tel. Co., 304 U.S. 333 (1938).

36. Harnischfeger Corp. v. NLRB, 207 F.2d 575 (7th Cir. 1953).

37. NLRB v. Tanner Motor Livery Ltd., 419 F.2d 216 (9th Cir. 1969).

38. NLRB v. Sunbeam Lighting Co., 318 F.2d 661 (7th Cir. 1963).

39. Comment, "Exclusive Representation and the Right of Employees to Engage in Concerted Activity—Conflicting Policies of the NLRA," 4 *University of San Francisco Law Review* 354 (1970).

40. NLRB v. Allis-Chalmers Mfg. Co., 388 U.S. 175 (1967); Atleson, "Union Fines and Picket Lines: The NLRA and Union Disciplinary Power," 17 *U.C.L.A. Law Review* 681 (1970).

41. 310 U.S. 88 (1940).

42. *See* AFL v. Swing, 312 U.S. 321 (1941); Cafeteria Employees v. Angelos, 320 U.S. 293 (1943).

43. Carpenters Union v. Ritter's Cafe, 315 U.S. 722 (1942).

44. Building Service Employees Int'l Union v. Gazzam, 339 U.S. 532 (1950); Cox, "Strikes, Picketing and the Constitution," 4 *Vanderbilt Law Review* 574 (1951).

45. 354 U.S. 284 (1957); Christensen, *supra* note 11.

46. NLRB v. Fruit & Vegetable Packers & Warehousemen, Local 760, 377 U.S. 58 (1964).

47. 391 U.S. 308 (1968).

48. Crown Cafeteria, 135 N.L.R.B. 1183 (1962). The Board has held that "area standards" picketing is not curtailed at all by Section 8(b)(7). Claude Everett Constr. Co., 136 N.L.R.B. 321 (1962). *See generally* Crowley, "Regulation of Organizational and Recognitional Picketing Under Section 8(b)(7) of the NLRA," 47 *Marquette Law Review* 295 (1964).

49. *See generally,* Ruark, "Labor's Political Spending and Free Speech," 53 *Northwestern University Law Review* 61 (1958).

50. 335 U.S. 106 (1948).

51. 352 U.S. 567 (1957).

52. Lane, "Analysis of the Federal Law Governing Political Expenditures by Labor Unions," 9 *Labor Law Journal* 725 (1958).

53. 367 U.S. 740 (1961).

54. Brotherhood of Ry. Clerks v. Allen, 373 U.S. 113 (1963).

55. 323 U.S. 192, 199, 204 (1944).

56. Ford Motor Co. v. Huffman, 345 U.S. 330 (1953).

57. Radio Officers' Union v. NLRB, 347 U.S. 17 (1954).

58. Brotherhood of R.R. Trainmen v. Howard, 343 U.S. 768 (1952).

59. Ford Motor Co. v. Huffman, 345 U.S. 330, 338 (1953).

60. *See generally* Sovern, "The National Labor Relations Act and Racial Discrimination," 62 *Columbia Law Review* 563 (1962); Wellington, "Union Democracy and Fair Representation: Federal Responsibility in a Federal System," 67 *Yale Law Journal* 1327 (1958).

61. Herring, "The 'Fair Representation' Doctrine: An Effective Weapon Against Union Racial Discrimination?" 24 *Maryland Law Review* 113 (1964).

62. Local 12, Rubber Workers v. NLRB, 368 F.2d 12 (5th Cir. 1966), *cert. denied,* 389 U.S. 837 (1967).

63. Conley v. Gibson, 355 U.S. 41 (1957).

64. Hughes Tool Co., 147 N.L.R.B. 1573 (1964).

65. Local 12, Rubber Workers v. NLRB, 368 F.2d 12 (5th Cir. 1966), *cert. denied,* 389 U.S. 837 (1967).

66. Hughes Tool Co., 104 N.L.R.B. 318 (1953).

67. Smith v. Evening News Ass'n, 371 U.S. 195 (1962).

68. Republic Steel Corp. v. Maddox, 379 U.S. 650 (1965).

69. Vaca v. Sipes, 386 U.S. 171 (1967); Humphrey v. Moore, 375 U.S. 335 (1964).

70. *See generally* Aaron, "The Labor-Management Reporting and Disclosure Act of 1959," 73 *Harvard Law Review* 851 (1960); Cox, "Internal Affairs of Unions Under the Labor Reform Act of 1959," 58 *Michigan Law Review* 819 (1960); Summers, "American Legislation for Union Democracy," 25 *Modern Law Review* 273 (1962).

71. S. Rep. No. 187, 86th Cong., 1st Sess. 20 (1959).

72. *See generally* Etelson & Smith, "Union Discipline Under the Landrum-Griffin Act," 82 *Harvard Law Review* 727 (1969).

73. *Cf.* Mitchell v. International Ass'n of Machinists, 196 Cal. App. 2d 796, 16 Cal. Rptr. 813 (1961).

74. Ryan v. IBEW, Local 134, 361 F.2d 942 (7th Cir.), *cert denied,* 385 U.S. 935 (1966).

75. NLRB v. Industrial Union of Marine & Shipbuilding Workers, 391 U.S. 418 (1968).

76. *See* Yanity v. Benware, 376 F.2d 197, 201 (2d Cir. 1967) (Lumbard, C.J., dissenting), *cert. denied,* 389 U.S. 874 (1967).

77. Scovile v. Watson, 338 F.2d 678 (7th Cir. 1964), *cert. denied,* 380 U.S. 963 (1965).

78. Allen v. Local 92, Iron Workers, 47 L.R.R.M. 2214 (N.D. Ala. 1960).

79. *See* Yanity v. Benware, 376 F.2d 197 (2d Cir.), *cert. denied,* 389 U.S. 874 (1967).

80. *See generally* Atleson, "A Union Member's Right of Free Speech and Assembly: Institutional Interests and Individual Rights," 51 *Minnesota Law Review* 403 (1967).

81. 316 F.2d 445 (2d Cir.), *cert. denied,* 375 U.S. 946 (1963).

82. *See generally* Beaird, "Union Officer Election Provisions of the LMRDA of 1959," 51 *Virginia Law Review* 1306 (1965).

83. Section 401(c) gives a candidate the right to inspect once within 30 days prior to an election a list of names and addresses of members subject to a union shop agreement.

84. Yablonski v. UMW, 305 F. Supp. 868, 876 (D.D.C. 1969).

85. Wirtz v. Hotel, Motel and Club Employees, Local 6, 391 U.S. 492 (1968).

86. Wirtz v. Local 169, International Hod Carriers, 246 F. Supp. 741 (D. Nev. 1965).

87. Wirtz v. Local 153, Glass Bottle Blowers, 389 U.S. 463 (1968).

88. Calhoon v. Harvey, 379 U.S. 134 (1964). *See generally* Comment, "Union Elections Under the LMRDA," 74 *Yale Law Journal* 1282 (1965); Comment, "Fair Election Procedures Under the LMRDA of 1959 and the United Mine Workers," 6 *Columbia Journal of Law & Social Problems* 76 (1970).

THE RIGHTS OF SERVICEMEN

EDWARD F. SHERMAN

CONCERN FOR SERVICEMEN'S RIGHTS IS A RELA-
tively recent phenomenon. Until well into this century, it was generally assumed that soldiers had duties and obligations, and in some
cases privileges, but few rights. Induction into the military was
viewed as a contract which necessitated, by the very nature of the
military establishment, that servicemen surrender civilian rights,
and even the fact that induction might have been involuntarily
induced by conscription did not lessen the rigor of the contract
theory logic. The military was considered a different world in
which, as General William Tecumseh Sherman described it, "a collection of armed men [are] obliged to obey one man," and in such a
world there seemed to be no place for rights or individuality.

This traditional view of the serviceman's status has been tem-
pered in the twentieth century by the influx of millions of drafted
civilians into the military and the effects of bureaucratization and
technology. The need for well-trained and highly specialized personnel has led to subtle changes in the harsh authoritarianism of the
old military. Despite these changes, a basically anti-individualist
tradition still persists. The word "rights," when used in the military context, still refers primarily to economic benefits and prerogatives of military status, rather than to constitutional protections.

*Edward F. Sherman is Assistant Professor of Law at the Indiana University School
of Law, a reserve Captain in the United States Army Judge Advocate General's Corps,
and the author of several articles on military law. He has served as appellate counsel
in several military free speech cases.*

The list of servicemen's rights, for example, described in the current edition of *The Officer's Guide* includes such protections as the right to wear a uniform, to draw pay and allowances, to receive medical attention, to be accorded the protections of the Uniform Code of Military Justice and the benefits of the Soldiers and Sailors Relief Act, to retire, and to be buried in a national cemetery, without mentioning the rights of speech, association, privacy, and constitutional due process which have come to represent the heart of American individual liberties in our day.

The current status of servicemen's rights, however, is neither as limited nor as static as *The Officer's Guide* suggests. Ferment for a broader application of constitutional guarantees to servicemen has characterized the era following World War II, with special impetus in the Vietnam war period. Congressional, administrative, and judicial actions have expanded the scope of servicemen's rights, and important battles are now being waged in all three of these areas for further extension.

The Legal Basis of Servicemen's Rights

Servicemen's rights have a different historical tradition from civilian rights. Despite some ambiguity as to the intent of the framers of the Constitution, it was determined early in the nineteenth century that the individual rights granted by the Constitution did not apply to servicemen and that servicemen's rights derived entirely from congressional statutes, executive orders, and military regulations. This conclusion that servicemen were not entitled to constitutional protections, although based on questionable legal precedents, had a tremendous negative impact on the future development of servicemen's rights. It was further strengthened by Supreme Court decisions holding that the civilian courts had no constitutional power to review military administrative determinations or courts-martial,[1] thus according the military virtual autonomy as regards its own personnel.

Since servicemen could not look to the Constitution for protection or to the civilian courts for redress, they were largely dependent for their rights upon the willingness of Congress and the disposition of the administrative and military bureaucracies to extend protections to them. Neither of these sources has provided a comprehensive grant of individual rights or a very effective check on military arbitrariness. Although the executive branch, through the President's constitutional powers as Commander in Chief, and Congress, through its constitutional powers to appropriate funds and "make rules for the government and regulation of the land and naval forces," have exercised broad control over the military, neither branch has displayed much interest over the years in interfering with the way the military handles its own personnel.

Administrative Regulations

Executive and military regulations (issued by the President, the Secretary of Defense, the secretaries of the services, and the military commands under them) provide the principal guidelines for the operation of the military and are a significant check on the powers of commanders. But these regulations are primarily concerned with housekeeping functions such as supply, maintenance, equipment, and personnel, and the extension of individual rights is only incidental to their principal objective of ensuring the uniform and efficient administration of military operations. Nevertheless, in the absence of more explicit and comprehensive statements of servicemen's rights, effective protections can sometimes be squeezed out of regulations. For example, regulations governing classification of conscientious objectors, complaint procedures, disciplinary actions, and matters relating to criminal prosecutions can sometimes be relied upon as sources of individual rights when violated by the military.[2] Sometimes an individual right emerges by negative implication from a regulation—for example, the once controversial Army regulation that servicemen's faces will be clean-shaven "with the exception that wearing a neatly trimmed mustache is permitted."

Most regulations establish broad standards for administrative action, leaving considerable discretion to the commander or official administering it. Thus, although regulations governing such subjects as administrative discharges, duty assignments, and promotions contain distinct requirements for administrative processing, it is often difficult for a serviceman who claims that the regulation has not been followed to obtain redress within the military. Also, some regulations extend not a right but a privilege (a popular term in the military lexicon); thus a commander's authority regarding such matters of granting of passes, permission to drive automobiles on post, training methods, and the requirements of discipline is virtually unlimited and, except in cases of extreme misuse cannot be successfully challenged by a serviceman.

The informal system of discipline serves as a sort of underlaw which gives commanders extensive control over the conduct of servicemen. Each commander is given broad discretion to discipline his men. The disciplinary requirements he imposes, unlike criminal laws, which are primarily negative, often demand conformity to a variety of positive acts and attitudes that he deems appropriate. Thus a commander's views on what constitutes proper dress, display of military attitudes, respect toward superiors, and even discussion of political and other matters, are often reflected in the requirements of discipline which he imposes on his men. A growing number of cases have challenged clearly arbitrary impositions of discipline by commanders, but most courts have not been willing to examine command discretion.

The demands of discipline can only be considered law in a broad sense, as they are usually not written or clearly defined in advance. They are ultimately supported by the threat of court-martial or nonjudicial punishment (if a serviceman consents to nonjudicial punishment rather than demanding a court-martial, a commander can assess forfeitures of pay, demotion, and from 7 to 30 days in custody, depending on the rank of the commander, for commission of a military offense).[3] The military justice code contains a number of provisions empowering a commander to court-martial for breaches of discipline, such as disobedience of any order of a superior; insubordinate conduct toward a superior; "conduct unbecoming an officer and a gentleman"; "disorders and neglects to the prejudice of good order and discipline in the armed forces"; and "conduct of a nature to bring discredit upon the armed forces." These military crimes have been challenged as unconstitutionally vague and overbroad, but they have thus far been upheld, and they provide an ultimate sanction in support of the informal system of discipline.

Because of the limited objectives of regulations and the traditional bias among military drafters for subordinating individual rights to command discretion, administrative regulations have provided little protection for what are usually called civil liberties. However, there has been some movement in the Vietnam war period toward extension of civil rights through administrative directives and regulations. Public reaction to harsh military treatment of servicemen who have dissented against the Vietnam war led to the issuance of an Army directive in May 1969, instructing commanders as to the scope of their discretion concerning dissent activities and generally encouraging a more lenient policy toward certain free speech activities by servicemen. Similarly, increased racial tensions in the military resulted in a Marine Corps directive in September 1969,[4] followed by directives in other services, which liberalized military policies concerning racial and cultural diversity in servicemen's appearance and dress and re-emphasized official prohibitions on discrimination in the service. But these limited extensions of rights, still little more than vague expressions of policy, are a far cry from the vigorous protection given First Amendment and other civil rights in civilian courts.

Congressional Acts

Although Congress, through its power to make rules for the military forces, could enact a comprehensive grant of rights to servicemen, it has never done so except for the passage of a code to govern courts-martial. Congress has passed extensive legislation governing the operation of the military (now contained in the Armed Forces section of the United States Code), but the rights which a serviceman can derive from these acts relate primarily to administrative matters—such as promotions, pay, and personnel procedures—rather than to individual civil liberties.

The Uniform Code of Military Justice of 1950 (UCMJ),[5] as amended by the Military Justice Act of 1968,[6] is the principal source of servicemen's due process rights in a military criminal prosecution. It sets up a system of criminal law binding on all servicemen, with its own substantive laws (there are 58 punitive articles making criminal both common-law crimes like larceny and homicide and military offenses like disobedience and desertion), its own courts and procedures (there is a hierarchy of courts-martial, including the summary court, whose sentence cannot exceed one month; the special court, whose sentence cannot exceed six months; and the general court, which can adjudge up to the maximum sentence for the crime, including death), and its own appeals system. The UCMJ extends a number of rights to servicemen, including some which are not related to the conduct of a court-martial, for example, rights relating to nonjudicial punishment, presentation of grievances, and claims against the government. It is supplemented by the *Manual for Courts-Martial*, written by the military but issued by Executive Order, which fills in the details of the procedures established by the UCMJ.

The due process rights provided by the UCMJ and the *Manual* in connection with a court-martial are roughly comparable to civilian due process, although sometimes quite different from civilian procedures (for example, there is no right to a grand jury, but there is a right in a general court-martial to a pretrial investigation). The UCMJ was notably ahead of civilian law in its guarantee of certain due process rights (such as the right to warnings prior to interrogation and the right to appointed counsel), but the Warren Court's revolution of criminal due process in the 1950's and 1960's has brought civilian procedures up to, and in some cases past, the UCMJ. The most criticized aspects of the UCMJ are not the due process guarantees but the structure of the court-martial system itself. Congress gave in to military demands that the traditional structure of courts-martial be retained; that commanders be left in control of court-martial machinery with the power to appoint court members and counsel from their officers, carry out certain administrative duties, and review the sentence; and that appeals only be permitted within the military justice system. A commander, for example, before trial, can reverse the decision of a military judge to dismiss a charge as a matter of law if he disagrees with the judge's interpretation of the law. The result, critics have argued, is that the due process rights provided a serviceman by the UCMJ are seriously weakened by command control, packed courts, and inadequate appeals.

Bills to reform the UCMJ have been introduced in almost every session of Congress since 1951 and a bill to remove commander's control over court-martial machinery is now pending, but congressional reform of military justice is a slow process. Since Congress has only acted to protect servicemen's rights in limited areas concerning courts-martial, and here only with considerable deference to the wishes of the military and reluctance to make changes, it is not surprising that there is continuing pressure for a larger role by the courts in providing remedies for servicemen.

The Court of Military Appeals

In 1951 the UCMJ established a civilian Court of Military Appeals to be the Supreme Court of the military. Since its inception this court has played the key role in interpreting and applying the requirements of the UCMJ and, more recently, of the Constitution to court-martial cases. The Court of Military Appeals originally took the position that the Bill of Rights did not apply directly to the military and that servicemen were only entitled to those elements of "military due process" which could reasonably be derived from the UCMJ in light of the nature of the military.[7] It altered its position after the Supreme Court ruled in 1953 that federal courts had jurisdiction to review denial of servicemen's constitutional rights in courts-martial, and it now holds that servicemen are entitled to all constitutional rights except those expressly or by implication inapplicable to the military.[8] As a result, the Court of Military Appeals has been primarily responsible, in the 1960's, for keeping military due process abreast of the developing constitutional standards of the civilian courts.

The Court of Military Appeals has limitations which have prevented it from developing into the type of forum which the federal courts provide for the protection of civilians' rights. Under its authority from Congress it is limited in scope of review, equitable powers, and availability on appeal, and thus its effectiveness in shaping and protecting servicemen's rights is considerably reduced. It has viewed its role as interpreting and applying the UCMJ, and despite a gradual acceptance of the obligation to apply the Constitution to courts-martial when applicable, its decisions are circumscribed by the limited scope of the UCMJ itself. It has been a cautious court, aware of its statutory limitations, conscious of its special relationship with the military, and hesitant to make the kind of precedent-breaking constitutional judgments which the Supreme Court, and even the circuit courts, are accustomed to making. As a result, these days the Court of Military Appeals is often behind the Supreme Court in announcing new protections in the area of criminal due process, and is even less reponsive in the area of affirmative individual liberties like free speech.

Federal Courts

By the latter part of the nineteenth century it had been firmly established that federal courts had no jurisdiction to review courts-martial or military administrative determinations except for the limited inquiry, on habeas corpus, as to whether a court-martial had proper jurisdiction over the person tried and the offense charged. However, chinks began to appear in the armor of non-reviewability by the middle of the twentieth century. The nature of the American military changed dramatically with the coming of World War II, and continued postwar conscription meant that there would be no return to the small, volunteer military of the prewar period. The rationale for altering the time-honored "hands-off" doctrine was expressed by Chief Justice Warren in a lecture at New York University Law School in 1962: "When the authority of the military has such a sweeping capacity for affecting the lives of our citizenry, the wisdom of treating the military establishment as an enclave beyond the reach of the civilian courts almost inevitably is drawn into question."[9]

In 1953, the Supreme Court made the first substantial breach in the doctrine of nonreviewability as to courts-martial. It held in *Burns v. Wilson*[10] that on habeas corpus by a serviceman who had exhausted his military appeals, a federal court was not merely limited to asking whether the court-martial had proper jurisdiction but could also review claims of denials of due process rights to which the military had not given full and fair consideration. There has been considerable dispute as to how broad a scope of habeas corpus review the Supreme Court authorized in *Burns*. Some decisions have held that if the federal court finds that the military gave full and fair consideration to the serviceman's claims of denial of due process, it can go no further and must deny relief; others have held that it should determine whether in fact he was denied any constitutional right.[11] The latter interpretation gives the federal courts broad authority to impose constitutional standards on military courts, much as the now liberalized scope of federal court habeas-corpus review of state court determinations had done.

A good example of the impact which broadened habeas corpus review of court-martial convictions can have on servicemen's due process rights can be found in the history, over the last decade, of the right to a lawyer in a special court-martial. The UCMJ did not provide for a right to legally trained counsel in a special court-martial (where the maximum sentence is six months confinement, forfeiture of pay, demotion, and a bad-conduct discharge). The Court of Military Appeals held in 1963 that the right to legally trained counsel in a special court-martial was not constitutionally required.[12] In 1965, a nineteen-year-old private, who had been refused a lawyer in a special court-martial and was represented by a captain in the Veterinary Corps who confused the elements of a key defense and incorrectly advised a guilty plea, brought a writ of habeas corpus in the United States District Court on grounds that his right to counsel under the Sixth Amendment and to due process under the Fifth Amendment had been violated. The Court held that because the charges involved moral turpitude and there was a risk of substantial incarceration, the Sixth Amendment right to counsel applied, and ordered him released from confinement because that right had been denied in the court-martial.[13] The military chose not to appeal, and its position that denial of legally trained counsel in a special court-martial is not constitutionally defective was upheld in two other cases.[14] But with the possibility that more court-martial convictions could be voided, Congress finally, in the Military Justice Act of 1968, provided a right to a lawyer in most special courts-martial.

Five years after *Burns* was decided, the Supreme Court also broadened federal court review of military administrative determinations. In *Harmon v. Brucker*,[15] a suit seeking review of an undesirable discharge issued to a serviceman on grounds that he was a security risk, it held that federal courts have jurisdiction to consider claims that the military has exceeded its statutory authority. Subsequent decisions have broadened the scope of court review of military administrative determinations, permitting review where the military's action exceeds statutory, regulatory, or other authority, is grossly discriminatory or beyond any rational exercise of discretion, is unconstitutional, or has a serious chilling effect on First Amendment rights.[16]

The Vietnam war has brought a variety of new situations in which federal court relief from military determinations has been sought. Military actions involving activation of reserves, rejection of requests for conscientious objector discharges, and suppression of antiwar dissent among servicemen have resulted in an avalanche of federal court suits. Suits have been filed to require discharge on the grounds that the military improperly determined conscientious objector status, medical fitness, and personal hardship; to avoid activation of reserve and National Guard units and individuals; to prevent transfer of units and individuals overseas; to rescind orders of duty assignments; to require a commander to permit distribution of antiwar literature, authorize an on-post meeting and other speech activities, and prevent various adverse actions regarding off-post coffeehouses; and to prevent the court-martial of servicemen. Many of the suits brought early in the war were dismissed for lack of jurisdiction on the grounds that federal courts will not review military determinations, but increasingly, as courts have become accustomed to suits against the military and educated as to the precedents, they have accepted jurisdiction. As a result the federal courts now offer a genuine forum for relief from certain types of military action, and the threat of federal court intervention can sometimes exert a significant deterrent effect on unreasonable and arbitrary actions of commanders.

The federal courts have also had a significant impact on military law through decisions limiting court-martial jurisdiction. The drafters of the UCMJ conceived of military justice as a total system of criminal law which applied to servicemen wherever they are, to reservists while on inactive duty training as authorized under orders, and to certain civilians with special relationships to the military. That broad jurisdiction has been gradually chipped away. The Supreme Court, in a series of cases, struck down court-martial jurisdiction over discharged servicemen, civilian dependents overseas in peacetime, and civilian employees of the military,[17] and administrative rulings have limited jurisdiction over reservists to summer-camp active duty and weekly meetings where use of dangerous or expensive equipment is contemplated.[18] Finally, in June 1968, the Supreme Court held, in *O'Callahan v. Parker*,[19] that courts-martial lack jurisdiction over offenses committed by servicemen which are not "service-connected." It found no court-martial jurisdiction over a serviceman charged with attempted rape while he was off post, off duty, and in civilian clothes. The effects of the *O'Callahan* decision have been enormous. Whereas the military previously claimed jurisdiction over a serviceman no matter where he was or what he was doing, wide areas of a serviceman's life may now be immune from court-martial jurisdiction. The rationale of the majority opinion in *O'Callahan,* quite clearly based on the belief that trial by court-martial deprives one of substantial rights available in a civilian trial, also leaves the possibility open that, unless the court-martial system provides rights to servicemen roughly comparable to those provided in civilian courts, expanded judicial review and further limitations on court-martial jurisdiction will continue.

CONSTITUTIONAL RIGHTS IN COURTS-MARTIAL

For an overall view of servicemen's due process rights in connection with court-martial prosecution, let us look at a typical case of a serviceman charged with theft in the barracks.[20]

First, he is entitled to the protection of the Fourth Amendment against unreasonable searches and seizures. Any search of his person, property, or belongings not made pursuant to a warrant based on probable cause or pursuant to the usual exceptions to the requirement of a warrant (such as consent or incident to lawful arrest) will result in exclusion of the evidence at the court-martial. However, search warrants are issued by the commander, who is not equivalent to an impartial magistrate as under civilian practice. Routine inspections and "shakedowns" are not considered searches subject to the Fourth Amendment. Thus, if a commander discovered the stolen property in the serviceman's wall locker pursuant to a routine inspection of wall lockers or in a "shakedown" in which the belongings of every person assigned to a room or barracks were inspected, there would have been no unreasonable search and seizure. The insulation of routine inspections and "shakedowns" from constitutional requirements is usually justified by the need for commanders to inspect men and equipment and to respond quickly to morale-endangering barracks thefts, but it points up the limitation on individual rights, even in the criminal context, occasioned by military status.

Second, the serviceman accused of theft is entitled to the protection of the Fifth Amendment right against self-incrimination, as formulated by the Supreme Court in *Miranda v. Arizona*.[21] The military rule as to criminal interrogations, established by Article 31 of the UCMJ as expanded by the Court of Military Appeals in *U.S. v. Tempia*,[22] is more protective in some ways than the civilian court rule. The obligation to give warnings is not limited to a custodial situation or to interrogation by police, and the right against self-incrimination has been held to include voice identifications, blood samples, and handwriting exemplars. However, the coercive element inherent in the relationship between servicemen and superiors can create a special threat to Fifth Amendment rights not present in civilian situations, which military courts have often failed to appreciate in ruling on the voluntariness of confessions and incriminating statements.

Third, he is entitled to a public trial and to a speedy trial, which has generally been applied more rigorously by military courts than by civilian courts. He is also protected by the Fifth Amendment right against double jeopardy, as far as second prosecutions for the same offense in a court-martial or a federal court, but not as to prosecutions in a state court. Under *The Manual for Court-Martial* the decision to confine a soldier prior to his trial is not made by a magistrate, as in the civilian practice, nor is there a right to bail. Normally, the defendant's lowest-level commander (usually the very person who accused him) will make this discretionary determination. Likewise, postconviction release pending appeal is also discretionary with the commander and is inadequate in comparison to civilian-court bail procedures.

Fourth, he is entitled, but only if he is to be tried in a general court-martial, to a "thorough and impartial" pretrial investigation by an investigating officer appointed by the commander. A serviceman or his counsel may request that witnesses be called to testify and may cross-examine witnesses and present evidence, and thus the pretrial investigation provides broader rights than the usual grand jury hearing. However, the commander makes the ultimate decision whether to court-martial or not, and so, unlike a civilian defendant, who cannot be prosecuted if the grand jury refuses to indict, a serviceman can be court-martialed by his commander despite the contrary recommendation of the investigating officer.

Fifth, he is entitled to a free military lawyer to represent him in all general courts-martial and, in most cases, in special courts-martial, and in all stages of military appeals.

Sixth, the serviceman, through his counsel, is entitled to discover evidence and subpoena witnesses for trial. Military discovery procedures are generally liberal. However, the trial counsel (prosecutor) plays an undesirably important role in ruling on defense requests for discovery and subpoenas.

Seventh, the court-martial trial itself provides most of the due process guarantees found in civilian courts. Military rules as to available defenses, sufficiency of the charges, conduct of counsel, admissibility of evidence, scope of cross-examination, and other procedural formalities are generally comparable to those of civilian courts. However, the method of selection of the court itself (who are generally chosen by the commander or his subordinates from among his officers rather than by random selection from the community at large as is a civilian jury) prevents the court-martial from providing a right to trial by jury of one's peers. Furthermore, the commander's control over various aspects of the court-martial (including the power to prosecute, select the court, appoint counsel and other personnel, exercise a number of administrative functions before and during the trial, and review the sentence) is an unfortunate vestige of the old disciplinary court-martial system which raises questions concerning the judicial quality of the proceedings. After the 1968 amendments the trial is now conducted by military judges, but it is still not clear whether such judges can exercise normal civilian duties such as the issuing of warrants for search and arrest and conducting hearings on the necessity for an individual's confinement both before a case is referred to trial and pending appeal after conviction and sentencing. "A court martial," as Justice Douglas wrote in *O'Callahan v. Parker,* "is not yet an independent instrument of justice but remains to a significant degree a specialized part of the overall mechanism by which military discipline is preserved."[23]

Finally, the serviceman, if convicted, is entitled to certain military reviews and appeals. All sentences of general and special courts-martial are reviewed by the commander, who can remit or reduce the sentence but has no power to increase it. Critics have argued that leaving this review power with a commander encourages courts to give higher sentences in the belief that the commander should have the option of reducing it. The second level of appeal is to the Courts of Military Review (formerly called boards of review), available in cases involving generals or flag officers or sentences of death, dismissal, dishonorable or bad-conduct discharge, or more than a year's confinement. These courts, usually made up of three military officers, have been criticized for their lack of independence from the Judge Advocate General. The final level of appeal is to the civilian Court of Military Appeals, but this is discretionary in most cases, and only a tiny percentage of court-martial convictions are finally reviewed by this Court.

FIRST AMENDMENT RIGHTS

The most controversial subjects of servicemen's rights today are in the First Amendment area. The traditional military attitude toward free speech rights has been extremely limited. Dwight Eisenhower, for example, was called before the chief of the infantry after World

War I for writing a paper for a military journal which was critical of army tactics, and observed in his autobiography, *At Ease:* "I was told that my ideas were not only wrong but dangerous and that henceforth I would keep them to myself. Particularly, I was not to publish anything incompatible with solid infantry doctrine. If I did, I would be hauled before a court-martial." Military constraints on free speech, which a professional soldier like Eisenhower could accept in an earlier period, have become more oppressive now when most servicemen are not in the military by choice. The Vietnam war added an ingredient not present to any degree in prior wars: serious political and moral opposition to the war and military policies by a sizable number of servicemen. As a result a variety of free speech cases have arisen. Servicemen have been court-martialed for offenses arising out of participating in off-post peace rallies, possessing or passing out anti-war literature on post, publishing underground antiwar GI newspapers, and making antiwar statements to civilians or other servicemen. Others have been subjected to a variety of unfavorable administrative actions after expressing dissenting views, ranging from petty harassment and unfavorable reassignments to court-martial on other charges and undesirable discharge. In light of these cases it may be useful to review, first, what free speech rights are recognized by military law, and second, what further rights now seem to be developing.

Free Speech Rights Recognized by Military Law

Despite the traditionally narrow military view of the First Amendment, certain free speech rights are recognized. One is the right to make complaints to superiors, protected by Article 138 of the UCMJ. Although military regulations implementing this article speak only in terms of making complaints through the chain of command, a 1966 army board of review decision has treated it as a more general right. There an army doctor, who was unhappy with his assignment to Vietnam and the medical facilities at his dispensary, complained to General Westmoreland when he was making an inspection tour. His commanding officer was outraged and had him court-martialed for conduct unbecoming an officer. The board reversed, saying:

> Complaining is indulged in by enlisted men and officers of all grades and rank. Complaints may be registered on any topic and

frequently are. "Bitching," to use the vernacular, may be expressed in gutter talk or in well-articulated phrases and has frequently been developed into a fine art. . . . The right to complain is undoubtedly within the protection of the first amendment of the Constitution of the United States guaranteeing freedom of speech.[24]

The right to make requests and complaints to one's commander has been applied to a variety of administrative situations, as shown by a 1969 decision by the Sixth Circuit Court of Appeals which reversed the punitive activation of a reservist because of the failure of his commander to consider his request under Article 138 to be given a hearing.[25] However, this right works better in theory than in practice. In the military environment, where officers and non-commissioned officers exercise immense discretion over such matters as assignments, details, passes, discipline, and punishments, assertion of individual rights can sometimes result in even more unfavorable treatment. Complaints through the chain of command or through the Inspector General are often ineffective in obtaining redress of individual rights because of the tendency of some members of the military to resist challenges to the system and to protect fellow officers and noncommissioned officers. Thus, despite the encouraging language of the board of review above, the army doctor who complained to General Westmoreland never received consideration at the command level (General Westmoreland told the hospital command: "Don't worry, Colonel. I can tell a psychotic just by looking at him.")[26] and only cleared himself at the appellate court level after being convicted in a court-martial.

A corollary of the right to complain to superiors should be the right to express complaints, dissatisfactions, and criticisms to others. The military has displayed a tolerance for "bitching" about such things as food, living conditions, and even superiors, but, as the court-martial of dissenters in the Vietnam war period indicates, it views criticisms of the war and military policies in a different light. A federal statute provides that nothing shall be deemed "to prohibit free discussion regarding political issues or candidates for political office,"[27] and military regulations state that servicemen have a right "to express their opinion privately and informally on all political subjects and candidates."[28] However, when expressions of opinion by servicemen have been highly critical of the military or government, inflammatory, or appeared to be influencing other servicemen, the military has tended to give a narrow interpretation to this right and to suppress such speech.

Another corollary of the right to complain is the right to communicate with members of Congress, which is specifically protected by a federal statute and service regulations.[29] A 1966 Court of Military Appeals decision involved a soldier who felt he was being harassed by his first sergeant for complaining to his senator about the food and living conditions at his post. He wrote a press release with the headline, FT. RILEY SOLDIER RECEIVES PUNISHMENT FOR EXERCISING RIGHTS and told his commander he was going to send it to the newspapers if the harassment did not stop. He was court-martialed and convicted of extortion and wrongful communication of a threat. The court reversed, and in a concurring opinion, Judge Ferguson wrote that discipline had been "perverted into an excuse for retaliating against a soldier for doing only that which Congress has expressly said it wishes him to be free to do," and that "it was open to him respectfully to make known his intention to air his just grievance publicly, without being subjected to adjudication as a blackmailer."[30]

When a serviceman's speech involves more than complaints to superiors or low-key, nonpolitical "bitching," official recognition of protected rights begins to fade. The civil rights movement in the South in the early 1960's presented a problem, for the first time, of participation by a significant number of servicemen in off-post free speech activities of a political nature. In response, the Army issued a regulation prohibiting "participation in picket lines or any other public demonstrations" during duty hours when required to be present for duty; when in uniform; when on a military reservation or in a foreign country; when the activities constitute a breach of law and order; or when violence is reasonably likely to result.[31] These limitations, which have since been adopted for all services by the Department of Defense, have also been used to curtail participation in antiwar marches and other dissent activities in the Vietnam war period. Nevertheless, the military has not attempted to enforce this regulation uniformly, as exemplified by the fact that servicemen have participated in peace demonstrations in uniform without being court-martialed, and is obviously concerned as to its constitutionality. Even under the regulation, it should be noted, there is a limited right by negative implication to participate in demonstrations if off duty, off post, and not in uniform, when the activities do not constitute a breach of law and order, and violence is not reasonably likely to result. (The military still claims absolute authority to ban any type of on-post demonstrations and has successfully resisted several recent injunctive suits to permit on-post speech activities.[32])

Another limited right recognized by the military involves the possession and distribution of political materials. The May 1969 Army Directive on Dissent emphasized that "mere possession of a publication may not be prohibited" and that "a commander may not prevent distribution of a publication simply because he does not like its contents," although he may prohibit distribution of publications which are "obscene or otherwise unlawful (e.g., counselling disloyalty, mutiny, or refusal of duty)" or "if the manner of accomplishing the distribution materially interferes with the accomplishment of a military mission (e.g., interference with training or troop formation)." The directive also provided that "in any event, a commander must have cogent reasons, with supporting evidence, for any denial of distribution privileges" and "the fact that a publication is critical—even unfairly critical—of government policies or officials is not, in itself, a grounds for denial." The September 1969 Department of Defense Directive,[33] aimed at mollifying congressional critics who felt the Army directive had made too many concessions, emphasized that prior approval must be obtained for any distribution on a military installation and that the commander can impound printed material if he determines that an attempt will be made to distribute it without authorization. Thus, the right of a serviceman to have an antiwar paper in his locker or to distribute printed materials was seriously undercut by a broad grant of command discretion. But the constitutionality of such stringent limitations and broad command discretion is subject to question, as is indicated by the fact that the legal corps have counseled against arbitrary refusals of requests to distribute literature and that commanders have been forced to permit limited distributions on threat of federal court action.

Another limited right is the right to join organizations, including servicemen's unions. The Army Directive on Dissent stated that commanders are not authorized to recognize or bargain with a servicemen's union, but conceded that "in view of the constitutional right to freedom of association, it is unlikely that mere membership in a servicemen's union can constitutionally be prohibited, and current regulations do not prohibit such membership." The Department of Defense Directive deleted this concession. Although there is not much doubt that a serviceman has a right to join a union, actions of the military such as harassment and frequent reassignment of known union members and threats of court-martial have been an effective depressant to the exercise of this right. Also, military law precedents upholding a court-martial conviction for association with "characters of known sexual deviation"[34] and an undesirable discharge for allegedly subversive associations[35] provide additional restraints on servicemen's freedom of association.

Servicemen have a limited right to write and publish. The Army Directive on Dissent provides that "the publication of 'underground newspapers' by soldiers off post, on their own time, and with their own money and equipment is generally protected under the First Amendment's guarantees of freedom of speech and freedom of press," but the DOD Directive emphasizes that "if such a publication contains language the utterance of which is punishable under Federal law, those involved in the printing, publication, or distribution may be disciplined for such infractions." The undesirable discharge of one underground newspaper editor and the court-martial of another indicates that the rights recognized by the military are tenuous.[36] The court-martial of Seaman Roger Priest, the editor of a Washington, D.C., underground paper, has raised a number of the constitutional issues which may be resolved on appeal.[37]

Military censorship requirements also impose substantial limitations on the right to publish. In a 1954 case in which a lieutenant colonel was court-martialed for publishing a book containing criticisms of General MacArthur, the Court of Military Appeals ruled that servicemen can be required to submit all manuscripts prior to publication to military censors to ensure that they do not contain security information.[38] After the decision, the services issued a joint directive indicating that censorship is only designed for deletion of security information in wartime and emergency situations, and, in light of later decisions, it is doubtful that advance censorship of writings by servicemen who have no access to security information is still permissible.

CURRENT LITIGATION INVOLVING FREE SPEECH RIGHTS OF SERVICEMEN

Vietnam war courts-martial for speech activities have created a number of cases in which basic First Amendment issues are being raised. The first important Vietnam war free-speech case arose in the fall of 1965 when a young second lieutenant, Henry W. Howe, Jr., carried a sign reading END JOHNSON'S FACIST AGRESSION IN VIETNAM and LET'S HAVE MORE THAN A CHOICE BETWEEN PETTY IGNORANT FACISTS IN 1968 (*sic*) in a peaceful off-post rally, while off duty and in civilian clothes. He was convicted in a general court-martial of two traditional military crimes applying only to officers, "conduct unbecoming an officer and a gentleman" (Article 133) and using "contemptuous words against the President" (Article 88), and was sentenced to two years at hard labor, forfeiture of pay and allowances, and dismissal. The Court of Military Appeals affirmed, rejecting his claim that the conviction violated the First Amendment. The court stated that, although the First Amendment applies to the military, the right to free speech is not an absolute, and proceeded to apply the "clear and present danger" test to Lieutenant Howe's speech activities:

> We need not determine whether a state of war presently exists. We do judicially know that hundreds of thousands of members of our military forces are committed to combat in Vietnam, casualties among our forces are heavy, and thousands are being recruited, or drafted, into our armed forces. That in the present times and circumstances such conduct by an officer constitutes a clear and present danger to discipline within our armed services, under the precedents established by the Supreme Court, seems to require no argument.[39]

The court's application of the "clear and present danger" test has some disquieting aspects. The court relied principally on the Supreme Court's 1951 decision in *Dennis v. United States*,[40] which upheld the conviction of Communist Party leaders under the Smith Act, but failed to note that the *Dennis* rationale was substantially modified by a 1957 decision, *Yates v. United States*.[41] In *Yates*, the Supreme Court reversed the convictions of a number of Communist Party members under the Smith Act, holding that mere advocacy or teaching of violent overthrow of the government is constitutionally protected and that speech can only be punishable if it is reasonably and ordinarily calculated to incite persons to prohibited action. It is difficult to imagine how Lieutenant Howe's participation in the peace rally could meet that test, for there was no evidence that he was recognizable as an Army officer at the rally or that the words on the sign were calculated to incite others to unlawful action. The Court's attempt to avoid the problem of an absence of circumstances relating to incitement by asserting that, since forces were committed to combat in Vietnam, "it requires no argument" that the "clear and present danger" test had been met was especially unsatisfying. However, the fact that Howe was an officer and that the military has always claimed the right to subject officers to stricter standards of conduct seems to have had an important effect upon the Court's decision, and it is arguable that the *Howe* case should be strictly limited to its facts and should not be viewed as a precedent governing free speech activities by all servicemen.

Since the *Howe* case, military courts have upheld convictions of servicemen, over claims that their First Amendment rights had been violated and that the court-martial charges were unconstitutionally vague and overbroad, for such activities as making antiwar statements to servicemen and civilians and refusing to teach medicine to Green Beret troops (Captain Howard Levy);[42] making antiwar statements to other servicemen during a noon "bull session" and encouraging them to talk to the commander about Vietnam (Corporal William Harvey and Private George Daniels);[43] distributing antiwar leaflets on post (Privates Ken Stolte, Jr., and Daniel Amick);[44] and making antiwar statements while in sanctuary (Privates Claude Gray, Thomas Met, and Victor Bell).[45] The charges varied considerably. The cases involving officers usually included charges, as in *Howe,* of "conduct unbecoming an officer" (Article 133) or "contemptuous words" (Article 88). Article 134, forbidding "disorders and neglects to the prejudice of good order and discipline in the armed forces, all conduct of a nature to bring discredit upon the armed forces," was frequently used, with a specification forbidding making "disloyal statements . . . with design to promote disloyalty among the troops," a popular charge. Finally, a number of cases have charged violation of a rarely used provision of the 1940 Smith Act, prohibiting advising, counseling, urging, causing, or attempting to cause insubordination, disloyalty, or refusal of duty, which is made a military crime by an assimilated crimes clause in Article 134.

The most significant decision of the military courts in the First Amendment area since *Howe* is *United States v. Daniels,*[46] which together with its companion case, *United States v. Harvey,*[47] was decided on July 10, 1970. Daniels and Harvey were court-martialed in 1967 for making statements to other black marines, primarily at an informal "bull session," that Vietnam was a white man's war and black men should not fight there. As a result, some fifteen black marines requested mast (a procedure for presenting grievances) to talk to the commander about their opposition to going to Vietnam. There were no incidents, breaches of discipline, or disobedience of orders resulting from the statements. Daniels was convicted of the Smith Act offense mentioned above, while Harvey was convicted of the lesser included offense of making "disloyal statements." They received ten-year and six-year sentences (later reduced to four years and three years).

The Court of Military Appeals reversed both convictions: in *Daniels*, because the court members had not been instructed that Daniels' statements must be found to have had a natural tendency to lead to disloyalty, disobedience, or refusal of duty; and in *Harvey*, because they had not been instructed that his statements must be found to have been disloyal to the United States and not merely to the Marine Corps. Thus the Court limited military prosecutions under the Smith Act to cases where the speech posed a clear and present danger in terms of its natural tendency, under the circumstances, to incite others, and limited the offense of "disloyal statements" to speech found to be disloyal to the United States itself. However, the salutary effect of the decisions was limited by the fact that the Court expressed its holdings in terms of instructional error rather than constitutional requirements, and, in broad dicta, indicated that it felt the evidence was sufficient to support both convictions. Thus, it continued to view the "clear and present danger" test in terms of an ad hoc balancing approach which gives great weight to the military interests of preserving order and discipline, and, despite the lack of evidence of illegal effects resulting from Daniels' and Harvey's statements, it endorsed conviction for such speech.[48]

Because of the restrictive view of the First Amendment which still prevails in the military courts, servicemen have increasingly turned to the federal courts in hope of obtaining broadened free speech rights. Petitions for habeas corpus or complaints for mandamus are now pending in United States district courts in *Howe*,[49] *Levy*,[50] *Stolte & Amick*,[51] and *Daniels*,[52] all of them with ACLU attorneys and all raising issues as to the vagueness and overbreadth of the military offenses involved as well as the constitutionality of the convictions. It is too early to predict how these cases will fare, but in light of recent Supreme Court decisions extending broader free speech rights to government employees, public school teachers, and students, it may not be overly optimistic to predict a more favorable judicial attitude toward servicemen's First Amendment rights in the future.

RIGHTS IN PRIVATE LIFE

The military structure necessitates the regulation of certain aspects of a serviceman's life which are usually considered private in civilian society. However, the traditional military view that a serviceman is on call twenty-four hours a day and that the status of a serviceman requires conformity to military standards of conduct at all times is now subject to serious question on constitutional grounds.

The military interest is most obvious in the regulation of servicemen's conduct on post. Post and command regulations usually govern a wide variety of on-post activities, such as the kind of dress which must be worn in various places, the personal property a serviceman may have in his wall or foot locker, and what servicemen can do and where they can go off duty. These rules are considered discretionary with commanders, and servicemen have never had much success in protesting harsh rules and arbitrary administration. However, recent directives granting blacks limited rights concerning hair styles and conduct of service clubs are examples of concessions granted in the face of racial unrest and indicate that pressures can sometimes accomplish liberalized policies on private rights. There seems to be no reason why regulation of servicemen's on-post lives should not be required to be reasonable and non-discriminatory in administration, and grievance procedures, political pressures, and lawsuits seem to be likely vehicles to accomplish this in the future.

The military interest in regulating servicemen's conduct off-post is more doubtful. *O'Callahan* laid to rest the military's claim of jurisdiction to court-martial servicemen for all acts committed off post by limiting court-martial jurisdiction to offenses which are "service-connected." The Court of Military Appeals has given the term "service-connected" a broad interpretation, holding that offenses are "service-connected," even though committed off post, when they involve drugs or are perpetrated against other servicemen, or when military rank is a moving force in victimizing the civilian community.[53] The retention of court-martial jurisdiction in such cases is questionable and will, no doubt, be the subject of further litigation in the federal courts.

Despite *O'Callahan,* the military still claims the right to regulate the places where servicemen can go off post through the power to declare establishments "off limits." The DOD Directive on Dissent deleted a reference in the Army Directive indicating that "the service should not use its off-limits power to restrict the exercise of freedom of speech and association," stating instead that "commanders have the authority to place establishments 'off-limits,' in accordance with established procedures, when, for example, the activities taking place there, including counselling members to refuse to perform duty or to desert, involve acts with a significant adverse effect of members' health, morale, or welfare." A new tough line on "off limits" was initiated in December 1969 when the Army undertook to declare the Shelter Half Coffee House in Tacoma, Washington, off limits on the grounds that it was "a source of dissident counselling and literature and other activities inimical to good morale, order and discipline within the Armed Services."[54] However, after threatened legal action by civil liberties attorneys, the "off-limits" action was indefinitely postponed, and no similar action has been taken against other coffee houses. GI coffee houses have also experienced difficulties with local law enforcement authorities, involving denials of permits to operate, police surveillance, and frequent raids. As a result, some have converted into "movement houses," catering to a small number of GI's with sympathetic political views rather than attempting to provide a public establishment open to all GI's.

The military also claims the right to control various aspects of servicemen's family and personal lives. Regulations provide that servicemen are responsible for proper control of their dependents on post, the proper support of their families, and the proper payment of their debts. Servicemen have been court-martialed for failure to abide by these regulations, and many a serviceman with genuine legal grounds for not paying contested alimony, child support, or bills has been badgered into paying them by his commander on threat of administrative harassment, stymied promotions, or disciplinary action. These actions are probably unconstitutional, but they are often difficult to raise in a judicial context, and most servicemen, particularly career men, are hesitant to pursue their rights.

Military law also places substantial restrictions on the right of association, permitting court-martial or discharge, as has already been mentioned, for associations with such groups as alleged homosexuals and subversives. Withdrawal of security clearance (often a serious detriment, since army NCO's cannot be promoted without such a clearance and many attractive assignments require one) can be based on such grounds as association with revolutionists or subversives and unreliable or untrustworthy behavior. Military regulations also considerably restrict a serviceman's political associations and activities, forbidding participation in partisan political campaigns, but permitting membership in a political club in an unofficial capacity and participation in nonpartisan campaigns. These restrictions, similar to the Hatch Act restrictions on civilian civil service employees, are of questionable constitutionality today.

The recent proliferation of servicemen's unions, GI coffeehouses, and GI underground newspapers and the continued participation by servicemen in antiwar demonstrations and peace activities indicates that the contemporary movement for expanded servicemen's rights still has vitality. Some have compared the GI rights movement, at this stage, to the civil rights movement in the South in the early 1960's. There have been, until now, more defeats than victories, but the groundwork which has been laid seems to portend an increasingly effective movement in the future. The struggle is taking place on a number of different planes—congressional, administrative, and judicial—and it now appears that significant expansions of servicemen's rights can and probably will be achieved.

NOTES

1. *E.g., Ex parte* Reed, 100 U.S. 13 (1876).
2. *See* Hammond v. Lenfest, 398 F.2d 705 (2d Cir. 1968); Schatten v. United States, 419 F.2d 187 (6th Cir. 1969); Clark v. Brown, 414 F.2d 1159 (D.C. Cir. 1969); Smith v. Resor, 406 F.2d 141 (2d Cir. 1969).
3. 10 U.S.C. §815 (art. 15 of the UCMJ).
4. Department of the Army, Office of the Adjutant General, AGAM-P (M) (27 May 1969) DSCPER-SARD, Subject: Guidance on Dissent.
5. 64 Stat. 107 (1950), *as amended,* 10 U.S.C. §801 *et seq.*
6. Pub. L. No. 90–632, 82 Stat. 1335 (Oct. 24, 1968).
7. United States v. Clay, 1 U.S.C.M.A. 74, 1 C.M.R. 74 (1951).
8. *E.g.,* United States v. Tempia, 16 U.S.C.M.A. 629, 37 C.M.R. 249 (1967).

9. Warren, "The Bill of Rights and the Military," 37 *New York University Law Review* 181, 188 (1962).

10. 346 U.S. 137 (1953).

11. *Compare* Palomera v. Taylor, 344 F.2d 937 (10th Cir.), *cert. denied,* 382 U.S. 946 (1965), *with* Kauffman v. Secretary of the Air Force, 415 F.2d 991 (D.C. Cir. 1969).

12. United States v. Culp, 14 U.S.C.M.A. 199, 33 C.M.R. 411 (1963).

13. Application of Stapley, 246 F. Supp. 316 (D. Utah 1965).

14. Kennedy v. Commandant, 377 F.2d 339 (10th Cir. 1967); Le Ballister v. Warden, 247 F. Supp. 349 (D. Kan. 1965).

15. 355 U.S. 579 (1958) (per curiam).

16. For discussion of decisions, see Sherman, "Judicial Review of Military Determinations and the Exhaustion of Remedies Requirement," 55 *Virginia Law Review* 483, 529–40 (1969).

17. McElroy v. United States *ex rel.* Guagliardo, 361 U.S. 281 (1960); Grisham v. Hagan, 361 U.S. 278 (1960); Kinsella v. United States *ex rel.* Singleton, 361 U.S. 234 (1960); Reid v. Covert, 354 U.S. 1 (1957); Toth v. Quarles, 350 U.S. 11 (1955).

18. *See* Note, "Court-Martial Jurisdiction over Weekend Reservists?" 44 *Military Law Review* 123 (1969).

19. 395 U.S. 258 (1969).

20. This brief discussion necessarily contains many generalizations. For a more precise analysis of military due process, see Sherman, "The Civilianization of Military Law, Part II," 22 *Maine Law Review* 3, 59 (1970); Moyer, "Procedural Rights of the Military Accused: Advantages over a Civilian Defendant," 22 *Maine Law Review* 105 (1970); Quinn, "The United States Court of Military Appeals and Military Due Process," 35 *St. John's Law Review* 225 (1961).

21. 384 U.S. 437 (1966).

22. 16 U.S.C.M.A. 629, 37 C.M.R. 249 (1967).

23. 395 U.S. at 265 (1969).

24. Wolfson, CM 413411, 36 C.M.R. 722, 728 (1966).

25. Schatten v. United States, 419 F.2d 187 (6th Cir. 1969).

26. F. Gardner, *The Unlawful Concert: An Account of the Presidio Mutiny Case* 4 (1970).

27. 50 U.S.C. §1474.

28. *See, e.g.* AR 600-20, Army Command Policy and Procedure (May 17, 1968), ¶42.

29. 10 U.S.C. §1034; AR 600-20, *supra* note 28, ¶41a.

30. United States v. Schmidt, 16 U.S.C.M.A. 57, 36 C.M.R. 213, 217 (1966).

31. AR 600-20, *supra* note 28, ¶46. *See also* DOD Directive No. 1334.1, "Wearing of the Uniform" (Aug. 11, 1969).

32. Dash v. Commanding General, 307 F. Supp. 849 (D.S.C. 1969); Yahr v. Resor (E.D.N.C., decided Jan. 2, 1970).

33. DOD Directive No. 1325.6, Sept. 12, 1969.

34. United States v. Hooper, 9 U.S.M.C.A. 637, 26 C.M.R. 417 (1958).

35. Olenick v. Brucker, 173 F. Supp. 493 (D.D.C. 1959). *But see* Harmon v. Brucker, 355 U.S. 579 (1958) (per curiam); Kennedy v. Secretary of the Navy, 401 F.2d 990 (D.C. Cir. 1968).

36. *New York Times,* April 15, 1969, at 1, col. 8; April 13, at 11, col. 1.

37. *See* "Seaman Priest," 162 *New Republic* 14 (Feb. 14, 1970).

38. United States v. Voorhees, 4 U.S.C.M.A. 509, 16 C.M.R. 83 (1954).

39. United States v. Howe, 17 U.S.C.M.A. 165, 37 C.M.R. 429, 437–38 (1967).

40. 341 U.S. 494 (1951).

41. 354 U.S. 298 (1957).

42. Levy, CM 416463, — C.M.R. — (Aug. 29, 1968), *petition for review refused by Court of Military Appeals* (Jan. 6, 1969).

43. Harvey, NCM 68-1734, — C.M.R. — (July 10, 1969); Daniels, NCM 68-1733, — C.M.R. — (May 15, 1969).

44. Amick & Stolte, CM 418868, — C.M.R. — (May 16, 1969).

45. Met, NCM 69-0987, — C.M.R. —; Gray, NCM 69-1171, — C.M.R. —.

46. 19 U.S.C.M.A. 529,—C.M.R.—(1970).

47. 19 U.S.C.M.A. 539, — C.M.R. — (1970).

48. *See also* United States v. Gray, No. 22,546 (USCMA, decided Aug. 28, 1970).

49. Howe v. Clifford, No. 622–68 (D.D.C. 1968).

50. Levy v. Parker (M.D. Pa.), *pet. for release on bail granted,* 90 S. Ct. 1 (1969) (Douglas, J.).

51. Stolte & Amick v. Laird, Civil No. 1764-70 (D.D.C. 1970).

52. Daniels v. Laird, HC 140-70 (D.D.C. 1970).

53. United States v. Beeker, 18 U.S.C.M.A. 563, 40 C.M.R. 275 (1969); United States v. Rego, 19 U.S.C.M.A. 9, 41 C.M.R. 9 (1969).

54. Letter from Captain H. W. Stauffacher, President, Armed Forces Disciplinary Control Board, Headquarters, 13th Naval District, Seattle, Washington to Proprietor, Shelter Half Coffee House, Dec. 11, 1969. *See also New York Times,* Jan. 22, 1970, at 9, col. 1.

THE RIGHTS OF
ALIENS

EDWARD J. ENNIS

THE UNITED STATES CONSTITUTION AND THE CON-
stitutions of the fifty states apply to all persons within their territories, including all aliens, whether permanent residents, visitors, or
even illegal entrants. This means that in the enforcement of laws
applicable to all persons generally, such as criminal laws, aliens are
protected from unreasonable arrest, search, and seizure and are entitled to due process of law and all other constitutional protections
in criminal trials. An alien's property cannot be taken without due
process of law or without just compensation, except in the special
case of detention of an alien enemy or seizure of his property in
time of war. In limited situations, by international law or treaty
or diplomatic protection of a foreign government of which an alien
is a citizen, an alien may have greater protection than a citizen in
the enforcement of laws.

The operation of laws, federal and state, designed to control the
conduct of aliens, rather than the general laws designed to control
all persons present on the territory of the sovereign, reveals the
constitutional rights of aliens as such. Federal laws determine which
aliens may enter the United States and which aliens are subject to
deportation, and the conditions under which aliens may be naturalized as citizens of the United States or may suffer the loss of

*Edward J. Ennis, Chairman of the Board of Directors of the American Civil Lib-
erties Union and a practicing lawyer in New York City, served for many years in
the Department of Justice and participated in numerous cases in the United States
Supreme Court involving rights of citizenship and other civil liberties issues.*

citizenship once acquired. State laws usually define the occupations which are barred to aliens. The operation of all these laws is subject to some constitutional restrictions, which will now be considered.

Admission of Aliens

The power of the United States as a sovereign independent nation to exclude classes of aliens by legislative enactment cannot be seriously questioned. This federal power over foreign commerce and the conduct of foreign relations excludes the exercise of the power of any individual state in the same area to regulate the entry of aliens. The early federal policy of an open door to the immigrant began to change in 1882 when Orientals were first excluded. Thereafter Congress gradually added to the excluded classes persons suffering from mental or physical disease, criminals, anarchists, and other classes. In 1891, Congress first authorized the deportation of illegal entrants within one year after entry, and in 1907, the deportation of women found engaged in prostitution within three years after entry. Quota limitations were not applied until 1921, when Congress became concerned about the immigration of as many as a million persons a year from war-torn Europe in 1919 and 1920 and applied the national-origins quota system designed to favor the first settlers, the English, German, and Irish, at the expense of later immigrant groups such as the Italians, Greeks, and Poles.

The present statute[1] excludes thirty-one categories of aliens from admission to the United States, among them the mentally ill, drug addicts, convicts, persons likely to become public charges, stowaways, anarchists, Communists, or aliens advocating a totalitarian dictatorship in the United States, and includes two seldom-used and somewhat vague provisions barring aliens believed by consular officers or the Attorney General to be coming here to engage in activities prejudicial to welfare or security or to engage in illegal activities.

In 1965 the national-origins quota system of about 154,000 a year was replaced by an annual quota of 170,000 for the Eastern Hemisphere as a whole (with a limit of 20,000 immigrants from any one country), and in 1969 the Western Hemisphere, which had been subject to no numerical quota, was placed under an annual quota of 120,000.

In the government fiscal year ending June 30, 1969 (the most recent official figures available), there were 350,000 immigrants,

comprising 120,000 from our Western Hemisphere, 170,000 from
the Eastern Hemisphere, and 60,000 not subject to numerical limitation, such as spouses of United States citizens. The immigrants
from Europe, Africa, and Asia (but not those from the other American countries) come in seven statutory preference categories, including 13,000 professionals or persons of exceptional abilities and their
families, 11,000 workers deemed in short supply and their families,
10,000 refugees, 18,000 nonpreference aliens, and the remainder in
several relative preferences for spouses, children, and brothers and
sisters of resident aliens or citizens. We also received over 1,750,000
visitors of various classes: 1,200,000 for business, pleasure, or both;
60,000 students; 58,000 exchange visitors on various programs;
crewmen, transients, and others.

A special class of immigrants have been refugees under the Displaced Persons Act of 1948, the Refugee Relief Act of 1953, and
other statutes.[2] The political crises in Hungary, Cuba, and Czecho-
slovakia resulted in a large movement of refugees. As many as
600,000 Cubans (10 percent of the population) became refugees;
500,000 have been admitted to the United States. It is to be expected that the United States will continue to accept its share of
the world's political refugees.

The governmental apparatus which applies the statutes and
regulations to control the flow of immigrants and alien visitors
consists of our hundreds of consulates abroad, which issue visas
under the supervision of the Visa Office of the Bureau of Security
and Consular Affairs of the Department of State; the Immigration
and Naturalization Service of the Department of Justice, which controls the ports of entry and conducts all exclusion and deportation
proceedings; and the Division of Immigration Certifications of the
Department of Labor, which issues individual certifications to
immigrants required to establish that they will not take jobs from
resident workers.

Registration of Aliens

The Alien Registration Act of 1940[3] first provided for registration and fingerprinting of all aliens thereafter issued either non-
immigrant or immigrant visas and of all aliens then in the United
States. This registration and fingerprinting of one minority of our
population was opposed as an unnecessary and discriminatory measure but was adopted in the war environment which then prevailed.

The present statutory provisions authorize the regulations which waive fingerprinting for nationals of countries which do not require United States citizens to be fingerprinted and for all other nonimmigrants who maintain their status and do not remain in the United States for more than one year.[4] The statutory provisions also require all aliens in the United States every January to file address report cards and to report all changes of address. Willful failure is not only a misdemeanor but is also grounds for deportation. Although these provisions do not appear to be rigorously enforced, they do subject resident aliens as well as visitors to this special control of annual registration not required of the remainder of the population.

A most important general consideration for individual aliens in understanding their rights is that only Congress can define the excluded or deportable classes of aliens. Congress has not authorized consular officers abroad to refuse visas required for entry, or immigration officials at port of entry to exclude aliens at their discretion as "undesirable" or on any ground not set forth by Congress in a specific statutory provision. Another fundamental protection for aliens subject to exclusion or deportation proceedings is that they must receive due process of law, which means a fair hearing to determine whether the facts establish that an alien is within one of the statutory excludable or deportable classes. The 1952 Act and regulations expressly recognize this constitutional requirement by providing[5] that in any exclusion or deportation proceeding an alien is entitled to a hearing, at which he may be represented by counsel, and the determination that he is excludable or deportable must be on the evidence produced at the hearing. The alien has an appeal from decision of the Special Inquiry Officer, who conducts the hearing, to the Board of Immigration Appeals established by the Attorney General and then to the courts.

Exclusion of Aliens

In exclusion cases the alien is either detained at the border or temporarily paroled into the United States pending decision. In deportation cases the alien is usually free on his own recognizance or on bail, although in some cases, usually involving persons with criminal records or those whose conduct indicates that they may abscond during the proceeding, the alien may be detained during the proceeding.

In applications for visas to our consular officers in foreign countries, aliens do not have the procedural protection of formal hearings or appeals from adverse decisions. A consular officer may deny a visa on the basis of information available to him that the applicant is in one of the many classes of excluded aliens. The alien may be refused access to this information and an adequate opportunity to refute it. In cases of doubt the consul may follow the practice of asking an advisory opinion on the case from the Visa Office of the Department of State in Washington, on the basis of which the consular officer then makes the final decision.

An alien and even his family in the United States have no appeal or resort to the courts from refusal of a visa. Because of the important human considerations involved, an amendment of the statute has been proposed by a large number of senators and congressmen to provide for review of denial of immigrant visas by a Board of Visa Appeals on the application of a citizen relative or permanent-resident alien relative of an applicant entitled to a preference on the quota by reason of the family relationship. Congress, in refusing to adopt such provisions in the past, has shown a reluctance to extend to aliens abroad the constitutional protection of administrative hearings and administrative and judicial review applicable to aliens present in the United States. But the time may have come to extend the benefits of administrative law and judicial review to the important matter of refusal of an immigrant visa.

In special cases judicial review is limited. If an alien is excluded on the basis of a certificate of a United States Public Health Service doctor that he is in one of the classes excluded for mental or physical health reasons, the only appeal is to the Surgeon General of the United States, and the courts will not grant an independent review of that determination.

Constitutional questions arise in particular cases in which aliens at ports of entry, by writs of habeas corpus in federal district courts, question administrative decisions of excludability. If an alien is excluded on the basis of confidential information, the disclosure of which the Attorney General concludes would be prejudicial to the public interest, he may be denied the usual statutory hearing before the special inquiry officer. In the *Knauff* case[6] a divided Supreme Court held that it was constitutional to exclude an alien seeking to immigrate as a war bride of a United States soldier on the basis of unrevealed confidential information that her entry would be prejudicial to internal security. Subsequently, after considerable public protest, the Attorney General decided to allow the alien a regular exclusion hearing, at which the information was revealed and the Board of Immigration Appeals concluded that the evidence did not support her exclusion.[7]

When the government sought to apply this regulation authorizing exclusion on withheld information to a permanent resident alien returning to the United States after a voyage abroad as a seaman, the Supreme Court in 1953 avoided the serious constitutional question presented by holding that the regulations did not apply to permanent resident aliens briefly absent abroad.[8] This regulation has been incorporated in the 1952 Act but has been severely criticized as unfair and unnecessary, and in fact it is very sparingly used even in respect of nonresident aliens. Shortly after the *Chew* decision, in the *Mezei* case in 1953 the Court distinguished *Chew* and affirmed the exclusion on confidential information of a permanent resident abroad for about nineteen months in Hungary and seeking to return on a new visa.[9] He was detained at Ellis Island for nearly two years because no country could be found who would accept him after he was excluded. A majority of the Supreme Court upheld the government's power to refuse him admission in these circumstances, although the minority of the Court insisted that procedural due process of law required that Mezei be given an opportunity to know and meet the evidence if he was to be continued in detention. As in the *Knauff* case, after succeeding in the assertion of its power to exclude, the government gave Mezei a hearing before a special board of inquiry which upheld the exclusion but recommended that he be paroled into the United States. This was done, and he was returned to his home in Buffalo.

The "strict entry" doctrine that every alien, new arrival or returning resident, is subject to every ground of exclusion on each entry caused great hardship to some returning residents until modified first by some Court decisions that aliens involuntarily leaving the United States briefly were not making new entries. In one case the alien seaman's ship was torpedoed in the Atlantic Ocean and when rescued he was brought first to Cuba. When he attempted to re-enter at Miami he was excluded because of a prior burglary conviction. But the Supreme Court refused to treat the return as an "entry" and held that the alien was not excludable.[10] Congress then modified the strict re-entry doctrine by defining "entry" as not including a permanent resident alien who proves that his departure was not intended or that his presence abroad was not voluntary. In

1963 the Supreme Court held that an alien resident who went across the border to Mexico at Ensenada for a couple of hours was within the spirit of this new provision and was not subject to exclusion as a homosexual allegedly within the excluded class of aliens afflicted with "psychopathic personality."[11] The Court avoided reviewing the decision of the lower court that the statutory phrase "psychopathic personality" when applied to include homosexuals was too vague to be constitutional.

Alien residents generally have the same constitutional rights of free speech as citizens, but the question has been raised and never fully resolved whether an alien's visit may be abruptly terminated because of public speech opposing official policy. Distinguished aliens believed to be politically hostile to the United States are occasionally denied visitors' visas to come here to attend meetings of various literary or scientific groups. This limitation on free speech and assembly and the right of American citizens to invite the views of visitors from abroad has been vigorously protested, but in the absence of any judicial remedy the court of public opinion is the only recourse from such official repression of speech.

United States citizens may visit the principal countries of Europe without obtaining visas, but the United States requires visitors' visas to be obtained by all aliens visiting the United States except citizens of Canada and Mexico. There has been some discussion of facilitating tourism from Europe by legislation eliminating visitors' visas for short visits of thirty or sixty days with special provisions that such visitors may not remain longer or attempt to change their status to that of permanent resident. These proposals have not been enacted, and in the meantime scrutiny continues of applicants for visitors' visas by consular officers, to be satisfied that they are not in reality immigrants. It is hoped that a favorable experience of alien visitors departing within the visit allowed will encourage the government to reciprocate at least with the countries which do not require visas from United States citizens and facilitate further travel to the United States.

Deportation of Aliens

Deportation, particularly of long-time residents who have retained no home abroad, is inescapably severe individual treatment

by the government which should satisfy all constitutional requirements. The Supreme Court has recognized that deportation, although not technically criminal punishment, is a harsh remedy
which may well result in the loss "of all that makes life worth
living."[12] The 1952 Act lists some fifteen categories of aliens subject to deportation, including aliens excludable at time of entry,
institutionalized at public expense within five years of entry for
mental illness not shown to have arisen after entry, or convicted of
one crime of moral turpitude committed within five years after
entry or two such crimes at any time, and aliens who at any time
after entry are anarchists, Communists, members of any organization advocating totalitarian dictatorship here, and narcotic addicts.
The statute provides that an alien may be detained or released with
or without bond pending a deportation proceeding, and relatively
few are detained (at present principally seamen who may abscond).
The statute expressly provides for representation by counsel, examination of witnesses, and cross-examination of government witnesses,
and requires a decision based on "reasonable, substantial, and
probative evidence."

Many of the substantive and procedural aspects of the deportation laws have been subjected to the judicial tests of constitutionality.

Deportation of alien members of the Communist Party, and
their detention during protracted deportation proceedings, raised
constitutional questions. In the leading case[13] the Supreme Court
held constitutional an amendment of the statute making past
membership in the Communist Party a ground for deportation and
rejecting the contention that this action violated constitutional
provisions guaranteeing due process of law and freedom of speech
and prohibiting any *post facto* laws. The Court expressed the view
that so long as alien residents choose not to become naturalized
citizens they remain subject to expulsion by deportation according
to the policy which Congress may adopt.

In another case decided at the same time as *Harisiades*, a
divided Court upheld the statutory power given to the Attorney
General to deny bail and hold aliens in detention during deportation proceedings and exercised to detain members of the Communist Party pending deportation.[14] The dissenting Justices expressed
in part the view that the statute, read in the light of the Eighth
Amendment prohibiting excessive bail, required the Attorney General to consider standards which he had not observed such as the

alien's availability for deportation if enlarged on bail. Subsequent court decisions have required bail pending deportation proceedings in the absence of a showing that the alien would be dangerous to public security if at large or might abscond.[15]

The 1952 Act attempts to enforce deportation by a provision making it a crime for an alien subject to a deportation order for six months to refuse information about his activities and associations requested by the Attorney General. The Supreme Court has upheld this provision by restricting the information to that concerning availability of the alien for deportation and ruling that other information cannot be required.[16] Another provision making it a criminal offense to willfully refuse to depart under a deportation order has been held by the Court to apply only when a country willing to receive the alien is identified.[17]

Discussion of the very limited constitutional restrictions on the deportation powers of Congress should also take note of *Flemming v. Nestor*[18] which narrowly upheld the power of Congress to terminate social security old-age insurance benefits being made to aliens deported as Communists or on selected other grounds. The minority of the Court dissented from this harsh decision on a number of grounds. It thought that the statutory provision was unconstitutional in that it deprived the alien, who had contributed social security taxes for many years, of his property without due process of law and was an unconstitutional bill of attainder—in effect, legislative punishment without judicial trial.

Section 243 of the 1952 Act provides for deportation to the country of the alien's choice if it will accept him, and otherwise to the country of his nationality, but if the latter will not accept him, then either to the country from which he last came or where he was born or has resided, or finally, to any country which will accept him. As a practical matter, refusal of countries to accept deportees limits the government's choice. It is very doubtful that it would be constitutional to deport an alien to a country where he had never been and with which he had no connection simply because its government acceded to our government's request to accept him.

The 1952 Act provides a humanitarian limitation on the deportation power by authorizing the Attorney General to withhold deportation to any country where, in the Attorney General's opinion, the alien would be subject to persecution on account of race, religion, or political opinion. Persons deportable to Communist countries or other totalitarian regimes have been able to persuade the Attorney General that deportation should be withheld indefinitely.[19]

Naturalization

National policy is to welcome and encourage resident aliens to become United States citizens but not to demand that they change their allegiance. Many permanent resident aliens, taxed here just as citizens are, prefer to retain their original nationality, particularly if it is citizenship in a favored country such as Canada, Great Britain, or France. Of course, they run the risk of changes in congressional policy which might cause them to fall within the deportation provisions or the exclusion provisions on departure. Or in time of war they might run the risk, on return to the United States, of being classified an "enemy alien," as were German, Italian, and Japanese aliens during World War II, and therefore subject to detention and confiscation of property. The Japanese aliens were in the especially unenviable position of being ineligible to become United States citizens because of their Asian ancestry until this discrimination was eliminated in the 1952 Act.

The 1952 Act defines as citizens at birth all persons who are born in the United States, as the Fourteenth Amendment decrees, and all persons born abroad of citizen parents or of one alien parent and a citizen parent who was present in the United States for not less than ten years of which five years were over the age of fourteen. The statute also prescribes the requirements for naturalization, including five years residence after admission for permanent residence (three years in the case of an alien living with a United States spouse). Aliens barred from naturalization include Communists, advocates of a totalitarian dictatorship in the United States, and persons obtaining release from military training because of noncitizenship. Before being admitted to citizenship an alien must renounce allegiance to any foreign sovereign and agree to bear arms or, alternatively, perform noncombatant service or work of national importance under civil direction if there is objection to military service by reason of religious training and belief.

Loss of Nationality

Section 349 of the 1952 Act provides numerous grounds upon which a United States national, by birth or naturalization, shall lose his nationality, including naturalization in a foreign state, declaration of allegiance to a foreign state, and renunciation of United States nationality. Loss of nationality by such voluntary conduct which has as its intention and purpose loss of United States nationality presents no problem. Our national policy has been, at least since 1868, that "expatriation is a natural inherent right of all people, indispensable to the enjoyment of the rights of life, liberty, and the pursuit of happiness." Our government has always insisted that immigrants from Europe might renounce allegiance to foreign sovereigns and become United States citizens alone, not subject to claims of allegiance by their former sovereigns. Claims of continuing allegiance by the Russian czars, German kaisers, and Italian kings have been protested. Equally, our government has taken the position that United States citizens may freely renounce nationality and has formally stated that "any declaration, instruction, opinion, or decision of any officer of the United States which denies, restricts, impairs or questions the right of expatriation is declared inconsistent with the fundamental principles of the Republic" (R.S. § 1999).

The Foreign Investors Tax Act of 1966 amends the Internal Revenue Code to limit the effect of renunciation of United States nationality to evade taxes by providing that a citizen who renounces for such a purpose shall continue for ten years to be subject to federal income and estate taxes on a basis different from other nonresident aliens in respect of property in the United States.[20]

Other statutory grounds for loss of nationality not constituting voluntary renunciation have been the subject of much litigation, and have been condemned as unconstitutional. Most recently the Court, overruling an earlier decision, held that a naturalized citizen, by voting in an election in Israel, did not by that action establish an intention to renounce United States citizenship.[21] The Court has ruled similarly where the citizen has remained out of the United States to evade military service, has engaged in involuntary service in the armed forces of a foreign state, or has been convicted by a court-martial of wartime desertion.[22]

These cases establish the principle that citizenship is conferred by the Constitution and can be lost only through the voluntary act of the citizen disclosing termination of allegiance and not by act of Congress as a penalty for criminal conduct such as desertion or evasion of military service.

In *Schneider v. Rusk*[23] the Court held unconstitutional a statutory provision which provided that a naturalized citizen, unlike a native-born citizen, lost nationality merely by residing abroad for three years in the country of his former nationality or for five years in any other foreign country. This decision establishes the principle that under the Constitution a naturalized citizen has all the rights of a native-born citizen and that special provisions cannot be made for his loss of nationality that are not applicable to all citizens.

State Regulation of Aliens

We have discussed the manner in which the federal government, subject to constitutional limitations, has regulated the entry, deportation, and naturalization of aliens and loss of nationality by naturalized and other citizens. There remains to be considered the manner in which state governments, subject to both federal and state constitutional limitations, have sought to control the entry or conduct of aliens within the state. Early in our history New York's attempt to tax arriving aliens was declared an unconstitutional attempt to regulate foreign commerce reserved to the federal government.[24]

The Pennsylvania Alien Registration Act of 1939, requiring the annual registration by all aliens within the state, was ruled an unconstitutional interference with the Federal Alien Registration Act of 1940 under which all aliens entering the United States are registered and required annually to file a current address and to report changes of address.[25] Federal regulation occupies this area and prohibits duplicate and burdensome state registration.

In the most vital area of efforts by aliens to earn a livelihood in the United States, hostile state statutes attempting to bar aliens, or particular classes of aliens, from ordinary occupations have been ruled unconstitutional. In the famous *Yick Wo* case[26] the Supreme Court held that a San Francisco ordinance requiring a license to operate a public laundry in a wooden building, although fair on its face, was enforced in an unconstitutionally discriminatory manner against Chinese laundrymen and therefore denied equal protection of the laws, which is guaranteed to aliens as well as citizens. An Arizona statute requiring that 80 percent of the employees of an employer having five or more employees be citizens was also held to be barred by the Fourteenth Amendment.[27]

The other side of the picture, however, is that the Supreme Court has upheld the right of states to bar aliens from certain occupations thought to be of special public interest. A Cincinnati ordinance prohibiting a poolroom license to an alien was upheld.[28] The public interest in denying such a license to the English alien involved in this case seems very tenuous, but this decision has encouraged state court decisions denying licenses to aliens to operate buses or even to sell soft drinks. A New York statute prohibiting the employment of aliens on public works projects has been upheld.[29] But the New York courts held unconstitutional a statute prohibiting a chauffeur's license to an alien who had not made a declaration of intention to become a citizen.[30] More recently the Supreme Court struck down a California statute which attempted to bar aliens ineligible for citizenship, which meant Japanese aliens, from fishing off the coast of California.[31]

In the other important area, the right to own land, the Supreme Court has conceded that in the absence of federal treaty, states may determine whether aliens can own, purchase, or inherit real property in the state.[32] Happily, the states have gradually withdrawn earlier restrictions on alien ownership of land, and with limited exceptions, aliens are free to own land throughout the United States.

There remain a large number of occupations which are traditionally licensed by the states, permission to engage in such work being treated, not as a right, but as a privilege only to be obtained by complying with state requirements. Such occupations as attorney, medical doctor, certified public accountant, architect, dentist, optometrist, engineer, and many others are barred to aliens, although in certain cases permanent resident aliens who file declarations of intention to become citizens may engage in some occupations temporarily pending citizenship.

Desirable Changes in Admission of Aliens

What of the future? Insofar as future immigration policy is concerned, strongly supported bills are pending in Congress[33] which would substitute for the present separate Western and Eastern Hemisphere quotas one world-wide quota available to applicants in the order of application, subject to preference classes based on close relationship to citizen or resident aliens, or on skills desired in the United States. Thus it would appear that for the immediate future, immigration will be limited to about 300,000 quota immigrants a year, plus some nonquota spouses, parents, and children of United States citizens and refugees, for a total of under 500,000 annually—a very small percentage of our population of 200,000,000.

A desirable change would be a return to the provision of the 1952 Act under which aliens seeking to enter in order to perform skilled or unskilled labor are excluded if the Secretary of Labor certifies that there are enough resident workers available to perform such labor. The 1965 amendment, urged by organized labor, bars an immigrant from coming here to work unless he obtains an individual certificate that his intended work will not adversely affect resident workers. This provision is not applicable to parents, spouses, or children of United States citizens or resident aliens, and in fact applies to less than one-half of the 350,000 annual immigrants who are not wage-earners but their dependents. This provision requires a cumbersome procedure to obtain the individual certification, which is wholly unnecessary for the protection of resident labor. It is to be hoped that organized labor and Congress will be convinced that this provision is unnecessary and may be repealed even if the result is that a few thousand immigrants may be admitted who have nothing to offer but their labor and ambition to succeed in the New World.

Another useful change would be the proposed Visa Review Board to review consular denial of immigration visas abroad, which at present leaves the applicant without any established remedy.

It is increasingly recognized that the poor need and deserve more legal services in civil and criminal matters. This is also true in exclusion or deportation proceedings, which determine the all-important question whether an alien shall live in the United States of his choice or elsewhere. Although the statute contains provisions for fair hearings and determinations on the evidence produced at the hearings, the proceedings are technical and an alien is completely unable to represent himself effectively. In fact, only a limited number of attorneys are familiar with immigration procedure because this is a field of the law which cannot attract attorneys by the lure of a lucrative return. Legal aid societies and other organizations, some with the help of federal funds from the Office of Economic Opportunity, fill part of the need for legal services to indigent aliens involved in immigration proceedings, but a great many still remain unrepresented as the future of their lives is being determined. Much remains to be done to remedy this situation.

Another persistent difficulty, which apparently can be remedied only by a change in the attitude of the officials of the State and Justice Departments charged with exclusion of visiting aliens, is the refusal of visitors' visas or admission to prominent aliens seeking to visit the United States to attend conventions or make speeches if they are politically *persona non grata* to the admitting officials. An example of such an exclusion on political grounds in 1970 was the refusal to admit Mrs. Shirley Graham DuBois, who was invited to address a meeting of Fisk University students in Nashville, Tennessee and was excluded by the Department of Justice apparently because of her political associations and admissions, including support of Nkrumah in Ghana. In 1969 a prominent Mexican literary figure, Dr. Carlos Fuentes, was refused temporary admission en route from Europe home to Mexico because of his alleged radical past. This kind of political exclusion is persistent. As long ago as 1935 the prominent English writer, John Strachey, who had written something favorable about communism, was granted a visitor's visa to visit the United States by State Department officials but was denied entry by officials of the Department of Justice. In all of these cases the Department of State was not opposed to temporary admission. The Department of Justice, however, insisted upon exclusion on alleged security grounds, although it later admitted Mrs. DuBois.

This kind of political exclusion, limiting the constitutional right of our citizens who invite such speakers in order to hear their views, are not very numerous, although not all of the incidents may come to public attention. But any such exclusion of an individual who is not barred for his actions but merely because his views are not acceptable to current official policy, is intolerable in a free society. The lack of an effective legal remedy makes the situation all the more irritating, and requires a mobilization of public opinion and political pressure on the officials concerned to persuade them that the rights of free speech and assembly include the right to invite the views of alien visitors without government censorship. In the present circumstances of our foreign relations, in which we admit annually hundreds if not thousands of official Communist visitors, it is ludicrous to exclude an occasional private visitor for fear that his politics might have serious security consequences.

It is hoped that as foreign travel by United States citizens abroad and by aliens to the United States increases, as it now is doing tremendously under the "go-now-pay-later" credit plan, the alien in our midst will be considered less and less a stranger. Interest in the culture of other lands and acceptance of the alien is a mark of our maturity and should result in less and less discrimination in public regulation and private attitudes.

.

NOTES

1. Immigration and Nationality Act of 1952, *as amended,* 8 U.S.C. §1101 *et seq.*
2. *As amended,* 50 U.S.C. App. §§1951 *et seq.; id.* §§1971 *et seq.; id.* §§1975 *et seq.*
3. Act of June 28, 1940, ch. 439, §§30–39, 54 Stat. 673.
4. 8 U.S.C. §§1201, 1301–06; 8 C.F.R. §264.1(e).
5. 8 U.S.C. §§1226, 1252; 8 C.F.R. §§236, 242.
6. United States *ex rel.* Knauff v. Shaughnessy, 338 U.S. 537 (1950).
7. *See generally* E. Knauff, *The Ellen Knauff Story* (1952).
8. Kwong Hai Chew v. Colding, 344 U.S. 590 (1953).
9. Shaughnessy v. United States *ex rel.* Mezei, 345 U.S. 206 (1953).
10. Delgadillo v. Carmichael, 332 U.S. 388 (1947).
11. Rosenberg v. Fleuti, 374 U.S. 449 (1963).
12. Ng Fung Ho v. White, 259 U.S. 276, 284 (1922) (Brandeis, J.).
13. Harisiades v. Shaughnessy, 342 U.S. 580 (1952).
14. Carlson v. Landon, 342 U.S. 524 (1952).
15. *E.g.,* Rubinstein v. Brownell, 206 F.2d 449 (D.C. Cir. 1953), *aff'd per curiam by an equally divided Court,* 346 U.S. 929 (1954). *But cf.* Kordopatis v. Hurney, 254 F. Supp. 70 (N.D. Ill. 1966) (burden of proof on alien).
16. United States v. Witkovich, 353 U.S. 194 (1957).
17. Heikkinen v. United States, 355 U.S. 273 (1958).
18. 363 U.S. 603 (1960).
19. *E.g.,* Matter of Janus and Janek, 12 I.&N. Dec. 866 (1968).
20. Int. Rev. Code of 1954, §§877, 2107.
21. Afroyim v. Rusk, 387 U.S. 253 (1967).
22. Kennedy v. Mendoza-Martinez, 372 U.S. 144 (1963); Nishikawa v. Dulles, 356 U.S. 129 (1958); Trop v. Dulles, 356 U.S. 86 (1958).
23. 377 U.S. 163 (1964).
24. Henderson v. Mayor of New York, 92 U.S. 259 (1876).
25. Hines v. Davidowitz, 312 U.S. 52 (1941).
26. Yick Wo v. Hopkins, 118 U.S. 356 (1886).
27. Truax v. Raich, 239 U.S. 33 (1915).
28. Ohio *ex rel.* Clarke v. Deckebach, 274 U.S. 392 (1927).
29. Heim v. McCall, 239 U.S. 175 (1915).
30. Magnani v. Harnett, 169 Misc. 697, 8 N.Y.S.2d 447 (Sup. Ct. 1938), *aff'd mem.,* 257 App. Div. 487, 14 N.Y.S.2d 107 (1939), *aff'd mem.,* 282 N.Y. 619, 25 N.E.2d 395, *cert. denied,* 310 U.S. 642 (1940).
31. Takahashi v. Fish & Game Comm'n, 334 U.S. 410 (1948).
32. Terrace v. Thompson, 263 U.S. 197 (1923).
33. *E.g.,* S. 3202, 91st Cong., 1st Sess. (1969) (introduced by Senator Edward Kennedy and 23 others).

INDEX